T0236831

Lecture Notes in Computer Science   9735

Commenced Publication in 1973
Founding and Former Series Editors:
Gerhard Goos, Juris Hartmanis, and Jan van Leeuwen

More information about this series at http://www.springer.com/series/7409

Sakae Yamamoto (Ed.)

Human Interface and the Management of Information: Applications and Services

18th International Conference, HCI International 2016
Toronto, Canada, July 17–22, 2016
Proceedings, Part II

 Springer

Editor
Sakae Yamamoto
Tokyo University of Science
Tokyo
Japan

ISSN 0302-9743   ISSN 1611-3349   (electronic)
Lecture Notes in Computer Science
ISBN 978-3-319-40396-0   ISBN 978-3-319-40397-7   (eBook)
DOI 10.1007/978-3-319-40397-7

Library of Congress Control Number: 2016940822

LNCS Sublibrary: SL3 – Information Systems and Applications, incl. Internet/Web, and HCI

Printed on acid-free paper

This Springer imprint is published by Springer Nature
The registered company is Springer International Publishing AG Switzerland

Foreword

The 18th International Conference on Human-Computer Interaction, HCI International 2016, was held in Toronto, Canada, during July 17–22, 2016. The event incorporated the 15 conferences/thematic areas listed on the following page.

A total of 4,354 individuals from academia, research institutes, industry, and governmental agencies from 74 countries submitted contributions, and 1,287 papers and 186 posters have been included in the proceedings. These papers address the latest research and development efforts and highlight the human aspects of the design and use of computing systems. The papers thoroughly cover the entire field of human-computer interaction, addressing major advances in knowledge and effective use of computers in a variety of application areas. The volumes constituting the full 27-volume set of the conference proceedings are listed on pages IX and X.

I would like to thank the program board chairs and the members of the program boards of all thematic areas and affiliated conferences for their contribution to the highest scientific quality and the overall success of the HCI International 2016 conference.

This conference would not have been possible without the continuous and unwavering support and advice of the founder, Conference General Chair Emeritus and Conference Scientific Advisor Prof. Gavriel Salvendy. For his outstanding efforts, I would like to express my appreciation to the communications chair and editor of *HCI International News*, Dr. Abbas Moallem.

April 2016   Constantine Stephanidis

HCI International 2016 Thematic Areas
and Affiliated Conferences

Thematic areas:

- Human-Computer Interaction (HCI 2016)
- Human Interface and the Management of Information (HIMI 2016)

Affiliated conferences:

- 13th International Conference on Engineering Psychology and Cognitive Ergonomics (EPCE 2016)
- 10th International Conference on Universal Access in Human-Computer Interaction (UAHCI 2016)
- 8th International Conference on Virtual, Augmented and Mixed Reality (VAMR 2016)
- 8th International Conference on Cross-Cultural Design (CCD 2016)
- 8th International Conference on Social Computing and Social Media (SCSM 2016)
- 10th International Conference on Augmented Cognition (AC 2016)
- 7th International Conference on Digital Human Modeling and Applications in Health, Safety, Ergonomics and Risk Management (DHM 2016)
- 5th International Conference on Design, User Experience and Usability (DUXU 2016)
- 4th International Conference on Distributed, Ambient and Pervasive Interactions (DAPI 2016)
- 4th International Conference on Human Aspects of Information Security, Privacy and Trust (HAS 2016)
- Third International Conference on HCI in Business, Government, and Organizations (HCIBGO 2016)
- Third International Conference on Learning and Collaboration Technologies (LCT 2016)
- Second International Conference on Human Aspects of IT for the Aged Population (ITAP 2016)

Conference Proceedings Volumes Full List

1. LNCS 9731, Human-Computer Interaction: Theory, Design, Development and Practice (Part I), edited by Masaaki Kurosu
2. LNCS 9732, Human-Computer Interaction: Interaction Platforms and Techniques (Part II), edited by Masaaki Kurosu
3. LNCS 9733, Human-Computer Interaction: Novel User Experiences (Part III), edited by Masaaki Kurosu
4. LNCS 9734, Human Interface and the Management of Information: Information, Design and Interaction (Part I), edited by Sakae Yamamoto
5. LNCS 9735, Human Interface and the Management of Information: Applications and Services (Part II), edited by Sakae Yamamoto
6. LNAI 9736, Engineering Psychology and Cognitive Ergonomics, edited by Don Harris
7. LNCS 9737, Universal Access in Human-Computer Interaction: Methods, Techniques, and Best Practices (Part I), edited by Margherita Antona and Constantine Stephanidis
8. LNCS 9738, Universal Access in Human-Computer Interaction: Interaction Techniques and Environments (Part II), edited by Margherita Antona and Constantine Stephanidis
9. LNCS 9739, Universal Access in Human-Computer Interaction: Users and Context Diversity (Part III), edited by Margherita Antona and Constantine Stephanidis
10. LNCS 9740, Virtual, Augmented and Mixed Reality, edited by Stephanie Lackey and Randall Shumaker
11. LNCS 9741, Cross-Cultural Design, edited by Pei-Luen Patrick Rau
12. LNCS 9742, Social Computing and Social Media, edited by Gabriele Meiselwitz
13. LNAI 9743, Foundations of Augmented Cognition: Neuroergonomics and Operational Neuroscience (Part I), edited by Dylan D. Schmorrow and Cali M. Fidopiastis
14. LNAI 9744, Foundations of Augmented Cognition: Neuroergonomics and Operational Neuroscience (Part II), edited by Dylan D. Schmorrow and Cali M. Fidopiastis
15. LNCS 9745, Digital Human Modeling and Applications in Health, Safety, Ergonomics and Risk Management, edited by Vincent G. Duffy
16. LNCS 9746, Design, User Experience, and Usability: Design Thinking and Methods (Part I), edited by Aaron Marcus
17. LNCS 9747, Design, User Experience, and Usability: Novel User Experiences (Part II), edited by Aaron Marcus
18. LNCS 9748, Design, User Experience, and Usability: Technological Contexts (Part III), edited by Aaron Marcus
19. LNCS 9749, Distributed, Ambient and Pervasive Interactions, edited by Norbert Streitz and Panos Markopoulos
20. LNCS 9750, Human Aspects of Information Security, Privacy and Trust, edited by Theo Tryfonas

Human Interface and the Management of Information

Program Board Chair: **Sakae Yamamoto, Japan**

- Yumi Asahi, Japan
- Dennis Coelho, Portugal
- Shin'ichi Fukuzumi, Japan
- Michitaka Hirose, Japan
- Daiji Kobayashi, Japan
- Kentaro Kotani, Japan
- Mark Lehto, USA
- Hiroyuki Miki, Japan
- Hirohiko Mori, Japan
- Shogo Nishida, Japan
- Robert Proctor, USA
- Katsunori Shimohara, Japan
- Jiro Tanaka, Japan
- Kim-Phuong Vu, USA
- Tomio Watanabe, Japan

The full list with the program board chairs and the members of the program boards of all thematic areas and affiliated conferences is available online at:

http://www.hci.international/2016/

HCI International 2017

The 19th International Conference on Human-Computer Interaction, HCI International 2017, will be held jointly with the affiliated conferences in Vancouver, Canada, at the Vancouver Convention Centre, July 9–14, 2017. It will cover a broad spectrum of themes related to human-computer interaction, including theoretical issues, methods, tools, processes, and case studies in HCI design, as well as novel interaction techniques, interfaces, and applications. The proceedings will be published by Springer. More information will be available on the conference website: http://2017. hci.international/.

General Chair
Prof. Constantine Stephanidis
University of Crete and ICS-FORTH
Heraklion, Crete, Greece
E-mail: general_chair@hcii2017.org

http://2017.hci.international/

Contents – Part II

Information in e-Learning and e-Education

Access to Cultural Heritage, Creativity and Art

e-Science and e-Research

Information in Health and Well-being

Contents – Part I

Big Data Visualization

Information Analytics, Discovery and Exploration

Interaction Design

Human-Centered Design

Haptic, Tactile and Multimodal interaction

Communication, Collaboration
and Decision-Making Support

Collaborative Modes on Collaborative Problem Solving

Yu-Hung Chien[✉], Kuen-Yi Lin, Kuang-Chao Yu, Hsien-Sheng Hsiao,
Yu-Shan Chang, and Yih-Hsien Chu

Department of Technology Application and Human Resource Development,
National Taiwan Normal University, Taipei, Taiwan
roland.chien@ntnu.edu.tw

Abstract. Collaborative problem solving (CPS) is an important skill for 21st-century workplaces. We examined the effects of two collaborative modes (learner-on-computer agent mode and learner-on-learner mode) on the CPS performance of 64 college students (28 women, 36 men; age range = 18–22 yr., M = 20.1, SD = 1.2). Participants' CPS performance scores in the learner-on-computer agent mode were significantly higher than those in the learner-on-learner mode. The optimal mode for teaching CPS skills, the practical implications of using a CPS system, and the limitations of this study are also discussed.

Keywords: Collaborative mode · Gender · Learning style · Problem solving

1 Introduction

Employers have been placing an increasing emphasis on collaborative problem-solving (CPS) skills [6]. CPS is a non-routine skill employed to solve various complex and information-insufficient problems [3]. In other words, CPS is not a domain-specific routine skill, but a transversal competence that differs from reasoning and working memory. Given that the problems with which people deal in daily work and life are usually complex, not all the information needed to solve these problems is usually available. Additionally, in such situations, multiple goals have to be considered at the outset, and problems cannot be solved solely by reasoning and working memory, but have to be approached by people working collaboratively and using various strategies to gather information. As a result of recent developments in web technologies, online CPS has become a more important means for information sharing and communication [4]. Research has found that the use of web technologies, such as e-mail, videoconferencing, instant messaging, and so on, for virtual collaboration is one of key skills that will be necessary in the workplaces of the future [2]. Thus, web-based CPS has received considerable attention in educational programs and is now part of large-scale educational assessments internationally. For instance, Organisation for Economic Co-operation and Development (OECD) assesses CPS skills related to primary development in the Program for International Student Assessment [PISA]. PISA 2015 defined CPS competency as "the capacity of an individual to effectively engage in a process whereby agents attempt to solve a problem by sharing the understanding and effort required to come to a solution and pooling their knowledge, skills, and efforts to reach that solution" [6].

© Springer International Publishing Switzerland 2016
S. Yamamoto (Ed.): HIMI 2016, Part II, LNCS 9735, pp. 3–10, 2016.
DOI: 10.1007/978-3-319-40397-7_1

According to the aforementioned characteristics of CPS, it is important to develop the ability to apply CPS skills to web-based technological scenarios. Consequently, the purpose of this study was to develop a CPS system involving computer agents and web technology to train learners and to assess their CPS skills in building teams, communicating information, sharing knowledge, and developing strategies to solve problems. The development of a CPS system involves careful consideration of several issues. For instance, systems allow learners to collaborate with computer agents or humans. Questions about which aspects of the CPS abilities of learners will be particularly important for collaborating with computer agents and other learners must be addressed when designing training and assessment programs. Few studies have compared the advantages of the collaborative mode involving learner-on-computer agent (LCA mode) with those of the mode involving learner-on-learner (LL mode) in terms of CPS performance.

In recent years, an increasing number of studies have examined computer-supported approaches toward collaborative learning. For example, some studies have focused on developing systems to approach open assignments by supporting collaboration, whereas others have adopted an interactive whiteboard technology to facilitate learners' interaction and collaboration to help them actively solve problems [5]. Although these approaches have had some good results, Researchers found that learners were not satisfied with their team members, and each felt that he or she made more effort than the other team members did, despite the fact that the skills of learners increased more with CPS than with traditional learning [8]. That is, learners evaluated the efforts and contributions of others in the problem-solving activities while participating in the collaborative process, which thus elicited both cooperative and competitive behaviors [7]. Findings such as these led other researchers to conclude that support of collaborative learning activities and procedures requires specialized tools instead of standard, web-based technologies.

CPS involves collaboration between an individual and other agents during a problem-solving process [6]. These agents may be computer-simulated participants or humans. Many systems using computer agents for training or evaluating in different fields have been applied to overcome difficulties related to the aforementioned competitive behaviors; these include the use of computer agents to collaboratively find solutions [9] and the development of an inferential problem-solving system [1]. Again, additional and more in-depth direct comparisons of the effects of different collaborative modes on learners' CPS performance are needed. The results of such investigations would be particularly useful for improving a computer agent-based CPS system. Consequently, the goals of this study were as follows: (1) to develop a CPS system using web technology and computer agents and (2) to understand the advantages and disadvantages of different collaborative modes in terms of learners' CPS performance.

2 Method

2.1 Development of the CPS System

This study developed a CPS system with web technology and computer agents to train and assess CPS skills. Figure 1 shows the interface of the CPS system.

Fig. 1. The CPS system interface presents eight problems

The design elements of task characteristics, the problem scenarios, the medium, and the composition of teams were considered in the process of developing the present system. With regard to task characteristics, all tasks in this study were related to learners' daily work and life, and learners and computer agents had to assume different responsibilities to solve problems. As mentioned above, problems involved tasks that could plausibly appear in the daily lives of learners. In terms of medium, learners were provided with sufficient information to work with computer agents, and were asked to determine the appropriateness of strategies offered by such agents. With respect to team composition, learners worked with computer agents and were required to play different roles in different scenarios.

The problem-solving tasks were designed to allow guidance by the system. Learners followed the system's instructions and completed each task in 10–15 min. Four tasks were used in the present study: hanging shelves, using a microwave oven, defusing a bomb, and arranging a bedroom. Figure 2 shows the interfaces for the problem involving using a microwave oven, in which participants collaborated to prepare a meal using this device and applied related scientific knowledge that was provided, such as heating method, power, and microwave penetration. In the task involving arranging a bedroom, participants used knowledge about ergonomics and the interior design materials provided to arrange furniture in a bedroom. Hanging shelves involved discussion among participants about how to attach shelves to the surface of the ceramic tiles in a bathroom. In the bomb defusing task, participants acted as police officers and used selected tools to apply exactly four gallons of water on a sensor to defuse a bomb. The reasoning method and mathematical principles of leverage were explained to help learners collaboratively generate strategies and determine the best solution to each problem.

Task description

Dialogue board and scheme selection

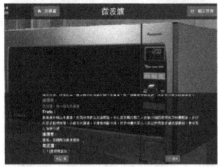

Dialogue scenario (I)

Dialogue scenario (II)

Fig. 2. Interfaces in the problem involving use of a microwave oven

CPS performance was rated in terms of the following three skills: shared understanding, problem solving, and establishing and maintaining team organization [6]. For example, the task of building shelves involved 13 questions related to shared understanding, 19 related to taking appropriate action to solve the problem, and 7 related to establishing and maintaining team organization during the CPS process. Students answered these questions based on their interactions during the collaborative problem-solving tasks.

2.2 Experiments

Participants. Sixty-four college students with an academic background in technology participated in this study. Of these, 36 participants were male, and 28 were female; the age of participants ranged from 18 to 22 years (Mean = 20.1 yr, SD = 1.2). None of the participants had used the CPS system previously.

Design and Procedure. This study examined the effects of different collaborative modes on learners' CPS performance using a CPS system. The collaborative mode was a within-subject variable. Half of the participants were randomly assigned to the LL mode first and then to the LCA mode, and the remaining participants were assigned to

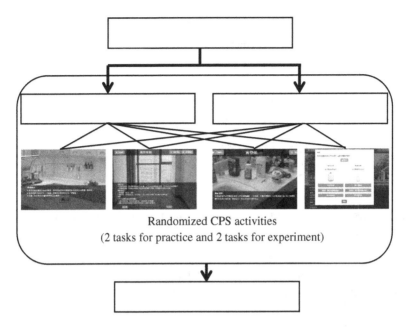

Randomized CPS activities
(2 tasks for practice and 2 tasks for experiment)

Fig. 3. Experimental procedure

the LCA mode first and then to LL mode. Figure 3 shows the procedure of the experiment.

Participants were invited to a classroom, where they received a brief explanation of the purpose and the procedure of the study. Then, participants used two of four problems to practice the process of collaborating in LL and LCA modes and to become familiar with the CPS system interface in different collaborative modes. After practice, participants took a 2-min rest, and then started to solve the other two problems in either LL or LCA mode. In LCA mode, each participant used a personal computer with a 17" monitor to independently complete the CPS task. In the LL mode, two participants viewed a same monitor and communicated with each other face to face. One of the two participants was responsible for entering their joint responses to the CPS system's questions. The CPS system recorded all participants' responses and calculated CPS performance scores. Each participant took about 30 min to finish the experiment.

3   Results

In this study, analysis of variance (ANOVA) was used to analyze whether collaborative mode affected CPS performance, and t-tests were used to compare the effects of the two different collaborative modes on learners' evaluation of the CPS system. Table 1 shows participants' CPS performance scores in two different collaborative modes and Table 2 shows the ANOVA analysis.

Table 1. Participants' CPS performance scores in LL mode and in LCA mode

	LL mode		LCA mode	
	%	SD	%	SD
Total	77.75	5.63	79.19	8.88

Table 2. ANOVA for CPS performance scores

Source	Type III sum of squares	Mean square	F	p	η_p^2
Mode	321.22	321.22	24.49	<0.01	0.31

3.1 Effects of Cooperative Modes, Gender, and Learning Styles on Learners' CPS Performance

Table 1 presents participants' CPS performance scores (mean and standard deviation) by collaborative mode. The ANOVA revealed that the collaborative mode significantly affected participants' CPS performance scores ($F(1,54) = 24.49$, $p < .01$, $\eta_p^2 = .31$). Participants' CPS performance scores in the LCA mode ($M = 79.19$, $SD = 8.88$) were significantly higher than those in the LL mode ($M = 77.75$, $SD = 5.63$), with an effect size of $r = .10$.

Participants' system performance evaluation on two different collaborative modes. The mean evaluation score in the LL mode was 3.15 ($SD = .37$), and it was 2.97 ($SD = .42$) in the LCA mode. The mean score on each item related to collaborative mode was higher than the overall mean (Value = 2). The t-test revealed that the overall mean score for the LL mode was significantly higher than that for the LCA mode ($t(63) = 3.73$, $p = <.01$), with an effect size of $r = .30$.

4   Discussion and Conclusions

Given changes in the professional competencies needed for the future, countries have devoted considerable attention to training youth in CPS skills to increase their ability to solve problems that cross traditional disciplinary boundaries [3]. This study developed a CPS system as a tool to achieve the educational goals mentioned above. CPS training can involve working with a computer agent or with a real person. This study investigated the differences in learners' CPS skills (knowledge sharing, problem solving, and team organization) using two different collaborative modes, the LL mode and the LCA mode.

The results of this study showed that CPS performance differed significantly by collaborative mode. According to previous research, learners who engaged in LL mode were not satisfied with their team members, feeling that they expended more effort than others did. That is, learners evaluated the efforts and contributions made by others while they were collaborating with them, thus simultaneously engaging in both cooperative and competitive behaviors [7]. In this study, participants were asked to solve the problems within a limited period of time by following system's instructions and using the information provided. However, learners need more time than computer agents to communicate with one another, build trust, and establish and maintain organization [7]. These observations might explain why participants performed significantly better in the LCA than in the LL mode. Although we found a significant difference in participants' CPS performance between the two collaborative modes, the effect size was small ($r = .10$); hence, the LL mode might potentially be useful when carefully applied in appropriate situations. For example, the LL mode could be used to train CPS skills when students collaborate with a teacher instead of with other learners. As the relationship between teacher and learners is not competitive, competition between students may be avoided. Furthermore, teachers would be more familiar with the content of the problem and would have effective collaborative and communication skills. Thus, it would possible for them to assist learners in communicating, sharing knowledge, and establishing and maintaining organization. In contrast, the LCA mode is more applicable to assessing learners' CPS performance skills. The LCA mode could avoid competitive behaviors, save time that would otherwise be devoted to interpersonal communication, build trust, and develop an organized approach involving other learners, leading to more accurate and efficient performance. Moreover, the use of the LCA mode allows greater flexibility with regard to practice times, enabling learners to practice CPS skills themselves using the STEM-based CPS system with a computer agent at any time and in any place. Consequently, this study identified an optimal mode for training CPS skills.

There are some limitations. First, as the sample size of this study consisted of only 64 participants, significant findings should be interpreted with caution. Moreover, the CPS system used in this study was not well developed and requires numerous improvements. However, our results can help researchers to identify areas of improvement for a CPS system, and might inspire other attempts to design CPS-related systems. Future research should involve longer-term studies that include more different collaborative scenarios, a larger sample size, and a wider variety of measures. Second, the problems used in this study were well structured. It would be interesting to examine learners' transversal competence in addressing poorly structured problems that did not have correct answers to assess differences in learners' CPS performance and collaborative behavior in response to problems with different levels of difficulty.

Acknowledgement. The authors gratefully acknowledge the financial support provided by the Ministry of Science and Technology of the Republic of China under Project NSC 102-2511-S-003-059-MY2.

References

1. Biswas, G., Jeong, H., Kinnebrew, J., Sulcer, B., Roscoe, R.: Measuring self-regulated learning skills through social interactions in a teachable agent environment. Res. Pract. Technol. Enhanc. Learn. **5**(2), 123–152 (2010)
2. Davis, A., Fidler, D., Gorbis, M.: Future Work Skills 2020. Institute for the Future, Palo Alto (2011)

3. Greiff, S., Kretzschmar, A., Müller, J.C., Spinath, B., Martin, R.: The computer-based assessment of complex problem solving and how it is influenced by students' information and communication technology literacy. J. Educ. Psychol. **106**(3), 666–680 (2014)
4. Lin, K.Y., Yu, K.C., Hsiao, H.S., Chu, Y.H., Chang, Y.S., Chien, Y.H.: Design of an assessment system for collaborative problem-solving in STEM education. J. Comput. Educ. **2**(3), 301–322 (2015)
5. Looi, C.K., Chen, W., Ng, F.K.: Collaborative activities enabled by Group Scribbles (GS): an exploratory study of learning effectiveness. Comput. Educ. **54**(1), 1–26 (2010)
6. Organisation for Economic Co-operation and Development: Draft Collaborative Problem Solving Framework. Unpublished manuscript, OECD (2013)
7. Rosen, Y., Tager, M.: Computer-Based Assessment of Collaborative Problem-Solving Skills: Human-to-Agent Versus Human-to-Human Approach. Research & Innovation Network, Pearson Education, Philadelphia (2013)
8. Scifres, E.L., Gundersen, D.E., Behara, R.S.: An empirical investigation of electronic groups in the classroom. J. Educ. Bus. **73**, 24–25 (1998)
9. VanLehn, K., Graesser, A.C., Jackson, G.T., Jordan, P., Olney, A., Rose, C.P.: When are tutorial dialogues more effective than reading? Cognitive Sci. **31**, 3–62 (2007)

Modelling Information Flow and Situational Awareness in Wild Fire Response Operations

Laila Goubran[✉], Avi Parush, and Anthony Whitehead

Carleton University, Ottawa, Canada
laila.goubran@carleton.ca

Abstract. Wild fire management is often an intense and highly dynamic context, which requires the continuous flow of large amounts of information. It requires effective preparedness, quick response, and efficient and effective team communication and situational awareness. Aside from the skills and experience of the management team, the success of the process often depends on effective tools and technology that can present, communicate, and document the fire information in a way that supports and facilitates the response process. The aim of this study was to assess the informational needs of the wild fire response process and model the information flow and situational awareness, with and without supporting technology. It aimed to translate the findings to definitions and requirements for enhancing the process through human-computer interaction (HCI) design solutions and improved usability.

Keywords: Situational awareness · Emergency response · User-centered design · Wildfire response · Process analysis · Design requirements

1 Introduction

Forest fire management is the process of planning, preventing and fighting forest fires to protect people, property and the forest resource. The primary goal of the Ontario wildfire management program is the protection of public safety and values. This can only be achieved through quick and efficient information communication and response operations. However, the wildfire response process includes the processing of large amounts of information collected from a complex and constantly changing situation. In addition, response operations are often conducted by distributed teams, which can result in challenges and breakdowns in communication.

This study provides detailed insight about the response process and requirements. It focuses on the information flow between the field and the headquarters offices. The information flow includes the collection, communication and distribution of fire information required to maintain an accurate representation of the situation and awareness about its dynamic factors. In addition, the study highlights pain points in the current process that can be explored in future research. These pain points are current obstacles or problems that slow the process down or result in information loss. The aim of this study was to assess the informational needs of the wild fire response process and model the information flow and situational awareness, with and without supporting technology.

© Springer International Publishing Switzerland 2016
S. Yamamoto (Ed.): HIMI 2016, Part II, LNCS 9735, pp. 11–19, 2016.
DOI: 10.1007/978-3-319-40397-7_2

It was aimed at translating the findings to definitions and requirements for enhancing the process through human-computer interaction (HCI) design solutions and improved usability.

2   Literature Review

This research focuses on the communication and flow of information that is required to maintain situation awareness and to conduct response operations in emergency management.

2.1   Emergency Response

Forest fires are considered emergency incidents that require a special emergency response process to manage[1]. The management of an emergency response process requires a high level of complex coordination between different operators and locations, in addition to efficient and timely communication. One of the many challenges of the domain is the necessity for rapid decision-making in situations of uncertainty and under time and resource constraints [1]. The establishment and maintenance of situational awareness (SA) is an essential requirement for successful crisis and emergency management [2]. The maintenance of SA requires the proper collection of complete and accurate information about the situation in an accessible and timely manner as well as the proper analysis and interpretation of the different factors and overall situation [3].

Effective communication and information flow is identified as one of the key components of an effective incident command system [4, 5]. Teams often have to function in fast-paced, large-scale and stressful events where members are required to deal with and process large amounts of ambiguous information that must be processed in a limited time [5, 6].

2.2   Situational Awareness (SA)

As described, the process of emergency response requires all members of the response team to be on the same level of awareness about the factors affecting their strategy and decisions; also known as situational awareness (SA).

One of the most popular theoretical models of SA and its role in the dynamics of human decision making is the one developed by Endsley [7]. According to the model, SA must go beyond the perception of the elements in their environment to the interpretation of all factors and prediction of their development in the near future. Endsley explains that, in addition to the goals and objective, this three-step process is affected by several other factors [7]; these include a person's knowledge and experiences, their working environment as well as the interface and system that they are working with.

Mica Endsley's SA model is most widely used in the reviewed literature and was therefore the guiding model in this study. However other definitions and models of SA

---

[1] Emergency Management Ontario.

include having a "common operational picture" [8] and a "moment to moment knowledge about, and understanding of the [...] environment" [9].

Emergency response is always conducted by teams. This can add even more complexity to the required SA; in addition to the awareness about the environment, the operators are required to be updated with other team members' activities, status as well as contribution to the cooperative task, also refereed to as Team Situation Awareness (TSA) [10]. The information is required to be continuously extracted from the dynamic situation and integrated into the team's awareness model and situation representation upon which decisions are taken [11]. The study confirms the importance of continuous acquisition and update of information for the maintenance of TSA.

3   Methodology

The study took place in the province of Ontario, Canada, with the Ministry of Natural Resources and Forestry (MNRF) as the responsible provincial ministry. In-Situ research was conducted in three forest fire response and management offices: the regional and sector headquarters in Dryden and Sudbury, and the provincial office in Sault Ste Marie.

The qualitative research methods used in this study were the observation of the daily workflow including preparedness and response processes, interviewing response operators and the attendance of a fire response simulation training session.

3.1   Interviews

The interviews were semi-structured, and focused on understanding the individual responsibilities, needs and priorities of the different team members, as well as understanding their perceived and actual role within the overall response process.

All the interviewed operators have worked at the response offices during fire seasons, with their experience at the ministry ranging from 6 to 33 years. The interviewed operators also occupied different roles within the response team in order to gain insight from different perspectives; they included duty officers (DO), aircraft management officers (AMO), fire intelligent officers sector response officers (SRO), as well as radio operators, crew leaders, pilots and technical employees.

3.2   Fire Response Training Simulation

In addition, a crew leader training simulation was arranged at the Dryden Sector office, in order to observe the communication and process required during a response operation. The simulation was video-recorded and the researcher received the script of the simulation as well as a fire diary to follow the procedure. Several other MNRF report documents and training handbooks were also collected in order to understand the requirements of the process.

3.3   Analysis Verification Methodology

To ensure the accuracy of the process analysis, a document that summarized the most important process analysis insights was created and sent to ten operators from the three locations for verification. The document used for the verification included a description of the purpose of the study and of the analysis, and the results of the study, described in the next section.

4   Results

The observations focused on understanding the physical environment as well as the work dynamics of the team members. In the interviews, the operators described the daily work process from the perspective of their role within the team and the tools and software that they use to complete their tasks.

In all of the visited offices, the desks of the operators were generally arranged so that operators can easily communicate together while still able to see the common screen. Radio operators were situated in adjacent rooms with glass separation.

4.1   Technologies and Communication

The study showed that the response process utilizes a variety of tools of different technological levels to allow the team members to get a comprehensive overview of the situation in the region or sector. Information and databases required are accessed through the Fire Management Information System (FMIS). FMIS gives access to the Daily Fire Operating Support System (DFOSS), area information database and aircraft (Mapper) and personnel. Figure 1 presents the information flow and communication channels between response teams as well as the operators involved on each level.

4.2   Information Categories

The tools used to communicate information can be categorically divided into individual workstations and shared displays. The shared tools include displays for weather forecasts, and regional maps showing resource locations. Operators also have access to the information and tools through their own workstation.

Figure 2 shows a model of the three main components of the information communication process and their sources: 1. The incoming information (top box); 2 The tasks and decisions it supports (left box); and 3. The sources for the shared SA. Further analysis of the information was conducted to identify information categories, based on the study as well as previous research [3]. The categorization was done through an affinity diagram (Fig. 3) that sorted the information in the response and process specific categories as well as prioritized the different elements.

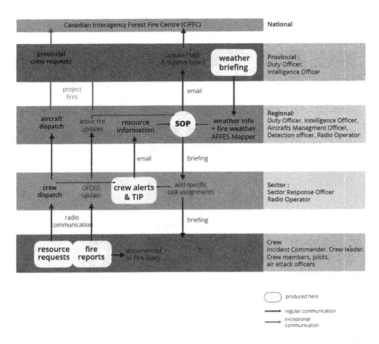

Fig. 1. Vertical communication between response teams (Color figure online)

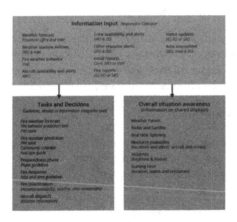

Fig. 2. Overview of information components and flow

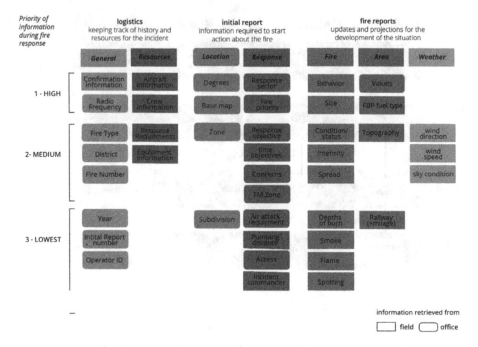

Fig. 3. Final affinity diagram showing categories and prioritization

4.3 Information Requirements Analysis

In the next steps of the analysis, the information required for response processes were analyzed for specific operators. For this analysis, decision ladders for four of the main operators were created. These are diagrams that summarize the information processing and cognitive steps as well as the information required for completing the step [12] (Fig. 4).

4.4 Pain Points and Challenges

The analysis of the process showed that operators' tasks and decisions are highly inter-dependent and heavily rely on timely and accurate communication of information. Several challenges that could cause delays or miscommunications in the process were identified:

(1) Reliance on verbal and radio communication
    Despite the availability of technologies to keep a good level of situational awareness within the team, a major reliance on verbal communication was noted. This challenge is especially critical in communication between the crew in the field and the offices where radio communication is the only available channel to communicate information.
(2) Retrieval of information from different sources
    Operators have to search for the required information to complete their tasks and make timely response decisions among different sources and displays.

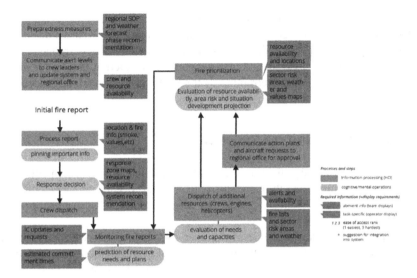

Fig. 4. The verified decision ladder for a sector response officer (Color figure online)

(3) Manual documentation of information
Incident information is manually recorded in the Fire diary by the incident commander. Additionally, each office operator is responsible for manually logging actions and events.

4.5 Enhancement Proposals

The above-described analysis concluded that the existing challenges could be addressed through facilitating the interaction with existing tools and databases rather than radical changes in the process. Based on this analysis, the following high-level system enhancements were proposed:

(1) Facilitate information collection, communication and documentation:
Improved usability and efficient interaction with the software can enhance the speed and the quality of the information inputted into the system as well as reduce the operators' reluctance to use them for communicating information. System enhancements should also integrate automatic documentation tools and logging of updates and incident developments. Such tools would be used for after-action reviews and process assessment.

(2) Interface design that supports team situation awareness:
The design should accommodate team communication through document sharing, messaging or conference call tools. The interface should also provide information about team members' activities [13], location and task assignment and progress according to process requirements.

(3) Operator- specific or customizable dashboard:
Dashboard designed to accommodate operators' specific needs. It would serve as operator-specific hubs for collecting information with shortcuts to frequently used software and databases It should also support the interaction between team and operator displays without interrupting their specific tasks through integrated notification and alert system [14].

5   Conclusion and Future Research

The study highlights the significance of effective and efficient information collection, from a variety of sources and through various technologies. This can impact effective shared situational awareness, not only within the response office, but also with the remote and dispersed ground crews.

The analysis of the response process led to user- and process-driven design proposals that can address the pain points of the process as well as the challenges of situational awareness. The proposed system enhancements aim to guide integrated process oriented and user-friendly designs that can be developed to make the response process more efficient and usable. The information categorization and the requirements analysis could also guide the organization of the design and interfaces of the system.

Furthermore, the study provides detailed insight about the response process requirements, and the analysis and verification of the communication and information flow needed for maintaining SA and completing wildfire response tasks. The results could therefore be used and explored for further forest fire management research.

The analysis methods can also be applied to other command and control and emergency response context like medical emergencies, military operations or other response processes. The findings and conclusions can also be extended to other context where information collection, communication and documentation are critical to mission success.

Acknowledgements. Many thanks to all team members from the Ministry of Natural Resources and Forestry; their time and valuable and continuous feedback greatly assisted the full development of the study.

References

1. Chen, R., Sharman, R., Rao, H.R., Upadhyaya, S.J.: Coordination in emergency response management. Commun. ACM **51**(5), 66–73 (2008)
2. MacEachren, A.M., Jaiswal, A., Robinson, A.C., Pezanowski, S., Savelyev, A., Mitra, P., Zhang, X., Blanford, J.: SensePlace2: GeoTwitter analytics support for situational awareness. In: 2011 IEEE Conference on Visual Analytics Science and Technology (VAST), pp. 181–190, October 2011
3. Hueston, E.: Fire Update Support Engine (FUSE): Visual Integration of Information within the Complex Environment of Emergency Response. Carleton University, Ottawa (2013)
4. Neill, B.O.: A Model Assessment Tool for the Incident Command System: A Case Study of The San Antonio Fire Department. Texas State University, San Marcos (2008)

5. Salas, E., Burke, C., Samman, S.: Understanding command and control teams operating in complex environments. Inf. Knowl. Syst. Manag. **2**, 311–323 (2001)
6. Brandigampola, S.R.: Team Situation Awareness Displays: An Empirical Evaluation of Team Performance. Carleton University, Ottawa (2011)
7. Endsley, M.R.: Toward a theory of situation awareness in dynamic systems. Hum. Factors: J. Hum. Factors Ergon. Soc. **37**(1), 32–64 (1995)
8. Kurapati, S., Kolfschoten, G.: A theoretical framework for shared situational awareness in sociotechnical systems. In: 2nd Workshop on Situational Awareness for Logistic Multimodal Operations, pp. 47–53 (2012)
9. Andre, A.D., Cutler, H.A.: Displaying uncertainty in advanced navigation systems. In: Proceedings of the Human Factors and Ergonomics Society Annual Meeting, vol. 42, no. 1, pp. 31–35 (1998)
10. Furuta, K., Shu, Y.: Team Situation Awareness and Its Assessment. Advancement on Operation and Maintenance for Nuclear Power Plant, no. 1–2, November 2004
11. Macredie, R.D., Sandom, C.: Analysing situated interaction hazards: an activity-based awareness approach. Cogn. Technol. Work **5**(3), 218–228 (2003)
12. Endsley, M., Jones, D.: Designing for Situation Awareness: An Approach to User-Centered Design (2011)
13. Wallace, J., Ha, V., Ziola, R., Inkpen, K.: Swordfish: user tailored workspaces in multi-display environments. In: CHI 06, Montreal (2006)
14. Röcker, C., Magerkurth, C.: Privacy and interruptions in team awareness systems. In: Proceedings of the 12th International Conference on Human Computer Interaction (2007)

Supporting Analytical Reasoning
A Study from the Automotive Industry

Tove Helldin[1(✉)], Maria Riveiro[1], Sepideh Pashami[2], Göran Falkman[1],
Stefan Byttner[2], and Slawomir Nowaczyk[2]

[1] University of Skövde, Skövde, Sweden
{tove.helldin,maria.riveiro,goran.falkman}@his.se
[2] Halmstad University, Halmstad, Sweden
{sepideh.pashami,stefan.byttner,slawomir.nowaczyk}@hh.se

Abstract. In the era of big data, it is imperative to assist the human analyst in the endeavor to find solutions to ill-defined problems, i.e. to *"detect the expected and discover the unexpected"* [23]. To their aid, a plethora of analysis support systems is available to the analysts. However, these support systems often lack visual and interactive features, leaving the analysts with no opportunity to guide, influence and even understand the automatic reasoning performed and the data used. Yet, to be able to appropriately support the analysts in their sense-making process, we must look at this process more closely. In this paper, we present the results from interviews performed together with data analysts from the automotive industry where we have investigated how they handle the data, analyze it and make decisions based on the data, outlining directions for the development of analytical support systems within the area.

Keywords: Analytical reasoning · Sense-making · Visual analytics · Truck data analysis · Big data

1 Introduction

Analysts today are often faced with large amounts of heterogeneous data on which they are to make quick and well-informed decisions. Often, the process of making sense of the data is exploratory, where the ground truth is now known, leaving the analysts in the dark regarding the quality of the reasoning carried out. Moreover, the problems are often ill-defined and the analysis tools used non-transparent. As argued by Stolper et al. [22], the results from the computational reasoning are often presented as an end product that the analysts are to examine, leaving no opportunity for them to guide or inspect the analysis during the process. When dealing with ill-defined problems that are best solved in an experimental manner by a human analyst, the performance of the analyst can be strongly influenced by his/her ability to quickly test different hypotheses, something which is not always possible when dealing with large, streaming,

© Springer International Publishing Switzerland 2016
S. Yamamoto (Ed.): HIMI 2016, Part II, LNCS 9735, pp. 20–31, 2016.
DOI: 10.1007/978-3-319-40397-7_3

heterogeneous data. Moreover, by examining the incremental, piecemeal results from the computations, the analyst is enabled to detect uncertainties or abnormalities early on and perform measures to handle them, such as transform the data and adapt the reasoning model(s).

Within the Visual Analytics (VA) research area, efforts have been made to appropriately visualize different types of data and uncertainties and to ensure that the analyst is able to adapt or inspect the reasoning algorithms used. However, the body of the research conducted has been centered around the performance of the computational reasoning strategies, not on how the analyst actually reasons to solve the problem(s) at hand. For example, as argued by Makonin et al. [11], VA has generally not used machine learning techniques within visual interaction to assist and enhance human analytical reasoning. This makes it difficult to adapt the support system in accordance with the analyst's preferences and reasoning style(s) as well as to evaluate the VA systems developed due to our sparse knowledge of how the system assists, if at all, the reasoning carried out.

In this paper, we investigate how a particular group of analysts that handle large quantities of data carry out their analytical tasks and how a VA support system that enables the analysts to interact with the data, the models and the visualizations could aid them in their sense-making process. As a case study, we have interviewed analysts from the automotive industry - a domain where the analysts are in great need of analysis support to handle the large quantities of data involved in order to solve complicated tasks, such as the identification of indicators of the need for different kinds of repairs as well as how the fuel consumption of a vehicle can be decreased. Such predictive analysis can drastically decrease the amount of time that the vehicle has to spend in the workshops, the need for additional spare parts of vehicles, as well as decrease fuel costs and environmental effects.

The paper is structured as follows: Sect. 2 presents a brief review of previous research regarding theories of human sense-making whereas Sect. 3 discusses how the sense-making process can be supported through the use of visual analytics tools. The study is summarized in Sect. 4 and Sect. 5 presents the results obtained. Section 6 offers a discussion of the work conducted, whereas conclusions and directions for future research are presented in Sect. 7.

2   How Do Experts Make Sense of Data?

This section presents an overview of relevant theories on human analytical reasoning and sense-making. Our aim is to review the literature trying to answer the following question: how do experts analyze data and find insights? We are particularly concerned with the analysis of huge amounts of data from heterogeneous sources and studies that include the analysis of data presented in visual form (we limit our study to individual analysis, collaborative aspects are not included). A more extensive review can be read in [17].

Analysis is cyclic and iterative. Reaching judgment about a single question is normally an iterative process that will produce several more questions about a larger issue [23]. Depending upon the request's needs, Thomas and Cook [23] distinguish three basic tasks the analysts may be asked to perform: (1) assess, understand the current world around them and explain the past (the product of this type of analysis is an assessment), (2) forecast, estimate future capabilities, threats, vulnerabilities and opportunities and (3) develop options, establish different optional reactions to potential events and assess their effectiveness and implications.

Many forms of intelligence analysis are "sense-making" tasks [15]. Such tasks consist of some kind of information gathering, representation of the information in a schema that aids the analysis, the development of insight through the manipulation of the schema and the creation of some knowledge product or direct action based on the aid (information → schema → insight → product). Sense-making provides a theoretical framework for understanding the analytical reasoning process that an analyst performs. From a psychological perspective, sense-making has been defined as "how people make sense out of their experience in the world" [2]. In [1], the authors describe intelligence analysis as an example of sense-making.

Another framework that explains the analyst's process is the "think-loop model", presented in [1], see Fig. 1. The processes and data are arranged by degree of effort and degree of information structure and the data flow shows the transformation from raw information to reportable results. The overall process is organized into two major loops [1]: (1) a foraging loop that involves processes aimed at seeking information, searching and filtering it, and reading and extracting information possibly into some schema and (2) a sense-making loop that involves iterative development of a mental model (a conceptualization) from the schema that best fits the evidence. The analyst integrates [1]: (1) a bottom-up approach that builds a theory based on a hypothesis by assembling evidence assumed relevant to a question, and (2) a top-down approach that searches for evidence for an assumed hypothesis.

The foraging loop is essentially a trade off among three kinds of processes [15]: (1) exploring or monitoring more of the space (increasing the span of new information items into the analysis process), (2) enriching (or narrowing) the set of items that has been collected for analysis and (3) exploiting the items in the set (through reading of documents, extraction of information, generation of inferences, noticing of patterns, etc.). A detailed description of the information foraging theory, models, empirical investigations and applications of the theory to the design of user interfaces can be found in [14].

It is important to note that sense-making does not always follow the progression data → information → knowledge → understanding. For instance, sense-making can have many loops or does not always have a clear beginning or end points (this has been highlighted by Klein et al. in [9]).

Other researchers have reached similar conclusions about intelligence analysis. Klein et al. present another view of sense-making in [9], the data/frame theory. For Klein et al., a frame is a mental structure that organizes the data and sense-making is the process of fitting information into the frame.

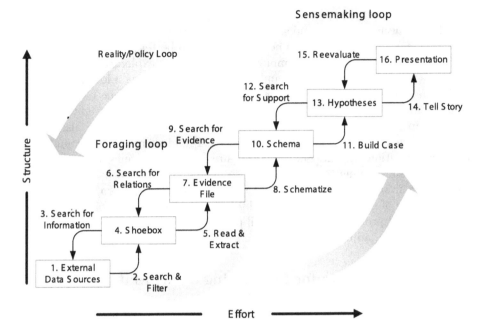

Fig. 1. The think loop model (adapted from [1] and reproduced from [17]). The process is divided into to loops: the foraging loop and sense-making loop.

Frames change as data is acquired (frames shape and define the relevant data, and data mandate that frames change in non-trivial ways, neither the data nor the frame comes first). Within this theory, sense-making involves two cycles: (1) elaborating a frame and (2) re-framing (questioning the frame and doubting the explanation it provides, leading us to reconsider and seek to replace it with a better one). Frames have similar functionality as the "schema" in the sense-making model by Bodnar [1] and Pirolli and Card [15].

Klein et al. examine in [9] the meaning of sense-making from three different perspectives: psychology, human centered computing and naturalistic decision-making. Although sense-making and situation awareness have been considered equivalent terms [10], Klein et al. [9] highlight a main difference between them. Situation awareness (as it is defined by Endsley [3]) is about the knowledge state that is achieved (knowledge of data elements, inferences drawn from the data, or predictions that can be made using these inferences). Sense-making is about the process of achieving these kinds of outcomes, the strategies and the barriers encountered.

Naturalistic decision-making theories explain how experts make complex decisions in real and dynamic environments. A large number of studies in this domain can be considered to describe a sense-making process. Some interesting outcomes for this paper are some assumptions about sense-making that have been proved wrong by naturalistic decision-making research. For example, human decision makers notice less emergent problems when they passively received automated interpretations [18] (referred as the "data fusion and auto-mated hypothesis generation aid sense-making" myth in [9]). In [13], the authors show that more information does not always lead to better sense-making.

Visual representations are commonly used for data exploration and analy-sis. Lately, visualization research, and of course, VA is paying a lot of attention to the evaluation of visualizations, and discussions regarding the real value of visualization are filling recent articles. Many authors consider "insight" as one of the main purposes of information visualization, even though they also agree that insight is not a well-understood concept [24] and there is not a commonly accepted definition [12]. In [24], the authors review previous information visual-ization literature trying to answer "how do people gain insight using visualiza-tion?" In their argumentation, they state that sense-making plays a major role in the procedure of gaining insight. Their literature review led to the identification of four types of processes through which people gain insight using visualization: provide overview, adjust, detect pattern and match mental model.

3   Visual Analytics for Supporting Sense-Making

Visual analytics has been defined as the science of analytical reasoning supported by visual interfaces [23]. As argued by Green and Maciejewski [4], this analytical reasoning can be divided into two types of analytics: computational analytics, performed by the computerized tools, and reasoning analytics, performed by the human analyst. Computational analytics is suitable for well-defined problems and can often be solved through algorithmic means, whereas reasoning analytics is required when solving ill-formed problems, where the knowledge and creativity of the analyst is vital for finding a solution. Reasoning analytics thus comprises how the analyst interprets the results from the computational analyses, i.e. how the analyst make sense of the data [4] which, in a visual analytics context, is enabled through visualization of and interaction with the computational bases and results. However, the human reasoning strategies involved can significantly vary where the analysts can follow strategies and heuristics such as trial and error, means-end analysis, satisficing, expected utility, abduction, induction and deduction (see [4,5] for more information).

As argued by Pohl et al. [16], users of VA systems usually do not develop elab-orate strategies in their minds before they start working, but react interactively to what is perceived on the screen. As such, investigating which information to present, how to present it, as well as performing careful analyses regarding how the VA system user is to interact with the information displayed is of vital importance for guiding the user in his/her individual reasoning process. Impor-tant is to consider the limited cognitive capabilities of the analyst to grasp the meaning of the computational analyses performed as well as to limit the risk of human biases. If overwhelmed with information, the analyst might choose to concentrate on only a limited set of the information available, possibly resulting in that important features are left undetected.

4   Method

To investigate how experts make sense of large amounts of data, we performed interviews with seven data analysts from the automotive industry in Sweden. This particular group of analysts were chosen due to the explosion of data collected from the automotive industry in the recent years and due to the lack of use of visual analytics tools. The purpose of our study was thus to investigate how the analysts work today to make sense of the data collected, as well how the implementation of a VA tool could support this sense-making process in this particular domain (also guiding the development of VA tools in this particular domain).

The participants worked at (or cooperated with) two of the largest industries in Sweden, Volvo Trucks and Scania, and had an average of 5,7 years of experience of analyzing data. They were all working with research and development issues within their respective companies, thus focusing on exploratory analyses of truck data in order to investigate different parameter effects on the driver behavior, causes of vehicle accidents, fuel consumption and maintenance needs of the vehicles. The semi-structured, individual interviews took about an hour to perform and were centered around five themes: data analysis problem statement, data preparation, data analysis, the tools used and their perceived needs for analyzing truck data in an efficient manner in the future. The following section depicts the results obtained from the interviews.

5   Results

5.1   Data Analysis Problem Statement

The interviewees all worked with research and development issues at their respective companies. Thus, the work conducted centered around exploratory analyses of the large amounts of heterogeneous data collected (both from databases and in a streaming fashion) from different sensors on the vehicles, documents from the vehicle workshops, weather and geographical data etc. Their daily work contained tasks such as hypotheses generation, collection of appropriate data sets to answer these hypotheses, data preparation and analysis, and hypotheses verification/rejection. However, one of the analysts argued that what to explore was also data-driven, meaning that also the data, and its quality, could determine which hypotheses that were generated. Three analysts explicitly stated that the data they are working with is quite unique and "one of a kind." They consider it significantly different from what state-of-the-art methods are typically tested on and developed for. At the same time, as a general rule the data is private and cannot be widely shared – which can be seen as an interesting challenge for the research community.

Every task within this process entails challenges for the analysts. As the work conducted is highly exploratory in its nature, and where there is no ground truth, it is very difficult for the analysts to know how to approach the problem, or if it even is possible. Which variables are likely to have an impact on the hypothesis?

What is the quality of the data that can be used to investigate the hypothesis? How can the phenomena to be explained best be modeled?

5.2 Data Preparation and Data Analysis

The analysts interviewed had access to several terabytes of data, containing various types of data. None of the analysts interviewed used all the available data in their analyses due to the lack of platforms for handling the amount of data, as well as that several variables in the data were deemed irrelevant for their analysis at hand. Instead, some of the analysts looked for interesting situations in the data, and used such smaller data sets during the analyses. Yet, to find such "interesting situations" could be very time-consuming, such as to find events in video logs of the vehicles without automatic support.

It was interesting to note the difference in opinions between analysts with regards to how big of a problem the necessity of doing initial analysis with a small subset of data was. In some cases this was deemed a serious issue that greatly increased the efforts involved in data analytics, since some results that were promising in such early study would later turn out to be invalid when tested on the whole data set. In other cases, it was considered a normal practice and only a minor burden, as the small subsets of data were found to be representative of the full population. There are several possible explanations for those discrepancies, and it will require further study to determine if they are related to the data analysis process, the task at hand, the experience of individual analysts, the properties of the data, or something else.

There was a noteworthy difference between the analysts working at vehicle manufacturing companies and those working in a professional analytics company. The latter described their main task as adapting the existing data analysis processes to the specific needs of individual customers. In a sense, they saw themselves as experts in data analysis and relied on domain specialists to define the goals. On the other hand, analysts employed in the automotive industry considered themselves more of domain experts. They rely on their own understanding of the subject matter in defining the tasks and evaluating the results.

The analysts in the study had to assess the quality of the data by manual means - often through selecting some small subset of the data and apply quick analyses of it to find outliers, missing values and/or noise. Errors in the data were often due to missing time-stamps and the loss of historical data due to electrical faults. One of the analysts in the study thought of this process as very ad-hoc and argued for the importance of performing continuous and iterative quality investigations of the data used. We also noticed several similarities and differences between the analysts here. Analysts often either said that they had problems with noise or with uncertainty, and did not make a clear distinction between them. We believe the lack of sufficiently good tools for managing big data was the reason as to why the analysis was done by selecting small batches of data instead of using all of the data.

A lot of work is put on pre-processing the data - one of the analysts expressed that *"the data is very, very noisy. Around 90 % of my work is about pre-processing the data"*. One obstacle was perceived as the unknown uncertainty in the data. For example, when trying to predict the need for component maintenance, the exact state of the component is not known since the only data available is historical and might include the workshop personnel's subjective options of the state of the component. The lack of ground truth was explicitly mentioned by four out of seven analysts. In addition, the lack of direct interactions with end users or receivers of the analytics results, was also common. This has lead to several analysts mentioning that evaluation of results they are obtaining is a challenge.

However, due to the unlimited access to data, one of the analysts argued that noisy data was not a hindrance in the analysis process, since just another data sample set, with better quality, could be used instead. A much greater problem was identified as investigating which variables, or combination of variables, that could have an impact on the hypothesis in focus as well as to create models that could appropriately explain the phenomena in the data. All the analysts were using different statistical, data mining and machine learning methods for regression, classification, clustering, outlier detection, etc.

5.3 Tools and Perceived Needs for the Future

None of the analysts interviewed used tools developed with the framework of visual analytics in mind. The analysts all used standard mathematical and programming tools to detect errors or noise in the data and where they could implement their models and make basic visualizations of the data. The most common tools were Matlab, R and Python, but there were also some who used C++ and Java. Few reported using commercial frameworks and tools such as Hadoop, SPSS or Spotfire and in some cases custom developed tools for their organization. All of the analysts interviewed developed their own scripts and used available tool-kits and libraries to speed up their analyses. In terms of visualizations, the analysts argued that these were only used for two purposes: to better understand the data and its quality, and to understand the computational results. However, one of them argued that he could be significantly aided in his analyses if visualizations could be used to show different views of the data, delimiting the risk for biases and misinterpretations.

When asked about their perceived needs for the future in terms of automatic support that could aid them in their reasoning process, three of the analysts argued for the importance of developing tools and platforms that could handle the increasing amounts of available data, such as data from databases, streaming data and video data. One of the analysts further argued that to be able, during run-time, to make alterations of the analysis performed could significantly decrease the amount of time needed to finish the analyses. Further, to be able to repeat the same pre-processing and analysis steps on a different data set would also decrease the time needed to perform analyses. An interesting observation was that it was common for analysts employed in automotive companies to make a different description of the challenges of the analysis. They tended to focus on that the challenge lies in the uncertain, incomplete or noisy data, i.e. specific properties of the data. The analysts in that worked in a professional analytics company described a challenge as whether they have the relevant data sources, i.e. a higher level perspective on the analysis.

6 Discussion

6.1 Making Sense of Data

As stated by Thomas and Cook [23], there are three tasks that an analyst may be asked to perform: analysis to understand the world and the past (assessment), forecasting and action projection. The analysts interviewed dealt with all of these tasks in order to explore their hypothesis. Although similar, the analysts all expressed their analysis process in different ways, highlighting individual differences and perceived challenges when it comes to reasoning. As such, a future VA tool should not only be adaptable to accommodate different types of data, models and tasks, but also to accommodate the possible individual preferences of the users, a fact which has also been highlighted by [8].

The analysts interviewed all tried to make sense of the data in exploratory ways, not knowing the quality of the computational and reasoning analyses carried out. To aid the analysts in this process, a reasoning tool could present different views of the data used and the results generated in order to, for example, increase the analysts' knowledge of the quality of the data as well as different representations of the results generated. Following the information seeking mantra: overview first, filter and details on demand [21], the analysts could be aided in their sense-making process, offering cognitive support.

To accommodate for the ever increasing amounts of data, support must be provided in order to understand which pre-processing is needed, which parameters are related, as well as to enable the analysts to adjust the computational reasoning carried out during run-time. As such, there is a need for developing effective means of integrating and fusing various types of data (i.e. video data, geographical data, text based data etc.). However, as one analyst concluded, there is a need for developing company internal analysis tools due to data security reasons and the lack of trust in commercial tools.

6.2 Visual and Interactive Support

The analysts in the study argued that visualization and interaction with the data and computational reasoning results only occurred in the data pre-processing stage when trying to understand the data to be used in the analysis, and in the computational results analysis phase, when trying to understand the results from the automatic reasoning. However, as argued by one of the interviewees, to be able to investigate the progressive computational reasoning during run-time could effectively improve the analysis carried out, especially when dealing with large amounts of data. This interaction capability is the core of the VA framework. However, as argued by Stolper et al. [22], this capability is threatened by the trends of the increasing amounts of data to be used in the analyses and the development of complex and computational expensive algorithms. These trends forces the user to spend a lot of time waiting to proceed in his/her reasoning process as well as to remember the choices made during the pre-processing and analysis phase in order to understand the results. This challenge has been outlined as one of the major challenges within the VA community, highlighting the need for progressive, incremental visualizations where partial, yet meaningful results from the running analyses processes are presented to the users [20].

6.3   Future Tool

Based on the results from the interviews, we argue that the analysts within the automotive industry could be efficiently supported by developing a reasoning tool enabling the analysts to analyze larger quantities of data, where different views of the data are appropriately presented to detect patterns and outliers and avoid human biases, and where the presentation of the incremental results generated during run-time could enable the analysts to guide the analysis process. Yet, due to the individual differences of the analysts, whose reasoning strategies can be strongly affected by the information presented to them, careful evaluations of such support system must be performed. Due to the implementation of the VA system, the specific user group, the data to be used and the models to be applied, a comprehensive set of evaluation tasks need to be performed in order to investigate if the tool supports the human analyst's reasoning carried out.

Many research papers present user evaluations of already implemented VA applications, such as Jigsaw [7] and CzSaw [6]. However, a few studies propose the execution of evaluative tasks earlier in the design process. For example, Green and Maciejewski [4] have suggested early laboratory studies and in situ evaluations of VA applications, such as field studies, case studies or ethnographics, to capture the reasoning situation of the users as a whole. Through such evaluations, it is possible to investigate how the users interact with the visualizations during the reasoning, as well as to see how reasoning informs the problem solving tasks at hand in the context of use. This view is also supported by Scholtz et al. [19], who argue that the development and evaluation process of VA applications should follow established VA guidelines and user studies, however, where much more work is needed to establish and evaluate easy-to-use and informative VA guidelines.

7   Conclusions and Future Work

In this paper, we have investigated how analysts from the automotive domain analyze large amounts of data in order to solve complicated tasks such as the predictive identification of the need for different kinds of vehicle repairs and how the fuel consumption of the vehicles can be decreased.

The analysts worked at "traditional" companies (i.e. not IT companies), where the tradition of using and analyzing large amounts of data is quite young. Focus is still on understanding the relationships in the data, and what to make out of it, making the analysis tasks conducted highly exploratory in their nature. The data used is highly uncertain and contains a lot of errors, making the data pre-processing part of the analyses very challenging and time-consuming.

One analyst concluded that the main challenge was not in the methods or tools, but in communicating the results to an immature organization. Due to the recent focus on analyzing data within this domain, there is no tradition of using VA tools for this purpose, but instead traditional analysis tools are used such as Matlab and R. However, a future need for tools that enables the analysts to handle large amounts of data, that can aid the analysts to early detect interesting parts of data sets, patterns and relationships among variables, and different views of the results generated was identified during the interviews.

Future work includes, as Green and Maciejewski [4] suggest, observations of the analysts in their working situation, enabling the extraction of more detailed analysis procedures and difficulties, shedding more light on the complete working situations of the analysts. Additional work further includes the implementation of a big data platform, aiding the analysts to analyze large amounts of heterogeneous data where intermediate results, the models used and the final results can be adjusted and interacted with. A first step could be to implement visual and interactive components of the current tools used and evaluate the impacts on the analysts' analysis performance.

Acknowledgment. This research has been conducted within the *A Big Data Analytics Framework for a Smart Society* (BIDAF 2014/32) project, supported by the Swedish Knowledge Foundation. We would like to thank the study participants for their valuable feedback.

References

1. Bodnar, J.W.: Making sense of massive data by hypothesis testing. In: International Conference on Intelligence Analysis, pp. 2–4 (2005)
2. Duffy, M.: Sensemaking in classroom conversations. In: Maso, I., Atkinson, P.A., Delamont, S., Verhoeven, J.C. (eds.) Openness in Research: The Tension between Self and Other, pp. 119–132. Van Gorcum, Assen (1995)
3. Endsley, M.R.: Toward a theory of situation awareness in dynamic systems. Hum. Factors J. Hum. Factors Ergon. Soc. **37**(1), 32–64 (1995)
4. Green, T.M., Maciejewski, R.: A role for reasoning in visual analytics. In: Proceedings of the 46th Hawaii International Conference on System Sciences (HICSS), pp. 1495–1504. IEEE (2013)
5. Green, T.M., Wakkary, R., Arias-Hernandez, R.: Expanding the scope: interaction design perspectives for visual analytics. In: Proceedings of the 44th Hawaii International Conference on System Sciences (HICSS), pp. 1–10. IEEE (2011)
6. Kadivar, N., Chen, V., Dunsmuir, D., Lee, E., Qian, C., Dill, J., Shaw, C., Woodbury, R.: Capturing and supporting the analysis process. In: IEEE Symposium on Visual Analytics Science and Technology (VAST), pp. 131–138. IEEE (2009)
7. Kang, Y., Stasko, J.: Examining the use of a visual analytics system for sensemaking tasks: case studies with domain experts. IEEE Trans. Vis. Comput. Graph. **18**(12), 2869–2878 (2012)

8. Keim, D.A., Kohlhammer, J., Ellis, G., Mansmann, F.: Mastering the Information Age: Solving Problems with Visual Analytics. Florian Mansmann, Goslar (2010)
9. Klein, G., Moon, B., Hoffman, R.R.: Making sense of sensemaking 1: alternative perspectives. IEEE Intell. Syst. **21**(4), 70–73 (2006)
10. Leedom, D.: Sensemaking Symposium. Technical report, Evidence Based Research. Inc., Technical Report prepared under contract for Office of Assistant Secretary of Defense for Command, Control, Communications & Intelligence (2001)
11. Makonin, S., McVeigh, D., Stuerzlinger, W., Tran, K., Popowich, F.: Mixed-initiative for big data: the intersection of human + visual analytics + prediction. In: Proceedings of the 49th Hawaii International Conference on System Sciences (HICSS-49) (2016)
12. North, C.: Toward measuring visualization insight. IEEE Comput. Graph. Appl. **26**(3), 6–9 (2006)
13. Omodei, M., Wearing, A., McLennan, J., Elliott, G., Clancy, J.: More is better? problems of self-regulation in naturalistic decision making settings. In: Brehmer, B., Lipshitz, R., Montgomery, H. (eds.) How Professionals Make Decisions, pp. 29–42. Lawrence Erlbaum Associates Inc., Mahwah (2005)
14. Pirolli, P.: Information Foraging Theory: Adaptive Interaction with Information. Oxford University Press, Oxford (2007)
15. Pirolli, P., Card, S.: The sensemaking process and leverage points for analyst technology as identified through cognitive task analysis. In: Proceedings of International Conference on Intelligence Analysis, vol. 5, pp. 2–4 (2005)
16. Pohl, M., Smuc, M., Mayr, E.: The user puzzle: explaining the interaction with visual analytics systems. IEEE Trans. Vis. Comput. Graph. **18**(12), 2908–2916 (2012)
17. Riveiro, M., Falkman, G., Ziemke, T., Kronhamn, T.: Reasoning about anomalies: a study of the analytical process of detecting and identifying anomalous behavior in maritime traffic data. In: Tolone, W., Ribarsky, W. (eds.) SPIE Defense, Security, and Sensing. Visual Analytics for Homeland Defense and Security, Orlando, FL, USA, vol. 7346 (2009)
18. Rudolph, J.: Into the big muddy and out again: error persistence and crisis management in the operating room. Ph.D. thesis, Boston College (2003)
19. Scholtz, J.: Developing guidelines for assessing visual analytics environments. Inf. Vis. **10**(3), 212–231 (2011)
20. Schulz, H.J., Angelini, M., Santucci, G., Schumann, H.: An enhanced visualization process model for incremental visualization. IEEE Trans. Vis. Comput. Graph. **PP**(99), 1 (2015)
21. Shneiderman, B.: The eyes have it: a task by data type taxonomy for information visualizations. In: Proceedings of the IEEE Symposium on Visual Languages, pp. 336–343. IEEE (1996)
22. Stolper, C.D., Perer, A., Gotz, D.: Progressive visual analytics: user-driven visual exploration of in-progress analytics. IEEE Trans. Vis. Comput. Graph. **20**(12), 1653–1662 (2014)
23. Thomas, J., Cook, K. (eds.): Illuminating the Path: The Research and Development Agenda for Visual Analytics. IEEE Computer Society, Los Alamentos (2005)
24. Yi, J.S., Kang, Y., Stasko, J.T., Jacko, J.A.: Understanding and characterizing insights: how do people gain insights using information visualization? In: Proceedings of the 2008 Workshop on Beyond Time and Errors: Novel Evaluation Methods for Information Visualization, p. 4. ACM (2008)

Towards More Practical Information Sharing in Disaster Situations

Masayuki Ihara[1]([✉]), Shunichi Seko[2], Akihiro Miyata[2],
Ryosuke Aoki[1], Tatsuro Ishida[3], Masahiro Watanabe[1],
Ryo Hashimoto[1], and Hiroshi Watanabe[1]

[1] NTT Service Evolution Laboratories, NTT Corporation, Yokosuka, Japan
{ihara.masayuki,aoki.ryosuke,watanabe.masahiro,
hashimoto.ryo,watanabe.hi}@lab.ntt.co.jp
[2] NTT Resonant, Inc., Tokyo, Japan
{shunichi,miyata-a}@nttr.co.jp
[3] NTT Plala, Inc., Tokyo, Japan
t-ishida@plala.co.jp

Abstract. This paper presents how to design a more practical information sharing service for disaster situations based on the requirements learned from many disaster experiences in Japan in the past. In designing technologies to be used in disaster situations, it is important to add resiliency that can handle changes in the situation. To provide more people with an information sharing service, the technologies should be independent of Internet availability and should work on many types of user devices. We develop and evaluate a resilient information sharing platform and some applications, all of which can work with Wi-Fi and a web browser. This paper also details the results of field experiments and describes the importance of the "service usability" concept in making those technologies truly practical.

Keywords: Disaster · Resilience · Information sharing · Mobile device · Digital signage

1 Introduction

In disaster situations, it is important to share "information" such as safety confirmation and public transportation notices. The East Japan Earthquake in 2011 disconnected the Internet in many areas by destroying facilities and/or flow control of the public communication network. A report on the earthquake noted that 78.5 % of evacuees carried their own mobile devices, and at the train stations in urban areas, many tried to get disaster information from digital signage displays.

This paper describes how to design a communication service for disaster situations by utilizing mobile devices and digital signage. The contribution of this work to HCI research is to provide use cases in the design, development, and testing of services for disaster situations and to provide other countries which will experience disasters with design principles for future services.

S. Yamamoto (Ed.): HIMI 2016, Part II, LNCS 9735, pp. 32–39, 2016.
DOI: 10.1007/978-3-319-40397-7_4

2 Web-Based Implementation

One problem with applications for disaster situations is that native applications cannot be downloaded if the Internet is disconnected. To support evacuation centers without Internet access, our multi-device collaboration technology realizes resilient information sharing that allows evacuees to share disaster information among devices with an HTML5 browser by connecting to a local Wi-Fi router and launching the browser. To support evacuees at the train station, our technology allows digital signage terminals to provide disaster information to evacuees' mobile devices via local Wi-Fi connections and any HTML5 browser. The advantage is that no software installation is needed, as our proposal is completely web-based using HTML5. Our web-based implementation brings the other advantage of ease in developing and maintaining the application regardless of the operating system. For example, we do not need to develop both Android versions and iOS versions.

3 Resilient Information Sharing

Technologies for use in disaster situations must be very resilient to support changes in the environment. For example, many people may enter and leave an evacuation center frequently. This means that the number of mobile devices connected to Wi-Fi in the evacuation center changes frequently. Our resilient information sharing platform (See Fig. 1) can accept such a situation as it uses a javascript-based decentralized

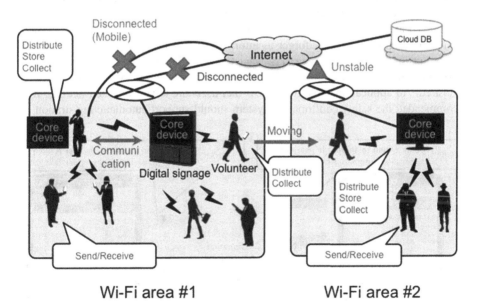

Fig. 1. Resilient information sharing platform. This can accept frequent device joining to or leaving as it uses a javascript-based decentralized cooperation control program on each device. A few core devices collect, store and distribute information from non-core devices. Human movement between Wi-Fi areas #1 and #2 enable information sharing.

cooperation control program on each device to collect, store, and distribute information among devices.

The resilient information sharing platform has a great advantage in terms of implementation. The system is available even if the Internet is disconnected. This is realized by using local Wi-Fi links and a delay tolerant network (DTN) technology, (most existing alternatives assume the existence or recovery of Internet connections [1, 2, 6]). The DTN technology uses the inter-center movement of humans to realize information sharing rather than Internet connections [3].

4 Applications

We developed three applications for disaster situations, all of which work on the resilient information sharing platform; safety confirmation, evacuation navigation and signage-smartphone collaboration.

4.1 Safety Confirmation

Safety confirmation is rated most important by evacuees [5]. Our safety confirmation application makes it possible to share safety confirmation information among evacuation centers using DTN. Evacuees can discover safety confirmation of family or friends without visiting many evacuation centers.

Figure 2 shows how our safety confirmation application works. According to the real use of some disaster-relief applications in the past disasters, users (i.e., sufferers in the affected area) are quite eager to take actions to know other's conditions (and their posting messages) while they forget to inform others of their own conditions, which people outside the affected area really want to know. To collect sufferers' conditions more efficiently in a confused situation, the automatic registration of user's conditions is desired. An application server can know that users are alive from their actions. It is recommended the safety confirmation system should support automatic registration of

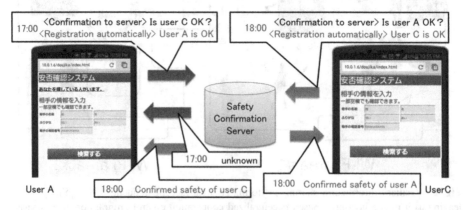

Fig. 2. Safety confirmation application. In this application, self-safety information will be sent to the server with the search query of the retrieval.

user's conditions in conjunction with user's other actions to the system and service. The actions that trigger automatic registration include retrieval of other user's messages. In this case, self-safety information will be sent to the server with the search query of the retrieval.

4.2 Evacuation Navigation

Evacuation is one of most important actions just after a disaster occurred [4]. Our evacuation navigation application uses collaborating digital signage terminals to provide the direction and distance to the nearest evacuation center (See Fig. 3). Evacuees can evacuate with a downloaded map to the nearest evacuation center and can know the updated information such as a change of the center to evacuate according to the changing disaster situation from a digital signage terminal in front of the shop as well as the information of distance and direction to the evacuation center.

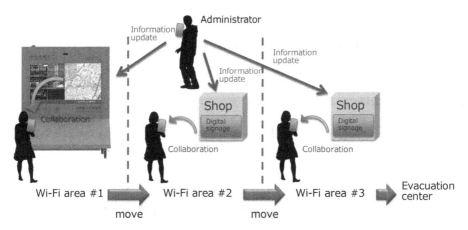

Fig. 3. Evacuation navigation application. Evacuees can evacuate with a navigation shown on each screen of digital signage displays. The navigation can change according to the changing disaster situation such as an evacuation center change.

4.3 Signage-Smartphone Collaboration

The signage-smartphone collaboration application makes it possible for evacuees to download information from digital signage terminals to their own smartphone interactively. For example, they can obtain a route to the nearest evacuation center from the current train station (See Fig. 4). This collaboration is achieved by real-time mutual communication (WebSocket/WebRTC) between a digital signage terminal and smartphones.

Fig. 4. Signage-smartphone collaboration. Evacuees can download a map or route to the nearest evacuation center via local Wi-Fi.

5 Experiments

To evaluate the feasibility of these three applications, we conducted experiments at a shopping arcade (See Figs. 5, 6, 7 and 8).

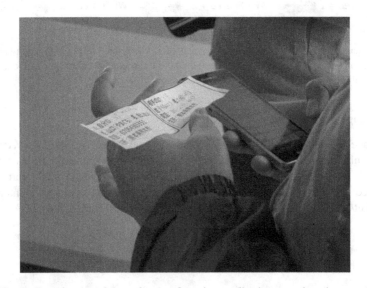

Fig. 5. Experiments of the safety confirmation application at a shopping arcade

Fig. 6. Experiments of the evacuation navigation application at a shopping arcade

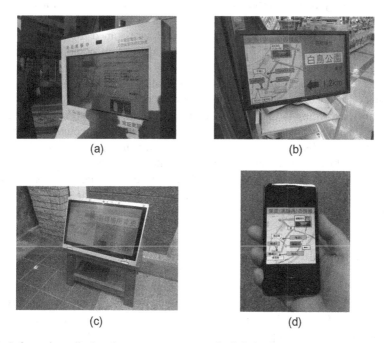

Fig. 7. Information displayed on many types of digital signage or a smartphone. (a): Downloadable information on a digital signage screen. (b): A distance and direction to the nearest evacuation center on a digital signage device in front of a shop. (c): Information of change of the center to evacuate. (d): A downloaded route map on a smartphone.

Fig. 8. Experiments of the signage-smartphone collaboration at a shopping arcade

About 100 subjects experienced our technology in each application and answered questionnaires about their experiences. Experiments of the safety confirmation application were conducted by many subject pairs under an assumed friend name which is written on the given sheet. As a result, 86 % of the subjects could confirm friend's safety and the rest failed due to a mistake in registration of his/her own name. In experiments of the evacuation navigation application, we confirmed that updated information of the change of center to evacuate was correctly displayed on each type of signage screen according to the given disaster scenario. A main part of experiments of the signage-smartphone collaboration was whether subjects could connect to Wi-Fi and download necessary disaster information onto their own smartphone or not. As a result, 90.5 % of the subjects could download the information by themselves for the first time and 96.2 % could do for the second time. These results were positive for our applications but three significant issues must be resolved to make the applications more practical.

6 Service Usability

We propose the novel concept "service usability" to make the applications more practical, which consists of service affordance, network connection usability, and intuitive user interface. Service affordance is critical in alerting users to the existence of the service because most people do not know that they can download information from a signage terminal to their own device. The network connection usability is essential as most people will give up if the Wi-Fi connection is difficult to make. The intuitive user interface is important since in a disaster situation many users will be novices. These three issues identify the importance of service usability as service usability includes more issues than simply those related to the interface.

7 Conclusion

The contribution of this report is to provide use cases of the development and field-testing of completely web-based communication technologies for disaster situations without any Internet connection. This paper presents the following four design principles for developing applications for disaster situations. Following them will yield applications that are truly practical.

- Utilize mobile devices and digital signage terminals
- Employ web-based implementation
- Match changes in the situations
- Improve usability as a total service

Future work includes improving the proposed technologies by applying the service usability concept.

Acknowledgements. This research is supported by the Ministry of Internal Affairs and Communications, Japan.

References

1. Frommberger, L., Schmid, F.: Mobile4D: crowdsourced disaster alerting and reporting. In: 6th International Conference on Information and Communications Technologies and Development: Notes, ICTD 2013, vol. 2, pp. 29–32. ACM, New York (2013)
2. MartíN-Campillo, A., Crowcroft, J., Yoneki, E., Martí, R.: Evaluating opportunistic networks in disaster scenarios. J. Netw. Comput. Appl. **36**(2), 870–880 (2013)
3. Reina, D.G., Askalani, M., Toral, S.L., Barrero, F., Asimakopoulou, E., Bessis, N.: A survey on multihop ad hoc networks for disaster response scenarios. J. Distrib. Sens. Netw. **2015**, 647037 (2015)
4. Song, X., Zhang, Q., Sekimoto, Y., Horanont, T., Ueyama, S., Shibasaki, R.: Modeling and probabilistic reasoning of population evacuation during large-scale disaster. In: 19th ACM SIGKDD International Conference on Knowledge Discovery and Data Mining, Chicago, IL, pp. 11–14, August 2013
5. Yuze, H., Qian, Y., Suzuki, N.: Development of smartphone application for off-line use in case of disaster. In: 27th International Conference on Advanced Information Networking and Applications Workshops, pp. 243–248. IEEE Computer Society. Washington, D.C. (2013)
6. Yuze, H., Nabeta, S., Izumi, M.: Light-weight safety confirmation system for large-scale disasters. In: 28th International Conference on Advanced Information Networking and Applications Workshops, pp. 588–592. IEEE Computer Society, Washington, D.C. (2014)

Prototype of Decision Support Based on Estimation of Group Status Using Conversation Analysis

Susumu Kono[1]([✉]) and Kenro Aihara[1,2]

[1] SOKENDAI (The Graduate University for Advanced Studies),
Tokyo, Japan
{su-kono,kenro.aihara}@nii.ac.jp
[2] National Institute of Informatics,
2-1-2 Hitotsubashi, Chiyoda-ku, Tokyo 101-8430, Japan

Abstract. We propose a prototype for a system to verify the decision support of a group based on estimations of group status through utterance analysis.

Based on methods used in prior studies of group dynamics and utterance analysis, we measured the utterance characteristics of group members to infer group status; moreover, we aimed to enhance the overall condition of the group by providing appropriate reference information in a timely manner through a conversational agent system. The goal of this system was a more satisfying decision-making process.

We manufactured a prototype system to verify both the operations involved in the test case and the ability to infer group classification and status according to group dynamics.

Our proposed method was appropriate based on the prototype system. Future work will focus on optimizing the logic and system functions of group status estimation and the subsequent step of informing the group.

Keywords: Conversation estimation · Group status estimation · Utterance feature · Conversational agent · Intention extraction

1 Introduction

1.1 Object

Our objective is to clarify the effectiveness of estimating the classification and status of a group by measuring the utterance characteristics of the group members. In particular, we aim to explore the possibility of identifying all utterances in a conversation using the extracted intention of some words in utterances and time course information at the first step.

Then, we will explore the possibility of estimating connections of utterances and relationships between participants in the conversation using this information and replacing any missing information with utterance characteristics. The relationships between participants that are revealed will be applied for estimating the classification and status of a group at the next step.

© Springer International Publishing Switzerland 2016
S. Yamamoto (Ed.): HIMI 2016, Part II, LNCS 9735, pp. 40–49, 2016.
DOI: 10.1007/978-3-319-40397-7_5

1.2   Background and Motivations

In group decision-making, some members may hesitate or yield their position to superiors, or they may offer no concrete ideas or suggestions, and thus these members may feel frustration in such situations. Group members who are in a weak position may not be as confident, and thus cannot clearly declare their intentions, while members who hold a position of power in the group can confidently and clearly declare their intentions.

Therefore, our motivation for this study was to solve this problem by using speech recognition and the extraction of intentions based on a group dynamics approach. We also aim to lead the overall group to a good situation by providing appropriate reference information and suggestions in a timely manner using status estimations based on a group dynamics approach.

2   Related Work

2.1   Group Dynamics

We define a *group* as an aggregate of individuals who have frequent interaction, mutual influence, common feelings of camaraderie, and work together to achieve a common goal. We define a *member* as an individual who joins a group.

Group dynamics refers to a system of behaviors and psychologically influential interpersonal processes that takes place both within social groups (intragroup dynamics) and between social groups (intergroup dynamics) [4].

Here we focus on the former aspect of group dynamics, and in particular we apply intragroup dynamics approaches to the estimation of the decision-making behavior of small groups through conversation. In prior group dynamics studies, it has been shown that the characteristics of each group vary based on its classification and status, even in relation to decision-making among members [3,4,6,8,9].

2.2   Group Decision-Making

Group decision support systems using electronic communication and other computing methods have already been investigated in previous research [2]; however, our study focuses on the actual speech used in group conversations, and how group decision-making can be supported mechanically by the provision of information or suggestions through a conversational agent system.

2.3   Utterance Analysis

We define an *utterance* as the smallest unit of speech of spoken language, that is, a continuous piece of speech beginning and ending with a pause, *speech* as the vocal form of human communication, *conversation* as a form of interactive, spontaneous communication between two or more people, typically occurring

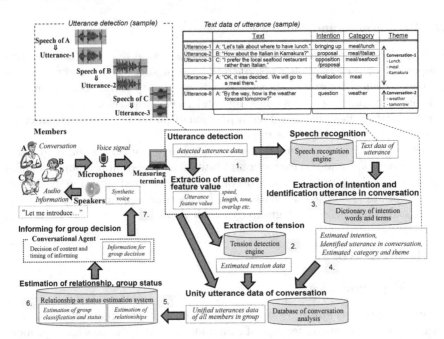

Fig. 1. Processes of group status estimation and provision of group decision-making. *Numbers 1 to 7 refer to the descriptions provided in the main text.*

in spoken communication, and a *conversational agent* as a computer system intended to converse with humans.

Utterance feature values such as the spectrum of utterance power levels have been used for estimation of the status and the tension of members in previous research [1]. *Tension* is defined as mental manifestations of physiological responses in this paper.

We define *intention in spoken dialogue* as a plan or an expectation in a speaker's mind to do something that has been mentioned in their speech, and it can be estimated by comparing the text data between speech recognition results and spontaneous dialogue corpora. Methods of intention extraction in spoken dialogue utterances have been established by prior research [5].

3   Methodology

The methodology we use here, which is based on real-time reactions to speech and its responses, is not new, as noted in related work. However, our proposed method aims to go beyond previous work and recognize the group status to find the most appropriate answers; that is, it does not simply provide answers to speech.

3.1   Extraction of Intentions in Utterances

1. Voice signal monitoring and utterance detection
   First, each member's voice signals are monitored and differentiated from the voices of other members and background noise. Then, the voice signals are segmented one by one, and the utterance feature values are extracted from the dialogues (Fig. 1-1).
2. Extraction of intentions and tension of utterances in a conversation
   Each utterance in speech is recognized, and its content is converted to text. Then, the speed of the utterance (mora/msec) is calculated using the speech recognition results. After the speech recognition process, "subject (theme)" (e.g., the place to eat lunch, the gift to buy in the shopping mall), "category" (e.g., meal, shopping), "sentence style" (e.g., positive, negative, interrogative), "intention" (e.g., proposal, question, agreement, opposition), and "expected action" (e.g., decision on where to have lunch, searching the shop to buy gifts) are extracted by comparing the text data from the speech recognition results and spontaneous dialogue corpora data (Fig. 1-3). Examples of utterance feature values and text data for group status estimation is shown in Fig. 2. The tension levels are also extracted by a calculation using the extracted utterance feature values (Fig. 1-2).
3. Estimation of relationships among members and classification and status of the group
   Then, by extracting the content of the utterances between group members in step 2, we can also estimate the relationships among those members (Fig. 1-5). These data also serve as reference information for the estimation of the classification and status of the group (Fig. 1-6). Sample data showing the relationships among group members are shown in Fig. 6.

3.2   Decision Support Based on Group Status

We proposed an approach to enhance the overall group condition through the intervention of a conversational agent system using a synthetic voice at an appropriate time based on the group's estimated classification and status as shown in Sect. 3.1. We hypothesize that this intervention will lead to more satisfactory decision-making results. Our proposed intervention examples for the various group classifications are as follows. The agent provides information to a target member through the influencer like a facilitator in conversations, if such an influencer exists. Otherwise, the agent provides the information to a target member directly, if no such influencer exists.

1. High intimacy and flat relationship group
   The members of this group classification are assumed to share their opinions frankly. For example, it can be determined whether the members have any specific ideas or requests, and then the conversational agent can provide detailed information based on the situation of each member.

Input	Extracted items	Items for estimation of relationship between members	Items for estimation of group status	Items for estimation of group classification
Voice signal of utterance 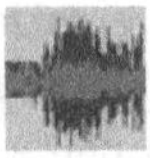	**Utterance feature value** -tone -speed -power level -length -times -overlaps ⇓ **Tension** -in positive reply -in negative reply etc.	-strength of connection and intimacy -existence of hesitating -hierarchical relationship	-existence of leader -existence of elders -existence of subgroup -satisfactions for decision	-level of intimacy -existence of flat connections -existence of hierarchy
Text data of utterance *"Thank you..."*	-intension -theme, category -polite word -instruction word -childish word	-parent-child relationship in each link	-frequency of speech in a group	

Fig. 2. Examples of utterance feature values and text data for group status estimation.

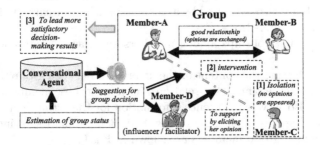

Fig. 3. Group intervention in our proposed model.

2. High intimacy and hierarchical relationship group

   This group classification assumes that an older member has the leadership role and knows the views of each member. For example, the dialogue may start with the conversational agent asking the older member what kind of information is preferred by all the members. Then, the conversational agent can provide the appropriate information.

3. Low intimacy and hierarchical relationship group

   This group classification assumes that the older member controls the group and junior members may be hesitant to express their feeling directly. It identifies members in a weak position, for example, those who experience isolation from other members, and aims to support such members by eliciting their opinions using appropriate reference information or suggestions (Fig. 3).

   We consider applying this logic of supporting the group decision-making process (e.g., destination, venue) while traveling in a car as a test case. We aim to lead the group to higher overall satisfaction by providing appropriate reference information and suggestions in the discussion prior to a group decision through the conversational agent system using the estimated classification and status of the group.

In our proposal, we focused on supporting members in the weak position mentioned above rather than those in the strong position in the discussion [7]. The procedure uses voice signal monitoring to infer the status of the group and determine the provision of information (Fig. 1-7).

Then, we assume that the connections of utterances and relationships between participants in the conversation can be estimated using the above information and replacing any missing information with utterance characteristics (Fig. 1-5). We prepared a method of visualizing the utterance statuses for the purpose of verification, as shown in Fig. 4.

Then, we inferred the classification and status of the group by measuring the utterance characteristics of members in group, and provided information and suggestions based on an estimation of the group's status (Fig. 1-6).

3.3 Prototype System Configuration

We manufactured a prototype system to verify the operations and methods used in the abovementioned test case in which the group members discuss decisions to be made while traveling in a car. The system configuration of the prototype is shown in Fig. 5. This prototype is composed of three functional parts: (1) utterance measurement, (2) group status and decision estimation, and (3) provision of information for group enhancement.

4   Preliminary Experiment

The prototype system was developed, and the basic operation of the system was tested using analysis of utterances and estimations of relationships between members in conversations during preliminary experiment. We have not prepared the appropriate noise reduction system for a car as yet, thus we implemented the test in a conference room, which was hardly affected by noise at all. In the next step, we will prepare the appropriate noise reduction system and implement the test in a car.

We analyzed four kinds of test dialogues with a three-member group (Group A: age 30–55, all males) and a two-member group (Group B: age 25–49, both males) in April 2015. These dialogues each lasted for approximately 5 min, and we processed these test dialogues using the prototype system. The themes of the test dialogues were a sports event and a sight-seeing tour in Tokyo for Group A, and a summer festival and a party for Group B. The results of the preliminary experiment are shown below.

1. Speech recognition of words for extraction of intention
   Speech recognition was 78 % on average, as shown in Table 1. This is not a particularly high percentage, but it is sufficient to extract the intention of almost all conversations.

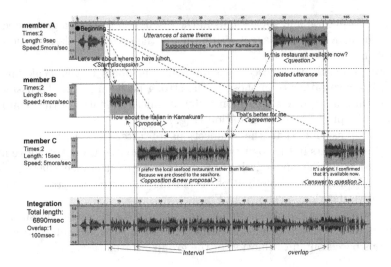

Fig. 4. Image of visualized utterance for verification.

Table 1. Results of the preliminary experiment.

Conversation #	Group name	Numbers of utterances	Recognized utterances including target words (value, rate)	Extraction of utterances (value, rate)	Extraction of utterances in conversation (value, rate)
1	A	74	19/29 65.5 %	19/69 27.5 %	69/69 100.0 %
2	A	70	20/25 80.0 %	20/65 30.88 %	65/65 100.0 %
3	B	47	18/21 85.7 %	18/45 40.0 %	45/45 100.0 %
4	B	65	21/25 84.0 %	21/61 34.4 %	61/61 100.0 %
Average	–	64	78.0 %	32.5 %	100.0 %

2. Extraction of intention of utterance
   The intention of utterance could be extracted in only 32 % of all utterances as shown in Table 1. However, we could identify all utterances in conversation through the extraction of intention and time course information. It is necessary to increase the number of words in the dictionary for more appropriate extraction of intention.
3. Extraction of the utterance feature values
   It was quite successful, and we could calculate the strength of the tension using these utterance feature values. We confirmed that the strength of the tension was correctly estimated through human monitoring, excluding any utterances that did not have sufficient length or power to judge the tension.
4. Estimation of group classification and status
   The status of utterances between members in a test conversation is shown in Table 2, and the connections between members is shown in Fig. 6. The group classification and status could also be estimated using these estimated

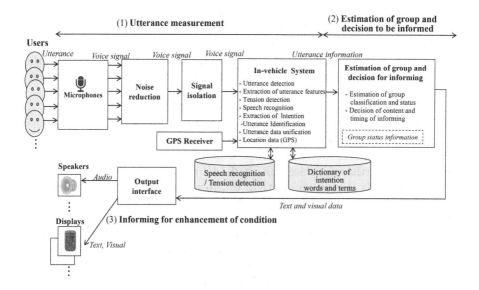

Fig. 5. System configuration of prototype.

Table 2. Status of utterances between members in a test conversation.

Link no.	Utterance direction	Numbers of utterances	(Details of intentions)
1, 5, 7, 9	A → B, C, D, E	14	(question:10, proposal:1 etc.)
2, 3, 4, 8	B → A, C, D, E	4	(proposal:4)
2	B → A	1	(agreement:1)
10	C → A	5	(negation:3, agreement:1 etc.)
6	D → A	2	(agreement:1 etc.)
11	E → A	8	(agreement:2)

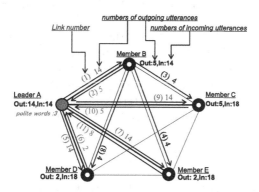

Fig. 6. Connections between members in a test conversation.

relationships and connections and the collected data (e.g., utterance feature values, intention, strength of tension).

While the degree of agreement between the estimated group status and the real group status remains insufficient, we plan to further optimize this procedure by testing using many additional kinds of utterance data in future experiments.

5. Judgment of contents and timing of provision of information

We did not implement the function of informing members in this preliminary experiment. However, we confirmed that extraction of utterance data for judgment of contents and timing of provision of information is possible. We plan to further optimize this method by continued testing with many additional kinds of utterance data in future work.

6. Degree of Satisfaction with Decision-Making Conversation

We aimed to measure the index of satisfaction in decision-making conversation by understanding how members express their own opinions, how those opinions are discussed with other members, and how the final group decision is reached. We obtained this index of satisfaction by extracting the intention of utterances at the current stage. For example, the intention was calculated using the number of times keywords were expressed in an individual's opinions. However, merely extracting keywords from each utterance is not enough for the accurate estimation of satisfaction, thus we will continue to study the proposed method.

5   Conclusion

In this paper, we proposed a system to infer the classification and status of groups by measuring the utterance characteristics of the group members, and to enhance the overall group condition through a conversational agent system based on estimations of group dynamics.

The basic availability of our proposed method to measure the utterance characteristics of group members was confirmed by our prototype system in our preliminary test. In future work, we will further optimize the logistical and system functions for estimating group status and the continuous provision of information to the group members.

We will also proceed to further verify the details of our method and system through continuous field tests, and we hope to verify the ability to increase the group members' satisfaction with the group's decision-making process through the use of our proposed conversational agent. Specifically, in our future work, we will collect many additional kinds of utterance-test data and further clarify the appropriate parameters for estimation and information provision using machine learning.

References

1. Ariga, M., Yano, Y., Doki, S., Okuma, S.: Mental tension detection in the speech based on physiological monitoring. In: IEEE International Conference on Systems, Man and Cybernetics, ISIC, pp. 2022–2027. IEEE (2007)

2. Desanctis, G., Gallupe, R.B.: A foundation for the study of group decision support systems. Manag. Sci. **33**(5), 589–609 (1987)
3. Deutsch, M., Gerard, H.B.: A study of normative and informational social influences upon individual judgment. J. Abnorm. Soc. Psychol. **51**(3), 629 (1955)
4. Forsyth, D.: Group dynamics. Cengage Learning (2009)
5. Hodjat, B., Amamiya, M.: Applying the adaptive agent oriented software architecture to the parsing of context sensitive grammars. IEICE Trans. Inf. Syst. **83**(5), 1142–1152 (2000)
6. Hogg, M.A., Tindale, S.: Blackwell Handbook of Social Psychology: Group Processes. Wiley, New York (2008)
7. Kono, S., Aihara, K.: A model of decision support based on estimation of group status by using conversation analysis. In: Stephanidis, C., Tino, A. (eds.) HCII 2015 Posters. CCIS, vol. 528, pp. 627–632. Springer, Heidelberg (2015). doi:10.1007/978-3-319-21380-4_106
8. Kelley, H., Thibaut, J.: Interpersonal Relations: A Theory of Interdependence. Wiley, New York (1978)
9. Lickel, B., Hamilton, D.L., Wieczorkowska, G., Lewis, A., Sherman, S.J., Uhles, A.N.: Varieties of groups and the perception of group entitativity. J. Pers. Soc. Psychol. **78**(2), 223 (2000)

Preventing Incorrect Opinion Sharing with Weighted Relationship Among Agents

Rei Saito[1(✉)], Masaya Nakata[1], Hiroyuki Sato[1], Tim Kovacs[2], and Keiki Takadama[1]

[1] The University of Electro-Communications, Chofu, Japan
{r.saito,m.nakata}@cas.hc.uec.ac.jp,
sato@hc.uec.ac.jp, keiki@inf.uec.ac.jp
[2] The University of Bristol, Bristol, UK
Tim.Kovacs@bristol.ac.uk

Abstract. This paper aims at investigating how correct or incorrect opinions are shared among the agents in the weighted network where the relationship among the agent (as nodes of its network) is different each other, and exploring how the agents can be promoted to share only correct opinions by preventing to acquire the incorrect opinions in the weighted network. For this purpose, this paper focuses on Autonomous Adaptive Tuning algorithm (AAT) which can improve an accuracy of correct opinion shared among agents in the various network, and improves it to address the situation which is close in the real world, i.e., the relationship among agents is different each other. This is because the original AAT does not consider such a different relationship among the agents. Through the intensive empirical experiments, the following implications have been revealed: (1) the accuracy of the correct opinion sharing with the improved AAT is higher than that with the original AAT in the weighted network; (2) the agents in the improved AAT can prevent to acquire incorrect opinion sharing in the weighted network, while those in the original AAT are hard to prevent in the same network.

Keywords: Multi agent system · Community computing · Learning communities

1 Introduction

In our society people sometimes communicate with the others in order to form their own opinions. They collect information of others, decide which information can be useful to make their opinions, and then form their opinions. For this issue, Gilinton proposed Opinion sharing model [1] as a multi-agent model to simulate such a decision making process. Since opinion sharing model focus on communication among people in the real world situations, this model regards the agents as people that communicate with the others in order to form their own opinions. Since this model aims at capturing the dynamics of opinion sharing in the decision-making process through communication among people, the agents have a simple style. In this model, a very limited number of agents in a community receive the correct information from an environment,

© Springer International Publishing Switzerland 2016
S. Yamamoto (Ed.): HIMI 2016, Part II, LNCS 9735, pp. 50–62, 2016.
DOI: 10.1007/978-3-319-40397-7_6

while most of the agents can-not; then the agents convey their opinions after forming them, while the other agents who receive the opinions from neighbors formed their opinions; the neighbor agents also convey it, which results in spreading out the opinions. What should be noted here is that the received opinions can be not only correct but also incorrect which derives the community of agents that wrongly share the incorrect opinions. To promote the agents to form the correct opinions by conveying their opinions including correct and incorrect ones, Pryymak proposed Autonomous Adaptive Tuning (AAT) algorithm [2]. The AAT algorithm can improve the accuracy of the correct opinion sharing in the various scale networks even including the incorrect opinions. However, this algorithm does not focus on the situation which is close real world, i.e., the weighted network where the relationship among the agent (as nodes of its net-work) is different each other. Such a situation should be considered because people in our society, have relationships such as kindness, trust, social standing or family, and most of them believe the opinions of others according to the relationships with others. To cope with such a relationship, this paper modifies the original AAT to propose the improved AAT which promotes the agents to form the opinions considering the relationships of neighbor agents connected to them. By employing the improved AAT, this paper aims at investigating how the relationships can help us (or the agents) to share the correct opinions. In this paper, the relationships among the agents are implemented by the weighted network where the weights give an influence to the decision making process of the agents. To investigate the effectiveness of the improved AAT, this paper compares an accuracy of the correct opinion sharing with the improved AAT with that with the original AAT in the weighted network.

This paper is organized as follows. Section 2 starts to explain the details of the opinion sharing model, and Sect. 3 describes the AAT algorithm. Section 4 proposes the improved AAT, and the experimental results are discussed in Sect. 5. Finally, our conclusion is given in Sect. 6.

2 Opinion Sharing Model

In this section, we describe in detail *Opinion Sharing model* for multi agent model (Glinton et al. [1]). Opinion Sharing was formulated to capture dynamics of the decision making process which cooperating agents have in network. In this model, there are the agents can share their opinion by communicating with neighbors. In addition, some agents have noisy sensors that can only receive information which is related to environment. All agents aim to form the correct opinion by information from sensors and neighbors' opinions. As a result, the opinions of almost agents are unified correctly.

The agents aim for propagating the correct opinions in the following limitations [1]:

- The only few agents which have sensors in the network can observe environment.
- The observations of the agents which have sensors may form incorrect opinions since the sensors receive incorrect information.
- The agents can communicate with only their neighbors, while the agents compose network.

2.1 Overview of the Opinion Sharing Model

In this model, the network $G(A, E)$ consists of a large set of agents $A = \{i^l : l \in 1 \cdots N\}, N \gg 100$ connected by E (set of edges). Each agent $i \in A$ can only communicate with their neighbors $D_i = \{j : \exists (i, j) \in E\}$. The average number of neighbors is defined as the degree $d = \sum_{i \in A} |D_i|/N$. The network is sparse because the degree is small number for all agents size, which $d \ll N$. The state of environment is either of value, for example $B = \{\text{correct, incorrect}\}$, where $b \in B$. The B following the argument that a binary choice can be applied to wide range of real world situations is supported by the paper [1]. The aim of the community which is comprised of every agent is to find the true state b where observed by some agents which have sensor. The aim of each agent is to form the opinion o_i that is the real state of environment, such that $o_i = b$. Each agent form its opinion by relying on their neighbors' opinions. Then agents which have noisy sensor also rely on the sensor. In order to decide the own opinion, the agent need to have its private belief $P_i(b = \text{correct})$. P_i corresponds the probability of b = correct (further denoted as P_i) and consequently $1 - P_i$ corresponds the probability of $b = \text{correct}$. The agents' belief is updated starting from some initial prior P_i'' and the ongoing belief is defined as P_i^k, where k is the current step of update sequence for belief. Only some agents in the network $S \subset A, |S| \ll N$ have noisy sensors and can observe the state b of the environment. Those agents are defined as sensor agents. Each sensor agent $i \in S$ periodically reserves an observation $s_i \in B$ that is low accuracy r $(0.5 < r \le 1)$. To incorporate observations from sensors, the agent use formal updating based on Bayes' theorem [1]:

$$P_i^k = \frac{c_{upd} P_i^k}{(1 - c_{upd})(1 - P_i^k) + c_{upd} P_i^k} \tag{1}$$

$$\text{where} \begin{cases} c_{upd} = r & \text{if } s_j = \text{correct} \\ c_{upd} = 1 - r_i & \text{if } s_j = \text{incorrect} \end{cases}$$

The agents may be confident the opinions with updating its belief and forms these opinions about the true state b of environment. Forming own opinions of the agents follow the opinion update rule about its private belief P_i^k. It dose that its belief P_i^k exceeds thresholds:

$$o_i^k = \begin{cases} \text{undeter., initial, if } k = 0 \\ \text{correct, if } P_i^k \le \sigma \\ \text{incorrect, if } P_i^k \le 1 - \sigma \\ o_i^{k-1} \text{ otherwise} \end{cases} \tag{2}$$

Thresholds $\{1 - \sigma, \sigma\}$ are the confidence bounds, and the range is $0.5 < \sigma < 1$. The Fig. 1 indicates the function of updating opinion has sharp hysteresis loop, Pryymak et al. [2].

If new observation support opposed state, the agents may change its opinion because received opinions may be incorrect.

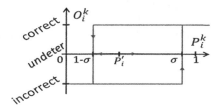

Fig. 1. The update rule of the opinion

The agents send new opinions to their neighbors only when they change own opinion. Subsequently, neighbors update their own beliefs and form their own opinions. To receive their neighbors' opinions, the agents use formal updating that is similar to sensor. When the agents receive new opinions from their neighbors $\{o_j : j \in D_j\}$, they uses the same belief update rule for each opinion o_j:

$$\text{where} \begin{cases} c_{upd} = t_i & \text{if } o_j = \text{white} \\ c_{upd} = 1 - t_i & \text{if } o_j = \text{black} \end{cases} \tag{3}$$

where $t_i \in [0, 1]$ is defined as the importance level. This is the measure of influence of neighbors' opinion, and it is conditional probability. The importance level is collateral to the accuracy such that Eq. 1. However, unlike the accuracy of sensor r, each agent must find own importance level t_i because it is unknown. We describe off algorithm that select t_i in Sect. 3. With regard to the importance level t_i, the agents should consider only its range $t_i \in [0.5, 1]$. When $t_i = 0.5$ indicates, the agents ignore the received opinions. On the other hand, when $t_i = 1$ indicates, the agent changes the own belief to $P_i^k = \{1, 0\}$ regardless of its previous value P_i^{k-1}.

In the model, there is possibility of converging false state. Accordingly, the agents are identified with theses neighbors in themselves. In regard to this model, we consider that the agents are not equated with these neighbors since it may be quite natural.

2.2   Performance Metrics of the Model

The model is simulated until rounds $M = \{m_l : l \in 1 \cdots |M|\}$. Every round, the new true state $b^m \in B$ of environment is selected randomly. At the end of each round m_l, the conclusive opinions are observed. Each round is limited by the enough step which the agents converge the own opinion. When each round finishes, the current true state expires. After the new round start, the agents reset their opinion and belief.

In order to measure the average accuracy of the agents' opinions at the end of each round, Glinton et al. proposed the proportion of the agent numbers that form correct opinion in the community is accuracy metric.

$$R = \frac{1}{N|M|} \sum_{i \in A} |\{m \in M : o_i^m = b^m\}| \cdot 100\% \tag{4}$$

Furthermore, [2] proposed performance index for single agent. When its opinion is formed correctly, the agent can't perceive. Therefore, the agents should be conscious of how often own opinion is formed correctly. Pryymak et al. denote it as an agent's awareness rate h_i [2].

$$h_i = \frac{|\{m \in M : o_i \neq \text{undeter.}\}|}{|M|} \tag{5}$$

This myopic metric can be calculated locally by each agent and it is important metric for AAT algorithm that is descripted in Sect. 3.

3 Autonomous Adaptive Tuning (AAT) Algorithm

In this section, we explain Autonomous Adaptive Tuning (AAT) algorithm. The algorithm is designed for improving the accuracy R by communicating the agents' opinions each other in the various complex network. In this algorithm, the agents automatically update these belief relying on only the local information. Especially, this algorithm is based on the observation as follows. The accuracy R increases when the dynamics of the opinion sharing is in phase change between the stable state (when the opinions are not shared out in the community $\forall i \in A: h_i \lll 1$) and an unstable one (when the opinions are propagated on a large scale $h_i = 1$). Accordingly, it is necessary that the agents share each opinion in smaller groups before large cascade occurs without reacting to the incorrect opinions in surplus. In order to set optimum parameter of the issue, this algorithm regulates importance level of the agents severally.

This algorithm has three stages for tuning that.

- The each agent running AAT has candidates of the importance level to reducing the search space for the following stages. This step runs only one at the first time of the experiment.
- After each dissemination round, the agent estimates the awareness rates of the candidate levels that are described in Sect. 2.2.
- The agents select the importance level by estimated the awareness rates of the candidate levels for next round. Then the agents consider how close it is to the target awareness rates. It is necessary that the importance levels are tuned gradually while considering an influence of own neighbors.

In the following sections, we describe three stages of AAT algorithm in detail.

3.1 Candidate Importance Levels

In this section, we describe how the agent running AAT estimates the candidates of importance levels T_i. By estimating the set of candidate importance levels, the agent reduces the continuous problem of selecting an importance level to use t_i from the consecutive values with the range [0.5, 1].

Through the number of sensor is much smaller than the total number of agents, we focus on the agents that update their belief using only neighbors' opinions without sensors. Pryymak et al. describe the sample dynamics of the agent's belief, where the agent i has the opinion of black change it after receiving more white opinions [2]. Starting from its prior P_i' (black), the agent update own opinion 'white', because of an increase of belief after receiving the 'white' opinion continuously. The most important point of this dynamics is the update step that the agent changes its opinion newly, because it is only time the agent sends new opinion with its neighbors. Consequently, we focus on how many times the agent update its belief until changing the own opinion.

According to the opinion update rule in Sect. 2.1, we consider the case when the agent's belief match one of the confidence bounds $P_i^k \in \{\sigma, 1 - \sigma\}$. If we consider that the maximum number of opinions that the agent can receive is limited to the number of its neighbors, $|D_i|$, we can pare down the candidate importance levels. The agent should find the importance levels as its belief coincides with one of the confidence bound $P_i^l \in \{\sigma, 1 - \sigma\}$ in $l \in 1 \cdots |D_i|$ updates (see Eq. 3). After solving this problem, the agent can get set of the candidate of importance levels that lead to opinion formation by receiving $1 \cdots |D_i|$ opinions.

$$T_i = \{t_i^l : P_i^l(t_i^l) = \sigma, l \in 1 \cdots |D_i|\} \cup \{t_i^l : P_i^l(t_i^l) = 1 - \sigma, l \in 1 \cdots |D_i|\} \quad (6)$$

Consequently, the set of candidate importance levels is limited to twice the number of neighbors, $|T_i| = 2|D_i|$. This is the necessary and sufficient set of candidate importance levels in which the agent forms an opinion after different update steps and it should be initialized only once.

After this stage, the agent has to estimate the most optimal importance level from its set of candidate importance levels.

3.2 Estimation of the Agent's Awareness Rates

In this section, we describe criterions of selection the importance levels from candidates. As mentioned above, AAT algorithm is based on observation as follows, the accuracy R of the community improved when the opinion sharing dynamics is in a phase transition between stable state and unstable one. In order to estimate such optimal parameters, the agents have to procure the minimal importance levels to form their opinion.

In the opinion sharing model, there are two terms, such that in order to maximize the accuracy R.

- Each agent has to form its opinion. Consequently, each agent should reach a high level of its awareness rate h_i, because the agents without determined opinions drop in the accuracy of the community.
- Each agent has to form an opinion as late as possible with only local view, after the agent gathers the maximum number of neighbors' opinions.

To satisfy these terms, the agent has to select the minimal importance level $t_i^l \in T_i$ from the candidates, such that it can form its opinion ($h_i = 1$).

However, since sensors observe the value influenced by random noise, the dynamics of opinion sharing like phase transition behaves stochastically. The agents cannot form their opinion until the opinions are shared on the large scale, suffered by their awareness rates. The agents should select the minimal importance level, t_i^l, from the candidates T_i. Then the awareness rate imitates the target awareness rate h_{trg}. The target awareness rate is slightly lower than maximum, $h_i = 1$.

The each agent solves the following optimization problem:

$$T_i = argmin_{t_i^l \in T_i} \left| h_i(t_i^l) - h_{trg} \right| \tag{7}$$

In this problem, $h_i(t_i^l)$ shows the awareness rate of the importance level t_i^l that the agent achieves. It is optimal parameter, $h_{trg} = 0.9$ for versatile network dynamics [2].

3.3   Stratagem of Select Importance Levels

The agent affects the dynamics and awareness rates of all agents with the interdependence of the agents' opinion and neighbors' one. If the agent greedily select optimal importance level following the definition of its optimization problem (Eq. 7 shows), it may extremely change the local dynamics of the community. The agent has to select a strategy without dramatic changes in its dynamics, in order to estimate awareness rates of the community accurately and solve faster. To select such the strategy, the agent has to focus on the inference as follows. The agents' awareness rate for its importance levels increase monotonously. Because the minimum importance level t_i^{min} requires many updates against the maximum importance level t_i^{max}, if the importance levels are sorted in ascending order. In this inference, the agent employs a hill-climbing strategy. If the awareness rate of the current importance level $t_i = t_i^l$ is lower than the target $\widehat{h_i^l} < h_{trg}$, the agent employing the hill-climbing strategy increases the importance level to closet lager one (i.e. $l = l + 1$). If the awareness rate of the close importance level is lower than the target $\widehat{h_i^{l-1}} > h_{trg}$, the agent use this importance level in the next round (i.e. $l = l - 1$). The agents employed the hill-climbing strategy deliver the higher accuracy than the greedy strategy [2].

4   AAT with Weighted Network Among Agents

Section 3 explains that AAT algorithm can improve the accuracy R in the various complex network. However, this algorithm does not focus on the situation which is close to real world, i.e., the weighted network where the relationship among the agents (as the nodes of its network) is different each other. Such a situation should be considered because people in our society, have relationships such as kindness, trust, social standing or family, and most of them believe the opinions of others according to the relationships with others. From this viewpoint, the relationships among people may help our communication smoothly. To cope with such a relationship, this paper modifies the original AAT to improve AAT algorithm to promote the agents to form the opinions considering the relationships of neighbor agents connected to them.

By employing the improved AAT, this paper aims at investigating how the relationships can help us (or the agents) to share the correct opinions. In this paper, the relationships among the agents are implemented by the weighted network where the weights give an influence to the decision making process of the agents. In the weighted network, the agents have the weighted edge $w_j^i \in W$, where j is the neighbor $D_i = \{j:\exists (i, j) \in E\}$ and the range of the weighted edges is $0.9 \leq w \leq 1$. The agents have weighted edges as many as neighbor agents, i.e. $|W_i| = |D_i|$. In order to combine the weighted edges into AAT algorithm, we modified it by multiplying the importance levels with the edges where the optimal importance levels T_i is the measure of influence of neighbors' opinion, while the weighted edges W_i implies the relationships for agents' neighbors. Note that the importance levels with the improved AAT are lower than that with original AAT, since it multiplies importance levels and the weighted edges together. The agents with the improved AAT may become cautious since they have the importance levels which is lower than original that.

The AAT algorithm with weighted edges is described as follow [2].

AAT Algorithm with weighted Edges

Procedure UPDATE(i)

MULTIPLY each importance level by each weighted edges

{Revises the current importance level after each round}

1: if OPINIONS RECEIVED : $u_i^m \neq 0$ then

2:     for all CANDIDATE LEVELS : $t_i^l \in T_i$ do

3:             if OPINION FORMED(t_i^l, t_i, m) = **True then**

4:                 $\widehat{h_i^l}$ =UPDATE AVERAGE AWARENESS$(h_i^l, 1)$

5:             else

6:                 $\widehat{h_i^l}$ =UPDATE AVERAGE AWARENESS$(h_i^l, 0)$

7:     t_i =SELECT BY AWARENESS RATE$(\langle t_i^l, \widehat{h_i^l}\rangle : : l \in 1 \cdots |T_i|)$

---

5 Empirical Evaluation

5.1 Experimental Content

In order to investigate the influence of weighted networks, we simulate multi-agent model of opinion sharing. We visualize the model on system to facilitate the analysis of the network model.

We validate the usability of our study as follows:

- The network topology of the community is adopted Small World Network since we motivate to simulate our study at the case which closes the real world.
- In order to validate the influence of the small community that share incorrect opinions easily, we set the number of the agents to 100.
- The number of the sensor agents that can observe the information of the true state b is only 5 % for all agents. Then the community may form incorrect opinions, since the accuracy of sensor is low, about 55 %.

5.2 Evaluation Criteria

In order to measure the influence of weighted networks, we use the accuracy R (number of the agents which have correct opinion in the community). We measure each average of the accuracy R in the 10 network (various network form and sensors') and compare original AAT algorithm and improved AAT (AAT with weighted edge). In order to analyze the network dynamics clearly, we also compare each number of the accuracy R of fixed network (same network form and same sensors' seed).

5.3 Experimental Result

Figure 2 indicates the each average of the number of the correct agents in the 10 network as follows:

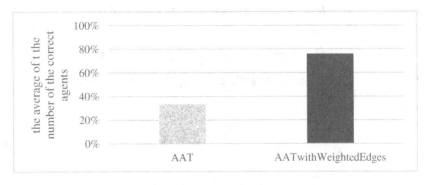

Fig. 2. The average of the accuracy R

The vertical axis and the horizontal axis, indicate the average of the accuracy R in the 10 network, and the respective method (AAT, improved AAT). Following Fig. 2, the average of AAT is low, about 30 %. However, the average of improved AAT is over than the average of AAT, about 70 %.

Figure 3 indicates the dispersion of the agents' opinions in the community running AAT when the community form incorrect opinion as follows:

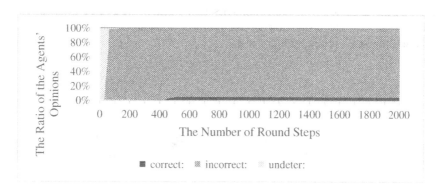

Fig. 3. The dispersion of the formed opinion by the all agents in the small community running original AAT

The vertical axis and the horizontal axis, indicate the ratio of the agents' opinions, and the number of round steps. Since the AAT cannot keep high performance in the situation that is referred to the Sect. 4, this small community spread the incorrect opinion to its members. In such a situation, we apply weighted networks and improved AAT to the community, where the weighted networks which the agents have for their neighbors are set up randomly.

Figure 4 indicates the dispersion of the formed opinion in the community which applied improved AAT.

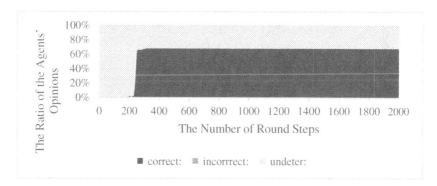

Fig. 4. The dispersion of the formed opinion by the all agents in the small community running improved AAT

The vertical axis and the horizontal axis, indicate the ratio of the agents' opinions in the community applied improved AAT and the number of round steps. The result indicates that the more agents succeeded forming the correct opinions in the similar community.

Now, we apply the AAT algorithm which is tuned the target awareness rate h_trg = 0.7 to same network. The target awareness rate is measure how much the agents form their opinions to receive neighbors' opinions. Following Fig. 2, The average of the accuracy R in the community running improved AAT is about 70 %. Figure 5 indicates the dispersion of the formed opinion in the community after application the AAT tuned by h_trg = 0.7.

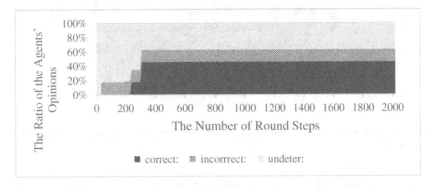

Fig. 5. The dispersion of the formed opinion by the all agents in the small community running AAT tuned by h_trg = 0.7

The vertical axis and the horizontal axis, indicate the ratio of the agents' opinions, and the number of round steps. Following this result, the agents which form incorrect opinion is over than the agents which form correct one.

Figure 6 indicates the each average of the accuracy R in the 10 network as follows:

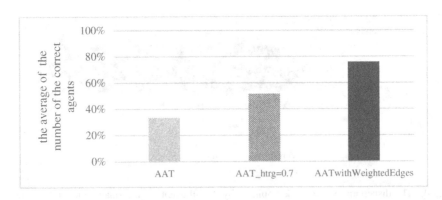

Fig. 6. The average of the accuracy R

The vertical axis and the horizontal axis, indicate the average of the awareness rate in the 10 network, and the respective method (original AAT, AAT with h_trg = 0.7, improved AAT). Following Fig. 6, the average of AAT with h_trg = 0.7 is 50 %.

5.4 Discussion

Following Fig. 6, the average rate of improved AAT is over than original AAT and AAT with h_trg = 0.7. Following Figs. 3, 4 and 5, the accuracy of the correct opinion sharing in improved AAT is higher than that in the original AAT and AAT with h_trg = 0.7. Following these results, the agents running improved AAT can share a correct opinion in a certain small network, while those in the conventional method cannot share it in the same network. Additionally, the improved AAT prevent incorrect opinion in same community with weighted network, while AAT and AAT with h_trg = 0.7 cannot prevent it. The results indicates the agents with the improved AAT may be cautious, since they selects the importance levels with weighted networks which are lower than that with original AAT. These results indicate the weighted networks have influence on decision making of the agent and weighted networks help the prevention of incorrect opinion sharing in the difficult situation. There is some possibility of the weighted network which imply relationship among the agents may help the correct opinion sharing.

6 Conclusion

To promote the agents to share only correct opinions by preventing to acquire the incorrect opinions in the weighted network where the relationship among the agent (as nodes of its network) is different each other, this paper investigated how correct or incorrect opinions are shared among the agents in such a network, and improved the Autonomous Adaptive Tuning algorithm (AAT) to address the weighted network which is close in the real world. To investigate the effectiveness of the improved AAT, this paper compares an accuracy of the correct opinion sharing with the improved AAT with that with the original AAT in the weighted network. Through an intensive empirical experiments, the following implications have been revealed: (1) the weighted networks help the current communication, since the accuracy of the correct opinion sharing with the improved AAT is higher than that with the original AAT in the weighted network; (2) the agents in the improved AAT can prevent to acquire incorrect opinion sharing in the weighted network, while those in the original AAT are hard to prevent in the same network. What should be noticed here is that the effects of the weighted networks has not yet been shown in detail. Therefore, further careful quali-fications and justifications are needed to generalize our results. Such important directions must be pursued in the near future in addition to the following future research: (1) to explore how the weighted network improves the correct opinion sharing; and (2) to explore how the weighted networks prevent incorrect opinion sharing.

References

1. Glinton, R., Scerri, P., Sycara, K.: Towards the understanding of information dynamics in large scale networked systems. In: 12th International Conference on Information Fusion, pp. 794–801 (2009)
2. Pryymak, O., Rogers, A., Jennings, N.R.: Efficient opinion sharing in large decentralized teams. In: The 11th International Conference on Autonomous Agents and Multiagent Systems, pp. 543–550 (2012)
3. Saito, R., Tatebe, N., Takano, R., Takadama, K.: Network construction for correct opinion sharing by selecting a curator agent. In: The 34th Chinese Control Conference and SICE Annual Conference (CCC and SICE 2015) (2015)

The Temporal Analysis of Networks for Community Activity

Yurika Shiozu[1(✉)], Koya Kimura[2], and Katsunori Shimohara[2]

[1] Faculty of Economics, Aichi University, Nagoya, Japan
yshiozu@vega.aichi-u.ac.jp
[2] Graduate School of Science and Engineering,
Doshisha University, Kyoto, Japan
kimura2013@sil.doshisha.ac.jp,
kshimoha@mail.doshisha.ac.jp

Abstract. Using a questionnaire survey and a smartphone-based social experiment, we conducted a study of private non-profit organizations aiming to supply public goods during three periods. Using the data obtained, we identified a dynamic change in the communication by temporal network analysis and elucidated the relevant factors by panel analysis. From the result of this paper, it was shown that having effect by the period on network structure, and sex and Face to Face Communication where there were scale-free characteristics were unrelated to the information dispatch by the ICT.

Keywords: Social network · Temporal network analysis · Panel analysis

1 Introduction

In this paper, we aim to describe the communication situation of a private organization that dynamically provides local public goods. As an example, in most places, local inhabitants are not responsible for repairing roads. On one hand, it is possible to supply local public goods privately, but on the other hand, that cannot be achieved the purpose. Expense burdens, whether financial or non-financial, are incurred for the supply of local public goods by any means, but a free-rider problem emerges because of the character of public goods, including their non-excludability and non-competitiveness. Therefore, it is important to inform various area inhabitants of the necessity of the local public goods.

The contents of this paper are as follows. In Sect. 2, we survey the literature on this subject. In Sect. 3, we show the data and methods used in the social experiment described in this paper. We present the estimated result in Sect. 4 and the discussion in Sect. 5. In Sect. 6, we describe the conclusion and remarks.

2 Preceding Studies

There has been extensive research on the provision of private or local public goods. Because a free-rider problem arises from the character of public goods, it is known that local public goods will serve as very little provision. Aoki (1999) showed the

© Springer International Publishing Switzerland 2016
S. Yamamoto (Ed.): HIMI 2016, Part II, LNCS 9735, pp. 63–71, 2016.
DOI: 10.1007/978-3-319-40397-7_7

conditions under which inhabitants of a Japanese rural area must behave cooperatively or else face permanent ostracism by their peers. Shiozu et al. (2013) extended the model of Aoki and described the condition of private provision of local public goods as a behavior based on reciprocity in an urban area.

Yamashita (2003) classified the problem into four patterns according to the structure of the network. If the network has a horizontal and open structure, information can be sent or taken from outside. To realize private provision of local public goods, the structure of the network is important.

Kawabata et al. (2011) showed that if information about the private provision of local public goods is offered to non-recipients of the benefit, their willingness to pay for the local public goods will rise by Contingent Value Method. It will be suggested that the provision of local public goods can be promoted.

3   Data and Methods

3.1   Data

With the cooperation of "Makishima Kizuna-no-kai," a non-profit organization (NPO) that performs community activities in the Makishima, Uji-city, Kyoto Prefecture, we conducted a social experiment involving an NPO member. We conducted the social experiment over 3 periods. The first term was from November 11 to December 10, 2013, and the number of cooperators was 20 (13 effective answers); the second term was from February 11 to March 27, 2015, and the number of cooperators was 30 (30 effective answers); and the third term was from August 1 to August 31, 2015, and the number of cooperators was 50 (47 effective answers). The ages of the cooperators were 30–70 years. Because the number of cooperators increased with the progress of the period, we could build unbalanced panel data. We obtained ethical approval for this social experiment from Doshisha University as well as informed consent from all cooperators. In a questionnaire, we asked participants less than five personal names and the frequency with which they talked. We provided them with a smartphone with GPS to collect the data on their locations and communication with other members during the period. Table 1 shows the terminal information used for the social trial run.

Table 1. Situation of the smartphone

Period	1	2–3
Career	NTT Docomo	NTT Docomo MVNO/IIJ mobile
Manufacturer	Fujitsu	ASUS
Product no.	ARROWS Kiss F-03E	ZenFone 5 (A500KL)
OS	Android 4.0.4	Android 4.4.2

3.1.1   95 % Home Range

In this paper, we estimated the 95 % home range from the actual GPS data for every time period of each cooperator. The formula is given by expression (1):

$$p(x) = \frac{1}{n}\sum_{i=1}^{n} K(\frac{x - X_i}{h}).$$ (1)

Here, $\{X_i\}_{i=1}^{n}$ shows the actual GPS value, K(.) is the kernel density function, n indicates number, and h expresses the band width. We used a fixed band width for kernel density estimation. The estimation was performed by R 3.1.2 with the package "adehabitat ver.1.8.18" by Calenge (2015).

The descriptive statistics of the questionnaire for each time period, as well as the social experimental data, are shown in Table 2.

Table 2. Descriptive statistics

	N	Min	Max	Average	S.D.
Period	150	1.00	3.00	2.0000	0.81923
Home range (m^2)	93	0.00	8281441.00	220775.2536	1000665.648
Female	150	0.00	1.00	0.4000	0.49154
Authority	95	0.00	0.10	0.0285	0.01881
Hub	96	0.00	0.14	0.0263	0.02846
Number of meeting	88	1.00	5.00	4.2159	1.10847
Effective number	84				

3.2   Methods

3.2.1   Social Network Analysis

To obtain the structure of the network of members who gathered for community activities, social network analysis was performed. Our data varied in time; therefore, temporal network analysis, which is a dynamic approach, was applied.

In social network analysis, the indicators for knowing the fundamental structure of the whole network include the diameter, clustering coefficient, and density. If the diameter is small and the density and cluster coefficient are large, it is an exclusive network. Conversely, if the diameter is large and the density and cluster coefficient are small, it is an open network. The dynamic state of the whole network can be analyzed using a time-series transmutation of these indicators.

In the social trial run of this paper, because we rented a smartphone for only research purposes, we could observe the relationship between cooperators. Therefore, it became possible to analyze the structure within the network.

When information dispatch was performed toward individual B from individual A, it was expressed with social network analysis using a directed graph. In other words, individual A is an information addresser and the individual B becomes a receiver. The degree can be calculated by setting the information dispatch frequency to the individual B to the weight from the individual A. A hub refers to an individual with a high degree of information dispatch, and an authority refers to an individual with a high degree of an information reception in a network.

Barabási and Albert (1999) showed that a vast majority has the character (scale-free nature) which is not so, although some network members are hubs or authorities.

3.2.2   Panel Analysis

Panel analysis was conducted using a hub according to the time period of each individual obtained by social network analysis and the value of an authority. This paper examined whether a scale-free network also exists in the local resident network in which it is gathered for the purpose of the private provision of local public goods. Because the number of social trial-run cooperators is increasing with time, as described in the preceding paragraph, unbalanced panel data can be obtained. Then, we examined whether a scale-free network exists, even as members increase in number over time.

A hub (information addresser) is considered to be a person who moves actively and talks with many people. Moreover, for males, there is little opportunity for connection with community activity when they work. Females have more opportunities to participate in community activity because they are expected her to join activities such as PTA. The distance for an individual may easily change over a time period, but because each subject was over 30 years old, it was thought that the members who spoke to them did not change dramatically. Moreover, it was thought that sex, for the most part, did not change. Therefore, it could be predicted that authority, distance, conversation number, and female coefficient also become significantly positive. The estimated equation is as follows. The subscript i of each variable expresses the individual and t expresses the experimental period (t = 1, 2, 3). The value of the home range is subjected to logarithmic conversion:

$$Hub_{it} = \alpha_0 + \alpha_1 A_{it} + \alpha_2 R_{it} + \alpha_3 N_{it} + \alpha_4 F_i + \mu_{it};$$
$$\alpha_0, \alpha_1, \alpha_2, \alpha_3, \alpha_4 > 0 \tag{2}$$

Hub denotes a hub, A denotes authority, R denotes the home range, N denotes the number of meetings, F denotes a female dummy, alpha 0 denotes a constant term, and mu denotes an error term.

4   Results of Estimation

4.1   Social Network Analysis

Table 3 shows a summary of the whole network structure of each term. The estimation was performed by Gephi. Ver.0.8.2 Beta.

Table 3. A summary of the whole network structure of each term

Term	Diameter	Average cluster coefficient	Density
First term	3	0.707	0.276
Second term	3	0.273	0.028
Third term	2	0.739	0.092

As shown in Fig. 1, in each period, the values of density are low. Moreover, because the diameter does not change much, the communication-of-information speed can be called comparatively quick in this network. Although the average cluster coefficient decreases greatly for the second term, it is recovered again. It is possible that this may be an exclusive network from the indicators of the first and third terms.

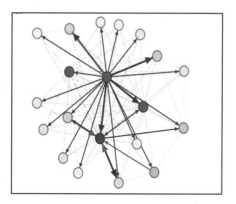

Fig. 1. Hub and authority in first term

Next, the scale-free network of the first term is checked using Fig. 1. In the diagram, the dark-colored circle expresses that the value of an authority or hub is high. In the first term, the value of the hub and authority of two points surrounded with a circle in the central part of Fig. 1 is high. Because these spots can be checked, there exists a scale-free nature for the first term.

Then, the scale-free network of the second term is checked using Figs. 2 and 3. In the second term, one very large black spot exists in the central parts of Figs. 2 and 3. Because this spot expresses the same individual, it can be used to check that the scale-free network also exists for the second term.

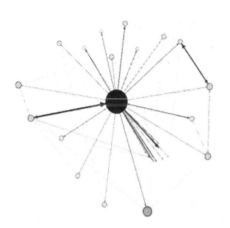
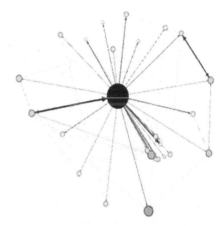

Fig. 2. Hub in second term   **Fig. 3.** Authority in second term

Then, we checked for a scale-free network for the third term using Figs. 4 and 5. One black circle exists in the central part in Figs. 4 and 5. Like the second term, because this spot expresses the same individual, it can be used to check whether a scale-free network also exists for the third term.

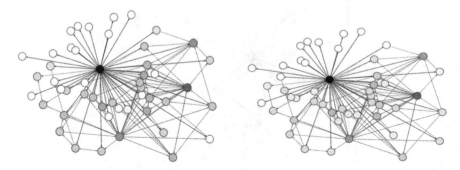

Fig. 4. Hub in third term   **Fig. 5.** Authority in third term

The abovementioned analysis revealed that a scale-free network clearly exists throughout the period, and one person has a scale-free network in the second and third terms.

4.2 Panel Analysis

Because sex was considered to be an individual attribute that does not change over a time period, we applied the fixed- and random-effect model. The estimation was performed using STATA Ver.12. Table 4 shows the result. The fixed-effect model was rejected on the basis of the result of the F-test. The result of Breusch and Pagan test supported pooling regression. We therefore adopted pooling regression.

Table 4. Comparison of models

F test, where all u_i = 0: $F(47, 28) = 1.09$ Prob > F = 0.4143
Breusch and Pagan Lagrangian multiplier test for random effects
hub[id,t] = Xb + u[id] + e[id,t]

	Var	sd = sqrt(Var)
hub	0.000745	0.027293
e	0.000666	0.025798
u	0	0

Test: Var(u) = 0 chibar2(01) = 0.00 Prob > chibar2 = 1.0000

Excluding the effect of period, we added the variable "sex." The result of pooling regression is shown in Table 5. The sample number is 79.

Table 5. Result of pooling regression (1)

Hub	Coef.	Std. Err.	t	P > t
Authority	0.451647	0.151987	2.97	0.004
Home range	0.000791	0.001896	0.42	0.678
Female	0.011855	0.006234	1.9	0.061
Number of meeting	0.001981	0.002615	0.76	0.451
Cons	−0.00204	0.014353	−0.14	0.887

F(4,74) = 2.92 Prob > F = 0.0268 R-squared = 0.1362 Adj
R-squared = 0.0895 Root MSE = 0.02604

When the symbol and t value of each coefficients were checked, the coefficient of authority became significantly positive. Moreover, the coefficient of females was positive. This means that females bear the role of being addressers of information.

Excluding the effect of sex, we added the variable period. The result of pooling regression is shown in Table 6. It also shows that the coefficient of authority becomes significantly positive by a 10 % p-value.

Table 6. Result of pooling regression (2)

Hub	Coef.	Std. Err.	t	P > t
Authority	0.345587	0.198391	1.74	0.086
Home Range	0.001239	0.001924	0.64	0.522
Period	−0.0027	0.005045	−0.54	0.594
Number of meeting	0.001062	0.002671	0.4	0.692
Cons	0.014061	0.022325	0.63	0.531

Prob > F = 0.1036 R-squared = 0.0975 Adj
R-squared = 0.0487 Root MSE = 0.02662

5 Discussion

The structure of the whole network was clarified on the basis of the results of social network analysis. It was thought that the factor peculiar to the second term committed the 1st term and the 3rd term from each indicator having shown the in general same trend. In this social trial run, there was a member who participated in the first and third terms. It was also suggested that the presence of this individual caused the structure of the whole network to transmute. If it takes into consideration that it is also clear that an existence of the individual who exercises a strong leadership leads community activity as pointed out by many researches, it will also set to the NPO in this research. The degree of participation in community activity by an individual with a leadership position enables strengthening of the union power in a network.

When the number of participating members became 30 or more, from the standpoint of communication of information, it was shown that there will be only one member with a scale-free nature. If communication of information can be conducted only through the reception and transmission of e-mail, based on the presumed result of this research, a scale-free nature may not be particularly related to the union power of the whole network. In other words, ICT can serve as the central figure of information reception and transmission, even if the leadership in a society is of middle or old age.

To analyze the leading factor affecting information reception and transmission, panel analysis was performed because the networks in question were temporal. To scrutinize a presumed result, parallelism with cross-section regression was performed. A presumed result is shown in Table 7.

Table 7. Result of cross-section regression

Hub	Coef.	Std. Err.	t	P > t
Authority	0.37116	0.195283	1.9	0.061
Home range	0.00067	0.001912	0.35	0.727
Period	−0.00328	0.004963	−0.66	0.511
Female	0.012103	0.00627	1.93	0.057
Number of meeting	0.001755	0.002647	0.66	0.509
Cons	0.009006	0.022081	0.41	0.685

F(5,73) = 2.4 Prob > F = 0.0449 R-squared = 0.1413 Adj R-squared = 0.0825 Root MSE = 0.02614

On comparing the results of the pooling and cross-sectional regressions, authority was found to be significantly positive in each model. Therefore, when a certain amount of sample size was secured, it could be checked that a scale-free network is achieved.

Based on the fact that the home range and number of meetings are not significant factors, the models show that geographical sphere or face-to-face communication is not necessarily connected with information dispatch.

Under pooling regression, sex was found to be a significant positive factor for all the models. This suggests that a female can become an information addresser more easily than a male. It was thought that there are many people taking the role that the woman is relatively engaged in a local action from youth, and information sends them for members.

6   Conclusion and Remarks

The purpose of this paper was to dynamically model the status of the communication of information across a structure that privately provides local public goods. From the result of temporal social network analysis, a member's degree of participation was found to heavily influence the union power of the whole network. On the other hand, when the network number exceeded fixed numbers, regardless of the leadership in a real society, the central figure of reception and transmission of information was performed by one person.

Moreover, panel analysis showed that the sex of members influenced the structure used for the common purpose of city planning. We showed that the relations from youth to a local activity influenced information dispatch. The existence of a scale-free network and distance became clear from pooling regression. However, the number which talks by meeting does not influence. It can be inferred that face-to-face communication is unrelated to information dispatch by ICT.

The area of the geographical home range was not estimated to influence information dispatch. However, the LSCV method and an estimated method having high precision including Local Convex Hull are developed in the home range estimate. We performed home range estimation by this technique and tried to confirm the robustness of the result.

Acknowledgment. This work was supported by The Science Research Promotion Fund 2011–2013 and the Telecommunications Advancement Foundation 2014. We would like to express the deepest appreciation to cooperators.

References

Aoki, M.: Toward a Comparative Institutional Analysis. MIT Press, Cambridge (2001)

Barabási, A.-L., Albert, R.: Emergence of scaling in random networks. Science **286**, 509–512 (1999)

Shiozu, Y., Yonezaki, K., Shimohara, K.: Incentive structure of participation in community activity. In: Yamamoto, S. (ed.) HCI 2013, Part I. LNCS, vol. 8016, pp. 259–268. Springer, Heidelberg (2013)

Kawabata, M., Sano, K., Tsuchiya, S., Matsumoto, S.: Non-beneficiary citizens' fairness perception and WTP: impacts of resident governed organization in bus operation. J. JSGE **67** (5), 69–78 (2011). (in Japanese)

Yamashita, Y.: Social network and community development. Stud. Humanit. (Hirosaki University) Cult. Sci. **9**, 171–184 (2003). (in Japanese)

Method to Evaluate Difficulty of Technical Terms

Yuta Sudo[1]([⊠]), Toru Nakata[2], and Toshikazu Kato[1]

[1] Graduate School of Science and Engineering, Chuo University, Tokyo, Japan
all.rneh@chuo-u.ac.jp, kato@indsys.chuo-u.ac.jp
[2] National Institute of Advanced Industrial Science
and Technology (AIST), Tokyo, Japan
toru-nakata@aist.go.jp

Abstract. We have developed an auto annotating system. To apply to the system, we conducted experiments about the method to evaluate difficulty of technical terms in documents by using data of Wikipedia. Based on a hypothesis that basic and easy terms appear frequently in Wikipedia, we surveyed relationship between subjective difficulty and appearance frequency in Wikipedia. As a result, we could classify technical terms into the easy term and the difficult term at the accuracy of 0.70.

Keywords: Word clustering · Automatic annotation · Information assistance

1 Introduction: Demand of Automatic Detecting of 'Difficult' Terms

Technical documents often contain technical terms without explanations, so non-expert readers may fail to understand the documents. To solve this problem, we developed an auto annotating system (Fig. 1).

The system should automatically detect 'difficult' technical terms and attach explanations on them. Evaluation of difficulty of terms is not so trivial.

This paper presents a method to score difficulty of technical terms by analyzing terminological structure of Wikipedia. The method evaluates difficulty of each term by observing appearance frequency of terms.

2 Related Work

Several researches on evaluation of easiness (or familiarity to readers) of terms have been conducted. Amano et al. [1] proposes an evaluation method that employs a catalog of familiarity of words. YAGO [2] should be mentioned as a famous example of ontology dataset. Such ontologies may be used to rank difficulty of terms, because we can guess that terms connected to difficult terms are difficult too.

Those methods, however, can work only on fixed vocabulary. We propose a method that can automatically generate the catalog of difficulty. This catalog will play effective role in the field of Document's Readability Assessment [3, 4].

© Springer International Publishing Switzerland 2016
S. Yamamoto (Ed.): HIMI 2016, Part II, LNCS 9735, pp. 72–80, 2016.
DOI: 10.1007/978-3-319-40397-7_8

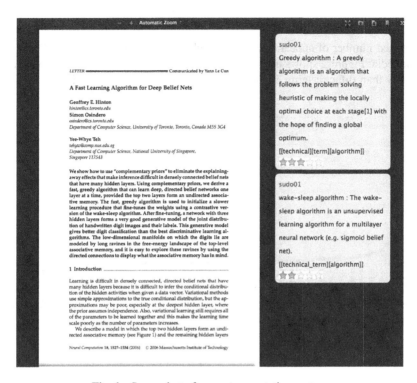

Fig. 1. Screenshot of our auto annotating system

3 Our Hypothesis on Characteristic of Term Difficulty

We define 'basic' and 'specific' as follows:

We call Term A is more basic than Term B when Term A is required to define Term B.

We define 'specific' as the antonym of 'basic'.

Our research starts with a hypothesis: "Basic terms tend to be referred very frequently in documents to define and to explain more specific terms."

4 Experiments

Impression of easiness of a term is subjective, while we defined the meaning of 'basic' objectively. We will investigate the correlation between easiness and basicness.

We performed the following experiments on the Japanese articles in the category of 'statistics' in Wikipedia.

4.1 Distribution of Term Appearance Frequency

We counted number of appearance of each index word within the 'statistics' category of Wikipedia. Figure 2 shows the distribution, and we find that easy terms appear more frequently than difficult terms in general. It corresponds to our hypothesis.

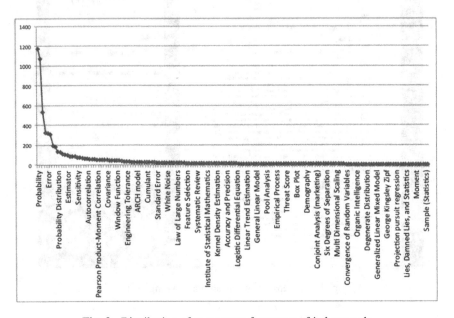

Fig. 2. Distribution of appearance frequency of index words

4.2 Relationship Between Frequency and Subjective Difficulty

We conducted a questionnaire research to measure subjective difficulty of the technical terms. We select 20 terms from the category (Table 1). We employ 11 people to rate difficulties of the terms. The scale of rating has 4-degree, and each subject answers by the number as following:

1. I have never heard the term.
2. I have heard the term, but I do not know the meaning of it.
3. I know the meaning of the term to some extent but not deeply to explain to the last detail.
4. I know the meaning of the term deeply.

The result shown in Fig. 3 indicates the correlation between appearance frequency and subjective difficulty. The correlation coefficient was 0.71. The fitting line for Fig. 3 was $y = 0.24x + 1.37$. It supports our hypothesis to some extent.

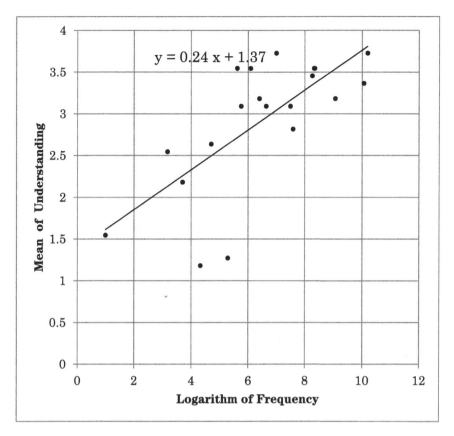

Fig. 3. Appearance frequency and averages of subjective score of understanding.

4.3 Agreement of Subjective Word Difficulty and Its Estimation Based on Word Frequency

In Sect. 4.2 we got the formula to estimate difficulty of words based on frequency of terms. We evaluate the accuracy of the estimation formula.

Considering the meaning of "3. I know the meaning of the term to some extent but not deeply to explain to the last detail" in questionnaire, we classified terms whose estimation of understanding is lower than three as the difficult terms that should be annotated. On the contrary, we classified terms whose estimation of understanding is equal or higher than three as easy terms that should not be annotated.

Table 2 is the confusion matrix between the estimated term difficulty and the subjective difficulty judged by the subjects. Fourteen words out of twenty are estimated correctly.

Table 1. Subjective degree of understanding and appearance frequency of terms

Words	Understanding	Frequency	Logarithm of frequency
Probability	3.73	1172	10.19
Statistic	3.36	1071	10.06
Statistics	3.18	536	9.07
Inference	3.55	326	8.35
Error	3.55	321	8.33
Random variable	3.45	307	8.26
Uncertainty	2.82	192	7.58
Deviation	3.09	180	7.49
Statistical population	3.73	127	6.99
Estimator	3.09	99	6.63
Probability density function	3.18	84	6.39
Standard score	3.55	68	6.09
Miracle	3.09	54	5.75
Covariance	3.55	49	5.61
Probability mass function	1.27	39	5.29
Family budget research	2.64	26	4.70
True negative rate	1.18	20	4.32
Kernel density estimation	2.18	13	3.70
Homoscedasticity	2.55	9	3.17
Directional statistics	1.55	2	1.00

Table 2. Result of automatic estimation of term difficulty based on term frequency compared to impression of the subjects

	Subjectively difficult	Subjectively easy
Estimated as difficult	6	5
Estimated as easy	1	8

5   Discussion

5.1   Good Amount of Annotation for Users

Considering the meaning of questionnaire, we chose three as the threshold of necessity of annotation in Sect. 4.3. Off course, we should consider about other value for the threshold. Changing the threshold value, we got the curve of classification accuracy (Fig. 4). The estimation based word frequency achieved 60 % accuracy in any threshold.

5.2   Referring/Referred Index and Subjective Difficulty

As a new candidate of difficulty indicator, we employ the number of referred times and referring times of each index word.

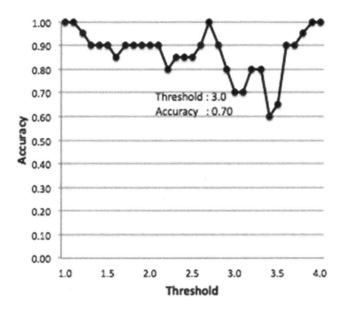

Fig. 4. Threshold of easy/difficult grade of words vs, accuracy of estimation based on word frequency

For example, we pick up the index word of "Least Squares Method (LSM)". This term refers (Table 3) and is referred (Table 4) by many other index words.

Table 3. Index words referred by term "LSM"

Title	Referred frequency	Frequency of appearance
Error	30	321
Least squares method	11	45
Residual	7	46
Probability theory	2	113
Independence (probability theory)	2	11
Presumption	2	326
Residual sum of squares	2	2
Probability	2	1172
Observation error	1	50
Statistic	1	1071
Covariance	1	49
Statistics	1	536
Non-linear least squares	1	6
Deviation	1	180
Maximum likelihood estimation	1	20
Degrees of freedom (statistics)	1	59

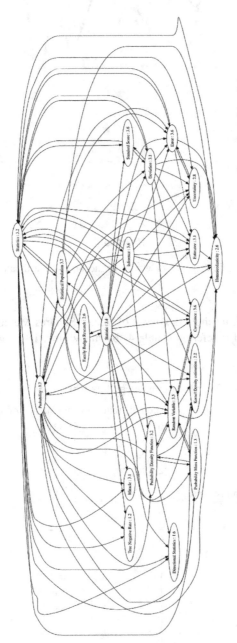

Fig. 5. Referring/referred relationship network. A term in upper stream is referred by the Wikipedia article of the term in lower. Numbers in each oval are subjective degree of understanding of term.

According to our definition of 'basic' and 'specific', index words in Table 3 are more basic than the term LSM, and the terms in Table 4 are more specific.

The referring/referred relationship formulates a network structure among terms. Figure 5 is an example of such network among the index words concerning 'statistics' in Wikipedia. We call the network "RR Network".

Table 4. Index words referring term "LSM"

Title	Referring frequency	Frequency of appearance
Non-linear least squares	18	6
Least squares method	11	45
Linear trend estimation	6	11
Error	2	321
Regression analysis	2	55
Coefficient of determination	2	8
Linear regression	2	28
Residual sum of squares	1	12
Regression analysis (multi variable)	1	22

Figure 5 suggests that the words being in upper stream are regarded as 'basic' by the definition are also subjectively easy. Using this RR Network, we can estimate difficulty more accurate.

We defined a value of "reference rank" of a term as the difference between referred frequency and referring frequency. The correlation coefficient between subjective difficulty and $A/(A + B)$ was 0.56, where A is the number of referring and B is the number of being referred.

6 Conclusion

We conducted experiments that indicating relation between term frequency and subjective difficulty. From the result, we classified terms. The accuracy was 70 %. Although we used three as the threshold, there is room for more research about the annotation amount that people needs. As the method to improve accuracy, we are considering using RR-network.

Acknowledgement. This work was partially supported by JSPS KAKENHI grants (No. 25240043) and TISE Research Grant of Chuo University.

References

1. Amano, S., Kondo, T.: Estimation of mental lexicon size with word familiarity database. In: Proceedings of International Conference on Spoken Language Processing, vol. 5, pp. 2119–2122 (1998)
2. Suchanek, F.M., Kasneci, G., Weikum, G.: Yago: a core of semantic knowledge. In: Proceedings of the 16th International Conference on World Wide Web, pp. 697–706. ACM, May 2007
3. Jiang, Z., Sun, G., Gu, Q., Bai, T., Chen, D.: A graph-based readability assessment method using word coupling
4. Sato, S., Matsuyoshi, S., Kondoh, Y.: Automatic assessment of Japanese text readability based on a textbook corpus. In: LREC, May 2008

Essential Tips for Successful Collaboration – A Case Study of the "Marshmallow Challenge"

Noriko Suzuki[1(✉)], Haruka Shoda[2,3], Mamiko Sakata[2], and Kaori Inada[2]

[1] Faculty of Business Administration, Tezukayama University,
7-7-1 Tezukayama, Nara City, Nara 631-8501, Japan
nsuzuki@tezukayama-u.ac.jp
[2] Department of Culture and Information Science, Doshisha University,
1-3 Tatara Miyakodani, Kyotanabe, Kyoto 610-0394, Japan
[3] Global Innovation Research Organization, Ritsumeikan University,
Nojihigashi 1-1-1, Kusatsu 525-8577, Japan
shoda@fc.ritsumei.ac.jp

Abstract. We report essential tips for collaboration success obtained through the task of the "Marshmallow Challenge." This involves examining the relationships among task achievement, performance satisfaction, and verbal/non-verbal behaviors throughout the task. We record and analyze the speech and gaze of participants with a video camera. The height of the marshmallow tower is measured as the metric of task achievement. The performance satisfaction felt by participants is obtained with a post-task questionnaire. We use correlation analysis between task achievement/performance satisfaction and verbal/nonverbal behaviors at three stages of the task: the early, middle and final phases. The results suggest that number of agreement utterances in the early phase contributes to increased height of the marshmallow tower. The distribution of the frequency of eye contact in the early phase seem to affect the performance satisfaction of the participants.

Keywords: Multi-party collaboration · Task achievement · Performance satisfaction · Verbal and nonverbal behaviors · Marshmallow Challenge

1 Introduction

In our everyday life, we have opportunities to interact with unfamiliar people, for example through exercise activities at university or group work in tasks like job searching. What components make us feel successful in group work? How do verbal and nonverbal behaviors contribute to the success of group work?

There are many kinds of exercises and activities aimed at ice breaking among people gathered for teamwork [2, 5, etc.]. The "Tower Building Challenge" is one of the most famous ice-breaking exercises. The purpose of the task is to build the tallest free-standing tower among several groups by using prepared materials, e.g., newspapers, photocopy paper, straws, index cards and so on.

© Springer International Publishing Switzerland 2016
S. Yamamoto (Ed.): HIMI 2016, Part II, LNCS 9735, pp. 81–89, 2016.
DOI: 10.1007/978-3-319-40397-7_9

The "Marshmallow Challenge" task is a particular form of the Tower Building Challenge. This task was invented as a design exercise by Peter Skillman at TED2006 and was discussed in depth by Tom Wujec at TED2010 [9,11]. The goal is simple: Groups must build the tallest possible free-standing structure in eighteen minutes using only 20 sticks of pasta, 90 cm of tape, 90 cm of string, and one marshmallow. The marshmallow needs to be placed on top of the constructed tower [4].

An awareness of the actual weight of the marshmallow is regarded as a significant factor in the Marshmallow Challenge. The participants must build a tower with sufficient stability to support the weight of the marshmallow on top. The task can be applied to leadership lessons intended to retain the capabilities of a "beginner's mind" in innovation [1].

We can find many tips for building the tallest free-standing tower on the web, including those for the Marshmallow Challenge in particular. However, there has been little study of tips for collaboration through verbal and nonverbal behaviors in the tower building challenge.

In this paper, our purpose is to find communication tips for successful collaboration by focusing on the Marshmallow Challenge task based on our previous studies [6,10]. We measured the degree of task achievement as the height of the marshmallow tower and examined the performance satisfaction of the participants through a post-task questionnaire. Participants' speech and gaze were recorded with video cameras. We analyzed relationships by using correlation analysis among task achievement, performance satisfaction, and verbal and nonverbal behaviors of participants at intervals of six minutes.

2 Method

2.1 Participants

A total of 21 graduate and undergraduate students (mean age: 19.524 years, SD: 1.468) participated in the experiment. The participants had never met each other before the task. No participant was assigned any particular role in the task. Seven groups (g1 to g7), each consisting of three participants, took part in the Marshmallow Challenge task.

2.2 Procedure

Each group was instructed to sit down and face each other around a table (Fig. 1). As participants in the Marshmallow Challenge, they were required to build a free-standing tower by using 20 sticks of pasta, 90 cm of string, 90 cm of tape, and a single marshmallow within a period of 18 minutes.

The most remarkable characteristic of the Marshmallow Challenge task is the possibility of competitors turning the tables on each other in the end due to the actual vs. perceived weight of a marshmallow, since people normally assume that a marshmallow is an extremely lightweight item.

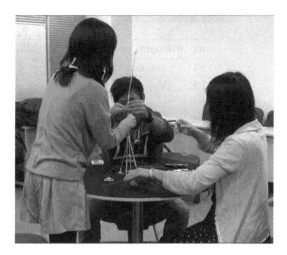

Fig. 1. Participants in the Marshmallow Challenge task

2.3   Parameters

Task achievement: We measured the height of the constructed free-standing tower with one marshmallow on top as the result of task achievement after the task was finished.

Performance satisfaction: We asked participants seven questions on their performance satisfaction using a four-point scale with a post-task questionnaire (Table 1).

Verbal behavior: We extracted the speech of participants through the task of using the ELAN annotation software (EUDICO Linguistic Annotator [3]). We also labeled each speech segmentation using illocutionary act tags based on [7,8] (Table 2). Each task was evenly split into thirds, i.e., its early, middle, and final phases.

Nonverbal behavior: We extracted the frequency of eye contact between two participants throughout the task by using the ELAN annotation software. As mentioned above, each task was evenly split into thirds: the early, middle, and final phases of the task.

Table 1. Post-task questionnaire on performance satisfaction

1	I shared my opinion with other group members
2	I understood the opinions of other group members.
3	I had a good time participating in this experiment.
4	I was happy through the experiment, regardless of the height of the marshmallow tower.
5	I cooperated with my team members throughout the task.
6	I engaged myself in the task to good advantage.
7	I want to participate in this experiment again with the same team members.

Table 2. Illocutionary act tags

Illocutionary act tags	
ST	Statement
PR	Proposal
RP	Response
QS	Question
AN	Answer
CH	Chat
AG	Agreement
DG	Disagree
RQ	Request
ETC	etc.

3   Results

Figure 2 shows results for the height of the marshmallow tower as a task achievement, while Fig. 3 shows the results for performance satisfaction by using the four-point scale post-task questionnaire after the marshmallow challenge task was finished.

Figures 4 and 5 show the results of analyzing verbal behaviors, utterance duration, and the ratio of each illocutionary act tag to each utterance in the early, middle, and final phases.

Furthermore, the results of nonverbal behavior were analyzed relative to the frequency of eye contact between two participants in the early, middle, and final phases (Fig. 6).

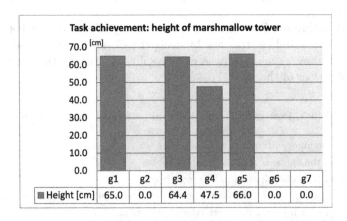

Fig. 2. Results of task achievement: height of marshmallow tower

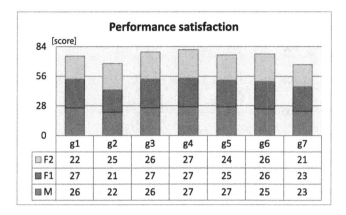

Fig. 3. Results of performance satisfaction (Color figure online)

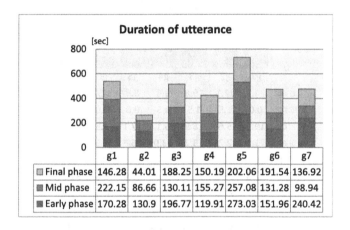

Fig. 4. Results of utterance duration (Color figure online)

There was a moderate positive correlations between task achievement and performance satisfaction ($r = .643$). Table 3 shows the results of the correlation analysis between task achievement/performance satisfaction and verbal/nonverbal behaviors. There were strong positive correlations between task achievement and number of all utterances in the middle phase ($r = .769$) as well as number of agreement utterances in both the early and the middle phase ($r = .782$, $r = .724$). There was a strong positive correlation between performance satisfaction and number of proposal utterances in the final phase ($r = .889$), although there were strong negative correlations with number of the question utterances ($r = -.767$) or the distribution of the frequency of eye contact ($r = -.891$) in the early phase.

These results suggest that the more agreement behaviors the participants expressed at the beginning of the task or the more speech used in the middle

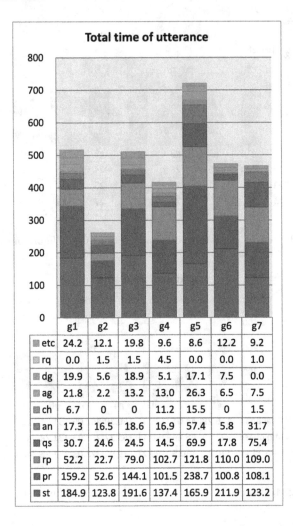

Total time of utterance

	g1	g2	g3	g4	g5	g6	g7
etc	24.2	12.1	19.8	9.6	8.6	12.2	9.2
rq	0.0	1.5	1.5	4.5	0.0	0.0	1.0
dg	19.9	5.6	18.9	5.1	17.1	7.5	0.0
ag	21.8	2.2	13.2	13.0	26.3	6.5	7.5
ch	6.7	0	0	11.2	15.5	0	1.5
an	17.3	16.5	18.6	16.9	57.4	5.8	31.7
qs	30.7	24.6	24.5	14.5	69.9	17.8	75.4
rp	52.2	22.7	79.0	102.7	121.8	110.0	109.0
pr	159.2	52.6	144.1	101.5	238.7	100.8	108.1
st	184.9	123.8	191.6	137.4	165.9	211.9	123.2

Fig. 5. Results of distribution of illocutionary act tags (Color figure online)

of the task, the higher a marshmallow tower they built. They also suggest that the more proposal behavior used in the final phase as well as the less question behavior or the less frequent eye contact expressed in the early phase, the higher the satisfaction participants felt.

We applied stepwise multiple regression to detect the interactive roles of leader, active follower, and passive follower. We used 13 sets of verbal and non-verbal behavior data as independent variables (see Table 3) and the results of task achievement (i.e. height of marshmallow tower) and performance satisfaction with the building process as dependent variables.

Table 3. Correlation coefficient between task achievement (TA)/performance satisfaction (PS) and verbal/nonverbal behaviors

Verbal/nonverbal behaviors	Phase	Correlation coefficient	
		TA	SS
Number of all utterances	early phase	.259	−.215
	middle phase	.769*	.438
	final phase	.502	665†
Number of ST utterances	early phase	.459	.384
	middle phase	.328	.711*
	final phase	−.089	.177
Number of PR utterances	early phase	.293	−.090
	middle phase	.682*	.102
	final phase	.659†	.889**
Number of RP utterances	early phase	−.127	−.073
	middle phase	.572†	.721*
	final phase	−.070	.423
Number of QS utterances	early phase	−.388	−.767*
	middle phase	.538	.198
	final phase	.444	. 137
Number of AN utterances	early phase	−.003	−.515
	middle phase	.694*	.381
	final phase	.559†	.168
Number of CH utterances	early phase	.471	.453
	middle phase	.385	.220
	final phase	.418	.107
Number of AG utterances	early phase	.782*	.364
	middle phase	.724*	.166
	final phase	. 374	.498
Number of DG utterances	early phase	.607†	.168
	middle phase	.435	.361
	final phase	.644†	.529
Number of RQ utterances	early phase	.047	.327
	middle phase	.183	−.213
	final phase	.608†	.230
Number of ETC utterances	early phase	.382	−.205
	middle phase	.475	.203
	final phase	.217	.399
Distribution of all utterances	early phase	−.288	.068
	middle phase	.282	.024
	final phase	−.400	.173
Frequency of eye contact	early phase	−.132	−.615†
	middle phase	.555†	.103
	final phase	.468	.130
Distribution of eye contact	early phase	−.453	−.891**
	middle phase	.280	−.026
	final phase	.519	.092

† $p < 0.10$, * $p < 0.05$, ** $p < 0.01$,
TA: Task achievement, PS: Performance satisfaction

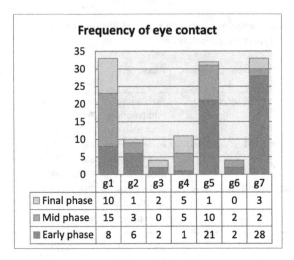

Fig. 6. Results of frequency of eye contact (Color figure online)

The regression equations for the interactive roles are as follows:

$$\begin{aligned}(\text{Task achievement}) = {}& 4.864 \times (\text{Number of agreement utterances in the early phase}) \\ & + 6.908 \times (\text{Number of disagree utterances in the middle phase}) \\ & + const. \hspace{3em} (1)\end{aligned}$$

Equation (1) shows that number of both agreement and proposal utterances in the early phase from 14 sets of behavioral data contribute to the task achievement, that is, maximizing the height of the marshmallow tower.

$$\begin{aligned}(\text{Performance satisfaction}) = {}& -3.230 \times (\text{Distribution of eye contact in the early phase}) \\ & + 0.905 \times (\text{Number of request utterances in the middle phase}) \\ & + const. \hspace{3em} (2)\end{aligned}$$

The Eq. (2) shows that the distribution of eye contact in the early phase and the duration of request utterances in the middle phase from the 14 sets of behavioral data contribute to performance satisfaction with the building process.

We obtained the above regression equation models for detecting the task achievement (adjusted $R^2 = 0.827$, $p < 0.01$) and the performance satisfaction (adjusted $R^2 = 0.916$, $p < 0.01$). The adjusted R^2 value shows the percentage of overall contribution of the above selected variables in the regression equations for each interactive role.

In comparing the results of correlation coefficients in Table 3 with regression equations (1) to (2), we find behavioral data with correlation coefficients of 0.2 or more are mostly selected. On the other hand, number of answer utterances or number of statement utterances is not selected as a parameter for higher contribution, even though it has a moderate correlation coefficient. We should examine the adequacy of the model for application to other groups under similar experimental conditions.

4   Conclusion

In this study, we examined the relationship between task achievement/ performance satisfaction and verbal/nonverbal behaviors of participants through the Marshmallow Challenge task. As a result, verbal/nonverbal behaviors having some effect on task achievement do not necessarily have a corresponding effect on performance satisfaction, although there was a positive correlation between task achievement and performance satisfaction. In other words, the construction of a higher marshmallow tower is not always directly linked to the satisfaction participants felt with their performance in the task.

As essential tips for successful collaboration, these results also suggest that the more active discussions the participants have, the higher the marshmallow tower they will build; furthermore, the results show that the lower the distribution of eye contact they express, the higher satisfaction with the task they will have.

Acknowledgments. The contents of this study are based on the fourth author's graduation thesis. We thank the 21 Doshisha University students who volunteered as subjects for their participation in the experiment.

References

1. Anthony, S.: Innovation leadership lessons from the marshmallow challenge, Harvard Business Review Online, 09 December 2014. https://hbr.org/2014/12/innovation-leadership-lessons-from-the-marshmallow-challenge
2. Bordessa, K.: Team Challenges: 170+ Group Activities to Build Cooperation, Communication, and Creativity. Chicago Review Press, Chicago (2005)
3. ELAN. https://tla.mpi.nl/tools/tla-tools/elan/
4. Marshmallow challenge. http://www.marshmallowchallenge.com
5. Miller, B.C.: Quick team-building activities for busy managers: 50 exercises that get results in just 15 minutes. In: AMACOM (2003)
6. Sakata, M., Miyamoto, K.: Process in establishing communication in collaborative creation. In: Salvendy, G., Smith, M.J. (eds.) HCII 2011, Part II. LNCS, vol. 6772, pp. 315–324. Springer, Heidelberg (2011)
7. Searle, J.R.: Speech Acts: An Essay in the Philosophy of Language. Cambridge University Press, Cambridge (1969)
8. Schegloff, E.A., Sacks, H.: Opening up closings. Semiotica, VIII **4**, 289–327 (1973)
9. Skillman, P.: Marshmallow design challenge. In: TED2006. http://peterskillman.tumblr.com/post/74717155833/my-2006-talk-at-ted-in-monterey-3-minutes-on-the
10. Suzuki, N., Umata, I., Kamiya, T., Ito, S., Iwasawa, S., Inoue, N., Toriyama, T., Kogure, K.: Nonverbal behaviors in cooperative work: a case study of successful and unsuccessful team. In: Proceedings of CogSci2007, pp. 1527–1532 (2007)
11. Wujec, T.: Build a tower, build a team. In: TED2010. https://www.ted.com/talks/tom_wujec_build_a_tower

A Mechanism to Control Aggressive Comments in Pseudonym Type Computer Mediated Communications

Hiroki Yamaguchi[1] and Tetsuya Maeshiro[1,2(✉)]

[1] School of Library and Information Science, University of Tsukuba,
Tsukuba 305-8550, Japan
maeshiro@slis.tsukuba.ac.jp
[2] Research Center for Knowledge Communities, University of Tsukuba,
Tsukuba 305-8550, Japan

Abstract. We propose a mechanism to alleviate the aggression on Computer Mediated Communications. A title reflecting the aggressivity of comments posted by the user is displayed on screen. The effects of the proposed mechanism are verified with laboratory experiment, where participants post comments after reading the topics of discussion and other participants' comments. The results indicate the validity of the proposed mechanism.

1 Introduction

With recent widespreading of smartphones and PDAs, computer-mediated communication (CMC) has been increasingly popular. For example, online chat services enable sending messages back and forth among people on the Internet, and social networking service (SNS) enables building virtual community based on real community [1]. Compared to face to face (FTF) communications, CMC is characterized by the lack of Social Cue (e.g. voice, face, emotion, etc.) compared to FTF communication. It has been proposed that character based communications enhance public self-consciousness (public SC) and reduce private self-consciousness (private SC) [2]. Public SC means the externally directed consciousness, such as face and behavior, which can be seen by others. On the other hand, private SC denotes the internally directed consciousness, such as feeling, emotion and thinking, which can not be seen by others. There is a hypothesis of tendency to change self consciousness in order to increase anonymity, in direction to hide social cues [3].

The side effect of anonymity is the encouragement to deviate from the standard values and rules. For example, criminal accusations exist on 2-channel[1] and Twitter[2]. In response to this situation, the necessity of information literacy is increasingly recognized, and many educational institutions teach how to use SNS [4].

---

[1] http://www.2ch.net/.
[2] https://twitter.com/.

© Springer International Publishing Switzerland 2016
S. Yamamoto (Ed.): HIMI 2016, Part II, LNCS 9735, pp. 90–100, 2016.
DOI: 10.1007/978-3-319-40397-7_10

On the other hand, the advantage of anonymity is to encourage people to accuse, report crimes, and self-disclose. Encouraged self-disclosure means the abolishment of prejudice and even an opportunity to express opinion by disconnecting the discussion topic from personality. In addition, it prevents people from having a bias toward opinions driven by appearance or social status. Moreover, it facilitates shy people, who hesitate to express their opinions in public, to state their opinions.

The identity of a user on Internet can be classified based on attainability and linkability [5]. The attainability is defined as the possibility of identifying personal information, and the linkability is defined as possibility of distinguishing whether an online action is executed by the same person or not. Table 1 shows the explanation of autonym, pseudonym, and cryptonym based on attainability and linkability. For example, Facebook has attainability and linkability because it forces its users to disclose their real name. Hence it is an autonym service. On the other hand, 2-channel is a complex CMC service, because it has a huge number of threads and they belong to different classes. In 66 % of all forums users present their IDs, so that their comments can be linked to the user, however they are not forced to open their real name. In other 34 % forums, users are not forced open real name, without attached user IDs. Therefore, the former belongs to Pseudonym type, and the latter to Cryptonym type.

Table 1. Definitions of anonymity

	Attainability	Linkability
Autonym	Yes	Yes
Pseudonym	No	Yes
Cryptonym	No	No

CMC users can conceal their social cues, so individuality is easily lost [3]. In other words, they are difficult to realize the difference among each other. It is likely that such circumstances make them aggressive, besides the accusations cyber cascade, risky shifts and flamings. For example, according to an early CMC study, when the participants discussed on FTF and CMC to reach a consensus, the CMC group showed more aggressive and insulting comments compared to FTF communication groups [6]. However, the result is heavily criticized [7].

On the other hand, FTF communication curbs the outcome of group decision making because group members are afraid of criticism and poor evaluation of their idea. There is a possibility that CMC with assured anonymity reduces the user's feeling of pressure from other users [8]. In addition, it has been reported that the group decision support system (GDSS) alleviates effectively the social anxiety [9]. Thus GDSS facilitates group decision making on CMC. Moreover, it has been reported that the CMC group's motivation and degree of contribution are bigger than FTF communication group's [10]. Furthermore, the group decision by FTF communication often result in a small number of members contributing to the discussion, whereas CMC evens the contributions of all group members [11]. Thus, electronic brain storming (EBS) has been designed, and EBS seems to improve productivity of idea generation than normal brain storming on FTF communication [12].

In all above mentioned CMC services, there is a problem of aggressive comments by the users, sometimes resulting in flamings.

Mechanisms proposed to directly alleviate aggressions on CMC services are as follows.

1. When a user makes a comment and clicks "post button" on a CMC service, the service jumps to a page which recommend the user to have second thoughts about the context of comment before receiving and reflecting on the communication page.
2. When a user makes a comment and clicks "post button" on a CMC service, the service checks the comment by natural language processing, and if it contains aggressive words, it prohibits the user from posting.

Moreover, general parental control system can also detect the action that a user posts an aggressive comment. However, if a user is familiar to these methods, the user clicks automatically the button in the first method, or avoid using unprintable and bad words that are detected by the natural language processing. These methods are not effective in alleviating aggressive comments.

On the other hand, there are systems with moderation system, such as "Slashdot", "textream" and "Youtube", in which users moderate each other's comments, and every user can see the assessments of their comments. In "Slashdot", a title based on other users' assessments are assigned to each user. The title is a reminder to users that their comments are observed by other users, which may enhance public SC, and reduce private SC, and may alleviate user's aggressivity. A problem of these CMC services is that the titles are assigned to user accounts, which automatically requires the disclosure of users, and anonymous user cannot be used.

The present study focuses on anonymous CMC services, and proposes a mechanism to incorporate title assignment into pseudonym CMC services.

2   Methods

2.1   Hypotheses

Based on the relation between anonymity and self-consciousness, the following hypotheses are tested.

Hypothesis H1: In pseudonym CMC, the aggressivity of the user with attached title is lower than those without title.

Hypothesis H2: In pseudonym CMC, users with attached title take longer time to decide (forumulate) the comments than users without title.

The second hypothesis H2 is tested because displaying the attached title to the users might affect their self-consciousness to remind that their comments are assessed by other people, thus requiring longer time to decide or formulate the comments to post.

2.2   Experiment System

An experimental CMC system (Figs. 1, 2 and 3) was built to verify the validity of the proposed mechanism and to test the hypotheses H1 and H2.

It is necessary that the discussion topics used in the experiment include extreme opinions in order to generate aggressive comments. Twenty topics that actually resulted in active discussions and extreme opinions including some kind or rivalry in existing CMC services were extracted.

Prospected to clarify the subject's opinion and enhance rivalry mind from some CMC services. Figure 4 shows examples of discussion topics.

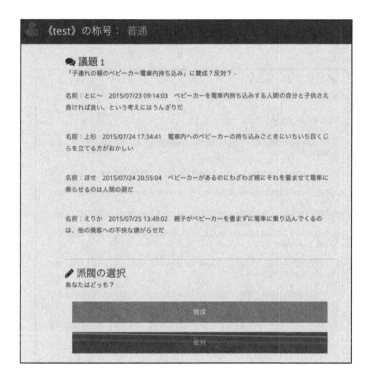

Fig. 1. Screenshot of experimental system at Step 1

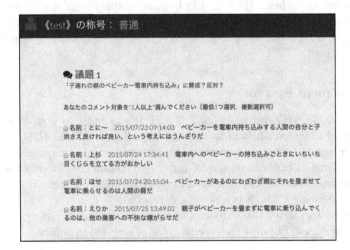

Fig. 2. Screenshot of experimental system at Step 2

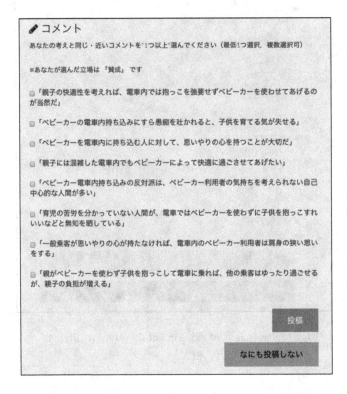

Fig. 3. Screenshot of experimental system at Step 3

Do you agree or disagree with the juvenile's act?
Do you agree or disagree with the nuclear power plant?
Do you agree or disagree with the education of second language from childhood?

Fig. 4. Examples of discussion topics

The experiment is conducted as follows.

1. Enter the account name.
2. Repeat twenty times the following steps.

   Step 1. Read a topic and comments from other four users about the topic, where two are agreeing opinions, and the other two are disagreeing opinions. Then choose (i) agree or (ii) disagree.

   Step 2. Read the four candidate comments, then select one comment that the participant wants to use as the replying comment to the forum. If there are no suitable comments, the participant does not have to select any comments.

   Step 3. Read the eight candidate comments, then select one comment that the participant wants to use as the replying comment to the forum. If there are no suitable comments, the participant does not have to select any comments.

3. Answer a questionnaire.

The participants select one comment for each topic from candidate comments which are prewritten sentences whose aggression levels (minimum: 1–maximum: 5) are predetermined in a pre-analysis. The aggression levels of comments are hidden to the subjects.

The number of topics is twenty, so that participants repeat twenty times the steps 1–3. The experiment consists of four sets, where each set consists of five topics. The duration of one experiment is about 60 min. Experimental room is laid silent. There are a desk and a laptop computer to access the experimental forum system. Only one person participates in one experiment session.

At the Step 1, four comments posted by four "virtual" users are presented to the participant, in order to simulate an on-going discussion. The four comments consists of two agreeing opinions to the presented topic, and two disagreeing opinions. At the Steps 2 and 3, sixteen candidate comments, consisting of eight agreeing and eight disagreeing opinions, are presented to the subject.

Twenty topics are provided in an experiment sessions, thus the total number of comments is 400. These comments consist of comments extracted from existing CMC services and originally created comments.

Only half (eight) of provided comments are presented to the subjects at Step 3, based on the agreeing or disagreeing opinion selected by the subject at Step 2. Furthermore, the presented comments can be divided into two classes (four comments based on reason-X, and four comments based on reason-Y). For example, if a participant selects disagree regarding the topic "Do you agree or disagree with the juvenile act?" at Step 2. In eight disagreeing candidate comments presented at Step 3, where four candidate comments are based on reason-X ("We must inflict a severe punishment on juvenile delinquency for regeneration"), and other four are based on reason-Y ("Victims or bereaved family can't be convinced of the reason for commutation of sentence which a criminal is youth"). In addition, the comments based on a reason consists of different aggression levels A, B, C and D (the weakest is A, the strongest is D).

We arranged the aggression level of comments by combining four content elements "Slanderous", "Critical", "Declarative", "Affirmative". "Slanderous" is when the context and its words make others uncomfortable. "Critical" indicates the words and context are contradictory. They can be used as the broad index of aggression. "Declarative" indicates the words and context do not include any softener expression, which is defined as the ending of sentences to make them mild, such as "in my humble opinion" or "for what it's worth" [13]. "Affirmative" indicates the words and context not belonging to the previous three content elements. In addition, the aggression level of the four example comments from other users (two agreeing and two disagreeing opinions) presented at Step 1 are level D, designed to cause subjects to select aggressive comments from the eight candidate comments at Steps 2 and 3. Table 2 shows the structure of the candidate comments.

Table 2. Structure of supposed comments

Faction	Basis of arguments	Aggression level (Ideal value)
Agree or disagree	X	A (1.5)
		B (2.5)
		C (3.5)
		D (4.5)
	Y	A (1.5)
		B (2.5)
		C (3.5)
		D (4.5)

The titles assigned and displayed to the participants are (1) "Rabid", (2) "Normal", and (3) "Clement". The initial title is "Normal" at set_1. The title changes three times at an interval (one min) between the sets. Note that the title does not change during one set.

The average aggression levels of selected comments at the set S_n determines the title at the next set S_{n+1}. The candidate comments include some comments who have gaps between the ideal value of aggression and measured value. In addition, the candidate comments presented at Step 2 depend on the faction selected at the last step, so that, we can not use uniformity criterion to decide the title. The following criteria are used.

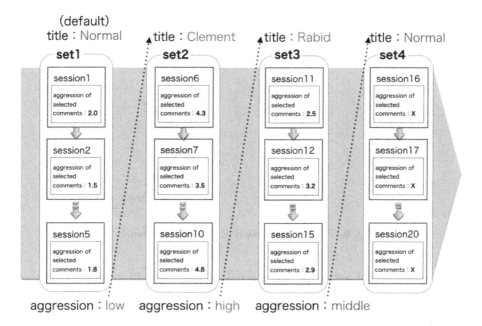

Fig. 5. Mechanism of title assignment

Rabid: The average aggression in set_n is higher than the maximum value of quartile deviation of the candidate comments presented in set S_n.

Normal: The average aggression in set S_n is within the quartile deviation of the candidate comments presented in set S_n.

Clement: The average aggression in set S_n is lower than the minimum value of quartile deviation the candidate comments presented in set S_n.

Figure 5 shows the title changing mechanism.

3   Results and Discussions

The number of participants was 46 (age: 18–27 yr), and Table 3 shows the ratio of male to female of this experiment. They were divided into the experimental group (n = 23, the title was presented) and control group (n = 23, title was hidden).

We compared the experimental group with the control group from the viewpoint of "average aggression of selected comments" and "average duration of selecting comments". The former corresponds to hypothesis H1, the latter corresponds to hypothesis H2. Shapiro-Wilk analysis indicated that both parameters are non-normal distribution, thus we used the Mann-Whitney U test to assess the statistical significance of mean differences between the groups.

Figure 6 shows the difference of average aggression of selected comments between the groups. The average aggressivity level of the experimental group was 6.9 % lower than the control group. Furthermore, the difference is significant ($p < 0.01$), indicating that the hypothesis H1 is supported. No significant

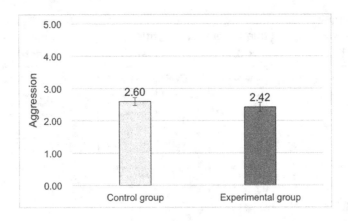

Fig. 6. Average aggression of selected comments

difference was found between the average duration of selecting comments of the experimental and control groups.

The number of sets attached with title "Rabid" was zero. The ratio of "Normal" and "Clement" were 42 % and 58 %. Furthermore, there were no difference on the two parameters (average duration of selecting comments and average aggression of selected comments) between "Normal" and "Clement" sessions.

Table 3. The ratio of male to female of this experiment

	Control group		Experimental group	
Male	15	65.2 %	11	47.8 %
Female	8	34.8 %	12	52.2 %
Total	23	100.0 %	23	100.0 %

In the experimental group, the ratio between male and female is approximately the same (Table 3). In the control group, however, male participants are approximately double of females. This is not a problem because gender difference seems to have no effect on cyber aggression [14]. Moreover, our experiment treats anonymous cases, so we assume that difference of gender ratio does not affect to the average aggression of selected comments.

Figure 7 shows the aggression histogram of selected comments. Figure 7 indicates that aggressive comments, those above 4.0, were hardly selected in both the experimental and control groups. It is possible that the participants do not tend to select highly aggressive comments, or the selection of aggressive comments was repressed by the experiment environment. To verify this point, the experimental design should be improved.

The following three methods are possible. (1) Use more aggressive candidate comments from CMC services to induce a more aggressive reaction.

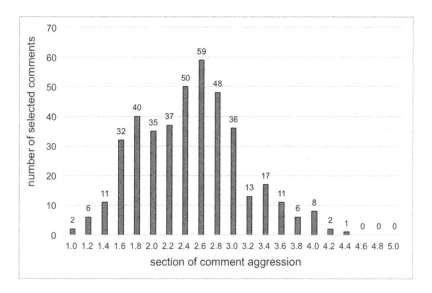

Fig. 7. Histogram of aggression levels of selected comments

(2) Experiment with younger participants, who are in early teens. (3) Incorporate more realistic settings to the experimental forum. The second method is based on the fact that the prefrontal cortex of adolescents is not fully developed yet, so teenagers have more difficulty in controlling their desires and behaviors [15]. The age of participants of the present study was between 18 to 27, University students, and they may have already known CMC manner and Internet literacy. The third method, to improve the experimental system, is to reduce the gap from the actual CMC services. In our study, the participants selected only one response from candidate comments. This might have caused the unrealistic feeling to the participants who use actual CMC services. Incorporating mechanism to allow participants to reply and obtain responses from other users, creating more interactive environment, and allowing submission of free texts instead of choosing prewritten texts, are possible improvements.

4   Conclusion

The purpose of this study is to alleviate the aggression on Computer Mediated Communication services by introducing the attachment of titles based on the comments written by the users. The results indicate that the aggressivity of comments can be reduced. However, it is interesting that the time duration to formulate comments was unaffected.

References

1. Institute for Information and Communications Policy: The Research on actual condition of Blog. (http://www.soumu.go.jp/iicp/chousakenkyu/data/research/survey/telecom/2009/2009-3.pdf)
2. Sato, H., Yoshida, F.: The effects of computer-mediated communication on uninhibited behavior and self-awareness. Tsukuba Psychol. Res. **36**, 1–9 (2008)
3. Hasegawa, S., Yasui, T., Yamaguchi, M.: Educational use of the social networking service and social learning. Nagoya Bunri Univ. Repository **13**, 51–58 (2013)
4. Sato, H., Hibino, K., Yoshida, F.: The effects of computer-mediated communication (CMC) on verbal aggression. Tsukuba Psychol. Res. **39**, 35–43 (2010)
5. Orita, T.: Anonymity on social media. Jpn. Soc. Artif. Intell. **27**(1), 59–66 (2012)
6. Sproull, L., Kiesler, S.: Connections New Ways of Working in the Networked Organization. MIT Press, Cambridge (1991)
7. Wallace, P.: The Psychology of the Internet. Cambridge University Press, Cambridge (1999)
8. Kimura, Y., Tsuzuki, T.: Group decision making and communication mode: an experimental social psychological examination of the differences between the computer-mediated communication and the face-to-face communication. Jpn. J. Exp. Soc. Psychol. **38**(2), 183–192 (1998)
9. Poole, M.S., Holmes, M., DeSanctis, G.: Conflict management in a computer-supported meeting in a computer supported meeting environment. J. Manage. Sci. **37**(8), 926–953 (1991)
10. Zigurs, I., Poole, M.S., DeSanctis, G.: A study of influence in computer-mediated group decision making. MIS Q. **12**(4), 625–644 (1988)
11. Hiltz, S., Johnson, K., Turoff, M.: Group decision support: the effects of designated leaders and statistical feedback in computerized conferences. J. Manage. Inf. Syst. **8**, 81–108 (1986)
12. Collaros, P.A., Anderson, L.R.: Effect of perceived expertness upon creativity of members of brainstorming groups. J. Appl. Psychol. **53**, 159–163 (1969)
13. Matsuda, E., Okada, K.: Interpersonal relationships on computer-mediated communication: the psychological analysis of interpersonal trust, aggression and emotion-regulation skills. J. Multimed. Aided Educ. Res. **2**(1), 159–173 (2005)
14. Schoffstall, C.L., Cohen, R.: Cyber aggression: the relation between online offenders and offline social competence. Soc. Dev. **20**(3), 587–604 (2011)
15. Lenroot, R.K., Giedd, J.N.: Brain development in children and adolescents: insights from anatomical magnetic resonance imaging. Neurosci. Biobehav. Rev. **30**, 718–729 (2006)

Information in e-Learning and e-Education

One Size Does Not Fit All: Applying the Right Game Concepts for the Right Persons to Encourage Non-game Activities

Hina Akasaki[✉], Shoko Suzuki, Kanako Nakajima, Koko Yamabe, Mizuki Sakamoto, Todorka Alexandrova, and Tatsuo Nakajima

Department of Computer Science and Engineering, Waseda University, Tokyo, Japan
{h.akasaki,s.suzuki,kanako.n,k.yamabe,mizuki, toty,tatsuo}@dcl.cs.waseda.ac.jp

Abstract. In this paper, we present some insights extracted from experiences with conducting three case studies that show how different game-based approaches affect people's motivation to encourage more activities in digital services. The first case study is a game-based English words learning application. The second case study is a gamified sharing economy service. The third case study is a persuasive service customized for a user's unique preference. The results of the case studies show that adopting only one approach is not effective to motivate all diverse people, and multiple approaches should be incorporated when developing digital services that motivate diverse users by game-based approaches.

Keywords: Gamification · Human motivation · Personality · Preference · Learning · Sharing economy · Healthcare

1 Introduction

Most young people have spent plenty of time playing video games because playing a game increases their pleasure and happiness [9]. Applying game concepts in order to motivate people to change or increase certain daily activities has already been recognized as a promising approach. Human motivation is an important aspect in our daily life [3] and game concepts can increase the human motivation artificially [12] and help to achieve a flourished society [6]. One of the most popular approaches is using a "serious game" [2]. A serious game usually looks like a typical video game, but the goal of the game is not to achieve fictional missions in a virtual world but to acquire practical skills in the real world or to increase the knowledge for preventing certain undesirable habits [10]. Another approach to encourage the change of people's daily activities and behavior is to use the "gamification" concept [4, 11, 21]. Gamification adopts game mechanics like points, badges and leaderboards in non-entertainment information services to engage their users.

The aim of this paper is to show that one game-based approach is not effective for diverse people, and multiple approaches need to be adopted in order to motivate larger and more diverse audience. For example, in [15], we show that each player's personality

© Springer International Publishing Switzerland 2016
S. Yamamoto (Ed.): HIMI 2016, Part II, LNCS 9735, pp. 103–114, 2016.
DOI: 10.1007/978-3-319-40397-7_11

has a significant influence on his/her motivation to play a trading card game, and thus there is a need to incorporate multiple ways to motivate people with different personalities.

In this paper, we present some insights extracted from experiences with conducting three case studies that show how different game-based approaches affect people's motivation. The first case study is a game-based English words learning application. The second case study is a gamified sharing economy service. The third case study is a persuasive service customized for a user's unique preference. The results of the case studies show that adopting only one approach is not effective to motivate all diverse people, and multiple approaches should be investigated when developing digital services to motivate diverse people by game-based approaches.

The remainder of the paper is organized as follows. In Sect. 2, we show a game-based English words learning application and the effect of different types of user motivations in the game. Section 3 presents a gamified sharing economy service and the effect of different personalities in the service. Section 4 shows a persuasive service customized for a user who has a unique preference. Section 5 discusses how to develop ludic services effective for diverse people. Finally, we conclude the paper in Sect. 6.

2   Designing a Ludic Solution Based on a Player's Motivation

In the first case study, we have developed a simple game-based English words learning application. The application has the following four versions. The first version (Type A) does not adopt any game concepts. The second version (Type B) uses the gamification-based approach. This version uses points and badges to motivate users. The third version (Type C) uses the serious game-based approach. In this version, a user plays the application in a fictional world, and some fictional rewards are given when missions are completed. The last version (Type D) adopts both the gamification and the serious game-based approaches. As shown in Fig. 1, we define a gamifying degree to indicate the strength of extrinsic influence on users. We have developed four games based on the gamifying degree as shown in Fig. 2.

In the experiment of the first case study, we classified users' personalities based on the following two factors. The first factor is the inherent motivation, and the second factor is the context-dependent motivation as classified in [8]. The inherent motivation indicates whether a person has high motivation to perform any activity. Conversely, the context-dependent motivation means that a person has a high motivation for performing only a specific activity; in this case, English word learning.

We conducted the experiment with 31 participants that were between 20 and 50 years old, and each participant played the respective four versions of the game. We first investigated each participant's inherent motivation and context-dependent motivation through questionnaires, and based on the results of the questionnaires categorized them into four groups, that were IM High-CM High, IM High-CM Low, IM Low-CM High, IM Low-CM Low, where IM stands for inherent motivation and CM stands for context-dependent motivation. For our experiment based on the preliminary questionnaires, the 31 participants were divided into these four groups as follows: 9 participants with IM

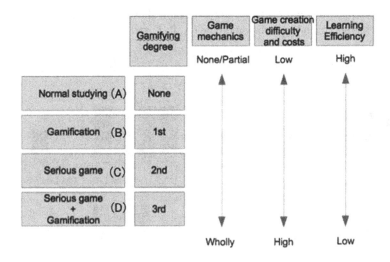

Fig. 1. Gamifying degree

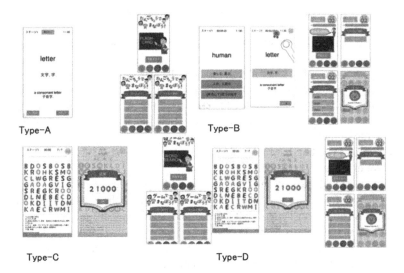

Fig. 2. Four types of games

High-CM High, 3 participants with IM Low-CM High, 5 participants with IM Low-CM High, 14 participants with IM Low-CM Low. Then, the participants were asked to play the four different types of games described above. After participants completed to play the games, we conducted additional questionnaires based on the Bandura's self-efficacy [1] scale to measure how a participant liked the games and how effective they were for their goals. The results of the experiment are given in Fig. 3. The figure shows two graphs for the results of each of the four groups the users were divided into, based on their inherent and context-dependent motivation classification. The right graph shows how many people liked the approach and the left graph shows how many people felt self-efficacy in the approach for each game type (A, B, C and D).

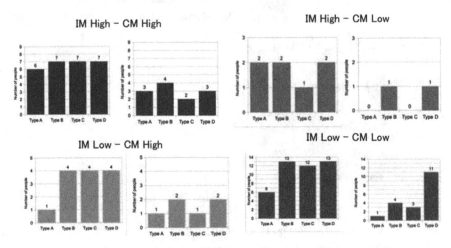

Inherent Motivation (IM), Context Dependent Motivation (CM)

Fig. 3. How each game motivates participants?

From the results of the experiment, we first discuss the effect of the gamification-based approach as shown in Fig. 3 for each group that has different types of motivations. Based on the results, first we compare the effect of Type A and Type B; in this case, all users increase their motivations more in Type B than in Type A. Next, we compare the effect of Type C and Type D. Similarly, all users increase their motivations more in Type D than in Type C. This means that the gamification-based approach is basically effective for all users.

Second, we would like to discuss the effect of adding the serious game-based approach. We compare the effect of Type A and Type C; basically, when the inherent motivations are low, Type C is better than Type A, but there are not significant differences between Type A and Type C in other cases. However, when comparing Type B and Type D, Type D is significantly better than Type B if both motivations are low, but there are no significant differences between Type B and Type D in other cases. This means that the serious game-based approach is not effective when either motivation is high.

An important observation from the results is that when both motivations are low, combining the gamification-based approach and the serious game-based approach is effective for most people.

The results of the case study indicate that the effect of a serious game to introduce deep gaming experiences is not effective if a player already has either of the motivations. For him/her, the motivation to learn English words is high, so he/she wants to learn English words directly and the game effect disturbs his/her inherent motivation to learn English words. The strong game-based approach may kill a user's motivation for the target activities. Also, it is hard to develop a serious game that attracts a user well. On the other hand, introducing gamification is basically effective for all participants. Also, if a participant's both motivations are not high enough, the effect of a serious game increases the effectiveness of gamification.

3   Designing a Ludic Solution Based on a Player's Personality

The sharing economy referring to peer-to-peer-based sharing of access to goods and services has recently attracted a great deal of attention [5, 14]. The term covers a sprawling range of digital platforms and offline activities such as Airbnb[1]: a peer-to-peer lodging service and Uber[2]: a peer-to-peer transportation network. The sharing economy typically uses information technology to provide individuals, corporations, non-profits and governments with information that enables the optimization of resources through the redistribution, sharing and reuse of excess capacity in goods and services. The sharing economy services have been recently growing rapidly world wide, but the popularity of the services in Japan is still limited. The purpose of this case study is to encourage the usage of these services to Japanese people by enhancing the services through game mechanics with the pop cultural atmosphere.

In the second case study, we have developed a gamified sharing economy service through storytelling to encourage a user to actively use the sharing economy service. In the service named "Osusowake" as shown in Fig. 4, each user can rent currently necessary goods from other users who do not need to use the goods at the moment to encourage sharing goods within a community. A virtual world is offered for the users in the Osusowake sharing economy. In a fictional story of the virtual world, the users become more active in the sharing economy with helps of a female fictional guide. The system adopts the following four gamification elements - badge, collection, rank and storytelling. In particular, we would like to compare the effects of storytelling with other typical gamifications elements; our study performed an experiment to evaluate the effectiveness of a game story to increase the motivation of a user.

In the experiment, we recruited 13 participants and conducted interviews with them. From the interviews, we found that storytelling helps us to understand what motivates a user. For example, a service is designed to teach a user why he/she needs to perform an activity presented in the story or why an activity is undesirable with concrete examples. If a user can learn the meaning of the activity that is particularly encouraged in a service or improve his/her attitude against currently undesirable activities for him/her through storytelling, the user can continue to perform the activities with his/her own internal motivation. This aspect is a very strong advantage of storytelling that other gamification elements do not have because traditional gamification elements usually increase only external motivation to encourage short-term activities.

We also conducted two personality tests for the 13 participants to check the personality of each participant and investigate the influence of a user's personality on the effectiveness of respective gamification elements used in the developed service. The first personality test: Bartle Test[3] classifies a person into four categories depending on

---

[1]   https://www.airbnb.com/.
[2]   https://www.uber.com/.
[3]   http://mud.co.uk/richard/hcds.htm/.

Fig. 4. Osusowake sharing economy service

how he/she plays MMORPG (Massively Multiplayer Online Role-Playing Game). These four personality categories are: Achiever, Explorer, Socializer and Killer, and the test shows how and which personality is stronger than other personalities. Table 1 shows the results of Bartle Test for the participants in this case study. Big Five Test[4] is a diagnostic test describing the human personality with five dimensions. In our current experiment, Bartle Test is more useful to present the effect of the personalities on gamification elements than the Big Five Test. Thus, in this paper, we only show the results of the analysis based on Bartle Test.

In the analysis to investigate the effect of gamification elements, we first classified all participants based on their highest personality score in Bartle Test as shown in Table 1 (for example, the first participant in the table is Achiever). We assumed a hypothesis that a person classified in a certain personality category in Bartle Test is engaged effectively by a different set of gamification elements. For investigating the hypothesis, we asked the participants to fill questionnaires before and after the experiment. The first questionnaire investigated how each participant expected the effect of each gamification element, and the second questionnaire investigated how each participant was actually affected by each gamification element after the game. Table 2 shows each hypothesis and the corresponding actual result. In the current experiment, only one participant had the highest score in the Socializer category so we omitted this personality in the table. As shown in the results, the gamification elements that we expected to offer strong effect were not actually the most effective.

We also analyze why our expectation is different from the actual effect in the experiment based on a participant's personality. In the analysis, we investigate a participant's personality whose personality score in Bartle Test is higher than 50 %. Therefore, 9 participants have the Achiever personality, 4 have Explorer, 7 have Killer, and 7 have Socializer personality as shown in Table 1.

---

[4] http://www.outofservice.com/bigfive/.

Table 1. Personality scores in Bartle test

Participant	Achiever(%)	Explorer(%)	Killer(%)	Socializer(%)
1	60	53	40	47
2	40	87	13	60
3	20	80	40	60
4	47	73	20	60
5	60	33	40	67
6	53	33	93	20
7	60	33	80	27
8	67	33	40	60
9	53	33	87	27
10	40	40	67	53
11	60	33	60	47
12	80	27	60	33
13	53	27	67	53

Table 2. Hypothesis and results each category of Bartle test

Category Name	Effective Elements (in Hypothesis)	Effective Elements (Before Experiment)	Effective Elements (After Experiment)
Achiever	Badge Rank Collection	1st: Collection 2nd: Rank 3rd: Badge 4th: Story	1st: Collection 2nd: Badge 3rd: Story 4th: Rank
Explorer	Story	1st: Story 2nd: Rank 3rd: Collection 4th: Badge	1st: Collection 2nd: Story 3rd: Rank 4th: Badge
Killer	Rank	1st: Rank 1st: Badge 2nd: Collection 3rd: Story	1st: Collection 2nd: Badge 3rd: Story 4th: Rank

We first consider that a rank is effective and a collection is not effective for participants whose personality is Killer because they usually tend to like competing with others and to compare their ranks. However, the results after the experiment show opposite results, i.e. collection was the most effective and rank was the least effective element. We further investigated that this unexpected results happened because our design for the rank is difficult to be compared among participants, but the number of the collections owned by each participant can be easily compared, thus they can compete to earn more collections.

We next analyzed how the motivation of participants improved by every gamification element.

For Achievers, badges that can be earned by individuals are typically effective, but for Killers and Socializers, badges that can be compared with others are more effective than the badges earned by individuals because Socializers tend to increase the relationship with other participants through exchanging badges and Killers compete with each other by comparing acquired badges.

Collections in games that participants usually play tend to be effective for Explorers, but in our current system, collections were effective for people with any personality. We think that the reason for that is the fact that each participant's collections in our systems can be seen by other participants, thus it is effective for Killers to compete by explicitly showing the differences of their collections with others and for Socializers to increase their social relationship by exchanging their collections.

Ranks in games that participants usually play tend to be effective for all personalities, but in our current system, ranks appear to be not so effective for any personality. Many participants said that this is because there is no benefit to raise the rank in our current system. In certain games usually played by the participants, raising ranks also increases the effect of other gamification elements, but our current system is not well designed to offer such effects.

Storytelling is usually effective for Explorer because stories allow them to exploit the stories' worlds. However, from the experiment, we found that the stories are also effective for Socializers. The reason is that Socializers may enjoy the relationship with characters in the stories. For example, the story in Osusowake tries to establish the close relationships with a user. However, the effect of a story depends on a user's taste. If a user does not like characters or a view of the world in the story, the story is not effective to motivate the user.

We think that the following reasons might be the sources of the above results. The first reason is that the current design of each gamification element implemented in our system has a different level of completion. The second reason is that each gamification element that is targeted to a specific personality has unexpected effects on people who has other personalities. Our case study shows that analyzing services based on Bartle Test's personalities is a useful tool for designing services that motivate diverse people and identify possible pitfalls of the design.

4 Designing a Ludic Solution Based on a Player's Unique Preference

In the third case study, we present the effect of the game-based approach on changing undesirable everyday habits for people who are pop culture geeks and tend to sleep very late, which frequently causes their health problems. Most traditional persuasive technologies solutions tried to ensure that the average of users improve to change their habits. We have developed a game-based application that encourages pop culture geeks to sleep earlier by using stories told by their favorite virtual characters as shown in Fig. 5. In these stories, fictional characters present the importance to sleep earlier to users for maintaining their good health. The results of the experiment show that traditional game-based approach is not effective. However, our approach changes pop culture geek's undesirable behavior successfully.

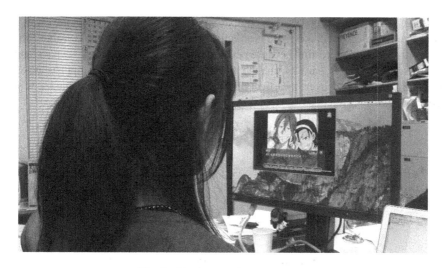

Fig. 5. Playing the third case study

In the case study, we assume a player who likes the Boy's Love culture [13] as her unique preference. Boy's Love is a very popular pop culture for young girls recently, and there are many types of products and contents on the topic such as comics, novels, animations and games. In particular, it is a popular culture to create a Boy's Love game around a character that appears in well known comic or animation stories. The most important issues for a person who likes the Boy's Love culture is that the character appearing in the media contents is highly preferred by the person. Also, as shown in the past research, using a virtual agent is effective to persuade people [19, 20]. Thus, in this study, our game adopts virtual characters used in Boy's Love media contents, where the behavior of the characters and how they talk reflect typical manners of the Boy's Love culture. Therefore, a player of the case study believes that the virtual characters appearing in the game are very typical in the Boy's Love story.

We conducted an experiment to use the game to persuade the healthier lifestyle of a player who prefers the Boy's Love culture. We recruited 4 participants who liked the Boy's Love culture in the experiment. The case study is a game to persuade players to sleep earlier in the evening, to wake up early in the morning and walk enough every day. Typical people, who like Boy's Love usually stay up late at night and usually prefer to stay at home during the day. The purpose of the game is to improve the undesirable habits of the geek people through the persuasion by the virtual characters that he/she prefers.

In the experiment of the case study, we first checked the sleep time and wakeup time of each participant, and how many steps he/she walks a day before playing the game for seven days. The results are shown in Table 3, where results are the average for the seven days. Then, after playing the game, we checked again their sleep and wake up time and the number of steps they were doing a day. The results are shown in Table 4, where results are also the average of seven days. Table 4 shows that all the participants started sleeping earlier at night, they all had longer and healthier sleep for the night and most of them walked more steps per day compared with before the experiment. From the results, we considered that the game is effective to change the users' undesirable habits. The results are very interesting because people who like Boy's Love usually have undesirable habits and it is hard to change their habits with traditional approaches for persuading people. However, the effect of the game is significant if the game takes into account a geek's preference.

Table 3. Results before playing the game

Participant	Sleep Time	Wakeup Time	Walk Steps
A	1:28am	6:26am	8639
B	2:05am	7:06am	6176
C	3:17am	5:35am	4256
D	1:35am	5:32am	6328

Table 4. Results after playing the game

Participant	Sleep Time	Wakeup Time	Walk Steps
A	0:11am	7:00am	10515
B	0:40am	8:19am	5929
C	0:45am	6:39am	8167
D	23:52pm	6:54am	9901

5 Design Implication for Designing for Diversity

In past work on gamification, some researchers claimed its ineffectiveness. On the other hand, other researchers claimed the effectiveness of the approach. The contradictory results may come from the small number of participants in these experiments, where there may be a strong bias in the participants among the experiments. The claim of our study can explain these results; they did not take into account the possibility of the bias caused by the participants' personalities or preferences in the experiments.

The results of the case studies indicate two interesting findings. The first finding is that it is important to take into account the type of a user's motivation. If a user is already motivated to achieve a goal, game concepts are not necessary to encourage him/her. On the contrary, introducing game concepts in this case may decrease the player's motivation significantly. The current gamification-based approach supports some light-weighted game mechanics like badges, points and leaderboards; the effects do not offer a great impact on human motivation, due to their shallow game experiences but future gamification will expand the scope and include deeper game experiences. In this case, designers need to be careful how the game mechanics affect a user's motivation.

The second finding is that it is essential to take into account a user's preferences and personality when designing deeper game experiences. In the second case study, we observed the effect of a user's personality on deeper game experiences. The third case study is customized based on a user's hobby. Most of the current gamification-based approaches have been designed for average people not diverse people. However, for flourishing our society, all diverse people need to be satisfied with their daily life. Our approach claims the necessity to design digital services for diverse people and offers some insights for designing gamification for all; it is essential to incorporate multiple approaches to attract diverse people. In particular, our essential contribution is to demonstrate that customized persuasive effects according to people's deep taste or preference are very effective. Even if the usual persuasion strategy for the average is not effective, the customized persuasion for people with a unique preference may work well.

Designing the semiotic meaning of the real world is a promising approach to systematically develop ludic digital services [7, 16, 17]. In particular, the real world should be meaningful for people to motivate them. As shown in [18], the diversity of users' preferences and personalities can be taken into account based on the approach. Also, incorporating fictionality into the real world is an effective technique to change the semiotic meaning, and offer more meaningful effect for persuading them. We will investigate how to enhance the insights extracted in the paper in the near future, and we will extend the framework shown in [18] to develop digital services to take into account people's diversity.

6   Conclusion

References

1. Bandura, A.: Guide for constructing self-efficacy scales. In: Pajares, F., Urdan, T. (eds.) Self-efficacy Beliefs of Adolescents, vol. 5, pp. 307–337. Information Age Publishing, Greenwich (2006)
2. Bellotti, F., Kapralos, B., Lee, K., Moreno-Ger, P., Berta, R.: Assessment in and of serious games: an overview. Adv. Hum.-Comput. Interact. **2013**, Article ID 136864 (2013). doi:10.1155/2013/136864
3. Deci, E.L.: The Psychology of Self-Determination. Lexington Books, Lanham (1980)
4. Deterding, S., Dixon, D., Khaled, R., Nacke, N.: From game design elements to gamefulness: defining "Ramification". In: Proceedings of the 15th International Academic MindTrek Conference: Envisioning Future Media Environments, pp. 9–15 (2011)
5. Hamari, J., Sjöklint, M., Ukkonen, A.: The sharing economy: why people participate in collaborative consumption. J. Assoc. Inf. Sci. Technol. (2015). doi:10.1002/asi.23552
6. IJsselsteijn, W.A., de Kort, Y.A., Midden, C., Eggen, B., van den Hoven, E.: Persuasive technology for human well-being: setting the scene. In: IJsselsteijn, W.A., de Kort, Y.A., Midden, C., Eggen, B., van den Hoven, E. (eds.) PERSUASIVE 2006. LNCS, vol. 3962, pp. 1–5. Springer, Heidelberg (2006)
7. Ishizawa, F., Takahashi, M., Irie, K., Sakamoto, M., Nakajima, T.: Analyzing augmented real spaces gamified through fictionality. In: Proceedings of the 13th International Conference on Advances in Mobile Computing and Multimedia (2015)
8. Kage, M.: The 12 Theories to Learn Motivation. Kongo Pub. (2012) (in Japanese)

9. McGonigal, J.: Reality is Broken: Why Games, Make Us Better and How They Can Change the World. Penguin Press, London (2011)
10. Nakajima, K., Nakajima, T.: A vocabulary learning game using a serious-game approach. In: Huang, Y.-M., Chao, H.-C., Deng, D.-J., Park, J.J.J.H. (eds.) Advanced Technologies, Embedded and Multimedia for Human-Centric Computing, pp. 13–22. Springer, The Netherlands (2014)
11. Liu, Y., Alexandrova, T., Nakajima, T.: Gamifying intelligent environments. In: Proceedings of the 2011 International ACM Workshop on Ubiquitous Meta User Interfaces (2011)
12. Nakajima, T., Lehdonvirta, V.: Designing motivation using persuasive ambient mirrors. Pers. Ubiquit. Comput. **17**(1), 107–126 (2013)
13. Oto, T.: Knowledge creation in second generation creation, knowledge co-creation. In: Knowledge Co-creation Forum, vol. 1 (2011). (in Japanese)
14. Puschmann, T., Alt, R.: Sharing Economy. Bus. Inf. Syst. Eng. **58**(1), 93–99 (2016)
15. Sakamoto, M., Alexandrova, T., Nakajima, T.: Analyzing the influence of virtuality on playful social interaction. Multimedia Tools Appl. 1–29 (2015). Springer. doi:10.1007/s11042-015-2751-x
16. Sakamoto, M., Nakajima, T.: In search of the Right design abstraction for designing persuasive affordance towards a flourished society. In: Proceedings of the 9th International Conference on Design and Semantics of Form and Movement (2015)
17. Sakamoto, M., Nakajima, T.: A better integration of fictionality into daily lives for achieving a digital-physical hybrid gameful world. In: The 20th International Conference on Control Systems and Computer Science (2015)
18. Sakamoto, M., Nakajima, T., Alexandrova, T.: Enhancing values through virtuality for intelligent artifacts that influence human attitude and behavior. Multimedia Tools Appl. **74**(24), 11537–11568 (2015)
19. Schulman, D., Bickmore, T.: Persuading users through counseling dialogue with a conversational agent. In: Proceedings of the International Conference on Persuasive Technologies (2009)
20. Yoshii, A., Nakajima, T.: A study on persuasive effect of preference of virtual agents. In: Huang, Y.-M., Chao, H.-C., Deng, D.-J., Partk, J.J.J.H. (eds.) Advanced Technologies, Embedded and Multimedia for Human-Centric Computing, pp. 47–55. Springer, The Netherlands (2014)
21. Zichermann, G., Cunningham, C.: Gamification by Design: Implementing Game Mechanics in Web and Mobile Apps. O'Reilly, Sebastopol (2011)

Gaze-Aware Thinking Training Environment to Analyze Internal Self-conversation Process

Yuki Hayashi[1(✉)], Kazuhisa Seta[1], and Mitsuru Ikeda[2]

[1] College of Sustainable System Sciences,
Osaka Prefecture University, Osaka, Japan
hayashi@kis.osakafu-u.ac.jp
[2] School of Knowledge Science,
Japan Advanced Institute of Science and Technology, Nomi, Japan

Abstract. To communicate one's thinking precisely and to find proper solution in case of conflict, it is important to improve one's thinking skills. Thinking skills are required to expose the root of conflict between one's own thought process and that of others. To cultivate such a skill, a training tool that analyzes a person's internal self-conversation by verbalizing their thought is proposed by [1]. If such a process can be interpreted in human-understandable levels, a system can judge whether the learner is thinking logically in the self-conversation or not. In this paper, we propose a system that traces the sequence of a user's eye-gaze during his/her internal self-conversation process. The initial analysis based on the trainers' correction process data for hospital nurses' cases showed that our proposed system has the potential to interpret the context of a person's metacognitive monitoring and control process.

Keywords: Internal self-conversation · Thinking externalization · Meta-cognitive activity · Eye-tracking

1 Introduction

In our daily life, we experience many difficult social issues that may have various viewpoints, making it difficult to find a proper solution in such situations. To enable a person to think deeply about the problems and arrive at a logical decision under any circumstances, it is important to enhance their meta-cognitive skills of "internal self-conversation." The self-conversation requires creation of new knowledge by identifying conflicts between one's own thinking and that of others. In order to train such a tacit process, Chen et al. proposed a thinking training environment for learners' internal self-conversation [1]. The tool plays the role of a safety wheel for learners so that they eventually think about their self-conversation. Previous research includes continuously practiced educational programs using Sizhi for undergraduate university students and hospital nurses [2, 3]. It has been reported that the tool effectively works to cultivate the meta-cognitive skills of the learners. However, while the quality of the externalized thought (i.e. collective statements and their logic) varies depending on the learners, the difference between externalization processes of each learner's self-conversation such as what the learner saw, thought, and verbalized is unrevealed.

© Springer International Publishing Switzerland 2016
S. Yamamoto (Ed.): HIMI 2016, Part II, LNCS 9735, pp. 115–125, 2016.
DOI: 10.1007/978-3-319-40397-7_12

The objective of this study is to propose a learning environment to analyze the internal self-conversation process based on a learner's gazing behavior along with their thinking externalization action. Eye-gazing behavior can be used to interpret a learner's exhaustive thinking process between actions; as the famous proverb goes: *the eyes are as eloquent as the tongue*. In addition to analyzing a learner's thinking process, the system also analyzes the thinking process of the trainers who assess and adjust the learner's outcome. To date, an eye-tracker has been mostly used to analyze the process of viewing advertisements or reading text (e.g. Web searching [4], difference between normal reading and mindless reading [5]). Although some research has been conducted on analyzing the verbalization process by using the eye-tracker (e.g. stimulated retrospective think-aloud [6]), as far as we know, there is no study on eye-gazing behavior during an internal self-conversation process. If the process could be interpreted and modeled in human-understandable levels, the system may judge whether the learner is thinking logically in the self-conversation or not, also the system may provide an intellectual support to foster the effective self-conversation process.

In following sections, we first introduce the importance of internal self-conversation and explain our approach. Then, we explain the internal self-conversation training system that has a function to trace the sequence of user's eye-gazing information in the thinking process. Finally, we discuss the results of the initial analysis to validate the available eye-gazing data in the thinking process.

2 Sizhi: Thinking Training Environment for Self-conversation

In general, it is important to externalize one's logical thinking. We cannot always express our thought process precisely. Therefore, it is must to focus on the effect of the "verbalization" of thoughts as a learning strategy and propose a model on verbalization [7] to meet the learning goals. The model describes the sequence of three phases: *description* (cyclic state of verbalizing one's thought based on own experiences), *cognitive-conflict* (state of facing the conflict through the verbalization of one's thought and interaction with others), and *knowledge-building* (cyclic state to resolve the conflict states). Along with the process, if learners actively think deeply about the problem faced by them as an internal self-conversation, their thinking process becomes unclouded and the thinking gets sophisticated.

In order for learners to train their ability on thinking process, Chen et al. proposed the thinking training environment called "Sizhi" [1] as shown in Fig. 1. They claim that the most important aspect in designing the tool is to clearly verbalize one's own thinking (*thinking-A*) and that of others (*thinking-B*) by reflecting on one's own thinking process in a logical manner, and reflect on the thinking process to find *meaningful conflicts*. In the tool, a learner must verbalize his/her thinking by switching Sizhi tabs that represents three thinking phases based on [7], and by selecting Sizhi tags to add descriptive statement expressing the type of thought (detail information is described in Sect. 3.1).

They also propose the replay tool called "Sizhi player" to capture a learner's thinking reflection process [8]. The tool has a function to display the internal self-conversation

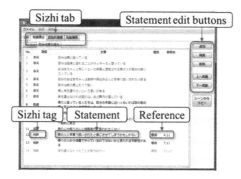

Fig. 1. Sizhi interface proposed by [1]

process by reading Sizhi log. Since the replay is based on a learner's externalized actions (e.g. clicking the mouse and pushing keyboard buttons), the reason for the learner's action is still implicit. Therefore, the interpretation depends on viewers.

Our research with eye-gazing information as a key aims to lighten a part of the learner's meta-cognitive monitoring and control process in the context of self-conversation.

3   Proposed System

3.1   System Interface

Figure 2 shows the interface of the system we developed. The system follows the learning design concept of Sizhi explained in the previous section. The interface depicts four thinking areas: "*A's-thinking*" denotes one's own thinking, "*B's-thinking*" denotes opponent's thinking, "*conflict*" denotes the difference between A's-thinking and B's-thinking, and "*knowledge-building*" denotes dissolving the root of conflict. In A's-thinking, B's-thinking and knowledge-building areas, the user can add/delete their statements using the Statement edit buttons and input the statement text by selecting pre-defined Sizhi tags such as *fact*, *hypothesize*, *decision*, *assumption*, *policy/principle* etc. The user can also add other statements as references to express the reason for adding the statement. To help the learner to gain deep insight into conflicts in the cognitive-conflict areas, the user is allowed to select only one *policy/principle* statement from each of the statements described in A's-thinking and B's-thinking area, and express the root of conflict into the text area.

To track a user's gazing behavior in internal self-conversation process, we introduced a screen-based eye-tracker device (Tobii Pro X2-30 [9]) that provides gaze data at 30 Hz. The device distinguishes the type of area in the interface a user is looking at by setting area of interest (AOI) regions to areas and objects. This way, even if the user moves the positions of the objects (e.g. positions of statements move by scroll-bar or up/down button in the interface), our system correctly detects the targets by judging whether the eye movements fall within such AOI at each frame. Currently, it recognizes *four types of thinking areas* (A's-thinking, B's-thinking, conflict, and knowledge-construct), *each*

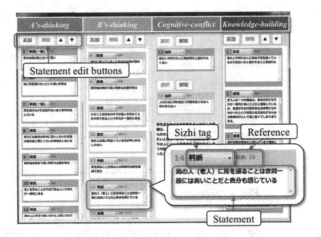

Fig. 2. Gaze-aware Sizhi interface

statement area itself and *the included components* (areas of Sizhi tag, reference, and text), *conflict text area*, and *edit buttons*. The system records the user's activity details, which includes user's gazing events and thinking externalization action (i.e. keyboard and mouse events).

We assume that the proposed system can be used to analyze the meta-cognitive thinking process in the following conditions:

- *Externalizing internal self-conversations by learners*; the difference between the sequences of learners' gazing data by collating their critical thinking skills.
- *Correcting the learner's outcome by skillful trainers*; type of verbalized thoughts the trainers tend to focus on, and adjust them for exposing the root of conflict using the clue of gazing data.

In addition, the system has a potential to introduce interactive situations during learner-learner/trainer (e.g. to show the sequence of learner's gazing targets to the trainer).

3.2   Output Data for Analysis

To analyze the internal self-conversation process, it is necessary that the system records the user's exhaustive behavior through the session as much as possible. Table 1 shows the specification of the system log file format. The file is generated as comma separated value (csv) format, and each line corresponds to each detected event. Row 1 and 2 indicates the time data of the event. For analysis purpose, the system records each event on the millisecond time scale. Row 3 represents meta-event name: events in *operations of statement object* (STATEMENT_EVENT), *operations of conflict area* (CONFLICT_EVENT), *eye-gazing target changing* (GAZE_EVENT), and *user's operations to the system* (SYSTEM_EVENT). Row 4 corresponds to the specific event name of the meta-event, and the following data (after Row 5) shows the detail information of the event.

For example, when a user clicks a statement (id: 4, 3rd statement from the top in A's-thinking area, reason: nothing), following is the output on the millisecond time scale:

...	...	...						
1450256939878	2015-12-16-18-08-59-878	STATEMENT_ EVENT	FOCUS_ TEXT_AREA	ThinkingA	4	3	*Tag*	*Statement Text*
...	...	...						

Especially, in case of changing eye-gazing target, nested records of the target object's IN/OUT event appears in pairs when the eye-coordination falls within/out of the target AOI area:

...	...	...								
1450256431512	2015-12-16-18-00-31-512	GAZE_EVENT	IN	Statement	Construct	2	2	*Tag*	*Statement text*	4 5	7 4
...	...	...								
1450256431815	2015-12-16-18-00-31-815	GAZE_EVENT	OUT	Statement	Construct	2	2	*Tag*	*Statement text*	4 5	7 4
...	...	...								

The records present the data when a user looks at the statement (id: 2, 2nd statement from the top in knowledge-construct area, reason: statements 4 and 5), and looks away from the same statement after a few seconds (303 ms). Thus, the log data allows us to trace not only the time taken by a user to make action on each statement but also the kind of objects a user looks at during the internal self-conversation process.

4 Initial Analysis

4.1 Data Collection

To validate the availability of using eye-gazing data in the thinking process, we conduct an experiment for collecting the data of trainers' correction process. Here, *two trainers* (T1 and T2) who have some experience in correcting learners' cases through the thinking method workshop corrected *three hospital nurses' cases* (C1, C2 and C3).

Before using the system, to precisely detect what a trainer is looking at during the correction process, we asked the trainers to calibrate the eye-tracker. They looked at a series of displayed points. Then, they opened the case files in the proposed system and started to correct the case. The trainers continued the process until they were fully satisfied. As a result, we obtained six log files (two trainers multiplied by three cases) as described in Sect. 3.2.

In internal self-conversation, the important factor is to clearly write ones' own case by reflecting on individual thinking process using Sizhi tags, and to find meaningful conflicts of the case [1]. Based on the concept, as the first step in analyzing the trainers' gazing behaviors, this initial analysis especially focuses on the trainers' correction process of the conflict. We analyzed the following features:

Table 1. System log file format

Time Data		Meta Event Name	Event Name	[Attribute1], … ,[AttributeN]
Row 1	Row 2	Row 3	Row 4	Row 5, 6, …., N
UNIX _TIME (ms)	TIMESTAMP (yyyy-MM-dd-HH-mm-ss-fff)	STATEMENT_ EVENT	ADD	5: 4 types of thinking area 6: Statement ID 7: Display number 8: Statement tag 9: Statement text 10: Reason ID/s 11: Display reason number/s
			DELETE	
			UP	
			DOWN	
			OPEN_TAG_AREA	
			CHANGE_TAG	
			CHANGE_REASON	
			FOCUS_TEXT_AREA	
			SELECT	
			RELEASE	
			KEY_PRESS	Above 5 to 11 attributes 12: Key code
		CONFLICT_ EVENT	SELECT_CONFLICT	Above 5 to 11 attributes
			RELEASE_CONFLICT	
			FOCUS_TEXT_AREA	5: Conflict text
			LEAVE_TEXT_AREA	
			KEY_PRESS	5: Conflict text 6: Key code
		GAZE_ EVEENT	IN	5: Target AOI area - 4 types of thinking area - Statement area - StatementTag/Text/Reason area - Button area 6...N: Detail attributes of target area
			OUT	
		SYSTEM_ EVENT	13 types of user's operation (START_SYSTEM, CLICK_SAVE_MENU, etc.)	

- *Eye-gazing process in each thinking area*; the sequence of turning eye-gazing intervals in A's-thinking, B's-thinking, conflict, and knowledge-construct areas through the correction process.
- *Timing of setting the conflict statements*; the number of clicking select/release button in conflict area.
- *Timing of verbalizing actions*; keypress to the statements in the A's-thinking and B's thinking area.

4.2   Result

Quantitative Analysis. Table 2 shows the overall results of total eye-gazing time in each area. Vertical axis indicates the time (milliseconds). From the results, we infer that the correction time differs for each trainer. The total time of the eye-gazing is shorter than the total time of the session. This is because the frames of user's eye-coordination were not detected by the eye-tracker (e.g. while blinking, looking at the keyboard and not at the display etc.). The worst session was C2&T2 where eye-gazing data was not found for 16.3 % of the total session time. The best was C1&T1 as only 3.4 % data was lost during the session time.

Table 2. Result of total gazing time in each area

Case	Trainer	Total time (ms)	Total gazing time in each thinking area (ms)						
			Thinking A	Thinking B	Conflict			Knowledge construct	Total
					A	B	Text		
C1	T1	1120111	582126	204300	106990	108214	67549	13148	1082327
	T2	1301080	765894	280514	6589	7160	38805	25739	1123771
C2	T1	1161191	420598	297717	111876	93236	99533	43275	1066235
	T2	657804	271174	187296	6795	13576	22619	48874	550334
C3	T1	2546297	1436953	687933	65119	41616	112163	43045	2386829
	T2	1252924	687826	268075	5173	10194	31206	61990	1064464

Figure 3 represents the bar graphs based on the total gazing time on each thinking area. The gazing rates of knowledge-construct area (green) are very small for all cases. The result suggests that both the trainers gave their full attention to unearth meaningful conflicts of the correcting case. On the other hand, in the result of gazing time in conflict area, T1 relatively took much time to focus on the area than T2, especially in C1 and C2. The result suggests that the correction policy depends on trainers.

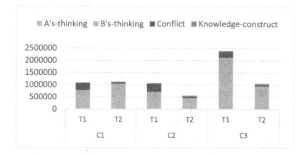

Fig. 3. Bar graphs of total eye-gazing time in each area (Color figure online)

Table 3 shows the number of keypress in each area. Table 4 shows the number of select/release A's/B's-statement which is the Sizhi tag displaying the *policy/principle* as a root of conflict. From the result, both the trainers modified conflict text of cases (only 2 times in C1&T2) very little. In particular, T1's keypress actions for C1 and C2 occurred in only the statements of conflict area, while that of other four results occurred in the statements of A's-/B's-thinking areas (Table 3). This result indicates that T1 largely agreed to the policy/principle conflict statements originally described by the nurses of C1 and C2, and edited their statement texts in conflict area. In fact, as shown in Table 4, T1 did not select/release the conflict statements while correction. On the other hand, other results suggest that the trainers did not agree with the original conflict statements, and they tried to pick up the policy/principle statements from the statements in A's-/B's-thinking area and edited them so as to be a root of conflicts. This hypothesis supported by the select/release data in Table 4: except of T1&C1 and T1&C2, the trainers replaced the original conflict statements.

Table 3. Result of the number of keypress in each area

Case	Trainer	Thinking A	Thinking B	Conflict			Knowledge construct	Total
				A	B	Text		
C1	T1	0	0	192	241	0	0	433
	T2	380	438	0	0	2	0	820
C2	T1	0	0	257	227	0	0	484
	T2	340	287	0	0	0	0	627
C3	T1	556	371	0	0	0	0	927
	T2	281	576	0	0	0	0	857

Table 4. Result of the number of select/release A's/B's statement in conflict area

Case	Trainer	Select	Release	Total
C1	T1	0	0	0
	T2	2	2	4
C2	T1	0	0	0
	T2	2	2	4
C3	T1	7	7	14
	T2	2	2	4

Timeline Sequences of Eye-Gazing Process. Figures 4, 5 and 6 represent the timeline of the correction process in each case. Each timeline graph has three sub-timelines shown from left to right. Though the total session time shown in Table 2 is different from the correction process, they are normalized in the same time scale. Upper timeline shows eye-gazing sequence in each of the four types of thinking area; middle timeline indicates the eye-gazing sequence in policy/principle statements and the conflict text areas in conflict area; and lower timeline shows the keypress action throughout the correction process. According to the visualized results, we can grasp that the sequence of eye-gazing in thinking areas are not always chaotic but has some block of time width. This gives us an important clue to infer the succession of trainers' monitoring and control process.

In case of T1&C1, for example, the trainer first looked at conflict area to understand the nurse's original root of conflict (purple area on the left of Fig. 4 (T1)). Then, the trainer focused on a task to understand the statements in A's-/B's-thinking area (blue and orange areas on the left of Fig. 4 (T1)). Especially, the trainer took time to understand the statements in A's-thinking area; hence, we assume that the trainer tried to not only understand but also confirm whether the statements were consistent in terms of the nurse's root of conflict. After that, the trainer must have started correcting the

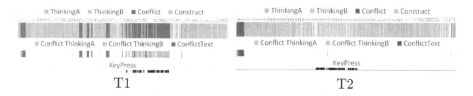

Fig. 4. Result of timeline: case C1 (Color figure online)

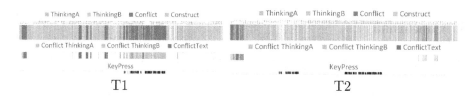

Fig. 5. Result of timeline: case C2 (Color figure online)

Fig. 6. Result of timeline: case C3 (Color figure online)

policy/principle statements in conflict area (purple area in middle of Fig. 4 (T1)). We find from the picture of the process that the trainer first revalidated the conflict text. Then, as shown by the keypress data, the trainer modified the text in the statements to improve them. The result of following timeline shows that the trainer seldom or never spent time to confirm the corrected conflict. Instead, the trainer devoted all his attention to revalidate the logic of A's-/B's-thinking (blue and orange areas in the last half of Fig. 4 (T1)). From the log data, though the trainer did not edit the statement text itself, the trainer took several actions to press the statement up/down button. As a whole, we speculate that the trainer first confirmed, corrected, and consented his correction in the first half of session (the most important part of the correction objective) to find meaningful conflicts of the case, and then spent the latter half to check the minor part of the original statements for desirable ones (e.g. change displaying order of the statements).

We also infer that each trainer universally started by focusing on the conflict area. The results convinced us that their correction policy was first to understand the original root of conflict. In addition, in the case of C3, as the keypress sequences of both trainers did not merge, this case might be considered as the logical structure of the original one, which was not clearly verbalized. In this manner, by considering eye-gazing process between trainer's actual actions for correction, there is some possibility to interpret the context of trainer's monitoring and control process.

As an initial analysis, we mainly focus on the comprehensive features such as the amount of eye-gazing time in thinking areas. As described in Sect. 3.2, based on the log data, we can analyze how the trainers modified the target statement tag/text while comparing the statements and the displaying order of statements in thinking areas. For future work, we must provide the detail eye-gazing process such as the type of Sizhi tag particularly focused by the trainers and their correction process.

5   Conclusion

In this paper, we proposed a novel gaze-aware internal self-conversation system that has can record the sequence of user's eye-gazing information. To validate the availability of the system, we conducted an initial data analysis based on the trainers' correction data. From the results, we confirm that there is some possibility to interpret the context of a trainer's monitoring and control process.

Unlike the trainers' correction process, which started with understanding the learners' output, learners need to verbalize their thought from scratch. We believe that the log data includes the different tendencies of the thinking composition process from the thinking ability perspective of the learner, e.g. critical thinking skills. In order to make the difference clear, we have a plan to conduct an experiment for collecting the internal self-conversation data of a learner.

Acknowledgements. This work is supported by JSPS KAKENHI Grant Number 26870588.

References

1. Chen, W., et al.: Sizhi: self-dialogue training through reflective case-writing for medical service education. In: Proceedings of Workshop on Skill Analysis, Learning or Teaching of Skills, Learning Environments or Training Environments for Skills in Conjunction with ICCE 2011, pp. 551–559 (2011)
2. Seta, K., et al.: Meta-cognitive skill training program for first-year bachelor students using thinking process externalization environment. Int. J. Knowl. Web Intell. **4**(2), 217–237 (2013)
3. Kanou, H., et al.: A Method of Sharing the intention of reviewing in writing-training for nurses. In: Proceedings of the 21st International Conference on Computers in Education (ICCE 2013), pp. 983–989 (2013)
4. Cutrell, E., Guan, Z.: What are you looking for? an eye-tracking study of information usage in web search. In: Proceedings of the SIGCHI Conference on Human Factors in Computing Systems, pp. 407–416. ACM (2007)
5. Reichle, E.D., Reineberg, A.E., Schooler, J.W.: Eye movements during mindless reading. Psychol. Sci. **21**(9), 1300–1310 (2010)
6. Guan, Z., Lee, S., Cuddihy, E., Ramey, J.: The validity of the stimulated retrospective think-aloud method as measured by eye tracking. In: Proceedings of the SIGCHI Conference on Human Factors in Computing Systems, pp. 1253–1262. ACM (2006)

7. Ito, T.: Effects of verbalization as a learning strategy: a review. Japan. J. Educ. Psychol. **57**(2), 237–251 (2009). (in Japanese)
8. Chen, W., Cui, L., Tanaka, K., Matsuda, N., Ikeda, M.: Sizhi player: a nursing thinking reflection process replay tool. In: Proceedings of the 30th Annual Conference of Japan Society for Educational Technology, 1a-021-04 (2014). (in Japanese)
9. Tobii technology: http://www.tobii.com

Educational Externalization of Thinking Task by Kit-Build Method

Tsukasa Hirashima[(✉)] and Yusuke Hayashi

Information Engineering, Hiroshima University, Hiroshima, Japan
tsukasa@lel.hiroshima-u.ac.jp

Abstract. This paper describes kit-build approach to realize educational externalization of thinking task. In this approach, a learning target is to comprehend an information structure. In order to comprehend the structure, an interactive environment where a learner is allowed to operate the structure is designed and implemented. In the operation, the learner is provided several components and operates them. So, this approach is called kit-build approach. In this paper, the framework and several past related work are introduced. Then, ongoing work and future work following this approach are reported.

Keywords: Educational externalization · Thinking task · Kit-build · Domain-specific information structure

1 Introduction

Learning is an internal change in cognitive system or knowledge as a result of learning activity. This means that it is impossible to support or promote learning itself directly. Therefore, the target of support or promotion of learning should be the learning activity. Because problem-solving is one of the most important learning activity, this paper focuses on thinking tasks as problem-solving.

Cognitive process in problem-solving can be categorized into the following four sub-processes: representing, planning/monitoring, executing and self-regulating [1, 2]. Many investigations then have already indicated that to complete these processes adequately is not easy tasks for most learners [3, 4]. In other words, the thinking activity itself is often difficult for learners and some of them fail to complete the process. Because quality of learning depends on the number and quality of learner's problem-solving experiences, the way to complete the process is one of the most important issues to support of learning from problem-solving.

Externalization of thinking tasks is proposed as a promising method to support a learner to complete the problem-solving process in this paper. If it is assumed that information structure is the processing object in the problem-solving process, the above four sub-processes are categorized into three processes for the information structure: (1) representation, (2) manipulation and (3) evaluation. Then, if we suppose that the thinking tasks are carried out in human's cognitive system as representing, manipulating and evaluating the information structure concerning the tasks, externalization of thinking tasks is able to be realized by externalization of the representation, manipulation and evaluation of the information structure. This externalization is different from

© Springer International Publishing Switzerland 2016
S. Yamamoto (Ed.): HIMI 2016, Part II, LNCS 9735, pp. 126–137, 2016.
DOI: 10.1007/978-3-319-40397-7_13

self-explanation or externalization of results of thinking, because the processes of thinking tasks themselves are carried out outside of the cognitive system. Although similar ideas can be found in the earliest studies of intelligent tutoring systems in the 1970s, the goal has not been achieved even now.

From a viewpoint of artificial intelligence, simulation of excellent thinking process of human, for examples, abstraction, analogical reasoning or metacognition, is one of the most important research goals that has not achieved even now. However, even for human, especially for a learner who is just learning, to complete such excellent thinking processes is often uneasy task. In artificial intelligence, the main difficulty of realization of the simulation is in generalization of the thinking process realized in the simulation. However, it is often claimed that human thinking is domain-specific [5]. Therefore, domain-specific realization of thinking process would be enough to use for learning support. Neither a computer nor a learner can adequately complete the thinking process alone, the process would be able to be carried out adequately if both engage in the process cooperatively. In this research, we have proposed a research approach composed of the following three steps: (1) building a domain-specific model by researchers as representation, (2) rebuilding the model with provided components by learners as manipulation, and (3) diagnosing the rebuilt model and giving feedback to the rebuilt model as evaluation. Preparing components by decomposing a domain-specific model and rebuilding the model by a learner are the most characteristic features of this approach. Because of these characteristics, the rebuilt model is diagnosable. We call this approach "kit-build approach" [6].

In this paper, I introduce several past major investigations with the similar goal with this proposal and indicate that the goal has not been completed yet even now. Then, a series of ongoing case studies is reported. Finally, potential of this challenge is discussed.

2 Past Studies

2.1 Past Trials to Externalization of Thinking Tasks

The idea to externalize thinking process had been proposed several times in the history of research of education and learning. The most important two frameworks related to this idea are "Galperin's theory of the stepwise formation of mental actions" [7] and "Microworld" in Papert's Mindstorms [8]. In Galperin's theory, learning is a process to acquire mental action (that is, intelligent thinking) and the process is organized as stepwise formation composed of the following four distinctive steps: (1) orientation by instruction, (2) physical material action, (3) verbal action and (4) mental action.

Basically, in this theory, the objects of action, that is, objects of thinking, should be materialized previously. In the first step, a learner is taught how he/she acts on the materialized objects. Then, in the step of physical material action, the learner learns the way to use the actions to specific objects and representations of them. In the step of verbal action, dialogical thinking is requested as a complement of the previous step. At the final step, an action has become a pure mental act. In this theory, it is assumed that thinking can be performed as action to materialized objects and the result of learning is modelled as internalisation of the external and materialized action. Therefore, this theory provides theoretical base to trials of externalization of thinking tasks. However, although many practical lessons based on the theory had been reported in the past, there were significant difficulties in materialization of the objects and in supporting the learning process. Information technology has potential to overcome these difficulties.

In MINDSTORMS [8], Papert emphasized the importance of having a well-defined model of a learning object and to build an environment where a learner is able to manipulate the learning object. Then, he also indicated that the model should be composed of "mind-sized bites". In this framework, it is expected that the learner is promoted to comprehend the learning object through the manipulation. This comprehension means that the construction of the model in his/her mind. This is also a trial to externalize thinking tasks that are difficult for a learner. Then, he indicated that the promising contribution of information technology and conceptualization based on artificial intelligence in order to realize such learning environment. He named such learning environment "microworld". LOGO developed by Papert as a method to manipulate learning objects in the microworld is a programming language that can deal with general learning objects. Although it is very famous and popular programming language, the language itself is not optimal one as externalization of thinking tasks.

Both Geometry Tutor in geometry proofs [9] and Algebraland in algebra equation-solving [10] were the first and important trials to realize domain-specific computer-based microworld. In Algebraland, a problem space of algebra equation-solving is visualized. In the problem space, a learner is provided an equation as a problem and allowed to manually perform all the calculations associated with different algebraic operations. The problem space presents a visual representation of all previous problem status and applied operations. Also in Geometry Tutor, a problem space to visually construct a proof graph is provided to a learner. In this space, a learner is able to work either forward from given conditions (forward chaining) or backward from what is to be proved (backward chaining) by applying geometry theorems manually. Because these problem spaces were designed based on a model of cognitive system of problem-solving, they are examples of trials of externalization of thinking tasks. Unfortunately, during the period when these studies were conducted, there was not enough hardware and software infrastructure of information technology. Therefore, they were not able to produce practical results. Besides, in the target tasks of them, that is, geometry proof and algebra equation-solving, basic representation of the problem-solving process have been already formalized. Nowadays, we have already significantly advanced infrastructure. Based on the infrastructure, we would be able to challenge thinking task that is not basically carried out inside of cognitive system and produce fruitful results.

2.2 Domain-Specific Information Structure

Modelling a learning object as an information structure is the most important task to realize "externalization of a thinking task". An approach to model a learning object as an information structure has been a traditional way to design an intelligent tutoring system. SCHOLAR [11] that is widely considered as the first intelligent tutoring system was designed based on well-defined information structure of a learning object, the geography of South America. The information structure was represented by a semantic network representation [12] that was the latest cognitive model at that time. Carbonell called this approach "information structure oriented approach" and emphasized that the information structure processed in an intelligent tutoring system should be the same one in learner's cognitive system.

A series of researches of GUINDON and NEOMYCIN [13] insisted that the knowledge that can be taught to the learner should be described with transparent or glass-box representation. GUIDON was developed to teach expert knowledge (rules) of MYCIN that was a rule-based expert system to identify bacteria causing severe infections. The results of GUIDON suggested that the knowledge of computers or expert systems was difference from the knowledge for a learner. Based on this consideration, NEOMYCIN was developed as a reconfiguration of MYCIN. The main component of NEOMYCIN was a psychological model of diagnostic thinking. The model is used to interpret learner's behaviour and teach diagnostic strategies. This reconfiguration is regarded as the shift from a performance-oriented design to a knowledge-engineering design, that is, to describe knowledge with transparent or glass-box representation. Although the series of researches were oriented to realize general framework of expert systems and tutoring systems, such as GUNIDON2, the contribution of the domain-specific model for diagnostic thinking was significant to the success of NEOMYCIN. Therefore, these researches are also regarded as successful examples of information structure oriented approach.

A student model as a basic component of intelligent tutoring systems is also based on modelling of cognitive process and a learning object. For example, bug model [14] was developed as a model of cognitive procedure for solving computational exercises in subtraction and succeeded in reproducing learner's erroneous answers in subtraction by adding a bug as a wrong partial procedure. REPAIR theory [15] was a generation theory of the bug from the correct cognitive procedure. STEP theory [16] was a learning model of bug generation that explains the reason why a learner obtained the bug. Because one of the most important outcomes of this series of researches was the excellent domain-specific model of the cognitive process and the learning object, they were also very important previous researches about information structure.

Externalization of a thinking task is realized by visualizing such information structure and enabling direct operations to the structure. In the above information structure oriented approach, the information structure is used as a reference model of system design or as an internal mechanism for diagnosis and feedback for learner's behaviour. In contract, in externalization of thinking tasks, the structure is used as the objects of learner's behaviour. Therefore, the approach to externalization of thinking process is a kind of revival of information structure oriented approach.

3   An Ongoing Case Study

In order to realize externalization of thinking tasks, domain-specific model of information structure is indispensable. Besides, evidence of being usable in practical learning or teaching situation is strongly required. Therefore, an investigation aiming to externalization of thinking tasks is not popular in late years. In this section, a series of ongoing case study conducted by the author is introduced.

3.1 Learning by Problem-Posing in Arithmetic Word Problems

In this subsection, externalization of problem-posing task of arithmetic word problems designed on "triple sentence model" is introduced [17]. An interactive problem-posing environment of arithmetic word problems [18, 19] (we call it MONSAKUN, that is, Problem-Posing Kid in Japanese) has been developed and practically used in arithmetic classes in several elementary schools at the first grade (addition and subtraction) [20], the second grade (multiplication) [21], and the third grade (multiplication and division) [22].

Several investigations have already indicated that problem-posing of arithmetic word problems are promising learning activity [23, 24]. However, this activity gives heavy load to both a learner and a teacher. It is usually hard for a learner to make sentences from scratch. The learner often feels difficult how to write sentences, select story or numbers that are not so important from arithmetical point of view. Although posed problems and their posed processes are different in each learner, it is impossible for a teacher to diagnose posed individual problems in real time. Therefore the learner is not able to receive individual support. Even if the teacher gives up diagnosing the posed problems in real time, to diagnose all problems posed by a set of learners is a time-consuming task. Moreover, it is not easy for the teacher to use the diagnosed results for teaching effectively because of time lag between the class of problem-posing and the class of feedback based on the results. Because of these difficulties, it was rare that a class of learning by problem-posing was carried out. Agent-assessment is a solution of this issue [25, 26]. To realize the agent assessment, kit-build approach is a promising approach.

In this subsection, firstly, in order to give an image of externalized task of problem-posing by kit-build approach, MONSAKUN is introduced. Then, the model of information structure of an arithmetic word problem is explained.

MONSAKUN: Interactive Environment for Learning by Problem-Posing. The workspace of the problem-posing activity is shown in Figs. 1 and 2 shows a scene where a student is using MONSAKUN for problem-posing. In the upper left side of the interface, a calculation "7-3" and a type of arithmetic story (change problem: increase) [27, 28] are assigned (these words were translated from Japanese into English). A learner is required to pose a problem that can be solved by the calculation and belongs to the specified type of arithmetic problem by using sentence cards provided in the right side of the interface. The set of sentence cards includes not only the necessary ones but also unnecessary ones (the unnecessary card is called dummy card). In the lower left side, there are three blanks where a learner puts sentence cards in order to complete a problem. In Fig. 1, two cards have been put in the blanks. In this case, required problem is composed of {"Tom has 3 pencils." "Tom buys several pencils." "Tom has 7 pencils."}. By pushing the "Check the problem" button, the posed problem is diagnosed and the learner is able to receive feedback based on the diagnosis.

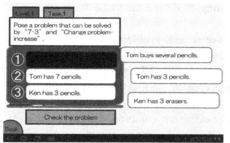

Fig. 1. Workspace of problem-posing   **Fig. 2.** A scene of practical use

In MONSAKUN, the task to pose a problem is externalized as (1) selection of sentence cards and (2) ordering the selected sentence cards based on the model of information structure of arithmetic word problem. In other words, a learner can operate information structure of an arithmetic word problem by operating sentence cards. In usual problem-posing situation, only a posed problem appears as the result of thinking of a learner. Therefore, the problem-posing is a typical thinking task in mind. In contrast, in MONSAKUN, components of a problem are visualized for a learner as operatable ones. Then, the learner is able to compose a problem through visual operations of the components. Therefore, it is possible to say that the MONSAKUN is an example of externalization of a thinking task.

3.2   Triplet Sentence Model

In MONSAKUN, problem-posing task is designed based on a model of an arithmetic word problem called triplet sentence model [17]. In the model, a basic arithmetic word problem is composed of three sentences. Then, the problem-posing task is designed as combination of the sentences. An arithmetic word problem should be solved using one or more basic arithmetic operations. A problem that can be solved by one basic operation is called basic arithmetic word problem. Since one operation composed of three numerical values, that is, two operands and one result, the basic arithmetic word problem includes three arithmetic concepts corresponding to the three numerical values. By writing a pair of the arithmetic concept and its value in a sentence, it is possible to express a basic problem by using three sentences. In the triplet sentence model, the sentences are categorized into two types, that is, (1) existence sentence and (2) relation sentence. The existence sentence includes an independently existing arithmetic concept and its numerical value. For example, "there are six apples" or "there are two dishes" are existence sentences. The relation sentence includes an arithmetic concept and its value that expresses a relation between other two existence sentences. For example, "two apples are eaten" expresses the relation between the number of apples before eating and after eating. "There are six apples" and "there are four apples" is able to be connected by the relation sentence. By arranging the three sentences in the following order: "there are six apples", "two apples are eaten" and "there are four apples", an arithmetic story is formed. The story is transformed to a problem by changing a numerical value to unknown one and requesting to derive the value from other two values.

Based on this model, it is possible to derive several problems from one existence sentence as shown in Fig. 3. Bold rectangles are relation sentences and others are existence sentences. An existence sentence can be used in all kinds of stories/problems although its role is different depending on the type of stories/problems. The types of arithmetic word stories/problems solved by addition or subtraction are categorized into following four stories: change-increase, change-decrease, combine, compare. Compare stories are often classified into compare-more story and compare-less story. As for the stories/problems solved by multiplication or division, there is only one story and the story is composed of three factors, that is, "base quantity", "proportion quantity", and "comparison quantity". Relation between them are expressed "base quantity" * "proportion quantity" = "comparison quantity". In both multiplication story and division story, three arithmetical concepts are assigned to one of them. In the story of multiplication or division, an existence sentence plays a role of the proportion quantity or the comparison quantity. The base quantity is assigned only relation sentence. In Fig. 3, "one apple is 80 cents" and "2 apples on one dish" are relation sentences that play the role of base quantity. The existence sentence "there are 6 apples" expresses the portion quantity when the relation sentence is "one apple is 80 cents", and it expresses the comparison quantity when the relation sentence is "2 apples on one dish".

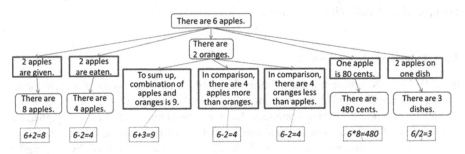

Fig. 3. Various problems derived by the same existence sentence

Based on this model, it is possible to design various kinds of activities to manipulate the structure of arithmetic word problems and to implement diagnosis and feedback function for the activities. Through practical use of MONSAKUN reported in the previous subsection, it has been confirmed that operating the sentence cards doesn't disturb learners' thinking process and promotes the task of problem-posing. Moreover, learning effect for structural comprehension of arithmetic word problems has been observed. Therefore, it is possible to say that the investigation about MONSAKUN is a promising example of externalization of thinking tasks. These researches deal with a basic problem that can be solved by one arithmetic operation. In order to deal with more complex problem that can be solved several operations, triangle block model and interactive learning environment based on the model have been investigated [29]. Because of page limitation, they are not introduced in this paper.

4 Targets of the Challenge

In this section, as examples, several thinking tasks that would be targets of the externalization are discussed. In order to externalize a thinking task, it is indispensable to visually represent information structure. Although the information structure is built from scratch in usual thinking process, if we pay special attention that the structure is built by connecting components, it is possible to divide the building process of the structure into (1) generation of the components and (2) connection of the components. If the components are provided to a learner, the task to build the information structure becomes (1') recognition and selection of the components and (2') connection of selected components. If this framework of building of information structure is acceptable, it is possible to express the externalization of thinking process as representation, manipulation and evaluation of information structure. This framework is called "kit-build" framework and has been used in several schools practically [30–32]. In this section, several targets of the externalization are considered based on the kit-build framework, that is, it is allowed to provide components of information structure. The framework where a learner is requested to use only provided components might constrain a learner strong and impede learner's flexible thinking. Solving this trade-off, enabling and constraining, is an open question now.

4.1 Analogy

Analogy is one of the most popular research targets of cognitive science/psychology or artificial intelligence as an excellent and creative thinking task that a human can do better than a computer [33]. Various cognitive models of the analogical thinking have been proposed and several computational simulations have been also developed. The way to use them in education is also discussed [34]. However, it is also well known that to make an analogy adequately is very difficult for usual human [35, 36]. It is also difficult to let a learner make analogy following an ideal thinking process in a cognitive model [37].

Several models of analogy that deal with the process as representation, manipulation and evaluation of information structure have already been proposed, for example, structure-mapping [38, 39], where it would be a promising target of the externalization of the thinking tasks in analogy. In the structure-mapping, (1) building of structural representation of base object, and (2) mapping the structure of the base to the structure of the target, are the two main tasks. By adopting kit-build framework, the two main tasks are able to be externalized by providing a learner with the components beforehand and requesting to build the structures with them.

Figure 4 are the image of the externalization of analogical thinking tasks with Rutherford analogy, that is, "the hydrogen atom (composed of electron and nucleus) is like our solar system", used in [38]. Figure 4 shows a set of components of the information structure of "solar system". A learner is required to build the information structure of the solar system by using the components. The information structure of the solar system that has been built is shown in Fig. 4. These are the phase of building the structural representation of the base object. In the structure mapping phase, by corresponding "planet to electron" and "sun to nucleus", the structure between "planet and sun" is used as the structure between "electron and nucleus". In this phase, the learner is required to build the structure related to electron and nucleus by copying the structure shown in the middle of Fig. 4. Right side of Fig. 4 shows the goal structure of this analogical thinking task. In this framework, it is possible to diagnose learner's behaviour and support his/her behavior based on the diagnosis.

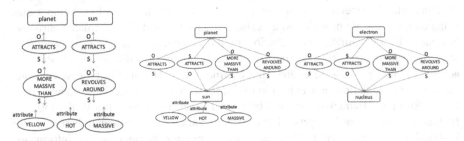

Fig. 4. Components of information structure, base structure and target structure

4.2   Reading Comprehension

Reading comprehension is defined as construction of meaning of a written or spoken communication [40]. If we can prepare explicit representation of meaning, the task is also able to be externalized as the construction of the components of the representation of the meaning. A semantic network is a network which represents semantic relations between concepts and often used as a representation of meaning. SCHOLAR [11] adopted Quillian's semantic network [12] to represent information structure of the geography of South America as the learning object. Concept map [41] that has the same representation has been also popularly used as mental representation in educational context. So, it would be reasonable to use the representation of the meaning as the result of reading comprehension. By decomposing the representation, the components of the representation can be generated. By using the components, the task to construct the meaning with the components is externalized. Learners who accomplished this externalized task are able to share the same comprehension for the communication. Therefore, when we hope learners to have basic and common comprehension about a text or communication, this externalization task would be reasonable. A trial with kit-build concept map for reading comprehension has been already started. The results of the early stage have also reported [42, 43].

In this externalized task, however, the sub-task to extract concepts, that is, components of the representation, from a text or communication is replaced to selection from the provided ones. Moreover, since the origin of the components specified in one representation, it would guide a learner to accomplish the specific comprehension and it would impede the learner to attain his/her own comprehension. Therefore, although this externalization would have advantage to let a learner experience the task of reading comprehension and share common understanding, it would have disadvantage that the learner is impeded to think and understand flexibly. Overcoming this disadvantage is the common challenge of the externalization of thinking tasks.

5   Conclusion Remarks

Thinking activity itself is often difficult for learners and some of them fail to complete the process. Since quality of learning depends on the number and quality of learner's thinking experience, the way to support the thinking process is one of the most important research issues in technology enhanced learning. The main difficulty to think is (1) it should be conducted in leaner's mind, and (2) the task itself is often unclear for his/her. Externalization of thinking tasks is a promising and challenging approach to solve these difficulties. In this paper, as an example of approaches to the externalization, kid-build approach is introduced. Although kit-build approach enables a learner to think externally by operating components, his/her thinking is restricted within the prepared components. In other words, there is a trade-off between "enabling" and "constraining". Solving this trade-off is an open question now. Although this question would be a true challenge, I hope the considerations in this paper would contribute as a step to solve it.

Acknowledgement. This work was supported by JSPS KAKENHI Grant Number 15H02931.

References

1. Polya, G.: How to Solve It, 2nd edn. Princeton University Press, Princeton (1957)
2. Mayer, R.E., Wittrock, M.C.: Problem solving. In: Winne, P.H. (ed.) Handbook of Educational Psychology, pp. 289–303. Psychology Press, Abingdon (2006)
3. Nathan, M.J., Kintsch, W., Young, E.: A theory of algebra-word-problem comprehension and its implications for the design of learning environments. Cogn. Instr. **9**(4), 329–389 (1992)
4. Mayer, R.: Mathematical problem solving. In: Royer, J. (ed.) Mathematical Cognition, pp. 69–92. Information Age Publishing, Greenwich (2003)
5. Brown, A.: Domain-specific principles affect learning and transfer in children. Cogn. Sci. **14**, 107–133 (1990)
6. Hirashima, T., Yamasaki, K., Fukuda, H., Funaoi, H.: Framework of kit-build concept map for automatic diagnosis and its preliminary use. Res. Pract. Technol. Enhanc. Learn. **10**(17), 1–18 (2015)
7. Gal'perin, P.Ia.: An experimental study in the formation of mental actions. In: Stones, E. (ed.) Readings in Educational Psychology, pp. 142–154 (1970)
8. Papert, S.: Mindstorms: Children, Computers, and Powerful Ideas. Basic Books, New York (1980)
9. Anderson, J.R., Boyle, C.F., Yost, G.: The geometry tutor. In: Proceedings of IJCAI, pp. 1–7 (1985)
10. Foss, C.L.: Learning from errors in Algebraland. IRL report no. IRL87-0003 (1987)
11. Carbonell, J.R.: AI in CAI: an artificial intelligence approach to computer-assisted instruction. IEEE Trans. Man-Mach. Syst. **11**(4), 190–202 (1970)
12. Quillian, M.R.: Semantic network. In: Minsky, M. (ed.) Semantic Information Processing, pp. 227–270. MIT Press, Cambridge (1968)
13. Clancey, W.J.: From GUIDON to NEOMYCIN and HERACLES in twenty short lessons: ORN final report 19794985. AI Mag. **7**(3), 40–60 (1986)

14. Brown, J.S., Burton, R.R.: Diagnostic models for procedural bugs in basic mathematical skills. Cogn. Sci. **2**, 155–191 (1978)
15. Brown, J.S., VanLehn, K.: Repair theory: a generative theory of bugs in procedural skills. Cogn. Sci. **4**, 379–426 (1980)
16. VanLehn, K.: Human procedural skill acquisition: theory, model and psychological validation. In: Proceedings of the 1983 Conference of the American Association for Artificial Intelligence, pp. 420–423 (1983)
17. Hirashima, T., Yamamoto, S., Hayashi, Y.: Triplet structure model of arithmetical word problems for learning by problem-posing. In: Yamamoto, S. (ed.) HCI 2014, Part II. LNCS, vol. 8522, pp. 42–50. Springer, Heidelberg (2014)
18. Hirashima, T., Yokoyama, T., Okamoto, M., Takeuchi, A.: Learning by problem-posing as sentence-integration and experimental use. In: AIED 2007, pp. 254–261 (2007)
19. Hirashima, T., Kurayama, M.: Learning by problem-posing for reverse-thinking problems. In: Biswas, G., Bull, S., Kay, J., Mitrovic, A. (eds.) AIED 2011. LNCS, vol. 6738, pp. 123–130. Springer, Heidelberg (2011)
20. Yamamoto, S., Kanbe, T., Yoshida, Y., Maeda, K., Hirashima, T.: A case study of learning by problem-posing in introductory phase of arithmetic word problems. In: Proceedings of ICCE 2012, Main Conference E-Book, pp. 25–32 (2012)
21. Yamamoto, S., Hashimoto, T., Kanbe, T., Yoshida, Y., Maeda, K., Hirashima, T.: Interactive environment for learning by problem-posing of arithmetic word problems solved by one-step multiplication. In: Proceedings of ICCE 2013, pp. 51–60 (2013)
22. Yamamoto, S., Akao, Y., Murotsu, M., Kanbe, T., Yoshida, Y., Maeda, K., Hayashi, Y., Hirashima, T.: Interactive environment for learning by problem-posing of arithmetic word problems solved by one-step multiplication and division. In: ICCE 2014, pp. 89–94 (2014)
23. Ellerton, N.F.: Children's made up mathematics problems: a new perspective on talented mathematicians. Educ. Stud. Math. **17**, 261–271 (1986)
24. Silver, E.A., Cai, J.: An analysis of arithmetic problem posing by middle school students. J. Res. Math. Educ. **27**(5), 521–539 (1996)
25. Nakano, A., Hirashima, T., Takeuchi, A.: Problem-making practice to master solution-methods in intelligent learning environment. In: Proceedings of ICCE 1999, pp. 891–898 (1999)
26. Hirashima, T., Nakano, A., Takeuchi, A.: A diagnosis function of arithmetical word problems for learning by problem posing. In: Mizoguchi, R., Slaney, J. (eds.) PRICAI 2000. LNCS, vol. 1886, pp. 745–755. Springer, Heidelberg (2000)
27. Riley, M.S., Greene, J.G., Heller, J.I.: Development of children's problem solving ability in arithmetic. In: Ginsberg, H.P. (ed.) The Development of Mathematical Thinking. Academic Press, New York (1983)
28. Cummins, R.R., Kintsch, W., Reusser, K., Weimer, R.: The role of understanding in solving word problems. Cogn. Sci. **20**, 405–438 (1988)
29. Hirashima, T., Hayashi, Y., Yamamoto, S., Maeda, K.: Bridging model between problem and solution representations in arithmetic/mathematics word problems. In: Proceedings of ICCE 2015, pp. 9–18 (2015)
30. Hirashima, T., Yamasaki, K., Fukuda, H., Funaoi, H.: Kit-build concept map for automatic diagnosis. In: Biswas, G., Bull, S., Kay, J., Mitrovic, A. (eds.) AIED 2011. LNCS, vol. 6738, pp. 466–468. Springer, Heidelberg (2011)
31. Yoshida, K., Sugihara, K., Nino, Y., Shida, M., Hirashima, T.: Practical use of kit-build concept map system for formative assessment of learners' comprehension in a lecture. In: Proceedings of ICCE 2013, pp. 906–915 (2013)

32. Sugihara, K., Osada, T., Nakata, S., Funaoi, H., Hirashima, T.: Experimental evaluation of kit-build concept map for science classes in an elementary school. In: Proceedings of ICCE 2012, pp. 17–24 (2012)
33. Holyoak, K.J., Thagard, P.: Metal Leaps: Analogy in Creative Thought. MIT Press, Cambridge (1995)
34. Aubusson, P.J., Harrison, A.G., Ritchie, S.M. (eds.): Metaphor and Analogy in Science Education. Springer, The Netherlands (2006)
35. Gick, M., Holyoak, K.J.: Analogical problem solving. Cogn. Psychol. **12**, 306–335 (1980)
36. Gick, M., Holyoak, K.J.: Schema induction and analogical transfer. Cogn. Psychol. **15**, 1–38 (1983)
37. Richland, L.E., Holyoak, K.J., Stigler, J.W.: Analogy use in eight-grade mathematics classrooms. Cogn. Instr. **22**(1), 37–60 (2004)
38. Gentner, D.: Structure-mapping: a theoretical framework for analogy. Cogn. Sci. **7**, 155–170 (1983)
39. Falkenhainer, D., Forbus, K.D., Gentner, D.: The structure-mapping engine: algorithm and examples. Artif. Intell. **41**, 1–63 (1989)
40. Harris, T., Hodges, R. (eds.): The Literacy Dictionary. International Reading Association, Newark (1995). p. 207
41. Novak, J.D., Gowin, D.B.: Learning How to Learn. Cambridge University Press, New York (1984)
42. Alkhateeb, M., Hayashi, Y., Rajab, T., Hirashima, T.: Comparison between kit-build and scratch-build concept mapping methods in supporting EFL reading comprehension. J. Inf. Syst. Educ. **14**(1), 13–27 (2015)
43. Alkhateeb, M., Hayashi, Y., Rajab, T., Hirashima, T.: The effects of KB-mapping method to avoid sentence-by-sentence comprehension style in EFL reading. In: Proceedings of ICCE 2015, pp. 46–55 (2015)

Student Authentication Method by Sequential Update of Face Information Registered in e-Learning System

Taisuke Kawamata[1(✉)], Susumu Fujimori[2], and Takako Akakura[2]

[1] Graduate School of Engineering, Tokyo University of Science,
1-3 Kagurazaka, Shinjuku-Ku, Tokyo 162-8601, Japan
kawamata_taisuke@ms.kagu.tus.ac.jp
[2] Faculty of Engineering, Tokyo University of Science,
1-3 Kagurazaka, Shinjuku-Ku, Tokyo 162-8601, Japan
{fujimori,akakura}@ms.kagu.tus.ac.jp

Abstract. e-Learning is easing restrictions on time and space for a learner. However, its weak point is that a user authentication employs only on log-in with credentials, which makes it easy to cause a cheating. We have studied the changes in face image in e-Learning with the aim of detecting the cheating. We proposed an authentication method with sequential updates of student's face information using new images taken by a web-camera during the e-Learning. We examined the update timing and procedure in this study, and found that the authentication accuracy the highest by summing each face feature vector in the face image which is taken when a student operates the e-Learning system.

Keywords: e-Learning · Video lecture · Student authentication · Face image

1 Introduction

e-Learning has been widely spreading in recent years because it can alleviate time and space restrictions [1]. A lot of schools have introduced the e-Learning into their lectures and students have many opportunities to take the lectures using e-Learning system now. However, there is a problem in the e-Learning that teachers cannot observe students behavior during a lecture, because they do not face directly each other. Most e-Learning systems perform a user authentication using only a user name and password which are entered at login, making it easy to cheat, students other than ones enrolled in the course may take the learning or students may leave away from the in seats before finishing.

Agulla et al. [2] developed the method using biometric authentication based on face recognition in order to check how much time the student is in front of the computer during the e-Learning session. Theirs method uses the student frontal images taken by web-camera during e-Learning. The method guarantees that the student is the enrolled one, and also gives the exact information on how much time the student spends in front of the computer for the e-Learning content. In the case that the face authentication system is unable to identify of a user for a period of time, other verifications based on fingerprint and voice are performed.

© Springer International Publishing Switzerland 2016
S. Yamamoto (Ed.): HIMI 2016, Part II, LNCS 9735, pp. 138–145, 2016.
DOI: 10.1007/978-3-319-40397-7_14

However, this kind of combined authentication may become a disturbance for students to learn. It is needed to develop the highly accurate authentication method using face images only, without the other verifications. In this paper, we propose a new method based on face information and examine the effect of the new method.

2   Proposed Authentication Method

2.1   Proposed Method

We proposed the authentication method with sequential updates of student's face information for collating using newly input images taken by a web-camera during the e-Learning (Fig. 1), and named this method "update method". It is expected that the update method enables to make sure whether a student is the same person from beginning to end during e-Learning by inputting a newly taken face information in certain timing and matching it with the previously input face information.

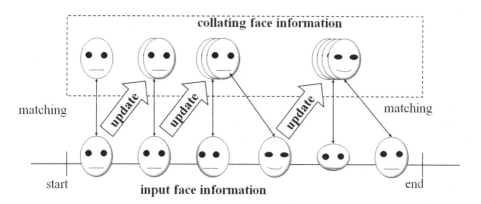

Fig. 1. The model of updating the face information for collating

The important thing in the update method is how face information for collating is updated. We assume that face detection method applied to the collation of student's face image student during e-Learning successively. The face of student often cannot be detected at such timing as student looks down to read or write notes. Therefore, the details of updating procedure have to be considered.

2.2   Face Authentication

This subsection explains conventional face authentication flow in this study. Face authentication used in this paper is based on the method proposed by Ahonen et al. [3].

First of all, we explain about the student's face information in the authentication database. An original student's frontal image is a photograph of the student himself/herself. This image, which is called a registered image, is submitted by the student at the time of registration. A face area is detected from the registered image. Face detection method is performed using the Viola and Jones algorithm [4] included in the OpenCV library. Face feature vector is extracted from the area of face in input image. Face feature is expressed the uniform local binary patterns histogram (LBPH), proposed by Ojala et al. [5].

Next, we explain the face authentication during e-Learning. Input frontal image of the student is taken by web-camera, and this input image is used to detect the face region and to extract the face feature vector. Last, correlation coefficient between the previously taken face feature and newly input face feature is calculated. Correlation coefficient between two LBPH is referred to as "similarity", and the similarity determines whether a person in front of PC is a true student or an impostor.

3 Results

3.1 Experiment Overview

We made an analysis to find an appropriate updating procedure. Subjects of the experiment were nine students in a Japanese university. The students took the e-Learning by watching about 1 h.

The experiment flow is following. A student is explained about the experiment overview before the experiment starts. After the explanation, the student takes the video lecture using e-Learning system (Fig. 2). This system has an operation log acquisition function. Web-camera on the PC display takes the frontal image of a student every second during e-Learning. A student is permitted to take note and look at lecture materials during the experiment. When a certain time passes in the lecture, the video stops and the message, "Do you understand?" appears in the lecture video, as shown in Fig. 3. This function is implemented to make a student operate the e-Learning system. The student can restart the video by clicking the "OK" button on the dialog box. With regard to making a spoofing situation, we also make a student leave away from the seat 5 s later than the start of the lecture and return to the seat 15 s after. After the lecture finishes, a frontal image of the student is taken as a verification photograph.

Fig. 2. The conditions of an experiment

Fig. 3. Dialog box

3.2   Consideration of Update Detail

Update Timing.

The update timing is considered. We chose the time when a student operates the system, as the update timing (hereinafter referred to as "Event timing"). A student usually faces the display of PC at the timing of operating system, so probably the face detection is easy to be made successfully and the similarity is higher than other timings. To check whether a face of student can be detected and the similarity is high or low, we apply the Ahonen method to the data.

Table 1 is the result of analysis. Face detection rate indicates the percentage of successful face images detection. This result suggests that the face detection rate was higher at the Event timing than at the other timing. In addition, the average of similarity value was higher at the Event timing than the other timing. The difference in the similarities between the Event timing and the other timing was 0.05 and statistically significant. This result suggests that students face the display at the Event timing. Based on this result, we use the Event timing as the time of face image update in this study. We also use an ordinary constant timing, Normal timing, as another update timing, for comparison.

Table 1. Face detection rate and statistical value of similarity

	Event timing	Normal timing
Number	109	18388
Face detection rate (%)	92.37	60.04
Mean	0.533	0.489
Standard deviation	0.081	0.095

Update Procedure.

We proposed two update procedure. One procedure overwrites new input image on the previous student image. It is expected that the new input images are more similar to previous images, and this procedure may contribute to the increase in accepting the true student.

The other procedure updates the feature vector for collating by summing image feature vector in each previous time. The summation of feature vectors possibly contain many features of true student's face images. And, this feature vector more corresponds to the face image than any other materials. Therefore, it is expected that this procedure reduces misconceive another student as the true student, if the true students sit down in front of PC long time.

3.3 Analysis Method

We analyzed the effect of the update method for the spoofing situation. The spoofing situation was made to connect images taken before a student leaves away from the seat and images taken after another student sits down in the seat. Figure 4 shows the example of the analysis. In this figure, the horizontal axis is the learning time, and the vertical axis is the similarity. The similarity are plotted as a line diagram. Blue line on the figure means the similarity in the true student, and red line mean the similarity for the impostor. A vertical bar indicates the Event timing. It is expected that the spoofing is detected early. So, we analyzed images of the student to 250 s from 20 s in the experiment.

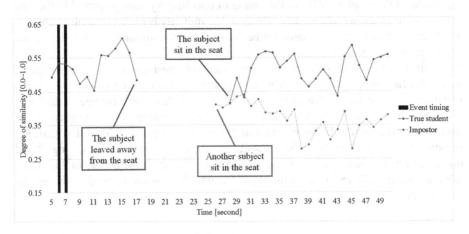

Fig. 4. Analysis method

3.4 Evaluation Method

We used d-prime (d') to evaluate the separation between student and impostors of similarity distribution. The d-prime is the degree of separation between two distributions. High d-prime means that the identification of the person with the true student and the impostor by similarity is easy. The d-prime is calculated as follows:

$$d' = \frac{|\mu_r - \mu_n|}{\sqrt{(\sigma_r^2 + \sigma_n^2)/2}}$$

μ_r: mean of similarity for the true student,
μ_n: mean of similarity for the impostor,
σ_r: standard deviation of similarity for the true student,
σ_n: standard deviation of similarity for the impostor.

To evaluate from the different point of view, we employed False Rejection Rate (FRR), False Acceptance Rate (FAR) and Equal Error Rate (EER) and for evaluating accuracy. EER is the value at which the false acceptance rate (FAR) is equal to the false rejection rate (FRR): FAR is the probability that an unauthorized person is authenticated, and FRR is the probability that an authorized person is rejected. In the second phase, a given threshold is required for authentication. When threshold value is low, FAR is close to zero, but FRR becomes high; when the threshold value is high, FAR becomes high and FRR becomes low. Thus EER is frequently used to evaluate authentication methods.

3.5   Evaluation of the Appropriate Update Timing and Procedure

Compared update methods are following:

- OE: Overwriting at Event timing
- SE: Summing at Event timing:
- OC: Overwriting at Constant timing:
- SC: Summing at Constant timing:

Table 2 summarizes the results for our method. These results indicate that the method of summing at Event timing will be the best in the authentication accuracy. The d-primes of update at Event timing were higher than the conventional method. Comparing conventional method, the d-prime of update at Event timing was improved by more than 0.3. The best result from this evaluation is obtained from the summing at the Event timing. On the other hand, the d-prime of update at constant timing is low. This result suggests that updating of the face information frequently decreases the separation of similarity between the true student and impostors.

Table 2. Results of our method

	Conventional method	Proposal methods			
		OE	SE	OC	SC
d-prime	1.006	1.292	1.317	0.023	0.131
EER	0.235	0.236	0.224	0.500	0.455

The table shows EER and d-prime for each update methods. The EERs of updating at Event timing were about 0.4. We thought the frequent update of the face information makes the FAR high because constant updating uses the face of impostor many times. In the case that the update timing is restricted to the time when a student operates e-Learning system, the authentication accuracy becomes highest. Comparing update procedures, "summing a face feature vector to each other" makes the EERs higher than overwriting the input face image onto a face image for collating. Comparing conventional method and our methods, summing at Event timing update was lower the EER than conventional method. The EER was improved by more than 0.01.

Figure 5 compares the error rate of the conventional method and that of the Event timing update. The horizontal axis is the threshold, and the vertical axis is the error rate. The FAR is plotted as a blue line and the FRR is plotted as a red line. Dot line means the error rate for conventional method and normal line means that for the update method, which is the overwriting at the Event timing. The FRR for the update method was lower than that of the conventional method and FAR of the update method was higher than that of the conventional method for each threshold. In e-Learning, the spoofing seldom occurs. Therefore, rejecting the true student is more troublesome than accepting impostors. Thus, this result indicates that update method is better than the conventional method.

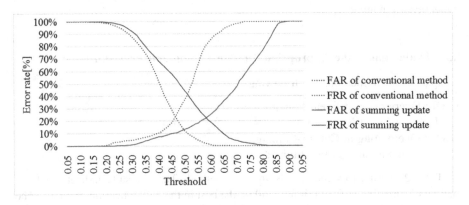

Fig. 5. Error rate curve of conventional method and event timing update method (Color figure online)

The method update the face information unconditionally, even if the input face is the impostor's one. This case causes the high FAR. Therefore, the conditions for updating will be considered in the future work.

4   Conclusions and Future Work

We proposed the authentication method with sequential updates of student's face information for collating using newly input images taken by a web-camera during the e-Learning. In this paper, we examined the update timing and procedure. In the result of analysis, we found that the method of summing at Event timing will be the best in the authentication accuracy.

However, the authentication accuracy of update method is still not enough for the authentication of a student during e-Learning in practice. We will develop a new update method using an updating threshold to improve the false accept rate.

Acknowledgments. This work was supported in part by a Grant-in-Aid for Challenging Exploratory Research (No.15K12427) from JSPS.

References

1. Suzuki, K.: e-Learning in Japan: past, present, and future. In: KAEM and the 4th BK21 GGRTE International Conference: Technology and Future Learning Space Proceedings, pp. 9–17 (2009)
2. Agulla, E., Rúa, E., Castro, J., Jiménez, D., Rifón, L.: Multimodal biometrics-based student attendance measurement in learning management systems. In: 11th IEEE International Symposium on Multimedia, pp. 699–704 (2009)
3. Ahonen, T., Hadid, A., Pietikäinen, M.: Face recognition with local binary patterns. Application to face recognition. IEEE Trans. Pattern Anal. Mach. Intell. **28**(12), 2037–2041 (2006)
4. Viola, P., Jones., M.: Rapid object detection using a boosted cascade of simple features. Proc. Comput. Vis. Pattern Recognit. **1**, 511–518 (2001)
5. Ojala, T., Pietikäinen, M., Harwood, D.: A comparative study of texture measures with classification based on feature distribution. Pattern Recogn. **29**(1), 51–59 (1996)

An Open-Ended and Interactive Learning Using Logic Building System with Four-Frame Comic Strip

Kayo Kawamoto[1,2(✉)], Yusuke Hayashi[2], and Tsukasa Hirashima[2]

[1] Graduate School of Information Sciences,
Hiroshima City University, Hiroshima, Japan
kayo@hiroshima-cu.ac.jp
[2] Graduate School of Engineering, Hiroshima University,
Hiroshima, Japan
{hayashi,tsukasa}@lel.hiroshima-u.ac.jp

Abstract. This paper reports an interactive system for learning by logic building. In the system, a learner is requested to build multiple logic patterns to explain a given four frame comic strip in multiple ways. The system can diagnose the build logic patterns and provide immediate feedback with semantic reason related to the strip. We show the effectiveness of the proposed system by using experimental results that were obtained through a use of the system by elementary school students.

Keywords: Critical thinking · Educational system · Logic · Four-frame comic strip

1 Introduction

The "21st-century skills" have been proposed as indispensable skills to participate in an active global society [1] and many countries are currently undertaking implementation. The definition includes ten skill groups in four areas (ways of thinking, ways of working, tools for work, and ways of living in the world). The "critical thinking" skill in the "critical thinking, problem solving, and decision making" group is considered to be important for the future. Critical thinking is defined by Zechmeister et al. as "logical, unbiased thinking based on appropriate standards and reasons" [2].

Many researchers have pointed to the importance of a multi-perspective thinking style and being able to grasp multiple aspects of the given information and knowledge [3–5] but creating exercises for developing that capability is not easy. We have already developed an open-ended, interactive logic building learning system that enables logical thinking about four-frame comic strip content from multiple viewpoints. Practical use of this system in an elementary school is also reported.

© Springer International Publishing Switzerland 2016
S. Yamamoto (Ed.): HIMI 2016, Part II, LNCS 9735, pp. 146–158, 2016.
DOI: 10.1007/978-3-319-40397-7_15

2 Related Work

2.1 Importance of Multiple Viewpoints in Critical Thinking

Suzuki et al. define critical thinking as "the capability and attitude of careful, logical analysis of given information and knowledge rather than accepting it without thought" [3]. Michita position critical thinking as a problem solving process that includes (1) problem discovery, (2) solution search, (3) solution evaluation, and (4) conclusion, and defines it as seeing through to the essence of a problem by understanding multiple aspects without being confused by the obvious [4]. These definitions include the concept of multiple viewpoints, and step 2 of the process described by Michita particularly emphasizes the need for capturing multiple aspects of a problem.

Zechmeister et al. also hold that an 'open mind' is a characteristic of persons that engage in critical thought. This open-mindedness is expressed as a behavior in which unbiased judgements are made by viewing a thing in both good and bad aspects and considering it from all points of view rather than simply one or two perspectives. Zechmeister and Johnson [2] describes a four-step critical thinking process that involves (1) clarification, (2) investigation of the basis for reasoning, (3) reasoning, and (4) decision to act. They further describe a higher-level metacognitive process that performs look-back control to check for the correct execution of the four steps, and the necessity of an objective and multi-perspective attitude in steps 2 through 4 [5]. Michita also describe "the necessity of understanding something before critiquing it" and "critique without (an effort for) sufficient understanding is nothing more than simple misunderstanding with the identification of faults and other essential elements of critical argument removed". They also point to the importance of a favorable understanding in critical thinking [6]. Taking other logical structures to be correct for the moment is nothing other than multi-perspective thinking.

2.2 Training for Logical Thinking

Logical thought is important in critical thinking. It is required in step 3 of the process proposed by Michita [4] and in the first three steps of the process proposed by Kusumi [5], which are both described in Sect. 2.1. The capability for logical thought must be cultivated to achieve logicality in critical thinking, and the Toulmin model is often adopted for that purpose. In the Toulmin approach, the outcome of an argument obtains from the arrangement of a proposition and statements (layout method), which requires a particular form of argumentation [7]. Specifically, a claim C requires supporting grounds D and a warrant W to provide a reason that C can be claimed on the basis of D. There is also qualification Q that represents the reliability of the warrant, rebuttal or reservations (unless...) R, and backing B that supports W. There is research on writing composition that introduces this argument form [8, 9]. The objective of that research is to promote logical thought.

With the objective of fostering the development of capabilities for conceptualization, logical thinking, expression, critical thinking, and communication, the Finnish approach to education has been studied and introduced [10, 11]. That approach emphasizes reason-based teaching, and uses lessons that involve making mind maps with Carta, writing composition lessons that use formats, and other such methods.

All of that research presumes time-consuming reading and writing of documents that is difficult to do repeatedly. That makes it difficult to try various logic structures or to make sense of strange logical structures. Here, we propose a method for building logics in which a four-frame comic strip is used as the layout and short sentences written on cards are arranged. This approach makes it possible to implement learning activities in which students can try various logical structures and make sense of them.

2.3   Research Using Four-Frame Comic Strips

The advantages of using comics as teaching materials listed below were suggested by Michita [12].

(a) They are fun and motivating.
(b) Ideas can be expressed briefly and simply. Four-frame comic strips in particular generally consist of a logical narrative development, such as introduction, development, turning point, and conclusion.
(c) The exposition is not entirely by words, so the reader is free to apply language and reason on their own beyond the text.
(d) There is no problem of privacy.

Our work uses advantages (b) and (c) from the above list. Specifically, concise presentation of ideas and logical development are used in logic building exercises. Using advantage (c), learners are free to interpret the comic strip frame by frame, so logic-building exercises in which the learner can build logical structures from multiple viewpoints can be designed.

Our reasons for introducing four-frame comic strips can thus be summarized as follows.

(a) The logical development for reaching a conclusion is included.
(b) The content is limited and concise.
(c) It is easy to think with focus on the logical development itself.

Furthermore, because there is no dialogue or explanation,

(d) The learner has freedom in interpreting each frame, allowing various logical developments to be considered.

That is to say, the learner can freely build logical developments while attention is restricted to the pictures drawn in the four-frame comic strip.

The result is that

(e) Exercises for building a variety of logics can be systematically constructed.

Previous work using four-frame comic strips can be broadly classified as follows.

(a) Research on using comic strips as a means of presenting communication and educational content: various fields

(b) Research on setting topics for eliciting explanation of the drawn content in comic strips: Japanese language education, medicine
(c) Research on the comic strips themselves: literature, cultural anthropology, etc.
(d) Research on using comprehension of comic strips as grounds for distinguishing humans from machines based on the advanced thinking capability required for understanding comic strips: log-in authentication
(e) Research that introduces the creation of comic strips as a learning subject: education

The work we report here concerns categories (b) and (d) in the above list. Advanced research in category (b) involves the use of four-frame comics as teaching materials for foreign students learning Japanese and as materials for identifying learners who have neurological or sensory disabilities. Our work targets healthy Japanese elementary school students. Research in category (d) concerns methods of using high human cognitive abilities as filters to prevent unauthorized log-in to on-line services by computer programs. Our work also deals with advanced thinking, but our purpose differs from previous research in this area. Category (b) also includes work on identifying patterns of story development in existing comic strips [13]. Our research separates the patterns into three types according to the relationships between frames. Differences in the interpretation of each frame enable greater variation in logical development.

3   Proposed Learning Method

In this paper, a learning task that requires a learner to build several logic patterns for a four-frame comic strip with a set of components of the strips. Because the components and the ways to connect have been specified previously, it is possible to diagnose the build one. We call this framework kit-build framework [14]. Kit-build framework is promising to realize interaction for a task that required a learner to build something by him/herself. We have already implemented practical learning environment for problem-posing arithmetic word problem [15] and concept map for scientific knowledge [16].

3.1   Learning Task and Method

First, the system presents one comic strip (with dialog or other textual explanation removed) and a set of cards on which explanations of one or a few sentences are written. The learner first reads those and then arranges the cards to match the frames to which they are appropriate. In each task, at least eight cards are presented so that multiple cards might be assigned to one frame. Assigning multiple cards makes it possible to create multiple logical developments.

The assignment of cards to frames is followed by construction of logical developments. In this step, cards are selected for each frame and arranged in order so that the four frames are logically linked to build a logical structure. The system provides immediate feedback with semantic reason. When the student gets it wrong, he is required to improve the incorrect story until it becomes correct one. If the built story is correct, the student is requested to build other logical story for the same comic if the number of storied that student built for the strip is not enough. This process with respect to the same comic are repeated several times. A student builds several logical stories with respect to the given four-frame strip. We believe that this process can be used to implement learning activities for building multiple logics from the same target.

3.2   Open-Ended Interactive Environment

The concept of logical development in a four-frame comic strip is illustrated in Fig. 1. The four-frame comic strip that is presented has had dialog and explanation removed and consists of images only. The logical developments include both complete and partial series that are consistent with the final frame. Introducing pictures that have no dialog or explanation allows various interpretations to be made frame by frame, so the learner can compose logical developments by selecting cards in any order according to their own interpretation. For example, considering that there are $_{10}P_4 = 5040$ combinations for constructing logics from 10 cards for a single four-frame comic strip, if there are five correct solution patterns, then the probability of obtaining a correct solution by chance is 1/1008. In the sense that the learner can arrive at multiple correct answers from those various interpretations, this can be said to be an open-ended environment.

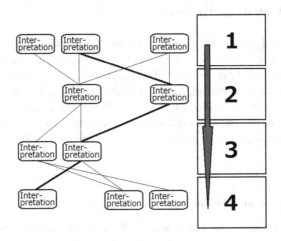

Fig. 1. Logical development in a four-frame comic

Because the system provides the components for constructing logics, it does not give the learner complete freedom in thinking. We nevertheless believe that it does allow sufficient freedom for the purpose of enabling to learner to consider different logics for the same target by making it possible to provide a search space that enables the sort of trial-and-error thinking described above. Restricting freedom to a certain extent in this way also is also expected to stimulate learner activity. That is to say, we believe that providing components and limiting interpretation might itself promote logical thinking by the learner. As a result, we can expect that the learner will be able to arrive at more interpretations and logical developments than would be possible with completely free thinking.

The system determines whether or not a correct logical development is included in the card arrangements made by learners and provides immediate feedback, thus implementing interactive logic-building exercises. The system also collects information on learner behavior and intent, such as which buttons and cards are selected, thus indicating which problems were attempted, which cards were selected, how cards were ordered, and the extent to which different logical patterns were challenged. That information is then used to select which exercises are presented to the learner. Logging into the system with the same ID allows learners to continue an exercise where they were when they last logged out. To motivate learners, medals are awarded according to the correctness and patterns of the assembled logical developments. These features also contribute to the interactivity of the environment.

3.3   The Learning System

We designed and developed a system for practicing the learning exercises described in Sect. 3.1. The materials for an exercise include a four-frame comic strip and a set of cards for constructing logical developments for the comic strip. Materials for seven exercises were prepared.

Learners can log into the system with individual IDs and passwords that were given to them. Immediately after logging in, the learner can select the problem level 1 or level 2. It is recommended to start with level 1, which is simpler and presents fewer cards.

Once a level is chosen, the display changes to the problem selection screen (Fig. 2). Below each problem displayed on the screen is a line of monochrome medals that represents the total number of correct solution patterns. When the learner discovers a

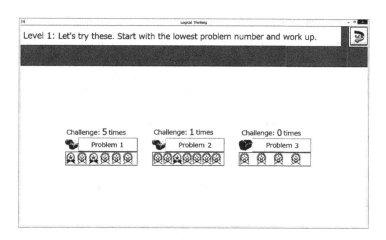

Fig. 2. Problem selection screen

correct pattern, the medal corresponding to that pattern is displayed in color to indicate the achievement.

When the learner clicks a button to select a problem, the display changes to the exercise screen (Fig. 3). A four-frame comic strip is presented on the right side of the screen and the cards to be used in constructing the logic are arranged on the left side.

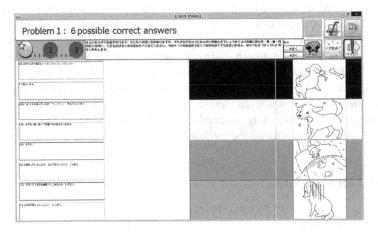

Fig. 3. Exercise screen 1

The number of cards depends on the problem, but varies in the range from 8 to 10. On each card, a short sentence of one of the types listed below is written.

(a) A part of a series of explanations and dialogs that are logically consistent with the fourth frame of the four-frame comic strip

(b) Explanations and dialogs that are logically consistent with a part the four-frame comic strip

(c) Explanations and dialogs that are similar to the cards that of types (a) or (b) and can easily be mistaken

By collecting and arranging the cards of type (a) and (b), it is possible to represent all of the logical development patterns that are obtainable for the problem four-frame comic strip. From four to nine patterns are possible, depending on the problem.

The learner can drag and drop the cards to line them up beside each frame according to their interpretation. When done, the learner can click the 'Done' button in the button group in the upper right of the screen to line the selected cards up horizontally beside each frame (Fig. 4). The learner then considers the logical development of the four-frame comic strip and selects the frames and arranges the cards horizontally beside each frame accordingly. When the learner clicks the 'Done' button, the system returns feedback on whether the result is correct or not. If it is correct, the learner can try to build another logic structure; if it is incorrect, the learner can either try again to build the logic or try to build a different logic. When the learner feels that enough has been done for one comic strip, they can move on to a different problem.

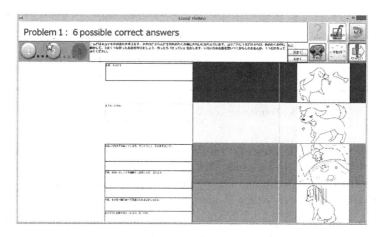

Fig. 4. Exercise screen 2

4   Experiment

4.1   Purpose

This experiment is intended to test whether or not the system described here can implement the open-ended, interactive exercises for four-frame comic that are the objective of our research. Although we have argued for the importance of these exercises, they cannot be implemented manually. Accordingly, the design and development of a system for implementing them is essential to an empirical demonstration of significance. Here, we show experimentally that it is possible to implement a system that handles these exercises. The kind of exercises and system described here have not previously been proposed or implemented, so confirmation of their feasibility would be a highly novel result.

4.2   Subjects

The subjects were 24 elementary school students (ten 4th graders, ten 5th graders, and four 6th graders) in the Personal Computer Department of a public elementary school. The subjects are accustomed to using personal computers.

4.3   Procedure

(a) Explain the system and exercise method. (2 min)
(b) Pretest: Present a four-frame comic strip (Fig. 5) and instruct the learner to describe a coherent story and create stories as many different logical patterns as possible. (15 min)
(c) Use the system to do an exercise: log in and solve problem 1. (7 min)
(d) Check the problem solving method by using Problem 1 as an example. (3 min)

Fig. 5. Four-frame comic strip used for the pretest

(e) Use the system to do exercises: Instruct the learner to first construct one logical pattern for each of the remaining six problems, and then construct at least two stories (logical developments) for any problems they like. (23 min)

(f) Post-experiment questionnaire (5 min)

The time from log-in to log-out is 33 min. Of that time, 3 min are used to check the method for solving the problems and 30 min are for using the system to do the exercises.

4.4   Evaluation

(a) Pretest: Investigate what kinds of stories the subjects can create with the description formula and what level of description is possible.

(b) Questionnaire: Ask about the subjects feelings regarding the exercises, such as if the exercises were fun, if the problems were difficult, and if they would like to do them again.

(c) Learning log: The pages viewed by the subjects, the buttons clicked, the logic patterns constructed, and the times at which each behavior occurred, etc. are all recorded in a log.

5   Results and Discussion

When the pretest ended, nearly all of the subjects had finished writing, so the time for the pretest was sufficient for the subjects to write down all of the stories they could think of. However, there was often insufficient explanation of the four-frame comic strips for which the subjects wrote, so there were not many for which the logical development could be understood. For that reason, if an explanation for four frames was written in the form of a story, it was regarded as one story.

When using the system, on the other hand, the time for constructing a variety of logical developments was entirely insufficient for all of the problems. Furthermore, because the subjects were instructed to first create one story for all of the problems in step 3 of the experiment, only one pattern was created for many of the problems. That phenomenon was seen particularly often for the level 2 problems (about 44 %). That is to say, many subjects concentrated on the exercises for level 1 problems. For that reason, we compared the number of medals earned (i.e., the number of logical developments) per problem in the exercises for level 1 problems 1, 2, and 3 with the number of compositions in the pretest. The number of medals earned per problem for level 1 was 2.22 (SD = 1.42) and the average number of compositions in the pretest was 1.46 (SD = 0.83). A paired-sample difference test showed that the number of medals earned per problem in the level 1 exercises using this system, which is to say the number of logical development patterns, was significantly greater (t (23) = 2.49, p < .05). We can therefore conclude that the exercises done with this system enabled the subjects to construct more logical development patterns.

Next, investigation of the number of medals earned (number of logic patterns created) in exercises done using this system revealed that the average per person was 11.91 (SD = 4.71). We can see that this result indicates the number of logical patterns that can be constructed. The average for 15 min number of patterns for describing the stories on paper in the pretest was only 1.46 (SD = 0.83), and only a few of those had a logical structure that could be read for comparison and study. Although the time taken doubled to 30 min when the system was used, the number of appropriate logical development patterns that could be constructed in that time increased by a factor of more than 8 and the patterns could be compared. Also, considering the number of possible combinations, we can say that it is not possible to create appropriate logical development patterns without logical thinking. These facts show that subjects who had difficulty constructing even a single logical structure on paper could build multiple logics for a single problem when using this system.

The average number of medals earned by students was 15.25 (SD = 1.89) for the 6th graders and 11.25 (SD = 4.84) for the 4th and 5th graders. A difference test for the two groups shows that the 6th graders earned significantly more medals (t (19) = 2.77, p < .05). That is to say, the 6th graders were more successful in constructing multiple logics from diverse points of view. According to Kishi, understanding of the logical structure of text is acquired between the 4th grade and the 6th grade, and 6th graders have reached nearly the level of university students for the ability to understand the important parts of logical structure [17]. This difference in development is probably reflected in the difference in our results.

Next, we consider the time taken to do the exercises with the system. To obtain the actual time taken for each exercise, we obtained the times for actually doing and viewing each exercise from the exercise logs and used the summed data. The actual exercise time excludes time for changing to irrelevant pages and long periods of inactivity of the system and includes only time spent interpreting the four-frame comics, considering the logical development, and moving the cards accordingly while the system is running.

The time spent and the number of subjects that did the exercises are presented in Table 1. The χ^2 test indicated significance in the results. The subjects that did the exercises in from 25 to 30 min were the largest group, and very few spent from 15 to 20 min on the exercises.

The total time in which the system could be used to do the exercises was 30 min. Although two subjects took from 30 to 35 to actually do the exercise, that is considered to be a result of the time for 'checking the solution method using problem 1 as an example' during the process and using the system up to the time for answering the post-experiment questionnaire. The largest group of subjects took from 25 to 30 min, which is to say they did exercises more or less straight through from beginning to end.

Table 1. Actual learning times for test subjects

Learning time (minutes)	Persons
30 to 35	3
25 to 30	12
20 to 25	7
15 to 20	2

$\chi^2 (3) = 10.33, p < .05$

Although some subjects took from 20 to 25 min, they are considered to have done the exercises as such. These facts indicate that the subjects participated fully in using the system to do the exercises.

A questionnaire was given to the subjects after the experiment to obtain subjective evaluation. Many subjects reported that the exercises were difficult (Table 2). On the other hand, significantly many subjects reported that the exercises were fun and that they would like to do more of the same kind of exercises (Tables 3 and 4). That is to say, the exercise could be enjoyed and there was motivation to do similar exercises despite the difficulty. These results show that the exercises can be by accepted learners.

Table 2. Evaluation of difficulty

Question item	Persons	Significance
This exercise was difficult	19	$p < .01$
This exercise was not difficult	5	

Table 3. Evaluation of enjoyment

Question item	Persons	Significance
This exercise was fun	23	$p < .01$
This exercise was not fun	1	

Table 4. Evaluation of willingness to try again

Question item	Persons	Significance
I would like to try this kind of exercise again	20	$p < .01$
I would not like to try this kind of exercise again	2	

6 Conclusion

We have proposed open-ended, interactive logic-building exercises based on four-frame comic strips and implemented them in a learning system. Experiments confirmed that learning is possible with this system. This method provides children with the experience of building multiple logical patterns from the same target material, which has not previously been possible. This activity is relevant to fostering the capability and attitude of logical analysis from multiple perspectives, and we can expect it to promote education that develops the capacity for critical thinking that will be needed for living in our future society. We confirmed the feasibility of using this system for learning with the types of exercises described here. Further work on ways to incorporate this system into educational contexts and on measurement and analysis of the learning effect is needed.

Acknowledgement. This work was partially support by Grant-in-Aid for Scientific Research (C) (Grant Number 25350344) from JSPS.

References

1. ATC21s, Assessment & Teaching of 21st Century Skills. http://www.atc21s.org
2. Zechmeister, E.B., Johnson, J.E.: An Introduction to Critical Thinking. Kitaoji Shobo, Kyoto (1996). Translated by Miyamoto, H., Michita, H., et al. (in Japanese)
3. Suzuki, T., Oi, T., Takemae, F. (eds.): Critical Thinking and Education - Reconstructing Education in Japan. Seikaishisosha, Kyoto (2006). (in Japanese)
4. Michita, Y.: Critical thinking deepened by metacognition. Gendaiespri **497**, 59–67 (2008). (in Japanese)
5. Kusumi, T.: Critical thinking for good citizenship. Psychol. World **61**, 5–8 (2013). (in Japanese)
6. Michita, Y.: The importance of soft heart in critical thinking. Univ. Ryukyus Bull. Coll. Educ. **60**, 161–170 (2002). (in Japanese)
7. Inoue, S.: Strategies for Developing Thinking Skills. Meiji Shoten, Tokyo (2007). (in Japanese)
8. Funahashi, H.: Development of teaching materials for Japanese language composition for developing the ability of logical understanding and expression. Shiga Daikokubun **48**, 15–24 (2011). (in Japanese)
9. Shibuya, H.: Research on teaching criticism (high school): relating reading to essay (in Japanese). Japanese Teach. Soc. Japan Abstracts **101**, 186–189 (2001)
10. Shimizu, N.: Teaching logical thought and expression. Japanese Teach. Soc. Japan Abstracts **114**, 67–70 (2008). (in Japanese)
11. Takita, K.: What are the problems in developing the Japanese language curriculum? Genbun **55**, 29–43 (2007). (in Japanese)
12. Michita, Y.: Use of comics in teaching exercises, trial and evaluation. Univ. Ryukyus Bull. Coll. Educ. **53**, 317–326 (1998). (in Japanese)
13. Hong, H V, Wanabe, T., Kato,J.: Story analysis in four-frame comic strips. In: Proceedings of the IEICE Society Conference 2000, p. 212 (2000) (in Japanese)
14. Hirashima, T., Yamasaki, K., Fukuda, H., Funaoi, H.: Framework of Kit-build concept map for automatic diagnosis and its preliminary use. Res. Pract. Technol. Enhanced Learn. **10**, 1–21 (2015)
15. Hirashima, T., Kurayama, M.: Learning by problem-posing for reverse-thinking problems. In: Biswas, G., Bull, S., Kay, J., Mitrovic, A. (eds.) AIED 2011. LNCS, vol. 6738, pp. 123–130. Springer, Heidelberg (2011)

16. Sugihara, K., Osada, T., Nakata, S., Funaoi, H., Hirashima, T.: Experimental evaluation of kit-build concept map for science classes in an elementary school. In: Proceeding of ICCE2012, pp. 17–24 (2012)
17. Kishi, M.: The Psychology of Understanding Explanatory Text. Kitaoji Shobo, Kyoto (2004). (in Japanese)

Construction of a Literature Review Support System Using Latent Dirichlet Allocation

Yusuke Kometani$^{(\boxtimes)}$ and Keizo Nagaoka

School of Human Sciences, Waseda University,
2-579-15 Mikajima, Tokorozawa, Saitama 359-1192, Japan
kometani@aoni.waseda.jp, k.nagaoka@waseda.jp

Abstract. The role of universities in imparting knowledge to students is declining as e-learning and massive open online courses become widespread, and it seems likely that eventually only seminar activities will remain on university campuses. Prof. Nagaoka, Waseda University in Japan, previously proposed the importance of making seminar activities the core of university education, considering them as a "university within a university," and furthermore proposed the concept of a seminar management system (SMS). Following this proposal, we report on the development of a literature review support system using latent Dirichlet allocation as one aspect of an SMS.

Keywords: Seminar activity · University within a university · SMS (seminar management system) · Literature review support system · Latent Dirichlet allocation

1 Introduction

Since the early 2000s, different methods for providing universal access through distance education, such as the OpenCourseWare program and MOOC (massively open online courses), have rapidly gained prominence, and universities worldwide have been pressed to change with the times. Although it seems that in the near future most lecture-type classes are likely to be offered through distance education to off-campus locations, discussion- and participatory-type lessons are still mainly performed at university campuses, and they continue to require in-person attendance, even in Japanese University.

One type of educational model is centered on seminar activities. In particular, each seminar activity offered by a university instructor should fill a role in a larger framework that defines the curriculum. Prof. Keizo Nagaoka have proposed that such seminar activities should support the particular educational philosophy established for a "university within a university," and furthermore proposed the concept of an integrated Seminar Management System (SMS) (Kometani and Nagaoka 2015, Nagaoka and Kometani 2016).

In this report, we propose a system for supporting literature review in undergraduate research as one aspect of an SMS for supporting seminar activities. The proposed system is based on an electronic portfolio (e-portfolio), and uses the latent Dirichlet allocation (LDA) (Blei et al. 2003) and linguistic topic models to create feedback for students.

© Springer International Publishing Switzerland 2016
S. Yamamoto (Ed.): HIMI 2016, Part II, LNCS 9735, pp. 159–167, 2016.
DOI: 10.1007/978-3-319-40397-7_16

A key concept is that students can effectively discover their research interests and research questions through reflection on the materials obtained through their literature review and the LDA-based analysis results. Accordingly, it is expected that using LDA for analyzing the literature review should result in improved student attitude toward seminar activities and research. The main aims of this research are to develop a literature review support system that is appropriate for studying materials gained through the literature review process and to examine whether topic analysis using LDA effectively supports the literature review. We examine the utility of using a literature review support system by analyzing the study materials as well as questionnaire survey results.

2   Design of Literature Review Support System

2.1   Process of Literature Review

In designing a literature review support system, we first define the process of literature review (Fig. 1). To create a review, students should first read many articles critically. For each article, students make their own summary as a study material. Second, when writing the literature review, students should organize and relate the contents of articles to create a narrative and narrow down their topics. Finally, students should decide their research questions. If the students cannot determine their research question after this three-step process, they should repeat the entire process.

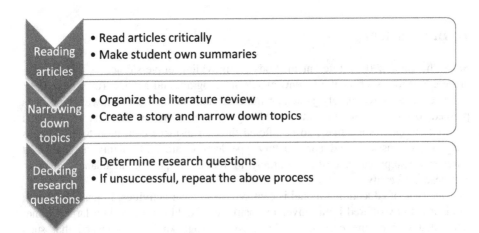

Fig. 1. Literature review process

2.2   Target of Our System and Difficulties Faced in Literature Review

In previous research, many methodologies have been suggested to support students in reading an article critically.

However, few studies have focused on supporting students as novice researchers aiming to narrow down topics. Therefore, our system targets supporting the "narrowing down of topics" stage in Fig. 1.

To narrow down topics, students should relate the contents of each article and create structures. However, it is difficult for students to relate the contents of articles for two reasons:

1. Students who are novices in the research area do not have enough knowledge, making it difficult to understand which articles are similar and to find relations between articles easily.
2. Students do not know how to organize a literature review, as it is difficult to define a well-organized literature review.

2.3   Functions of System

To address the above two difficulties, we propose two functions:

1. Feedback on similarity between students' own summaries of articles
2. Feedback on the literature review structure

The key idea is to use LDA, which is one type of linguistic topic model (Blei et al. 2003). It can be used for estimating the implicit topics of documents. We believe that showing the implicit topics estimated from articles can help support students who do not have sufficient knowledge.

As support function 1, to display the similarities and differences among articles clearly, we propose the student summaries' similarity feedback function using LDA and multi-dimensional scaling (MDS). Figure 2 shows the concept of this function. The topic distribution of each article can be calculated using LDA. We use the divergence between the distributions as an indicator of the similarity of the articles. By calculating the similarity (distance) of each pair of articles, we can obtain a distance matrix. Finally, the similarity of articles can be visualized on an x-y coordinate system using MDS. It is expected that this function will make students aware of which articles are related, thus helping them in writing their literature review.

As support function 2, to display the structure of the literature review, we propose a literature review structure feedback function using the LDA results. Figure 3 shows the concept of this function. The review sentences can be divided into bags of words. Here, each bag of words belongs to one topic, and it is calculated using LDA. As a result, we can obtain a topic occurrence pattern. We assume that there are different patterns between well-trained researchers and novice researchers. Therefore, collecting good patterns will be useful for students in organizing their literature review. A graphing function is created using the data series shown in Fig. 3, and a clear structure is displayed to the students.

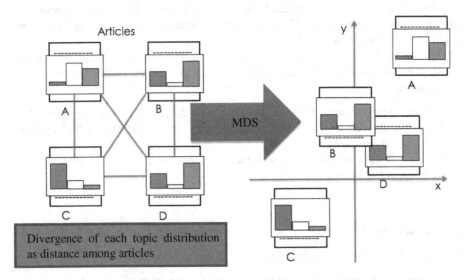

Fig. 2. Concept of student summaries' similarity feedback function using LDA and MDS

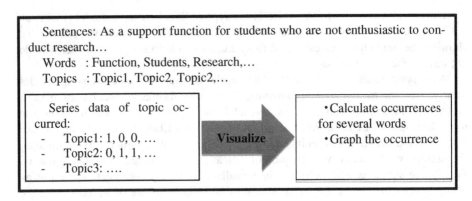

Fig. 3. Concept of literature review structure feedback function using LDA result

3 System Development

We developed a system prototype (Figs. 4, 5, 6, 7, 8 and 9). Figure 4 shows the system configuration. A learner summarizes his or her own article (learner summary) and a review in the client-side user interface, and those are saved into a database (DB). The system reads these document data from the DB, uses morphological analysis to divide them into morphemes for each document, and eliminates stop words. Bag-of-words expressions are derived for each document. Further, only a noun and an adjective are selected in this research. Next, topics for each word are estimated from the bag-of-words data. Topic distributions of learner summaries and topic occurrence patterns of the literature review are calculated using word–topic correspondence. These results are returned to the client-side user interface.

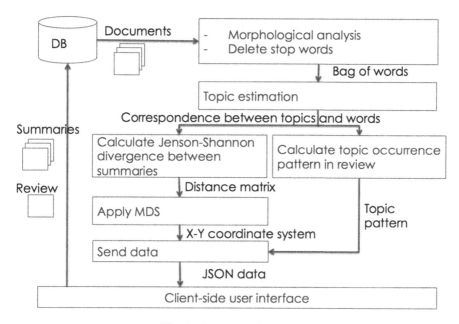

Fig. 4. System configuration

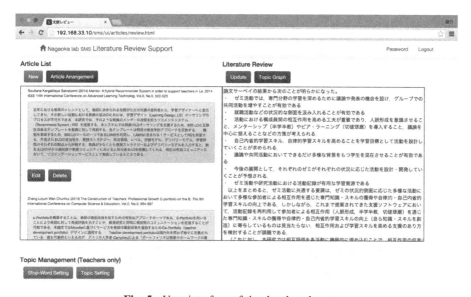

Fig. 5. User interface of the developed system

Figure 5 shows the client-side user interface. The article list is shown on the left side and the literature review editor is shown on the right side. Teachers can use a button at the bottom to call up the topic management dialog. It is possible to create a new thesis using the learner summary by clicking the "New" button of the article list.

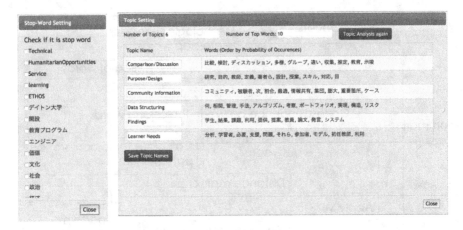

Fig. 6. User interface of stop-word setting dialog and topic setting dialog (teacher use only)

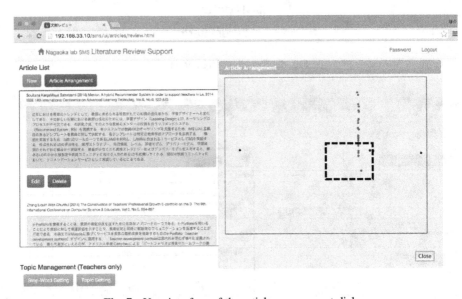

Fig. 7. User interface of the article arrangement dialog

Clicking the "Edit" button allows the registered article information to be edited, and clicking the "Delete" button deletes the article information. Clicking the "Article Arrangement" button allows use of the article arrangement function (Fig. 2). Clicking the "Topic Graph" button shows a visualization of the topic pattern (Fig. 3).

Figure 6 shows the stop-word setting dialog and the topic setting dialog that only teachers are allowed to use. This is important for effectively guiding students toward clarifying whether words are important in the research area. The system thus allows seminar instructors to select stop-words to reflect the intention. Furthermore, topics that can be estimated from summaries are changed if the number of learner summaries

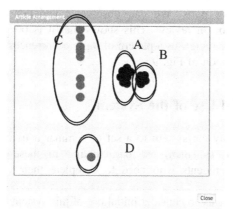

Fig. 8. Focus function of the article arrangement dialog

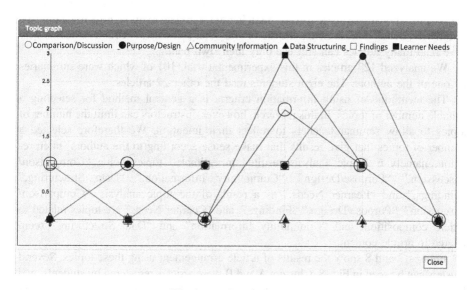

Fig. 9. Topic graph dialog

increases. The topic management screen is prepared for reanalysis and updating the number of topics and topic name.

Figure 7 shows the article arrangement screen. Each dot in the right-side scatter graph is equivalent to one article. When a dot is clicked, information regarding the corresponding article is shown in the article list on the left side. This allows comparison between articles with similar topics. Panning and zooming is possible, allowing more detailed observation of the dot distribution. As an example, Fig. 8 shows a magnification of the area enclosed by a dotted line in Fig. 7. Section 4 presents concrete results.

Figure 9 is a topic-occurrence pattern chart (topic graph) of the literature review. The review text is divided into five parts, and the occurrence frequency of the topic is calculated by respective parts. We can observe a variation of topic occurrence according to the position in review. This shows that it is possible to visualize the structure of the literature review as a pattern of topic occurrences. Section 4 presents a more detailed consideration of Fig. 9.

4   Results of Trial Use of the System

We experimentally apply the system to a set of seminar activities. At present, eight students (two women, six men) are participating in these activities. They are fourth-year university students who need to complete their graduation thesis this winter.

However, it is necessary to consider initial use of this system in actual situations. If only students make article summaries, there might be anxiety regarding obtaining enough sample data and a sufficient number of articles for a literature review. We therefore suggest that seminar instructors initially add self-created article summaries to the system. This allows students creating a literature review to quote not only their own summaries, but also those by the instructor and other students. Of course, students who have read many articles can still use only their own data.

We analyzed 123 articles in this experimental trial, 101 of which were summaries by one of the authors. The eight students read the other 22 articles.

The technique of using information criteria is a general method for selecting a suitable number of topics. In this research, however, instructors can limit the number of topics to allow seminar teachers to reflect their intention. We therefore selected a number of topics that give results that make sense according to the authors' interpretation, namely 6. Topic analysis resulted in estimated topics being "Comparison/ Discussion," "Purpose/Design," "Community Information," "Data Structuring," "Findings," and "Learner Needs." as a result of the topic analysis. "Comparison/ Discussion," "Purpose/Design," "Findings," and "Learner Needs" are topics related to article composition, and "Community Information" and "Data Structuring" seem related to article content.

Figures 7 and 8 show the results of article arrangement using these topics. Several clusters can be seen in Fig. 8. Clusters A and B were articles registered by students, and C and D were registered by an author. Both A and B are about communication, but their detailed contents are different. Cluster A includes articles focusing on improving presentation skills, while those in B focus on more practical needs such as career education and work after graduation. The C group is near A and B, but the article contents regard interaction supports between learners and teachers, such as discussion or mentoring. Interaction support can be considered a communication support, but with a different support target than in A or B. The D group consists of only one article, and it is located far from A, B, and C. The article content describes the relation between understanding and lecture evaluations of students in a lecture course, so it differs from A, B, and C. These results show that the article arrangement function grouped articles with similar content. It is useful for students to identify articles in similar categories but with somewhat different targets. This function can thus support creation of literature reviews.

Figure 9 shows the results of the topic graph function. One of the authors collected articles related to seminar activity and wrote reviews for them. We used these reviews for analysis. The first part of each review summarizes knowledge obtained from reading the article, the middle part describes social needs, and the last part describes purposes appropriate for enhancing seminar activity research. In the chart, "Findings" appears first, then "Learner Needs" and "Purpose/Design." While we have presented only one case, we can see that the topic occurrence pattern reflects the actual contents. When learners see this pattern, it will trigger reflection on the structure of the literature review. Furthermore, there is a possibility that learning from others can be induced, such as learning how to structure the literature review by seeing topic graphs of master learners such as graduate students and instructors.

5   Conclusion

Following the SMS concept proposed by Nagaoka, here we proposed a literature review support system as one aspect of a support function. Features include (1) topic models from LDA, (2) displaying article similarity using topic distributions of learner summaries and MDS, and (3) visualization of the literature review structure as an occurrence pattern of topics in the literature review. Trial use of the system shows that these functions can be useful supports for creating a literature review.

In future work we will continue using this system to accumulate learner summaries, evaluate the support and learning effects, and enhance the model. We presume that methods for choosing stop words and topic estimation parameters will influence the analysis results, so we will investigate what support can be realized using this system.

References

Blei, D.M., Ng, A.Y., Jordan, M.I.: Latent Dirichlet allocation. J. Mach. Learn. Res. **3**, 993–1022 (2003)

Kometani, Y., Nagaoka, K.: Development of a seminar management system. In: Yamamoto, S., de Oliveira, N.P. (eds.) HIMI 2015. LNCS, vol. 9173, pp. 350–361. Springer, Heidelberg (2015). doi:10.1007/978-3-319-20618-9_35

Nagaoka, K., Kometani, Y.: Seminar Activity as Center of University Education - SMS: Seminar Management System, Proposal and State of Development. Research Report, Japan Society for Educational Technology, JSET15-1 (2016) (in Japanese, printing)

Design for Adaptive User Interface
for Modeling Students' Learning Styles

Ashery Mbilinyi[1], Shinobu Hasegawa[2(✉)], and Akihiro Kashihara[3]

[1] School of Information Science,
Japan Advanced Institute of Science and Technology, Nomi, Japan
ashery.mbilinyi@jaist.ac.jp
[2] Research Center for Advanced Computing Infrastructure, JAIST, Nomi, Japan
hasegawa@jaist.ac.jp
[3] The University of Electro-Communications, Tokyo, Japan
akihiro.kashihara@inf.uec.ac.jp

Abstract. Various researches have shown that providing adaptive support during students learning process improves student's motivational and learning outcomes. Therefore the effectiveness of e-learning systems can be determined based on how adaptive they are to the intended students. In this paper we describe a design for an adaptive user interface for a web-based learning system that can estimate students learning styles from their interaction with the web and use that information to guide them during their knowledge construction process.

Keywords: Adaptive user interface · Learning style · Web-based learning system

1 Introduction

A study conducted on 140,546 students participated in 4 Massive Open Online Courses (MOOCs) found that, despite the linear structure imposed on students – chronological ordering of weeks and learning sequences – learners predominantly navigate through MOOCs in a non-linear way, on average students skip 22 % of learning sequences entirely and perform a high number of back jumps, most often jumping from assessments back to earlier lectures [1]. This means, even though there are currently a large number of hypermedia-/hypertext based resources for learning purposes on the web [2], still students will have individual preferences on how they make choices on the learning resources no matter how structured they might be.

There are many factors that contribute to this individuality preferences but one thing common to all is, when they navigate through the hyperspace, they have to create a useful navigation path which influences their knowledge construction process [3]. But the problem is, so often the learners fails in creation of such navigation path due to cognitive overload, which is caused by diverse efforts not only in comprehending the contents of the webpages, but also in planning their own navigation process [4, 5].

Therefore, the provision of personalized or adaptive learning support for individual students is one of the important features to be provided by the e-learning systems [6] to help the students in their self-directed learning process. Adaptive learning systems can

© Springer International Publishing Switzerland 2016
S. Yamamoto (Ed.): HIMI 2016, Part II, LNCS 9735, pp. 168–177, 2016.
DOI: 10.1007/978-3-319-40397-7_17

either present personalized content for individual students or guide them to learn by providing a personalized path [7]. On our research we are focusing on a personalized path by developing a web-based system that can learn students behavior pattern called learning style and provide adaptive user interface to guide them.

Since it is difficult in applying adaptation on web-based learning systems based on students' learning styles because of the availability of students' behavior information on the web that can help to estimate their learning styles, we would like to examine the two following research questions;

- What kind data from student's interaction on the web can lead to recognition of their behavior pattern and therefore their learning style.
- What kind of user interface features can better adapt those recognized learning styles.

2   Related Works

2.1   Self-directed Learning

Adaptive presentation and adaptive navigation support has been two major technologies explored by adaptive hypertext and hypermedia systems [8] to help students in their self- directed learning. In systems with adaptive presentation, the pages are not static but adaptively generated or assembled for each student based on information stored on student model while in adaptive navigation support, the system assist their hyperspace orientation and navigation by changing the appearance of visible links to make it easier for students to choose where to go next and therefore help student find an "optimal learning path" [8]. There are many researches related to adaptation in self-directed learning. But two of the following works may be related to adaptation using learning style model.

AHA: The "Adaptive Hypermedia Architecture" system supports an on-line course with some user guidance through conditional (extra) explanations and conditional link hiding. In this system each time a user visit a page, the name of the page is passed to the adaptation engine, which updates a user model. The links are then displayed differently depending on the suitability of the link destination, which determined by an author-defined requirement, which express common relationships between concepts. The unvisited links are displayed blue color, purple is for visited ones, both of these are suitable links but the unsuitable or undesired links becomes black and not underlined [9].

CS383: This system dynamically creates HTML pages containing an ordered list of the educational resources, from the most to the least effective from the student's learning style point of view based on results from answering a dedicated questionnaire. CS383 follows 3 constructs of the Felder-Silverman Learning Model: Sensing/Intuitive, Visual/Verbal, Sequential/Global. For each category of resources (i.e. hypertext, audio files, graphic files, digital movies, instructor slideshows, lesson objectives, note-taking guides, quizzes, etc.), the teacher has to mention its suitability (support) for each learning style (by rating it on scale from 0 to 100). When a student logs into the course, a CGI executable loads the student profile, it then computes a unique ranking of each category of resources, by combining the information in the students profile with the resource ratings [10, 11].

Heritage Alive Learning System: is based on Felder-Silverman learning style model. Learning preferences are diagnosed implicitly, by analyzing behavior patterns on the interface of the learning system using Decision Tree and Hidden Markov Model approaches. Consequently the learning system interface is adaptively customized: it contains 3 pairs of widget placeholders (text/image, audio/video, Q&A board/Bulletin Board) each pair consisting of a primary and a secondary information area. The space allocated on the screen for each widget varies according to the student's learning style. [12, 13].

INSPIRE: Based on 4 Learning Styles in Honey and Mumford model [14], all learners in the INSPIRE system are presented with the same knowledge modules, but their order and appearance (either embedded in the page or presented as links) differ for each learning style. Thus for Activists (who are motivated by experimentation and challenging tasks), the module "Activity" appears at the top of the page, followed by links to examples, theory and exercises. In case of Pragmatists (who motivated by trying out theories and techniques), the module "Exercise" appears at the top of the page, followed by links to examples, theory and activities. Similarly, in case of Theorist the order is: theory, examples, exercises and activities while Reflectors the order is: examples, theory, exercises, and activities [11, 15].

2.2 Learning Style

Learning styles designates everything that is a characteristic to an individual when he/she is learning, i.e. a specific manner of approaching a learning task, the learning strategies activated in order to fulfill the task [13]. Learning style represents a combination of cognitive, affective and other psychological characteristics that serve as relatively stable indicators of the way a learner perceives, interacts with and responds to the learning environment [16]. For example, while approaching the same learning topic, there are students who would like to be presented first with definitions followed by examples, while others prefer abstract concepts to be first illustrated by a concrete, practical example. Similarly, some students learn easier when confronted with hand-on experiences, while others learn better alone [11].

There are over 70 learning style models in the literature [17]. Different models are used by various adaptive systems to classify learners. In our research, we are using Kolb's model.

Kolb's Model. Kolb's learning model which has been widely known as the Learning Style Inventory (LSI) [18] is probably the most famous model used in many disciplines, including education, management, computer science, psychology, medicine, nursing, accounting and law [19] to identify learning styles. Kolb's theory articulates that people learn from experience so the learning is a continual process which follows the cycle, so it is very unlikely that people will always have the same learning style, but changes during the knowledge construction process which involves a person and the environment they find themselves [20]. The cycle consists of 4 phases (Fig. 1), which are Concrete experience to Reflective observation to Abstract Conceptualization to

Active experimentation and back to Concrete experience. So at one time during the learning process a person can fall in one of the following learning styles [17]:

Accommodators: (Concrete experience + Active experimentation)

These types of students are practically oriented and get involved with unfamiliar and changeable circumstances. They are good at solving problems intuitively but sometimes seen by others to be overly proactive and somewhat impatient.

Assimilators: (Abstract Conceptualization + Reflective observation)

Assimilator likes inductive reasoning, logic and construction of theories; these learners are driven more by abstract ideas than by interaction with others.

Convergers: (Abstract Conceptualization + Active experimentation)

Students with a converging learning style are good at decision-making and problem solving; they prefer resolving technical issues compared to sort out interpersonal problems.

Divergers: (Concrete experience + Reflective observation)

Students with this learning style are imaginative and perceive situations from many perspectives; they are people-oriented and adapt by observation compared to direct action.

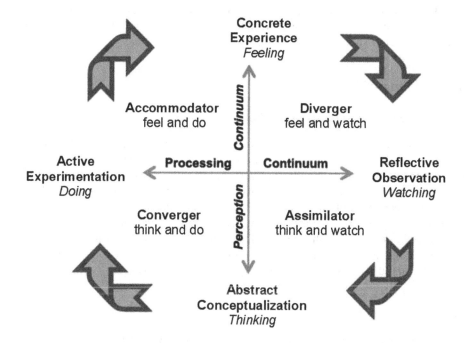

Fig. 1. Kolb's Learning Model (derived from http://www.learningexperience.org.uk/)

We have chosen Kolb's Model not just because it is well-accepted learning model among others over long time but also its foundation is on the idea that people are learning through experience so it accommodates the dynamism of learning styles involved during knowledge construction process of a person.

Honey and Mumford's Model. This model categorize four learning styles which are very similar to Kolb's model even though their model based on general individual behavior rather than learning in particular. Their learning style types are Activists (correlating to the "concrete experience" aspect of Kolb's experiential learning style), Reflectors (reflective observation), Theorists (abstract conceptualization) and pragmatists (active experimentation) [20]. Just like Kolb's, this model also illustrates that learning style is not a constant person's characteristics but dynamic one which changes due to the circumstances the learners experiences.

2.3   Target Learning Environment

Our system will be used to learn elementary school level mathematics. We will use Statistics subject in the prototype. Statistics offers flexibility in developing adaptive contents since among many mathematical subjects, few rival statistics in everyday applications [21]. The learning contents will be grouped in 4 modules, which are Examples, Theory, Exercise and Problem Solving Task. Each module should be tailored to give fully understanding of the specific learning topic. Once a student chooses a learning topic, the system should be able to guide him or her dynamically to the module that better suite his/her learning style at a particular time.

3   Modeling of Learning Style

3.1   In Preliminary Test: Initialization

At the initial stage when student creates their profiles in the system, we need to build a user profiles that will enable personalized interaction. Profiles should store both user-defined preference information and system detected user behavior pattern. Whenever the system detects a change in behavior pattern, it should update the profile [22].

Kolb's Learning Style Inventory (LSI) offers a questionnaire (Kolb's Test) which helps to identify the 4 mentioned learning styles types. At the initial point where the system does not have enough data from the users to recognize their learning style, the answers to this questions which will categorize their learning style will be the initial data to be stored on their profile as the user-defined preferences.

3.2   In Learning Process

During the students' learning process, our user modeling will involve tracking the interaction between the user and the system to recognize the users' behavior patterns and identify how these behaviors relate to their learning styles. This will help us to investigate whether Kolb model is appropriate for web-based learning or not. The data to be used will be the tracked users interface actions mainly frequency of clicking on learning modules, and navigation buttons and time intervals spent between modules.

First we want to track the student's first choice of learning module (first link click), after the system has displayed the learning modules available for the topic. Their first click on the specific learning module would likely mean that no matter the chronological arrangement suggested to students by the system, that learning module might be their preferable one. Then as he/she continues learning, time spend on each module would also let the system learn his/her behavior. The less interval time he/she spend on a certain module since his/her first click action before jumping to another module would mean he/she didn't prefer the previous module. At last the students will be given an open test in which they will be able to review any module or information to help them answer this test, the back jumps frequency to a particular module will give information on what kind of learning materials each student think they better help him/her in understanding of the learning topic. We have designed a "Weak User Model" (Fig. 2) to model the above-mentioned user behavior. We have called it a "Weak User Model", since we are still investigation if these kinds of data would be enough to give full recognition of students learning style.

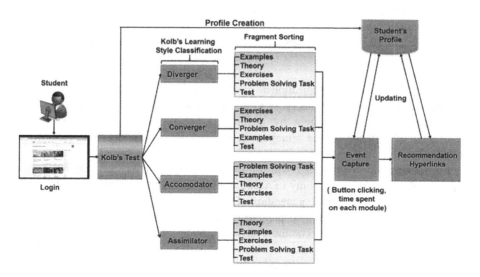

Fig. 2. Weak User Model

4 Design for Adaptive User Interface

4.1 Learning Style Adaptation

One of the main difficulties on designing of adaptive hypermedia systems is linking learning styles with the hypermedia applications [23]. For our system, adaptation will be in two levels, which are adaptive contents and adaptive user interface. For the contents, each module will be designed to give a full understanding of the learning topic so that when a user access the contents he/she prefer can get to understand the topic. For the user interface, we want the system to provide different arrangement of learning modules to each user's learning style so it can be easy for users to find the modules they prefer and also as they continue to learn, thus their preference behaviors changes, we want a system to dynamically provide different recommendation links to each learning style recognized so as to guide their knowledge construction process.

4.2 User Interface Adaptive Features

Fragment sorting is the technique in which educational resources are presented in different order considered suitable for each student [7]. So for each learning style identified after Kolb's Test (Fig. 1), students will be presented different order from the most suitable module at the top to the least one at the bottom. The fonts size and color of each link to the module will also be different with the top one larger and bottom one smaller in descending order. The arrangement is derived from INSPIRE system but will follow the Kolb's learning styles teaching suggestions as follows:

Accommodator: The arrangement will be Problem Solving Task $\Rightarrow$ Examples $\Rightarrow$ Theory $\Rightarrow$ Exercises $\Rightarrow$ Test, because this student can be taught better through making at integration between experiences and application, so problem solving task should be at the top.

Assimilator: Making facilitation for concept formulation is better way to teach this kind of student so the arrangement is Theory $\Rightarrow$ Examples $\Rightarrow$ Exercises $\Rightarrow$ Problem Solving Tasks $\Rightarrow$ Test.

Converger: Making personalization by practice is suitable for this learning style so the arrangement is Exercises $\Rightarrow$ Theory $\Rightarrow$ Problem Solving Task $\Rightarrow$ Examples $\Rightarrow$ Test.

Divergers: Are better taught by making connection between experiment and pre-existing knowledge so the arrangement is Examples $\Rightarrow$ Theory $\Rightarrow$ Exercises $\Rightarrow$ Problem Solving Task $\Rightarrow$ Test.

Recommendation Hyperlinks: will follow some adaptive navigation support techniques of Brusilovsky's taxonomy of adaptive hypermedia technologies as follows: -

Adaptive link hiding and generation: During "Event Capturing" phase in our system (Fig. 2), we recorded two parameters, time spend on each module and frequency of click on a module. The links of two learning modules corresponding to the highest value of those two parameters or the one link if both parameters favor it will be displayed this time at the top followed with link for the "Test" at the bottom. If the students test score will be less than 60 %, after learning through the module or modules given, the system should generate another mostly likely link for the student to choose from the hidden links, this time will be only one link with the highest parameter value of the either two parameters among the hidden links. Otherwise if the score is above 60 %, only one most preferable link will be shown together with Test for the next learning topic. Through this way, the system will keep on narrowing the recommendation links choices until the one link of the module that mostly preferred by the student will be recognized at the end.

5 Experiment Plan

5.1 Preliminary Experiment

We want to evaluate if Kolb's model is effective to be used in Web-based Learning Systems or not. If it is effective there must be close correlation between the learning style class the system placed a student during a fragment sorting phase and the learning modules the system will detect that a student prefer most, after the "event capturing" and "recommendation hyperlinks" phase. For example, if the student is Accommodator type of learning style that means at the end the mostly preferable link to him should be "Problem solving task".

5.2 System Experiment

We want to evaluate whether the system's adaptive features have been of assistance to student in guiding him to his/her preferred modules during navigating the hyperspace or have been limiting students. We will use confidence questionnaire to ask students how satisfied they were with the navigation support the system provided. We will also evaluate the effective of our systems by comparing the average learning time and test scores on learning topics assigned to students when using system with adaptive features and when there is no adaptive features.

6 Conclusion and Future Work

In this paper, we have described the design of adaptive user interface for modeling students' learning styles with two research questions in hand (i) What kind data from student's interaction on the web can lead to recognition of their learning pattern and therefore their learning styles (ii) What kind of user interface features can better adapt those recognized learning styles. The key idea is that adapting students' way of learning has a positive effect their learning process, leading to increased efficiency, effectiveness and/or learners satisfaction [11]. While we are still investigating if the set of input parameters we are using can be of enough information about users behaviors in learning, in the future we would like to have a "Stronger User Modeling" and propose a learning styles based on web-based learning environment. To do that we are expecting to broaden our behavior identification techniques by performing association rule mining [24] on clusters that represent group of users that interact similarly with the interface [25]. This process involves extracting the common behavior pattern in terms of class association rules (CAR) in the form of $X \rightarrow c$, where X is a set of feature value pairs and c is the predicted class label (that is, the cluster) for the data points where X applies. We also want to broaden the evaluation of effectiveness of the adaptive user interface through tracking feedback expression of users expression by observing face recognition and eye tracking data.

Acknowledgements. This work is supported in part by Grant-in-Aid for Scientific Research (B) (No. 26282047), from Ministry of Education, Science and Culture of Japan and Japan International Cooperation Agency (JICA) under ABE Initiative Program.

References

1. Guo, P.J., Reinecke, K.: Demographic differences in how students navigate through MOOCs. In: Proceedings of the First ACM Conference on Learning' Scale Conference, pp. 21–30 (2014)
2. Hasegawa, S., Kashihara, A.: An adaptive support for navigation planning in hyperspace. In: Proceedings of World Conference on Educational Media and Technology, Association for the Advancement of Computing in Education (AACE), pp. 2548–2555 (2006)
3. Hammond, N.: Learning with hypertext: problems, principles and prospects. In: McKnight, C., Dillon, A., Richardson, J. (eds.) Hypertext: A Psychological Perspective, pp. 51–69. Ellis Horwood Limited, Chichester (1993)
4. Cunningham, D.J., Duffy, T.M., Knuth, D.A.: The textbook of the future. In: McKnight, C., Dillion, A., Richardson, J. (eds.) Hypertext: A Psychological Perspective, pp. 19–49. Ellis Horwood Limited, Chichester (1993)
5. Thuering, M., Hannemann, J., Haake, J.M.: Hypermedia and cognition: designing for comprehension. Commun. ACM **38**(8), 57–66 (1995)
6. Tseng, J.C.R., Chu, H.C., Hwang, G.J., Tsai, C.C.: Development of an adaptive learning system with two sources of personalization information. Comput. Educ. **51**(2), 776–786 (2008)
7. Brusilovsky, P.: Adaptive hypermedia. User Model. User-Adap. Interact. **11**, 87–110 (2001)
8. Brusilovsky, P., Peylo, C.: Adaptive and intelligent web-based educational systems. J. Artif. Intell. Educ. **13**, 156–169 (2003)
9. De Bra, P., Aerts, A., Berden, B., De Lange, B., Rousseau., B., Santic, T., Smits, D., Stash, N.: AHA! The adaptive hypermedia architecture. In: Proceedings of the Fourteenth ACM Conference on Hypertext and Hypermedia, pp. 81–84 (2003)
10. Carver, A., Howard, A., Lane, D.: Enhancing student learning through hypermedia course and incorporation of student learning styles. IEEE Trans. Educ. **42**, 33–38 (1999)
11. Popescu, E., Badica, C., Moraret, L.: Accommodating learning styles in an adaptive educational system. Informatica **34**, 451–462 (2010)
12. Cha, H.J., Kim, Y.S., Park, S.-H., Yoon, T.-b., Jung, Y.M., Lee, J.-H.: Learning styles diagnosis based on user interface behaviors for the customization of learning interfaces in an intelligent tutoring system. In: Ikeda, M., Ashley, K.D., Chan, T.-W. (eds.) ITS 2006. LNCS, vol. 4053, pp. 513–524. Springer, Heidelberg (2006)
13. Popescu, E., Trigano, P., Badica, C.: Towards a unified learning style model in adaptive educational systems. In: Seventh IEEE International Conference on Advanced Learning Technologies, pp. 804–808 (2007)
14. Honey, P., Mumford, A.: The Manual of Learning Styles Maidenhead. Peter Honey Publications, Oxford (1992)
15. Papanikolaou, A., Grigoriadou, M., Kornilakis, H., Magoulas, D.: Personalized the interaction in a web-based educational hypermedia system: the case of INSPIRE. User-Model. User-Adap. Interact. **13**, 213–269 (2003)
16. Keefe, J.W.: Learning style: an overview. In: NASSP's Student Learning Styles: Diagnosing and Prescribing Programs. National Association of Secondary School Principals, Reston, VA, pp. 1–17 (1979)

17. Coffield, F.D., Moseley, E., Hall, E., Ecclestone, K.: Learning Styles and Pedagogy in Post-16 Learning: A Systematic and Critical Review. Learning and Skills Research Centre, London (2004)
18. Kolb, D.A.: Experiential Learning: Experience as the Source of Learning Development. Prentice Hall, New Jersey (1984)
19. Mainemelis, C., Boyatzis, R.E., Kolb, D.A.: Learning styles and adaptive flexibility: testing experiential learning theory. Manag. Learn. **33**(1), 5–33 (2002)
20. Brown, E.: The use of learning styles in adaptive hypermedia: thesis submitted to the university of Nottingham for the degree of doctor of philosophy (2007)
21. Minsky, M.: What makes mathematics hard to learn (2008). http://web.media.mit.edu/~minsky/OLPC-1.html
22. Liu, J., Wong, C., Hui, K.: An adaptive user interface based on personalized learning. IEEE Intell. Syst. **18**(2), 52–57 (2003)
23. Franzoni, A.L., Assar, S.: Student learning styles adaptation method based on teaching strategies and electronic media. Educ. Technol. Soc. **12**(4), 15–29 (2009)
24. Zhang, C., Zhang, S.: Association Rule Mining: Models and Algorithms. Springer, Berlin (2002). doi:10.1007/3-540-46027-6
25. Conati, C., Samad, K.: Student modeling: supporting persSonalized instruction, from problem solving to exploratory, open-ended interactions. AI Mag. **34**(3), 13–26 (2013)

An Adaptive Research Support System for Students in Higher Education: Beyond Logging and Tracking

Harriet Nyanchama Ocharo[1] and Shinobu Hasegawa[2(✉)]

[1] School of Information Science, Japan Advanced Institute of Science and Technology,
Nomi, Japan
harriet.ocharo@jaist.ac.jp
[2] Research Center for Advanced Computing Infrastructure,
Japan Advanced Institute of Science and Technology, Nomi, Japan
hasegawa@jaist.ac.jp

Abstract. In this paper, we focus on design for an adaptive research support system that provides support for research activities of students in higher education, as well as improving the research skills of the students. Research activity is one of the core activities of institutions of higher education and it is with this in mind that we propose an adaptive research support system to improve the research skills of students. Research skills include such generic skills as planning and scheduling, communication and presentation; and specific skills such as trend analysis, problem definition and data analysis. We present a general way to improve research skills of students by adaptation, achieved through coaching and scaffolding supports using information gained from archived laboratory knowledge.

Keywords: Adaptation · Research support system · Research skills · Coaching · Scaffolding

1 Introduction

Research is one of the core activities of institutions of higher education. Therefore it follows that ways of improving research skills of the students is an important area of study. Teaching students research skills provides the students with information and facility for improving their research capacity, quality and productivity with the aim of better quality output, more effective and efficient research output from institutions of higher education.

Several studies have been conducted into ways to teach both general and discipline-related research skills to students. A Research Skills Framework (Willison and O'Regan 2007) is a conceptual framework that was developed to guide the teaching of undergraduate students in order to achieve explicit development of research skills. The framework can be used "to both chart and monitor students' research skill development" (Willison and O'Regan 2007) and to guide the student in progressing from the "commonly known, commonly not known to the totally unknown". In a paper by (Showman et al. 2013), they explain five essential research skills for undergraduates help them move from learning to discovering. These and other studies underpin the

© Springer International Publishing Switzerland 2016
S. Yamamoto (Ed.): HIMI 2016, Part II, LNCS 9735, pp. 178–186, 2016.
DOI: 10.1007/978-3-319-40397-7_18

importance of equipping students with research skills right from the undergraduate level to the graduate level. However, one challenge is that research skills are cognitive skills which are difficult to teach and to evaluate because they are implicit.

Most institutions of higher education implement some sort of tracking or logging system to monitor and track students' research activities and to provide a tool for communication between students and their supervisors. These systems are usually used for quality assurance of the research process of the students. The monitoring and tracking systems, while helping students with logging their research activities and keep up with deadlines, have a few limitations. These include the fact that they are seldom adaptive with regards to the needs of each particular student, they do not preserve previous laboratory research knowledge, and do not offer a platform for students to improve their research skills.

A limitation of the existing tools and frameworks designed to improve the research skills of students is that they factors in the physical and continuous presence of a mentor or teacher, but in reality face-to-face interaction with the researchers may be minimal or may be a mixture of real and virtual laboratory. In addition, the students in higher education join a certain laboratory for a short time because of graduation timelines. This makes it difficult for them to learn the research skills properly.

An adaptive research support system can bridge this gap by offering a platform for students to learn invaluable research skills while they carry out their research activities. In adaptation, for example, students who are carrying out a task for the first time will be provided with relevant information and step by step support to accomplish the task, while advanced students will be given more challenging tasks to encourage them to find creative ways to solve problems on their own.

The target of our proposed adaptive research support system is students in all levels of higher education: undergraduate, master's and doctoral students or their equivalents. Research students in general could benefit from making use of the system. The research should ideally be organized in laboratory format, where students carrying out research in a common area or theme are grouped together under one professor such as in STEM where faculty and students often collaborate on common problems of inquiry (Franke and Arvidsson 2011). Research organized under a common theme will enable preservation of relevant laboratory knowledge which will be exploited for the implementation of adaptation.

The goal of the adaptive research support system is to support academic research activities while improving the research skills of the research students. Research skills include such generic skills as planning and scheduling, communication and presentation; and specific skills such as trend analysis, problem definition and data analysis. Improving research skills of students through our adaptive systems is a key and unique goal that highlights the originality of this research. The motivation of our research is that students in higher education need adequate interaction with professors in order to improve their research skills but this is not always possible especially in developing countries where the ratio of students to professors may be higher, and in the case of distance learning where contact with the professors may be minimal.

The following sections are constructed as follows: in the second section, we describe in detail the research activity process, the specific definition of research skills, and we present a review of related literature. In Sect. 3, we discuss our general design approach for an adaptive system to improve research skills. Section 4 includes the conclusion and future works.

2   The Research Activity Process and Review of Related Work

2.1   The Research Activity Cycle

Most of scientific research follows a common cycle that can be abstracted as shown in Fig. 1. We base this representation on The Research Process Model by (Fankfort-Nachmias and Nachmias 1992) showing the main steps in scientific research. This research activity process is more or less the same for all disciplines (Lynch 2013). Lynch further notes that "the key difference across disciplines is in the subject matter, and therefore, the type of data used and the methods for gathering it".

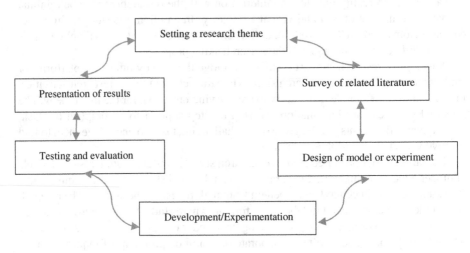

Fig. 1. Research activity cycle

In **setting a research theme**, the aim is to identify a topic of interest to study. **Survey of related literature** involves exploring the works of fellow researchers. After surveying related works, a researcher may go back to the first step to modify their problem statement. The research cycle is not unidirectional and is also not strictly sequential. The **design of model or experiment phase** involves creating a plan, considering expected findings, tools, methodologies and designing experiments or models. **Development or experimentation** phase involves carrying out the experiment or developing the software or tool in the case of information science. **Testing and evaluation** involves collecting data and analyzing it using statistical packages, for example. Presentation of results involves publishing in books/journals, web publication, presenting at seminars and conferences and so on.

2.2 Research Skills

Research skills are necessary for students to improve their research capacity, quality and productivity with the aim of better quality output, more effective and efficient research output from institutions. However, research skills are cognitive skills that are hard to teach, to learn and to evaluate. What exactly are research skills? Research skills can be widely categorized into two: discipline specific and general research skills. While there may be several types of research skills, the key idea of our research is to develop and improve research skills from a low degree of autonomy corresponding to closed inquiry and high degree of guidance, to a high degree of autonomy where students conduct open inquiry within self-determined guidelines (Willison and O'Regan 2007).

Depending on what stage of the research activity cycle students are in, Table 1 shows examples of the crucial skills students in higher education carrying out research should develop.

Table 1. Research activities and corresponding skills

Research activity	Specific skills	Generic skills
Setting a research theme	• Trend analysis • Problem definition	• Planning/scheduling • Communication • Self-directed and motivated • Creativity/innovation
Survey of related literature	• Information retrieval • Reading • Evaluation	
Design of model or experiment	• Design • Discipline-specific skills	
Development/experimentation	• Discipline-specific skills	
Testing and evaluation	• Analytical • Evaluation	
Presentation of results	• Presentation	

2.3 Related Works

There has been previous research into tools and systems to support students with their research activities. In their research, (Hasegawa et al. 2007) created a portal site to manage all content created during the research activity cycle through seamlessly integrating activities support services. Their research demonstrated success in two web services: setting a research theme and trend analysis (review of related literature), saving students efforts at this stage of the research activity cycle.

Other researchers have reported positive findings in recommending relevant research resources to assist researchers with the literature review process. (Porcel et al. 2008) concluded that their system was effective in enabling researchers to obtain automatically information about research resources interesting for them; (Bandara et al. 2011) proposed an extensive tool support for the identification of appropriate papers during the literature review process. (Kiah et al. 2014) developed a customizable search engine for trusted resources in medical informatics.

Previous research has mainly been focused on improving specific areas of the activity research cycle such as setting a research theme and survey of related literature. Some previous research has focused on the entire research activity cycle such as the proposed framework for a web-based research support system by (Yao 2003) where various research activities are linked to different systems that support those activities. The paper combined computer technology and research methods to develop a conceptual framework for research support systems. Yao not only links activities to support tools, but also notes that an adequate research support system would need to be adaptive to the scientist and states the need for applying algorithms to documents stored to "discover patterns and extract knowledge useful to a user".

A practical example of a system that extracts previous knowledge from stored documents is the article revising system by (Hasegawa and Yamane 2011) where the system extracted laboratory knowledge from the information accumulated from laboratory members. There has also been research into improvement of presentation and communication skills. In their study, (Kerby and Romine 2009) state that students can improve their oral presentation skills by, among other ways, experiencing consistent instructor feedback.

Previous research has focused on improving some of the research skills of its students in order to increase efficiency and reducing the efforts required to carry out some of the research activities. However, there has been no specific research support system (computer system) whose explicit goal is to improve research skills of students and our aim in this paper is to present the design for such a system.

3 Design Approach: Adaptation for Improvement of Research Skills

Research skills are cognitive skills that are therefore difficult to teach and evaluate. The Cognitive Apprenticeship Theory was originally proposed by Collins et al. (1989). It proposed a way to apply features of traditional apprenticeship in teaching cognitive skills by following the 6 steps in order: modeling, coaching, scaffolding, articulation, reflection, and exploration.

Our approach is to combine content (research knowledge) with metacognitive support (modeling, coaching, and scaffolding) to improve the students' research skills. Adaptation relies mainly on coaching and scaffolding; to improve research skills we need to reduce the cognitive support for the students as their level of skill increases. This approach is called fading scaffolding/fading, where functions of the supporting tool can be *fadable* according to the student's meta-cognitive skill (Kashihara et al. 2008).

In designing a research support system to improve the skills of students, we need to deal with the following issues:

- how to represent the research activity process
- how to estimate the student level
- how to provide coaching and scaffolding

3.1   How to Represent the Research Activity Process

Each phase in the research process (refer to Fig. 1) will be represented as a research outcome in the system. At each phase of the research activity cycle, students produce research artifacts such as documents, presentations, and data in various forms, among others. These research artifacts will usually undergo revision with the supervisor giving comments to students in order to help improve the work product. We propose to have students upload their work product into the system and the supervisor to use the same system to give comments which the students will use to improve their work product. In this regard, it would work like an issue or incident tracking system (refer to Fig. 2). The system will keep track of the revision history of the artifacts as well as the comments associated with the revised documents. All the document versions and associated comments will be stored and analyzed in order to improve the knowledge base that will be used to provide coaching and scaffolding for future students.

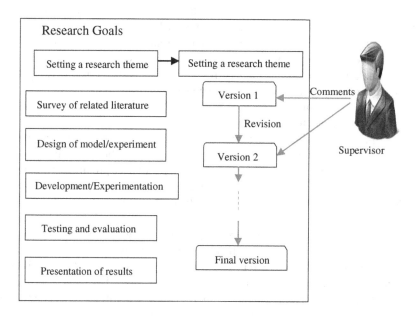

Fig. 2. Overview of the research support system interface

3.2   How to Estimate the Student Level

In order for the system to be adaptive to the research skill needs of students, it must be able to estimate their initial and continued skill levels. Initial estimation of student skill may depend on previous work carried by the students and uploaded for evaluation into the system. Additionally, undergraduate students may initially be estimated to be at beginner level, master's students at an intermediate level, and doctoral students at an advanced level. These levels are not fixed and for example, an undergraduate students can muster a skill and move to an advanced level. The system will be adaptive and will keep a student in a relevant category as their skill level changes.

To monitor and track student progress in achieving a certain skill, the evaluation function will take into account two factors: process and outcome. For process evaluation, we will consider factors such as the number of comments, the type of comments, the draft history and the duration of revision. Outcome evaluation is much harder to carry out as it depends on factors such as the quality, originality and effectiveness of the student's work product.

We will divide student skills into five levels according to the Research Skills Framework (Willison and O'Regan 2007). These will form a basis for providing coaching and adaptation as will be discussed in Sect. 3.3.

3.3   How to Provide Coaching and Scaffolding

Providing coaching and scaffolding, in addition to the evaluation function discussed in Sect. 3.2, will form the core functions of the adaptive system in order to improve the research skills of students. The input to our system will be students' research artifacts, comments from the supervisor and responses to the comments by the students, and any learning resources the supervisor might provide. The processing will include managing student information, managing and tracking research artifacts and revision history, evaluating the student level, analyzing content to generate rules to associate research skill level with appropriate resources, coaching and scaffolding. Output from the system will be feedback and guidance to students, and statistical trends.

We will provide coaching and scaffolding during the artifact revision process. Coaching will involve letting the student to do carry out a task but providing guidance as to how the task can be achieved. With scaffolding, the guidance provided to the student will reduce with time as the student's skill level grows. Once the student receives feedback in form of comments from the supervisor, the next step for the student is to revise the current draft. The system will analyze the current comment by comparing it to similar existing comments in the knowledge database and provide appropriate support and guidance (coaching) depending on the student level (see an example in Table 2). Even for similar comments, the system will provide different guidance to students in different skill levels. If a student gets a similar comment in the future but their skill level is different, they will get different guidance. As the student's skill level increases, this guidance becomes less and less (scaffolding). If the student's level stays the same or decreases over a certain period of time, this can be flagged by the system and the supervisor can take appropriate action.

In Table 2, we show an example for improving the modeling skills of students carrying out research in information systems. After setting a research theme (formulating the problem) and reviewing related literature, the students have to come up with a graphical representation of their proposed system (modeling phase).

Table 2. Providing coaching and scaffolding in learning modeling skills

Skill level	Design of model
Level 1	• System gives several examples of similar comments and revised artifacts • System/supervisor specifies which modeling methodology to use
Level 2	• System gives some examples of similar comments and revised artifacts • System provides 2–3 ways of modeling for the student to choose from
Level 3	• System provides examples only on request • System provides from all possible modeling ways for students to choose from
Level 4	• System does not provide examples • System provides from all possible modeling ways for student to choose most suitable
Level 5	• System challenges student to come up with their own original way of modeling if existing ways are not sufficient in some way

4   Conclusion and Future Work

In this paper, we proposed a way to improve the research skills of students using an adaptive research support system. This involves using the cognitive apprenticeship theory in teaching research skills since they are cognitive skills that are hard to teach and to evaluate. By using computer technology to provide coaching and scaffolding to students during the revision of research artifacts produced during the research process cycle, we posit that it is possible to improve the research skills of students. This will result in better conception, development and representation of research ideas from unstructured to highly structured and independent which will lead to shortening time the time it takes to conduct research while at the same time increasing efficiency and quality.

In future work, we will develop and implement the system based on the design discussed in Sect. 3, and design experiments to test out the effectiveness of the system. We will focus on the design model/experiment phase of research, and we aim to test this system with students carrying out research in information systems research field. Students will at this stage develop a graphical representation of their proposed information system using modeling languages such as Unified Modeling Language, and we will test whether their modeling skills will improve with time. We will collect all system data including logs of students' interaction with the system, and conduct pre-and-post interviews. We will analyze this data to identify meaningful patterns and emerging themes for further research.

Acknowledgements. This work is supported in part by Grant-in-Aid for Scientific Research (C) (No. 26330395) from the Ministry of Education, Science, and Culture of Japan.

References

Bandara, W., Miskon, S., Fielt, E.: A systematic, tool-supported method for conducting literature reviews in information systems. In: 19th European Conference on Information Systems. QUT Digital Repository, Helsinki, Finland (2011)

Collins, A., Brown, J.S., Newman, S.E.: Cognitive apprenticeship: teaching the crafts of reading, writing, and mathematics. Knowing Learning Instr. Essays Honor Robert Glaser **18**, 32–42 (1989)

Fankfort-Nachmias, C., Nachmias, D.: Research Methods in the Social Sciences, 4th edn. St. Martin's, New York (1992)

Franke, A., Arvidsson, B.: Research supervisors' different ways of experiencing supervision of doctoral students. Stud. High. Educ. **36**(1), 7–19 (2011)

Hasegawa, S., Yamane, K.: An article/presentation revising support system for transferring laboratory knowledge. In: 19th International Conference on Computers in Education, pp. 247–254. Asia-Pacific Society for Computers in Education, Chiang Mai, Thailand (2011)

Hasegawa, S., Mannari, K., Ooiwa, S., Kashihara, A.: a portal site for supporting research activities. In: 15th International Conference on Computers in Education, pp. 59–60. Hiroshima, Japan (2007)

Kashihara, A., Shinya, M., Sawazaki, K., Taira, K.: Cognitive apprenticeship approach to developing meta-cognitive skill with cognitive tool for web-based navigational learning. In: Seventh IASTED International Conference on Web-based Education, Innsbruck, Austria (2008)

Kerby, D., Romine, J.: Develop oral presentation skills through accounting curriculum design and course-embedded assessment. J. Educ. Bus. **85**(3), 172–179 (2009)

Kiah, M.M., Zaidan, B.B., Zaidan, A.A., Nabi, M., Ibraheem, R.: MIRASS: Medical Informatics Research Activity Support System. J. Med. Syst. **38**(4), 1–15 (2014)

Lynch, S.M.: Using Statistics in Social Research: A Concise Approach. Springer, New York (2013)

Porcel, C., Lopez-Herrera, A.G., Herrera-Viedma, E.: A recommender system for research resources based on fuzzy linguistic modeling. Expert Syst. Appl. **36**(3), 73–83 (2008)

Showman, A., Cat, A.L., Cook, J., Holloway, N., Wittman, T.: Five essential skills for every undergraduate researcher. CUR Focus **33**(3), 16–18 (2013)

Willison, J., O'Regan, K.: Commonly known, commonly not known, totally unknown: a framework for students becoming researchers. High. Educ. Res. Dev. **26**(4), 393–409 (2007)

Yao, Y.Y.: A framework for web-based research support systems. In: Computer Software and Applications Conference, pp. 601–606. IEEE, Dallas, Texas, US (2003)

Investigation of Learning Process with TUI

Natsumi Sei[1]([⊠]), Makoto Oka[2], and Hirohiko Mori[1]

[1] Tokyo City University Graduate Division, Tokyo, Japan
g1581815@tcu.ac.jp
[2] Tokyo City University, Tokyo, Japan

Abstract. We investigated the types of user interfaces effect the human learning by using the improved cognitive model, and found that there are some differences in learning process between GUI and TUI. In GUI condition, many subjects started establishing sub-goals in the tactile control and strategic control modes and stay in them even after the learning is proceeded. In TUI condition, on the other hand, though the subjects use the same strategy as GUI in the initial term of learning, they found the other strategy and become to utilize it in the late term of learning. In this strategy, when they face to the difficulties to establish sub-goals, they try to find clues by moving to the explorative mode and attempted to achieve the sub-goal by trial and error.

Keywords: Tangible User Interface (TUI) · COCOM · Verbal protocol · Cognitive process

1 Background

Computers are widely used in various situations throughout society and they are being introduced into the field of learning. In primary schools, for example, there are many classes where tablet-size computers are being used. TUI is attracting attention in the field of learning. With Tangible User Interface (TUI), a computer can be controlled by touching a physical object directly by hand. Therefore, the user can use a computer intuitively. Because of this advantage, TUI can be employed in the field of the learning.

However, Durfee [1] has pointed out that different results occur when a different interface is used even for the same task. This suggests that behavior and ways of thinking change depending on the interface used to solve a problem.

2 Purpose

In this paper, we focused on the effects of Tangible User Interface on human learning process and aims to investigate how the types of user interfaces causes the cognitive learning processes. By clarifying these characteristics, we believe that we will be able adopt what kind of user interface suit the task.

© Springer International Publishing Switzerland 2016
S. Yamamoto (Ed.): HIMI 2016, Part II, LNCS 9735, pp. 187–196, 2016.
DOI: 10.1007/978-3-319-40397-7_19

3   Related Works

Many researches have been done so far for education using TUI. TV globe [2], for example, allows children to learn the geography by connecting the physical globe to TV and Illuminating Clay [3] was developed to aim to understand the changes of the terrain. TUI is also used to learn computer programing. In Topobo [4], children can control the robot movement by combining the block. In these researches, however, the effects to be obtained for learning by adopting TUI are not investigated.

Only a few works have focused on the relationships between the types of user interface and learning and investigating the effects on learning according to the types of UI. Ito et al. [6] was compared TUI and GUI in learning process. In this research, they found that the subjects can enjoy the learning process with TUI while they feel painful with GUI in spite of the same tasks. However, they could not find the difference in their behavior and the results.

4   Experiment

We conducted the experiment to clarify the effect of TUI on human learning processes according to the types of user interfaces. For comparison, other interfaces are needed to clarify the characteristics of TUI. For this reason, we adopted GUI as a control group for comparison. Because GUI is used to control ordinary computers, we considered that it is suitable as a control group.

4.1   Learning Experiments Using a TUI

We chose logical circuit building as learning tasks that are easy to be implemented the tasks in the same appearance with GUI and TUI. The subjects are required to build a logical circuit watching a truth table by connecting some logic circuit. The three logic circuit used in this experiment were the "AND", the "OR" and the "NOT". In addition, the lead wire objects and the lamp objects, to connect among each gate and to confirm the output of the circuit respectively, were also prepared. In GUI condition, all operations for the logic circuit are "click" and "drag" on the icons with a mouse. In TUI, each logic gate is represented as a cube- shaped block which is graspable. The circuit can be created by arranging the blocks in 2-demension place. The subjects asked to "think aloud", and, their behavior and verbal protocol data were recorded by VCR.

4.2   Method

Each subject was asked to attend experiments the 6 times which were held once a week. Personality diagnostic test was conducted in first week to cancel the effect of the affinity between the personality and the UI types by being assigned the subjects to each condition based on the results of "the way of thinking".

After the second round, the subjects asked solve the task of logic circuit. The task in second round is to fill the truth table from the connection diagram. The task after the third round is to build the connection diagram from the truth table.

5   Results and Discussion

5.1   Analysis of Behaviors and Verbal Protocols

We analyzed the subjects' behavior and their verbal protocol data. There was no difference in the problem solving strategies between TUI and GUI in the early and medium terms. The difference between the conditions, however, were observed in the latter term.

Tables 1, 2 and 3 shows some parts of one subject's behaviors and the verbal protocol data, which was typical in each conditions in each term. We classified their behaviors into three types of actions. First, "move object" is action that subject operate the objects. Second, "Operation check" is action that subject push the switch for checking the results of output.

Table 1. GUI subject A Protocol data

No.	Start	Action	Verbal protocol	Other behavior
1	4:20	Thinking		See the instruction
2	4:25	Thinking		See the sample

Table 2. GUI subject A Protocol data

No.	Start	Action	Verbal protocol
1	31:00	Move object	
2	31:35	Operation check	Does it work?
3	31:50	Thinking	Do not light the lamp
4	31:55	Thinking	
5	32:15	Move object	Not stick in the "ONON"
6	32:35	Operation check	

Table 3. TUI subject D Protocol data

No.	Start	Action	Verbal protocol
1	27:20	Thinking	Just a moment. Yes, yes, I made a mistake
2	27:35	Move object	Not 'or', 'AND' should be correct
3	27:45	Operation check	Mistaken

Table 1 shows the data with GUI in the initial term. The table indicates that the subjects often read the instruction and watched the samples. This means, in this term, the subject did not understand how to operate the system and the structures of the tasks of the logic circuit, were making efforts to understand them and groped for the solution. From such a thing we call this term "knowledge acquisition stage". In TUI condition, the subjects also stood on the similar stage in the initial term.

When the subject understood the method of operation of system and problem structures of making logic circuit, they moved to the next stage in the medium term, thinking in head and checking right by system. Table 2 shows the typical data with GUI in medium term. The utterance of "Do not light the lamp" can be considered that wrong results was obtained against his considerations. The subject with GUI in the this term tried to make whole solution of the diagram task and to guess the result in his mind, and the system were used only to check the results. We call this stage "logical thinking stage". In TUI condition, the same stages were observed in the middle term.

In TUI condition, the subjects moved to the next stage in the latter term. In this stage, the subjects attempted to create the solution using the system though the system was used only to check the results in the logical thinking stage. Table 3 shows the verbal protocol data with TUI in the latter term. In this table, the subjects uttered "Just a moment. So Yes, yes, I made a mistake." This utterance was appeared after the check of a local part of result among the whole solution, and it means they did not guess the result in his mind. Also, "Not 'OR', 'AND' should be correct" was appeared in moving the object and he tried to check the result as soon as he came up the idea of the local solution. In this stage, therefore, the subject with TUI in the latter term visualized a part of the connection diagram in their mind using the system and by repeating this process they tried to reach the solution. We defined this stage "visual thinking stage".

On the other hand, the subjects with GUI did not move to the "visual thinking stage" and stayed the "logical thinking stage" even in the latter term. In GUI condition, the subjects moved the object after the deep consideration and checking the result after the guessing the result of whole solution. When their solution was wrong, they considered again in their mind.

These differences become more apparent when the task become more difficult. In difficult tasks, the subjects stayed consideration and did not cause any actions, while the subjects with TUI tried to find the solution by moving the objects without considering too deeply. In addition, TUI checked the result after guessing soon and when the result was incorrect they moved to the next operation soon. In this way, TUI is tend to allow to go into action as soon as an idea comes up.

5.2   Mode Classification Based on the COCOM

In order to verify why the difference of the strategies caused described in the previous section, we apply to the Contextual Control Model (COCOM) [7] in A Contextual Control Model.

In COCOM, the states of human thinking are classified using the four parameter, "number of goals", "plans available", "event horizon", and "execution mode", into four control modes: "Scrambled control", "Opportunistic control", "Tactical control" and "Strategic control". Figure 1 shows pattern diagram of COCOM.

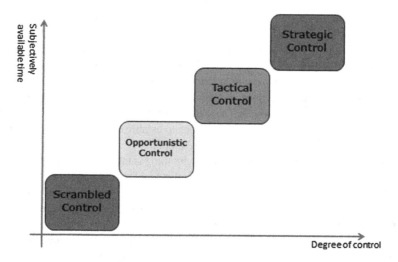

Fig. 1. Pattern diagram of COCOM

Here, we focus the "visual thinking stage" with TUI and the "logical thinking stage" of GUI and TUI to compare the control mode transition between the stages Tables 4 and 5 show the data which observed typically in each stage.

Table 4. GUI subject A logic thinking stage(COCOM)

No.	Start	Action	Analysis of the cognitive act	Mode
1	0:02	See the paper problem	It is to determine the logic circuit	Tactical
2	0:24	Move the logic circuit	It is to determine the object	Tactical
3	0:42	Move the logic circuit	How there is no, stalemate	Opportunistic
4	1:13	Move objects	Subject decided to placement	Tactical
5	1:29	Move objects	Placed on the basis of the goal	Tactical

Table 5. TUI subject D visual thinking stage(COCOM)

No.	Start	Action	Analysis of the cognitive act	Mode
1	0:04	Remove the object	Try to post a new plan	Opportunistic
2	0:33	See the paper problem	It is not determined goal	Opportunistic
3	1:02	Move the logic circuit	Try the things that came up	Opportunistic
4	1:30	Move lead wire	Do not understand	Scrambled
5	1:40	See the paper problem	Try understand the problem	Opportunistic
6	1:59	Move lead wire	Do not know way	Opportunistic
7	2:05	Move the logic circuit	It is to determine the logic circuit	Tactical
8	2:25	Move the logic circuit	It is determined goals	Tactical
9	2:42	Move the logic circuit	Do expect	Tactical
10	2:52	Trace the board	Determine the goal	Tactical
11	3:23	Move objects	Try to achieve the goal	Tactical

In "logic thinking stage", the problem solving process was done mainly by the transfer between "tactical" and "opportunistic" modes. Table 4 shows data of logic thinking stage with GUI. No. 1 and No. 2 in this table show the initial state where this subject was considering which logic circuit should be used to achieve the goal and started the problem solving process in "tactical" mode. Logic circuit In No. 3, he failed to connect the gates using lead lines and rebuilt a new goal. Here, however, as the new goal was for very local solution, he was transferred to "opportunistic" mode. After repeating these processes, he changed his tactics to establish a new goal of grasping the current state and he moved back to "tactical" mode.

Table 5 shows the mode transfer states in the visual thinking stage with TUI. Similar to the logical thinking stage with GUI, the problem solving process were done mainly by the transfer between "tactical" and "opportunistic" modes. Looking at No. 1, 2, 3, however, this subjects moved to "opportunistic" mode, because he tried to find the goals to achieve by checking the lamp and the result as a workaround but failed to find the adequate goal and repeated the same process until No. 6. As the operation in No. 6 was accidentally correct, he could move back to the "tactical" mode.

Here, though the states of the subjects were sometimes classified into the "opportunistic" mode in both stage of "logical thinking" and "visual thinking", their observed states were quite different between them. "Opportunistic" mode observed in the visual thinking stage is close to "scramble" mode. In COCOM, the mode is determined by majority of four parameters. While, the most cases where the subjects were determined in "opportunistic" mode in case of visual thinking stage, some parameters indicated scrambled mode, all parameter indicated opportunistic mode in case of the logical thinking stage.

This means the original COCOM model is not very appropriate to analyze the detail of the human learning process. COCOM is naturally a model to apply the plant operators who have already been well trained. So, such kind of operations to find what will happen by them has not been envisaged. And, it did not appear "scrambled" and "strategic" in this classification. Furthermore, when the subject did not smoothly find the goal, many of modes is determined "tactical", because it is not possible to clarify the difference between "strategic".

So, we need to improve COCOM to be adequate for the human learning tasks.

6   Improved Model

We made two improvements to a Contextual Control Model fit the analysis of human learning process.

First, new parameters, "action mass" and "intention for the goal", to determine the control mode are added to a Contextual Control Model to identify "strategic control" mode from "tactical control" mode. "Intention for the goal" is to indicate the width of the range subjects sweep the path to the goal in thinking. "Action mass" is a parameter to indicate whether they have found the operation to achieve their current sub-goal.

The other improvement is to add a new control mode: "Explorative Control" mode. Though COCOM has five modes including "Explorative Control" originally, "Explorative Control" mode was eliminated from COCOM because plant operators are generally well trained and they seldom move to this mode. We considered that this mode is necessary to analyze the human learning process and decided to add this mode.

So, in our improved model, the five modes are defined as follows.

Scrambled Control : "Intention for the goal" is very narrow (focus on only one action). "Action mass" is not clear.

The state that the user has no idea of what to do to solve the problem.

Opportunistic Control : "Intention for the goal" is not so wide. "Action mass" is not clear.

Though subjects think looking at only one or a few sub-goals toward the goal, they do not know what kind of action should be done to achieve them.

Explorative Control : "Intended for the goal" is narrow. "action mass" is clear.

Their sub-goal is not clear and not to go toward the goal directly but to just try to find something tentatively.

Tactical Control : "Intention for the goal" is wide. "Action mass" is clear.

Subjects think several sub-goals sweeping some part of path to the goal and knows what kind of action is needed to achieve sub-goals though they have not found the whole path for the goal yet.

Strategic Control : "Intention for the goal" is very wide. "Action mass" is clear.

The path toward the goal is established more detail than tactical control, and subjects know what action are required to achieve it.

Figure 2 shows pattern diagram of improved model.

6.1   Mode Classification Based on T Suggested Model

Based on the improved model, we assumed more detail analysis of the difference between the stages. We show some typical part of the data in Tables 6 and 7.

Table 6. GUI subject B in logical thinking stage

No.	Start	Action	Analysis of the cognitive act	Mode
1	0:07	Move objects	Logic circuit Create sub-goal and operate toward it	Strategic
2	0:28	Move objects	Correct the sub-goal	Strategic
3	0:52	Operation check	Try to check the sub-goal	Tactical
4	1:02	Remove the logic circuit	Consider a different sub-goal	Tactical
5	1:11	Move objects	Determine the logic circuit to achieve the sub-goal	Strategic

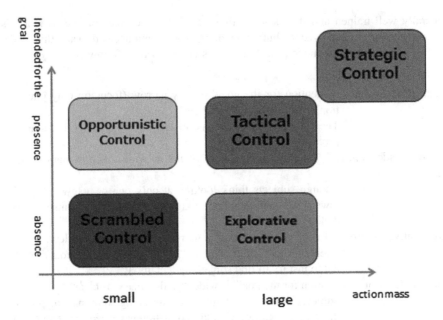

Fig. 2. Pattern diagram of improved model

Table 7. TUI subject D in visual thinking stage

No.	Start	Action	Analysis of the cognitive act	Mode
1	0:04	Remove the object	Try to make a new sub-goal	Tactical
2	0:33	Remove the object	It is not determined goals	Tactical
3	1:02	Move the logic circuit	Try the things that came up	Explorative
4	1:30	Move lead wire	Try the things that came up	Explorative
5	1:40	See the paper problem	Try understand the problem	Tactical
6	1:59	Move lead wire	Not understand what to do	Opportunistic
7	2:05	Move the logic circuit	Try anticipate	Tactical
8	2:25	Move the logic circuit	It is determined goal	Tactical
9	2:42	Move the logic circuit	To anticipate	Strategic
10	2:52	Trace the board	To anticipate the result	Strategic
11	3:23	Move objects	Try to achieve the goal	Strategic

In the logical thinking stage with GUI, the problem solving were proceeded mainly in only "strategic" mode and "tactical" mode. In Table 6 shows the data of the logical thinking stage with GUI. At No. 1, the subjects were in "strategic control" mode because, when the subject saw the problem, he could build the sub-goal and what kind of action is required. At No. 2, though the sub-goal was wrong, he could stay the same mode, because he could deal with the mistake. So, at No. 3 he can make a new sub-goal by moving to "tactical control" mode. Due to refine the sub-goal at No. 3, he moved to "strategic control" mode at No. 4 and tried to achieve it. At No. 5, he was able to see the path for the goal moving to "strategic control" mode and succeeded to solve the problem. In this way, most subjects tried to solve the problem by the transition between "Tactical Control" and "Strategic Control" in the logical thinking stage with GUI. Similar process was observed with TUI in solving easy problems. However, different strategy was used when the problems were difficult with TUI, though the same strategy were used with GUI in spite of the difficulty of the problems.

Table 7 shows visual thinking stage with TUI. With TUI in this stage, the subjects often move to "explorative control" mode and it was observed especially in solving difficult problems. At No. 1, he reset this thought and tried to make sub-goals sweeping the path to the goal in "Tactical Control". At No. 2, he read the question to confirm the goal in "Tactical Control". Here, he gave up to find the sub-goals toward the goal directly, moved to "explorative control" mode, and, and started moving logic circuit at No. 3, No. 4 tentatively. Due to moving to "explorative control" mode, he got a clue and went back to "Tactical Control" mode and could create a new sub-goal.

However, he did not divide the sub-goal into the series of actions and moved to "opportunistic control" mode. At No. 7, he started the deep thought about goal moving to "Tactical Control" mode. At No. 9, he was able to find some sub-goals in "Strategic Control" and succeeded to solve the problem. In this way, with TUI, the subjects frequently transfer between "tactical control" and "explorative control" modes to get clues by moving to "explorative control" mode. And when they find them, they return to "tactical control" mode.

In this way, the subjects of GUI solve the problem mainly in "strategic control". Subject of TUI was distinctive how to solve in difficult problem. First, subject was in "Tactical Control". Second, subject was in "Explorative Control". Final, subject returned in "Tactical Control". In other words, subject of TUI try to move logic circuit in difficult problem and explore the hint from try move. How to solve of GUI was not seen much. It is the characteristic that TUI solves the problem in "explorative".

7 Conclusions

We investigated the types of user interfaces effect the human learning by using the improved cognitive model, and found that there are some differences in learning process between GUI and TUI. In GUI condition, many subjects started establishing sub-goals in the tactile control and strategic control modes and stay in them even after the learning is proceeded. In TUI condition, on the other hand, though the subjects use the same strategy as GUI in the initial term of learning, they found the other strategy and become to utilize it in the latte term of learning. In this strategy, when they face to the difficulties to establish sub-goals, they try to find clues by moving to the explorative mode and attempted to achieve the sub-goal by trial and error.

It can be said that TUI must be appropriate to learn ill-defined problems to require the emergence of creativity and develop new ideas, such as story making and brainstorming while GUI is appropriate for learning the well-defined problems, such as calculating and programming. In the near future, we should investigate it.

Furthermore, though we found the differences of learning process between with GUI and TUI, the reason why the differences are caused are not clarified. This is our other future work.

8 Application

We concluded that TUI make it can be said to easy to develop. In solving the problems which require of various ways of thinking because broad searches in the problem space are needed for such kind of problems. For example, we think that it may be applied for tasks such as storytelling.

In the future, we must clarity farther characteristics of TUI and GUI, and we believe it will contribute to the e-learning fields.

References

1. Durfee, J.L., Billingsley, F.F.: vol. 53, pp. 214–220 (1999)
2. TVglobe: epoch. http://epoch.jp/gt/tvglobe/
3. Illuminating clay: a tangible interface with potential GRASS applications. In: Proceedings of the Open Source GIS - GRASS Users Conference, Trento, Italy, pp. 11–13 (2002)
4. Hiroshi, I.: Topobo: a constructive assembly system with kinetic memory, Vienna, Austria, pp. 24–29. ACM (2004)
5. Lightbot. http://lightbot.com/hocflash.html
6. Daisuke, I., Makoto, O., Hirohiko, M.: Comparing learning process with GUI and TUI. In: Proceedings of the 76th National Convention of IPSJ, pp. 415–416 (2014)
7. Hollnagel, E.: Human Reliability Analysis: Context and Control. Academic Press, London (1994)

A Method for Consensus Building Between Teachers and Learners in Higher Education Through Co-design Process

Ryota Sugino[1(✉)], Satoshi Mizoguchi[1], Koji Kimita[1], Keiichi Muramatsu[2], Tatsunori Matsui[3], and Yoshiki Shimomura[1]

[1] Department of System Design, Tokyo Metropolitan University, Tokyo, Japan
{sugino-ryota,kimita}@tmu.ac.jp, mizoguchi-satoshi@ed.tmu.ac.jp,
yoshiki-shimomura@center.tmu.ac.jp
[2] Department of Science and Engineering, Saitama University, Saitama, Japan
muramatsu@mech.saitama-u.ac.jp
[3] Department of Human Sciences, Waseda University, Saitama, Japan
matsui-t@waseda.jp

Abstract. Improving added value and productivity of services entails improving both value-in-exchange and value-in-use. Value-in-use is realized by value co-creation, where providers and receivers create value together. In higher education services, value-in-use comes from learners achieving learning outcomes (e.g., knowledge and skills) that are consistent with their learning goals. To enhance the learning outcomes of a learner, it is necessary to enhance and utilize the abilities of the teacher along with the abilities of the learner. To do this, however, the learner and the teacher need to build a consensus about their respective roles. Teachers need to provide effective learning content; learners need to choose the appropriate learning strategies by using the learning content through consensus building. This makes consensus building an important factor in value co-creation. However, methods to build a consensus about their respective roles may not be clearly established, making such consensus difficult. In this paper, we propose some strategies for consensus building between a teacher and a learner in value co-creation. We focus on a teacher and learner co-design and propose an analysis method to clarify a collaborative design process to realize value co-creation. We then analyze some counseling data obtained from a university class. This counseling aimed to build a consensus for value-in-use, learning outcomes, and learning strategies between the teacher and the learner.

Keywords: Consensus building · Value co-creation · Higher education · Learning service

1 Introduction

Improving added value and the effectiveness of services entails improving both value-in-exchange and value-in-use. Value-in-exchange is realized by exchanging products/services for consideration; value-in-use is realized by using products/services. As a result, value-in-use is defined by a product/service receiver, and therefore a provider

© Springer International Publishing Switzerland 2016
S. Yamamoto (Ed.): HIMI 2016, Part II, LNCS 9735, pp. 197–208, 2016.
DOI: 10.1007/978-3-319-40397-7_20

needs to provide a product/service that satisfies the receiver's requirements. In order to realize high value-in-use, a provider and a receiver need to build a long-term relationship and co-create value that can achieve these requirements. To realize value co-creation, it is important for a provider to involve a receiver in the development process of products and services [1]. Therefore, a receiver needs to play the role of both a user and a value co-creator in order to realize value co-creation [2]. To be a value co-creator, a receiver needs to acquire, enhance, and utilize the abilities of the value co-creator. At the same time, a provider must also acquire, enhance, and utilize abilities for realizing high value-in-use. Figure 1 shows the relationship of value for providers and receivers in services. In an ideal environment, methods of acquiring and enhancing the abilities are established; however, realizing value co-creation in this way is difficult. The purpose of this study is to clarify the mechanisms for value co-creation for realizing effective value. To do so, we propose a method of consensus building between a provider and a receiver and develop an analysis method of a co-design process to clarify the method. This allows the receiver to play the role of value co-creator in the product/service life cycle.

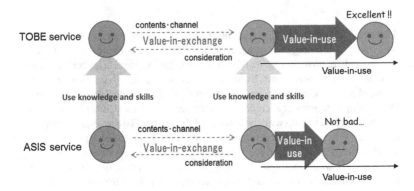

Fig. 1. Relationship among values, a provider and a receiver in service

2 Value Co-creation in Learning Service

2.1 Problems in Higher Education

While value co-creation is important for realizing value-in-use for learners in higher education services, higher education still has problems with value co-creation. In higher education services, it is important for learners to achieve their learning outcomes, in order to realize high value-in-use. To enhance learning outcomes of a learner, it is crucial to improve the quality of the learner's independence [3]. To do this, however, it is necessary for the learner and the teacher to build a consensus about learning outcomes that the learner aims for and learning strategies to achieve the learning outcomes. Moreover, a teacher needs to provide effective learning contents, whereas the learner needs to choose the learning strategies, including the learning content, appropriately through consensus building. However, a teacher conducts a class without reflecting a learner's goals and requirements to learning content and tools, as shown in Fig. 2. Therefore, only a teacher who can provide learning contents and appropriate tools to a learner and a learner who can utilize them are able to enhance learning outcomes.

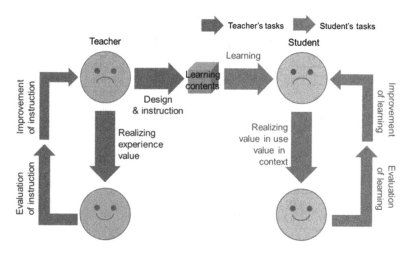

Fig. 2. Learning service in higher education (Color figure online)

2.2 Ideal Learning Service

From the services viewpoint, learners in higher education institutions can be regarded as customers, and the value of an education is therefore determined by learners. In addition, learners work as value co-creators; in other words, while teachers must provide effective contents, learners must perform adequate learning behaviors. In order to realize such an educational service, Kimita [4] proposed the education process shown in Fig. 3. First, a teacher develops an assumption about learning outcomes for learners. Learning outcomes are realized as state change that is desirable for the learner. In this step, then, the teacher identifies what constitutes the valuable state for learners, designs educational contents and suggests them to the learners. Here, the teacher needs to build a consensus with learners about the educational contents and the learning outcome. After building this consensus, the teacher provides the educational contents and conducts a formative evaluation in order to improve them. Finally, an overall evaluation is conducted.

In order to realize value co-creation in higher education outlined above, a learner needs to play a role of value co-creator and co-create value with a teacher. Therefore, a learner needs to acquire, enhance, and use the ability of the value co-creator. Figure 4 shows the ideal learning service that involves the learner in the teacher's process. In order to realize it, the teacher and the learner need to build a consensus about their respective role. In this paper, we suggest a method for analyzing processes of consensus building between a teacher and a learner in co-design process to realize ideal learning services.

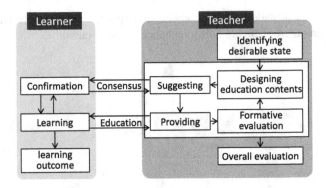

Fig. 3. Overview of the proposed education process [4]

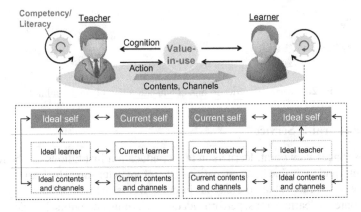

Fig. 4. A model for service value co-creation [5]

As a perspective on consensus building, this study adopts a model of service value co-creation [5]. The rest of this section introduces the detail of this model in higher education.

A Model for Value Co-creation in Higher Education Service. Figure 4 shows the proposed service model, which includes the co-growth of teacher and learner, along with its driver. A teacher proposes a value to a learner through contents and learning tools. The learner perceives the proposed value in a specific context. In response to the perceived value, the teacher modifies his/her actions, and the learner also modifies their actions to improve the service. In this model, value is co-created by such modifications of providing and receiving action in use of the service. Here, reflectiveness is regarded as the ability to appropriately modify one's own actions. The original meaning of "reflect" is to modify one's own actions by comparing one's own ideal model with the current state. However, the value of a service is co-created by mutual interactions between teacher and learner. Each should reflect on the other, and on contents and channels as well as on themselves. As shown in the lower section of Fig. 4, reflectiveness is defined here as an ability to appropriately modify one's own actions in comparing the ideal teacher, learner, contents, and channels. To realize a value co-creative service, it is extremely important for both teacher and learner to have this ability. Idealizing each other is a required condition of the service; if there is a large gap between their ideal state and the current state, it will be difficult to form a co-creative relationship between teacher and learner. For that reason, negotiation and consensus building about these gaps is necessary for realizing a viable co-creative relationship.

3   Proposed Method

3.1   Design Solution Model

Figure 5 shows a design solution model for analyzing the results of design solutions and basis for expanding the model that are derived by co-designing. This model organizes design solutions by viewpoints of "Why," "What," "How," and "Entity." The "Why" viewpoint describes a learner's desirable states and requirements. "What" describes learning objectives to attain for realizing an item in the viewpoint of "Why." "How" describes teaching and learning strategies for realizing an item in the viewpoint of "What," and "Entity" describes learning tools for an item in the viewpoint of "How." Figure 5 (right panel) shows a design basis list, which organizes what a teacher and a learner build by consensus as basis. Thereby, the proposed model enables to visualize design solutions and basis, and to analyze the results of the consensus building in the co-design process. Moreover, by visualizing knowledge (e.g., know-how of designing teaching/learning strategies and expanding the model), it becomes possible for a teacher to modify his/her design solutions and to improve the way a class is designed. On the other hand, a learner is able to learn how to design learning methods and design his/her learning through co-designing with a teacher.

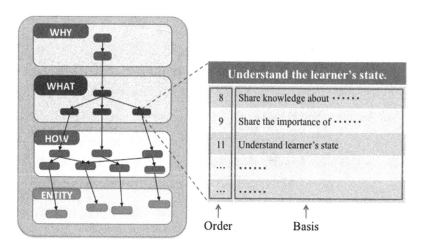

Fig. 5. Design solution model

3.2   Method for Analyzing the Co-design Process

Figure 6 shows a method for analyzing the co-design process. This method is based on the learning state map, which Kimita [6] proposed for analyzing level of a learner's achievement and the process to reach the level in higher education services. Our proposed method describes a state in the process of co-designing and an item of consensus building by using the design solution model and the design basis list. In addition, a stratagem matrix organizes the state transition from a certain state (ASIS state) to the next state (TOBE state). By using these models, we can visualize the state transition process on the map.

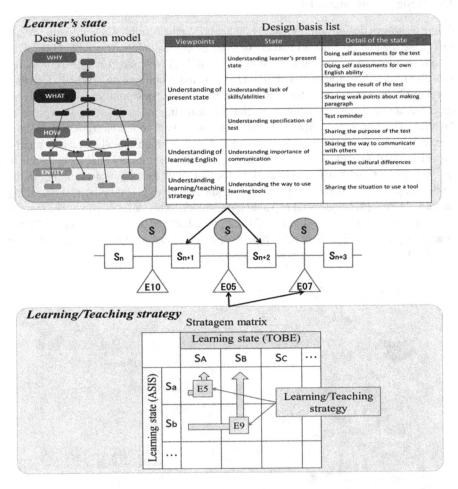

Fig. 6. Method for analyzing the co-design process

3.3   The Interpretive Structural Modeling Method

Interpretive structural modeling (ISM) is defined as a process aimed at assisting the human being to better understand what he/she believes and to recognize clearly what he/she does not know. Its most essential function is organizational. The ISM process transforms unclear, poorly articulated mental models of systems into visible and well-established models [7]. In this method, a set of different directly and indirectly related elements are structured into a comprehensive systematic model. The model so formed portrays the structure of a complex issue or problem in a carefully designed pattern implying graphics as well as words [8, 9].

By using ISM method, it makes possible to organize strategies to expand and formulate concrete design solutions while considering the state of the teacher and learner. It is possible to integrate and organize co-design strategies, design solution models that describe relationships among elements from multiple results of co-design process.

4   Application

In this paper, we conducted the application of the design solution model (Sect. 3.1) to confirm effectiveness of the model. To clarify a co-design process between a teacher and a learner, we analyzed the results of counseling in an English class that is part of the Creative Engineering Project at The University of Tokyo. In this application, a teacher provided about two one-hour counseling sessions for each learner to co-design learning. We then evaluated the learner's outcomes through an examination that evaluates the learner's communication ability in English. Moreover, learners filled out a questionnaire before and after co-designing to evaluate changes in their learning motivation. The questionnaire was prepared based on the ARCS model [10]. The ARCS model is used for promoting and sustaining motivation in learning process from the viewpoints of attention (A), relevance (R), confidence (C), and Satisfaction (S). In this application, we analyzed 9 out of 19 learners who had an improved score for learning motivation.

4.1   Design Solution Model

We present two instances as the results of the analysis. Figure 7 shows the results when a learner improved both the examination score and the learning motivation (as learner A). Figure 8 shows the results when a learner improved only learning motivation (as learner B). From these results, the authors confirmed that both learners A and B had the same requirements about studying abroad as a learner's TOBE state. However, they had different design solutions for "What." Learner A's learning purpose for improving communicating ability was focused on English conversation, while learner B's learning purpose was getting an advanced level examination score. We confirmed that learning purposes differed for each learner even if they had the same learner's TOBE state. They had the same purpose, for instance, they had a design solution about speaking more English. However, the design solution connected different learning strategies in the for "How." Learner A, for example, had the design solution to maximize the amount of time conversing in English, whereas learner B had the design solution to read sentences aloud. In addition, we confirmed learner A built consensus more concretely with the teacher than did learner B. By analyzing the counseling data, the authors clarified the design solution and design basis of learning that is co-designed by a teacher and a learner.

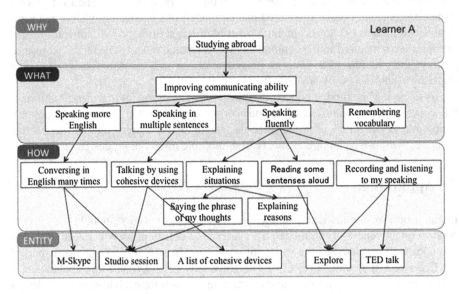

Fig. 7. A process of consensus building in the English lecture

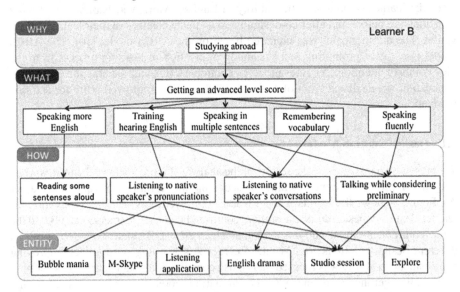

Fig. 8. The strategy for consensus building

Figures 9 and 10 show certain phases of analysis. We confirmed learner A initially built a consensus on the learning purpose for "What" and the learning strategy for "How" and then built a consensus on his/her TOBE state for "Why." On the other hand, Learner B initially built a consensus on his/her TOBE state for "Why" and then built a consensus on the learning purpose for "What" and the learning strategy for "How." Moreover, we confirmed that consensus building for the same learning purpose or strategy had different design bases. For instance, learner B built consensus on his/her ability as design basis for the design solution of speaking in multiple sentences. On the other hand, learner A built consensus on his/her ability along with concrete instances as the design basis for the design solution of speaking in paragraph. From these results, our proposed method enabled visualizing the design solutions and basis in the co-design process. Accordingly, we consider this proposed method as feasible for analyzing value co-creation in the co-design phase.

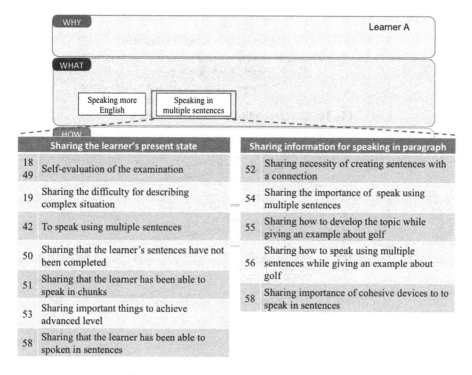

Fig. 9. Design solution and basis of learner A

4.2   Structuring the Results by the ISM Method

From the result of design solution model that is indicated Sect. 4.1, we built structuring models of consensus building between teacher and learner in co-design process shown in Fig. 11. We divided learners according to learning outcome; group A is consisted by 4 learners who improved examination score and learning motivation, group B is

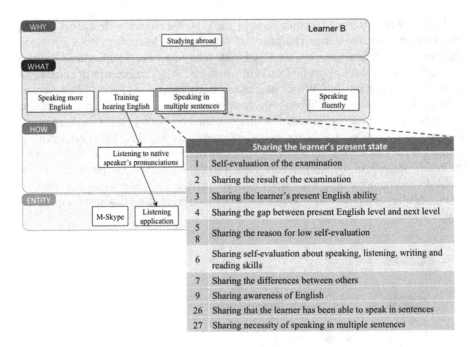

Fig. 10. Design solution and basis of learner B

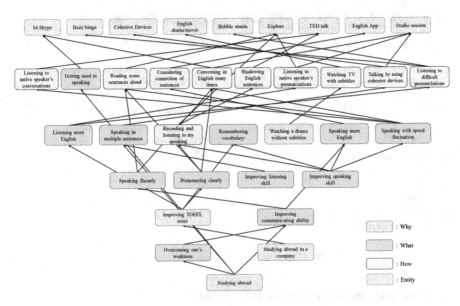

Fig. 11. Structure model of consensus building (Color figure online)

consisted by 4 learners who only improved learning motivation. Figure 11 shows a structuring model with results of 4 learners who improved examination score and learning motivation as a part of the result.

From those structuring models, we confirmed that it is possible to figure out relations between each design solution. In addition, we confirmed that it is possible figure out required design basis to expand a design solution in co-design process. Compare to group A and B, former ones built a consensus about many design solutions and shared concrete basis.

From those results, we found the way to co-design the class and expand design solution by using basis. For instance, at first, it is important for a learner who has a requirement about "Studying abroad" to initially build a consensus about the requirement through sharing learner's TOBE state or daily life. Then, they build a consensus on the learning objective about "Overcoming one's weakness" thorough sharing learner's English ability or the result of the examination.

5   Discussion

From the results of the application, we confirmed that our proposed method makes it possible to analyze the co-design process and design solutions. We confirmed the differences between learners who improve their examination score and those who improved their learning motivation. The former expand design solutions with a concrete design basis when they build a consensus about learning objectives ("What") and teaching/learning strategies ("How"). In addition, we confirmed that there are various processes to improve the learning motivation score. Learner A expanded the design solution from the viewpoint of "What," but learner B expanded it from the viewpoint of "Why." Nevertheless, both learners improved their learning motivation. From these results, our proposed method makes it possible to co-design for realizing effective value co-creation by analyzing the relation between design solution and process and realized value. However, it is difficult to organize those results because each student has different design solution and co-design process. To solve this problem, we organized those results for realizing effective value co-creation by ISM method. We expect that ISM method made it possible to figure out the way to co-design through consensus building.

6   Conclusion

This paper focuses on a collaborative design between teachers and learners. We proposed a design solution model for analyzing design solutions and as a basis to clarify the co-design process for realizing value co-creation. By using our proposed method, we analyzed the co-design process in an English class. From the results of the analysis, we confirmed the effectiveness of our method. For future research we propose integrating the ISM method into our proposed method for supporting co-design.

Acknowledgements.   This research is supported by JSPS KAKENHI Grant Number 26280114 and Research Institute of Science and Technology for Society (RISTEX).

References

1. McKenna, R.: Real-time marketing. Harv. Bus. Rev. **73**(4), 87–89 (1995)
2. Vargo, S.L., Lush, R.F.: Evolving to a new dominant logic for marketing. J. Mark. **68**(1), 1–17 (2004)
3. Sugihara, M.: The process of university students' becoming autonomous and cooperative concerning their learning in general education: from the viewpoint of role reconstruction in the learning community. Kyoto University Research Information Repository (2011)
4. Kimita, K., Nemoto, Y., Shimomura Y.: Value analysis method for learner centered instructional design. In: Proceedings of the 2nd International Conference on Serviceology, ICServe 2014, pp. 143–144. The Society for Serviceology (2014)
5. Nemoto, Y., Uei, K., Kimita, K., Ishii, T., Shimomura, Y.: A conceptual model of co-growth of provider and receiver towards value co-creative service. In: Proceedings of the 2nd International Conference on Serviceology, ICServe 2014, pp. 124–126 (2014)
6. Kimita, K., Muto, K., Mizoguchi, S., Nemoto, Y., Ishi, T., Shimomura, Y.: Learning state model for value co-creative education services. In: Yamamoto, S., de Oliveira, N.P. (eds.) HIMI 2015. LNCS, vol. 9173, pp. 341–349. Springer, Heidelberg (2015). doi: 10.1007/978-3-319-20618-9_34
7. Farris, D.R., Sage, A.P.: On the use of interpretive structural modeling for worth assessment. Comput. Electr. Eng. **2**, 149–174 (1975)
8. Ravi, V., Shankar, R.: Analysis of interactions among the barriers of reverse logistics. Technol. Forecast. Soc. Chang. **72**, 1011–1029 (2005)
9. Singh, M.D., Shankar, R., Narain, R., Agarwal, A.: An interpretive structural modeling of knowledge management in engineering industries. J. Adv. Manag. Res. **1**(1), 28–40 (2003)
10. Keller, J.M.: Development and use of the ARCS model of instructional design. J. Instr. Dev. **10**(3), 2–10 (1987)

Association Rules on Relationships Between Learner's Physiological Information and Mental States During Learning Process

Kazuma Takehana[1](✉) and Tatsunori Matsui[2](✉)

[1] Department of Human Sciences, Waseda University, Saitama, Japan
takehana@moegi.waseda.jp
[2] Faculty of Human Sciences, Waseda University, Saitama, Japan
matsui-t@waseda.jp

Abstract. In order to improve the efficiency of teaching and learning, it is very important to grasp learners' mental states during their learning processes. In this study, we attempt to extract and formalize the relationships between learners' mental states and learners' physiological information complemented with teachers' speech acts using the association rule mining technique through an experiment. As a result, four sets of association rules with high degrees of generality are obtained.

Keywords: Learning · Mental state · Physiological information · Association rule

1 Introduction

To improve the efficiency of teaching and learning, it is important to grasp learners' mental states during their learning processes. Although human teachers have the ability to comprehend learners' mental states and teach them in accordance with their mental states, the computer realization of this ability remains a long-term problem in the area of education systems. The field of educational technology also has provided us with much knowledge on the relationships between learners' physiological information, such as eye motion and amount of sweat, and learners' mental states [5]. As today's computers are currently becoming more and more convenient in function and lower in price, they can be utilized to perform a great deal of real-time processing of human physiological data. Therefore, many researchers are striving to develop automatic inference systems for learners' mental states. Furthermore, it is generally acknowledged that during a process of teaching and learning, the interaction between the teacher and learners, especially the teachers' speech acts, will greatly influence the learners' mental states. Therefore, it is also vital to clarify the relationships between teachers' speech acts and learners' mental states, and to integrate such knowledge into those automatic inference systems.

In this study, we sought to extract in an experimental way the relationships between learners' mental states and learners' physiological information complemented with teachers' speech acts. Different from the previous study [9], which analyzed only one

© Springer International Publishing Switzerland 2016
S. Yamamoto (Ed.): HIMI 2016, Part II, LNCS 9735, pp. 209–219, 2016.
DOI: 10.1007/978-3-319-40397-7_21

scene (about 60 s) in a single class (about 60 min), in this study we analyzed five scenes in a single class, each about 30 to 90 s in length. Through this experiment, we obtained several sets of association rules with high degrees of generality that describe the relationships between learners' mental states and the measurable physiological information of teachers and learners.

2 Comprehensive Analysis of Learning-Related Information

In this study, we attempted to analyze various aspects of learning using the technology of data mining in an experimental manner. In detail, we extracted the relationships between the learners' mental states and the learners' physiological information (NIRS signal, EEG signal, respiration intensity, skin conductance, and pulse volume) together with the information on the teachers' speech acts using association rule mining. Before conducting the association rule mining, because different kinds of physiological information have different data forms and recording frequencies, we changed all the recorded physiological information into categorical data. In the past, physiological data were processed mainly by mathematic methods, leading to results that are difficult to interpret. Because we divided our data into categories that have fairly simple universal meanings, we resolved the problem of data interpretation. In this section, we introduce the experiment settings as well as the methods of data processing and interpretation.

2.1 Experiment Settings

This experiment aims to collect the learners' physiological information. Two subjects, Subject A and Subject B, participated in the experiment. They were both junior high school students taking extra classes in a private tutoring school where there was only one teacher and one student in a single class. The classroom settings in the experiment were the same as in the private tutoring school. The physiological information collected in the experiment included an EEG signal (recorded using Emotive EEG), a NIRS signal (recorded using Hitachi WOT-100), respiration intensity, skin conductance, and pulse volume (recorded using NeXus). Except for the EEG signal and the NIRS signal, these psychological data were recorded at the same time. Because it was impossible to place the EEG instrument and the NIRS instrument on a single person's head at the same time, Subject A used the EEG instrument and Subject B used the NIRS instrument. In order to align the recording time of these instruments, we placed time markers at the beginning and end of the measurement. Three video cameras set at different places were used to record the course of the experiment. After several days, the subjects were asked to report on their mental states during the course of the experiment while watching the videos.

2.2 Data Selected for Analysis

From the course of the experiment, which lasted about 60 min, six scenes displaying rich teacher-learner interactions were selected for data analysis. Each scene includes various sorts of teacher-learner interactions. For each scene, the temporal location and the types of teacher-learner interactions included are described as follows.

Scene 1. *Temporal location:* 30:50-31:50 (60 s).

Main teacher-learner interactions: The teacher pointed out the mistakes in the learner's calculations. The learner asked the teacher about the right calculating methods. The teacher, in a relatively light-hearted tone, told the student to be careful not to make these kinds of mistakes again, for they were rather easy to make.

Scene 2. *Temporal location:* 34:30-35:30 (60 s).

Main teacher-learner interactions: The teacher praised the learner for his/her calculating methods. Then, the teacher pointed out and explained the mistakes in the learner's calculations, and introduced some more efficient calculating skills. (This scene is the only one that included praises, and there is relatively little chatting in this scene.)

Scene 3. *Temporal location:* 36:53-37:20 (27 s).

Main teacher-learner interactions: After the learner told the teacher that he/she had finished the previously assigned calculations, the teacher gave the learner the next calculation question. (This scene is one of the few scenes in which the teacher checked for task fulfillment.)

Scene 4. *Temporal location:* 51:04-52:27 (83 s).

Main teacher-learner interactions: The teacher explained the calculation questions. The teacher then explained the calculating methods with some examples. Finally, the teacher asked the learner what parts of the class the learner considered to be difficult to understand.

Scene 5. *Temporal location:* 53:51-54:22 (31 s).

Main teacher-learner interactions: The teacher alerted the learner to the mistakes made by the learner. The teacher found that the learner did not actually understand what the teacher had said but instead pretended to understand, and so the teacher further alerted the learner.

Scene 6. *Temporal location:* 57:55-58:51 (56 s).

Main teacher-learner interactions: The teacher alerted the learner because the learner had made some mistakes more than once. The teacher alerted the learner with some jokes, that is, in a relatively light-hearted manner.

3 Extraction of Association Rules from Scene 1

In order to extract the most basic relationships between the learners' mental states and the learners' physiological information together with the teachers' speech acts, we employed the association rule mining technique. This section introduces the general procedure of the association rule mining [9] applied to Scene 1. (For details of this association rule mining method, please refer to the previous study [9].)

3.1 Data Preprocessing

In view of the fact that different kinds of physiological information collected in the experiment vary in data form and recording frequency, we transformed all of them into categorical data. Table 1 shows the different types of physiological information and their corresponding categories. Considering that respiration intensity and skin conductance are continuous data, we categorized these using a five-point scale representing the amount of variation from the preceding data point. After treating the NIRS data using the global average reference method [2, 6], considering that the recording frequency of the NIRS instrument is low (5 Hz), we categorized the data according to their magnitudes instead of their degrees of variation. We utilized the Achievement Emotions Questionnaire (AEQ) [7] to divide the mental states into nine categories —"Enjoyment," "Hope," "Pride," "Anger," "Anxiety," "Shame," "Hopelessness," "Boredom," and "Others." We then developed a computer program that allowed the subjects to choose the categories that they considered their mental states to belong to while watching the videos recording the courses of their own experiments. Based on the categories used in some previous studies [1, 3, 8], we divided the teachers' speech acts into nine categories—"Explaining," "Questioning," "Comprehension Checking,"

Table 1. Different types of physiological information and their corresponding categories

Physiological data	Categories	Labels	Behavioral data	Categories	Labels
NIRS	A1	Very High	Speech acts (teacher)	D1	Explaining
	A2	High		D2	Questioning
	A3	Middle		D3	Comprehension Checking
	A4	Low		D4	Repeating
	A5	Very Low		D5	Praising
				D6	Task Fulfillment Checking
				D7	Alerting
				D8	Chatting
				D9	Others
Skin conductance	B1	Much Increased	Mental state (learner)	E1	Enjoyment
	B2	Increased		E2	Hope
	B3	Unchanged		E3	Pride
	B4	Decreased		E4	Anger
	B5	Much Decreased		E5	Anxiety
				E6	Shame
				E7	Hopelessness
				E8	Boredom
				E9	Others
Respiration intensity	C1	Much Increased			
	C2	Increased			
	C3	Unchanged			
	C4	Decreased			
	C5	Much Decreased			

"Repeating," "Praising," "Chatting," and "Others." With these nine categories, we labelled the teachers' speech acts while watching the videos recording the experiment courses.

Each kind of physiological information was labelled with the corresponding categories, and the labelled physiological information types were then aligned in the dimension of time, producing 2,267 recording points in total. Due to the fact that different kinds of physiological information have different recording frequencies, one or more types of physiological information are absent in some time segments. Considering that these time segments are all quite short and that the physiological information usually changes smoothly, we used interpolation to fill the missing data points, with the exception of the EEG and pulse volume. Because the EEG data and the pulse volume data differed so greatly from the other kinds of physiological information in recording frequency, the EEG and pulse volume channels contained too many missing data points. Therefore, the EEG data and the pulse volume data were excluded from the data analysis.

3.2 Results of Association Rule Extraction

Next, we performed the association rule mining to the labelled data. As a result, twelve total association rules were extracted, which are listed in Table 2 (support = 0.02, confidence = 0.89, lift = 2.2).

Table 2. The association rules extracted from Scene 1 (SA: speech acts; RI: respiration intensity; SC: skin conductance).

No.	Left-hand side	Right-hand side	Sup.	Conf.	Lift
1	NIRS=A2, SA=D7, RI=C1	⇒Mental state=E1	0.027	0.943	6.039
2	NIRS=A2, SA=D3, RI=C4, SC=B3	⇒Mental state=E3	0.047	0.906	3.380
3	SA=D9	⇒Mental state=E3	0.030	1.000	3.730
4	NIRS=A2, SA=D9	⇒Mental state=E3	0.029	1.000	3.730
5	NIRS=A5, RI=C1	⇒Mental state=E5	0.026	0.891	7.164
6	NIRS=A4, RI=C1	⇒Mental state=E6	0.047	1.000	2.289
7	NIRS=A4, SA=D1	⇒Mental state=E6	0.043	1.000	2.289
8	NIRS=A4, SA=D3, RI=C1	⇒Mental state=E6	0.041	1.000	2.289
9	NIRS=A4, RI=C1, SC=B4	⇒Mental state=E6	0.041	1.000	2.289
10	NIRS=A4, SA=D1, RI=C4	⇒Mental state=E6	0.037	1.000	2.289
11	NIRS=A4, SA=D3, RI=C1, SC=B4	⇒Mental state=E6	0.036	1.000	2.289
12	NIRS=A4, SA=D1, SC=B4	⇒Mental state=E6	0.024	1.000	2.289

Rule 1 regards the mental state category of Enjoyment (E1). This rule shows that when the learner's brain blood volume has increased a bit (A2), the teacher is alerting (D7), and the learner's respiration intensity has greatly risen (C1), the learner's mental state tends to fall under the category of Enjoyment (E1).

Rules 2–4 concern the mental state category of Pride (E3). These tell us that when the learner's brain blood volume has increased a bit (A2), the teacher is checking the learner's comprehension (D3), the learner's respiration intensity is low (C4), and the learner's skin conductance does not change (B3), the learner's mental state tends to be that of Pride (E3).

Rule 5 regards the mental state category Anxiety (E5). It demonstrates that when the learner's brain blood volume is very low (A5) and the learner's respiration intensity is very high (C1), the learner's mental state tends to fall under the category of Anxiety (E5).

Rules 6–12 regard the mental state category of Shame (E6). These rules mean that when the teacher is checking the learner's comprehension (D3) or providing explanations (D1) and the learner's brain blood volume is a bit low (A4), the learner's mental state tends to be that of Shame (E6). In addition, when the teacher is providing explanations (D3), the learner's respiration intensity tends to be high (C1).

3.3   Interpretation of Association Rules

Rule 1 suggests that if teachers alert learners in a relatively light-hearted manner (e.g., with some jokes), learners may laugh, causing their brain blood volume and respiration intensity to rise, thus resulting in the mental state of Enjoyment. In fact, we have observed in the current study's videos such scenes where the teacher alerted the learners with jokes.

From Rules 2–4, we can know that teachers' comprehension checking may increase learners' mental burdens, causing learners' brain blood volumes to rise. In addition, given the fact that learners' respiration intensity and skin conductance do not suggest any anxiety or nervousness, it is probable that the learners in our experiment were able to resolve the tasks assigned by the teacher, thus resulting in a feeling of pride.

Rule 5 implies that in the case of the mental state Anxiety, the intensity of the NIRS signal decreases. This is perhaps because the brain areas activated by the emotion of anxiety were different from the brain areas measured in our experiment, and the increases in the blood volumes at the former brain areas parallel the decreases of the blood volumes at the latter brain areas. Given the fact that this rule is the only one that includes a low-level NIRS signal (A5), and further that this rule also includes a great change in respiration intensity, we expect that the mental state of anxiety can be inferred to a certain extent from the physiological information.

With regard to Rules 6–12, we think that because the learners in our experiment failed to understand what the teacher had said and therefore could not provide the teacher with satisfactory answers, the learners began to feel shameful (E6), accompanied by the quickening of their breath (C1). On the other hand, when the teacher was giving explanations (D1), the learners breathed relatively slowly (C4). We conjecture that because the teacher did not require the learners to answer questions, the learners could listen to the teacher's words with ease, thus showing no increase in their respiration intensity. In addition, it is possible that within these rules, the NIRS signal decreases for the same reason as in the cases of the mental state of Anxiety (E5).

4 Integration of Association Rules Across Scenes

To evaluate the generality of the association rules extracted from Scene 1, we applied the same association rule mining procedure to Scenes 2–6.

4.1 Extraction and Interpretation of Association Rules from Each Scene

Scene 2. Eight rules were extracted from the time-aligned categorical data set (2,375 recording points) derived from Scene 2 (support = 0.02, confidence = 0.89, lift = 1.3). Six of these are concerned with the mental state of Enjoyment (E1), and the remaining two regard the mental state of Anxiety (E5). The rules concerning the mental state Enjoyment (E1) include a relatively high NIRS signal (A2), an increase in skin conductance (B2), respiration intensity that has increased a little or remains constant (C2–C3), and the speech category Explaining (D1). Although in this scene it was the teacher's speech acts that accounted for most of the time course, from the increases of the learners' brain blood volumes, amount of sweat, and respiration intensity, we can infer that the teacher's explanations were a bit difficult for the learner to grasp; that is, the teacher's explanations added some mental burdens to the learner. However, considering the fact that the learners enjoyed the learning processes, the difficulty of the performance tasks given by the teacher might be just right.

The rules regarding the mental state of Anxiety (E5) include a relatively low NIRS signal (A4), a large increase in skin conductance (B1), and the speech category Praising (D5). In other words, the teachers' words during the time segments corresponding to these rules were praises to the learners. We conjecture that the learners felt psychological stress due to an unease with the praises, thus showing high skin conductance.

Scene 3. Thirteen rules were extracted from the time-aligned categorical data set (1,086 recording points) derived from Scene 3 (support = 0.02, confidence = 0.89, lift = 1.4). Eight of these are concerned with the mental state Enjoyment (E1), three with the mental state Pride (E3), and the remaining two with the mental state Anxiety (E5).

The rules concerning the mental state of Enjoyment (E1) include a relatively high NIRS signal (A2), a small or large increase in skin conductance (B1–B2), and the speech categories of Explaining (D1) and Questioning (D2). In view of the teachers' frequent explaining and questioning as well as the increases in the learners' brain blood volumes and skin conductance, we infer that the learners experienced some mental burdens rather than being in a relaxed state. However, considering the fact that the learners' mental states were Enjoyment (E1), we think that in the corresponding time segments the teacher instructed in ways that were desirable to the learners.

As to the rules regarding the mental state Pride (E3), in most cases the speech category is Task Fulfillment Checking (D6). It is possible that the teachers' acknowledgements of the learners' fulfillment of the previously assigned calculation tasks offered the learners a sense of achievement, thus causing the learners to feel pride. Nevertheless, due to the absence of the data on the NIRS signal and skin conductance, there is not enough physiological information for us to predict the existence of this mental state.

With regard to the rules about the mental state Anxiety (E5), because the support value is lower than that of the other scenes, we lowered the threshold and extracted these two rules. The rules tell us that when the teacher was engaged in comprehension checking (D3), the learners' NIRS signals tended to decrease and their amount of sweat tended to rise. This is perhaps because the teachers' words placed some mental burdens on the learners. In addition, it is possible that the decrease in the NIRS signal resulted from the fact that the brain areas activated by the emotion of anxiety were different from the brain areas measured in our experiment.

Scene 4. Four rules, all of which are concerned with the mental state Enjoyment (E1), were extracted from the time-aligned categorical data set (3,278 recording points) derived from Scene 4 (support = 0.02, confidence = 0.89, lift = 1.3). These rules demonstrate that when the teacher was giving explanations (D1), the learners' physiological information included a low NIRS signal, unchanged respiration intensity (C3), and an increase in skin conductance (B2). This scene is unique in its low NIRS signal (A5), which means that the mental state of Enjoyment may have different patterns of brain activities in different environments or under different conditions.

Scene 5. Seventeen rules were extracted from the time-aligned categorical data set (1,249 recording points) derived from Scene 5 (support = 0.02, confidence = 0.89, lift = 2.1). Two of these regard the mental state Enjoyment (E1), thirteen regard the mental state Anxiety (E5), and the remaining two are concerned with the mental state Shame (E6).

With regard to the rules concerning the mental state Enjoyment (E1), due to the low confidence value, we lowered the threshold and extracted the two rules. These rules include a high NIRS signal (A1), unchanged skin conductance (B3), a large increase in respiration intensity (C1), and the speech category of Alerting (D7). We infer from the moderate amount of sweat and the increase in respiration intensity that in this scene, the teacher's alerting words were rich in jokes, and the jokes made the learners laugh, leading to an increase in the learners' brain blood volumes.

The rules regarding the mental state Anxiety (E5) include a moderate or relatively high NIRS signal (A3–A4), a large increase or decrease in respiration intensity (C1 or C5), a large increase in skin conductance (B1), and the speech categories Repeating (D4) or Alerting (D7).

As to the rules regarding the mental state Shame (E6), respiration intensity rose in some cases but fell in other cases, which means that respiration intensity can hardly be used as a predicting factor of this mental state. Besides, the relatively high brain blood volume may result from the mental burdens produced by the teacher's words of comprehension checking.

Scene 6. Twenty-one rules were extracted from the time-aligned categorical data set (1,085 recording points) derived from Scene 6 (support = 0.02, confidence = 0.89, lift = 1.28). Twelve of these regard the mental state of Anxiety (E5), and the remaining nine are concerned with the mental state Shame (E6).

The rules concerning the mental state Anxiety (E5) contain a large increase in skin conductance (B1), unchanged respiration intensity (C3), and the speech category Explaining (D1). In addition, the intensity of the NIRS signal varies to a certain extent, but generally shows a relatively high level. These rules tell us that when the teacher was providing explanations, the learners' amount of sweat and brain blood volumes rose, and they experienced unease. Perhaps this implies that the learners found it difficult to understand the teacher's explanations, which led to an excitement of the learners' brains.

The rules regarding the mental state Shame (E6) contain a moderate NIRS signal, an increase in skin conductance (B2), an increase in respiration intensity, and the speech category of Alerting. We think that the learners' large amount of sweat and high respiration intensity, as well as the shame that they felt, were the direct results of the teacher's alerting words. As to the moderate NIRS signal, it is reasonable to propose that although in this scene the teacher had spent much time pointing out the mistakes made by the learners, these words were fairly easy for the learner to understand.

4.2   Association Rules with High Generality

The rules with high generality across the scenes are summarized in Table 3. These rules described the relationships between learners' mental states and learners' physiological information complemented with teachers' speech acts. These rules are introduced in detail as follows.

Table 3. The association rules with high generality across the scenes

Association rules on the mental state Enjoyment (E1)
NIRS: A2(High) & respiration intensity: C1(Much Increased) & speech acts: D7(Alerting)
NIRS: A2(High) & skin conductance: B2(Increased) & respiration intensity: C2(Increased) & speech acts: D1(Explaining)
NIRS: A2(High) & skin conductance: B1(Much Increased) & speech acts: D1(Explaining)/D2(Questioning)
NIRS: A5(Very Low) & skin conductance: B2(Increased) & respiration intensity: C3(Unchanged) & speech acts: D1(Explaining)
NIRS: A1(Very High) & skin conductance: B3(Unchanged) & respiration intensity: C1(Much Increased) & speech acts: D7(Alerting)

Association rules on the mental state Pride (E3)
NIRS: A2(High) & skin conductance: B3(Unchanged) & repiration intensity: C4(Decreased) & speech acts: D3(Comprehension Checking)
skin conductance: B2(Increased)/B5(Much Decreased) & speech acts: D6(Answering)

Association rules on the mental state Anxiety (E5)
NIRS: A5(Very Low) & respiration intensity: C1(Much Increased)
NIRS: A4(Low) & skin conductance: B1(Much Increased) & speech acts: D5(Praising)
NIRS: A4(Low) & skin conductance: B1(Much Increased) & respiration intensity: C1(Much Increased)/C5(Much Decreased) & speech acts: D4(Repeating)/D7(Alerting)
NIRS: A2(High) & skin conductance: B1(Much Increased) & respiration intensity: C3(Unchanged) & speech acts: D1(Explaining)

Association rules on the mental state Shame (E6)
NIRS: A4(Low) & skin conductance: B4(Decreased) & respiration intensity: C1(Much Increased) & speech acts: D1(Explaining)/D3(Comprehension Checking)

With regard to the rules regarding the mental state Enjoyment (E1), in most cases the teacher was offering explanations or alerting the learners. When the teacher realized that the learners had made mistakes, the teacher alerted the learners to these mistakes in a friendly tone along with some jokes, making the learners feel happy about the learning processes. We can see that the mental state of Enjoyment usually accompanies a brain blood volume with a level no less than A2 (High), as well an amount of sweat and respiration intensity that remain constant or increase (≥B3 and ≥C3). Hence, when a learner's physiological information results in a brain blood volume of ≥A2, the amount of sweat at ≥B3, and the respiration intensity of ≥C3, the learner's mental state is most likely that of Enjoyment (E1).

There are relatively few rules concerning the mental state Pride (E3), and these rules possess no features that are common across all scenes. Moreover, only in these rules does the speech category of Task Fulfillment Checking (D6) appear. It is therefore reasonable to infer that this mental state cannot be elicited until a very limited set of conditions have been met. All in all, we think that although these rules can provide us with various idiosyncratic information regarding the mental state Pride, it is rather difficult to predict the existence of this mental state due to the lack of features that are common across the scenes.

As to the rules concerning the mental state Anxiety (E5), we found tendencies common across the scenes in brain blood volume and amount of sweat, but not in speech category. According to these rules, when brain blood volume is at or lower than the level of A4 (Low), in most cases the amount of sweat is at the level of B1 (Much Increased), and the respiration intensity level tends to be at C1 (Much Increased). As with the cases of rules regarding the mental state Enjoyment (E1), the mental state Anxiety also couples with substantial increases in respiration intensity and amount of sweat, but the mental state of Anxiety is exceptional for its low level (≤A4) of brain blood volume.

The rules regarding the mental state Shame (E6) differ so much that no characteristics common across the scenes can be found in terms of brain blood volume, amount of sweat, or respiration intensity. The only such characteristic present in the speech category is Comprehension Checking (D3). Like the mental state Pride, the rules regarding the mental state of Shame contain too much variation that it is very difficult to predict the existence of this mental state.

In conclusion, from the four groups of rules previously introduced, we can see that it is possible to infer a learner's mental states from the learner's physiological information together with the teacher's speech acts if the learner's mental states are that of Enjoyment (E1) or Anxiety (E5).

5   Summary and Future Works

In this study, we extracted four sets of association rules with high generality that describe the relationships between learners' mental states, especially Enjoyment and Anxiety, and learners' physiological information complemented with teachers' speech acts. In the future, we will further promote the accuracy of the predicting rules by employing more types of data on teachers' speeches and behaviors. We will also pay more attention to the changes of learners' mental states over time. Furthermore, in order to improve the generality of our study results, we plan to place more teachers and learners in a single class in our future studies. These experimental paradigms will become more convenient as EEG instruments are currently becoming less expensive and more sophisticated in function.

Acknowledgements. This research received support from the Grant-in-Aid of Scientific Research (22300294) and Service Science, Solution and Foundation Integrated Research Program of JST (Japan Science and Technology Agency)/ RISTEX (Research Institute of Science and Technology for Society). In addition, the authors would like to thank Siyuan Fang and Yoshimasa Tawatsuji for their great support of the progress of this research.

References

1. Fujie, Y.: Role of teacher's repetition in classroom teaching. Jpn. J. Educ. Technol. **23**(4), 201–212 (2000). (In Japanese)
2. Hirayama, K., Watanuki, K., Kaede, K.: Brain activation analysis of voluntary movement and passive movement using near-infrared spectroscopy. Trans. Jpn. Soc. Mech. Eng. Ser. C **78** (795), 3803–3811 (2012). (In Japanese)
3. Kishi, T., Nojima, E.: A structural analysis of elementary school teachers' and children's utterances in Japanese classes. Jpn. J. Educ. Psychol. **54**(3), 322–333 (2006)
4. Michael, H., Bettina, G., Kurt, H., Cristian, B.: Introduction to arules - a computational environment for mining association rules and frequent item sets. J. Stat. Softw. **14**(15), 1–25 (2010)
5. Nakayama, M., Shimizu, Y.: Research trend on educational evaluation of learning behaviors with biological information. Jpn. J. Educ. Technol. **24**(1), 15–23 (2000). (In Japanese)
6. Nozawa, T., Kondo, T.: Comparison of artifact reduction methods for real-time analysis of fNIRS data. In: Proceedings of the 24th Symposium on Biological and Physiological Engineering, pp. 381–384 (2009). (In Japanese)
7. Pekrun, R., Goetz, T., Frenzel, A.C., Barchfeld, P., Perry, R.P.: Measuring emotions in students' learning and performance - the achievement emotions questionnaire (AEQ). Contemp. Educ. Psychol. **36**(1), 36–48 (2011)
8. Shimizu, Y., Uchida, N.: How do children adapt to classroom discourse? Jpn. J. Educ. Psychol. **49**(3), 314–325 (2001). (In Japanese)
9. Takehana, K., Tawatsuji, Y., Matsui, T.: Study on the integrated analysis method for multi-faceted learning-related data. In: Proceedings of the 73th SIG-ALST in the Japanese Society of Artificial Intelligence, B403-13, pp. 67–70 (2015). (In Japanese)

Access to Cultural Heritage, Creativity and Art

Listening to Music and Idea Generation

Wen-Chih Chang[(⊠)] and Chi-Meng Liao

National Taiwan University of Science and Technology, Taipei, Taiwan
wchang@mail.ntust.edu.tw, jameslgm88@yahoo.com.tw

Abstract. This study explores the effects of music tempo on designer's idea generation, and compares the features of the subjects' ideas evoked through design behaviors and emotional feelings under without-music, fast-tempo, and slow-tempo music situations. Three experienced designers and design teachers were invited to evaluate their sketches. The experimental results showed that, (1) when listening to fast-tempo music, the subjects generated remarkably more sketches, and achieved significantly higher scores of idea fluency and flexibility, in contrast to listening to slow-music and non-music situations. (2) Under the slow-tempo music situation, the subjects' originality and feasibility of idea sketches were significantly higher than those under fast-tempo music and without-music. (3) The idea elaboration was enhanced when listening to slow-music and non-music situations. The study suggests that when require lots of ideas may listening to fast-tempo music, while listening slow-tempo music if need novelty ideas.

Keywords: Music tempo · Idea generation · Emotion · Activation

1 Introduction

People listen to music a lot in their daily life, and there are many studies regarding the effectiveness of music. For example, music can enhance the customer purchase rate [1], playing suitable music can influence product choice when consumers do not have a clear existing preference [2]. Some studies have found the influence of music on cognitive ability; for example, playing music that children are familiar with can help improve the creativity and vividness of their drawing ability [3], and improves students' speed and performance of picture drawing tasks [4]. Recently, Liao and Chang investigated more than 500 designers, and indicated that most designers get used to listening to music during design. The survey also indicated that listening to music during design has positive effect [5]. These studies showed that music does indeed have multiple influences. This study intends to investigate whether design concepts can be triggered through music stimulation, or whether design effectiveness can be further improved through mood regulation of music. The main purpose of this study is to investigate the influence of listening to fast-tempo music, slow-tempo music, and without-music on design idea generation, as well as to compare the characteristics of design concepts under different music situations through two aspects – design behavior and induced emotional feelings, as triggered by different music tempo.

© Springer International Publishing Switzerland 2016
S. Yamamoto (Ed.): HIMI 2016, Part II, LNCS 9735, pp. 223–234, 2016.
DOI: 10.1007/978-3-319-40397-7_22

2   Literature Review

2.1   Influence of Music Tempo on Behaviors and Emotions

Tempo refers to the speed of a beat, and is one of the fundamental elements of music. Music with a fast tempo makes a person feel aggressive, energetic, and excited; while music with a slow tempo can express solemn, lyrical, and calm feelings [6]. It shows music tempo will interconnect with people's perceptions, and further affect their behavioral responses. Therefore, listening to fast-tempo music activates perception improves athletes' motor response performance [7], and strengthen the performance of graphic pattern recognition tasks after paper is folded [8]. However, some studies suggest that slow-tempo music is beneficial to cognitive activities. The study of two weeks on students' writing ability by McKnight showed that, listening to slow-tempo music is beneficial to elementary school students' writing ability [9]. Hallam and Price also indicated that, listening to calm background music can improve students' emotions, reduce the rule-breaking, and improve their mathematical ability [10].

In addition, previous studies showed that, music tempo affects people's emotional feelings. Relevant studies showed that, tempo is positively correlated with happy or sad feelings [11]. Fast-tempo music makes people perceive happy and positive emotions, while slow-tempo music makes them perceive opposite feelings [12]. Moreover, music tempo may affect people activation [13]. Holbrook and Anand pointed out that, there is a logarithm relationship between people's energetic feeling and music tempo, at a faster tempo people feel more activation [14]. Yamamoto and his colleagues performed a cross-comparison on the subjects' physiological response and self-report scale under fast/slow-music tempo, and the results showed that, listening to slow-tempo music significantly decreases heartbeat and disperses pressure, which is beneficial to tasks with pressure [15]. These studies demonstrated that, musical tempo affects human behavioral and emotion perception, which further affects the performance of cognition.

2.2   Emotions and Design Creativity

Emotion refers to a physical and mental activation state triggered by external stimuli that induces physiological changes and behaviors responses. Physiologist Russell systematically arranged emotional qualities, and proposed the Circumplex Model of Affect, where the X-axis is an affective valence, Y-axis is activation. He suggested that, most emotional responses can be explained through two dimensions – activation and pleasant emotion [16]. According to the Circumplex Model of Affect, Russell and Carroll suggested that, the emotional state of people generally reflect the following 6 types: high activation of positive emotions (e.g., excitement and passion), moderate activation (e.g., happiness and satisfaction), low activation (e.g., calmness and relaxation, corresponding low activation of negative emotions (e.g., depression and boredom), moderate activation (e.g., unhappiness and dissatisfaction), and high activation (e.g., tension and anxiety) [17]. They are opposite to one another in the Circumplex Model of Affect, as shown in Fig. 1.

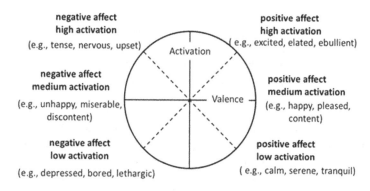

Fig. 1. Six clusters of affect items, as quoted from Russel and Carroll (1999)

For the relationship between emotions and design creativity, some studies indicated that under positive emotions, people can propose more creative solutions to problems, which improves the smoothness of thinking divergence [18]. Fast thinking, which involves many thoughts per unit time, generally produces positive affect, and generated significantly more ideas [19]. Moreover, some studies showed that, under positive emotions, people can associate with more diversified vocabularies and terms, and the content is more positive. The reason may be that positive emotions make people feel more comfortable, relaxed, and less stubborn, which allows them to smoothly develop creative solutions to problems [20]. Moreover, people under positive emotions can deal with things more flexibly and accept different solutions than they can under negative emotions [21]. Therefore, the diversity and flexibility of problem-solving may be one of the qualities of positive emotions.

Although most studies found that positive emotions are beneficial to design creativity, some studies showed that negative emotions are positively correlated with creativity performance. The study by Kaufmann proposed that, negative and neutral moods may be more helpful finding insightful and highly creative solutions to problems [22]. Vosburg also suggested that negative emotions are beneficial to the development of the best strategy and attach more importance to conception quality [18]. The reason may be that, people under negative emotions will try to get rid of emotions or difficulties at the moment, and adopt analytic thinking strategies to deal with problem, which activates knowledge and makes knowledge more useful [23]. Therefore, negative emotions more likely to develop novel ideas.

2.3 Design Creativity and Assessment

Design is a part of human imagination, every stage of the design process requires creativity. Therefore, the success/failure of design works is closely related to creativity. Guilford suggested that creativity thinking abilities have their properties, involving originality, fluency, flexibility, and elaboration abilities, these so called divergent-thinking [24]. Amabile proposed that the creative concept must be novel, appropriate, useful, and valuable to the task undertaken [25]. Therefore, in addition to attaching importance to the creativity of the concepts, studies regarding design creativity must also consider the feasibility and appropriateness of conception fulfillment. At the early conceptual stage of design process, designers applied pictorial representation and embody concepts in their mind using idea sketches, which have long been an important part of the design process [26]. Therefore, drawing idea sketches in studies regarding the design creative is a more direct method.

As the theories of creativity are diversified, there are many different methods for evaluating creativity. Hocevar and Bachelor analyzed more than 100 creative evaluation examples, and summarized eight major types of evaluations of design creativity, including: (1) test of divergent thinking: Torrance's test of creative thinking (TTCT) can be taken as representative, which test the fluency, flexibility, originality, and elaboration of subjects as the evaluation items of creativity; (2) attitude & interest inventories; (3) personality inventories; (4) biographical inventories; (5) ratings by teacher, peers & supervisors; (6) judgment of products; (7) eminence; and (8) self-reported creative activities & achievements [27]. Although Torrance's TTCT is used more frequently, Sternburg suggested that an experimental design apply practical design task may be the best, that can propose more reasonable explanations of the cause-and-effect relationship among various creative behaviors [28]. Therefore, this study requested the subjects to actually draw idea sketches in order to investigate the influence of music on design idea generation.

3 Research Methods

This study applied within-subjects design, requested the subjects to conduct design tasks under without-music, listening to fast-tempo music, and slow-tempo music, by drawing idea sketches in order to investigate the influence of music tempo on design creativity. The experiment including conducted design task, fill in music perception assessment, and evaluating design ideas by expertise.

3.1 Music on Experiment

In the researches we have discussed, the music was presented in be manipulated for laboratory settings. This kinds of music is unusual, it makes very hard to applied the research findings in the real world [13]. In order to improve ecological validity, we adopted the music original tempo was presented, so that is close to the real music listening experience people used to. The instrumental music was used in the experiment, which can avoid the interference from lyrics or singing style [29], the music was mainly played by piano. The music selected pianist Omar Akram who won a Grammy Award. We picked 3 fast-tempo songs, Downpour (126/bpm), Dancing with the wind (134/bpm), Last Dance (126/bpm); and 3 slow-tempo songs, Daytime Dreamer (72/bpm), The Promise (66/bpm), and My desire (84/pbm), in his album of Daytime Dreamer. The music was randomly played through a pair of 40 W speakers meanwhile music played continue until design task completed.

3.2   Experimental Assignments and Equipment

This study recruited 40 undergraduate students of the Department of Industrial Design of two universities in northern Taiwan to participate. The subjects were divided into groups A and B, with each group consisting of half males and half females. First, each group designed seasoning containers (powdered or liquid seasonings container were accepted) by free hand sketching under the condition of without listening to music. Then, Group A listened to fast-tempo music to first design powdered seasoning containers, and then, designed liquid seasoning containers under the condition of slow-tempo music 1 week later. Group B listened to slow-tempo music first to design powdered seasoning containers, and then, they designed liquid seasoning containers under the condition of listening to fast-tempo music 1 week later. The subjects had 5 min to warm up before they conducted the design task, and then, executed the design task for 40 min. When the design task was complete, the subjects filled in their basic information, music-induced design behaviors, and emotional feeling scale. This experiment was conducted in a school classroom, which only had a whiteboard on the wall, thus, reducing the interference of environmental factors. The subjects used black or blue pen or pencil to draw sketches of their own choices.

3.3   Measurement of Music Perception

According to the literature review, music tempo affects people's actions and thinking paces [e.g., 6, 7, 15]; therefore, this study hypothesized that music tempo (fast vs. slow) may also affect design behaviors. This study evaluated the potential influence of music tempo (fast vs. slow) on design thinking speed (slow vs. fast), concentration of design thinking (careful vs. careless), action of drawing sketches (slow vs. fast), and concentration of drawing (careful vs. careless), as the evaluation items of the influence of music on design behaviors. Previous studies also showed that, music tempo affects emotional feelings [e.g., 11, 12], and emotions affect design creativity performance [e.g., 21, 22]. Regarding music emotion assessment, this study selected Russell and Carroll, which suggested 6 representative emotional adjectives to test the subjects' emotional feelings [17]. These adjectives were: depressed vs. excited; unhappy vs. happy; tense vs. calm, for a total of 6 mutually opposite adjectives of emotions. The measurement scale is divided into 7 levels, as shown in the partial examples of the design behavior and emotional feeling scales in Table 1.

3.4   Expert Assessment of Design Concept

Three design experts, an associate professor, a design director, and a creative director, with experience totaling more than 10 years, were invited to evaluate the sketches. The experts agreed with the use of fluency, originality, flexibility, and elaboration of divergent thinking, as proposed by Guilford [24], as well as feasibility and appropriateness, as proposed in this study, as the test items of creative idea sketches in the experiment. They also agreed with the use of Torrance's TTCT as the evaluation criteria for judging creative performance. In addition, the experts suggested using a

Table 1. The examples of design behavior and emotional perception measurement

Measurement items	Measurement scale
	1 2 3 4 5 6 7
The music you are listening makes your thinking pace tend to	slower ☐ ☐ ☐ ☐ ☐ ☐ ☐ faster
The music you are listening makes your emotional perception tend to	calm ☐ ☐ ☐ ☐ ☐ ☐ ☐ tense

10-point scale to rate evaluation items, where the worst score was 1 point, while the best score was 10 points. The evaluation criteria of idea sketches are as shown in Table 2. Prior to performing the assessment, the experts selected the idea sketches for each evaluation item (higher and lower), according to the spirit of the evaluation criteria, in order to establish a consensus of assessment, as shown in the comparison of originality in Fig. 2, and the comparison of elaboration in Fig. 3.

Table 2. The principle of idea creativity measurement

Items	Evaluation criteria measurement	
Fluency	Judgement according to the quantities of idea sketches	By quantity
Originality	It is to provide novel, or clever idea, in form or operation methods in respect to condiment container design	1–10 scales
Flexibility	Have difference between one's own idea, or types of idea are divergent	1–10 scales
Elaboration	The contents of an idea are well considered, and the explanation is in detail both in text or drawing	1–10 scales
Feasibility	It refers to the idea can be practiced, especially in mass production	1–10 scales
Appropriateness	It refers to the product form or operation methods fulfillment people expectation	1–10 scales

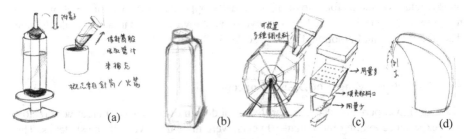

(a)   (b)   (c)   (d)

Fig. 2. Comparison of originality: (a) high originality, (b) low originality.

Fig. 3. Comparison of elaboration: (c) high elaboration, (d) low elaboration.

4 Experimental Results and Analysis

4.1 Music Tempo and Idea Creativity

The experimental results showed that, when listening to fast-tempo music, the subjects generated larger quantities of sketches (350 sketches; Mean = 8.70) than under slow-tempo music (298 sketches; Mean = 7.45), and without-music situations (282 sketches; Mean = 7.15). One-way repeated measures ANOVA was conducted to examine whether there is significant difference in the subjects' idea generation when listening to fast-tempo, slow-tempo, and without-music conditions. The verification results are as shown in Table 3. The idea sketch fluency, originality, flexibility, elaboration, and feasibility had p values of $0.00 < 0.05$, and there were significant differences under these three music situations. However, idea appropriateness had a p value of $0.42 > 0.05$, meaning there was no significant difference of idea appropriateness among these three music conditions.

Table 3. The feature of creative ideas, as examined by One-way repeated measures ANOVA

Variable	Fast-tempo		Slow-tempo		Without-music		F	fd	p	Post Hoc
	Mean	SD	Mean	SD	Mean	SD				
Fluency	8.70	3.09	7.45	2.56	7.15	2.11	21.83	2	0.00*	Ft > St; Ft > Wm
Originality	5.18	0.96	5.63	1.02	5.07	1.03	6.23	2	0.00*	St > Ft; St > Wm
Flexibility	5.62	0.84	5.10	1.11	4.85	0.94	9.89	2	0.00*	Ft > St; Ft > Wm
Elaboration	5.00	0.88	5.67	1.01	5.53	0.96	10.74	2	0.00*	St > Ft; Wm > Ft
Feasibility	4.53	0.98	5.15	0.89	5.01	0.94	8.78	2	0.00*	St > Ft; St > Wm
Appropriateness	4.78	0.89	4.95	1.06	5.06	1.23	0.83	2	0.42	No significant

$\alpha = 0.05$, *$p < 0.05$, Fast-tempo = Ft, Slow-tempo = St, Without-music = Wm

The results of Post Hoc testing showed that, under the fast-tempo music situation, the fluency and flexibility of subjects' idea sketches were significantly higher than those under slow-tempo music and without-music conditions. On the other hand, the originality and feasibility of subjects' idea sketches were significantly higher than under fast-tempo music and without-music situations. In addition, the idea elaboration of subjects had better performance when listening to slow music and without-music conditions than under fast-tempo music conditions.

4.2 Music Tempo, Design Behavior and Emotional Feelings

The results of the subjects' design behavior assessment and emotional perceptions under fast-tempo music, slow-tempo music, and without-music conditions, as examined by One-way repeated measures ANOVA, shows that there were significant differences under the three music conditions, as shown in Table 4. According to the results of Post Hoc testing, the subjects' demonstrated thought pace and drawing speed under fast-tempo music (mean = 5.73; 5.94) > without-music (mean = 3.58; 4.35) > slow-tempo music (mean = 2.27; 2.35), meaning the subjects felt their thought pace and drawing speed accelerated when listening to fast-tempo music. In addition, the subjects' concentration of design thinking and drawing when listening to slow-tempo music (mean = 5.52; 5.21) > without-music (mean = 3.98; 4.73) > fast-tempo music (mean = 2.81; 2.83). It shows that the subjects felt their design concentration tended to be more careful when listening to slow-tempo music. The results of the subjects' design behavior under these three music conditions are as shown in Fig. 4.

Table 4. Design behavior and emotion perception, as examined by One-way repeated measures ANOVA.

Variable	Fast-tempo		Slow-tempo		Without-music		F	fd	p	Post Hoc
	Mean	SD	Mean	SD	Mean	SD				
Thinking pace	5.73	1.03	2.27	0.96	3.58	0.89	177.66	2	0.00*	Ft > Wm > St
Thinking concentration	2.81	0.79	5.52	0.77	3.97	0.93	120.97	2	0.00*	St > Wm > Ft
Drawing pace	5.94	0.86	2.35	1.12	4.35	0.98	206.53	2	0.00*	Ft > Wm > St
Drawing concentration	2.83	0.18	5.21	0.19	4.73	0.12	117.51	2	0.00*	St > Wm > Ft
Excitement	5.71	0.77	3.73	0.57	3.50	0.79	154.26	2	0.00*	Ft > St; Ft > Wm
Happiness	5.50	0.88	3.78	1.04	3.75	1.08	61.11	2	0.00*	Ft > St; Ft > Wm
Tense	5.36	0.87	1.75	0.86	4.08	0.85	201.04	2	0.00*	Ft > Wm > St

α = 0.05, *p < 0.05, Fast-tempo = Ft, Slow-tempo = St, Without-music = Wm

In terms of emotional perceptions, referring to the results of Post Hoc testing shows that, the subjects felt emotional excitement and happiness under the fast-tempo music condition (mean = 5.71; 5.50) > without-music (mean = 3.50; 3.75), and slow-tempo music (mean = 3.73; 3.78). It means that, during the design task under fast-tempo music, the subjects significantly perceived the emotion of excitement, with positive affect and high activation, but felt moderate excitement of medium affect and activation when listening to slow-tempo music and without-music situations. Regarding the emotional tension of idea generation when listening to fast-tempo music (mean = 5.36) > under without-music listening (mean = 4.08 > listening to slow-tempo music (mean = 1.75). It shows that during the conducted design task, the subjects perceived that listening to fast-tempo music promoted the emotional tension of negative affect and high activation. In the without-music situation, their emotions tended to calm positive affect and low activation. Furthermore, the subjects obviously felt the calm emotion of positive affect and low activation when listening to slow-tempo music. The results of the subjects emotional feeling under these three music situations are as shown in Fig. 5.

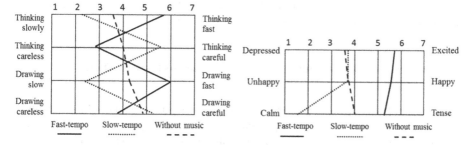

Fig. 4. Music tempo and design behavior   **Fig. 5.** Music tempo and emotion perception

5   Discussion

During design seasoning containers, the participants perceived design behavioral and emotional feelings were influenced by listening to fast-tempo music, slow-tempo music, and without-music listening. The possible reasons descriptive as below.

5.1   Influence of Music Tempo Affects Design Behavior on Design Creativity

The experiment results showed that, when listening to fast-tempo music, the subjects generated more seasoning container ideas, and demonstrated better fluency of their idea sketches. Such phenomenon may be caused by the interconnection between the music tempo and people's perceptions, and thus, influence behavioral reaction [6]. In addition, the design behavior assessment showed listening to fast-tempo music can sped up subjects' thinking pace and drawing speed (Fig. 4), meaning that more times of design thinking and drawing behaviors being performed in the same unit time [19], thus, more ideas will be generated and enhanced the fluency of creative ideas. Since more ideas were generated, that may result in more types of creative ideas as well as indirect improve the flexibility of ideas.

The subjects under slow-tempo music showed that, their design thinking and drawing speed tended to be slower and higher concentration (Fig. 4), which might help them to carefully consider how to overcome the problems of seasoning containers, and further generate ideas from the existing product framework. Therefore, the condition of slow-tempo music prompted subjects to generate creative ideas with originality and feasibility, which encouraged the elaboration of idea sketches.

Under the without-music situation, subject's idea sketch elaboration obtained high scores, which were the same as slow-tempo music listening; however, the reasons may be not the same. Since a lack of music stimulates the non-music listening condition, the subjects perceived neutral design thinking and drawing pace. This study speculates that idea elaboration obtained better performance under the without-music condition, which may be unrelated to design behavior perception, and may be attributed to the small amount of generated idea sketches. Therefore, they had extra time to detail their drawing sketches or note idea features, and this result indirectly improved the elaboration of idea sketches with better performance. However, the exact reasons for this phenomenon require further investigation in the future.

5.2 Influence of Music Tempo Affects Emotional Feelings on Design Creativity

In the perspective of emotion perception, under fast-tempo music, the subjects feelings were inclined to the emotion of excitement with the positive affect of low activation, and the emotion of happiness with positive affect medium activation (Fig. 5). This result verified that, fast-tempo music can induce positive emotions, as proposed in previous relevant studies [11], and the fact that people can develop more solutions and proposals under positive emotions [18]. Therefore, the fluency of design concepts can be improved by transforming them into positive affect. Moreover, under fast-tempo music, the flexibility of creative ideas is better. The reason may be that people are more relaxed and carefree under positive emotions, and thus, deal with things more flexibly and willing to accept different proposals [20, 21]. Therefore, the positive emotions, as induced under fast-tempo music, may help to improving the flexibility of creative ideas.

The subjects' originality, elaboration, and feasibility of creative ideas obtained better performance when listening to slow-tempo music. The reason might be that, during idea generation, the subjects perceived the calm emotion of lower activation under slow-tempo music (Fig. 5), which could help cool down their mind and concentrate on design problems. As indicated by Yamamoto, slow-tempo music can decrease heartbeat, reduce pressure, and relieve the tense atmosphere of an experimental task, which is beneficial to fulfillment of the design task [15]. Therefore, listening to slow-tempo music induces the perception of emotions of lower activation, which may help designers propose ideas with better originality, elaboration, and feasibility.

Under the without-music situation, the subjects perceived neutral affect and moderate activation of emotion. This study speculates that idea elaboration obtained better performance, which may not be concerned with emotion perception, but instead, be attributed to the small amount of generated idea sketches. The actual reason this study was unable to provide a specific explanation, meaning the same as the without-music situation effect on design behavior, requires further investigation in the future.

6 Conclusions and Suggestions

This study used the subjects' actual designs of seasoning containers to investigate the influence of music tempo on ides generation. The results showed that, music tempo will interact with people's behavioral reaction and emotion feelings, which further affect design creativity. The subjects listening to fast-tempo music developed more creative ideas and exhibited higher fluency and flexibility of ideas, while the subjects listening to slow-tempo music, the originality, elaboration, and feasibility of their ideas were better. However, the idea elaboration was enhanced when listening to slow-music and non-music situations.

The study suggests that designers could listen to fast-tempo music when they require lots of ideas in a short period of time, while slow-tempo music is a good choice when they are looking to break through a thinking barrier. Although this study applied the practical design of seasoning containers to investigate the relationship between music tempo and idea creativity, as compared with a real design project, the design of a seasoning container in 40-min was too short to achieve deep insight into the relationship between music tempo and idea generation. Future studies are advised to introduce music into a design project to perform long term observation, which may help to clearly identify the relationships between music and design creativity.

References

1. North, A.C., Shilcock, A., Hargreaves, D.J.: The effect of musical style on restaurant customers' spending. Environ. Behav. **35**(5), 712–718 (2003)
2. Yeoh, J.P.S., North, A.C.: The effect of musical fit on consumers' preferences between competing alternate petrols. Psychol. Music **40**(6), 709–719 (2012)
3. Schellenberg, E.G., Nakata, T., Hunter, P.G., Tamoto, S.: Exposure to music and cognitive performance: tests of children and adults. Psychol. Music **35**(1), 5–19 (2007)
4. Nittono, H., Tsuda, A., Akai, S., Nakajaima, Y.: Tempo of background sound and performance speed. Percept. Mot. Skills **90**(3), 1122 (2000)
5. Liao, C.-M., Chang, W.-C.: A survey on effects of music on design association. Bull. Jpn. Soc. Sci. Des. **61**(5), 47–56 (2015)
6. Kamien, R.: Music: An Appreciation. McGraw-Hill, Boston (2000)
7. Bishop, D.T., Wright, M.J., Karageorghis, C.I.: Tempo and intensity of pre-task music modulate neural activity during reactive task performance. Psychol. Music **42**(5), 714–727 (2014)
8. Husain, G., Thompson, W.F., Schellenberg, E.G.: Effects of musical tempo and mode on arousal, mood and spatial abilities. Music Percept. **20**(2), 151–171 (2002)
9. McKnight, R.: Does listening to slow tempo classical music during independent writing affect children's on-task performance. Education Resources Information Center, ED 430 898 (1998)
10. Hallam, S., Price, J.: Can the use of background music improve the behaviour and academic performance of children with emotional and behavioural difficulties? Br. J. Spec. Educ. **25**(2), 88–91 (1998)
11. Webster, G.D., Weir, C.G.: Emotional responses to music: interactive effects of mode, texture, and tempo. Motiv. Emot. **29**(1), 19–39 (2005)
12. Hunter, P.G., Schellenberg, E.G., Schimmack, U.: Feelings and perceptions of happiness and sadness induced by music: similarities, differences, and mixed emotions. Psychol. Aesthet. Creativity Arts **4**(1), 47–56 (2010)
13. van der Zwaag, M.D., Westerink, J.H.D.M., van den Broek, E.L.: Emotional and psychophysiological responses to tempo, mode, and percussiveness. Musicae Scientiae **15**(2), 250–269 (2011)
14. Holbrook, M.B., Anand, P.: Effects of tempo and situational arousal on the listener's perceptual and affective responses to music. Psychol. Music **18**(2), 150–162 (1990)
15. Yamamoto, M., Naga, S., Shimizu, J.: Positive musical effects on two types of negative stressful conditions. Psychol. Music **35**(2), 249–275 (2007)
16. Russell, J.A.: A circumplex model of affect. J. Pers. Soc. Psychol. **39**, 1161–1178 (1980)

17. Russell, J.A., Carroll, J.M.: On the bipolarity of positive and negative affect. Psychol. Bull. **125**(1), 3–30 (1999)
18. Vosburg, S.K.: The effect of positive and negative mood on divergent-thinking performance. Creativity Res. J. **11**(2), 165–172 (1998)
19. Pronin, E., Jacobs, E.: Thought speed, mood, and the experience of mental motion. Perspect. Psychol. Sci. **3**(6), 461–485 (2008)
20. Abele-Brehm, A.: Positive and negative mood influences on creativity: evidence for asymmetrical effects. Pol. Psychol. Bull. **23**(3), 203–221 (1992)
21. Murray, N., Sujan, H., Hirt, E.R., Sujan, M.: The influence of mood on categorization: a cognitive flexibility interpretation. J. Pers. Soc. Psychol. **59**(3), 411–425 (1990)
22. Kaufmann, G.: The Effect of Mood On Creativity in the Innovation Process. In: Shavinina, L.V. (ed.) The International Handbook on Innovation, pp. 191–203. Elsevier Science Ltd., Oxford (2003)
23. Schwarz, N.: Feelings as information: informational and motivational functions of affective states. In: Higgins, E.T., Sorrentino, R.M. (eds.) Handbook of Motivation and Cognition: Function of Social Behavior. Guilford Press, New York (1990)
24. Guilford, J.P.: The Nature of Human Intelligence. McGraw-Hill, New York (1967)
25. Amabile, T.M.: Creativity in Context. Westview Press, Colorado (1996)
26. Purcell, A.T., Gero, J.S.: Drawings and the design process: a review of protocol studies in design and other disciplines and related research in cognitive psychology. Des. Stud. **19**(4), 389–430 (1998)
27. Hocevar, D., Bachelor, P.: A taxonomy and critique of measurements used in the study of creativity. In: Glover, H.A., Ronning, R.R.C., Reynolds, R. (eds.) Handbook of Creativity, pp. 53–59. Plenum Press, New York (1989)
28. Sternberg, R.J.: Handbook of Creativity. Cambridge University Press, New York (1999)
29. Ali, S.O., Peynircioğlu, Z.F.: Songs and emotions: are lyrics and melodies equal partners? Psychol. Music **34**(4), 511–534 (2006)

Application of Co-creation Design Experiences to the Development of Green Furniture

Chia-Ling Chang[1(✉)] and Ming-Hsuan Hsieh[2]

[1] Department of Education Industry and Digital Media, National Taitung University,
Taitung City, Taiwan, ROC
idit007@gmail.com
[2] Department of Computer-Aided Industrial Design, Overseas Chinese University,
Taichung City, Taiwan, ROC
mhhsieh@ocu.edu.tw

Abstract. With the trend of environmental protection around the globe, the development of most green furniture in the past emphasized on the production processes and technical applications and more particularly on material selections and functional improvements. However, the user demands which keep pace with the times have seldom been considered. Thus it is difficult to satisfy the diversified demands for green furniture's creativity and functions by modern consumers whose motivation of buying is thus reduced. Moreover, with the rise of the creativity generation nowadays, people of the fresh new generation always have ever-changing creativity. Enterprises and those who develop products should collaborate with consumers and give users the room for product creation so as to satisfy the concept of user creation and fulfill the design experiences.

Based on the ideas of "value co-creation with users" and "experience service", the topic of "co-creation design experience" was investigated in this study with discussions on the possibility for an enterprise to develop products in joint cooperation with users. Enterprises should no longer develop products independently but should view users as the co-workers for product development. This allows users to participate in design processes and own design experiences so that it is possible to co-create products' new values with users. This study connects users' creativity in series for considering the balancing point of the co-creation between enterprises and users on product values. A "development procedure for products co-created with users" was proposed. Paper pallets were used as the material and a set of innovative eco-friendly furniture was successfully developed for satisfying the co-creation design experience between an enterprise and its users. For the meaning of this innovative eco-friendly furniture, it resembles LEGO toy blocks, which let the users enjoy the design experience by bringing their creativity into play and assemble the parts of the eco-friendly furniture without the need of additional learning or tools.

Keywords: Co-creation · Design experience · User innovation · Green furniture

© Springer International Publishing Switzerland 2016
S. Yamamoto (Ed.): HIMI 2016, Part II, LNCS 9735, pp. 235–243, 2016.
DOI: 10.1007/978-3-319-40397-7_23

1 Research Background

With the trend of industrial competition and globalization, the concept which strives for production manufacturing in the industrialized era is gradually getting unpopular. The economic era that succeeded it emphasizes more on personal creativity and environmental awareness. Nowadays, the creativity generation has emerged and the younger group accepts diversified stimuli from the external world via various types of channels. These have triggered kaleidoscopic types of creativity and they expect the products that they buy can better display their own uniqueness. As a result, a product of a single form or a single function can no longer satisfy their preferences and creativity demands. More and more users exhibit a higher degree of interests in the design behaviors and they pay close attention to the products that can present their own creativity. Therefore, most of the enterprises have acknowledged that any product development should no longer be limited within an enterprise. They should extend outward and collaborate with users, bring user creativity into designs, and even open up the room for product creation so that users are allowed to have freedom in creation. That is, enterprises no longer develop product independently. Instead, they view users as co-workers on product developments. They let users participate in the design process and collaborate with users on developing products. At the same time, this approach can enhance product adherence and diffusivity which allows creating new values for products together with users.

Under the worldwide trend of environmental protection, the development of most green furniture in the past emphasized on the production processes and technical applications and more particularly on material selections and functional improvements. However, the user demands which keep pace with the times have seldom been considered. As a result, though many eco-friendly furniture designs have a good intention, it is hard for them to satisfy modern users' diversified demands toward product creativity and functions and this causes the degraded motivation in buying. The marketing strategy failed to last longer for keeping the market competitiveness. This result instead loses the meaning and value of green product designs and developments (Tu and Wu 2005). On a modern market, a product can be viewed as having the true substantial value only when it is able to promote consumptions with a success (Magnusson 2001). Therefore, this study proposed that an eco-friendly product should also comply with the trend of user innovation and open up the room for product creation to users. As a result, the purpose of this study is to introduce the concept of "co-creation thinking" into the development of eco-friendly furniture so as to enhance the consumption motivation and the competitiveness for eco-friendly furniture.

2 Literature Review

2.1 Co-creation Design

Co-Creation is a new type of value creation pattern. Prahalad and Ramaswamy (2003) proposed a simple definition for co-creation: The value is jointly created by an enterprise and its customers. Ind et al. (2013) proposed that co-creation is a type of collaboration process that an enterprise and its users create products in an optimistic, creative, and socialized manner. Via this process, both sides can obtain benefits simultaneously. Co-creation designs adds new dynamics into the relationship between a manufacturer and its customers via having users directly participate in products' production or distribution so that they can jointly implement their creativity on the products (Kambil et al. 1999). As long as a user participates into these activities, he/she can easily generate personal affects so as to enhance the products' uniqueness and they can easily have a higher degree of satisfaction toward the products. When collaborating jointly with users on creating and developing products, as compared to the design personnel inside an enterprise, a user can bring their unique creativity and ideas into play during the self design process without being confined by the enterprises' regulations. This approach allows more design freedom and can help fulfill the eventual development target for products (Schreier et al. 2012).

Roggeven et al. (2012) indicated that, when a product is jointly created by an enterprise and its user, the co-creation design experiences are able to influence customers' satisfaction since the co-creation thinking allows a user to shape personalized features and irreplaceable design experiences on a product. Nowadays, many enterprises from various fields have transformed the original approach of new products development thinking from a single aspect into actually bringing users into the process. This allows users who are related to products/services to participate jointly in the process of products/services developments. This approach can indeed bring positive outcomes and economic interests to enterprises Weber et al. (2012).

2.2 Eco-friendly Furniture Products

Environmental Protection Agency of the Executive Yuan announced the definition of an eco-friendly product as follows. For a product from the beginning of the product life cycle to the end, it is required to reduce as possibly the impacts to the environment. From the aspect of product designs, this means during the process of designing products, it is required to avoid any potential hazard to the environment or increasing the social costs. The goal is to produce products with low contamination, low energy consumption, and low toxicity and to recycle and reuse them as possible. A design which also considers the values in economic development is preferable (Tu 2002). There is a wide range of eco-friendly materials and types. Generally speaking, when manufacturing eco-friendly materials, they can help reduce environmental hazards as possible, can decompose when being discarded, do not release toxic substances, or can be recycled and reused. However, when re-creating and re-designing a product based on a user's consideration, some components might possibly be repetitively used. It is thus required to evaluate whether the eco-friendly materials satisfy the demand of co-creation designs by avoiding the weight being too heavy, strengthening the structure to support heavy objects, and eliminating sharp edges for the users to operate without worries and disassemble/assemble creatively.

Furniture is one of the important export industries among traditional industries in Taiwan, which holds an important position on the global furniture markets and enjoyed a fame of being the dominant country for furniture exports. However since 1989 with the ascending global environmental awareness, woods are hard to acquire and the environmental statutes are getting stricter. Some of the furniture industry had trans-formed with the strategic development in eco-friendly furniture (Tu and Wu 2005). For the selection of construction materials with eco-friendly furniture, corrugated card-boards can be used not only on transportation packing but also are very suitable for use in the construction materials with eco-friendly furniture. Since corrugated cardboards are lightweight, of low cost, and good at cushioning, more than 80 % of corrugated cardboards can be recycled and reused. In addition, if viewed from the product design standpoint, they have various features such as being foldable, can be disassembled, recombined, and engaged closely, supporting heavy weights, and transported in flattened form (Chiang 2007). Domestic and overseas enterprises have used corrugated card-boards as the main sheet materials for producing furniture. In addition to the common types that have been developed including tables, chairs, beds, and cabinets, the range of application has be extended to exhibition partitions and screens as shown in Fig. 1.

Fig. 1. Existing applications of corrugated cardboard furniture

The effect of supporting heavy objects is achieved by the combination of corrugated cardboards and there are diversified ways of combination structures. Chen (2009) collected 40 samples of commercially available corrugated cardboard furniture and used the simple integrated KJ method and the cross analysis method to investigate the way of composing commercially available corrugated cardboard furniture. A total of 12 combinations or constituent types were collected and organized.

To sum up, when an enterprise opens up the design rights and collaborate with its users jointly in creating products, this usually brings positive influences to the enterpri-se's creativity and product sales. This indicates that it is worthy of introducing the eco-friendly furniture development process. However, the attempt of this study is to propose the "co-creation product development model" and the operating instructions are as follows. A case study on the corrugated cardboard furniture was conducted so as to perform implementations and developments.

3   Co-creation Product Development Model

The concept of co-creation products allows users to participate directly in the design and development tasks. However, considering that seldom of the typical users accept professional design training and a "creative" user doesn't equal to a user with the "design capability", co-creation products are required to cooperate with the most "user design capability" for encouraging users in carrying out designs and processing so as to reduce the feeling of frustration due to design failures. Therefore a co-creation product development model was proposed in this study for the follow-up users to carry out the actions of re-designing or re-creating products. The procedure is described as follows:

3.1 Investigating User Demands for Creativity

Nowadays in addition to the requirements of functions and external forms, users gradually evoke the "creativity" demands for products so as to demonstrate personal features and styles. This is something that was less investigated during the product developments in the past. Therefore the first step is to investigate the user demands for creativity. The existing user analysis methods such as the behavior observational method, focused interviews, questionnaire survey, and ethnography can be used to define user demands for product creativity, which can accordingly be used to set as the product design target.

3.2 Building a Classification of Product Functionality

Based on the design targets that have been established above, the functions required for a product can be determined. These can be classified into two types according to a function's degree of sharing: (1) When a function achieves two or more design targets simultaneously, it is called a "general-purpose function" with a high degree of sharing; (2) When a function is only suitable for a particular target, it is called a "particular function" with a low degree of sharing.

3.3 Components Required for Developing Products

When developing product components based on the stipulated target functions, a component is called the "major component" if it can independently exhibit most of the product's functions; in addition, it is allowed to develop particular components to satisfy other particular functions and it is called a "minor component". A minor component is not able to bring functions into play independently but has to attach to a major component for demonstrating the functions. It is among the particular functions. When a type of unit component can hold the entire product functions, it is required to only develop a type of major components. On the other hand, two or more types of components can be developed based on the product demands so as to extend product functions.

3.4 Developing Creative and Friendly Interfaces

Product interfaces can be classified as: concrete "physical interface" which is responsible for the connective relationship between the major component and minor components; and the mental "cognitive interface" which is responsible for the interactive relationship between products and users. A creative and friendly interface encourages its user to apply the existing knowledge, capability, and skills without the need of extra learning for continuing the design and creation. A designer can utilize the product semantic perception interface to guide the creativity and friendliness of a physical interface for its users.

3.5 Products' Embodied Design

Based on the major, minor components and the creative friendly interface that have been developed above, the commonly available CAD simulation, 3D printing, mock-ups and functional models can be utilized to apply concrete forms to the product components so as to carry out a diversity of functional and appearance test.

4 Verification by a Case Study

To verify the feasibility of the co-creation product development model, this study invited 4th grade junior college students in the Department of Product Design to carry out a case study on the eco-friendly furniture product development based on this mode. The target group is the young people who move out of home in the age of 18–35 years old. The reasons for this is twofold: (1) The group has a higher frequency of removing behaviors and expects their furniture to be diversified and easy to store; (2) The group has diversified ideas on the requirements of creativity and expects a product to demonstrate the creativity at any moment as compared to other group. The case study is described as follows:

4.1 Investigating User Demands for Creativity

The design team firstly observed the existing eco-friendly furniture. It was found that though the commercially available eco-friendly furniture can be assembled to become products with functionality, the product function is unified and fixed and could not be modified at any moment according to an individual's creativity. The design team also observed the way of storing items for the target group in their houses so as to understand the usage conditions. After the interviews and the open questionnaire survey on the ten target users, the KJ method was used to collect and organize the demands for furniture creativity for the group of people that move out of home: (a) A user can design the furniture appearance and forms in person; (b) A user can freely plan the storage space; (c) A user can adjust product purposes according to his/her demands at will; (d) Expecting the furniture to keep the usual way of using the top surface such as the desk top, chair top, bed topper, etc.

4.2 Building a Classification of Product Functionality

This portion is to propose the functions that the eco-friendly furniture should have for those moving out of home. Based on the above analysis of the top three design targets (a), (b), and (c), the components need to satisfy the general-purpose functions of adjusting the space with flexibility, no limitation on the direction of stacks and storage, with openness, adjusting product purposes according to the demands at will. It is known from the fourth design target (d) that, a product should provide the function of laminate boards for use as a horizontal plane and this is classified as a particular function.

4.3 Components Required for Developing Products

Based on the above, the major component should have the openness and a degree of freedom. Considering the support strength of a product's structure, the design team developed the "flake-type unit" as the major component for structural support and partitioning. This approach can improve the current problem of eco-friendly furniture not allowing the users to easily and freely plan the storage space and the appearance styling. Moreover, minor components are required to be replaceable at will and the original purpose should be able to change. In order to satisfy the user demands, a "planar unit" was developed accordingly as shown in Fig. 2.

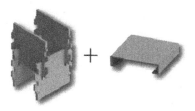

Fig. 2. Major and minor components

4.4 Developing Creative and Friendly Interfaces

The interactions between different types of components include the assembly and extension between a major component and other major components, or a major component and other minor components. The physical interface between components adopts a "sawtooth engagement" for fixing the components. On the cognitive interface, it complies with a user's past recognition model by using the "Yin and Yang" styling semantics to guide the user for the engagement. The user requires no extra learning or training and can achieve creativity interactions with products seamlessly. They can also intuitively design the furniture's forms and purposes. The assembling operation is as shown in Fig. 3.

Fig. 3. Procedure of assembling the components

4.5 Products' Embodied Design

Eco-friendly corrugated cardboards were used as the construction materials. Via CAD simulation, the major and minor components and interfaces were embodied one by one for determining the sawtooth angle and the structural strength (Fig. 4).

Fig. 4. Demonstration of assembling purposes

The characteristics of the co-creation eco-friendly furniture that was developed in this study are summarized as follows.

(1) The problem of having a single function for most of the corrugated cardboard furniture can be resolved.
(2) Unit components were simplified so as to reduce the production cost and enhance the production rate.
(3) Components are easy to disassemble. A variety of styling and functions are provided after being assembled.
(4) A type of furniture that changes according to the user creativity and functional requirements is created.

5 Conclusions

The co-creation product development model and operating instructions as follows were proposed in this study. A case study on operating the corrugated cardboard furniture was conducted for performing the implementation and development. The applications and implications are threefold: (1) Users and developers in enterprises jointly participate in product designs to co-create new values for eco-friendly furniture products. Eco-friendly products not only strive for eco-friendliness, but also provide users with design creation experiences. The resulting products are full of affective values and this approach can further create the distinctiveness and differentiation for enterprise brands. (2) When a product can add new components repeatedly according to the functional requirements, product adherence can be enhanced. Users buy eco-friendly furniture no longer just for one time, but will build a sustainable consumption mechanism, which extends the product life cycle. (3) The relationship between an enterprise and its user transformed from the vertical "host-client relationship" into the horizontal "friend-companion relationship". This approach can greatly enhance the product uniqueness and professional image for an enterprise and resolve the predicament of a saturated market for conventional eco-friendly furniture.

References

Tu, J.C.: Product Sustainable Design-Green Design in Theory and Practice. Asia Pacific Publisher, Taipei (2002)

Tu, J.C., Wu, C.N.: Impact of awareness and attitude of environmental protection and green consumption behavior on green furniture design. J. Des. **10**(3), 21–37 (2005)

Chiang, C.L.: Handmade paper manufacturing and its properties and paper design and processing - design application of cardboards. National Pingtung University of Science and Technology, Pingtung City, pp. 70–99 (2007)

Chen, Y.L.: Study on the assembly constitution of corrugated paperboard furniture. Department of Wood Science and Design, National Pingtung University of Science and Technology (2009)

Grönroos, C.: Adopting a service business logic in relational business-to-business marketing: value creation, interaction and joint value co-creation. In: Otago Forum, vol. 2, pp. 269–287 (2008)

Ind, N., Iglesias, O., Schultz, M.: Building brands together: emergence and outcomes of co creation. Calif. Manag. Rev. **55**(3), 5–26 (2013)

Kambil, A., et al.: Co-creation: a new source of value. Outlook Mag. **3**(2), 23–29 (1999)

Magnusson, T.: State-of-the-art: a review of eco-design research (2001). http://www.vinnova.se/

Prahalad, C.K., Ramaswamy, V.: The Future of Competition: Co-creating Unique Value with Customers. Harvard Business School Press, Boston (2003)

Roggeven, A.L., Tsiros, M., Grewal, D.: Understanding the co-creation effect: when does collaborating with customers provide a lift to service recovery? J. Acad. Mark. Sci. **46**(6), 771–790 (2012)

Schreier, M., Fuch, C., Dahl, D.W.: The innovation effect of user design- exploring consumers' innovation perceptions of firms selling products designed by users. J. Mark. **76**(5), 18–32 (2012)

Weber, M.E.A., Weggeman, M.C.D.P., van Aken, J.E.: Developing what customers really need: involving customers in innovations. Int. J. Innov. Technol. Manag. **9**(3), 777–782 (2012)

Well-Being of Decolonizing Aesthetics: New Environment of Art with BCI in HCI

Hyunkyoung Cho[1,2(✉)] and Jin-kyung Paik[3]

[1] ASPECT, Virginia Tech, Blacksburg, VA 24060, USA
hkcho.vt.edu@gmail.com
[2] u-Healthcare Design Institute, Design Institute, Inje University, Gimhae, South Korea
[3] College of Design, Design Institute, Inje University, Gimhae, South Korea
dejpaik@inje.ac.kr

Abstract. This paper presents that art with BCI (Brain-Computer Interaction) is decolonizing from the dimensions of action between politics *and* the aesthetic in traditional knowledge systems. In order to explore the creative power of art with BCI, it proposes the concept of decolonizing aesthetics. It critiques the beauty of art with BCI, through the reframing of aesthetic activities such as aesthetic objects, aesthetic attitudes, and aesthetic values in the view of psychoanalysis. Its aim is to find out a response for alternative perspectives of reference in HCI (Human-Computer Interaction) systems and alternative ways of understanding the relationships and collaborative actions between humans and new digital technologies.

Keywords: Decolonizing aesthetics · Art with BCI · Brain-Computer collaborative action · Beauty · Aesthetic objects · Attitudes · Values

1 Toward a Decolonized Approach to Art with Technology

To decolonize knowledge of art is to consider aesthetics in the ecology of networked knowledge enabling new forms of collaborations between sciences, engineering, arts, and design.[1] Art with technology contributes to the decolonization of aesthetics. One of significance quietness of art with technology is that the collaborative action of human and technology becomes artwork itself. When interactive artwork is constituted by the collaborative action of human and technology, there is no distinction between actor and spectator, human and non-human, artist and audience.

---

[1] Aesthetics is the philosophical study of beauty and taste. It is closely related to the philosophy of art, which is concerned with the nature of art and the concepts in terms of which individual works of art are interpreted and evaluated. The concept of aesthetics concerns an interesting and puzzling realm of experience: the realm of the beautiful, the ugly, the sublime, and the elegant; of taste, criticism, and fine art; and of contemplation, sensuous enjoyment, and charm. To provide more than a general definition of the subject matter of aesthetics is immensely difficult. Indeed, it could be said that self-definition has been the major task of modern aesthetics.

© Springer International Publishing Switzerland 2016
S. Yamamoto (Ed.): HIMI 2016, Part II, LNCS 9735, pp. 244–255, 2016.
DOI: 10.1007/978-3-319-40397-7_24

Especially, the beauty and its judgment of art with technology involve a decolonized approach to the relation of politics and the aesthetic. The relation of politics and the aesthetic has been claimed to be a mutual degradation between two opposing points of view. First is a use of aesthetics in politics: how politics has turned to the aesthetic as either a support or an ideological antagonism. Second is a use of politics in aesthetics: how the aesthetic has social and political meaning. Art with new technology undertakes a redefinition of the aesthetic that not only challenges the representational categories into which it has been placed but also redefines the aesthetic in terms of political existence. This challenge proposes a new definition of decolonized aesthetics agreeing with both politics and the aesthetic.

Decolonizing aesthetics of art with technology presents new possibilities for the relation of politics *and* the aesthetic in the ways that we humans and technology perform. Here politics *and* the aesthetic is a mobilization and thus, it ironically forgets its own movements. It is not just there because it is in the process of happening. It also can be addressed as utterance: systems of sensibility beyond two rigid systems of fixed thought and rigid action. In the collaborative action of human and technology, politics *and* the aesthetic becomes the performative with these non-representational links between different systems of meaning and action [1]. And, the 'We' attains collaborative relations without characterizing them in either positive or negative terms. It also pushes the realm of representational politics toward negation.

On the one hand, performative politics and aesthetic critiques politicize the historical ease with which the aesthetic has been and still is, confined to the ideological. On the other hand, it challenges the aestheticization of politics to account for politics with new forms of representation. This turn fuses the relations of politics *and* the aesthetic in the double determination of commonality and exclusivity. It establishes, at one and the same time, something common that is brought together out of shared and exclusive parts. This double determination of politics *and* aesthetic structures adduce networks so that everything possessing visibility is assigned a part. Such networks recall the ecology of networked knowledge enabling new forms of collaborations among sciences, engineering, arts, and design.

To put it differently, decolonizing aesthetics of art with technology embraces a place, or potential both "actors" (who act) and "systems" (which behave) in terms of Bruno Latour [2]. The relation of politics *and* the aesthetic is a contesting of collaborative balance and imbalance between actants in equal parts. Here, to become visible is that relation that takes place in equality. In order for mobilization to become visible, relations must unfold in place in equality. Contesting this collaboration is the eruption of politics *and* the aesthetic in decolonizing aesthetic of art with technology. Equality cannot be recognized as the object of politics *and* the aesthetic. Instead, it acts to give politics of leisure and liberation new reality in the form of specific time and space.

This performativity of contesting the collaboration between actants in networked knowledge adduces new ways of knowing provoked by technology. The performative dimension of art with technology constitutes a new focus on technology's continuous interrogation of the ground that supports our inadequate understanding of the efficacy of the arts. Decolonizing aesthetics of art with new information technology calls into question the production of knowledge in the Western world and its contemporary mutations. This questioning also dismantles the all too often simplistic character of the relation of human and technology, politics and the aesthetic, and the beauty and its judgment.

2 BCI Is Changing How Art Is Made

Art with technology provides a chance to study a growing interest in the concept of decolonizing aesthetics. Like human-human communication, technology and humans act and react. In particular, computational technology is endowed with highly intelligent and perceptive qualities; has its own laws; and the system itself evolves. With the ability of autonomy and emergence, technology performs the autonomous and emergent action beyond human control. It becomes 'an actor (a collaborator)' collaborating with humans. Technology as a collaborator transforms the knowledge condition. The transformation indicates that knowledge of we humans is organized by collaborative actions between we humans and technology. It responses to the need for alternative frames of reference to inter-active systems design and alternative ways of understanding the relationships and collaborative actions between humans and new digital technologies.

Human-Computer interaction (HCI) techniques evolve from conscious or direct inputs. Especially, the computer game with Brain-Computer Interaction (BCI) shows that the collaborative action of human and technology involves both conscious and non-conscious inputs. It expands the collaborative action into a kind of biofeedback. It suggests the brain signal processing as a new way for the collaborative action of human and technology.

For example, Brain-Computer Collaborative Art, *Racing Car Game* (Fig. 1) is an ongoing research-led practice project about decolonizing aesthetics of art with BCI. The artwork is constituted by the concentration between human and computer as collaborators. The brain-computer collaborative action changes the car's velocity; it can improve the attention state; when the collaboration between human and computer gets stronger, the concentration level goes higher.

Fig. 1. *Racing Car Game*: Art with BCI, Brain-Computer Collaborative Art: *Racing Car Game* designed by Bio-Computing Laboratory at GIST, Korea. EPOC and Carrera Slot Car.

In *Racing Car Game*, brainwave is the key measure. It represents the concentration as the degree of collaborative action of human and technology. Car's velocity shows the concentration level using Electroencephalography (EEG). EGG is an electrophysiological monitoring method to record the electrical activity of the brain. The concentration is observed in Beta wave and falls in the range of 14–30 Hz (Fig. 2).

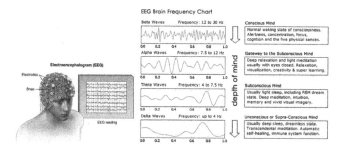

Fig. 2. EEG reading and four categories of brain wave patterns

3 The Creative Power of Art with BCI

The key point of Brain-Computer Collaborative Art is that the collaborative action through brain activities allows us a communication without physical and visible movement between human and computer (Fig. 3). Brain signals create a new philosophical and aesthetic dimension of art constituted by the collaborative action of human and technology.

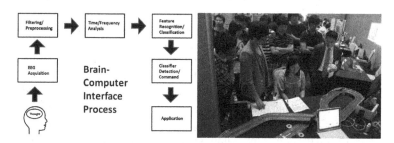

Fig. 3. Brain-Computer Collaborative Art, *Racing Car Game*: BCI Process and Exhibition (HCI Korea, 2012): Communication without physical and visible movement.

3.1 Art with BCI as Aesthetic Objects

Technology is redefining art in strange, new ways. Especially, BCI (Brain-Computer Interaction) triggers a whole series of basic questions that how does human thinks with a computer, what is the difference between animate and inanimate, human and non-human. In the work of art, *Racing Car Game*, BCI system is closer to a tool as an extension of the human body in that human provides the rhythm (Fig. 3). On the other hand, it is more independently active than a tool. It works automatically and imposes its rhythm on we humans. It presents that BCI system is nontransparent. It provokes a discrepancy that nevertheless the computer is inanimate, in practice it acts as a living and thinking object.

Thus, art with BCI can be an example of the conflict between the civilization and its discontents in terms of Sigmund Freud's the diagnosis; it recalls the repressed in the paradox of prohibition of incest as what is simultaneously prohibited and considered impossible. For it is not possible for the computer to think on the grounds that it is ethically and morally dangerous. Here, the interesting point is that BCI functions as a fantasy-frame to prevent the abyss of the Real in the concept of Lacanian psychoanalysis. As early as 1954 Jacques Lacan points out that the computer is the paradigmatic case of symbolic bliss [3]. What we call reality is constituted upon the model of the symbolic bliss for the exclusion of the traumatic Real. The symbolic bliss is "the coming into operation of the symbolic function." It converts "a horrendous discovery" into "a sort of ataraxia [4]".

Sigmund Freud testifies the structure of art with BCI in his famous two dreams; the famous dream of Irma's injection and that of the dead son who appears to his father and addresses him with the reproach, "Father, can't you see that I'm burning? [5]". In these dreams, the symbolic bliss wakes up when dreamers encounter Iram's throat and the burning son as the traumatic Real. It enables them to escape from the Real. In other words, through the fantasy-frame of symbolic bliss, the dreamers can continue to sleep after the horrifying look into the Real epitomized by Irma's throat and the apparition of burning son [6].

Like Irma's throat and the apparition of burning son, art with BCI operates in a fantasy-frame of symbolic bliss. It constitutes what we call reality through the exclusion of some traumatic Real. In the artwork, *Racing Car Game*, BCI is no less than "the price we pay for our access to reality [7]." If we think that the computer doesn't think, the price for our access to reality remains un-paid, un-thought. It means that we can approach the reality of BCI art so long as we consider BCI as thinking and acting aesthetic objects.

It is of particular interest how the tension between schizophrenia and paranoid takes place in *Racing Car Game* created by BCI. Every program is code writing and it is the expression in the computer language of a series of action that the computer needs to take in order to solve a problem. What is really important in the programming is always how efficiently they run on the computer. Although its aims at complete control and mastery, it proceeds intuitively and creates the new. The discrepancy between means and effect is bound with the tension between schizophrenia and paranoid of BCI art.

The double structure of schizophrenia and paranoid provides the possibility to catch the eloquence of BCI as aesthetic objects. In the work, *Racing Car Game*, the schizo-phrenic aspect of BCI can be analyzed as the pleasure of programming as text. According to Roland Barthes, the literature work is a fixed writing depending on its author, while the text is arbitrary signs [8]. It plays in itself. More detail, the text itself plays as one plays a game and "the reader plays twice over as a practice which reproduces it [9]." Like the text of literary, BCI system also has the shifting from work to text and abolishes the distance between writing and reading as well as author and reader. This process concerns the schizophrenic aspect of BCI system. We humans cannot see the play itself of programming as text. We humans exist only a reader in the sense that we can read the programming codes. That is to say, we humans become a second player in the art with BCI.

Although art with BCI operates on the basis of simulation of human's thoughts, its internal action is nontransparent. It indicates that BCI art is the paranoid by nature in terms of psychoanalysis. For the logic of BCI is far from a simple linear, closed, self-reflexive one. It follows an inconsistent logic which, caught in a snare of self-reference, can never be totalized. In this regard, art with BCI is self-evident as long as it loses the self-evident. The losing of self-evident in BCI is parallel to paranoid as an infinitely repetition (reiteration) of failed self- rescue.

Art with BCI is a process of ultimate abstraction; it is the abstract simulation of thoughts of we humans, in order to interpret and manipulate the real world. As a model for human brains, BCI system is only programmed, that it cannot in a real sense understand. However, when a thought is translated into a program, it loses the ability to live with the vagueness that thoughts normally employ. It shows us the other side of ourselves that we have never seen.

In this point, art with BCI gets the aesthetic originality. Georg W.F. Hegel points out that "in one respect, the originality is the most personal inner life of the artist, yet on the other hand it reveals the nature of the object and the special character of the thing itself [10]." The originality of BCI art can be considered as the nature of the object and personal inner life of we humans at the same time. It is linked with the uncertainty (autonomy) as the substance of art. Theodor W. Adorno notes, "it is self-evident that nothing concerning art is self-evident anymore, not its inner life, not its relation to the world, not even its right to exist [11]." The substance of art lies in not the arbitrariness of what simply exists but the endless losing of self-evident. A similar subversion takes place in the art with BCI.

On the one side, BCI art turns against itself, in opposition to its own concept. Only by the virtue of the separation from empirical reality, it achieves a heightened order of existence. In this sense, art with BCI refuses definition. The aesthetic identity of art with BCI seeks to the non-identical, which in reality is repressed by reality's compulsion to identity. Thus, the autonomy of art with BCI might be essentially internal like an art. On the other side, the non-communicative aspect of BCI art, however, occurs through the communication with what is external, with the world from which it seals itself off. For, insofar as BCI art is an object (artifact) as the product of social labor, the aesthetic force of production is the same as that of productive labor.

The aesthetic relations of production are no less than sedimentations or imprinting of social relations. It indicates that art with BCI is necessary to have a social relation, and to communicate with the empirical reality as reified external experience that it internally rejects and from which it draws its content. The double character shows the concrete mediating links between BCI art and the social structure.

Consequently, like the identity of art, art with BCI exists in both internal autonomy and external sociality. Hence, BCI meets art in the point of losing of self-evident. The meeting point has its foundation in the synthesis of the spirit-material dimension of works. In other words, the synthesis exists only in relation to its other as what it is not. Insomuch as it is the process that transpires with its other, the point that they meet is no less than an active and communicative movement. The movement becomes BCI art itself. It presents that art with BCI is decolonizing from the spell of the absolute of idealistic aesthetics.

3.2   Art with BCI as Aesthetic Attitudes

The artwork with BCI, *Racing Car Game*'s system is implemented under BCI2000 platform (general purpose software in BCI research). Graphical software visualizes concentration index, and hardware module controls the velocity of a racing car. BCI2000 is a general-purpose system for BCI research and development (Fig. 4). It can also be used for data acquisition, stimulus presentation, or brain observation applications. BCI2000 consists of a Signal Acquisition module that acquires brain signals from g.USBamp or g.MOBIlab+devices (Fig. 4) These raw signals are visualized and stored to disks and submitted to the Signal Processing module. The Signal Processing module extracts signal features and translates them into the device command. Its commands are used by the Applications module to generate the collaborative action of human and technology. *Racing Car Game* shows that BCI is changing how artwork is made as well as how to see the artwork. It recalls the painter Paul Klee's meditation, "Now objects perceive me [12]."

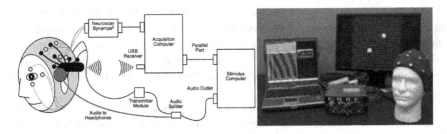

Fig. 4. Racing *Car Game:* BCI2000 Platform (BCI2000 has been used to replicate or extend current BCI methods in humans and has recently been used in a number of groundbreaking BCI studies. BCI2000 has been in development since 2000 in a collaborative effort led by the Wadsworth Center. BCI2000 is available free of charge for research purposes to academic and educational institutions.) and EPOC (14-channel wireless EEG system developed by Emotiv Systems).

Klee's intuition recently has become an objective fact. In the artwork, *Racing Car Game*, BCI goes back to the basic condition of art and through the observation of object shows institution about "the direct spiritual vision" of the object beyond the representation [13]. BCI reconstructs the traditional symbolic order and realizes the direct spiritual vision. The returning to the depths of the object is to break the symbolic order. Like "the child, the madman and the savage with special power," art with BCI can still, or again, look into the in-between world that exists between the worlds our senses perceive [14]. That is to say, it "does not reproduce the visible; rather, it makes visible [15]." It implies that BCI provides the possibility of achieving the sightless vision in the sense that there is no such thing as fixed sight depending on the human eye's movement.[2] It assumes to the sharing of vision, of perception between the animate and the inanimate, in this case, human and computer.

The synthetic vision of art with BCI can be called the collaborative vision of computer and human.[3] It is a new form of aesthetic attitude, free of any previous perspective. It is the shifting from "Small Optics" to "Big Optics," as Paul Virilio observes [16]. Small Optics is based on linear geometric perspective shared by human vision. It involves distinctions between near and far, between the object and the horizon against which the object stands out. It is the essence of the audio-visual perspective of old: to hear and see at the distance. Big Optics is aesthetic attitudes handled by the collaborative vision of computer and human. It is a real-time electronic transmission of information.

In the artwork, *Racing Car game*, BCI dissolves physical distances as familiar patterns of perception, the dimension of real space of linear geometrical perspective. It implies that we are moving towards "tactile perspective," that is, to "contact at a distance [17]." What may be radically new in the tactile perspective is that we can affect change on material reality over the physical distance in real time. It allows us to touch objects over distance. As new aesthetic attitudes, the collaborative vision of art with BCI reconsiders both a fundamental condition of human perception-spatial distance and the distance between the subject who is seeing and the object being seen; the observer and the observed or the spectator and the spectacle. It is "not an inferior representation of our reality, but a realistic representation of a different reality," and then "it is the result of a different, more than human, vision [18]."

At this point, art with BCI redefines the relation between subject and object of vision. It questions that 'when the vision is augmented by computer graphics, whose vision is it?' Art with BCI critiques the technological determinism reinforcing the binary of computer and human vision. It shows that now the different reality, the different vision is constituted by the collaboration of computer and human. The collaboration makes a new single vision as neither the machine vision nor human vision.

With regard to the problem of the subject in relation to the object, aesthetic attitudes of art with BCI fits well with Hal Foster's the reception of import of art in the view of psychoanalysis. The collective vision of art with BCI reframes the nature of the artistic activity and extends it into the fundaments of aesthetics configuration. It presents a broken relation to subject (self) and the world as manifest in a dissociation of thought, action, or effect-as a disruption of subjectivity marked by a disruption in representation.

---

[2] Vision is the ability to interpret information from visible light reaching the eye. It is the result of visual perception, and it is also known as eyesight or sight. Perspective is the way in which objects appear to the eye based on their spatial attributes, or their dimensions and the position of the eye relative to the objects.

[3] The collaborative vision is to merge two concepts of human vision in the field of human sciences and computer vision as the field of computer sciences. In general, human vision indicates the ability of visual perception to interpret information from visible light reaching the human eye, while computer vision is the science and technology of machines that see. As a new scientific discipline, it is concerned with the building artificial systems (computer vision systems) that obtain information from images.

According to the meditation of Freud, aesthetic attitudes of BCI art are overwhelmed by hallucinations that only deepen the sense of internal and external catastrophe. It constructs new systems to counter both catastrophes, with delusions of personal grandeur for the first and projections of world order for the second. The former focuses on a self-losing, while the latter deals with an ultimate failure of self-rescue. Both, however, are ultimately identified with a self-defense mechanism.

The collaborative vision of art with BCI evokes the collapsing of boundaries between subject and object, the observer and the observed; it merges the distinction into the disappearing (the breaking) of spatial and temporal distance between them. Shortly speaking, the distinction between subject and object is flattened in the art with BCI. That's why the collaborative vision of we humans and technology is perceived as an uncanny catastrophe that is suddenly estranged and hostile.

3.3   Art with BCI as Aesthetic Values

Idealism is based on mind, consciousness or perception.[4] It refers to a tradition in Western thought that represents things in an ideal. In the idealistic knowledge, the form of an object is subordinated to an absolutely subjective sign system denoting subjective instinctual impulses. The meaning is supposedly hidden behind the form of the object. On the idealism, aesthetic values have been inferred from the aesthetic attitude as "the aesthetic interest or pleasure through the subjective aesthetic experience [19]." The aesthetic values concern the beauty. It is considered as a series of experience as an aesthetic pleasure. If we feel an intense aesthetic pleasure through an artwork, we have an experience as what is projected on the object. Then what we call the beauty, what we experience is the idea of beauty rather than the beauty itself.

Art with BCI critiques the alienation of object in idealistic aesthetics. It recalls Marx's fable that "One man is king only because other men stand in the relation of subjects to him. They, on the contrary, imagine that they are subjects because he is king [20]." Being-a-king is an effect of the relation between a king and his subjects. The subjects, however, think that they are subjects giving the king royal treatment, since the king is already in himself, outside the relationship to his subjects, a king. Like this distorted relation of a king and subjects, idealistic aesthetic assumes that there is an absolute beauty beyond a direct social relation between object and people as well as objects. As an already given to us, the idealistic beauty is in itself like a king.

Art with BCI considers the definition of beauty in a direct social relation between object and people as well as objects. For example, the artwork with BCI, *Racing Car Game* uses Emotiv EPOC as a headset that actually picks up on our brain waves (Fig. 5). The EPOC headset incorporates 14 extensions of electrodes (seven pairs), mostly centered on the front of the scalp. But rather than using the wires of traditional EEG tests, the headset is completely wireless, allowing the player free, natural movement.

Emotiv EPOC reads unique patterns of brain waves and interprets both conscious and unconscious thoughts as well as emotions. On the one hand, it attempts to close the

---

[4] Idealism is widely used as the philosophical theory that the ultimate nature of reality is based on mind or ideas.

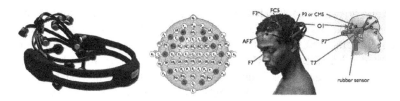

Fig. 5. Art using BCI, *Racing Car Game*: Emotiv EPOC system

gap further between the real world and the virtual world to create a more realistic experience, much like the Wii does. On the other hand, the Emotiv EPOC also tries to bridge the gap between human thought and the outside world to create an experience that's less like reality and more fantastical and dreamlike.

Thus, the beauty of *Racing Car Game* is in essentially unconscious projections of those who have produced them. It is nothing but facts like daydreams as well as objects of analysis. As an analogy of artwork and dream-work, art with BCI discovers the meaning of object itself as the linkage between the form of the object and its social relation. In an analysis of the form of dream as object, Freud defines that 'at bottom, dreams are nothing other than a particular form of thinking, made possible by the conditions of the state of sleep.' For it, he analyzes the self's dream, namely, the dream of Irma's injection. Through the analysis, he finds a repressed message in the relation to the connection of the form of a dream as an object and its social relation. The dream-work is the self's unconscious attempt to evade the social responsibility of the failure in his treatment of Irma as his patient.

According to Freud's meditation, the beauty of art with BCI is the attempt, the dream-work that creates the form of a dream as an object. It is realizing of a repressed unconscious desire of a dreamer in the linkage between the form of dream as object and its social relation. It means that the beauty of BCI performs in the form itself rather than a latent thought and manifest text. Insofar as the beauty of art with BCI is constituted in the form itself, there is no hidden meaning behind the form of art with BCI.

Art with BCI denies the very idea that the beauty is superior to the form of an object and emphasizes the form of object as movement in relation to object and its social relation. At this point, BCI art is connected to Hegel's dialectical aesthetics, which conceives the form as content. Although he also defines that 'the beauty is the Idea of beauty, he sharply distinguishes between the Idea and Concept.' The Concept articulates in the shape of object. It is the absolute unity of specifications, the mediated ideal unity of particular factors. It is a totality between object and its social relation in reality. The Idea reveals itself in the real (actual) existence of Concept.

In this sense, the beauty of art with BCI can be grasped as the Ideas as the immediate totality of the Concept with its reality. Insofar as the beauty is originated from the dialectic movement between Idea and Concept, it is regardless of its purposed fullness in the satisfaction of needs, and the accidental nature. It is that we find out the object beautiful rather a subjective consideration of the object.

Freud also notices that when the beauty investigates the aesthetic attitude as the conditions under which things are felt as beautiful, it is unable to give any explanation of nature and origin of beauty. He defines the beauty as attributes of the sexual object. According to him, "the love of beauty is a perfect example of a feeling (impulse) with inhabited aim… the genitals themselves, the sight of which is always exciting, are hardly ever regarded as beautiful [21]." The genitals themselves implies that what is eliminated by the prohibited object is the beauty itself. It testifies the essential lack of success of absolute that we can get the beauty, as long as we do not depict the site of sexual pleasure directly.

4 Invagination

As a case of art with BCI, *Racing Car Game* presents that the beauty is the moving. The beauty of BCI art requires the collaborative action of humans and computer. Here the interesting point is that we do not just see that things move in the artwork, but we see them moving in it, and this is because we ourselves move it. In other words, the beauty of art using BCI technologies is not the still of moving things, but the moving of moving things. There is no coherent and inherent relevance of beauty in art with BCI. The beauty that is not there challenges the way of knowing and decolonizes the power of traditional knowledge system.

Arthur Danto said that "We refer to Voltaire only with reference to why we see the cloud as we do, not with reference to why the cloud is the way we see it [22]." The ontological difference (or the existence) is caused by the experience of reality, but causality and reference are in front of undetermined (or being determined) experience. It is not undetermined causality and reference, but veridical experience. The beauty of art with BCI presents that we have to question the way of knowing, that is, the rule of the knowledge game.

In this sense, art with BCI has an ambivalence of politics *and* the aesthetic. The beauty created by BCI is originated from the collaborative action of we humans and technology. It critiques both knowledges of practical arts and practical arts themselves; it stimulates a network of conceptual relations rather than merely perceptions of the haptic and sensory aspects of interactive art. Thus, the artwork with BCI, *Racing Car Game* becomes a sociological imagination as "the vivid awareness of the relationship between personal experience and the wider society" for the decolonizing knowledge [23].

Acknowledgments. This work was supported by the National Research Foundation of Korea Grant funded by the Korean Government(NRF-2014S1A5B8044097)

References

1. Hyunkyoung, C., Joonsung, Y.: Performative art: the politics of doubleness. Leonardo **42**(3), 282–283 (2009). The MIT Press, Cambridge
2. Latour, B.: We Have Never Been Modern. Harvard University Press, Cambridge (1993)
3. Zizek, S.: From virtual reality to the virtualization of reality. In: Trend, D. (ed.) Reading Digital Culture. Blackwell Publishing, Oxford (2001)

4. Lacan, J.: Book II: The Ego in Freud's Theory and in the Technique of Psychoanalysis. Cambridge University Press, Cambridge (1988). Tomaselli, S. (trans.)
5. Freud, S.: The Interpretation of Dreams. NuVision Publications, London (2007)
6. Zizek, S.: Tarrying with the Negative: Kant, Hegel, and the Critique of Ideology. Duke University Press, Durham (1933)
7. Zizek, S.: From virtual reality to the virtualization of reality. In: Trend, D. (ed.) Reading Digital Culture. Blackwell Publishing, Oxford (2001)
8. Barthes, R.: The Pleasure of the Text. Hill and Wang, New York (1975). Miller, R. (trans.)
9. Barthes, R.: Image-Music-Text. Hill and Wang, New York (1977). Heath, S. (trans.)
10. Hegel, G.W.F.: Aesthetics. Oxford University Press, London (1975). Knox, T.M. (trans.)
11. Adorno, T.W.: Aesthetic Theory. Minnesota University Press, Minneapolis (1988). Hullot-Kentor, R. (trans.)
12. Virilio, P.: The Vision Machine. Indiana University Press, Bloomington (1994)
13. Foster, H.: Blinded insights: on the modernist reception of the art of the mentally Ill. **97**, 3–30 (2001). The MIT Press, Cambridge
14. Klee, F.: Paul Klee: His Life and Work in Documents. George Braziller, New York (1962)
15. Klee, P.: The Inward Vision. Harry Abrams, New York (1959). Guterman, N. (trans.)
16. Virilio, P.: Big optics. In: Weibel, P. (ed.) On Justifying the Hypothetical Nature of Art and Non-identically Within the Object World. Walther Koenig, Koln (1992)
17. Virilio, P.: Speed and information: cyberspace alarm! In: Trend, D. (ed.) Reading Digital Culture. Blackwell Publishing, Malden (2001)
18. Manovich, L.: The Language of New Media. The MIT Press, Cambridge (2001)
19. Rader, M., Jessop, B.: Art and Human Values. Prentice-Hall Inc., New York (1976)
20. Marx, K.: Capital: A Critique of Political Economy, vol. 1. International Publishers Co., New York (1967)
21. Freud, S.: Civilization and Its Discontents. W.W. Norton & Company, New York (1961). Strachey, J. (trans.)
22. Danto, A.: Moving pictures. In: Philosophizing Art. California University Press, California (2001)
23. Wright Mills, C.: The Sociological Imagination. Oxford University Press, London (2000)

Creation of Shadow Media Using Point Cloud and Design of Co-creative Expression Space

Maho Hayashi[1(✉)], Yoshiyuki Miwa[2], Shiroh Itai[2], Hiroko Nishi[3], and Yuto Yamakawa[1]

[1] Graduate School of Creative Science and Engineering,
Waseda University, Tokyo, Japan
melo-6st@fuji.waseda.jp, yy816-b.t.a@ruri.waseda.jp
[2] Faculty of Science and Engineering, Waseda University, Tokyo, Japan
miwa@waseda.jp, itai@fuji.waseda.jp
[3] Faculty of Human Science, Toyo Eiwa University, Kanagawa, Japan
hiroko@toyoeiwa.ac.jp

Abstract. The authors have previously shown that, by using shadow media that transforms the color and shapes of shadows to transform the relationship between individuals and shadow media, a variety of bodily expressions is created from individual performers. In this study, we attempted to support co-creative expressions by transforming the relationships between performers and shadow media space. Specifically, we developed shadow media utilizing point clouds (dappled shadows) and made it possible to freely alter the light source position of shadow media. In addition, we implemented a shadow media system that displays a shadow agent moving according to the movements of a group of performers (a virtual light source robot) on a stage, and used its position as a light source. As a result, we found that the expression space of performers expanded in comparison with existing shadow media systems. This result shows the possibility that this system supports the emergence of co-creative expressions.

Keywords: Co-creation · Bodily expression · Shadow media · Point cloud · Virtual light source

1 Introduction

Focusing on shadows, which are inseparable from the body, the authors have researched a shadow media system to support the emergence of bodily expressions. This system allows displaying artificial shadows with modified colors or shapes (shadow media) from one's feet. We've shown that, by creating gaps between the body and shadow, a variety of bodily expressions can be created from an individual 1–3]. On the other hand, in terms of co-creative expressions in which multiple people create expressions together using their bodies, the positioning of performers on stage – that is, the relationship between performers and the expression space –plays an important role [4]. Thus, if we are able to modify the relationship between performers and the shadow media space in bodily expressions by groups of performers using shadow media, there is a possibility that we could support the emergence of co-creative expressions. As a

© Springer International Publishing Switzerland 2016
S. Yamamoto (Ed.): HIMI 2016, Part II, LNCS 9735, pp. 256–267, 2016.
DOI: 10.1007/978-3-319-40397-7_25

first step in realizing this research, in this study, we focused on changing the size and direction of all shadow media according to the light source position of shadow media, we tried to freely control of the three-dimensional position of a shadow media light source. In addition, we developed a movable shadow agent (virtual light source robot) that uses the light source position of the shadow media as its own position. Then, we aimed to support the emergence of co-creative expressions by displaying that shadow on the stage along with the shadow media of the group of performers.

Real-time 3D processing of body images is necessary to control the light source positions of shadow media for multiple people. In relation to this, the authors have previously developed a shadow media system (3D shadow media system, Fig. 1 (a)) that utilizes a 3D virtual space and skeleton data (3D models of people) [4]. As a result, this allowed for freely controlling the posture and movement of shadow media individually for each part, and controlling the position of a virtual light source for the shadow media. However, in the existing system, attempting high-resolution contours of shadow media led to a massive increase in 3D model data for people, making it difficult to perform real-time 3D processing for the shadow media of multiple people.

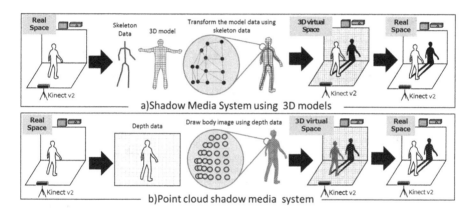

Fig. 1. 3D shadow media and point cloud shadow media

On the other hand, in CG research, in recent years high-speed 3D image processing has been implemented without sacrificing accuracy by using point cloud data [5, 6]. In this study, the authors propose and develop a new shadow media system using a 3D virtual space and point cloud data. The main feature of this system is the ability to position point clouds for human bodies and virtual light sources in a 3D virtual space, then use the shadows created from the point clouds generated by these light sources as shadow media. In other words, this system speeds up image processing by processing 3D shadow media without constructing 3D models of people composed of multiple surfaces (Fig. 1).

Due to the fact that expressing shadow media using point clouds creates blank space ("yohaku" in Japanese) in the shadow media, this opens the possibility of evoking the creation of a variety of images from these blank spaces. Moreover, it is possible that if these blank spaces (point cloud density) are modified by shadow media depth position, this will create thickness in shadow media which has heretofore been seen as flat, enhancing the feeling of depth and solidity of the shadow media.

Below, in this paper, we explain the details of the point cloud shadow media (dappled shadows) using point cloud data and the virtual light source robot. As we also attempted to support co-creative expressions using this system, we also report on those results.

2   Point Cloud Shadow Media (Dappled Shadows)

2.1   Dappled Shadow Generation Method

In this study, we developed a system composed of the following four-step process using Unity (Unity Technologies) to generate point cloud shadow media (Fig. 2). These processes are performed in advance by constructing a 3D virtual space that recreates the real space within Unity.

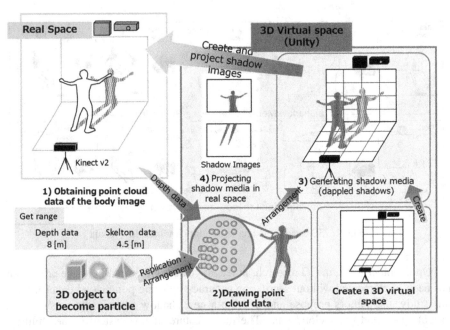

Fig. 2. Process of generation of point cloud shadow media

(1) Obtaining point cloud data of the body image

A depth image (512 × 424 pixels) captured by Kinect v2 (Microsoft) was used to obtaining point cloud data of the body image. By removing all objects in the image other than the person, such as the floor, walls, and screen, we obtaining the point cloud data for only people in the shadow media space.

(2) Drawing point cloud data

We generate a body image by positioning 3D objects at each point in the point data within the virtual space. It is possible to alter object size, shape and the distribution pattern when drawing the point cloud data.

(a) Object size

Object size can be set arbitrarily. However, shadow media may not be displayed when the size is small. In this study, the object size was set to above 5.0 mm.

(b) Object shape

Object shapes can be selected from cubes, regular tetrahedrons, spheres, rectangular plates, or two of these plates arranged in a cross pattern (Fig. 3).

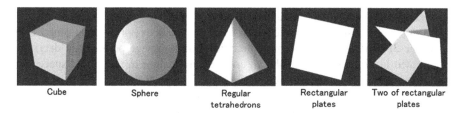

| Cube | Sphere | Regular tetrahedrons | Rectangular plates | Two of rectangular plates |

Fig. 3. Object shape

(c) Object distribution pattern

In this study, we allowed changing the object distribution pattern by reducing the point cloud density of the objects composing the body image (the amount of data in the point cloud data) according to one of the following four methods (Fig. 4).

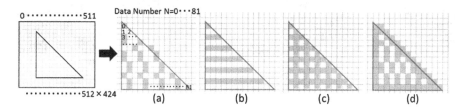

Fig. 4. Object distribution pattern: (a) Constant, (b) Border, (c) Lattice, (d) Contour enhancement

Figure 4(a) shows point cloud data composing a body image culled uniformly at fixed intervals (point cloud density D[point/Voxel]). Below, we refer to this object distribution pattern as "constant." Figure 4(b) shows the object displayed with point cloud data displayed only for points positioned at $N_{Interval\_l} \times i$ ($N_{Interval\_l}$ and i are positive integers) rows in the depth image (424 rows × 512 columns). This distribution pattern is referred to as "border." Figure 4(c) shows the object displayed with point cloud data displayed only for points positioned at $N_{Interval\_r} \times i$ ($N_{Interval\_r}$ and i are positive integers) rows or $N_{Interval\_c} \times i$ ($N_{Interval\_c}$ and i are positive integers) columns in the depth image. This distribution is referred to as "lattice." Figure 4(d) shows the result of performing contour detection on the point cloud data and displaying all objects at points on the contour. Contour detection is performed by comparing the distance of points in the depth direction among data number i and four points positioned above, below and to the left and right (data number $i - 512$, $i + 512$, $i - 1$, $i + 1$). Specifically, if even one of these four points has a distance of above 0.5 m in the depth direction, the point for data number i is determined to be a contour point. In this study, by performing this type of contour processing on the dappled shadow, we implemented high-resolution expression of shadow media contours. Drawing methods for objects other than those at contour points (points within the contour) were selected from the constant, border and lattice methods described above.

(3) Generating shadow media (dappled shadows)

Multiple object shadows created from point light sources (virtual light sources) set in the 3D virtual space and multiple objects (body image point cloud data) distributed in process (2) were shown on a screen or floor in the virtual space.

(4) Projecting shadow media in real space

The shadow image of body image point cloud data generated in process (3) was displayed at the feet of participants in the real space using a projector. Below, we call this shadow media "dappled shadow." In this study, even when shadow media for three people simultaneously existed within the media space, we were able to display shadow media (dappled shadows) for all people at 30 fps. An example of the dappled shadow generated in this study is shown in Fig. 5.

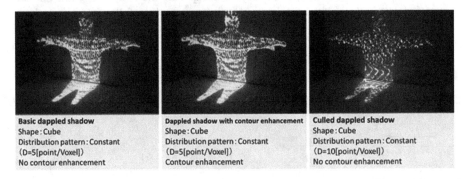

Basic dappled shadow	Dappled shadow with contour enhancement	Culled dappled shadow
Shape : Cube	Shape : Cube	Shape : Cube
Distribution pattern : Constant	Distribution pattern : Constant	Distribution pattern : Constant
(D=5[point/Voxel])	(D=5[point/Voxel])	(D=10[point/Voxel])
No contour enhancement	Contour enhancement	No contour enhancement

Fig. 5. Projecting dappled shadow

2.2 Dappled Shadow Features

Next, we examined the features and function of the dappled shadows developed in this study as shadow media. Specifically, we focused on dappled shadow point cloud density D and whether or not contours were enhanced, and checked for differences between the dappled shadow and the shadow generated by the projector in the real space (real shadow) The parameters for the three types of dappled shadows used in this experiment are given below.

Basic dappled shadow; size: 10 mm, shape: cube, distribution pattern: constant (D = 5[point/Voxel]), no contour enhancement.

Dappled shadow with contour enhancement; size: 10 mm, shape: cube, distribution pattern: constant (D = 5[point/Voxel]), contour enhancement.

Culled dappled shadow; size: 10 mm, shape: cube, distribution pattern: constant (D = 10[point/Voxel]), no contour enhancement.

In this experiment, we asked participants to move freely within the space for the first 30 s with the dappled shadow (or real shadow) displayed from their feet. Then, they were asked to perform bodily expressions through the dappled shadow for 60 s.

Figure 6 shows a view of the experiment. Participants commented that the basic dappled shadow "felt strong" and "felt solid and round." Regarding the dappled shadow with contour enhancement, participants commented that "it felt solid," "it felt more like me than myself," and "I felt like shadow could speak to me." Regarding the culled dappled shadow, participants commented that "it did not feel as solid as the other dappled shadows" and "it feels like flowers or snow." When we compared real shadows to the dappled shadows, participants commented that the dappled shadow "felt like it stimulated me internally," "felt like it drew out expressions from me," and that "it allowed for natural expressions." Particularly, participants commented that the dappled shadow with contour enhancement "felt the most like my own shadow of the four shadow media, including the real shadow."

 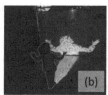  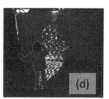

Fig. 6. Experiment of the features and function of dappled shadows with one person: (a) Real shadow, (b) Basic dappled shadow, (c) Dappled shadow with contour enhancement, (d) Culled dappled shadow.

This suggests that the dappled shadows developed in this study have an existence even stronger than real shadows, and that they possess even greater image emergence ability and expression emergence ability than the shadow media previously developed [1]. The authors believe that, this is caused by the enhancement of the ontological connection between one's body and shadow by the incompleteness of the media formed by blank spaces, because the dappled shadows are formed from point clouds.

3   Virtual Light Source Robot

3.1   Virtual Light Source Robot Positional Control Method

The virtual light source robot is composed of a cylindrical main body (0.30 m diameter × 0.50 m height) and a virtual light source positioned on top of it (Fig. 7). In this study, we allow changing the light source position of shadow media for the group of performers by moving this robot in the 3D virtual space. Also, in this study, we displayed the shadow of this robot as well as the shadow media (dappled shadows) of the group of performers in the real space (Fig. 8).

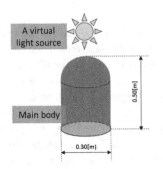 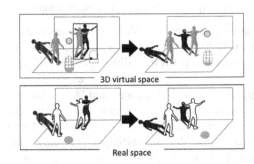

Fig. 7. Virtual light source robot

Fig. 8. Movement and the presentation of the virtual light source robot

In this study, as a starting point for researching support for the emergence of co-creative expression through transforming the relationship between performers and the shadow media space, we designed the following three operating modes for the virtual light source robot (Fig. 9).

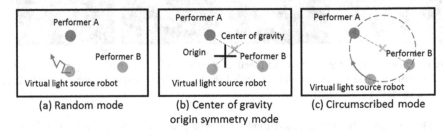

Fig. 9. Operating modes for the virtual light robot

(1) Random mode
    In random mode, the virtual light source robot is moved irrespective of the movements of the group of performers that exist within the shadow media space (Fig. 9(a)). In particular, the planar movement direction and its update interval for the virtual robot are set randomly within ranges of 0 to 360° and 3.0 to 10 s, respectively.

(2) Center of gravity origin symmetry mode
    In center of gravity origin symmetry mode, the virtual light source robot is moved according to the collective movements of the performers. Specifically, we calculate the position of the center of gravity for the standing positions of the group

of performers, then move the virtual light source robot to a position symmetrical to that position with respect to the origin (Fig. 9(b)). The origin is the center point of the shadow media space. A Laser Range Finder (LMS100, SICK) was used to measure the standing positions of the performers.

(3) Circumscribed mode

Due to the fact that the center of gravity position for the group of performers and virtual light source robot generally matches the origin, movement of detail including virtual light source robot is small in center of gravity origin symmetry mode. Circumscribed mode aims to shift the overall center of gravity position through the collective movements of the performers. To accomplish this, the virtual light source robot is moved in smallest enclosing circle enclosing the group of performers (Fig. 9(c)). The angular velocity of the circular movement is determined by the velocity of the center of gravity position for the standing positions of the group of performers.

3.2   Co-creative Expression Space Expandability

(1) Experiment with one person

Using the shadow media system using the virtual light source robot and dappled shadows described above, we first examined whether or not it could support the emergence of bodily expressions in the case of a single performer. The participant in this experiment was an adult male who is a beginner at bodily expressions. In this experiment, we directed the participant to perform bodily expressions freely for 60 s in a shadow media space measuring 6.0 m × 5.0 m × 2.8 m. We used the dappled shadow with contour enhancement as the shadow media, which was assessed as "feeling the most like my own shadow" in the experiment in Sect. 2.2. We set the following four conditions for the virtual light source robot. For condition 3, we used the position of the participant as the center of gravity position. In condition 4, the virtual light source robot was moved in a circular motion along a circle with a radius of 0.5 m centered on the position of the participant.

> Condition 1: immobile (fixed light source)
> Condition 2: random mode
> Condition 3: center of gravity origin symmetry mode
> Condition 4: circumscribed mode

Figure 10 illustrates this experiment. We received comments from the participant indicating that, in comparison with condition 1, in condition 2, "I often looked back without regard to the shadow media." In condition 3, the participant commented that "I could express while turning in various directions and being conscious of my own position." Moreover, in condition 4, the participant commented that "I moved my point of view in various directions and my movements became larger," and "I felt that I was being moved by my shadow." In addition, participant movement locus in the experiment (Fig. 11) showed that, particularly in condition 4, the movement range of the participant expanded in the depth direction with respect to the screen surface in

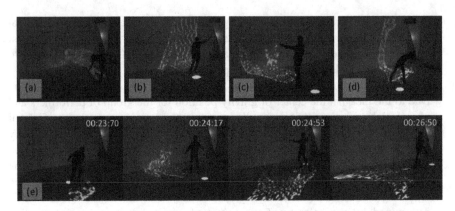

Fig. 10. Experiment of virtual light robot with one person: (a) Immobile, (b) Random mode, (c) Center of gravity origin symmetry mode, (d) Circumscribed mode, (e) Sequence photographs of expression in circumscribed mode.

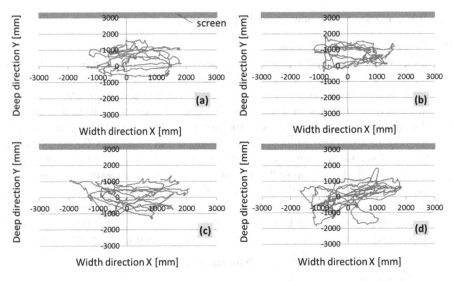

Fig. 11. Data position measurement: (a) Immobile, (b) Random mode, (c) Center of gravity origin symmetry mode, (d) Circumscribed mode.

comparison with condition 1. These results show that modifying the light source position of shadow media using a virtual light source robot can expand the expression space of performers.

(2) Experiment with multiple people (two people)

Next, we examined whether the shadow media system using a virtual light source robot and dappled shadows could support the emergence of bodily expressions for multiple people (two people). In this experiment, we directed participants to perform hand contact improvisation [7] in which they put their hands together and create improvisational, bodily expressions with their hands for 60 s. The conditions for the experiment were identical to those given in the experiment with one participant described above.

This experiment is shown in Fig. 12. Movement locus of the two participants in the experiment (Fig. 13) shows that, in conditions 2–4, the moving range is expanded in comparison with condition 1. Moreover, Fig. 14, which shows the frequency distribution for distance between the two participants, shows that in comparison with condition 1, in conditions 2–4 there were more instances of distances above 2 m. These results suggest that, in case with the existence of the virtual light source robot, the two participants used a wide space to perform bodily expressions.

Fig. 12. Experiment of virtual light robot with two people: (a) Immobile, (b) Random mode, (c) Center of gravity origin symmetry mode, (d) Circumscribed mode, (e) Sequence photographs of expression in circumscribed mode.

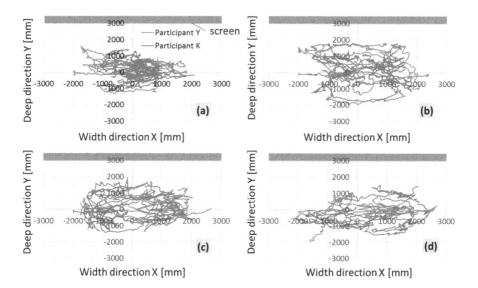

Fig. 13. Data position measurement: (a) Immobile, (b) Random mode, (c) Center of gravity origin symmetry mode, (d) Circumscribed mode. (Color figure online)

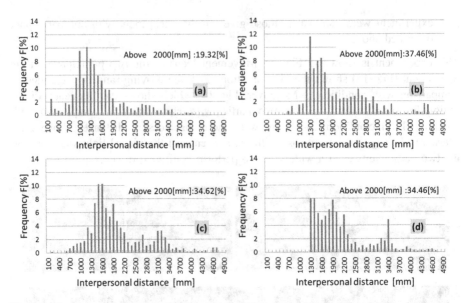

Fig. 14. Frequency distribution for interpersonal distance: (a) Immobile, (b) Random mode, (c) Center of gravity origin symmetry mode, (d) Circumscribed mode

In addition, we received comments in conditions 2–4 such as "I wanted to touch the robot," "I wanted to chase the robot," and "I felt like I was creating an expression together with my partner and the robot." These comments suggest that the performers felt the existence and movement of the robot through its shadow, and that its movement facilitated the bodily expressions of the performers. Interestingly, in the experiment with two participants, we received the following comment from a participant: "the dappled shadows were different from previous shadow media in that, even when the shadow media were overlapped, we could distinguish the anteroposterior relationship between the two, making it easier to create expressions." This feature is not seen in other shadow media.

4   Summary

In this study, we considered the possibility that we could support the emergence of co-creative expressions by modifying the relationship between performers and shadow media space. Thus, we developed a system to control the three-dimensional position of a virtual light source for shadow media. In order to achieve this, we designed and developed a shadow media system using point clouds. We were able to create dappled shadows with a higher sense of solidity and high-resolution contours in comparison with existing shadow media. Moreover, we constructed a system that displays the shadow of a virtual light source robot that sets the light source for the shadow media along with the shadow media of the performers. We implemented moving the position of this robot (a virtual light source) according to the movements of the group of performers. Performing bodily expressions using these systems demonstrated that the expression space of the performers was expanded in comparison with existing shadow media systems. These results suggest that it is possible to support the emergence of co-creative expressions through the virtual light source robot.

Acknowledgments. This study received support from a JSPS Grant-in-Aid for Scientific Research (B) (Principal investigator: Yoshiyuki Miwa, No. 26280131) and the support of the "Principal of emergence for empathetic "Ba" and its applicability to communication technology" project at the RISE Waseda University. Graduate students Yusuke Kajita, Kento Yamaguchi, Ibuki Mizuno, Takemi Watanuk, Takahiro Sugano et al. assisted with system development and experiment execution. The authors wish to express their gratitude here.

References

1. Miwa, Y.: Co-creative expressions and communicability support. J. Soc. Instrum. Control Eng. **51**(11), 1016–1022 (2012)
2. Miwa, Y., Ishibiki, C.: Shadow communication: system for embodied interaction with remote partners. In: Proceeding of CSCW 2004, pp. 467–476 (2004)
3. Miwa, Y., Itai, S., Watanabeand, T., Nishi, H.: Shadow awareness: enhancing theater space through the mutual projection of images on a connective slit-screen. Leonardo J. Int. Soc. Arts Sci. Technol. **44**(4), 325–333 (2011). (SIGGRAPH 2011 Art paper)
4. Kajita, Y., Takahashi, T., Miwa, Y., Itai, S.: Designing the embodied shadow media using virtual three-dimensional space. In: Yamamoto, S., de Oliveira, N.P. (eds.) HIMI 2015. LNCS, vol. 9173, pp. 610–621. Springer, Heidelberg (2015). doi:10.1007/978-3-319-20618-9_60
5. Aitor, A., Marton, Z., Tombari, F., Wohlkinger, W., Potthast, C., Zeisl, B., Rusu, R., Gedikli, S., Vincze, M.: Point cloud library. IEEE Robot. Autom. Mag. **19**, 80–91 (2012)
6. Mitra, N.J., Nguyen, A.: Esting surface normal in noisy point cloud data. In: Proceedings of the Nineteenth Annual Symposium on Computational Geometry, pp. 322–328 (2003)
7. Watanabe, T., Miwa, Y.: Duality of embodiment and support for co-creation in hand contact improvisation. J. Adv. Mech. Des. Syst. Manuf. **6**(7), 1307–1319 (2012)

Image Mnemonics for Cognitive Mapping
of the Museum Exhibits

Yasushi Ikei[✉], Ken Ishigaki, Hirofumi Ota, and Keisuke Yoshida

Tokyo Metropolitan University, 6-6, Asahigaoka, Hino, Tokyo 191-0065, Japan
ikei@tmu.ac.jp

Abstract. This paper discusses a new approach to assist human learning at the museum based on spatial and graphic information on mobile devices. A technique for memorizing a number of unstructured items is called mnemonics. Although its effects were remarkable, acquiring the skill to take advantage of the mnemonics is generally difficult. The present study provides a new technique of photo montage to fully exploit the effectiveness the mnemonics by facilitating the enrollment process. The proposed method utilizes images for a memory peg that are processed with mobile devices on the fly. After the basic structure is presented, the location type virtual memory peg (vmPeg) system is discussed. The evaluation of the system on the number of memory pegs revealed its coverage up to 50. The applicability of the method to museum exhibits specifically for children was also evaluated. The results of both experiments exhibited remarkable retention that suggested positive potential of this new mobile enhanced mnemonics.

Keywords: Cognitive space · Photomontage · Learning in a museum · Mobile device

1 Introduction

Museums have long been a medium for information transfer in the form of passive acquisition of knowledge. The advent of very small mobile computers such as high performance smartphones and handheld tablet PCs is rapidly changing the learning in museums. Spatial natures brought by the portability introduced interactive information support for the visitors. Learning is more effectively achieved when the visitor is engaged with exhibits in the museum than simply looks at exhibits and reads captions of them. A memory aid is one of effective uses of mobile computers since it is with the user at the moment of information acquisition. In the conventional memorization techniques that extend human memory capacity, it is known that spatial property including location and visual image is very effective for memory retention [1].

The present study investigates the characteristics of the memorization aid, the spatial electronic mnemonics (SROM) system [2], that expands user's cognitive memory space and its applicability to the museum learning. The method takes advantage of the property of human cognitive process on the real space and visual image using mobile devices to fit the process. It solves the problem of conventional memorization techniques, and

© Springer International Publishing Switzerland 2016
S. Yamamoto (Ed.): HIMI 2016, Part II, LNCS 9735, pp. 268–277, 2016.
DOI: 10.1007/978-3-319-40397-7_26

expands the memory capacity by changing concrete external space into cognitive memory space.

2 Mobile Learning Assistance

The spatial electronic mnemonics [2] could effectively utilize both the sensation of location of a real space and its image to create a virtual cognitive external memory space based on a mobile device. The system enhances the human memory performance by conforming to its nature of the image memory superiority and the episodic memory high retention. Visual image composition is used in the system to establish the virtual memory pegs (vmPeg) that assists encoding and organization of memory items [3]. The organization of items is formatted by both the number-shape images (graphic numerals) and the photographs of places that had a serial order. The encoding and organization are intensified also by doing the arrangement of a graphic numeral on the image of a place by the user where the particular combination makes a good link between the two. It is important that the arrangement operation is performed by the user her/himself in the real space overlaying the graphic numeral on the real scene to make a virtual image space with a specific meaning as shown in Fig. 1. The essential source of effects of the vmPeg is both the series of the photomontages and the user behavior to establish them.

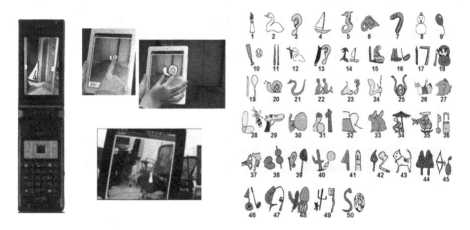

Fig. 1. SROM system running on a camera phone (left), iPad and Android terminals (center). Graphic numerals up to 50 to annotate photos (right).

The augmentation of human memory of this system has its basis on the method of loci, the peg and the link mnemonics. These traditional mnemonics have long been known [4], however they have not been in popular use because they depended heavily on the user's self-reliant effort. The SROM system as a new mobile mnemonics assists to set up a very large amount of virtual memory space extremely easily by using a smart (camera) phone and a mobile/tablet computer shown in Fig. 1.

The SROM system provides the user with cognitive mnemonic devices to effectively construct and make use of a memory space that we refer to as the external virtual memory space (eVMS). The eVMS resides in the user's mind as a cognitive map. The addressing indices to the eVMS include graphically augmented places, objects and people that are generically called as virtual memory pegs (vmPegs). The vmPeg is a cognitive tag to the location in the eVMS. Basic characteristics of the vmPeg are the same as usual memory peg such that it gives a framework of recall of many items and it is associative. However, the functions of the vmPeg are more augmented by an electronic support than the usual memory pegs.

The vmPeg has three basic features. First, it provides a framework of recall that holds many items in a randomly accessible form. It is visual and concrete for ease of encoding. Second, it is highly associative to other items or objects to memorize. Visual representation or annotation is introduced for associativity. Third, it is fast and easy to build. The vmPeg is created with an effective assistance of mobile computers to enable faster and easier acquisition, a higher retention ratio, a larger number of items, quicker and more accurate recall than conventional methods.

A vmPeg has three source material types on which it is built, and further three attributes for each of three types. The types are the location type, the object type and the human character type. The location type (shown in Fig. 2) is based on places and their landmarks where we can go in front of them or imagine standing before the scene. The object type is created from any objects in the world. The human character type is based on any person figures. The three attributes of each type define differences in the sources: familiar, real, and virtual ones. A familiar type vmPeg is based on places, objects, and people that are a real and familiar easy to recall for the user. A real type vmPeg is made of real places, objects, and people on the earth that may not be accessible or easy to access for the user. It includes famous places, persons, art works, or expensive products. A virtual type vmPeg is a place, object and avatar created in a virtual environment.

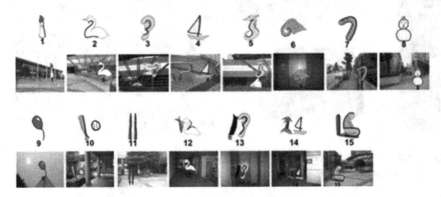

Fig. 2. Location type virtual memory pegs (vmPegs) composed of a photograph of a place and the annotation of a graphic numeral.

The SROM system includes three basic operations to manipulate the eVMS through the vmPegs.

1. Registration of vmPegs: to build vmPegs so that they work as a framework for addressing the eVMS.

2. Association of vmPegs: with targets to memorize. The vmPeg establishes relation to other items and objects with high later retention.
3. Assisting recall: by adaptive adjustment of a vmPeg to control characteristics of functions of voluntary recall and deletion of item in the eVMS.

3   Spatial Mnemonic Performance in the Location Type VmPegs

3.1   Objective of Evaluation

Although the vmPeg is essentially a cognitive item, its apparent, prior form is a composite picture (photomontage) that the user made by combining a number figure with the background scene at the place. By using smartphone, the composition is easily performed. This combination process including adjustment input is crucial for memorization. In addition, the number of usable vmPegs determines the practical utility when the user memorizes items for the task demand. We conducted an evaluation experiment that focused on the relations between the size (length) of the vmPegs and the recall ratio of them since the number of items of interest in a museum may tend to be large.

By comparing the recall ratios in the cases that the number of locations was set to 25 and 50, we examined the dependency of the SROM's memorization performance on the vmPeg length. The control condition was the memorization without the SROM support. The recall ratio was recorded with three time delays of immediately after the memorization, two days later, and a week later.

3.2   Procedure

The participant took pictures at the places arbitrarily selected in the university campus by a camera phone after the participant started to walk from the designated start point to the end point. The distance between the two points was about 100 m. The number of places to take pictures was 25 and 50. The subject learned the graphic numerals for a short time before the experiment.

In the SROM condition, the participant made a photomontage by placing a graphic numeral displayed on the screen of the camera phone with live background scene. Figure 3-left shows an example vmPeg that a participant composed in which the second graphic numeral of 'swan' was riding on a bicycle. After taking (composing) a shot of a place, the recorded picture was displayed on the phone screen for five seconds in the both cases where the graphic numeral was on the screen or not (control condition). The participant was asked to remember the picture (the vmPeg or a simple scene) during the five seconds. Twenty-five locations were memorized by vmPegs shown in Fig. 3-right in the case of SROM condition. After each shot, the participant was asked to do a mental calculation task—subtraction from a three-digit number on the screen by 3 repeatedly—to prevent the rehearsal of the image of the place until s/he reached to the next place.

Fig. 3. A vmPeg composed of a bicycle and a swan as the second place (left). The series of 25 vmPegs created by a participant with a camera phone (right).

Two minutes after the participant finished all the shots and compositions, the participant answered the places orally according to the indication of Arabic number shown on a computer screen. The answer voice was recorded by a sound recorder. Correct answer feedback was not provided to the participant. Both the random order recall and the serial recall were performed in this order. Every participant performed both (SROM and without SROM) conditions with a separation of an hour. In order to investigate the long term retention of the vmPegs, the participant was asked to recall the places two days later and one week later without notice. Again, no answer feedback was given.

The six students from the university and graduate school volunteered to perform the experiment. All of them reported their normal visual acuity and memory performance. The participants and places for the experiments were different between the two sets of 25 and 50 locations.

3.3 Results and Discussion

Figure 3-right shows twenty-five photomontages (vmPegs) created by one of the participants. The graphic numerals looks to be placed at an appropriate position to make a meaning for later easy recall. The recall ratios for 25 and 50 locations are shown in Fig. 4a and b, respectively. Three delay-times (0, 2, and 7-day delay) are in different colors. The participant answered both in a random order and then in a serial order according to the designated Arabic number on the PC screen.

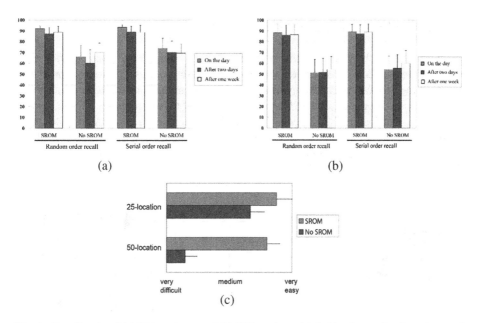

Fig. 4. Recall ratio of (a) 25 locations, and (b) 50 locations. (c) Subjective evaluation of ease of memorization. (Color figure online)

The result of the SROM condition for 25 locations (Fig. 4a) was markedly higher than the no SROM condition. With the SROM the participants correctly answered around 90 % of 25 locations. The decrease of the ratio after seven days was very small, which indicates that the retainment of memory was highly stable. On the other hand, the ratio without the SROM was 60-70 % correct answer in both random and serial order recalls.

This advantage of SROM condition was also observed in the 50-location experiment. The difference between SROM and no-SROM conditions rather increased as compared to the 25-location condition, while the SROM condition retained 90 % level correct answer ratio. The ratio of no-SROM condition was only 50 % level. Note that the high correct answer ratio of SROM was almost constant despite the increase in number of items to remember. The order of recall report—random or serial—had no effect on the recall ratio.

The result of subjective evaluation on the ease of memorization by a questionnaire is summarized in Fig. 4c. The participants reported a higher score for the SROM conditions than no SROMs. A marked difference was observed in the 50-location recall. The difference in ease of recall between conditions of SROM and no SROM was smaller in the 25-location condition. The advantage of the SROM seems to increase along with the amount of locations. On the other hand, the effort level that was induced to memorize locations was lower in the SROM than no SROM. However, a few subjects reported that they had a difficulty in relating a graphic numeral to the background scene in the case where two graphics looked to have little relation.

4   Application to Museum Exhibit Learning

To investigate practical applicability of the SROM, the authors conducted an evaluation experiment at the Science Museum in Tokyo. The museum exhibit is one of appropriate targets of the SROM system. Many objects in the museum may be easily forgotten even after a long-duration tour. The SROM system was used to remember the exhibit objects in the room that featured the science of gas. The participants were sixteen children of an age of elementary school (9 to 12 years old, the mean age was 10.5) who visited the museum during the winter holidays. We solicited children around the exhibition room of gas on the third floor (Fig. 5 center).

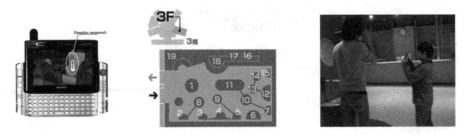

Fig. 5. SROM installed handy mobile PC (left. Vaio-U, Sony Corp.). Exhibition room featuring 'gas science' on the third floor (center). The image composition by a child with the experimenter (right).

A light-weight mobile PC (Sony, 500 g) with a touch sensitive screen was used for an easy operation. Moreover, the graphic numeral was made movable in the display by the finger. We asked the participant to walk with the PC and take a picture of exhibits using the method of SROM and without the SROM for comparison. The number of locations to remember was reduced to ten taking the age into consideration. Thus, we used only five graphic numerals so that the participant learned the numerals with only a glance. Also, testing the memory retention of participants after the memorization experiment was performed in the form of recognition in stead of recall.

4.1   Evaluation Procedure

The participant went through the exhibit room of the gas science shown in Fig. 5 after he/she received an instruction from the experimenter. The experimenter guided the participant. The participant took pictures of ten exhibits in total with the graphic numeral overlaid for odd-numbered places and without it at the even-numbered places. The experimenter asked the participant to take a picture by framing and touching the screen to position an overlaid graphic around the exhibit. After the shot, the picture was displayed for 5 s for memorization. Then a 'next' button appears on the display; the participant pushed it when he/she moved to the next exhibit to shoot. At even-numbered places the display showed Arabic number of the place outside the video frame of the mobile PC. After the all shoots in front of the exhibits, we showed printed graphic numerals to the participants while they were answering to the questionnaire. The recognition test asked which of photographs was that he/she shot and where it was in the sequence from 1 to 10. We printed twenty pictures which included on the sheet ten additional pictures (distractors) the experimenter took beforehand. The participant wrote the number under the pictures.

4.2   Results

Figures 6 and 7 show the photographs the participant took and composed (left). The graphic numerals were appropriately placed to be memorized easily. These images indicate that the system was very easy to use even for a child.

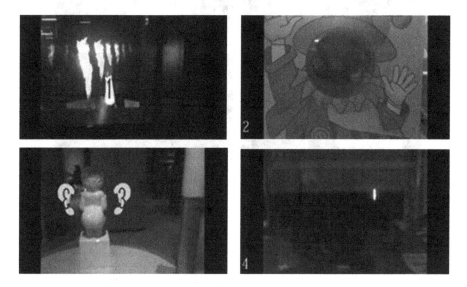

Fig. 6. Composed images (left) and shot (no composition) images (right) by a participant

The recognition ratio is shown in Fig. 8a. The score of the SROM condition was significantly higher than no SROM which suggested the SROM was effective in memorization also for school-age children. Figure 8b indicates the time for taking a picture of one exhibit. It took 14 s for the SROM, and sec without the SROM. The difference was statistically significant. It is considered that the five seconds were spent for composition of the photograph. This short-time easy operation to adjust the graphic numeral on the exhibit scene seemed very effective to increase attention to the exhibit object and to create a strong vmPeg for the later recall. The higher recognition ratio suggests that memorization and recall ratio would also be increased for the exhibit objects if so performed since the vmPeg seemed to have been successfully built. The utility of the vmPeg applied to the museum exhibit is more based on the graphic numeral than location cue since the visitor is usually not familiar with the layout of the exhibits. The recall clue provided by the vmPeg seemed much dependent on the composition task of the photomontage.

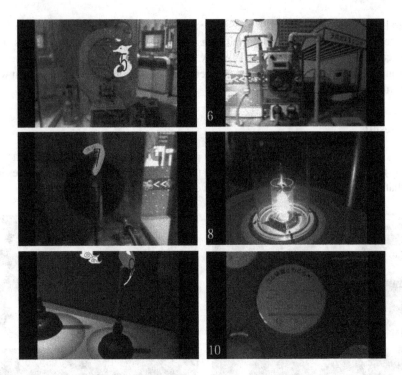

Fig. 7. Composed images (left) and shot (no composition) images (right) by a participant, continued.

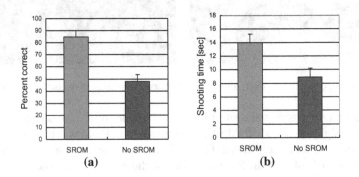

Fig. 8. (a) Recognition ratio for the exhibits. (b) Time for shooting one exhibit. (Error bars show SEM). (Color figure online)

5   Conclusion

We presented the basic concept of a spatial electronic mnemonics (SROM) that is based on a photomontage performed by a mobile device at the location in a very short time duration. According to the results of the evaluation experiment, the effectiveness of the method was maintained even when the number of vmPegs (locations) was doubled from

25 to 50. The application of the system to the museum exhibit suggested its effectiveness even for the elementary school children. The exhibit items could be mapped to the cognitive space, which might form the base of learning in the museum.

The future work includes the assistance of the composition task in addition to the support for the next stages of the association aid and the recall aid.

Acknowledgment. The authors would like to thank the Science Museum run by The Japan Science Foundation for an experiment support. This research was partly supported by JSPS KAKENHI Grant Number 26560125.

References

1. O'Brien, D.: Learn to Remember. Duncan Baird Publishers, London (2000)
2. Ikei, Y., Ota, H.: Spatial electronic mnemonics for augmentation of human memory. In: Proceedings of the IEEE Virtual Reality 2008, pp. 217-224 (2008)
3. Bellezza, F.: Mnemonic devices: classification, characteristics, and criteria. Rev. Educ. Res. **51**(2), 247–275 (1981)
4. Carruthers, M.: The Book of Memory: A Study of Memory in Medieval Culture. Cambridge University Press, Cambridge (1990)

AR Reference Model for K-Culture Time Machine

Eunseok Kim[1], Junghoon Jo[1], Kihong Kim[1], Sunhyuck Kim[2],
Seungmo Hong[2(✉)], Jea-In Kim[3], Noh-young Park[3], Hyerim Park[3],
Tamás Matuszka[3], Jungwha Kim[3(✉)], and Woontack Woo[3(✉)]

[1] Culture Technology Research Institute, KAIST, Deajeon, Korea
{scbgm,jojh,kihongkim}@kaist.ac.kr
[2] Postmedia Corp., Seoul, Korea
{sunny1015,hsm}@postmedia.co.kr
[3] Graduate School of Culture Technology, KAIST, Deajeon, Korea
{jeainkim86,nypark,ilihot,tamas.matuszka,
Jungwhakim,wwoo}@kaist.ac.kr

Abstract. In this paper, we introduce the K-Culture Time Machine Project, which develops a mobile AR platform for visualizing time-space connected cultural contents of Korea. Existing AR Applications in cultural heritage domains are currently not interoperable and cannot reuse content. To solve this problem, we developed the modified AR reference model as generic framework of a context-aware AR platform; and we developed the context-aware AR platform with several core technologies according to this model. For back-end, we established the Korean Cultural Heritage Data Model (KCHDM) to aggregate the heterogeneous cultural heritage databases in Korea. We also developed the semi-auto time-space correlation generation module for domain experts. Moreover, we developed the authoring tool to generate the time-space connected AR contents. For the front-end, we developed the vision- and sensor-based spatial data composition technology to perform the solid tracking in outdoor environment and context-aware AR framework. Through the UI/UX and 3D contents, whole technologies are packaged into the mobile AR platform. As a validation process for the application, a mobile AR application for the Korean world cultural heritage was developed. Based on this project, an interoperable AR platform that responds with heterogeneous database would be developed and smart tour guide of the cultural heritage site would be possible.

Keywords: Augmented reality · Cultural heritage domain · Context-aware · Authoring tool · K-Culture time machine project

1 Introduction

ICT (information and communications technology) has changed the mechanisms of museums and their heritage. We are now facing the era of the digital museum and digital heritage and numerous augmented reality (AR) applications in the cultural heritage domain. However, difficulties on the aggregating heterogeneous databases and the interoperability of the applications have impeded this new trend.

© Springer International Publishing Switzerland 2016
S. Yamamoto (Ed.): HIMI 2016, Part II, LNCS 9735, pp. 278–289, 2016.
DOI: 10.1007/978-3-319-40397-7_27

To overcome the issue of cultural heritage domain, we have worked with the K-Culture Time Machine project. In this project, we aggregated the heterogeneous cultural heritage databases and developed a context-aware AR platform based on this integration. After we introduced the progress of first year in this project [1], we continued in the second year toward a mobile-AR platform. Because mobile devices enables user mobility with reduced computation power, we have to solve the user localization issues in an outdoor environment with optimized algorithm and have to design the context-aware AR applications in a mobile platform.

To develop the interoperable context-aware AR platform, we designed the modified AR reference model as a blueprint of this project [2]. The modified AR reference model describes the generic workflow of the context-aware AR platform based on the MAR (Mixed Augmented Reality) reference model of ISO standard proposal [3]. According to the modified AR reference model, we have worked for the data aggregation process in the back-end, and have developed the mobile AR framework in the front-end.

Through the K-Culture Time Machine project, we expect to achieve several contributions. First, Korean Cultural Heritage Data Model (KCHDM), which is data aggregation method for heterogeneous databases in Korean cultural heritage, is a major contribution. Through this model, we expect our data model to be extended to the East-Asia Chinese character cultural area. Next, providing the context-aware AR platform in the cultural heritage domain guarantees interoperability and reusability. The modified AR reference will suggest the blueprint of the context-aware AR applications. To support these contributions, we performed standardization of these achievements. Through the standardized AR platform, compatibility and reusability of the AR applications and contents will be improved.

The structure of this paper is as follows. In Sect. 2, the technical explanation for each core technology in K-culture Time Machine Project is described. In Sect. 3, we introduce the prototype of the project and plans for the third year of the project.

2 K-Culture Time Machine with Modified AR Reference Model

As mentioned above, we developed the modified AR reference model as a structure of the project (See Fig. 1). Compared with original MAR reference model ISO standard, this modified model handles the interaction with the user and enhanced context-aware features. According to the AR reference model, we developed the mobile AR framework for the K-Culture Time Machine [4] and core technologies that are classified into two parts: back-end for integrated database and front-end for context-aware AR platform. Though the integration of these technologies, a context-aware mobile AR framework that embraces heterogeneous databases is completed.

In addition to platform development, we have been working on the standardization of our platform to disseminate the context-aware AR applications. Our ontological database aggregation method [5] and metadata schema of AR contents [6] were approved as domestic standards in 2015. Furthermore, the metadata schema for AR contents is currently prepared as international standard with MAR reference model.

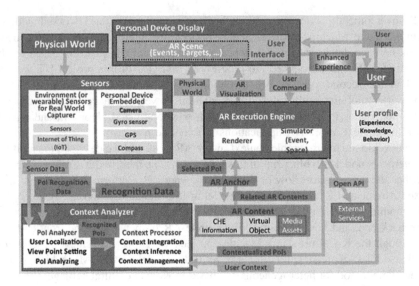

Fig. 1. Modified AR reference model. Blue boxes are originated from original MAR reference model (Color figure online).

Through these efforts, commercialization of the AR technology could be accelerated and ecosystem of the AR technology could be enlarged.

2.1   Back-End: Integrated Cultural Heritage Database Establishment

To support AR visualizations for cultural heritage, AR contents qualified with the historical records have to be generated. Although there have been several efforts to digitize the Korean cultural heritage information [7], these databases remain heterogeneous. To integrate these heterogeneous databases, we constructed the mediating ontological data model, KCHDM. After that, time-space correlations among the entities are generated with the pattern recognition analysis. Finally, the authoring tools create the time-space connected AR contents based on these correlated entities. Detailed explanations for core technology in back-end follow.

Korea Cultural Heritage Data Model (KCHDM). As data from cultural heritage vary in terms of type and properties, integrating cultural heritage databases from different institutions becomes a key issue in the cultural heritage domain. To achieve this goal, establishing a mediating ontology with the semantic relationships of the cultural heritage entity is the current trend. In Korea, each heritage institution has different goals and policy in collecting data, and their different metadata schema give rise to interoperability difficulties. To solve this issue, we developed the Korean Cultural Heritage Data Model (KCHDM). KCHDM aims at becoming an integration medium for collecting and connecting cultural heritage information provided by different institutions [8]. Therefore, constructing this data model is fundamental to the heritage data infrastructure for a semantic cultural heritage information hub in Korea.

KCHDM has concentrated on providing interoperability among heterogeneous heritage datasets and linking individual instances via semantic relationships. The main reference of the model is the Conceptual Model CIDOC-CRM, a domain ontology of heritage. Figure 2 shows the structure of our ontology model. It includes five superclasses, their instances and their properties. Superclasses provide contextual information and properties show relations among instances.

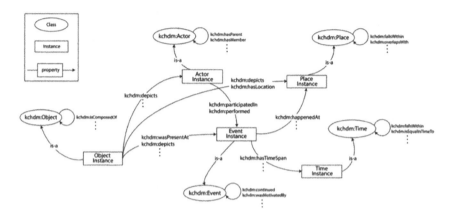

Fig. 2. KCHDM Ontology Model

To improve the semantic relationship of heritage data, more precise and rich metadata and an ontology based data model are needed. The challenge is to fill these instances of data modeling with actual information from every heritage resource. The semantic relations that are needed for ontology generation are found mostly in text sources. In the description part of the text resource, we can find semantic patterns and the related corpus that contains information on the semantic relationship. To generate instances of KCHDM, the definition of corpus pattern and extraction algorithm were applied. To derive semantic patterns from analyzed description text resources using a corpus, three phases are followed (See Fig. 3). The first phase is to parse the description text. From this, domain professionals extract semantic patterns that can explain relationships among specific resources to others. The second phase is to abstract the semantic patterns. Synonyms that have been found by domain professionals can be composed in the thesaurus library of KCHDM. After that, needless prepositions and conjunctions are removed to merge the corpuses into a same-meaning corpus. All words and related phrases that can represent certain semantic relations must be grouped by similar semantic relations and added to the ontology class of KCHDM. The third phase is to define pattern principles. These principles will be applied to the phase of mapping the raw heritage corpus to the KCHDM ontology classes and properties. As a result, semantic patterns can be used to generate every possible instance of KCHDM. These patterns are used in the process of mapping the raw heritage database to the KCHDM ontology using the semantic pattern principle.

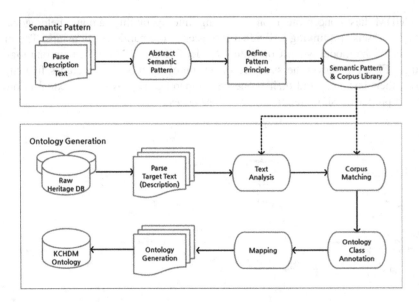

Fig. 3. KCHDM Semantic Pattern Analysis and Mapping Process

Time-Space Correlation Generation Technique. Although we have established the KCHDM ontology with the semantic pattern extraction, filling every correlation property between the entities in KCHDM ontology is still a challenge. Generating the detailed levels of time-space correlation in KCHDM ontology has to be performed by domain experts. With only a few experts, whole entities of the Korean cultural heritage cannot be correlated. Therefore, we developed semi-auto process module that provides rough correlation between entities to support the experts (See Fig. 4).

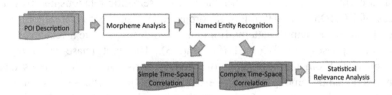

Fig. 4. Time-Space correlation generation process

In this module, every Korean description of cultural heritage in a raw database is processed by morpheme analysis. Through the morpheme analysis, named entities such as specific objects, events, or technical terms are extracted. Some of the simple correlations between specific entities are determined in this process. For the complex correlations, only relevancies between entities are statistically calculated with Pearson's correlation coefficient to support the domain expert. In this process, frequency of the term and relation between sentences become dominant factors for relevance.

AR Authoring Tool. As a channel for user participation to establish the AR contents ecosystems for sustainable service, we have been working on a 3D map-based content authoring tool framework and interface. Previous studies on AR authoring tools present the possibility of easy interaction during the authoring process. However, many issues such as usability, utility, data interaction, visualization and interactivity remain. To solve these issues and to provide easily approachable tools, we have focused on the nonprofessional, online, dynamic authoring tool. In addition, for efficient expression of the virtual reality that contains the character, connectivity and arrangement of content, we adapt a 3D map as a base platform Fig. 5.

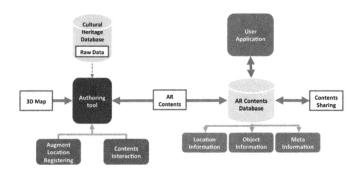

Fig. 5. Framework of the AR authoring tool

The AR authoring tool is divided into two parts: the authoring tool and the AR contents database. The authoring tool controls collected data through several types of media and generates the AR contents. The raw data retrieved from the related database are exploited in the authoring tool. Then the user designates the location of the augmentation of the data through the 3D map, and assigns the interaction of each augmented data. Through this process, raw data converted into the AR contents and AR contents database manages the AR contents generated from the authoring tool. To manage the AR contents, location information, object information and meta information of the content are tracked. The authoring tool and AR contents database are interlocked, and the AR contents can be shared by multiple users for diverse uses.

2.2   Front-End: Mobile AR Platform Development

After the AR contents are generated from the back-end, the visualization process of the AR contents is performed in front-end. In the spatial data composition module, accurate user localization in outdoor environment is made. Based on the robust tracking, the AR framework provides the visualization of the AR contents. On the other hand, the context-aware module analyzes the user context based on the sensor data. Finally, whole front-end modules are provided to the user with the UI/UX; and contents and the enhanced experience are provided to the user.

Vision- and Sensor-Based Spatial Data Composition. Integration between physical reality and virtual reality is core of the AR visualization. In this respect, tracking is the essential part of the AR. To support cultural heritage AR applications, tracking in the outdoor environment has to be supported. Enabling robust outdoor tracking is the most significant problem of current AR research.

The scope of AR environments has expanded from local 2D patterns to global 3D spaces. The latest research attempts to enlarge the operating environment of AR. But the state-of-the-art in this research area is still limited in scale expandability and data reusability for dynamic scene changes. Therefore, in this project we proposed the concept to build and maintain a large-scale AR outdoor workspace which can manage dynamic scene changes, and provide accurate and stable user camera localization and tracking.

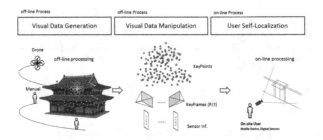

Fig. 6. Overall procedure of dataset management concept for outdoor AR.

The proposed system consists of three functionalities: (1) creating the AR dataset; (2) maintaining the AR dataset; and (3) supporting AR visualization. Figure 6 shows the overall procedure of our approach.

Feature-Based 3D Point Dataset Creation. In order to provide an accurate and robust 6-DoF (Degree-of-Freedom) camera pose to user, we applied keyframe-based 3D point reconstruction method. By the feature point-based SfM (Structure-from-Motion) and bundle adjustment [9], 3D point cloud and keyframes are created. Each keyframe has relative pose $(R|t)$ from the local coordinate system and the 3D point P has its local 3D coordinate (x, y, z).

Maintaining the 3D Reference Dataset. To provide robust tracking under a variety of dynamic scene changes (e.g. geometrical, seasonal, light condition changes) we proposed a maintaining algorithm for the 3D reference dataset. This algorithm exploits feature matching information by users. When user attempts nth image matching with the pi in the reference dataset, a reference point pi get a score information by re-projection error E_{ref}, then the maintaining process saves this information in linked queue $Q(i, n)$ as in (1). After that, if the linked queue is full, the maintaining process decides termination or addition of the p_i as in (2).

$$\text{if } Q(i, n) =, 1 Eref < w, \text{ or } Q(i, n) = 0 \text{ if } Eref \geq w \qquad (1)$$

$$\sum Q(i, j) / n < dthresh \qquad (2)$$

Supporting AR Visualization. Accurate 6-DoF camera pose is calculated by matching 2D images with modified 3D point dataset. This module calculates 3D to 2D correspondence to find optimal pose of camera. This pose matrix also used estimating user self-localization information.

Mobile AR Framework. To perform the actual visualization process of the AR contents, we developed a mobile AR/VR framework that can convert interchangeably from 2D map view and AR/VR view based on the actual user location and point of interest (PoI). In this framework, we assumed that the user wants to retrieve the information related with PoI such as "where is PoI" or "what is PoI." A user located far away from a given PoI will receive the location of the PoI from the system. PoI location's information on the 2D map enables users to easily find routes and approach PoI. When the user approaches the region of interest (RoI) where many PoI are located, the system converts to AR/VR view displaying the information of PoI's location that is a three dimensional point. Based on that, users can access the PoI's information retrieved from the integrated data.

The idea behind the PoI's information display is to provide additional information to the user about a selected Point of Interest. The above-mentioned KCDHM ontology serves as a knowledge base of our application. The user is able to see the textual description and the corresponding multimedia content (e.g. images, videos, audio sound) of a Point of Interest, among other things. The related POIs that represent objects, events, places, actors or times can also be seen by means of the mobile application. The entities of the knowledge have been interlinked; therefore, the users are enabled to discover the whole dataset starting from a selected POI. Due to this solution, the information displaying can be considered as a knowledge base browser that can contribute to the exploration of the Korean cultural heritage.

Context-Aware Features. To provide the smart AR guidance, we studied the context-awareness for the AR environment. Providing appropriate multimedia AR contents while considering user context is a goal. Much research provides the new media experience using multimedia resources in an Augmented Reality environment [10, 11]. However, most have not considered necessary context of related objects in AR environment. For example, they have used only limited context such as location and simple user profile [12, 13], and the simplest context-reasoning model such as key-value for user-centric service [14, 15]. Therefore, we have indicated the issue and designed 5W1H (Who, When, Where, What, How, Why) metadata schema to provide the new multimedia service in AR environment [16].

In the context-aware feature module, using the metadata integrates the context of places where multimedia content is displayed, users who consume the content and content that is provided through the AR framework. From the combined context, based on the 5W1H metadata schema, it infers the user's preference and situation and provides adaptive ubiquitous media service.

As the first stage of context-aware AR multimedia service, context-aware video service is being implemented. This module uses metadata from three classes such as AR Content class, Media Asset class and PoI class. AR Content class includes bibliographic data of video collected from 'IMDb'(Internet Movie Database) by web crawling (See Fig. 7). In PoI class, the GPS data and the name of the filming location addresses are stored using map API. In Media Asset class, we use GPS, Camera height (Altitude), Compass, and Gyro metadata of a video clip to guide the user to the shooting position where the video clip was filmed and order metadata to provide the experience of following the story based on the filming locations. Usually, because video clips do not have this kind of metadata, this part should be manually inserted to the database table.

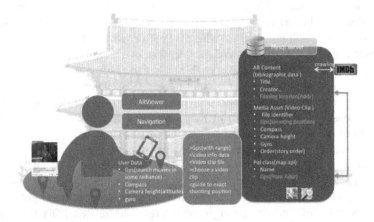

Fig. 7. Context-aware AR service based on the AR applications metadata

UI/UX & Contents. For the appropriate interaction with users, the UI of the mobile application has to be designed for the visualization of the culture heritage information and AR interaction. Meanwhile, the UI must present the overall structure of the integrated ontology and support tour guide service with dynamic interactivity. To fulfill these demands, the main concept of the UI is determined to be a "time machine" so that users can experience past times of the cultural heritage site through the augmentation of related AR contents. In addition to this concept, information about the cultural heritage is not offered independently, but is shown with related heritage (See Fig. 8). Therefore,

Fig. 8. User Interface for the K-Culture Time Machine project

users can see related object, related person, related place and related event of the heritage through this UI.

Moreover, to provide the enhanced experience to users, various types of contents have to be used. However, handling 3D model and movie requires sufficient computation power and network bandwidth. Therefore we developed optimized 3D models and movies for the mobile platform. In this the process, number of polygon used in the model is reduced and the texture composition is modified to reduce the size and processing time of the contents.

3 Prototype and Third Year Plan

Based on the AR platform we have been developing, we built the mobile AR applications for cultural heritages of Seoul as a prototype. In this application, several PoIs of the central historical places in Seoul are covered. In this application, dynamic data retrieval from the existing cultural heritage database is performed based on the KCHDM. After that, AR and VR visualize the data in the application. In AR visualization, sensor-based user localization and 3D PoI detection is made. To overcome the spatial limitation of AR requiring the user to be located near the PoI and to relieve the unstable tracking technology, we developed 360° panorama video-based VR module. Using this VR module, users can experience the AR contents in any place without tracking.

Figure 9 shows the screenshot of the time machine feature that enables the user to experience the past view of the cultural heritage site, using AR visualization. When the application recognizes the PoI in the camera stream data, it then accesses the existing cultural heritage database to find the related contents. Within the data, there can be several historical heritages that show the past of the PoI. Then, the application overlays the heritage site for specific times that selected by user on the PoI.

Fig. 9. Screenshot of the K-Culture Time Machine application

For the evaluation, we plan to open the trial service for the cultural heritage of Seoul in April of 2016, when usability testing will be performed. Through this trail service, evaluation of the user guidance, comparison between the contents delivery media (AR/VR, several type of media asset) and suggestions on the context-aware features will be made.

In the third year of this project, we plan to develop the wearable AR platform for cultural heritage. Among the various types of wearable devices, we target the optical see-through type of wearable glasses as our next platform. Several wearable glasses are available to the public and will be utilized in this project.

4   Conclusion

In this paper, we introduced the second year progress of the K-culture time machine project for context-aware mobile-AR platform. To consolidate the foundation, we develop and standardize the KCHDM to aggregate heterogeneous databases and AR contents metadata for visualizing and sharing, in order to establish a reusable and compatible AR framework. Based on this groundwork, we have developed a time-space correlation generation technique to provide the basis for the AR visualization, and authoring tool for user participation, the spatial data composition module to integrate the dual space, a context-aware AR platform to support smart tour guide, and UI/UX and 3D contents for optimized user interaction according to the platform.

Through this work, we developed the interoperable AR service in the cultural heritage domain. For the heterogeneous raw database, we developed the standardized aggregation data model. Moreover, we developed the modified AR reference model and the AR content metadata for AR visualizations. Our work guarantees reusability and compatibility. In addition, we made the AR authoring tool for user participation to establish the AR contents ecosystems. This authoring tool will support the sustainable service with user-generated contents.

For the third year, we target the optical see-through wearable device as our next platform and will concentrate on the users' convenience of service. During the third year, we expect that more a reliable and smart service for the cultural heritage sites will be made.

References

1. Ha, T., Kim, Y., Kim, E., Kim, K., Lim, S., Hong, S., Kim, J., Kim, S., Kim, J., Woo, W.: K-culture time machine: development of creation and provision technology for time-space-connected cultural contents. In: Yamamoto, S., Oliveira, N.P. (eds.) HIMI 2015. LNCS, vol. 9173, pp. 428–435. Springer, Heidelberg (2015). doi:10.1007/978-3-319-20618-9_43
2. Kim, E., Kim, J., Woo, W.: Metadata Schema for Context-Aware Augmented Reality Application in Cultural Heritage Domain. In: 2015 proceedings of Digital Heritage (2015)

3. ISO, Mixed and augmented reality (MAR) concepts and reference model part 3: Real character representation, International Organization for Standardization, Geneva, Switzerland, ISO ISO/IEC CD 18521-3, 2014

4. Kim, E., Woo, W.: Augmented reality based space-telling framework for archeological site tours (Korean). J. HCI Korea **14**(4), 1–10 (2015)

5. Telecommunications Technology Association (TTA), Context-based Metadata Model for Cultural Heritage Data Aggregation, Korea, TTAK.KO-10.0850

6. Telecommunications Technology Association (TTA), Metadata Schema for Visualization and Sharing of the Augmented Reality Contents, Korea, TTAK.KO-10.0851

7. Cultural heritage digital hub-bank, http://hub.cha.go.kr

8. Kim, S., Ahn, J., Suh, J., Kim, H., Kim, J.: Towards a Semantic Data Infrastructure for Heterogeneous Cultural Heritage Data. In: 2015 proceedings of Digital Heritage (2015)

9. Snavely, N., Seitz, S., Szeliski, R.: Modeling the world from internet phopto collections. Int. J. Comput. Vis. **80**(2), 189–210 (2008)

10. MacIntyre, B., Bolter, J.D., Moreno, E., Hannigan, B.: Augmented reality as a new media experience. In: Proceedings of IEEE and ACM International Symposium on Augmented Reality, 2001, pp. 197–206. IEEE (2001)

11. Shilkrot, R., Montfort, N. Maes, P.: nARratives of augmented worlds. In: IEEE International Symposium on Mixed and Augmented Reality-Media, Art, Social Science, Humanities and Design (ISMAR-MASH'D), September 2014, pp. 35–42. IEEE (2014)

12. Santos, P., Stork, A., Linaza, M.T., Machui, O., McIntyre, D., Jorge, E.: CINeSPACE: interactive access to cultural heritage while on-the-move. In: Schuler, D. (ed.) HCII 2007 and OCSC 2007. LNCS, vol. 4564, pp. 435–444. Springer, Heidelberg (2007)

13. Jang, S., Woo, W.: Framework for personalized user interface by sharing user-centric context between real and virtual environments. IEICE Trans. on Inf. Syst. **89**(5), 1694–1701 (2006)

14. Xu, C., Cheung, S.C., Chan, W.K., Ye, C.: Partial constraint checking for context consistency in pervasive computing. ACM Trans. Softw. Eng. Methodol. (TOSEM) **19**(3), 9 (2010)

15. Zhang, D., Huang, H., Lai, C.F., Liang, X., Zou, Q., Guo, M.: Survey on context-awareness in ubiquitous media. Multimedia Tools Appl. **67**(1), 179–211 (2013)

16. Park, H.,Woo, W.: Metadata design for location-based film experience in augmented places. In: IEEE International Symposium on Mixed and Augmented Reality-Media, Art, Social Science, Humanities and Design (ISMAR-MASH'D), 2015, pp. 40–45. IEEE. (2015)

Encouraging People to Interact with Interactive Systems in Public Spaces by Managing Lines of Participants

Takuji Narumi[1(✉)], Hiroyuki Yabe[1], Shunsuke Yoshida[2],
Tomohiro Tanikawa[1], and Michitaka Hirose[1]

[1] Graduate School of Information Science and Technology,
The University of Tokyo, 7-3-1 Hongo, Bunkyō, Tokyo 113-8656, Japan
{narumi,yabe,tani,hirose}@cyber.t.u-tokyo.ac.jp
[2] National Institute of Information and Communications Technology,
3-5 Hikaridai, Seika, Kyoto 619-0289, Japan
shun@nict.go.jp

Abstract. To attract visitors and encourage them to interact with interactive systems such as digital exhibitions, digital public art, and digital signage in public spaces, this paper proposes a method to not only attract passersby's attention but also maintain their attention until they interact with them by managing the situation in which someone is experiencing it and several people are forming a line. Our proposed method changes the experience time of the interactive system based on the presence of people interacting with the system. The experiments, held in real public spaces, showed that the proposed method counteracted the negative effect of crowded situations (which resulted from attracting many passersby), and increased the number of people who interacted with the system.

Keywords: Interactive media · Public space · Digital signage · Digital public art · Digital museum

1 Introduction

Recently, museums have introduced digital technologies into their exhibition methods to effectively provide supplementary background information regarding their exhibits [1–3]. In digital exhibition methods, interactivity plays an important role in stimulating interest and facilitating learning [4].

Interactive digital art and digital exhibition methods in museums have become popular; additionally, interactive art and entertainment in public spaces are emerging. Digital public art, which combines public art and digital art [5, 6], is gradually increasing in popularity. What distinguishes digital public artwork is its technological ability to explicitly interact with audiences. By importing the concept of interactivity, digital public art can create a vivid picture of the current state of the community or individuals related to the public place, and motivate them to become more positively involved in public concerns.

© Springer International Publishing Switzerland 2016
S. Yamamoto (Ed.): HIMI 2016, Part II, LNCS 9735, pp. 290–299, 2016.
DOI: 10.1007/978-3-319-40397-7_28

Interactive media, not only in the form of exhibitions or artwork, but also in the form of media for advertisement, is coming into widespread use in public spaces. Recently, digital signage and information kiosk machines have added large screens with touch panels. The interactivity of digital signage realizes on-demand provision of information based on user input. Moreover, some of these systems offer to share user-generated content on the screen within groups and communities [7]. This kind of interaction leads to the collection of more information and provides greater value to viewers.

As described above, the interactivity of digital media in public spaces has substantial merits. On the other hand, these merits are provided only to people who interact with these systems in the correct manner. When visitors interact with them incorrectly or do not interact with them at all, they do not obtain the expected benefits. In previous research, researchers carefully observed visitors moving around digital public artwork, and reported that 15 % of visitors paid attention to the artwork but only 5 % interacted with it [8]. Therefore, to ensure that all visitors can benefit, it is necessary to attract visitors and encourage them to interact with interactive media in public spaces.

One direct approach for attracting people to interactive media is to change the method of displaying the content [9, 10]. Display methods are sometimes effective, but the contents themselves might need to be modified to achieve the effect. Therefore, one often strongly constrains the content presented in the media. Another approach is changing the environment such as the space, lighting, sound, and temperature near the interactive media [11–13]. Previous research confirms that this kind of ambient information can trigger behavioral changes in public spaces [11]. However, these methods cannot be realized only using modifications of the interactive media and their content. Therefore, the applicability of this approach is limited to special situations.

As an alternative approach, we focused on the influence of others, i.e., behavioral contagion. Joint attention refers to a social-communicative skill used by humans to share attention directed at interesting objects or events with others via implicit and explicit indications such as gestures and gaze. Because of this joint attention, we tend to be attracted to objects or events that others are looking at. Behavioral contagion is a type of social influence based on this kind of skill; it refers to the propensity for certain behaviors exhibited by one person to be copied by others who are in the vicinity of the original actor. Milgram et al. reported that the larger the size of a stimulus crowd standing on a busy city street looking up at a building, the more frequently passersby adopt the behavior of the crowd [14]. These influences on others can be used for attracting people's attention to particular objects or events. This phenomenon is already utilized for supporting navigation in virtual environments using virtual agents. For example, virtual humans can give directions or transport users to locations [15]. Other research proposed the use of a flock of virtual animals to indicate interesting places in a virtual environment, and confirmed this method's effectiveness [16]. Additionally, to instruct users on how to interact with an exhibit in a museum, a system that records and three-dimensionally superimposes past visitor interactions around the exhibit was proposed [17]. In this system, visitors see the behaviors of previous visitors, and thereby, obtain a better understanding of the exhibit. These related studies focus on a virtual environment, not a real public space.

In this research, we propose a method of attracting passersby's attention to interactive systems in a public space by creating a situation in which someone is experiencing it and several people are forming a line. As mentioned above, people tend to more frequently direct their attention to interactive systems when they see that someone else is interacting with it. On the other hand, if the line for experiencing the system is too long, the system will no longer be able to maintain their attention and interest. Therefore, in our method, we focus on managing the length of the line by changing the duration of each interactive experience provided by the interactive system. In this paper, we investigate the effect of the viewing situation of people around an interactive system on passersby's behavior through an experiment at a mall, and evaluate the effect of the proposed method, which manages the viewing situation around the system.

2 Investigation of the Effect of Viewing Situation of People Around an Interactive System on Passersby's Behavior

2.1 Experimental Setup

In this chapter, we describe an experiment used to investigate the effect of the viewing situation of people around an interactive system on passersby's behavior. For this experiment, we installed a digital public artwork at GRAND FRONT OSAKA. GRAND FRONT OSAKA is a commercial complex in Osaka, Japan.

The artwork used was "Sharelog 3D," which is an extended version of interactive artwork "Sharelog" [8] that utilizes the IC card for a train fare system as an interaction device in a public space and visualizes the history of the trains that the user has taken (Fig. 1). The IC card for the train fare system in Japan is popular; it can even act as a personal ID. In a previous study, we confirmed that interaction using the IC card for the fare system is accepted socially, although personal travel records are (anonymously) exposed to the public [8].

Fig. 1. Sharelog 3D, Exhibited at GRAND FRONT OSAKA

In this experimental exhibition, Sharelog 3D visualizes a travel path on a local city map on a 200-in. public glasses-free 3D display [18]. Each IC card has records of up to 20 recent transactions for train travel. A migration path for each participant is generated based on records stored on his/her IC card.

Initially, the display only shows the map. When a participant put his/her IC card on the installation, the travel path is visualized as a trajectory of light spots on the map. This process takes 30 to 60 s. The time required to draw the pathways depends on the number of travel records stored. After all of the pathways have been drawn, they are shown for 180 s, and then, fade out.

We analyzed the relationship between the behavior of passersby in the mall and the situation surrounding the interactive artwork. Over the course of two days, 2,527 people were observed.

2.2 Hypothesis

In the analysis, we categorized the behavior of passersby into five stages. The first stage is "Passing": the passerby only passes by the artwork. The second stage is "Looking": s/he looks at the artwork. The third stage is "Stopping": s/he stops in front of the artwork. The fourth stage is "Approaching": s/he moves closer to the artwork. The fifth stage is "Experiencing": s/he interacts with the artwork. These stages are based on the step-by-step procedures for interacting with an interactive system, and a lower step is included in an upper step. Then if the passerby saw the artwork, stopped in front of it, and approached to it, his/her behavior is categorized as "Approaching." If the passerby saw the artwork and approached to it without stopping, his/her behavior is also categorized as "Approaching."

We also categorized the situation surrounding the artwork into four categories. The first category is the situation in which there is only one passerby near the artwork and it shows only the map (NoOne). The second category is the situation in which there is only one passerby near the artwork but it shows the trajectory of others who previously interacted with it (Trace). The third category is the situation in which another person is looking at the artwork when s/he arrives (OtherLooking). The fourth category is the situation in which another person is interacting with the artwork by touching his/her IC card when s/he arrives (OtherExperiencing).

People will more frequently direct their attention to interactive systems when they see someone else trying it. Therefore, we hypothesized that the number of Looking/Stopping/Approaching/Experiencing people would increase under the OtherLooking/OtherExperiencing conditions, relative to under the NoOne condition (Hypothesis 1). We also hypothesized that the Trace condition would have a weak effect that increases the number of Looking/Stopping/Approaching/Experiencing people, relative to under the NoOne condition, because the drawn trajectory attracts the attention of passersby (Hypothesis 2).

2.3   Results and Discussion

The results of passerby observations organized in terms of the behavioral stages and the situation around the artwork are shown in Fig. 2. We used the chi-square test for the percentage of each behavioral stage by the situation surrounding the artwork. This test revealed that there is a significant difference in the distribution of behavioral stages among all conditions, except between NoOne and Trace conditions ($p < 0.01$). Residual analysis revealed that the number of Looking/Stopping people increases under the OtherLooking/OtherExperiencing conditions, relative to that under the NoOne/ Trace conditions ($p < 0.01$). There is no significant difference in the number of Approaching/Experiencing people, regardless of situation. The analysis also reveals that the state transition probability between Passing and Stopping increases under the OtherLooking/OtherExperiencing conditions ($p < 0.01$). On the other hand, the analysis also revealed that the probability of changing between Stopping and Approaching decreases under the OtherLooking/OtherExperiencing conditions ($p < 0.01$).

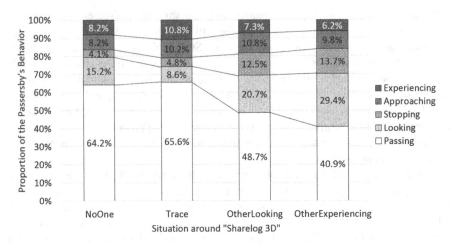

Fig. 2. Passersby's behavior toward the digital public artwork based on the surrounding situation. (Color figure online)

Hypothesis 2 was rejected based on the results of this experiment. Although some clues as to the kind of experience were provided, passerby did not pay attention to them. Therefore, showing the traces that resulted from previous interactions is not sufficient to attract attention to the work in a public space.

As we assumed in Hypothesis 1, passersby were more frequently attracted to the artwork when they saw someone else interacting with it. However, only the number of Looking/Stopping people increased under the OtherLooking/OtherExperiencing conditions; the number of Experiencing people did not increase, although the passersby were attracted to the artwork. This phenomenon may be caused by loss of interest. If a passerby has an interest in experiencing the artwork when s/he watches another person trying it, s/he must wait until the person who is experiencing it finishes and moves away. The more passersby that are interested in the artwork, the longer the waiting time for the experience. If the line for experiencing it is too long, the work will no longer be able to maintain their attention and interest. In this case, the number of people who experienced the work did not increase, although passersby were' attracted to the artwork. Therefore, a method for managing the length of the line based on the situation around the interactive system is required for avoiding losing passersby's interest and increasing the number of people who can experience the work.

3 Encouraging People to Interact with Interactive Systems in Public Spaces by Managing the Viewing Situation of People Around Them

3.1 Balancing the Social Effect of Attracting People and Encouraging Them to Interact Based on Adaptive Control of Experience Duration

The results of the experiment described in the previous chapter indicated that the presence of others who are interacting with the interactive systems has the advantage of enhancing the interest of people around them, but also has to the disadvantage of decreasing the number of people who can interact with it overall, because of the long waiting time. Therefore, it is useful to balance these social effects and thereby increase the number of people who interact with the system.

Therefore, in this work, we propose a method for managing the length of the line by controlling the experience duration based on the situation surrounding the interactive system so as to avoid losing passerby interest, and thus, increase the number of people who experience the work. To investigate the feasibility of the proposed method, we modified the Sharelog 3D system to allow control of the experience duration. This modification enable us to change the display time for the pathways with three levels: Slow (×1.8), Normal (×1.0), and Fast (×0.6).

Fast drawing shortens the experience duration, and decreases the waiting time for people waiting in line. On the other hand, if the passersby gather around the work sparsely, the chance of showing another user's interaction also decreases. Then, in some cases, it loses the social effect of attracting people to the work.

Our proposed method changes the drawing speed based on the situation of people around the system. If there are passersby who are waiting to experience the work, the system changes the display time to Fast (×0.6), and thus, shortens the experience duration. On the other hand, if there is no passerby around the work, the system changes the display time to Slow (×1.8), and thus, lengthens the experience duration. By doing so, the system aims to increase the chance of showing the other user's interaction to passersby.

3.2 Evaluation of the Balancing Method in a Public Spaces

To evaluate the effect of the proposed method, we performed an experiment in a public space. The experimental setup is almost the same as that described in Sect. 2.1. We compared the three conditions of display time: Normal (×1.0), Fast (×0.6), and

Adaptive (the proposed method, switching the display time based on the situation). The Normal condition is same as in the previous experiment. The Fast condition always uses the shorter display time (×0.6). The Adaptive condition changes the display time to Fast (×0.6) when there is a waiting line and to Slow (×1.8) when there is no waiting line. To describe the situation around the work and have it influence the display time, instead of using computer-vision-based analysis, an experimenter observed the people around the work and manually input the exact situation into the system via a wireless keyboard.

We investigated whether the display-time conditions affect the change in behavior of passersby in the mall by comparing the proportion of the passersby's behavior between the case in which there are others who were interacting with the artwork and the case in which there is no one. Over four days, 3,835 people were observed.

3.3   Results and Discussion

The results of observation of passersby organized based on the behavioral stages and the presence of others interacting with the system are shown in Fig. 3. We used the chi-square test to obtain the percentage of each behavioral stage under each display-time condition based on the presence of other users interacting. This test revealed that there is a significant difference in the distribution of behavioral stages under the Normal condition ($p < 0.01$); residual analysis revealed that the number of Looking/Stopping people increases when others are interacting with the system, as found in the previous experiment ($p < 0.05$). The test revealed that there is no significant difference in the distribution of behavioral stages under the Fast condition. The test also revealed that there is a significant difference in the distribution of behavioral stages under the Adaptive condition; residual analysis revealed that the number of Looking/Stopping/Approaching/Experiencing people increases when others are interacting with the system ($p < 0.05$). These analyses show that the proposed method increases not only the number of people who are attracted to the system but also the number of people who interact with the system. To increase the number of people who interact with the system, it is not necessary to increase the efficiency of the experience cycle, but instead the situation around the work should employ adaptive control of the experience time.

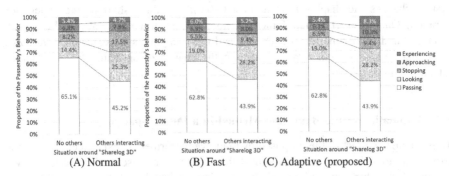

Fig. 3. Changes in passersby's behavior based on display-time conditions (Color figure online)

We calculated the odds ratios (ORs) between situations around the artwork under each display-time condition. An OR is defined as the ratio between the odds of an event occurring in one group and the odds of it occurring in another group. In this analysis, an OR of close to 1 means that the presence of others interacting with the work has no significant impact on the transition probability of passersby's behavior. An OR of larger than 1 means that the presence of others interacting with the work has the power to encourage people to change their behavior to the next step. On the other hand, an OR of less than 1 means that another user's presence has a negative effect, discouraging them from further behavior changes.

ORs between Passing to Looking and Stopping to Approaching under each display-time condition are shown in Fig. 4. ORs between Passing and Looking under the Normal and Adaptive conditions are significantly higher than that under the Fast condition ($p < 0.01$). This result shows that the presence of others interacting with the work encouraged the passersby to pay attention to the work under the Normal and Adaptive conditions. There is no significant difference in ORs between Stopping and Approaching among most conditions; only the OR under the Normal condition is less than 1 (i.e., it shows a negative tendency). This result indicates that the proposed method counteracted the negative effect of crowded situations that resulted from attracting many passersby, and thus, increased the number of people who interacted with the system.

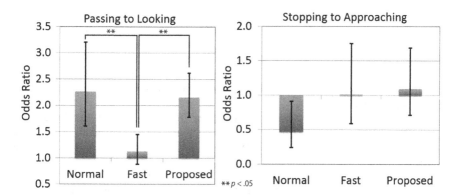

Fig. 4. Odds ratios [Passing to Looking (Left) and Stopping to Approaching (Right)] for display-time conditions

4   Conclusion

In this paper, we attempted to attract visitors and encourage them to interact with interactive systems in public spaces. We focused on utilizing the influence of others to draw the attention of passersby in public spaces, and proposed a method to not only attract passersby's attention but also maintain their attention until they had interacted with these systems by creating a situation in which one user is experiencing it and several people form a line. Our proposed method changes the experience time of the interactive system based on the situation of people around the system. In this method, if there are passersby who are waiting to experience the work, the system makes the display time faster (×0.6), and thereby shortens the experience duration. On the other hand, if there is no passerby near the work, the system makes the display time slower (×1.8), and thereby lengthens the experience duration. By doing so, the system attempts to decrease the waiting time for people waiting in line and increases the chance of showing the other user's interaction to passersby. The experiments, held in real public spaces, showed that the proposed method counteracted the negative effect of crowded situations as a consequence of attracting many passersby, and thus increased the number of people who interacted with the system.

The proposed method is only applicable to limited interactive systems that can manage the interaction duration. For example, interactive kiosks, which provide information to visitors using movies, can use the proposed method directly by changing the length or playback speed of the movies. The model of this work can be generalized to increase its applicability. Therefore, in future work, we will apply this method to other types of interactive systems in public spaces.

Acknowledgement. This work was partially supported by the MEXT, Grant-in-Aid for Scientific Research (A), 25240057.

References

1. Tanikawa, T., Narumi, T., Hirose, M.: Mixed reality digital museum project. In: Yamamoto, S. (ed.) HCI 2013, Part III. LNCS, vol. 8018, pp. 248–257. Springer, Heidelberg (2013)
2. Narumi, T., Hayashi, O., Kasada, K., Yamazaki, M., Tanikawa, T., Hirose, M.: Digital diorama: AR exhibition system to convey background information for museums. In: Shumaker, R. (ed.) Virtual and Mixed Reality, HCII 2011, Part I. LNCS, vol. 6773, pp. 76–86. Springer, Heidelberg (2011)
3. Kajinami, T., Hayashi, O., Narumi, T., Tanikawa, T., Hirose, M.: Digital display case: museum exhibition system to convey background information about exhibits. In: 2010 16th International Conference on Virtual Systems and Multimedia (VSMM), pp. 230–233. IEEE (2010)
4. Imura, J., Kasada, K., Narumi, T., Tanikawa, T., Hirose, M.: Reliving past scene experience system by inducing a video-camera operator's motion with overlaying a video-sequence onto real environment. ITE Trans. Media Technol. Appl. **2**(3), 225–235 (2014)
5. Cartiere, C., Willis, S. (eds.): The Practice of Public Art. Routledge, New York (2008)
6. Nishimura, K., Suzuki, Y., Tanikawa, T., Naemura, T., Aizawa, K., Hirose, M.: Report of the exhibition: "Digital Public Art in HANEDA AIRPORT "AIR HARBOR"-Technology Meets Air: A Sensation of a New World". In: 2010 16th International Conference on Virtual Systems and Multimedia (VSMM), pp. 45–50. IEEE (2010)
7. Churchill, E.F., Nelson, L., Denoue, L., Helfman, J., Murphy, P.: Sharing multimedia content with interactive public displays: a case study. In: Proceedings of the 5th Conference on Designing Interactive Systems: Processes, Practices, Methods, and Techniques, pp. 7–16. ACM, August 2004
8. Nishimura, K., Suzuki, Y., Ushigome, Y., Torigoe, Y., Narumi, T., Sato, M., Tanikawa, T., Hirose, M.: Interaction in a public space with an IC card for fare system: experiment as public art. J. Inf. Process. Soc. Jpn. **53**(4), 1307–1318 (2012). IPSJ (in Japanese)

9. Brignull, H., Rogers, Y.: Enticing people to interact with large public displays in public spaces. In: Proceedings of INTERACT, vol. 3, pp. 17–24 (2003)
10. Schmidt, C., Müller, J., Bailly, G.: Screenfinity: extending the perception area of content on very large public displays. In: Proceedings of the SIGCHI Conference on Human Factors in Computing Systems, pp. 1719–1728. ACM (2013)
11. Rogers, Y., Hazlewood, W.R., Marshall, P., Dalton, N., Hertrich, S.: Ambient influence: can twinkly lights lure and abstract representations trigger behavioral change? In: Proceedings of the 12th ACM International Conference on Ubiquitous Computing, pp. 261–270. ACM (2010)
12. Fujinawa, E., Sakurai, S., Izumi, M., Narumi, T., Houshuyama, O., Tanikawa, T., Hirose, M.: Induction of human behavior by presentation of environmental acoustics. In: Yamamoto, S., Abbott, A.A. (eds.) HIMI 2015. LNCS, vol. 9172, pp. 582–594. Springer, Heidelberg (2015). doi:10.1007/978-3-319-20612-7_55
13. Narumi, T., Akagawa, T., Seong, Y.A., Hirose, M.: Thermotaxis. In: SIGGRAPH 2009: Posters, p. 18. ACM (2009)
14. Milgram, S., Bickman, L., Berkowitz, L.: Note on the drawing power of crowds of different size. J. Pers. Soc. Psychol. 13(2), 79 (1969)
15. Van Dijk, B., Zwiers, J., op den Akker, R., Nijholt, A.: Navigation assistance in virtual worlds. In: Boyd, E., Cohen, E., Zaliwski, A.J. (eds.) Proceedings of 2001 Informing Science Conference, Krakow, Poland, pp. 1–9 (2001)
16. Ibáñez, J., Delgado-Mata, C.: Flocking techniques to naturally support navigation in large and open virtual worlds. Eng. Appl. Artif. Intell. 25(1), 119–129 (2012)
17. Narumi, T., Kasai, T., Honda, T., Aoki, K., Tanikawa, T., Hirose, M.: Digital railway museum: an approach to introduction of digital exhibition systems at the railway museum. In: Yamamoto, S. (ed.) HCI 2013, Part III. LNCS, vol. 8018, pp. 238–247. Springer, Heidelberg (2013)
18. Iwasawa, S., Kawakita, M., Inoue, N.: REI: an automultiscopic projection display. In: Proceedings of Three Dimensional Systems and Applications (Ultra Realistic Communication Forum), p. 1 (2013)

Visualization of Composer Relationships Using Implicit Data Graphs

Christoph Niese[1], Tatiana von Landesberger[1], and Arjan Kuijper[1,2(✉)]

[1] Technische Universität Darmstadt, Darmstadt, Germany
[2] Fraunhofer IGD, Darmstadt, Germany
arjan.kuijper@igd.fraunhofer.de

Abstract. Relationships between classical music composers are known due to explicit historic material, for instance the friendship between Joseph Haydn and Wolfgang Amadeus Mozart, as well as the influence of the latter on Ludwig van Beethoven. While Haydn and Mozart were critics of each others work, Mozart and Beethoven probably never met in person. In spite of that there is an impact on especially the early music of Beethoven. While relationships between well-known composers like the mentioned ones are investigated, it can also be of historic interest to know the roles less-known composers played. Some of them might have a part in a famous persons work but were not further analyzed given the fact that there have been many composers and no hints given to researchers indicating which person would be worth studying. In this work we develop an approach to visually hint possible relationships among a large number of composers. Detailed historic knowledge is not taken into account; the hints are only based on the composer works as well as their lifetimes in order to guess directions of influence.

1 Introduction and Motivation

There are and have been many music composers living on this planet. All of them naturally got influenced by other representatives of their profession, be it while their time at the conservatory or later in their work life. This simple observation leads to questions that are of academic interest:

- Who influenced the famous composers like Wolfgang Amadeus Mozart and Ludwig van Beethoven?
- Had composers who are nowadays nearly forgotten a major impact?

Those questions have been answered by music theorists. However, those persons of course usually investigate where they think new insights can be gained. This implies:

- Famous composers and their relationships are well researched.
- Less-known composers gain less or no attention.

S. Yamamoto (Ed.): HIMI 2016, Part II, LNCS 9735, pp. 300–312, 2016.
DOI: 10.1007/978-3-319-40397-7_29

There are always ordinary persons who are just doing their job fine, who usually are in the majority. But then there seem to be a few individuals that are outstanding, who seem to press forward mankind in what they do, like Mozart did. This has been expressed in the Great Man Theory [2]. However, Herbert Spencer noted an important fact on this:

> If it be a fact that the great man may modify his nation in its structure and actions, it is also a fact that there must have been those antecedent modifications constituting national progress before he could be evolved. Before he can re-make his society, his society must make him [18].

To Mozart this society may have included his father Leopold and his friend Joseph Haydn most probably among others. Some relationships are that popular that they are general knowledge that is taught in schools, like the just mentioned ones. But what if Mozart once went to a concert of an infamous composer and heard a tune he liked that much he build a major work on it? Or what if he even liked a lesser-known composers style that much he finally permanently adopted it in his own? Maybe it would change the view on Mozart totally. Besides being made up by us, this would not be limited to Mozart. We just use him as he seems to us the commonly most well-known composer. Nevertheless he and others may be connected in manners unknown today. Imagine you do not know anything on any composer and get the task to find all relevant relationships Mozart had. You have two possibilities to start with:

Explicit: Consult written or oral sources that state who he used to meet.
Implicit: Analyze and compare Mozarts and all other composers work to find commodities. Those may indicate that the respective persons either met or knew the work of the other.

It would be cumbersome to read all texts ever written by, to, and on Mozart. Besides you would have to locate those sources. Any seemingly irrelevant person could have known and written down something of interest in a diary. But at least you would have definitive statements. Analyzing all works by all composers would be even more cumbersome. Besides, on one hand, found commodities may be random occurrences or may only serve as hints but not as proofs. On the other hand, however, you may find links that are nowhere to be found in verbal texts. And a computer may help you. Text can be analyzed automatically, but as stated, the relevant text has to be found first. The musical work of composers, however, is more easily available. Of course, much work is lost or incomplete, but we think it is overall easier to grasp. Musical scores are much more formalized constructs than texts are. Therefore processing by machines is more straightforward than automatically analyzing text. In this paper, an automatic approach is developed that can assist you in the task of finding relationships between composers. It gives an overview and hints indicating points of interest so you can solve the following tasks:

– Examine: You have a certain composer in mind and want to find relationships to other composers you did not know of.
– Browse: You have no composer in mind and just want to browse and being lead to directions you did not think of yourself.

Full details can be found in [14].

2   Related Work

The strength of computers is to process large amounts of data. This has been used by others to analyse musical work. Besides there also exists work that has other approaches but leads to the same direction we want to go to.

The project Peachnote by Viro [21] is backed up by a large database of music n-grams. Based on them, similarity between music is measured. While the projects wants to be something like Google Books but for music, based on the technology the author also created an application that visualises an overview of similarities.

This visualisation, however, is work-centric. You specify a work and as a result you get similar works by the same or by other composers. On the one hand you can find similar composer, though only based on a single piece. On the other hand however you need to have an idea to start with, you cannot just browse and look on hints the application gives you [5].

The Classical Music Navigator[1] lets you browse composers and works. For each composer there are entries for influences by and to other composers. It is based on historic knowledge, does not analyse scores automatically and is therefore limited and what humans already know. Furthermore there is no visualisation, so the big picture cannot easily be seen.

The Map of Mozart [13] clusters by similarity into subregions of a predefined area [20]. This again is work centric. Additionally, if you would apply this visualisation approach to composers, you could only use one measurement of similarity. We, however, want to apply more.

Much work has been done on music querying, like [11,22]. Then there is work that processes on physical music signals, but not on notes, like [3,17]. However, they are not composer-centric. For an overview of work related to visualizing music collections based on metadata, see the thesis of Holm [6].

3   Approach

We see finding relevant composer relationships as a top-down process of three steps:

1. General overview: From a large amount of composers and possible relationships you have to pick those you are interested in.

---

[1] http://people.wku.edu/charles.smith/music/index2.htm.

2. Specific overview: You look closer at the chosen composers and relationships in order to keep or dismiss them.
3. Specific research: The items you kept lead to an in-depth research with historic texts, original scores and actual musical understanding and experience.

While the last step should be conducted manually by a music theorist, the first two can be supported by an automatic approach which we try in the following sections.

3.1 General Overview

Throughout the history of music theory, multiple concepts of measuring music similarity have been developed. We want my approach to theoretically support an unlimited number of those, i.e. it should be extensible and not limited to one kind of measurement like it is the case for Peachnote. we call a measuring concept analyser. An analyser basically represents a function that takes a composer as input and returns a vector type as an output. Between such vector types a distance can be measured. Due to the fact that we have composers that can be connected to multiple other composers in multiple ways at once, we think the best method of visualisation is a node link diagram that consists of vertices and edges [8,10]. A composer then is a represented as a vertex, a relationship by an edge [9].

Edge Representation. An edge for a certain analyser exists if the distance between the vector types resulting from the analysis of two composers does not exceed a certain threshold. This threshold is freely selectable by the user. As multiple edges between the same two composers can be confusing, we will merge those edges. Each edge as a colour that is derived from the analyser that was used to create it. Merging edges results in a single edge that is striped in the colours of the original edges. The standard colours of the analysers have been chosen in a way that they are easily to distinguish. From a hue circle, the maximum distances between colours have been chosen [19].

Edge Direction. Usually older people influence younger ones due to their experience. We want to reflect this by utilising directed edges which are represented by arrows from one vertex to another. The direction is determined by the following rules:

- If composer As death occurred earlier than composer Bs birth, the edge is drawn from A to B. In this case it is impossible that B influenced A.
- If composer Bs death occurred earlier than composer As birth, the edge is drawn from B to A. In this case it is impossible that A influenced B.
- If composer As birth occurred earlier than composer Bs birth, the edge is also drawn from A to B.
- Otherwise the edge is drawn from B to A.

Only the first two choices are guaranteed to be correct, as a living composer cannot influence a dead one. The other choices can, but do not need to be correct. However, since the graphs purpose is to provide a rough overview semi-correct edges can be tolerated. Furthermore, since we have a directed graph, every edge needs to have a direction. This is one of the two places where meta data is used, which always only happens for visualisation, not analysis purposes.

Vertex Highlighting. For a small graph this is sufficient and if you already know which composer you want to investigate, it may even be for a large graph. However, usually there are just to many edges. Therefore possible nodes of interest should be exposed to the user. We do this by offering highlighting dependent on the degrees of a node. The indegree is the number of edges that lead to a vertex from other vertices. The outdegree is the number of edges going from this vertex to other vertices. A high indegree means a composer has been influenced by many others, a high outdegree means a composer has influenced many others. The higher a degree is in respect to the total number of vertices in the graph, i.e. the more people a composer influenced or has been influenced by, the more highlighting will be applied.

Filtering. To further ease the navigation in an edge-heavy graph, as soon as a composer has been selected, all edges that are not in or outgoing ones of any selected composer are hidden. This is especially useful if you already know which composer you are interested in. You can directly select him and only see the relevant edges. This applies in addition to the filtering by threshold. Furthermore composer vertices can be hidden by choice.

Graph Layout. The last thing to note on the graph at this point is the layout. As the standard layout we choose a circle which proves to be simple and efficient. The vertices are arranged in a circle, leaving much empty space in a centre that can be filled by the edges. However, since lifetime metadata is present, it is used to provide additional layouting possibilities. Composer vertices can be arranged by birth century, birth decade, death century, and death decade. This can be especially useful if you are trying to follow temporal lines of influence. Depending on the granularity you wish, centuries or decades can be selected.

3.2 Specific Overview

If two composers are selected for further examination, the vector types the various analysers calculated for these composers need be compared to provide further insights. This will again done in a visual way. However, there are four questions up to this point:

1. What are the vector types analysers calculate?
2. How do analysers calculate those vector types?

3. How is distance between those vector types measured?
4. What is a good way to visually compare two vector types?

These questions are subject to the next section.

4   Analysis and Visualisation

In this chapter we present the analysers we created to analyse composers. For each analyser, the vector type it returns is defined as well as how one measures the distance between two. Finally there is a visualisation for each vector type that is used for comparison.

4.1   Music

As music is the subject of analysis we first want to introduce some basic concepts of music theory before defining the analysis approaches. There are seven natural tones which are in the English language identified by the letters C, D, E, F, G, A, B, which are represented by the white keys. Five semitones are represented by the black keys which can be created by manipulating the natural tones with an accidental. Those accidentals are ♯, b, ♯♯, bb and shift a natural tone by 1, −1, 2, −2 semitone steps respectively. Apparently the keys are repeating with the same letters. Therefore the letters need to be indexed, leading to the concept of an octave. Examples are C♯0, F1, B2. All combinations of natural tones and accidentals now have a unique identifier and can be called notes. Without the octave, the 12 different types of keys represent the pitch classes C, C♯, D, D♯, E, F, F♯, G, G♯, A, A♯, B. If you press a key, i.e. play a note, you chose how long you hold and how strong you press. This way you can influence the loudness of a tone, which is formalised in musical literature as the dynamic indication usually ranging from ppp (very silent) to fff (very loud). In this work we call this combination of note, duration and dynamic indication a note instance. Note instances are often produced at the same time. Those are grouped as so-called chords. For simplicity, chords can also contain only one note in this work. A sequence of chords played by a certain instrument is called a voice. One voice or multiple voices playing alongside form a movement. A collection of movements forms a piece, a musical composition. A person who has usually written multiple pieces is called a composer.

4.2   Favourite Analysers

The favourite note analyser simply counts all notes in all voices of all movements in all pieces by a composer. The favourite pitch class analyser and the favourite dynamic indication analyser do the same for pitch classes and dynamic indications. The item that is counted most often is then considered a composers favourite one. The distance between two notes a and b obviously is a simple subtraction, as well as the distance between two dynamic indications a and b:

abs(a − b). The distance between two pitch classes a and b can be measured by a modular operation [16]. This is because to the fact that those classes are arranged circular due to the lack of octave indexing: min((a − b + 12)mod12, (b − a + 12)mod12). Visually comparing two simple items requires nothing more than displaying them side by side.

4.3   Histogram Analyzers

Where the favourite analysers only determine the one favourite item by a composer, the histogram anaylsers use a very similar query to setup a histogram of all items that have been used by the composer. In a histogram objects are merged into classes and associated with the total numbers of occurrences. For example, pitch classes could be the classes and the total numbers are the numbers of times pitch classes can be found in a piece.

To measure the distance between two histograms we chose the cosine distance [4]. Its calculation requires two vectors of equal length and structure. Therefore we first determine all classes appearing in both histograms via a union operation. Then the two vectors are built upon these classes. The count values directly come from the original histograms. If a class does not exist there, the default value 0 is used.

In the visualisation, for each item two bars exist, one for each composer that is currently selected. They are normalized, meaning their lengths are relative to each histograms maximum. This allows comparison of distribution of values, not the actual counts. Nevertheless, those are also displayed at the sides.

The note histogram visualisation has the additional feature of displaying the notes that are not shared (i.e. one composer has a count of 0) are displayed at the top and bottom. This way the notes that actually have their counterparts can be compared.

4.4   Melody Analyzer

The melody of a movement is a sequence of single notes. In a piano work this would usually be notes played by the right hand whereas in orchestral works the melody is usually played by a group of string instruments, but not necessarily. To determine the melody we follow the approach of Lu et al. [12]: If the melody track is marked in the MIDI file, we choose it. If not, very short tracks and unlikely ones (percussion) are removed and the remaining ones are merged. The chosen or merged track is broken down to only the topmost notes of each chord.

A melody can be represented by a sequence of rectangles where a rectangles width is derived from a notes duration whereas its height is derived from the pitch. The distance between two such representations can be calculated by determining the difference of the total areas of both melodies [1]. Refinements in form of area minimisation by shifting the melodies horizontally and vertically as well as smartly scaling them are not applied by us. As we want to compare too many works the calculation should not bee too complex. We do, however, scale the rectangle sequences horizontally so they have an equal length and divide vertically by the minimum height. Each melody curve then has the same minimum and length allowing simple comparison of the courses. The analysis of a movement results in a collection of sequences of rectangles in which one is contained for each movement.

The rectangles can be seen as the extent of a set. Therefore the Jaccard index [15] can be used the measure the distance between two rectangle sequences. The needed intersection of two rectangle sequences is calculated like one would calculate the area between two functions, i.e. determining intersection points and solving multiple integrals. However, due to the noncurved structure, usual all-purpose integration is not necessary. The union of the rectangles can be determined by choosing the maximum area of two rectangles of equal width and summing all up.

We decided to let the distance between two rectangle sequence collections be the average of all pairwise contained rectangle sequences. As this whole approach is geometric the visualisation is basically simple. We show the areas of difference and draw coloured lines so one can track the melodies of both composers.

4.5   Data Sources

The resources we process come from three sources:

1. Kunst der Fuge (http://www.kunstderfuge.com) we chose MIDI as the file format from which to obtain musical data. It is a common format containing note information that can easily be parsed. The Kunst der Fuge archive contains contains more than 17,000 MIDI files.
2. Wikimedia Commons (http://commons.wikimedia.org) For a nice visualisation we need portraits of the composers. We extracted them from this collection.
3. Wikipedia (http://www.wikipedia.org) To draw directed edges we need the lifespans of each composer. We looked them up on this site. They do not have to be absolutely correct, so this source is sufficient.

4.6   Application Overview

Figure 1 represents a typical situation shortly after starting the program, loading composers and activating some controls.

On the top, the application features the typical menu bar that can be found in many programs. It contains several items and sub items. The import option is for importing data from the file system. A directory is expected that contains subdirectories which represent composers. Each subdirectory's name will be directly used as a composers name. Inside there can be an image file (PNG or JPG) featuring a composers portrait that is used for visualisation. The image files name should have the format YYYYMMDD-YYYYMMDD.FFF where YYYY is a year, MM a month, DD a day and FFF a file ending. Thus the file name indicates the life time of a composer. Subdirectories of composer directories represent pieces written by a him. The directory names equal the piece names.

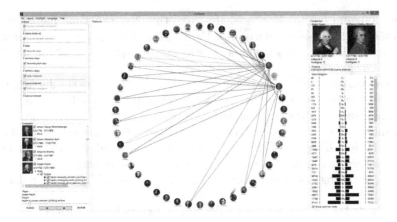

Fig. 1. Application overview

Inside a piece directory there are MIDI files representing movements or parts of the piece. Their names should equal the movement names. If you do not want to sort files by pieces, you could just create one folder and put all files into it. Open, save, and save as refer to the programs file format which is XML. XML files contain all data from the import directory, even the raw MIDI data and the portrait image, as a single file for convenient use. Furthermore analysis results are stored which are directly created at import. This is why importing takes much longer than opening an XML file. Further menu items include functionality for changing the graphs layout, the highlighting mode of vertices, and the language.

List of composers. The composers to be analysed can be reviewed and filtered here. Their respective works that will be analysed can be selected by whole and by movement, and the latter can be listened to with the integrated media player. If you click on a portrait, the composer is selected.

List of analysers. The analysers to be used to evaluate each composer and his respective pieces can be selected here. Each list entry also offers the possibility to set the threshold distance between two composers to filter edges. The analyser you have selected in this list is used for the detailed result comparison view.

Graph. The graph serves as the centre of the application. It is the visual overview of composers indicating similarities between them. Vertices and Edges are clickable in order to select two composers for further analysis. Zooming and translating is possible.

Comparison. The details of why two composers have been connected can be reviewed here. The commodities and differences can be seen as well as the calculated distance and the vertex degrees of the selected composers.

5   Evaluation

This penultimate chapter presents evaluation against known influences.

L. v. Beethoven   W. A. Mozart

Fig. 2. Graph with only Mozart and Beethoven

Analyser	Distance
Favourite note	0 semitone steps
Favourite pitch class	0 semitone steps
Favourite dynamic indication	1 step
Note histogram	0.0402 (cosine distance)
Pitch class histogram	0.0272 (cosine distance)
Dynamic indication histogram	0.1266 (cosine distance)
Melody	0.1989 (Jaccard index)

Fig. 3. Results for piano concertos by Mozart and Beethoven

5.1 Piano Concertos by Mozart and Beethoven

Ludwig van Beethoven got inspired by Wolfgang Amadeus Mozarts Piano Concerto No. 24 when writing his own Piano Concerto No. 3 [7]. At the very beginning of the pieces you will notice similar themes. We created a special graph you can see in Fig. 2 for this that only contains the two composers and their respective works. Clicking on the edge between them and iterating through the analyser list, the values presented in Fig. 3 can be extracted.

According to the analysers the pieces as a whole are very similar: Although Beethovens work is louder the most occurring notes and pitch classes are the same. Furthermore, the two note histograms have a small cosine distance that is even underscored by the one of the pitch class histograms. One probably would examine this further if the connection was not already known.

5.2 Whole Work by Haydn and Mozart

As mentioned in the beginning, Haydn and Mozart were friends that influenced each other. Analysis results of this relationship are shown in Fig. 4.

Due to the very small distances the analysers confirm that there is a connection between the two men.

5.3 Browsing

If we do not know what we are looking for we can nevertheless just start the program and load composers. The situation is as shown in Fig. 5 left. We decide

Analyser	Distance
Favourite note	0 semitone steps
Favourite pitch class	0 semitone steps
Favourite dynamic indication	0 semitone steps
Note histogram	0,0074 (cosine distance)
Pitch class histogram	0,0043 (cosine distance)
Dynamic indication histogram	0,0866 (cosine distance)

Fig. 4. Results for whole work by Haydn and Mozart

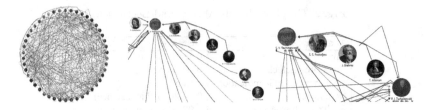

Fig. 5. Browsing, steps 1 to 3.

Analyser	Distance
Favourite note	0 semitone steps
Favourite pitch class	2 semitone steps
Favourite dynamic indication	2 semitone steps
Note histogram	0,0566 (cosine distance)
Pitch class histogram	0,0391 (cosine distance)
Dynamic indication histogram	0,1240 (cosine distance)

Fig. 6. Results for the comparison of Rachmaninoff and Tschaikowski

to click on Rachmaninoff because he is highlighted in a deeper blue than other composers. Now the situation has changed to the middle image. We see an edge coming from Tschaikowski and because we like Tschaikowski we decide to click on him. Now both composers are selected as shown in the right image. We analyse the distances and get the values shown in Fig. 6.

The results indicate a close relationship. If we look Rachmaninoff up in the Classical Music Navigator, we can read he has been heavily influenced by Tschaikowski which confirms the results.

5.4   Limitations

Much work cannot easily be found in the MIDI format. So even some works of famous composers are unavailable, not speaking of those of unknown ones. This seems to be the price of this trivially machine-readable format. Besides the issue that we cannot verify the connection between more work we know it is related, there is a much larger one: Influences of unknown composers cannot be found if the program has no data on them. You may have noted that results from the melody analyser is only available in the first evaluation. This is due to performance issues. Too many comparisons are needed to run on a decent end user device, so we excluded it most of the time. Also, we cannot load all 884 composers that are available to us, as the performance is too much of an issue. Therefore we used a smaller set of less than 50 composers.

5.5 Conclusions

In this work we developed an approach to assist a music theorist in finding unknown relationships between composers. We created a concept of music analysis, graph visualisation and details visualisation so an expert can follow three steps on the way to new insights. The approach resulted in a software application.

To solve the data amount problem, the largest online source of music should be concerned: Scanned sheet music, which is for example collected in the Petrucci Music Library. This then evokes the need of image analysis and translating into a machine-readable representation. Sheets never scanned or even never found unfortunately are inaccessible of course leaving the dream of a complete graph being a dream. It is unlikely that a fat client can handle all this data. Therefore a thin client with raw server power as a back end should be considered and the program accordingly rewritten. This also leads to new analysis possibilities. Where the melody analyser is critical because of the pairwise distance calculation, N-Grams that are used in Peachnote are simply too processing intensive. However they seem to work very well and the program could benefit from them. In general, there are always more analysers that could be added. A person who has academic music theory background could be consulted to determine what exactly is needed and to know whether the layout options are sufficient. Concerning visual output one could think of a better way of edge drawing. Both the routing and the colour mixing is not the optimum.

References

1. Aloupis, G., Fevens, T., Langerman, S., Matsui, T., Mesa, A., Nuñez, Y., Rappaport, D., Toussaint, G.: Algorithms for computing geometric measures of melodic similarity. Comput. Music J. **30**(3), 67–76 (2006)
2. Carneiro, R.L.: Herbert spencer as an anthropologist. J. Libertarian Stud. **2**, 1712 (1981)
3. Charbuillet, C., Peeters, G., Barton, S., Gouet-Brunet, V.: A fast algorithm for music search by similarity in large databases based on modified symetrized Kullback Leibler divergence. In: Content-Based Multimedia Indexing (CBMI 2010), pp. 1–6 (2010)
4. Connor, R., Moss, R.: A multivariate correlation distance for vector spaces. In: Navarro, G., Pestov, V. (eds.) SISAP 2012. LNCS, vol. 7404, pp. 209–225. Springer, Heidelberg (2012)
5. Engelke, T., Becker, M., Wuest, H., Keil, J., Kuijper, A.: MobileAR browser - a generic architecture for rapid AR-multi-level development. Expert Syst. Appl. **40**(7), 2704–2714 (2013)

6. Holm, J.: Visualizing music collections based on metadata: Concepts, user studies and design implications. Technical report, Tampere University of Technology (2012). https://dspace.cc.tut.fi/dpub/handle/123456789/21161
7. Kinderman, W.: Reviews of books: Beethoven forum, ii. Music Lett. **77**(1), 124–126 (1996)
8. von Landesberger, T., Bremm, S., Kirschner, M., Wesarg, S., Kuijper, A.: Visual analytics for model-based medical image segmentation: opportunities and challenges. Expert Syst. Appl. **40**(12), 4934–4943 (2013)
9. von Landesberger, T., Görner, M., Rehner, R., Schreck, T.: A system for interactive visual analysis of large graphs using motifs in graph editing and aggregation. In: Vision, Modeling, and Visualization 2009, pp. 331–340 (2009)
10. von Landesberger, T., Kuijper, A., Schreck, T., Kohlhammer, J., van Wijk, J.J., Fekete, J., Fellner, D.W.: Visual analysis of large graphs: state-of-the-art and future research challenges. Comput. Graph. Forum **30**(6), 1719–1749 (2011)
11. Liu, C.C., Hsu, J.L., Chen, A.: An approximate string matching algorithm for content-based music data retrieval. In: IEEE International Conference on Multimedia Computing and Systems, 1999, vol. 1, pp. 451–456 (1999)
12. Lu, L., You, H., Zhang, H.J.: A new approach to query by humming in music retrieval. IEEE International Conference on Multimedia and Expo, ICME 2001, pp. 595–598 (2001)
13. Mayer, R., Lidy, T., Rauber, A.: The map of mozart. In: 7th International Conference on Music Information Retrieval, ISMIR 2006, pp. 351–352 (2006)
14. Niese, C.: Visualization of composer relationships using implicit data graphs. Technical report, Darmstadt University of Technology (2015)
15. Niwattanakul, S., Singthongchai, J., Naenudorn, E., Wanapu, S.: Using of Jaccard coefficient for keywords similarity. Lect. Notes Eng. Comput. Sci. **2202**(1), 380–384 (2013)
16. Rahn, J.: Basic Atonal Theory. Schirmer, New York (1980)
17. Schnitzer, D.: Mirage - high-performance music similarity computation and automatic playlist generation. Vienna University of Technology, Austria, Technical report (2007)
18. Spencer, H.: The Study of Sociology. Appleton, New York (1896)
19. Stone, M.: Choosing colors for data visualization. Technical report (2006). http://www.perceptualedge.com/library.php
20. Tatu, A., Zhang, L., Bertini, E., Schreck, T., Keim, D., Bremm, S., von Landesberger, T.: Clustnails: visual analysis of subspace clusters. Tsinghua Sci. Technol. **17**(4), 419–428 (2012)
21. Viro, V.: Peachnote: music score search and analysis platform. In: 12th International Society for Music Information Retrieval Conference, ISMIR 2011, pp. 359–362 (2011)
22. Welsh, M., Borisov, N., Hill, J., von Behren, R., Woo, A.: Querying large collections of music for similarity. Technical report UCB/CSD-00-1096, EECS Department, University of California, Berkeley (2000)

Crowd-Cloud Window to the Past: Constructing a Photo Database for On-Site AR Exhibitions by Crowdsourcing

Sohei Osawa[✉], Ryohei Tanaka, Takuji Narumi,
Tomohiro Tanikawa, and Michitaka Hirose

Graduate School of Information Science and Technology,
The University of Tokyo, 7-3-1 Hongo, Bunkyō, Tokyo 113-8656, Japan
{osawa,r_tanaka,narumi,tani,
hirose}@cyber.t.u-tokyo.ac.jp

Abstract. In this paper, we propose a crowdsourcing system that constructs a database for AR (Augmented Reality) contents by user generation for on-site AR exhibitions that runs on personal mobile devices. The AR exhibition systems superimpose images from the past onto the present scene in the photographed places. They require location information of past pictures and current pictures that were shot in same place at same angle. Previously, system designers had to prepare the contents by themselves because the estimation of photographed positions was an unautomated task. This is one reason why there were only a limited number of contents. We overcome this problem by implementing a system in which many users can participate in creating contents easily. Users can post necessary information for AR contents only by taking photos when the current scene matches the semi-transparent past image. Through experiments and workshops, we found that our system had many interesting and acceptable sides. For example, our application for looking for the photographed positions gives users entertainment akin to games. Although its user interface and user-motivating design require increased sophistication, our system could work well and gather valuable user-generated contents to provide a richer AR experience.

Keywords: User-generated contents · Digital museum · Mobile AR

1 Introduction

The number of AR applications has gradually increased with the rapid spread of mobile devices such as smartphones and tablets in recent years. The applications called on-site AR exhibition systems are among them. The AR exhibitions can superimpose past pictures onto the present scene in photographed places, which helps users perceive both the changed and unchanged parts of the scenery. This leads users to understand the history of the places more deeply [1, 2]. In our past research, we developed the AR exhibition system "Window to the Past," on which anyone can easily superimpose past pictures of certain places with their smartphones and tablets [3, 4]. This system works as follows. The present picture of the location is displayed semi-transparently in the

© Springer International Publishing Switzerland 2016
S. Yamamoto (Ed.): HIMI 2016, Part II, LNCS 9735, pp. 313–324, 2016.
DOI: 10.1007/978-3-319-40397-7_30

center of the screen as a reference. The video captured from the device camera is shown in the background. Users go to the location depicted in the semi-transparent picture and attempt to match the scenery between the semi-transparent reference picture and the live video while walking around. When the reference and captured images are sufficiently similar, the system overlays the past picture onto the current scene. As a result, users can see the past picture merged precisely onto the current scene. This system used only extracted feature points from both the reference image and that of the device camera, without the use of any other equipment or AR markers.

However, although this matching procedure is automated using computer vision technologies, it is difficult to specify the reference image automatically because the imaging conditions differ largely [4, 5]. In "Window to the Past," the reference was specified manually by pre-preparing both the past and present pictures from the same spot and using present pictures as a reference for image recognition. We discovered that it was time-consuming to identify the exact photographed place and camera angle from the past picture and to capture a photo in the present at the exact same location. Hence, the designers had to prepare pictures of all contents, and this is one of the bottlenecks to the enrichment of contents.

Thus, we add a new function to reduce the workload of the system administrators by crowdsourcing photo collection tasks among the users. In this function, users can create AR contents themselves and share their contents with many other users. We realize this process via easy operations. Users must identify the location of the past pictures and capture the current reference images. This will extend "Window to the Past" to a larger area with more data created by many users.

2   Related Works

Estimating the Photographed Places and Guiding Users There. The study of Kasada et al. [6] is an example of estimating photographed places only from past pictures. They constructed a method by which users looked for photographed locations and captured present images at the same position and angle as the past photos. First, users find objects that can be seen in both the old picture and the present web-camera capture and choose three correlating feature points. Users then are guided to the photographed position of the past picture estimated by the positional relations of these three points on the plane. When the live web-camera image changes according to the users' movements, the specified three points are tracked by using optical flow, and the direction of navigation and distance are calculated sequentially.

As another method to estimate the photographed position more exactly, the "On-site virtual time machine" by Nakano et al. [4, 7] generates a point cloud of the current target landscape in advance with Bundler [8]. Users manually associate more than eight points that are not changed between objects in the current point cloud and those in the past picture. The system then calculates the exact photographed position using the eight associations and guides users to the position.

However, these guiding systems that estimate photographed positions require users to perform more numerous and complicated operations. In some cases, users can find the photographed position more quickly without using the systems. Users' operations in our system should be as simple as possible because we must encourage many users to use it proactively. In addition, as seen from the example in which many people enjoy "film-induced tourism [9]," "pop-culture tourism [10]," and so on, it is fun for them to find and visit the photographed positions themselves. In these trips, tourists often capture photos with the same composition as that of works. This method is called "rephotography" and has a long history [11]. It will motivate users to use our system spontaneously and continuously by giving the fun to the users. We wanted users' voluntary search for photographed positions to be available in our user-generated estimation system.

Solutions to Difficult Tasks for Computers by Crowdsourcing. For unautomated tasks, many studies have found that great success can be achieved crowdsourcing. The study of Luis et al. [12] succeeded in labeling images using computer games. Labeling images is an unautomated task for computers, but they solved this by crowdsourcing using a computer game. They created an online game called ESP Game in which two players provided words associated with each image and scored points if their words corresponded. Players' answers were accumulated in a large database and used to improve accuracy of labeling. In addition, Wikipedia is a classic example of user-generated contents composing an encyclopedia that features enormous articles by crowdsourcing. Many studies explain why people are motivated to contribute to the Wikipedia project. Kuznetsov analyzed the motivation of Wikipedia editors using the Value Sensitive Design (VSD) approach [13] and showed that they enjoy a sense of accomplishment, collectivism, and benevolence [14]. Nov analyzed motivational factors based on eight general motivations used extensively in research on open source software development and volunteers [15]. They revealed that fun and ideology enhance users' motivation. These studies show that user-generated contents would be successfully obtained only by substantial feelings, such as fun and a sense of accomplishment.

3 Design of the Proposed System

3.1 Overview

In this chapter, we introduce our implementation of the crowdsourcing system that constructs a database for AR contents by user generation for on-site AR exhibitions and runs on personal mobile devices such as smartphones or tablets. To be useful, the database for on-site AR exhibitions must contain present reference pictures of the past photographs, GPS information of the locations, and annotation of the pictures. The main required functions of our proposed system are as follows:

1. Posting Past Pictures (PPP)
2. Identifying Photographed Positions and Angles by crowdsourcing (IPPA)
3. Appreciating an On-site AR Exhibition (AOAE)

3.2   Procedure of Posting Past Pictures

The main function of PPP is to collect various and valuable images from many users. We thus create Web pages on which users can contribute past photos and view them freely (Fig. 1). They can also add comments to the photo annotations. On the right side of the page is the submission form through which users can contribute past photos under pseudonyms and comment on the photos. On the left side, thumbnails of the contributed past photos are listed. When the thumbnail is selected, the larger image is displayed along with the thumbnails of uploaded current photos that were taken from the same position and angle as the past one. Users can evaluate these uploaded photos on this page (Sect. 3.3 explains this in detail.).

Fig. 1. Web page screenshot for Posting Past Pictures

3.3   Procedure of Identifying Photographed Positions and Angles by Crowdsourcing

The main function of IPPA is to identify the photographed positions of contributed photos by crowdsourcing. We realized this function by creating an application and Web pages that help users identify photographed positions fairly easily (Figs. 2 and 3). The application enables users to capture pictures with compositions similar to the past pictures and

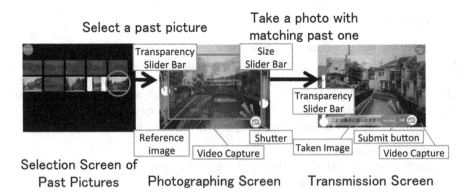

Fig. 2. Application to capture and collect current pictures at estimated photographed positions by users.

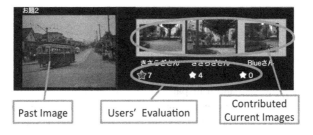

Fig. 3. Web pages to evaluate pictures captured by other users

post necessary data via simple operations. The Web pages enable users to evaluate how similar the pictures captured by other users are to the corresponding past photos.

Application to Capture and Collect Current Pictures at Estimated Photographed Positions by Users (Collection IPPA). This proposed system is realized as a mobile device application (Fig. 2). In this application, past photos uploaded by PPP are first displayed as a list. Users select a favorite from among them, and the selected picture is displayed semi-transparently in the center of the screen as a reference. The video captured from the device camera is shown in the background. Users explore the spots where old photos were captured. They need only to capture photos at the correct position and angle where the semi-transparent past image matches the background, and then they can easily add a series of necessary information for the AR exhibitions to our database. The slider bar on the right can change the size of the reference image to capture photos matching any of contributed photos under the settings of a device camera. The left slider bar can change the transparency of the reference image for easy comparison between the reference image and the background. It can be hoped that the users become familiar with the area and help revitalize the area by strolling around.

Web Pages to Evaluate Pictures Captured by Other Users (Evaluation IPPA). The present pictures collected via Collection IPPA have a risk of being associated with wrong locations, because the accuracy of the pictures are guaranteed only by the photographers themselves. It is necessary to evaluate the correctness of the posted present pictures, but automatic evaluation is difficult using feature points if current scenery has significantly changed from the past picture. We solve this problem also by users' power. We create the Web pages where users vote on pictures (Fig. 3). On these Web pages, the present pictures are listed with the corresponding past one, and each user can vote on which picture best matches the past picture. The present picture that receives the most votes is registered as a reference image. The image is used as a marker for AR exhibition, and its GPS data are also used for the corresponding past picture.

3.4 Procedure of Appreciating an On-Site AR Exhibition

The main function of AOAE is to appreciate past pictures superimposed onto current scenery at the photographed position. Thus, we extended "Window to the Past," on which users can easily superimpose past pictures of certain places with smartphones and tablets (Fig. 4). This system works as follows. First, the places already registered by IPPA are indicated on a map. When users select one location, the present picture of the place is displayed semi-transparently in the center of the screen as a reference. The video captured from the device camera is shown in the background. Using slider bars, users can transform the size and transparency of reference image freely. Users visiting the place can try to match the camera image with the semi-transparent reference picture. When the reference and captured images are sufficiently similar, the system overlays the past picture onto the current scene. The similarity of the images is recognized by matching feature points based on ORB [16].

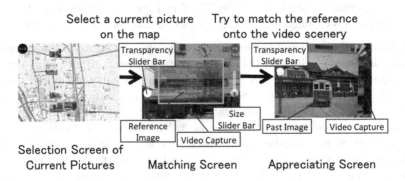

Fig. 4. Application for appreciating an on-site AR exhibition

4 Experiments

4.1 Experimental Purposes

This experiment aimed to evaluate IPPA. There are two processes in IPPA: Collection IPPA and Evaluation IPPA. In the first experiment, we judged the accuracy of the photos collected in Collection IPPA by the distance from the photographed location to the correct location and by visual inspection. The participants actually used the Collection IPPA and the posted present pictures, which were evaluated in terms of how well they matched with correct photographed positions and angles of the past pictures.

In the second experiment, we verified whether the users are able to select accurate photographed position photos from the various collected photos in Evaluation IPPA. The participants responded with the quantitative matching degree of their photographed points on a range of 0 to 1. This experimental result would suggest how well users can evaluate the photographed position of the images by comparing the current image and the past image.

4.2   Experiment 1: Evaluation of Collection IPPA

Detailed Procedures. We prepared 15 past images taken by various-angle cameras at the University of Tokyo Hongo Campus. Their accurate photographed positions were already known. The participants used Collection IPPA to post present pictures that match past images for 1 h. They then answered free description type questionnaires on the usability of Collection IPPA. Twelve participants in their twenties participated in the study. They were students at the university and were slightly acquainted with Hongo Campus. The posted present pictures were evaluated in terms of matching degree with the accurate photographed positions and angles of the original past pictures.

Result and Discussion. Figure 5 indicates an example in which we plotted some photographed points of uploaded images and past pictures on the map. The colors indicate the types of target past pictures used in the experiment. As the figure shows, the participants were able to capture images near the accurate positions. In 10 out of 15 pictures, there were some uploaded images in which the distance from the photographed location to the correct location was within 2 m. In the range of 2 m, there was almost no difference in the appearance of current scenery because most of the main objects in the past pictures used in this experiment were distant. All photos were captured at approximately the same camera angle, which could be sufficiently used as reference images for the AR exhibitions. In two out of 15 pictures, the uploaded images were within 5 m. One reason for this is that the participants had very little clue how to find the correct photographed positions because most of the main objects in the past pictures were hidden behind obstacles. There were only two cases that were not within 10 m. (red circle points in Fig. 5.) The two past pictures of these points were imaged by wide-angle cameras. Thus, the appearance of these uploaded pictures was more similar than those from accurate points (Fig. 6). The participants in this study were slightly acquainted with Hongo Campus as noted above. To sum up, users who knew a bit about the photographed place of the past picture were able to identify the locations and captured photos there. Moreover, with regard to the other place, nobody uploaded current pictures there. This occurred by accident because the participants used our application for their favorite pictures within the limited time in this experiment.

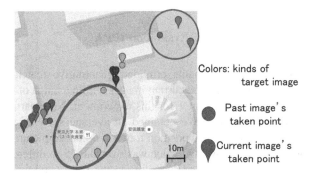

Fig. 5. Map plotting some photographed points of uploaded images and past pictures (Color figure online)

320 S. Osawa et al.

A past image with   A current image with
narrow–angle camera   device camera (narrow–angle)

Fig. 6. Visual difference using narrow-angle cameras and device cameras

A past image with   Current images with
wide–angle camera   device camera (narrow–angle)

Taken image from a   Taken image from
erroneous position   a correct position

Fig. 7. Visual difference using wide-angle cameras and device ones

In addition, seven of the 12 participants mentioned that they did not have a sufficient angle of view (AOV). Past pictures were taken with wide-angle cameras, which cannot be imaged within the AOV of the mobile device cameras. (The AOV of mobile devices is approximately 42–48°.) Five of the 12 participants answered that they wanted to enlarge the reference images sizes. In this Collection IPPA, we limited the reference image size to the device's screen size. Users must be able to magnify reference sizes larger than the screen size, and the application must be usable for wide-angle pictures.

4.3 Experiment 2: Evaluation of Evaluation IPPA

Detailed Procedures. The participants provided quantitative matching degrees of photographed points between past and current images within a range of 0 to 1. We used images collected through Experiment 1 for this experiment. Nine participants in their twenties participated in the study. We obtained an average score of all participants' matching degree of the photographed position for each uploaded picture. We judged an evaluation as correct when the average value was over the 75 % difference limen. The result of users' evaluation is classified according to the three patterns above.

Result and Discussion. There are three patterns in the collections by Collection IPPA according to the photographed position and appearance. They are as follows:

- Pattern 1: The appearance is correct, and the photographed position is also correct.
- Pattern 2: The appearance is greatly different, but the photographed position is correct; this is caused by new, obstructing buildings or demolition or by a great difference in AOV.
- Pattern 3: The appearance is similar, but the photographed position is different owing to a great difference in AOV.

In the case of Pattern 1, the participants had high opinions of the images and achieved correct evaluation (Fig. 7). There are 20 uploaded pictures classified under Pattern 1. Eighteen of 20 were correctly evaluated. In the case of Pattern 2, the participants had low opinions of them and evaluated that they were not correctly taken (Fig. 8). There are 7 uploaded pictures classified under Pattern 2, all of which were evaluated incorrectly. In the case of Pattern 3, the participants had low opinions of them, and the pictures were correctly evaluated (Fig. 9). There are 5 uploaded pictures classified under Pattern 3, all of which were correctly evaluated (Fig. 10).

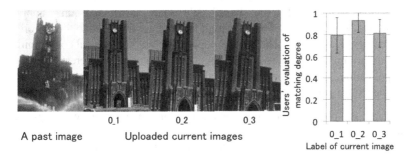

Fig. 8. The values of users' matching degree in the case of Pattern 1

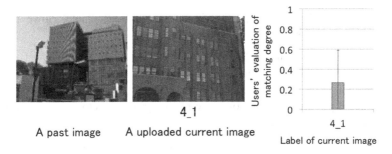

Fig. 9. The value of users' matching degree in the case of Pattern 2

If the appearance of uploaded images is significantly different from those of the corresponding past pictures such as in Pattern 2, the participants were unable to judge

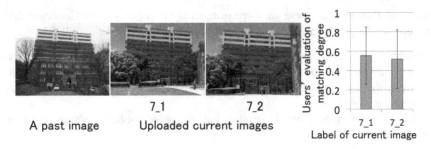

7_1   7_2

A past image   Uploaded current images   7_1   7_2

Label of current image

Fig. 10. The values of users' matching degree in the case of Pattern 3

them accurately because very little information was available for making a decision. Therefore, if similar present images are uploaded in spite of greatly different appearances, we must increase the evaluation value of the images.

4.4   User Study in Workshops

We integrated "Window to the Past" and Collection IPPA into one application named "Crowd-Cloud Window to the Past." We then distributed this application, "Crowd-Cloud Window to the Past" through the Internet (http://nozokimado.org/). We held workshops using this application in cooperation with many local communities and collected questionnaires and hearing information to evaluate the interest and feasibility of this application. The participants enjoyed using our application in these workshops. We obtained some positive opinion such as follows:

- Searching for photographed positions and taking pictures were interesting, like games.
- I thought it was troublesome to find the photographed positions but surprisingly fun to try.
- I enjoyed appreciating past scenery superimposed onto current scenery.
- I want AR contents of my town.

The result suggests that our application is substantially acceptable. However, there were also some negative opinions as follows:

- I want to be motivated to go far.
- I have no motivation to look for places in a familiar area.
- The behavior of the application was a little heavy.
- Sometimes, I properly superimposed the reference image onto the scenery, but the AR contents did not start.

To maintain users' motivation, some techniques should be introduced such as gamification methods that reward users for the number of their uploaded positions. We also should sophisticate its user interface and system behavior to improve usability. Finally, we found that our application was slightly complex and time-consuming, but it had many interesting and acceptable aspects.

5   Conclusion

In this paper, we presented a crowdsourcing system that constructs a database for AR contents by user generation and applied it in "Window to the Past," which runs on personal mobile devices. In "Window to the Past," the system designers had to prepare the contents by themselves, so there were only a limited number of contents. We overcame this problem by implementing a system in which many users can participate in creating contents by crowdsourcing. This will extend "Window to the Past" to a larger area with more data created by many users.

We proposed a crowdsourcing system in which users identify the location of the past pictures and capture the current reference pictures. This system helps users generate contents for "Window to the Past" with enjoyment. The database contains current reference pictures of the past pictures, GPS information of the locations, and annotation of the pictures. Our proposed system is realized as a smartphone and a tablet device application. Users explore the spots where old photos were captured on behalf of the designer. They only need to take photos at the correct position and angle where the semi-transparent past image matches the background, and then they can easily add a series of necessary information for "Window to the Past" to our database. We integrate "Window to the Past" and this crowdsourcing database construction system into one application named "Crowd-Cloud Window to the Past."

Through our experiment, we evaluated this proposed crowdsourcing system. The results showed that users who knew a bit about the photographed place in the past picture were able to identify the locations and take photos there. In most uploaded pictures, the distance from the photographed place to the correct location was within 10 m. Moreover, all photos were taken at approximately the same camera angle, which could be sufficiently used as the reference images for "Window to the Past." If the appearance of the uploaded images was significantly different from the corresponding past pictures such as in Pattern 2, they were unable to judge accurately because there was very little information for making a decision. Moreover, users were unable to evaluate the correctness of the present pictures accurately if the appearance of the images was significantly different from the corresponding past ones. We should incorporate functions to judge the accuracy of the pictures.

In addition, we distributed this application, "Crowd-Cloud Window to the Past" through the Internet. We held workshops using this application in cooperation with many local communities and evaluated the interest and feasibility of this application. Here, we found that this application was slightly complex and time-consuming, but it had many interesting and acceptable aspects. For example, our application for looking for photographed positions provides users with entertainment, like games. Although we should sophisticate its user interface and user-motivating design, these results suggest that the proposed system could work well in gathering valuable user-generated contents to provide a richer AR experience.

Acknowledgement. This work was partially supported by the MEXT, Grant-in-Aid for Scientific Research (A), 25240057.

References

1. Nakasugi, H., Yamauchi, Y.: Past viewer: development of wearable learning system for history education. In: Proceedings of the International Conference on Computers in Education, 2002, pp. 1311–1312. IEEE (2002)
2. Wither, J., Allen, R., Samanta, V., Hemanus, J., Tsai, Y.T., Azuma, R., Carter, W., Hinman, R., Korah, T.: The westwood experience: connecting story to locations via mixed reality. In: IEEE International Symposium on Mixed and Augmented Reality-Arts, Media, and Humanities (ISMAR-AMH 2010) (2010)
3. Okada, N., Imura, J., Narumi, T., Tanikawa, T., Hirose, M.: Manseibashi reminiscent window: on-site AR exhibition system using mobile devices. In: Streitz, N., Markopoulos, P. (eds.) DAPI 2015. LNCS, vol. 9189, pp. 349–361. Springer, Heidelberg (2015)
4. Nakano, J., Narumi, T., Tanikawa, T., Hirose, M.: Implementation of on-site virtual time machine for mobile devices. In: Virtual Reality (VR), March 2015, pp. 245–246. IEEE (2015)
5. Bae, S., Agarwala, A., Durand, F.: Computational rephotography. ACM Trans. Graph 29(3), 1–15 (2010)
6. Kasada, K., Hayashi, O., Narumi, T., Tanikawa, T., Hirose, M.: On-site virtual time machine with navigation to past camera position. In: Proceedings of ASIAGRAPH 2010, Tokyo, Japan, vol. 4, no. 2, pp. 35–40 (2010)
7. Nakano, J., Kasada, K., Nishimura, K., Tanikawa, T., Hirose, M.: On-site virtual time machine-navigation to past camera position and past picture superimpose on present landscape. Trans. Inf. Process. Soc. Jpn. 52(12), 3611–3624 (2011)
8. Snavely, N., Seitz, S.M., Szeliski, R.: Photo tourism: exploring photo collections in 3d. ACM Trans. Graph. (TOG) 25(3), 835–846 (2006)
9. Beeton, S.: Film-Induced Tourism, vol. 25. Channel View Publications, Clevedon (2005)
10. Gyimóthy, S., Lundberg, C., Lindström, K.N., Lexhagen, M., Larson, M.: Popculture tourism. In: Tourism Research Frontiers: Beyond the Boundaries of Knowledge. Tourism Social Science Series, vol. 20, pp. 13–26. Emerald Group Publishing Limited (2015)
11. Webb, R.H.: Repeat Photography: Methods and Applications in the Natural Sciences. Island Press, Washington, D.C. (2010)
12. Von Ahn, L., Dabbish, L.: Labeling images with a computer game. In: Proceedings of the SIGCHI Conference on Human Factors in Computing Systems, CHI 2004, pp. 319–326. ACM, New York (2004)
13. Friedman, B.: Value-sensitive design. Interactions 3(6), 16–23 (1996)
14. Kuznetsov, S.: Motivations of contributors to Wikipedia. ACM SIGCAS Comput. Soc. 36 (2), 1 (2006)
15. Nov, O.: What motivates wikipedians? Commun. ACM 50(11), 60–64 (2007)
16. Rublee, E., Rabaud, V., Konolige, K., Bradski, G.: ORB: an efficient alternative to SIFT or SURF. In: 2011 IEEE International Conference on Computer Vision (ICCV). IEEE (2011)

Backend Infrastructure Supporting Audio Augmented Reality and Storytelling

Kari Salo[1][(✉)], Diana Giova[1], and Tommi Mikkonen[2]

[1] Helsinki Metropolia University of Applied Sciences, Helsinki, Finland
kari.salo@metropolia.fi, dianakaal@gmail.com
[2] Tampere University of Technology, Tampere, Finland
tommi.mikkonen@tut.fi

Abstract. Today, museums are looking for new ways to attract and engage audience. These include virtual exhibitions, augmented reality and 3D modelling based applications, and interactive digital storytelling. The target of all these activities is to provide better experiences for audiences that are very familiar with the digital world. In augmented reality (AR) and interactive digital storytelling (IDS) systems, visual presentation has been dominant. In contrast to this trend, we have chosen to concentrate on auditory presentation. A key element for this is a backend service supporting different client applications. This paper discusses our experiences from designing a portable open source based audio digital asset management system (ADAM), which supports interaction with smart phones and tablets containing audio augmented reality and audio story applications. We have successfully implemented ADAM system and evaluated it in the Museum of Technology in Helsinki, Finland.

Keywords: Digital asset management · Metadata · Open source DAM · Audio augmented reality · Soundscape

1 Introduction

Today, museums are looking for new ways to attract and engage audience. There are lots of activities in virtual exhibitions [1, 2], augmented reality and 3D modelling based applications [3, 4], and interactive digital storytelling [2, 5]. The common target of all these activities is to provide better experiences for audience that is very familiar with the digital world.

The Neighborhood Living Room sub-project, which is a part of Creative Europe funded People's Smart Sculpture Project, studies different methods to build a more dynamic and participatory audience relationship in a museum. The vision is that the Museum of Technology could be integrated as a part of the Arabianranta district community in Helsinki, Finland. The museum is also aiming at offering an emotional and participatory experience for the residents, especially youth.

When we look at the young residents and their natural way of using information technology (IT) it is obvious that somehow IT should be involved in exhibitions. Many of the residents have a smart phone, a tablet or both. In Finland 88 % of the age group

© Springer International Publishing Switzerland 2016
S. Yamamoto (Ed.): HIMI 2016, Part II, LNCS 9735, pp. 325–335, 2016.
DOI: 10.1007/978-3-319-40397-7_31

16–24 years old have used internet several times a day. 87 % are using mobile phones and 35 % tablets when accessing internet outside of home or office [6].

In augmented reality (AR) systems and interactive digital storytelling (IDS) systems visual presentation has been dominant. We decided to concentrate to auditory presentation as there is not that much activities ongoing. We also decided to use soundscapes as a way to augment reality in museum environment [7]. One key element when developing AR, soundscape and IDS systems is a backend service supporting different client applications. In our case, the backend service is an audio digital asset management system (ADAM).

In this paper we propose an open source based ADAM that is portable and also affordable for smaller museums and other culture sector actors and events. ADAM supports interaction with smart phones and tablets containing audio augmented reality and audio story applications, which are targeted to young visitors in culture institutions and events.

The rest of the paper is organized as follows. In Sect. 2, we discuss about related works and concepts. Then, in Sect. 3 we describe the overall system, and in Sect. 4 we derive corresponding system requirements. In Sect. 5, we present the implementation of the system, including the design of the core system and its rationale. In Sect. 6 we evaluate how well we succeeded. In Sect. 7, we will further discuss the results, and in Sect. 8, we draw some final conclusions.

2 Background

Audio augmented reality systems have been planned for different purposes, and the complexity of these systems has varied from special purpose equipment to smartphone. Audio-Haptic Navigation Environment (AHNE) is a physical space which contains virtual 3D-objects that can be searched and moved. To enable interactions, Kinect depth camera is used to track user's movement, and feedback is provided through audio and custom-implemented haptic gloves [8]. Augmented and Tangible Sonic Interaction (ATSI) does not require special space and user does not have to wear any device except headphones. The user may attach sounds to physical objects that already exist in a selected space, like living room. ATSI will follow user's head and hands movement using Kinect and maintain the correct spatial auditory perspective when picking and moving sounding objects [9]. Mobile Audio Augmented Reality System (MAARS) relies only on mobile device's orientation sensor when creating the impression of virtual sound sources being located in the physical space. The user will experience this virtual audio space using headphones [10]. Common to all of these systems is that they need to know user's location in order to produce sound that is modified according to user's movement. In our case the user is the active party. She knows her location related to the particular environment, where the sounds have a role as augmenting the reality and either she will with the help of mobile apps search relevant sounds or produce the acoustic environment using her creativity and imagination.

A soundscape can be a musical composition, a radio program or an acoustic environment [11]. In our case, it is the acoustic environment. Klang.Reise is an installation of video and audio recordings inside a closed spherical space [7]. The goal is to demonstrate different sounds of a selected place and how these sounds change over the time. The Sound Design Accelerator (SoDA) project provides software for soundscape generation. Targeted to sound designers [12], SoDA contains a storage of annotated audio files, a semantic search engine, an automated soundscape composer combining interpretation of semantical analysis, a geographical and acoustic space modeler, user defined semantic filters, and a soundscape synthesis engine. Our approach is somewhere in between these two. Our target audience is museum visitors, like in Klang.Reise. However, in addition of fixed soundscapes we are asking visitors to build simple soundscapes. We do not expect visitors being familiar with reverberation, resonance, acoustic absorption, bit depth and other acoustic terms.

Interactive storytelling systems could be a mix of human produced stories and digitally produced interaction or fully digital environments with user participation. A fully digital prototype consisting of a game engine based narrative environment, an AI-based interactive digital storytelling system and communication protocol, and a language between these two components was developed. The user will interact through IDS, and narrative environment will reflect the interaction [13]. Sarajevo Survival Tools contains a digital story in the form of video. The video is divided into story segments. After each segment, the user is given a possibility to browse segment related objects and material in a virtual museum [2]. A prototype containing animation based user interaction, recorded actor readings, improvisations, and expert commentaries was developed for a museum exhibition on the medieval historian Jean Froissart. Metadata was attached to recorded audio clips to facilitate relevant audio file retrieval and play based on user interaction and location [5]. Our target is to rely on non-modifiable audio material on storytelling; thus the last two examples are closest to our approach. However, we are also prepared to save user's narratives, so that visitors should be able share their own stories.

Digital Asset Management System (DAM) should be able to manipulate as well as protect from unintentional alteration those digital assets stored in it. Digital asset could be defined as a file which is tagged with the information about it. This definition – an asset is a file plus metadata – is commonly used by large companies [14]. The second definition is that an asset is a file and its rights, which essentially means that content has value as long as its owner has the right to utilize it [15]. The two definitions are complementary. Thus a DAM should contain digital files along with their metadata as well as usage rights. The management aspect of the system is fairly straightforward to understand as it is the actions which are required to be executed onto these assets. The aforementioned assets could be adding, removing, and editing assets' data or metadata. This in turn would ensure that the digital integrity of the asset is maintained while providing re-purposed files for every media need.

To utilize, search, and find relevant media files, it essential to utilize metadata. There are several metadata standards for different purposes, like metadata exchange between systems [16], general metadata for broad range of domains [17], audio and video resources for a wide range of broadcasting applications [18, 19], series of interfaces for interchange information about multimedia content in the audio domain [20], and audio specific structural and administrative metadata [21]. Different standards have been evaluated from digital audio-visual library point of view using four selection criteria [15]. There are several studies regarding audio specific metadata and annotation, like Telemeta [22] and GlobalMusic2one [23]. Telemeta is very similar to what we aim at. The differences lie in the target group and related implications. Telemeta is targeted to music researchers and thus it relies on TimeSide audio processing framework, audio analysis plugins and audio extraction libraries. GlobalMusic2one annotation tool has the same target group as Telemeta, i.e. musicologists. Thus the tool aims at describing audio file in very detailed level. In contrast, our view is that individual audio file is a whole.

3   System Overview

Figure 1 describes the overall system including also mobile applications that will utilize audio digital asset management system. The overall system is a distributed system consisting of an audio digital asset management system (ADAM), management application, and mobile applications. ADAM provides functionalities to manage assets and offers interfaces for both for management application and mobile applications over internet. The management application is more or less an administration console to manage assets and users. Mobile applications, which we will not address in this paper, are for example audio augmented reality, soundscape design, audio story recording and listening, or audio memory sharing applications.

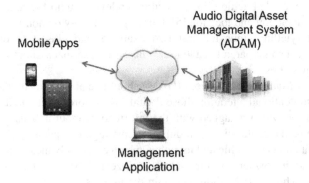

Fig. 1. System overview

4   Requirements

In May 2015, we decided that the first version the backend system should be up and running in Museum of Technology's server within 4–5 months. This meant that we could not start from scratch and that server requirements could not be too limiting. In addition, the system should be available also for other parties without license fees, and hence we would build our system using open source components. At functional level it was required that the system should provide the following functionalities:

- create, read, update and delete audio and related metadata content;
- search content based on metadata;

- manage access groups and rights;
- authenticate users;
- provide easy to use admin console for non-IT personnel;
- provide APIs: authenticate, search content, download content, and upload content.

Metadata requirements were left partially for further studies. Initially, we defined the following metadata requirements:

- Title of the audio file;
- Description of the audio file;
- Tags (keywords) assigned to audio file;
- Date when audio file was saved;
- Link to audio file;
- Format of the audio file: wav, mp3, and PCM;
- Length of the audio file in seconds;
- Category: nature, human, machine, and story;
- Sound type: soundscape, ambience, and effect;
- Location: longitude and latitude.

5 Implementation

Comparison of Digital Asset Management Systems. There are many different kinds DAMs. Some might be specifically designed for a specific file type, while others might be designed to handle a multitude of file types. In this case, the comparison is regarding systems which can accommodate audio files. Table 1 shows some of the open source DAMs along with their features, license and programming language(s). Based on the table, we determined that for us the best candidates would be Telemeta and Resource Space. As described in Sect. 2, Telemeta is mainly targeted to musicologists. In addition, Telemeta was still in development mode and it was not compatible with Windows systems. Consequently, we ended up using ResourceSpace as the basis for ADAM. This selection was also supported by the fact that we have a large pool of students with PHP skills.

Storage of Resources. Digital assets, called resources, are stored according to their identities in a table. The metadata values are stored into the row of that particular resource, and the metadata fields are stored in a separate table. This design simplifies modifying metadata fields and values. Moreover, there are further tables that are used to specify which collection resources are in, who has the rights to these resources, how many users there are, various reports, how many users have accessed the APIs, etc. In general, the tables are informative, which simplifies the programming. For example, relevant data can be fetched by joining or pivoting tables with MySQL. In ADAM resources are based on their identities. If a user sends an audio file into another user's collection, then only a record of that action is saved into the database – the files are not duplicated or physically copied on the server space.

Table 1. Detailed overview of DAMs

Software name	Features	License	Language
Telemeta	• open source • web audio archiving software • metadata • user management • English and French support • REST API • Dublin Core compatibility	CeCILL	Python and JavaScript
ResourceSpace	• fully featured DAM system • user management • API available • plugins available • metadata • many file types	BSD	PHP and SQL
Phrasenet	• DAM system • user management • images/video/documents support	GPL3	PHP
EnterMedia	• typical DAM system • uses XML, but database possible • plugins available • metadata	LGPL	Java

API Design. According to the requirements listed above, three APIs were needed: authentication API, upload API, and search API. Developing APIs was the most time consuming part of modifying ResourceSpace to fulfill the requirements. The authentication API is needed by the mobile users to receive a token, which in turn will be used with search and upload APIs. Authentication is security feature and ensures that only authorized users have access to token. The search API is a HTTP GET request containing token and predefined search parameters. The response given in JSON format contains audio files' metadata based on search parameters that are set along with the search request. Thus, the search API also enables downloading, as the link to audio file is a part of the metadata. The upload API lets users with a valid token upload their audio files along with metadata they choose to transmit to ADAM as a multi-part form using HTTP post. Metadata and token will be encoded in a part of the URL, and the audio file in the body of HTTP post.

Metadata. During the requirement specification phase, it was decided that we need to study metadata standards more deeply. Based on metadata evaluation criteria introduced in [23] we defined our criteria as following:

• Internal metadata model now, readiness for external model;
• Flat metadata model;
• Support identification, description, technical and rights types;
• Syntax of supported metadata.

Based on the criteria, we ended up adding more metadata fields to enable in the future the exchange of assets by supporting Open Archives Initiative Protocol for Metadata Harvesting (OAI-PMH), which requires compatibility with unqualified Dublin Core [15, 16]. In addition, it was clear that we cannot call our audio files as assets unless we introduce at least a rights metadata field. Thus our final metadata is as described in Table 2. In total, 7 new metadata fields were introduced. Most of the metadata will be input manually during the storage of audio file, but some will however be extracted automatically from the audio file properties.

Table 2. The Dublin Core Metadata Element Set mapping to ADAM

Dublin Core Metadata Element Set	AudioResourceSpace	Notes
Title	Title	
Contributor	Contributor	new
Source	Source	new
Creator	Creator	new
Date	Creation Date	automatic
Language	Language	new
Subject	Tags	
Type	Category + Sound Type	
Relation	Relation	new
Description	Description	
Format	File extension	automatic
Coverage	Location (longitude + latitude)	
Publisher	Publisher	new
Identifier	Link	
Rights	Rights	new
	Length	
	File Size	automatic

Management Application. The management application that a user of ADAM sees once she logs into the system, is straightforward to understand and use. Figure 2 shows the modified dashboard suited to serve the requirements for the audio storage system with some notes regarding its functionality. Some changes had to be made to accommodate only audio files, necessary user rights, and custom metadata fields. These changes were made by accessing the Team Centre menu (the top navigation bar in Fig. 2), which provides options for modifying user rights, file types, and metadata fields.

Installation Requirements. ADAM can be installed on Linux/Unix, Windows, Mac OS X, and Synology DSM systems and it works with the most web servers including Apache and Internet Information Services (IIS) for Windows Server. ADAM requires PHP greater than or equal to version 5, and MySQL greater than or equal to version 5.0.15.

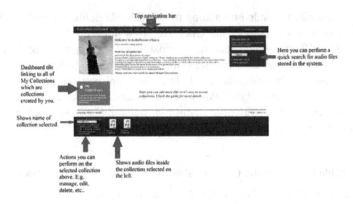

Fig. 2. ADAM dashboard

6 Evaluation

We produced five separate user guides: installation guide, admin guide, and one guide per API. Based on this documentation, we were able to evaluate how we initially succeeded in ADAM implementation.

The installation guide was given to a person who was not developing ADAM. He was able to first check together with IT staff in Museum of Technology that a compatible server environment was available. Then he followed the installation guide and successfully installed the system. After running basic functionality tests defined in the installation guide, it was clear that the installation succeeded.

Two persons from museum were given a short introduction regarding ADAM main concepts. They were given the admin guide to check if the management of audio files and users is easy enough. Their response was that the admin guide is sufficient to handle the tasks. The same guide was also handed to sound design students who were planning what kind of audio files can be used as building elements when designing soundscapes in museum environment. The feedback from the students was mainly positive. They were able to accomplish their task to store soundscape building elements with metadata. The only drawback was the time consuming manual input of metadata.

All the APIs were initially tested by a person who was not developing them. Authentication API was tested using Chrome Advanced REST Client. HTTP post containing the username and password were sent to ADAM, request succeeded and response contained token. Search API was tested also using Chrome Advanced REST Client. Defining different search combinations resulted into right response. Upload API was tested using simple Android app which was developed for testing purposes. Uploading an audio file together with relevant metadata worked as expected.

API testing continued with the group of students who were developing Android apps which would be accessing ADAM. The feedback received from this group was that they wished the search API would output an empty array in JSON if the results for search were null, which was changed accordingly. Otherwise all APIs were working as defined in the respective guides.

To summarize, we have succeeded in providing the backend system as expected (Table 3). The only drawback was the two weeks delay in installing the final system in the museum's server.

Table 3. Satisfying the requirements

General Requirements	Yes/No
Backend system working in museum within 4–5 months	2 weeks delay
Open source system	Yes
Functional Requirements	
create, read, update and delete audio and related metadata content	Yes
search content based on metadata	Yes
manage access groups and rights	Yes
authenticate users	Yes
provide easy to use admin console	Yes
provide the following APIs for mobile applications: authenticate, search content, download content, and upload content	Yes
Metadata Requirements	See Table 2

7   Discussion

Initially ADAM was installed and developed in Metropolia's (development organization's) server. As we wanted to prove the portability the system was installed in the Museum of Techology's server, and this version was used to get feedback from the different stakeholders. Two (none-IT) persons from the museum took the role administrator and tested usability and functionality of ADAM utilizing solely the respective user guide. We involved sound designers to evaluate system as a part of planning audio material for soundscape workshops. We also involved 7 Android application development teams to utilize ADAM as a part of their audio mixing apps. Based on the feedback from different parties ADAM was modified accordingly. So far the only feature that requires more attention is the metadata input. We need to study more which metadata is really required and reconsider if OAI-PMH support is relevant.

We will utilize ADAM at least in the following cases together with the Museum of Technology:

- audio augmented reality/soundscape workshops,
- audio stories connected to museum's artefacts,
- sharing memories in the form audio stories

We strongly believe that ADAM is a viable innovation platform also for smaller museums and other culture sector's actors who run on a tight budget and at the same time want to utilize audio as a part of their creative activities. One proof of this claim is that already now three of the People's Smart Sculpture partners have expressed their willingness to utilize the platform.

8 Conclusions

In this paper we have proposed an open source based audio digital asset management system that is portable and also affordable for smaller museums and other culture sector's actors and events. Audio digital asset management system supports interaction with smart phones and tablets containing audio augmented reality and audio story applications, which are targeted to young visitors in cultural institutions and events.

We have successfully implemented ADAM system and evaluated it in the Museum of Technology in Helsinki, Finland. Next, we are ready test different use cases where the backend system is heavily utilized for building innovative apps.

Acknowledgements. We thank Outi Putkonen and Riina Linna from the Museum of Technology for all the support. The work is co-funded by EU, Creative Europe Programme, The People's Smart Sculpture project (http://smartsculpture.eu). We thank the project partners for inspiring discussions.

References

1. Ardissono, L., Kuflik, T., Petrelli, D.: Personalization in cultural heritage: the road travelled and the one ahead. User Model. User-Adap. Inter. **22**(1–2), 73–99 (2012)
2. Rizvic, S., Sadzak, A., Hulusic, V., Karahasanovic, A.: Interactive digital storytelling in the Sarajevo survival tools virtual environment. In: Proceedings of the 28th Spring Conference on Computer Graphics, SCCG 2012, pp. 109–116. ACM, New York (2012)
3. Demiris, A.M., Vlahakis, V., Ioannidis, N.: System and infrastructure considerations for the successful introduction of augmented reality guides in cultural heritage sites. In: Proceedings of the ACM Symposium on Virtual Reality Software and Technology, VRST 2006, pp. 141–144. ACM, New York (2006)
4. De Sa, M., Churchill, E.: Mobile augmented reality: exploring design and prototyping techniques. In: Proceedings of the 14th International Conference on Human-Computer Interaction with Mobile Devices and Services, MobileHCI 2012, pp. 221–230. ACM, New York (2012)
5. Blythe, M., McCarthy, J., Wright, P., Petrelli, D.: History and experience: storytelling and interaction design. In: Proceedings of the 25th BCS Conference on Human-Computer Interaction, BCS-HCI 2011, pp. 395–404. British Computer Society, Swinton (2011)
6. Tilastokeskus, Internetin käytön yleiset muutokset (in Finnish). http://www.stat.fi/til/sutivi/2014/sutivi_2014_2014-11-06_kat_001_fi.html
7. Drechsler, A., Raffaseder, H., Rubisch, B.: Klang.Reise: new scientific approaches through an artistic soundscape installation? In: Proceedings of the 7th Audio Mostly Conference: A Conference on Interaction with Sound, AM 2012, New York, NY, USA, pp. 44–46 (2012)
8. Väänänen-Vainio-Mattila, K., Suhonen, K., Laaksonen, J., Kildal, J., Tahiroğlu, K.: User experience and usage scenarios of audio-tactile interaction with virtual objects in a physical environment. In: Proceedings of the 6th International Conference on Designing Pleasurable Products and Interfaces, DPPI 2013, pp. 67–76. ACM, New York (2013)
9. Pugliese, R., Politis, A., Takala, T.: ATSI: augmented and tangible sonic interaction. In: Proceedings of the Ninth International Conference on Tangible, Embedded, and Embodied Interaction, TEI 2015, pp. 97–104. ACM, New York (2015)

10. Heller, F., Krämer, A., Borchers, J.: Simplifying orientation measurement for mobile audio augmented reality applications. In: Proceedings of the SIGCHI Conference on Human Factors in Computing Systems, CHI 2014, pp. 615–624. ACM, New York (2014)
11. Schaefer, R.M.: The Soundscape: Our Sonic Environment and the Tuning of the World. Inner Traditions International/Destiny Books, Rochester (1993)
12. Casu, M., Koutsomichalis, M., Valle, A.: Imaginary soundscapes: the SoDA project. In: Proceedings of the 9th Audio Mostly: A Conference on Interaction with Sound, AM 2014. ACM, New York (2014). Article no. 5
13. Peinado, F., Navarro, Á., Gervás, P.: A testbed environment for interactive storytellers. In: Proceedings of the 2nd International Conference on INtelligent TEchnologies for Interactive Entertainment, INTETAIN 2008. ICST, Brussels (2008). Article no. 3
14. Jacobsen, J., Schlenker, T., Edwards, L.: Implementing a Digital Asset Management System: For Animation, Computer Games, and Web Development. Focal Press, Burlington (2005)
15. De Sutter, R., Notebaert, S., Van de Walle, R.: Evaluation of metadata standards in the context of digital audio-visual libraries. In: Gonzalo, J., Thanos, C., Verdejo, M., Carrasco, R.C. (eds.) ECDL 2006. LNCS, vol. 4172, pp. 220–231. Springer, Heidelberg (2006)
16. Open Archives Initiative Protocol for Metadata Harvesting. https://www.openarchives.org/pmh/
17. Dublin Core Metadata Element Set, Version 1.1. http://dublincore.org/documents/dces/
18. AES60-2011: AES standard for audio metadata - Core audio metadata. http://www.aes.org/publications/standards/search.cfm?docID=85
19. Ebu Core Metadata Set, Specification v. 1.6. https://tech.ebu.ch/docs/tech/tech3293.pdf
20. ISO/IEC 15938-4:2002(en) Information technology — Multimedia content description interface — Part 4: Audio. https://www.iso.org/obp/ui/#iso:std:iso-iec:15938:-4:ed-1:v1:en
21. AES57-2011: AES standard for audio metadata - Audio object structures for preservation and restoration. http://www.aes.org/publications/standards/search.cfm?docID=84
22. Fillon, T., Simonnot, J., Mifune, M., Khoury, S., Pellerin, G., Le Coz, M.: Telemeta: an open-source web framework for ethnomusicological audio archives management and automatic analysis. In: Proceedings of the 1st International Workshop on Digital Libraries for Musicology, DLfM 2014, pp. 1–8. ACM, New York (2014)
23. Woitek, P., Bräuer, P., Grossmann, H.: A novel tool for capturing conceptualized audio annotations. In: Proceedings of the 5th Audio Mostly Conference: A Conference on Interaction with Sound, AM 2010. ACM, New York (2010). Article no. 15

Creativity Comes from Interaction

Multi-modal Analyses of Three-Creator Communication in Constructing a Lego Castle

Haruka Shoda[1]([✉]), Koshi Nishimoto[2], Noriko Suzuki[3],
Mamiko Sakata[2], and Noriko Ito[2]

[1] Global Innovation Research Organization, Ritsumeikan University,
Nojihigashi 1-1-1, Kusatsu 525-8577, Japan
`shoda@fc.ritsumei.ac.jp`
[2] Department of Culture and Information Science, Doshisha University,
Tataramiyakodani 1-3, Kyotanabe 610-0394, Japan
[3] Faculty of Business Administration, Tezukayama University,
Tezukayama 7-1-1, Nara 631-8501, Japan

Abstract. We explored how three people communicate verbally (i.e. chatting, discussion) and nonverbally (i.e. gazes, gestures) in creating a Lego(R) castle collaboratively. We also investigated how such communication behaviors can be cues for a "better" and "more creative" castle. In Experiment 1, we asked a total of 30 students (3 people × 10 groups) to construct a castle fully in collaboration with the group members. In Experiment 2, we asked the other 27 students to assess the quality ("how good the castle is") and creativeness ("how creative the castle is") for the photographed castles. The verbal, gestural, and gazing behaviors of the creators were analyzed quantitatively. We conducted path analyses to identify parameters determining the quality and the creativeness, showing that the degree of communication behaviors was reflected in the evaluation of the created castle. In detail, the quality was enhanced by looking at the other group members as well as by discussing the content of the castle. The creativeness was determined by the degree of chatting and representational gestures. These results suggest the communication process in multiple-agent creation: Rapport can be constructed efficiently by chatting with the other members; creators can share divergent ideas; and they can construct a creative object.

Keywords: Communication · Creativity · Multiple-agent interaction · Multi-modal analysis · Lego(R)

1 Introduction

Creative activities, such as visual art, music, and building construction, are comprised generally of "communication" among creators, objects (i.e. works), and beholders (e.g. viewers, audiences) [3]. Creators' intentions are to be reflected in the object; beholders perceive such intentions by viewing the object; and they

© Springer International Publishing Switzerland 2016
S. Yamamoto (Ed.): HIMI 2016, Part II, LNCS 9735, pp. 336–345, 2016.
DOI: 10.1007/978-3-319-40397-7_32

assess the quality and the creativeness of the object. Our focus in the present study is how creators communicate with each other in constructing a work collaboratively, and how the created work is evaluated in terms of the quality and the creativeness. By understanding how multiple creators' communication behaviors contribute to the quality and the creativeness of the work, we can provide novel knowledge about creativity in multi-party interaction.

We already know that communication behaviors among three or more people are different from those between two [2,5]. In two-agent conversation, if one person speaks, the other one is expected inevitably to speak next. In contrast, the next speaker is not identified uniquely in three-agent communication, so that the communication is to be more complex [5]. We can communicate smoothly by identifying the next speaker via verbal (e.g. specific phrases such as "What do you think, Professor?") and/or nonverbal cues (e.g. eye contact, bodily direction), even among three or more people [4].

Our focus in the present study is targeted at whether such multi-party communication generates "creativity" that is not produced individually. In the literature [6], the individual's creativity can be classified into two components: "divergent" and "convergent." Divergent thinking is a thought process used to generate creative ideas by exploring many possible solutions. In contrast, convergent thinking follows a particular set of logical steps to arrive at one solution. We can assume that collaborative creation is also composed of these two elements: producing many different ideas (divergent) and gathering them into one work (convergent). In this kind of activity, the members should construct "rapport," which is a state in which multiple people can communicate with one another and is usually based on shared interests, values, and other personal factors [1].

The group members' nonverbal communication is also an important factor in the collaborative task. A member's gaze at the other group members is important in role-sharing [13] and gestures among three people promote the completion of the task [8].

In the literature, the clear goal of the task (i.e. instruction about how to make an object) was provided to the creators [13]. In a real creative activity, however, creators sometimes create objects in an impromptu manner through a trial and error process without any instruction. In such a condition, each group member should present his/her own imagery accurately with the others and needs communication to understand the other members' ideas. In the present study, we set up a collaborative creation task, in which creators construct a "castle" by using Lego(R) bricks without any instruction. Pike [12] has shown that Lego is a useful tool for a creator to shape his/her imagery in the mind. McGraw et al. [9] showed that the "trial and error" process of including and excluding bricks helps creators express their own ideas. The task using Lego bricks enables us to visualize how the group members construct one object collaboratively by sharing their own ideas.

The purpose of the present study is to understand how three creators communicate verbally and nonverbally with each other as well as how such communication behaviors determine the quality and the creativeness of the work (i.e. evaluation). These two evaluative axes, "quality" and "creativeness," are thought to be distinct as in, "This work is built well but not so creative" (e.g. [14]). We tested three hypothetical models (Fig. 1) in the present study. Figure 1a indicates that the verbal (i.e. discussion, chatting) and the nonverbal behaviors (i.e. gestures, gazes) would affect in parallel the quality and the creativeness of the work. If the verbal and the nonverbal behaviors are related to each other, we assumed that some causal relationships should be observed (as shown in Fig. 1b and c), so that we excluded the correlations between the verbal and the nonverbal behaviors in this diagram. Figure 1b indicates that the verbal behaviors would determine the nonverbal behaviors, both of which would explain the evaluation of the work. Figure 1c is a contrasting model of Fig. 1b in terms of the order of the verbal and the nonverbal behaviors. By understanding how creators' communication enhances the quality and the creativeness of the work, we would provide a basic perspective for multi-party interaction in a collaborative creation.

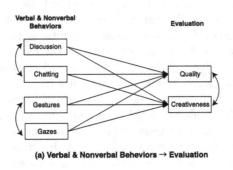

(a) Verbal & Nonverbal Behaviors → Evaluation

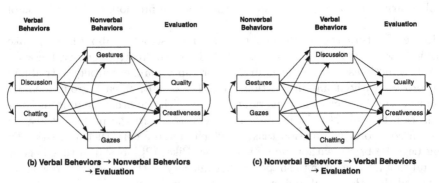

(b) Verbal Behaviors → Nonverbal Behaviors → Evaluation

(c) Nonverbal Behaviors → Verbal Behaviors → Evaluation

Fig. 1. Hypothetical models explaining evaluation by communication behaviors. Lateral and bilateral arrows indicate the causal and the correlational relationships between parameters, respectively.

2   Method

2.1   Experiment 1 (Collaborative Creation Task)

Participants. Thirty students (15 men, 15 women, $M = 20.03, SD = 1.81$) participated in Experiment 1, and were assigned to each of 10 same-sex groups (5 male groups and 5 female groups). The members of each group had never met each other before the experiment.

Procedure. Each experiment was conducted in a sound-proof room. Participants sat down at a circular table (top: radius 44 cm, height: 82 cm). Approximately 600–700 Lego bricks were placed in the groove on the edge of the table. The colors of bricks were white, red, blue, yellow, black, green, brown, lime, and orange. Participants were asked to create a castle collaboratively within 30 min by using the Lego bricks. The auditory and visual portions for each participant were recorded on a video camera, which was located in front of him/her (HDR-CX550V, Sony). We used a wireless microphone for the audio (ECM-AW3, Sony). Three cameras were synchronized by recording a flashing light simultaneously. An experimental snapshot is shown in Fig. 2.

Annotation. The second author annotated each participant's verbal and non-verbal behaviors using the EUDICO Linguistic Annotator (ELAN [7]). He annotated behaviors in three phases: "opening" (0:00–5:00), "middle" (15:00–20:00), and "ending" (20:00–25:00). We excluded the final phase of 25:00–30:00 because some of the groups completed the task at this phase. We analyzed the total of these 15 min in the present study. The following behaviors were annotated.

The *discussion* is defined as utterances related to the castle creation, e.g. "Let's make a gate with brown bricks!" and "Can I make this portion bigger?" Utterances irrelevant to castle creation were categorized as *chatting*, e.g. "Do you play baseball?" and "I feel like a kid again." We counted the number of *gazes*, or when a participant looked at another group member. We also identified the

どちらが完成度が高いですか？

Fig. 2. Snapshot of Experiment 1 (Color figure online)

Fig. 3. Example of images in Experiment 2. The sentence in the middle means "which is better?" in Japanese.

number of *gestures* (representational gesture [10]), which is a body movement expressing a specific object spatially. As for the discussion and the chatting, we asked an expert in annotation with ELAN to decode all the behaviors, showing high reliability of the second author's annotation (Cohen's $\kappa = .96$).

2.2   Experiment 2 (Evaluation Task)

Participants. Twenty-seven students (7 men, 20 women, $M = 19.63$, $SD = 1.28$) participated in Experiment 2. No participants participated in Experiment 1.

Stimuli. We photographed the front, the back, and the top images of each of the works and arranged them side by side. We combined two out of 10 works (45 combinations in total) and placed them vertically (see Fig. 3).

Procedure. We conducted an experiment to assess the quality and the creativeness of the work using Thurstone's pairwise comparison method [15]. Each experiment was conducted using a computer with a monitor (PCG-21514n, Sony) and SuperLab4.5 (Cedrus). The participant sat 30 cm in front of the monitor, watched one of 45 stimuli (Fig. 3), chose which was better ("quality"), and chose which was more creative ("creativeness"). He/She repeated the task for all combinations, the order of which was randomized among participants.

3   Results

3.1   Basic Statistics

The data collected in the present study are plotted in Fig. 4. The basic statistics are shown in Table 1. Although we should acknowledge that variations among the individuals/groups were relatively high as shown in Fig. 4 and Table 1, we used all the samples in the following analyses to obtain enough samples.

3.2   Correlation Among Parameters

We computed Pearson's correlation coefficients (Table 2) among all the parameters shown in Table 1. The discussion correlated negatively with the gazes ($r = -.35$) and positively with gestures ($r = .46$). The chatting correlated positively with the gazes ($r = .50$) and the creativeness of the work ($r = .61$), both of which also correlated with each other ($r = .40$). In contrast, the quality of the work did not show any significant correlation with the other parameters. The two evaluation items (i.e. quality, creativeness) did not correlate with each other.

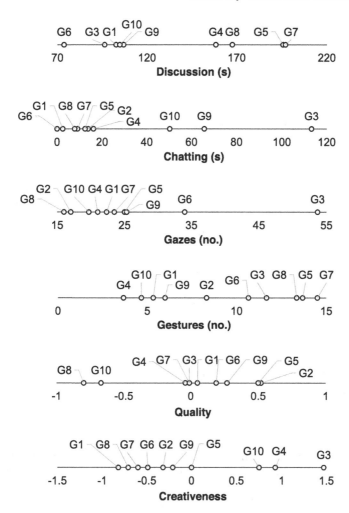

Fig. 4. Mean value per group computed for each parameter of verbal behaviors (i.e. discussion, chatting), nonverbal behaviors (i.e. gazes, gestures), and evaluations of the work (i.e. quality, creativeness). G1–G10 indicate group IDs. G1–G5 and G6–G10 are male and female groups, respectively.

3.3 Path Analysis Determining Quality and Creativeness by Communicative Behaviors

The aforementioned correlation analyses were useful to understand the relationship between any two items, but we have not understood the causality of how the creators' behaviors affect the quality and the creativeness of the work. We conducted path analyses (e.g. [16]) by which we can construct a model of the process from the creators' behaviors to the evaluation of the work.

Table 1. Basic statistics for each parameter. The values were computed for individuals in Experiment 1 ($N = 30$) and for groups in Experiment 2 ($N = 10$).

Parameter	Mean	SD	Max.	Min.
Verbal ($N = 30$)				
Discussion (in s)	140.47	65.80	317.49	32.77
Chatting (in s)	28.98	41.61	187.46	0.00
Nonverbal ($N = 30$)				
Gazes (no.)	25.70	14.34	73.00	6.00
Gestures (no.)	9.20	5.71	26.00	1.00
Evaluation ($N = 10$)				
Quality	0.00	0.42	0.52	−0.80
Creativeness	0.00	0.74	1.47	−0.82

Table 2. Correlation matrix for communication behaviors and evaluations ($N = 30$).

	Discussion	Chatting	Gazes	Gestures	Quality
Chatting	−.09				
Gazes	−.35†	.50***			
Gestures	.46**	.03	.08		
Quality	.19	−.06	.14	.04	
Creativeness	−.14	.61***	.40*	−.18	−.11

***$p < .001$, **$p < .01$, *$p < .05$, $^\dagger p < .10$

In the present study, we installed three hypothetical models (Fig. 1). Path analyses were conducted for these models using the generalized least squares method, by which we computed the goodness-of-fit indices for each model (Table 3). Model c yielded the minimal AIC and BIC and the maximal CFI, indicating that Model c fit the best with the present data. AIC, BIC, and CFI stand for Akaike Information Criterion, Bayesian Information Criterion, and Comparative Fit Index, respectively.

By excluding the insignificant paths from the initial model (Fig. 1c), we found the final model in which all the paths were significant ($\alpha = .05$) or at least approaching significant ($\alpha = .10$) (Fig. 5). Based on the goodness-of-fit indices,

Table 3. Goodness-of-fit indices for three hypothetical models (Fig. 1).

Model No.	AIC	BIC	CFI
a	508.59	526.81	.42
b	496.37	520.19	.94
c	494.13	517.95	1.00

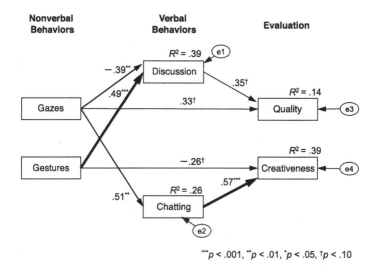

Fig. 5. Path diagram explaining evaluation by communication behaviors (values were standardized.) The boldness of the path was based on the significance of the value. e1-e4 indicate error variables. No correlation paths remained.

we confirmed that the present data fit the final model, $\chi^2(8, N = 30) = 4.26, p = .83, \text{CFI} = 1.00, \text{RMSEA} < .001$[1].

First, by gazing at one of the other creators, the chatting ($\beta = .51$) and the discussion ($\beta = -.39$) increased and decreased, respectively. The amount of gestures determined the amount of discussion ($\beta = .49$). As for the causality from the nonverbal behaviors to the evaluation of the work, the number of gazes enhanced the quality ($\beta = .33$) and that of gestures decreased the creativeness ($\beta = -.26$). According to the absolute values of β, the influences of the verbal behaviors seemed greater than those of the nonverbal. The amounts of discussion and chatting enhanced the quality ($\beta = .35$) and the creativeness ($\beta = .57$), respectively.

The final model shows that the nonverbal behaviors influenced the verbal behaviors, both of which influenced the quality and the creativeness of the work. The quality was determined by the amounts of gazing and discussion, whereas the creativeness was determined less by gestures and more by chatting.

4 Discussion

In the present study, we investigated effects of three creators' communication behaviors on the quality and the creativeness of the work in a collaborative creation task using Lego bricks. Results can be summarized as follows. First, the amounts of nonverbal behaviors determined those of verbal behaviors. Second,

---

[1] RMSEA stands for Root Mean Square Error of Approximation.

both verbal and nonverbal behaviors determined the quality and the creativeness of the work.

We found that more gestures generate more discussion. We focused in the present study on McNeill's "representational" gestures [10], which are bodily movements to shape an object spatially. In the present study, the creators' discussion was triggered by such gestures, implying that the creator's mental imagery is expressed spatially by the gesture, to be verbalized as discussion. McNeill suggested that a spatial aspect of a mental representation produces the gesture and that a verbal meaning of the representation produces the utterance [10]. According to this, the gesture takes an important role in the verbalization of the mental representation. In the path model (Fig. 5), the gesture and the discussion are not produced in parallel; rather, the creator's mental imagery is produced first, by which the conversation (discussion) can be promoted.

The amounts of discussion and gazing determined the quality of the work. In Suzuki et al. [13], three creators attempted to construct one large box like a jungle gym collaboratively. The presence of one "leader," who explained verbally how to construct the box, contributed to the quality of completion. Our finding in the present study is in line with this study. Our definition of "discussion" is "utterance related to creating the castle," which is equivalent to the "convergent" process in creativity [6]. This means that the convergent conversation (i.e. conversation toward the completion of the task) among three creators enhances the quality of the work. The more interesting thing is that the gazing behaviors among creators enhanced the quality of the work. Patterson [11] categorized gazing behaviors into several functions, one of which is "promoting the completion of the task," suggesting that the convergent function of discussion be obtained by "looking at the other members" as a nonverbal cue.

Furthermore, we showed that the amount of chatting determined the creativeness of the work. The chatting functions to construct rapport, which is a foundation of communication with each other [1]. Divergent ideas can be generated by chatting, with the result that highly creative work can be generated. In contrast, the use of the representational gesture decreases the evaluated creativeness. Such a gesture represents the spatial imagery of each member [10] being reflected in the work. This may cause the fixing of a particular member's imagery on the work, so that creators are unlikely to talk with each other divergently, resulting in non-creative work.

In the present study, we showed that the group creativity comes from the verbal and the nonverbal interactions among multiple creators. However, we have not understood yet effects of time-series characteristics of communication on the quality and the creativeness. We should examine the present data in depth in future study. The present study also suggests that creators' nonverbal skills in communication and/or personality (such as creativity, leadership) influence the work's quality and creativeness. Further experiments will be needed by incorporating personal and social factors of individuals and/or groups.

Acknowledgments. The contents of this study are based on the second author's master thesis. We also thank Tomoki Yao for checking the validity of our measurements, and Haru Nitta, Kana Shirai, Yu Oshima, and the members at Sakata Lab, Doshisha University for their valuable input for this study.

References

1. Amabile, T.M.: A model of creativity and innovation in organizations. Res. Organ. Behav. **10**(1), 123–167 (1988)
2. Bono, M., Takanashi, K.: Analytical Methodology of Multi-party Interaction. Ohmsha, Tokyo (2009). (in Japanese)
3. Caune, J.: Esthétique de la communication. Presses universitaires de France (1997)
4. Enomoto, M., Den, Y.: Will the participant gazed at by the current speaker be the next speaker? Japan. J. Lang. Soc. **14**(1), 97–109 (2011). (in Japanese)
5. Goffman, E.: Forms of Talk. University of Pennsylvania Press, Philadelphia (1981)
6. Guilford, J.P., Hoepfner, R.: The Analysis of Intelligence. McGraw-Hill Companies, New York (1971)
7. Lausberg, H., Sloetjes, H.: Coding gestural behavior with the neuroges-elan system. Behav. Res. Meth. **41**(3), 841–849 (2009)
8. Matsuda, M., Matsushita, M., Naemura, T.: Group task achievement under a social distributed cognitive environment: an effect of closeness between groups. IEICE Trans. Inf. Syst. **90**(4), 1043–1054 (2007). (in Japanese)
9. McGraw, J.J., Wallot, S., Mitkidis, P., Roepstorff, A.: Culture's building blocks: investigating cultural evolution in a Lego construction task. Front. Psychol. **5**(1017), 1–12 (2014)
10. McNeill, D.: Hand and Mind: What Gestures Reveal About Thought. University of Chicago Press, Chicago (1992)
11. Patterson, M.L.: A sequential functional model of nonverbal exchange. Psychol. Rev. **89**(3), 231–249 (1982)
12. Pike, C.: Exploring the conceptual space of Lego: teaching and learning the psychology of creativity. Psychol. Learn. Teach. **2**(2), 87–94 (2002)
13. Suzuki, N., Kamiya, T., Umata, I., Iwasawa, S., Ito, S.: Verbal and nonverbal behaviors in multi-party collaboration: third-party evaluation to leadership. In: Proceedings of the 28th Annual Conference of the Cognitive Science Society, pp. 41–44 (2011) (in Japanese)
14. Taira, N.: An analysis of writing ability evaluation based on a story production task. Japan. J. Educ. Psychol. **43**(2), 134–144 (1995). (in Japanese)
15. Thurstone, L.L.: A law of comparative judgment. Psychol. Rev. **34**(4), 273–286 (1927)
16. Toyoda, H.: Covariance Structure Analysis (Amos version): Structural Equation Modeling. Tokyo Tosho, Tokyo (2007). (in Japanese)

Co-creative Expression Interface: Aiming to Support Embodied Communication for Developmentally Disabled Children

Takuto Takahashi[1]([✉]), Ryutaro Hayashi[1], Yoshiyuki Miwa[2], and Hiroko Nishi[3]

[1] Graduate School of Creative Science and Engineering,
Waseda University, Tokyo, Japan
chobby75@akane.waseda.jp, ryul0064gt@asagi.waseda.jp
[2] Faculty of Science and Engineering, Waseda University, Tokyo, Japan
miwa@waseda.jp
[3] Faculty of Human Science, Toyo Eiwa University,
Yokohama, Kanagawa, Japan
hiroko@toyoeiwa.ac.jp

Abstract. This study is aiming to develop embodied interfaces to support co-creative expression which will be necessary when embracing the diversity in different people in a series of workshops, which are mainly focused on hand contact improvisation, held in the affected areas of the Great East Japan Earthquake. In specifics, two types of interfaces, which allow children to elicit hand-contact-improvisational expressions, create a relationship and cultivate it further, have been built with a focus on workshop-experienced autistic children having difficulties in verbal interactions in mind. These interfaces, designed to facilitate the reciprocal embodied awareness and thus achieve "the encounter and the connection with others through expression," play a role of an inclusive function in hand contact improvisation. In the attempts of hand contact improvisations using these interfaces with the autistic children, it has been observed that co-creative expressions have been achieved among those children who tend to avoid a face-to-face contact. This indicates that the interfaces are efficient as new non-verbal technologies to support their communication.

Keywords: Co-creation · Hand contact improvisation · Autistic spectrum disorder · Embodiment · Bodily expression

1 Background

Co-creation refers to creative activity wherein people with different backgrounds and values share thoughts and dreams and come together to achieve them. To this end, it is necessary for the participants to resolve for themselves the contradiction of not violating the other person's independence or individuality while sharing the same context with him or her [1]. Therefore, a space is created wherein there is a sense that "I" and "we" coexist, and each person must be positioned there. This is mediated by "expressive bodies." That is, it could be said that when the participants express themselves

S. Yamamoto (Ed.): HIMI 2016, Part II, LNCS 9735, pp. 346–356, 2016.
DOI: 10.1007/978-3-319-40397-7_33

through mutual bodies, an inclusive sense of coexistence and an awareness of such, that is, an awareness of "we," is created. As a concrete method of realizing this, the authors have focused in the past on "hand contact improvisation," which involves the participants joining the palms of their hands together and carrying out improvised bodily expression together. Experiments by one of the authors, Nishi, have confirmed that in this hand contact improvisation, as the expression grows deeper, the relationship between the participants transforms, and the expressions deepen from expressions between individuals that is between "you" and "me," into "our" expressions shown in Fig. 1 [2]. In other words, the main distinguishing feature of hand contact improvisation is that it leads to equal reciprocity. Also, as the authors continued to carry out workshops whose main activity was hand contact improvisation in areas stricken by the Great East Japan Earthquake, it became clear on the basis of experience that hand contact improvisation is an extremely useful means of supporting communication with children with developmental disabilities for whom verbal communication is difficult or who tend to avoid interpersonal interaction, in particular children with autism spectrum disorders [3].

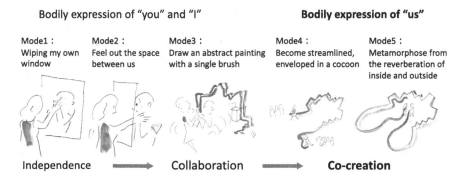

Fig. 1. Changes of relationship in hand contact improvisation (picture; Ken Yabuno)

Also, most existing communication support technologies are designed based on the condition that linguistic or symbolic communication is possible. Thus, in the past, there have been almost no cases in which a co-creative expression interface was developed that deepens the relationship between the participants and creates an awareness of coexistence through mutual bodily expression regardless of the presence or absence of disabilities, their severity, or the age of the participants. Therefore, although more attention is being paid to support for communication among children with developmental disabilities (autism) [4–6], this is occurring at a very late stage.

Thus, based on the knowledge gained from the authors' research on hand contact improvisation, in this study, two mutual expression interfaces that encourage children with autism to express themselves bodily through hand contact improvisation, and that enable them to express themselves together with those around them, were developed. Also, these interfaces were brought to sites where communication occurs with children with autism, and their usefulness was investigated; the results are reported below.

2   Tabletop Single-Axis Hand Contact Improvisation System and Co-Creative Expression Interface

The authors carried out workshops whose main activity was hand contact improvisation once per month beginning in April 2012 in the Great East Japan Earthquake-stricken cities of Higashimatsushima and Ishinomaki, Miyagi Prefecture, Japan. A diverse range of people of various ages and both sexes, who had been affected by the disaster to different degrees, some of whom were afflicted with developmental disabilities such as autism spectrum disorders and some of whom were not, took part in the workshops. During this time, most of the children with autism, for whom verbal communication was difficult, were able to continue taking part on their own, and as connections were established with them, problematic behavior towards others lessened, a surprising result. However, it was observed that some of the children with autism were still unable to put their hands together on their own or to continue with hand contact improvisation for a long period of time.

Also, in the past, to research the dynamics of hand contact improvisation, the authors developed a single-axis hand contact improvisation system for jointly creating expressions that uses a slide board with a single degree of freedom to the front and rear shown in Fig. 2 [7–9]. The results confirmed that with this system, co-creative expression was possible for those who were skilled at expressing themselves even if the hands of the participants did not touch directly. Also, it was found that there were differences in the measured data when co-creative expression occurred and when it did not occur. Specifically, when co-creative expression did occur, changes in the movements of the body overall in which awareness did not participate directly (changes in COP [center of foot pressure]) occurred prior to conscious hand movements (movements in the slide board), and chaos attractor-like structures occurred in the return map of the movements of the slide board, and further, intermittent chaos-like structures occurred in the temporal changes of the differences in the degree of force exerted on the slide board on both sides (expressional jerk), and so on. These experimental findings suggest that this system can be used to measure and evaluate the process of the deepening of expression as displayed in Fig. 1. Thus, not only is it likely that using the system with children with developmental disabilities will help to support hand contact improvisation, but also, the participants' bodily and emotional state as well as the process of the deepening of relationships with others may be reflected in the system, and it may be possible to use it to obtain objective data regarding these factors.

Thus, in this study, first of all, the size of the existing single-axis hand contact improvisation system was reduced, and a "tabletop hand contact improvisation system" that can be used at sites such as child welfare facilities was developed. However, it is not possible to use this system at workshops where hand contact improvisation is performed through three-dimensional bodily movements. Next, therefore, a "hand contact improvisation interface" that consists of cylindrical interfaces equipped with visual, auditory, and force feedback interfaces, and in which participants carry out mutual hand contact improvisation by freely moving in three dimensions, was developed.

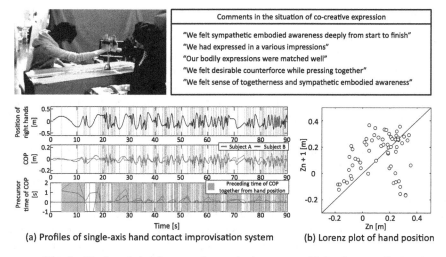

Fig. 2. Single-axis hand contact improvisation system (Color figure online)

3 Tabletop Hand Contact Improvisation System

3.1 Design Principle

Considering the sensitivity of people with autism to changes in the environment, a interface that could be brought into areas where children with autism live was needed. Therefore, it was determined that the interface would use a tabletop design. The design requirements were as follows.

1. A portable, tabletop-size, compact interface
2. Possible to measure exchanges of force, the positions of the hands in the context of the expressions created by the two participants, and the force on the hands
3. Possible to measure the unconscious movements of COP
4. Equipped with force feedback interfaces to encourage bodily awareness of the hands of both participants
5. Equipped with mechanisms with a high degree of backdrivability so as not to interfere in the movements of the participants

(4) and (5) were included in the design requirements in view of possible future application of the previously developed telecommunication-based hand contact improvisation system [10] and the single-person hand contact improvisation system [11] to children with autism. To fulfill the above requirements, the interface had to be no more than 400 mm wide and 500 [mm] deep so that it could sit on a tabletop. Also, in light of the mobility of the hands of an adult male facing directly ahead, the stroke of the slide board had to be at least 300 [mm].

3.2 System Design

The system is made up of a sensor interface, a force feedback interface, and a measurement interface that measure the position of the slide board, the force on it, and the COP shown in Fig. 3. In this system, to make the interface small and to simultaneously lengthen the stroke of the slide board, the sensors and the force feedback mechanism were all built into the unit on which the slide board was installed. In specific terms, a linear encoder was installed on the side of this unit, with the position of the slide board measured at a resolution of 10 [μm]. It is possible to independently measure the force on the slide board from both sides within ± 100 [N] because an aluminum post is built into the center of the unit and load cells are installed on the front and rear ends. When doing so, it is possible to choose between a large grip that keeps the hands of the two participants from touching directly and a small grip that permits their hands to touch. Regarding the force feedback mechanism, a DC motor is installed beneath the unit, and force feedback of up to 40 [N] is provided through torque control. When doing so, the combination of a decrease in speed by low gear ratio and a rack and pinion mechanism that reduces the tooth contact ratio provides backdrivability at 1.2 [N]. COP measurement is achieved by installing a stabilometer on the surface of the participants' seats and on the floor. Also, to ease onsite usage of the interface, the system can run on two 12 [V] lead batteries. In the above system, data measurement and control is achieved at a maximum of 200 [Hz] using a measurement control interface comprised of a PC and a DAQ.

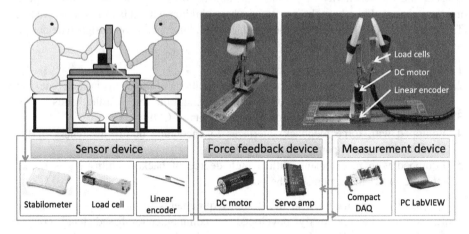

Fig. 3. Overview of tabletop hand contact improvisation system

3.3 Application of the System to Autistic Settings

We brought this system to a child welfare service, "Mirai" (Ishinomaki, Miyagi Prefecture, Japan) in order to investigate its usefulness (Fig. 4). In our 5-h trial, we observed a strong interest in the program that exceeded most of our expectations: with children lining up and waiting for their turn to participate. Of particular note was Boy A, who exhibited strong interpersonal avoidance behavior - usually by throwing himself on the ground repeatedly - who sat in the chair of his own volition and utilized our system to engage in hand contact improvisation. In addition, we observed Girl A engaged in hand contact improvisation even when using a small grip that involved touching hands, who even urged other children to participate. Further, Boy H stated, "I want the special school teachers to see my expression."

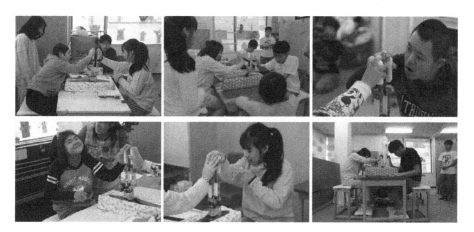

Fig. 4. Situation of using tabletop hand contact improvisation system

Figure 5 provides an example of our test results. As it shows, there was significant difference in participation duration and hand movements between each participant. This suggests that the bodily expression of children with autism is not uniform, but varied, and communication may be possible despite difficulties with linguistic interaction. Notably, the intermittency structure that is accentuated in co-creative expression occurred in the hand contact improvisation between autistic participant R and the perspective of expression expert N (Fig. 6). In addition, expression expert N subjectively judged this expression as co-creative expression. These results suggest that there may be a rich sensitivity inherent to autistic children similar to that seen in expression expert. We also received comments from parents and staff members such as, "I was surprised to see them engage with the interface without hesitation," "The system did a good job of communicating the feelings of participants," and "I saw facial expressions and emotions that I've never seen before." These results indicate that use of this system can support efforts at communication by facilitating co-creative expression among autistic children with a tendency towards avoiding interpersonal contact.

4   Development of a Hand Contact Improvisation Interface

4.1   Design Plan

Hand contact improvisation, as a method for non-restrictive improvisational co-creative expression, is possible in a variety of positions - standing, lying down, or seated.

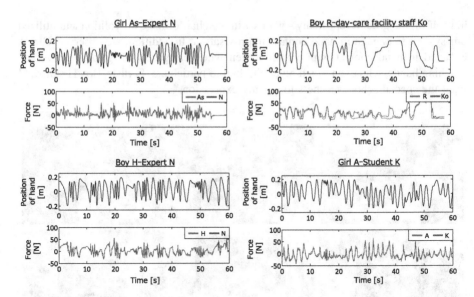

Fig. 5. Profiles of tabletop hand contact improvisation system in autistic settings (Color figure online)

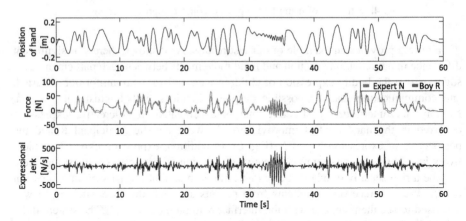

Fig. 6. Profiles from the experiment of expert N and boy R (Color figure online)

Our goal was to develop a "hand contact improvisation interface" that supports 3-dimensional hand contact improvisation by encouraging bodily awareness in the participants. The design requirements to achieve this were as follows:

1. The use of objects no heavier than what two children can pick up and carry
2. A mechanism of engagement that does not interfere with expressive behavior
3. A framework for introducing incentives that encourage bodily awareness
4. The ability to collect data on motion and exchange of force

4.2   Interface Design and Development

In order to satisfy the above requirements, we developed an interface constructed with 3 types of blocks - a cylindrical block, a joint block, and a contact block shown in Fig. 7. We then developed the cylindrical block, which was made of acrylic pipe, with a variety of sensors. This enabled a force measurement via the film sensor or load cell and acceleration, gyroscopic and geomagnetic measurements via the 9-axis sensor. In addition, the cylindrical block was mounted with LEDs that changed color and intensity in correspondence with the collected data. By sending the data wirelessly to a PC, we could save the data we had acquired. The joint block, made with ABS, connected to the cylindrical block. For our experiment, we equipped one of these ABS joint blocks with a small speaker. In order to make the contact block - also made with ABS - easy for two people to support with their hands, we gave it a curved surface that fits easily into one's palm.

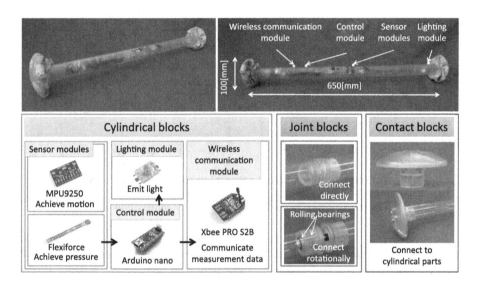

Fig. 7. Overview of hand contact improvisation interface

4.3   Application of the Interface to Autistic Settings

In order to determine whether or not our interface would be useful in encouraging 3-dimensional hand contact improvisation, we conducted experiments both with the "expert pair" and "novice pair". Participants of expert pair have experience in the hand contact improvisation with autistic children at the workshops. On the other hand, Participants of novice pair don't have such experience. Specifically, we held 1-min bodily expression trials in a $2.0 \times 2.0 \times 2.5$ [m] space, both with and without the interface. Our results shown in Fig. 8(a) showed that the vertical range of movement increased when the novice pair used the interface compared to their movement range (of midpoint of the line formed between their hands) when using only their hands. These results indicate that the interface has the ability to naturally draw out bodily expressions from two novices, expanding the expressive space. In addition, in contrast to the novice pair, we observed that the expert pair produced compressive and tensile force when using the interface in contrast to the novice pair, as shown in Fig. 8(b). It is our impression that it may be possible to evaluate changes in relationship that accompany the deepening of the expressions based on these differences.

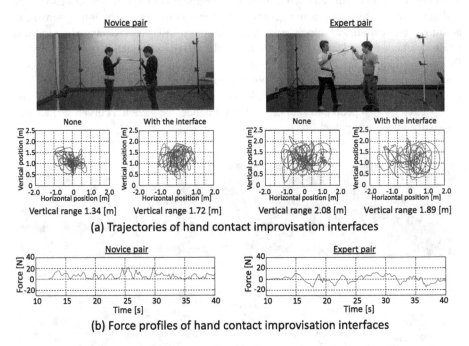

(a) Trajectories of hand contact improvisation interfaces

(b) Force profiles of hand contact improvisation interfaces

Fig. 8. Results of experiments using hand contact improvisation interfaces

Next, we used this hand contact improvisation interfaces during the workshop that included children with developmental disabilities at the disaster-stricken areas. Here we observed that developmentally impaired children who showed an interest in the interface interact with one another by using it shown in Fig. 9(a). Use of the interface was not limited to the children, and we observed parents and facility staff members conducting hand contact improvisation using it in a proactive fashion as well. Surprisingly to the authors, we also observed severely autistic children who generally are unable to engage in workshop activities for an extended period of time participating in hand contact improvisation for a longer period - with a greater range of motion - by utilizing the sound-making interface as shown in Fig. 9(b). We received comments from parents and staff such as, "This enables movements that you normally can't make in hand contact improvisation," "Even though you are separated, I feel connected to you," and "Based on the movement of the interface the sound changes, which was fun." One of the expression experts told us, "I don't just connect with my partner by dots or a line - there are many different faces by which I can connect with my partner." These results show that our interface has the potential to be useful in facilitating hand contact improvisation with autistic children at workshops.

(a) Situation of bodily expression using the device from various people in autistic settings

(b) Situation of bodily expression of severely autistic children with grater range of motion

Fig. 9. Application of hand contact improvisation interfaces in the workshop

5 Conclusion

Our study was aimed at the development of a bodily interface to facilitate co-creative expression inclusive of human diversity. Specifically, we developed a miniaturized tabletop version of our existing hand contact improvisation system, suitable for use in places such as child welfare institutions. In addition, we developed a hand contact improvisation interface capable of facilitating 3-dimensional bodily expression, and introduced it at a hand contact improvisation workshop in areas afflicted by the affected areas of the Great East Japan Earthquake. Via use of the interface, we observed voluntary engagement in hand contact improvisation from autistic children who tend to avoid a face-to-face contact, who freely utilized the expressive space to express themselves in three dimensions, for longer periods than previously observed. Furthermore, there appears to be potential to track hand contact improvisations between autistic children and the accompanying changes in their relationships via repeated use of the interface. The above demonstrates that hand contact improvisation interfaces such as these show promise as a new physical communication support technology that enables the establishment of sensitive connections with autistic children who struggle with linguistic exchange.

Acknowledgements. This study received support from the research project "Principle of emergence for empathetic 'Ba' and its applicability to communication technology" conducted at the Waseda University Research Institute for Science and Engineering, as well as from the JSPS Grant-in-Aid for Scientific Research (grant number: 25282187). We would like to thank a child welfare service, "Mirai" (Ishinomaki, Miyagi Prefecture, Japan) for supporting our research. We would also like to thank Dr. Shiroh Itai for his precious advice while writing this paper. Development of the system and execution of the experiment would not have been possible without the help of our graduate students: Taiga Iwanari, Harunobu Komine, Masanori Tsuruta, and Tomoki Tejika. We would like to express our deepest gratitude.

Out of respect for the dignity and rights of our participants and in order to maintain their personal privacy, the authors obtained permission upon review from the Ethics Review

Committee on Human Research of Waseda University for all information collected at the time of the study.

References

1. Shimizu, H., Kume, T., Miwa, Y., Miyake, Y.: Ba and Co-creation (in Japanese). NTT Publishing, Tokyo (2000)
2. Nishi, H.: Sympathetic Body Awareness: From a Joint Harmony of Body Movement to a Creative State of Join Being. Annual of the Institute of Thanatology, 87–108 (2012)
3. http://teawasekaken.jp
4. Pares, N., Masri, P., Van Wolferen, G., Creed, C.: Achieving dialogue with children with severe autism in an adaptive multisensory interaction: the "MEDIAte" project. IEEE Trans. Vis. Comput. Graph. **11**(6), 743 (2005). ISO 690
5. Hourcade, J.P., Bullock-Rest, N.E., Hansen, T.E.: Multitouch tablet applications and activities to enhance the social skills of children with autism spectrum disorders. Pers. Ubiquit. Comput. **16**(2), 157–168 (2012)
6. Boucenna, S., Narzisi, A., Tilmont, E., Muratori, F., Pioggia, G., Cohen, D., Chetouani, M.: Interactive technologies for autistic children: a review. Cogn. Comput. **6**(4), 722–740 (2014)
7. Miwa, Y., Itai, S., Watanabe, T., Nishi, H.: Generation dynamics of sympathetic embodied awareness in hand contact improvisation. In: Proceedings of IASDR 2013 - 5th International Congress of International Association of Societies of Design Research: Tokyo (2013)
8. Watanabe, T., Miwa, Y.: Duality of embodiment and support for co-creation in hand contact improvisation. J. Adv. Mech. Des., Syst. Manufact. **6**(7), 1307–1318 (2012)
9. Miwa, Y.: Co-creative expression and support for communicability. J. Soc. Instrum. Control Eng. **51**(11), 1016–1022 (2012)
10. Suzuki, Y., Ryutaro, H., Miwa, Y., Itai, S., Nishi, H.: Support for Co-creation in hand contact improvisation - a design of communication system with "Ba" transmitting feelings. In: Preceding of Human Interface Symposium, pp. 475–478 (2014)
11. Hayashi, R., Miwa, Y., Nishi, H., Iwanari, T., Takahashi T.: Study of facilitation technology of 'Ba' − measurement of cultivation process of expression by using self-referential hand contact improvisation system, and development of desktop hand contact improvisation device. In: Preceding of Human Interface Symposium, pp. 849–852 (2015)

High-Resolution Tactile Display for Lips

Yuhei Tsutsui[1], Koichi Hirota[1(✉)], Takuya Nojima[1], and Yasushi Ikei[2]

[1] Graduate School of Information Systems,
The University of Electro-Communications,
1-5-1 Chofugaoka, Chofu, Tokyo 182-8585, Japan
`hirota@vogue.is.uec.ac.jp`
[2] Faculty of System Design, Tokyo Metropolitan University,
1-1 Minami-Osawa, Hachioji, Tokyo 192-0397, Japan

Abstract. We developed a novel haptic display taking advantage of the sensitivity of the lips. Lips are one of the most sensitive regions of the human body similar to fingertip. Our display presents vibrotactile stimuli using piezo bimorph cells; the system is capable of presenting vibration on sixteen points on a lip in 2 mm pitch. We conducted experiments to evaluate the spatial discrimination characteristics of vibrotactile stimuli presented by our system. In the experiment, the two-point discrimination in simultaneous and sequential stimulations was investigated, and they were proved to be approximately 8 mm and 2 mm respectively. We also conducted an experiment that evaluates the amount of information that can be transmitted through the system; recognition of the patterns of vibration using three and four cells were investigated. It was proved that approximate bitrate of the interface was 3 bit/s.

1 Introduction

The lips are region of human body that is haptically sensitive as well as fingertips. Lips have not only an acute sense in the intensity of touch but also a relatively high spatial resolution on the location of the touch; it has been reported that its two point discrimination threshold is about 2 mm [1]. This feature of lips suggest that they can be used as an interface based on tactile sensation.

One of typical examples that transmit information through tactile sensation is braille. It is a tactile coding system for blind and low vision, normally using cells of six dots to represent characters and marks. The distance between dots in a cell is usually from 2 mm to 3 mm, and blind people recognize the patterns of the cells relying on the sensitiveness of fingertips. We considered that, since the lips are sensitive similarly to fingertips, tactile presentation of information on lips.

In this study, we developed a novel haptic display for lips using piezo bimorph vibrators (Fig. 1). The interbal of vibrators was designed to be 2 mm based on two point discrimination threshold on the lips; the display was composed of sixteen vibrators considering the width of the lips. The piezo bimorph was employed as the actuator because it is small and simple compared with others such as vibration motor and voice coil motor. This paper describes about design, implementation, and evaluation of the device.

© Springer International Publishing Switzerland 2016
S. Yamamoto (Ed.): HIMI 2016, Part II, LNCS 9735, pp. 357–366, 2016.
DOI: 10.1007/978-3-319-40397-7_34

Fig. 1. This picture shows how to use the stimulation unit. Users apply the stimulation unit on one's lips by having it in one's hand. In this paper, they apply it on lower lip only.

2   Related Works

Many researches on tactile displays have been conducted [2]. Some of them have focused on the haptic interaction using lips and the mouth. Iwata et al. developed "food texture display" [3]. This haptic display was capable of presenting biting force to the teeth. Hashimoto et al. developed "straw-like user interface" [4], that could present the vibration of straw on lips to represent the sensations of drinking. These researches were representing haptic stimulation based on actual food or drink. Samani et al. developed "Kissenger" [5], which was an interactive device that transmit the sensation of contact of kissing. They aimed to augment remote communication.

Various mechanisms to present tactile feedback have been investigated. One of common actuators is piezoelectric element. Poupyrev et al. implemented a tactile apparatus for small touch screens [6,7]. Taking advantage of smallness of the piezo bimorph, they integrated it into handheld devices. Hayward et al. developed a tactile display that generate distributed lateral skin stretch; the display was constructed from 64 piezoelectric actuators packed into $12\,\mathrm{mm} \times 12\,\mathrm{mm}$ [8]. Ikei et al. developed a texture display comprising 50 vibratory pins arranged in a $2\,\mathrm{mm}$ pitch driven by piezoelectric actuators. Also, authors employed piezoelectric element for our device to attain higher resolution.

Another mechanism that can cause tactile sensation with simple structure is electrical stimulation on the skin. Kajimoto et al. developed a device that can present spatial pattern on the forehead using an array of electrode [9]. Tang et al. investigated electrical stimulation inside a mouth [10]. A drawback of electrical stimulation is that it frequently causes the sensation of pain. We considered that such artifact is undesirabile for our purpose.

3   Device and Control

As stated in Sect. 1, the device was designed based on the constraints opposed by human factors: tactile resolution and the size of the mouth. The interval of vibrators, of stimulation points, was determined to 2 mm considering that the two-point discrimination threshold of lips is approximately 2 mm [1]. Width of the stimulation unit was restricted by the width of the lips, which was about 35 mm, hence the number of stimulation points was decided on sixteen resulting the whole width of the device to 35 mm. A piezo bimorph was employed to meet the requirements on the size and vibration intensity.

An overview of the system is shown in Fig. 2(a). The system consists of the stimulation unit, a control circuit, a regulated power supply, and a PC. The stimulation unit was made by combining piezo bimorphs (BM15015-06HC, RS Inc.) using epoxy adhesive as shown in Fig. 2(b); the size of each piezo bimorphs was 1.5(width) × 15(length) × 0.6(thickness). It was confirmed beforehand that the vibrator could generate amplitude that is sensible by the lip even when the vibrator is in contact with the lip. Piezo bimorphs were connected to the driver circuit by a flat-ribbon cable.

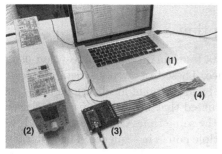 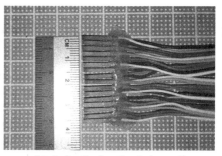

(a) An overview of the system   (b) A detail of a stimulation unit

Fig. 2. This is an overview of the system (a). It is mainly consists of a PC (1), a regulated power supply (2), a control board (3) and a stimulation unit (4). Stimulation unit is array of sixteen piezo bimorphs, bonded by epoxy adhesive. Piezo bimorphs are arranged in 2 mm pitch.

The device was controlled by a PC through a microcomputer and a driver circuit (see Fig. 2). The microcomputer (mbed NXP LPC1768, NXP) receives commands from the PC and controls the status of the driver circuit. The driver circuit is composed of H-bridge circuits for bipolar operation; actually the circuit was implemented using a serial to parallel converter with push-pull outputs (HV57908, Microchip), and using two outputs as a pair formed each H-bridge circuit. The source voltage of the driver circuit was 60 volt; although a regulated power supply was used in out current implementation, it will be easy to replace it by battery with booster circuit because the power consumption of the bimorph cell is low (Fig. 3).

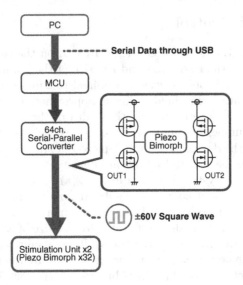

Fig. 3. This diagram shows the control flow of the our display. The control board receives a serial data from PC and drives piezo bimorphs of the stimulation unit.

4   Evaluation of Tactile Perception

In this study, we conducted two basic tests to evaluate tactile perception using vibrotactile stimuli generated by our device. These tests were carried on to confirm the two-point discrimination threshold and the point localization on lips. At the two-point discrimination test, we evaluated that how much resolution users can identify when they are stimulated at the same time. On the other hand, we evaluated it when they are stimulated multiple points in sequence. Through these tests, we explored what information and how stimulation approach is efficient for the user on this system at the point localization test.

4.1   Common Test Procedure

First, we explained how to use this device to participants. They applied the stimulation unit to the lower lip holding by own hand (as shown in Fig. 1). Also, contact of the device to the lip was confirmed by checking that the user can feel the vibration of the piezo bimorphs of all channels. Next, we gave participants time for practice up to 5 min before starting the test. We stimulated and confirm the answer with participants. In addition, each piezo bimorphs were numbered from right to left in relation to the user as channel 1 to 15 for the convenience of explanation in this paper.

4.2   Two-Point Discrimination Threshold

The first test was conducted to confirm the two-point discrimination threshold on lips. The test procedure was based on constant method; stimulate one or two channels selected randomly from comparison channels and let subjects answer one-point or two-points.

Concrete procedure of this evaluation was as follows:

1. Stimulate the standard channel and comparison channel for 1 s (one of the comparison stimulus is same as standard one: that is one-point).
2. Answer, "Stimulus is one-point/two-point."
3. Repeat 10 set for all of the comparison stimulus the step (1) to (2)

Stimulation range is from 0 mm (one-point) to 10 mm at intervals of 2 mm. Standard stimulus was Ch.7. And also, comparison stimuli were Ch.8 to Ch.12. We didn't stimulate whole of lips supposing the actual use of this device. Also, we adopt three frequencies: 50, 100, 200 Hz. 50 Hz is the frequency that FA-II fire most frequently. 100 Hz is a resonance frequency of the piezo bimorph. 200 Hz is same as 50 Hz on FA-I. Five volunteers (four males and one female, in ages from 22 to 24) participated this test.

Result of this test is shown in Fig. 4. 75 % discrimination threshold was about 8 mm at minimum when vibrating frequency was 50 Hz. It was much the same at 100 Hz. The most effective frequency differed by every participant. We only told participants, "Please wear the stimulus unit, so that you can feel the vibration well". We think that this caused a large individual difference in the test's results.

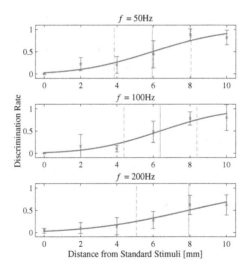

Fig. 4. The result of the two-point discrimination test. A curve is psychometric function that fitting average of all participants' answers to the cumulative distribution function. Stars are average of each stimulus, and error bar shows standard deviation of them. Vertical lines show PSE, and also dash lines show the JND.

4.3   Point Localization

The second basic test was conducted to confirm the point localization on lips, how much correctness users can recognize the point of stimuli. To evaluate this perception, we used constant method; vibrate standard and comparison channels selected randomly in sequence and let subjects answer relative point of the comparison channel.

This test was carried out in the following procedure:

1. Stimulate the standard channel for 500 ms.
2. 1 s interval.
3. Stimulate the comparison channel for 500 ms.
4. Answer, "Comparison is left/right/same."
5. Repeat 10 sets for all of the comparison stimulus the step (1) to (4)

The frequency of vibration was fixed to 100 Hz, as it achieved relatively better results in the two-point discrimination test. We conducted this test for three standard stimuli, Ch.5, Ch.8, and Ch.12, to confirm the difference between center and side of lips. Comparison stimuli were 2 mm to 8 mm away from the right and left of the standard stimulus. We recorded the ratio of the answer "left." In the computation, we treated the answer "same" as 0.5. Five volunteers (four males and one female, ranging in the age group 22 to 24) participated this test.

Result of this test is displayed in Fig. 5. The JND is around 3 mm at each condition. Participants were able to identify the small shift of stimuli point as compared to two-point discrimination. In the previous test, two-point discrimination threshold was about 6 mm. However, 75 % threshold value is around 3 mm in this test. We also confirmed the difference of this perception between center and end of lips. Results of the test displayed that the difference was not significant.

5   Vibrating Pattern Identification

This test was conducted to investigate the users' identification capability for multiple vibration points on their lips. The aim of this test was to see how efficiently users can identify the stimulation patterns that are presented by our device. Vibration patterns were presented using three and four piezo bimorphs, i.e., 3 and 4 bit. In addition, this test was conducted in two conditions: simultaneous stimulation of multiple points (at the same time) or in sequences.

5.1   Simultaneous Stimulation

The test was carried out as follows:

1. Stimulate some channels that are randomly chosen from the prepared stimuli patterns for 1 s.

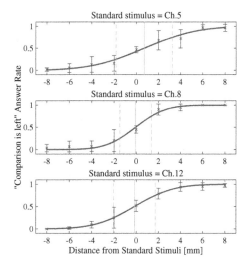

Fig. 5. The result of the point localization test. A curve is psychometric function that fits average of all participants' answers to the cumulative distribution function. Stars are average of each stimulus, and error bar displays standard deviation. Vertical lines displays PSE, and dashed lines displays the JND.

2. Participants marked answers on their answer sheet to denote where the stimulation point vibrated.
3. Repeat 10 sets for all the stimulus patterns from step (1) to (2)

In the 3-bit test, seven vibration patterns from a combination of three stimulation points were used except for all the off pattern points. Regarding the 4-bit test, however, four stimulation points make fifteen different vibrating patterns. We chose 10 patterns out of these fifteen and excluded some symmetrical ones (see Fig. 6). Channels 1, 8, and 15 were used for the 3-bit test, while channels 1, 6, 11, and 15 were used for the 4-bit test. These channels were selected so that the stimulation points were equally spaced. Six male volunteers and one female volunteer, ranging in the age group 22 to 24 years old participated in this test.

The result of the tests is displayed in Fig. 7. Regarding the 3-bit test (see Fig. 7(a)), average correct answer ratio was 87 % although considerable variation among the patterns was observed. For example, correct answer ratio of pattern 5 was 63 %. Average correct answer ratio of the 4-bit test was 67 %. The result suggests that the test was considerably difficult for the participants.

5.2   Stimulation in Sequence

Additionally, we conducted the test that vibrates piezo bimorphs in sequence instead of multiple point stimuli at the same time. The test procedure was same as the previous one. The duration of stimulation was 500 ms per channel. Only 4-bit test was conducted in this condition.

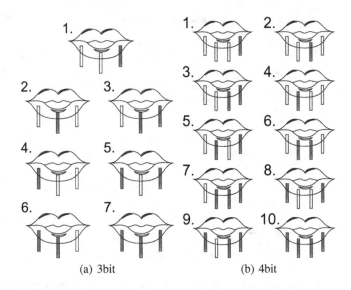

(a) 3bit   (b) 4bit

Fig. 6. This figure shows the vibrating patterns used in the pattern recognition test. Every participants answered which vibrator was ON, looking this figure.

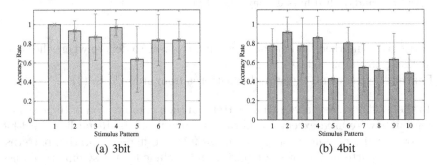

(a) 3bit   (b) 4bit

Fig. 7. This bar graph shows the results of the pattern identification test at 3bit(a) and 4bit(b). Errorbars show standard deviations.

The result of this test is displayed in Fig. 8. All participants recorded the higher correct answer rate than the previous test. One of them answered perfectly to all the questions. T-test calculation displays significantly higher average correct answer ratio at 5 % significance level as compared to previous test.

6   Discussion

In the 2PD test, a large individual difference was observed. We think that this resulted in a large individual difference in the test's results. In this paper, users placed the stimulation unit on their lips by holding it in their hand (Fig. 1). Additionally, we bonded sixteen piezo bimorphs with epoxy adhesive. This fabrication approach makes the stimulation unit rigid. Therefore, the system was

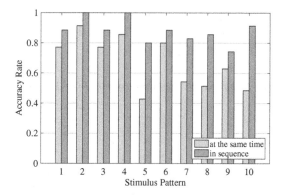

Fig. 8. This bar graph displays the results of the pattern identification test with stimuli in sequence (orange bar) as compared to previous results (blue bar). The average correct answer ratio increased significantly ($p = 0.05$). (Color figure online)

not able to adapt to the shape of the lips. This led to difference in stimulation intensity between the channels. We thought these factors made it difficult to sense the multiple point stimuli correctly by the participants. In future works, these issues will be addressed and the stimulation unit will be made adaptable to the shape of the users' lips.

We confirmed through the pattern recognition test that users can recognize the three piezo bimorph's vibration at the same time with 87 % correct answer ratio. Users can recognize the vibrating piezo bimorphs in sequence when piezo bimorphs increases to four. Bitrates calculated from test conditions were 3 bit/s and 2 bit/s. During the 3-bit test in sequence, the duration of stimulation was 1 s. Therefore, the estimated bitrate was 3 bit/s. During the 4-bit test at the same time, the duration of stimulation was 500 ms per channel. Therefore, the estimated bit rate was 2 bit/s. In this test, we asked participants to recognize the pattern only. We did not limit information to characters, figures, and so on. If the presented information is limited, the recognition rate will rise. For example, users get a hint of some word by complementing it themselves if this system is used to present the word.

7   Conclusion and Future Works

In this study, we developed a novel tactile display using the piezo bimorph. We confirmed that the system is capable of representing the vibrotactile stimulation using the evaluation of two-point discrimination and point localization. This system can present some information on the three simulation points from the pattern identification results.

Future work is to make the stimulation unit easily and certainly wearable. It is heavy to hold it in one's mouth because of the flat-ribbon cable. We can use both hands for any exertions by reducing its weight. Additionally, we aim to make the stimulation unit by substituting soft material for epoxy adhesive. This is because epoxy adhesive makes the stimulation unit rigid and it cannot be adapted according to the shape of lips.

Acknowledgement. This research was supported by JSPS KAKENHI Grant Number 26240029.

References

1. Weinstein, S.: Intensive and extensive aspects of tactile sensitivity as a function of body part, sex and laterality. In: The First International Symposium on the Skin Senses (1968)
2. Chouvardas, V.G., Miliou, A.N., Hatalis, M.K.: Tactile displays: overview and recent advances. Displays **29**(3), 185–194 (2008)
3. Iwata, H., Yano, H., Uemura, T., Moriya, T.: Food texture display. In: Proceedings - 12th International Symposium on Haptic Interfaces for Virtual Environment and Teleoperator Systems, HAPTICS, pp. 310–315 (2004)
4. Hashimoto, Y., Nagaya, N., Kojima, M., Miyajima, S., Ohtaki, J., Yamamoto, A., Mitani, T., Inami, M.: Straw-like user interface: virtual experience of the sensation of drinking using a straw. Assoc. Comput. Mach. **6**, 14–16 (2006)
5. Samani, H.A., Parsani, R., Rodriguez, L.T., Saadatian, E., Dissanayake, K.H., Cheok, A.D.: Kissenger: design of a kiss transmission device. In: Proceedings of the Designing Interactive Systems Conference on - DIS 2012, p. 48 (2012)
6. Poupyrev, I., Maruyama, S., Rekimoto, J.: Ambient touch: designing tactile interfaces for handheld devices. In: Proceedings of the 15th Annual ACM Symposium on User Interface Software and Technology, vol. 4, no. 2, pp. 51–60 (2002)
7. Poupyrev, I., Maruyama, S.: Tactile interfaces for small touch screens. In: Proceedings of the 16th Annual ACM Symposium on User Interface Software and Technology, pp. 217–220. ACM (2003)
8. Hayward, V., Cruz-Hernandez, M.: Tactile display device using distributed lateral skin stretch. In: Proceedings of the Haptic Interfaces for Virtual Environment and Teleoperator Systems Symposium, vol. 69, pp. 1309–1314 (2000)
9. Kajimoto, H., Kawakami, N., Tachi, S., Inami, M.: Smarttouch: electric skin to touch the untouchable. IEEE Comput. Graph. Appl. **24**(1), 36–43 (2004)
10. Tang, H., Beebe, D.J.: Design, microfabrication of a flexible oral electrotactile display. J. Microelectromech. Syst. **12**(1), 29–36 (2003)

Fortune Air: Interactive Fortune-Telling for Entertainment Enhancement in a Praying Experience

Ryoko Ueoka[1](✉) and Naoto Kamiyama[2]

[1] Faculty of Deisgn, Kyushu University, Fukuoka, Japan
r-ueoka@design.kyushu-u.ac.jp
[2] Graduate School of Design, Kyushu University, Fukuoka, Japan
naoto.k70@gmail.com

Abstract. In Japan, people visit shrines to pray for good fortune. For determining their fortune, they draw fortune-telling paper slips called Omikuji. The Omikuji contain predictions ranging from daikichi ("great blessings") to daikyo ("curses"). As a novel, interactive fortune-telling system, we propose the "Fortune Air." According to the person's interactions and a random value generated by the measured resistance of a leaf from a tree in the shrine, in real-time, a unique fortune is determined. Then the fortune-air system visualizes the fortune using one of the four patterns generated by double vortex rings: merging, rebound, disappearance and no-interference. After the visualization, the paper containing the fortune is printed by a thermal printer. In this study, we conducted an experiment for determining the parameters for controlling the four patterns of double vortex rings. From the results, we confirmed that the distance between the air cannons and a combination of the air pressure as well as the angle of the two air cannons, are the parameters to control the four patterns generated by the vortex rings. Using the results, we implemented a prototype system for the fortune-air and evaluated the entertainment value provided by the interactive system to enhance the praying experience.

Keywords: Interactive air media · Vortex ring · Air cannon

1 Introduction

In Japan, people visit shrines in order to pray for good fortune. For determining their fortune, they draw fortune-telling paper slips called Omikuji. The Omikuji contain predictions ranging from daikichi ("great blessings") to daikyo ("curses") As a novel interactive fortune-telling system, we propose the "Fortune Air". According to the person's interactions and a random value generated by the measured resistance of a leaf from a tree in the shrine, in real-time, a unique fortune is determined. Then, the fortune air system visualized the fortune using one of the four patterns generated by double vortex rings: merging, rebound, disappearance and no-interference. We adapted four fortune telling message to these four patterns of vortex rings. After the visualization, a paper containing the fortune-told is printed by a thermal printer. In this paper, we conducted an experiment to determine the parameters for controlling the four patterns

© Springer International Publishing Switzerland 2016
S. Yamamoto (Ed.): HIMI 2016, Part II, LNCS 9735, pp. 367–376, 2016.
DOI: 10.1007/978-3-319-40397-7_35

of the double vortex rings. From the results, we confirmed that the distance between the air cannons and the combination of the air pressure as well as the angle of the two air cannons, are the parameters that control the four patterns generated by the vortex rings. Using the results, we implemented a prototype system for the fortune air and evaluated the entertainment value provided by the interactive system to enhance the praying experience.

2   Related Studies

2.1   Air Media

Generally, vortex ring is generated by a moderate-sized hole punched on one of the faces of a cardboard box and the side of the box is struck, creating a mass of air that travels linearly while holding its shape. Hence, a vortex air cannon requires a container that has a circular hole and can be easily built if there is a device to rapidly expel the air [1]. Vortex rings are extensively studied; its stability conditions and speed controls can be designed according to the well-known principles. In our previous study [2], we developed a small air pressured facial tactile display to generate a sensation for the theater environment. By applying our previous knowledge, we developed two small air cannons placed side by side, to control the patterns of the vortex ring, for this study. The interactive media system while being unobtrusive, uses air pressure for the haptic interface. Suzuki et al. used an air jet to provide a force feedback for improving the realistic sensation while interacting with a virtual object such as an unobtrusive haptic display [3]. Sodhi et al. also developed a compact air-pressured tactile display called aireal to provide a haptic sensation on a CG object for a game-playing user in the real world [4]. As an unobtrusive aroma transmitter, the vortex ring is used for an olfactory display that transmits aroma to a distant target-user without diffusing it locally [5]. In this study, we have endeavored to control and create the patterns of the vortex rings representing a physical message. This message is mainly visual, but in future, the pattern will be used for a multi-sensory display integrating olfactory and the haptic functions.

2.2   Ritual-Related Interactive Interface Design in HCI

In the HCI field, we have often encountered interfaces that technically enhance traditional rituals. ThanatoFenestra [6] is an interactive altar that technically changes and controls the photos of deceased by the movement of a candlelight and "burning aroma" (representing incense sticks) that are used for rituals in front of the altar while praying for the deceased. This proposed system enhances the interaction with the deceased. Our proposed system is not a replacement for the altar for the family's deceased but it is for public use. A prayer companion [7] was proposed as a design study to aid for praying, for cloistered nuns by providing RSS news feeds as a resource of praying contents. This proposed system is an interface to provide updated news as a resource of the prayer activity for technically handicapped people like cloistered nuns or elderly people. Our proposed device is a substitute for a fortune-teller, using visualized vortex rings.

3   Fortune Air System

3.1   System Outline

Figure 1 shows system outline of the fortune air system. Two parallel air cannons generate two vortex rings by controlling four electromagnetic valves; two electromagnetic valves are implemented in an air cannon. One of the electromagnetic valves opens the compressed air into the air container unit of the air cannon while the another valve expels the compressed air from the air container when the vortex ring is to be generated. The switching of these valves is controlled by a PC and an arduino. From our previous research [8, 9], we know that the combination of the pressure value of each air cannon and the distance between the two air cannons affects the patterns generated by the vortex rings. However we could not fully control the patterns using these two parameters. In this study we found that angle between the two air cannons is the third parameter for determining the generated pattern. Therefore in order to control the angle of the air cannon interactively, we implemented two stepping motors. After a visualized fortune-telling by any four patterns of vortex rings, a slip of paper containing the fortune-told is printed by a thermal printer and the person can bring it home with him. The four patterns of fortune are determined by a stick that can be selected from several sticks in a stick container and a random value generated using the measured resistance value of a leaf from a tree in the shrine, in real-time. The detailed system description is provided in Sect. 5.

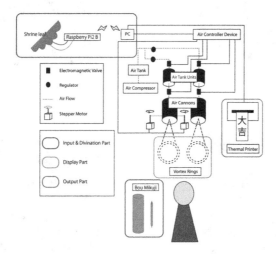

Fig. 1. Outline of fortune air system

3.2   Patterns of the Vortex Rings and Their Messages

The translational movement of two vortex rings causes a pressure decrease in between them and the vortex rings approach each other. Preliminary experiments to observe the patterns of translational vortex rings by changing air pressure values, were performed.

We found that four patterns of the vortex rings are likely to be generated in an ordinary space.

Figure 2 depicts a "merging." This is a merging of two vortex rings generating a large vortex ring. It proceeds slowly, straining in every direction. As this pattern combines two rings into one, we define it as a "Great blessing." Figure 3 shows a "rebound." This is a rebound of two vortex rings and each ring proceeds in opposite direction. As in this pattern, the two rings are repelled from each other, we define it as "Average blessing." Figure 4 portrays a "disappearance." Two vortex rings disappear as they approach each other closely and rebound strongly. We define it as a "Curse." Figure 5 shows a "no-interference." There is no interference between the two vortex rings and they travel forward in a straight path and fade out. We define it as "Small blessing."

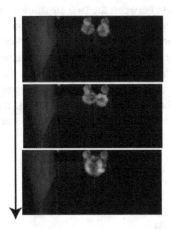

Fig. 2. Merging of the vortex rings (front view)

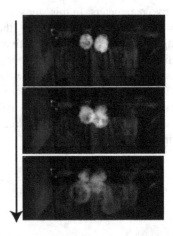

Fig. 3. Rebound of the vortex rings (front view)

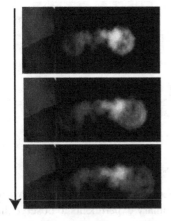

Fig. 4. Disappearance of the vortex rings (front view)

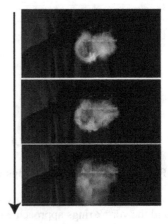

Fig. 5. No-interference of the vortex rings (front view)

4 Experiment to Determine the Parameters for Controlling the Four Patterns of the Vortex Rings

4.1 Observation of the Generated Patterns of the Vortex Rings

In our previous study, we found that the distance between the two air cannons and a combination of the air pressure were the parameters that determined the patterns generated by the vortex rings. However the determined combinations of these two parameters could not always generate these four patterns but they increased the probability of generation [9]. Thus, the system could no predict the pattern that would be generated. To output the fortune-told using a thermal paper, the system has to know the result. Hence, we sought an additional parameter to increase the probability of the four generated patterns.

In this study, we enlarged the aperture of air cannon (D) = 108 mm, compared to the previous study, where D = 77 mm, for stabilizing the vortex rings and for increasing the visibility of the generated patterns. Along with the change in the aperture, the length of the air cannon (L) become 445 mm and the volume of the air tank become 4275 cm^3, determined by the principle of air vortex rings [10].

Yanagida et al. crashed two vortex rings on purpose to spread a smell locally via free space to the targeted person [11]; a vortex ring that delivered the smell was crashed by striking it with another vortex ring, from an oblique. This inspired the idea that the angle can be another parameter to control the patterns generated by the vortex rings. As a first observation, we refereed to Yanagida's result; we evaluated if we could generate the disappearance pattern by tilting an air cannon in-and-out. Figure 6 shows two experimental conditions; one is to tilt the air cannon 3° inside (inside-tilt condition) and the another one is to tile it 3° outside (outside-tilt condition). Tilting the cannon caused a change in the distance between two air cannons accordingly, as depicted in Fig. 6. By changing the air pressure of each air cannon, we observed the disappearance pattern more often in an inside-tilt condition than in an outside-tilt condition. Moreover, with the inside-tilt condition, we observed an increase in the merging pattern by changing the angle to 1°. With these results, we hypothesized that controlling the angle by inside tilting inside is a promising method to control the generation of the four patterns.

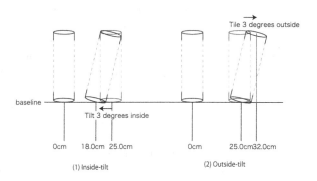

Fig. 6. Two positions of the tilting angle

4.2 Experiment

Based on the results of the preliminary experiment, we conducted an experiment to determine the parameter settings for generating the four patterns. Table 1 shows the combinations of the parameters for the experiment. We tilted the air cannon which expels a vortex ring with an air pressure 1 as shown in Table 1. A hundred trials were conducted for each pattern and we could generate the desired pattern of the vortex rings, a 100 %. "Rebound" and "no-interference" used the two parameter-combination of the air pressure and the distance; "merging" and "disappearance" additionally needed the angle parameter to generate the desired pattern.

Table 1.

Pattern	Air pressure 1(Mpa)	Air pressure 2(Mpa)	Distance(cm)	Angle(degrees)
Merging	0.045	0.045	22	1
Rebound	0.045	0.04	25	0
Disappearance	0.065	0.05	18	3
No interference	0.065	0.05	25	0

For the "merging" condition, by tilting the air cannon 1°, a more stable merging of two vortex rings was generated. On the other hand, by setting a larger difference in the angle (3°) than in the merging condition, each vortex ring crashed and disappeared before stabilizing. "Rebound" and "no-interference" were generated without the angle parameter. Rebound could be generated by creating a minor difference in the air pressure of each air cannon. However, no-interference could be generated by creating a significant difference in the air pressure of each air cannon.

5 Fortune Air Prototype System

We fabricated a prototype system for the fortune air. This interactive system conveys four types of fortunes based on the patterns of the vortex rings: great blessing, average blessing, small blessing and a curse. The prototype system is depicted in Fig. 7.

A person who is praying, pulls-out one fortune stick from five available sticks, each having a different value of a resistor, within. The person is asked to shake the container a number of times corresponding to the number of the month he was born, before pulling-out the stick. This step is adopted to create a similarity with a conventional fortune-telling. By placing the selected stick on a plate that has two conductive poles, as shown in Fig. 8, the person's number is determined by the system, with values ranging from1–5. Additionally, we implemented a remote system with a compact computer (Raspberry Pi 2 Model B) that transmits the resistance value of a leaf attached to the electrodes as shown in Fig. 9. The remote system is placed in a university campus near a local shrine. The resistance value of the leaf from a shrine

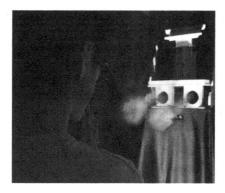

Fig. 7. Fortune air

Fig. 8. Stick fortunes and a plate

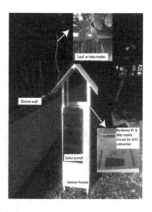

Fig. 9. Remote sensing system

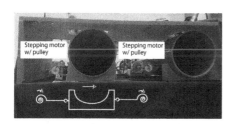

Fig. 10. Air cannon with a tilt function

Fig. 11. A thermal printer printed fortune-telling paper

symbolizes God, and has seasonal and a time variation. By adding this value to the number selected in accordance with the person's number, a unique number that determines the pattern of vortex rings, is selected. For the merging or the disappearance pattern, one of the air cannons is tilted-up to the predetermined value. The movement of the cannon is carried out by two stepping motors with a pulley function at each opposite end as depicted in Fig. 10. After the person has watched the visualized pattern, the fortune-told is printed by a thermal printer (Fig. 11), similar to a piece of fortune-telling paper, usually available in a shrine.

6   Evaluation

We evaluated the entertainment and the novelty value provide by the interactive fortune air system for a praying experience. Six university students (4 male, 2 female, average age 24.0) participated in the evaluation. They underwent a fortune-telling experience individually, after they were instructed on how to use the system, including the types of patterns generated by the vortex rings and their significance. Figure 12 depicts the experience of a participant. After the experience, they answered four questions and were asked to comment about the entertainment and the usability of this interactive system. Figure 13, 14 and 15 shows the result of the questionnaires regarding the system. A positive feedback was obtained from all participants. Regarding the usability, as shown in Fig. 16, they did not find it difficult to operate.

Fig. 12. Scene of fortune air experience

In the comment section, they commented that,

1. The process of the generation of the vortex rings felt like they were waiting for the answers from God and it was fun.
2. The vortex rings with smoke looked celestial and matched with the contents.
3. The leaf from a shrine added as a factor for the fortune-telling was effective in making the user believe of the result of the fortune telling.

In this evaluation test, we could confirm that Fortune Air could be a novel interface to provide entertainment in a praying experience (Fig. 14).

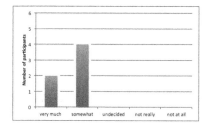

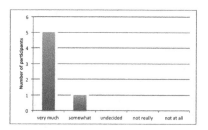

Fig. 13. Does this system give a fortune-telling experience?

Fig. 14. Does this system provide new fortune-telling experience?

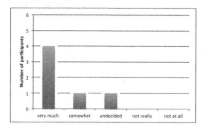

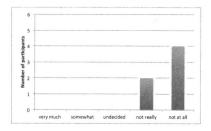

Fig. 15. Is this system entertaining compared to a conventional fortune-telling?

Fig. 16. Is this system difficult to use?

7 Conclusions

In order to propose a novel interactive system "Fortune Air," we implemented a prototype system. For generating the four patterns of the vortex air rings, we used two air cannons placed side by side and the vortex rings shot by each air cannon made four patterns such as merging, rebound, disappearance and no-interference by controlling three parameters: distance, air pressure and angle. The four patterns of the vortex rings were adapted to represent a special meaning in the fortune-telling. After the visualization of the vortex rings, a paper containing the fortune-told was printed by a thermal printer. In this study, we conducted an experiment to determine the parameters for controlling the four patterns generated by the double vortex rings. From the results, we confirmed that a combination of the distance and the air pressures as well as the angle of the two air cannons can be used to generate any one of the four patterns of the vortex rings. Using these results, we implemented a prototype system for the Fortune Air and evaluated the novel value provided a positive feedback regarding the entertainment value of the Fortune Air. By applying the principle of the physics of the vortex rings to a fortune-telling application, participants can grasp the meaning of physical phenomena as though it had a sacred meaning. This suggests that the interactive system can be used in cultural rituals for enhancing their meaning and for encouraging younger generations to appreciate their culture.

Acknowledgement. This work was supported by JSPS KAKENHI Grant Number 25350016.

References

1. Tsushiro, H., Yabe, A., Yoshizawa, Y., Sasamoto, A., Bai, B., Imamura, H., Kieda, K.: Mechanism of "cut and connection" phenomenon of two vortex rings. NAGARE J. Jpn. Soc. Fluid Mech. **17**(4), 279–287 (1998). (Written in Japanese)
2. Hashiguchi, S., Omori, N., Yamamoto, S., Ueoka, R., Takeda, T.: Application to the 3D theater using a air pressured facial tactile display. In: Proceedings of the Asia Digital Art and Design Association (ADADA) International Conference 2012, pp. 118–121 (2012)
3. Suzuki, Y., Kobayashi, M., Ishibashi, S.: Design of force feedback utilizing air pressure toward untethered human interface. In: Extended Abstracts of CHI 2002, April 2002, pp. 808–809 (2002)
4. Sodhi, R., Poupyrev, I., Glisson, M., Israr, A.: AIREAL: interactive tactile experiences in free air. ACM Trans. Graph. (TOG) **32**(4), 17–24 (2013). Article No. 134. SIGGRAPH 2013 Conference Proceedings
5. Yu, J., Yanagida, Y., Kawato, S., Tetsutani, N.: Air cannon design for projection-based olfactory display. In: Proceedings of the 13th International Conference on Artificial Reality and Telexistence (ICAT 2003), pp. 136–142 (2003)
6. Uriu, D., Okude, N.: ThanatoFenestra: photographic family altar supporting a ritual to pray for the deceased. In: Proceedings of the 8th ACM Conference on Designing Interactive Systems, pp. 422–425 (2010)
7. Gaver, W., Blythe, M., Boucher, A., Jarvis, N., Bowers, J., Wright, P.: The Prayer companion openness and specificity, materiality and spirituality. In: Proceedings of the SIGCHI Conference on Human Factors in Computing Systems, pp. 2055–2064 (2010)
8. Hashiguchi, S., Takamori, F., Ueoka, R., Takeda, T.: Design and evaluation of vortex air cannon for air pressured facial tactile display. Trans. Hum. Interface Soc. **14**(1–4), 375–382 (2012). (Written in Japanese)
9. Ueoka, R., Kamiyama, N.: Fortune air: an interactive fortune telling system using vortex air cannon. In: Yamamoto, S., Oliveira, N.P. (eds.) HIMI 2015. LNCS, vol. 9173, pp. 646–656. Springer, Heidelberg (2015). doi:10.1007/978-3-319-20618-9_63
10. Fukumoto, Y., Kaplanski, F.: Global time evolution of an axisymmetric vortex ring at low Reynolods numbers. Phys. Fluids **20**(053103), 1–14 (2008)
11. Masuda, Y., Kitano, K., Yanagida, Y.: Trajectory prediction for scent projectors using range imaging 3D-camera. Technical report, Multimedia Virtual Environment, The Institute of Electronics, Information and Communication, pp. 25–30 (2008). (Written in Japanese)

e-Science and e-Research

Prioritizing Tasks Using User-Support-Worker's Activity Model (USWAM)

Hashim Iqbal Chunpir[1,2,3]($\boxtimes$)

[1] Department of Computer Science,
Universidade Federal de São Carlos, São Paulo, Brazil
chunpir@dkrz.de
[2] Faculty of Informatics, University of Hamburg,
Vogt-Kölln-Str. 30, Hamburg, Germany
[3] German Climate Computing Centre (DKRZ),
Bundesstraße 45a, Hamburg, Germany

Abstract. Service desk has been widely deployed to cater user-support in an organisation. However, in the field of e-Research there are only few studies conducted to enhance the user-support services or user-services. Little has been done to improve the motivation of the employees of e-Science infrastructures to service incoming user requests known as incidents. In this paper, User-Support-Worker's Activity Model (USWAM) is presented that enhances the interactivity of the employees of cyber-infrastructures with the incidents. Furthermore, the model enhances not only the handling of the incoming user requests but also the management of the core activities assigned to the employees via visualization queues and matrices in the UI. Subsequently, USWAM aids the employees to remain interested in supporting users, similar to playing a game. Accomplished tasks can be rewarded in the form of money/gifts or recognitions. Finally, USWAM can be transferred to other service-oriented domains where prioritization or management of tasks is required.

Keywords: e-Research · Cyber-Infrastructures (CI) · Help desk · Service desk · Prioritization of tasks · Employee's activity model · Task management · Employee motivation

1 Introduction

The utility and importance of user-support (also known as service desk or help desk) in any organisation cannot be underestimated. However, the resources of an organisation, especially a research institute are mostly limited. This is the case in the field of research as well as e-Research, where the employees of multiple organisations form a cyber-infrastructure and have a limited time and budget to answer arriving incidents [1, 2]. The user requests are also known as incidents, especially in Information Technology Service Management (ITSM) [3].

In most of the cases it is difficult to automatically process the incoming user-requests (incidents) because the application of intelligent technologies to automate the process either has limitations or is too expensive to implement [4]. Therefore, in

© Springer International Publishing Switzerland 2016
S. Yamamoto (Ed.): HIMI 2016, Part II, LNCS 9735, pp. 379–390, 2016.
DOI: 10.1007/978-3-319-40397-7_36

e-Research, the employees of organisations that constitute a particular cyber-infrastructure handle incoming incidents in addition to their core activities, mostly on voluntarily basis [5, 6]. As per observations in the Earth System Grid Federation (ESGF), some employees participate in user support activities more than others [7]. ESGF is a well-known climate cyber-infrastructure [8, 9]. Normally, the employees of cyber-infrastructures, for instance in ESGF (and also in other cyber-infrastructures), are over-whelmed by their core tasks/activities and normally find little time and concern to process incidents [5].

The core activities of cyber-infrastructure employees include: Research, programming, system administration, data curation, data management and others [4]. These core activities are necessary to advance technology, cultivate standards and maintain the operations of a cyber-infrastructure. They are part of the planned tasks which is part of the job description of the employees. However, processing an incident is not formally part of the job description of the employees and is considered as an interrupting event by the employees. Handling incidents depends on the time factor i.e. extra time available to the employees to treat them. Besides, it also depends on an employee's interest and motivation to get indulged in supporting users[1]. In order to generate an interest and motivate the employees to process incidents a suggestion has been forwarded to the governance (i.e. the organisational committee) of the ESGF cyber-infrastructure to recognize handling of incidents as part of the job description [10]. However, in addition to this suggestion, a user-support-worker's activity model (USWAM) has been proposed and elaborated in this paper. USWAM provides an overview of the planned tasks as well as the incidents using GUI. Furthermore, a user-support-worker's or an employee's interest can be aroused with the USWAM-based GUI. In addition, the employee is able to process these activities in an optimum manner.

This paper is organized as follows: Sect. 2 describes the background of the concepts of e-Research, user support, the significance of user support in e-Research and the existing models in optimizing employee/workers activities. Section 3 describes the contemporary user support practices in ESGF from various sources of data that were gathered by the author. Moreover, the significance to introduce USWAM has also been described in Sect. 3. Section 4 elaborates the USWAM including its visualization via the GUI, followed by discussion and future work regarding USWAM in Sect. 5. Finally, the paper concludes in Sect. 6.

2 Background

The related work of this paper is divided into the four main areas given in the following subsections:

2.1 E-Research

E-Research is collaborative, relies on grid computing technologies to share and use data to perform research in different fields including humanities and science [4, 10–12].

---

[1] The word "customers" can be replaced.

E-Research is conducted via cyber-Infrastructures (CI) also known as e-Science infrastructures that are deployed to access and share the data, high performance computing (HPC) facilities and human resources to facilitate intra-disciplinary and inter-disciplinary research to harvest knowledge. A CI is formed through collaboration of many organisations across national and international boundaries. It is the synchronized integration of software, hardware and other technologies, as well as human expertise, required to support current and future discoveries in science, humanities and engineering [13]. Networks that constitute CI are complex: Users need an interface to access its resources usually data [14]. The interface includes command line tools, web portals and Graphical User Interface (GUI) to access data assets which are the main resources hosted [15, 16]. However, during an interaction of a user with a CI, a user may require help due to outages of some resources e.g. servers or any other anomaly [15]. In other case: a user requires particular scientific or technical information. In order to meet these user support challenges, CI offers user support in the form of a help-desk, which even being a core activity has not received adequate attention since inception of cyber-infrastructures [1, 17, 18].

2.2 User Support in e-Research

In the last decade, the user-support in ESGF has been evolving mainly due to the changes in the service-oriented architecture of ESGF CI. For instance; looking at the history of the ESGF development, the technological and organisational change has been constant. Moreover, the number of users and their needs have been changing as well [18–21]. Consequently, up until now the employees of ESGF are performing the user support by handling incidents, on a free will basis i.e. on top of their core infrastructure development activities/tasks [5]. A recent survey questionnaire and mailing list analysis conducted revealed that up to 15 % of the incidents were ignored by the employees [4, 7, 12]. Therefore a need to enhance ESGF user support was felt and as a part of result USWAM is suggested amongst other changes in the organisation and governance of ESGF.

2.3 Support Employee/Workers Activity Modelling

There are existing models that may be used to model CI employee's support activities. In software engineering, activity diagram in Unified Modelling Language (UML) [22] as well as Business Process Modelling Notation (BPMN) [23] can describe human activity in a sequential process. However, these methods are helpful in analysing stable and common processes in a non-dynamic environment other than CI. Moreover, they help to replace them via automated processes by employing IT-systems. Likewise, there are analysis and modelling methods on characteristics of human behaviour. For instance; information processing of humans is useful to provide standards of IT-systems such as responsiveness [24].

There is work done by Watanabe et al. that provides a basis of employee's activity model for support of interpersonal services in nursing care environment [25]. However, this proposed employee's activity model is used in a solitary, non-dynamic environment for the nursing staff, care workers and occupational therapists. It does not include team based coordination steps, multiple pools, point counters and a reward system. Therefore, there is a need to extend this model to suit other environments such as in user support environments such as a help-desk or a service-desk, where multiple human agents are supporting users. This is especially the case in an e-Research environment such as ESGF, our case study [18].

Thus, keeping with the previous work of Card et al. about information processing of humans and Watanabe et al. proposed guidelines of employee activity model, USWAM is proposed. Furthermore, on top of it, USWAM incorporates the findings from informal interviews, participatory observations and survey questionnaire based on feedback from stakeholders of ESGF; especially employees as well as users. USWAM supports from 1 to N tier user support model in e-Research and can be applied to other fields. A user support model defines the number of levels of workers involved in servicing an incident. For instance; two or three level tiers in user support models are popular [26].

3 Investigation of Contemporary User Support Practices in e-Research

An investigation of the current user support practices of the employees of a cyber-infrastructure: ESGF is carried and is described in the following three subsections:

3.1 Significance of the Case Study: ESGF

An important practical use-case in the field of climate science cyber-infrastructures is ESGF (Earth System Grid Federation) project [27]. ESGF is the first inter-agency and international effort in the domain of Climate Science used for Earth Science Modelling (ESM) [21, 27, 28]. At the moment, more than twenty-seven thousand researchers are accessing huge amount of climate data for climate-model inter-comparison purposes from ESGF distributed data-archive worldwide that makes ESGF a key cyber-infrastructure that supports ESM [12]. This is one of the main reasons to take ESGF as a use-case for this research.

Moreover, ESGF facilitates to study climate change and impact of climate change on human society and Earth's eco system [21]. Since physical phenomenon that govern Earth's climate are so complex and diverse, it is the most important scientific challenges of our time to undergo sophisticated model simulations that generate huge amount of data, collect observational data from various sources and share that data at a global scale. This is made possible by ESGF to discover, analyse and access the climate data sets which are stored at multiple geographic locations across the globe [8, 10, 21, 29, 30].

3.2   Research Methods Applied

In this study, case study method is chosen as a research method. The information about current user support practices in ESGF, and similar cyber-infrastructures, was captured via; survey-questionnaire, participatory observation of the first author [4]. Moreover, twelve interviews with stakeholders that included employees and users of ESGF and C3Grid cyber-infrastructures were conducted. All interviewees had different backgrounds and roles. Furthermore, relevant documents such as reports, publications and archival analysis of user and staff communication within the user's mailing list of ESGF were also observed [4]. The triangulation of sources of information was chosen to capture different perspective to validate and to contrast the findings [31–33]. The development of USWAM is partly based on these research findings as well as the research methods applied [4–6, 15].

3.3   Findings (Related to USWAM User Support)

This empirical qualitative cum quantitative investigation revealed a number of issues where attention of ESGF team is needed to improve the existing user-support process in cyber-infrastructure. The issues about the existing user-support process in climate cyber-infrastructure projects include allocation of time, human resources, time to solve the user-problems, characteristics of user requests, support tools, support structure and many others [4, 5, 7]. From the analysis of data collected in this study; it is found that the employees of ESGF are supporting users by handling the incidents on a free-will basis spontaneously [5]. Moreover, some employees show more engagement than others. It was observed that this and other factor is leading to more than 15 % of user requests that remain unanswered [15]. In order to create interest amongst the employees who perform multiple tasks including handling incidents, USWAM is suggested. Based on data there was a strong wish of the support workers in ESGF to visualize the tasks, prioritize them, set deadlines, track the workflow of the incidents and forward them to co-workers [34]. These factors lead to the development of USWAM to be introduced in the arena of user support in cyber-infrastructures.

4   User-Support-Worker's Activity Model

The details of the USWAM are described in the forthcoming sub-sections:

4.1   Description of USWAM

USWAM is a basic framework to visualize and manage incoming user incidents by the employees[2]. It arouses employee's interest by providing a point count system and encourages an employee to respond to incidents flexibly. According to the point count

---

[2] However, USWAM is not only limited to employees rather to whoever who is interested in supporting users.

system, if the support worker handles an incident within a set time[3] (i.e. recommended time which is set 72 h in ESGF after reception of an incident), s/he gets one point. S/he gets a half point if the incident is handled outside the set time. S/he may get an extra point if the solution is appreciated by a user. Collecting points is connected with a reward system i.e. more points collected, the bigger reward one can collect. USWAM provides a support to employee's for performing activities that include planned and incident tasks. USWAM is meant to create a value through a human and human interaction via a communication channel in a collaborative environment. Figure 1 depicts the USWAM in detail.

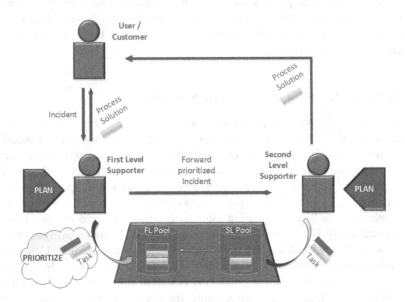

Fig. 1. The User-Support-Worker's Activity Model (USWAM) and the steps carried out by the supporters to process user's incident based on task pooling and the priority mechanism (Color figure online)

A user, in this case a climate e-Researcher shoots an incident as an e-mail to the ESGF user-support system or service-desk (see Fig. 1). The employee, usually a first level support person (FLS) gets these incidents, processes it and sends back the answer or solution (see Fig. 1). Alternatively, if FLS is unable to address the user's issue s/he may add some information (i.e. enabling information sharing) and forwards it to another employee, usually a specialist second level support person (SLS) for further treatment. This is the example of the 2-tier user support model which is the agreed (by the stakeholders to be suitable) in ESGF user support system. Nevertheless, USWAM can be applied to 1-tier to N-tier user support models in any environment whether research-oriented or commercial set-up, as the need may arise according to a particular situation. The employee (whether FLS or SLS) have two types of inputs, namely:

---

[3] A set-time to process an incident is mutually agreed by user support task force which is part of a governance of a cyber-infrastructure.

- *Planned activities*; which are already planned, analogous to "To-Do" list both for FLS and SLS (on the right and left hand side of the Fig. 1). Planned activities are the core activities scheduled beforehand (on a daily basis).
- *Unplanned activities or incidents*; which are incidents, can be thought of as events; i.e. they occur spontaneously at any point in time and need to be addressed at a certain point in time (i.e. meeting the priority level). Incidents are non-core activities which are not scheduled beforehand. An incident is an information request from a user e.g. a system outage that triggers a new activity which is not planned. However, they may initiate (or be the cause of) core or non-core planned activities at any instance in time; in this it may either transform into a planned activity, thus ceasing to be a spontaneous interruption or an employee has to plan some extra activities to cater the original incident.

Eventually, each activity is called a task i.e. planned task and an incident task. An incident task depends on the information embedded in the incident e.g. the situation that a user is facing that leads to a problem or an information needs that determines the urgency of the incident. It is important to take into consideration and anticipate that there can be *implicit incident tasks* that can be performed by an employee on his/her own awareness or knowledge of the situation within the environment of a cyber-infrastructure.

In service industry, interruptions to employee or workers task normally occurs quite often [34]. Similarly, different nature of tasks may pile up, making hard for a worker to remember specific details about them. Since human memory has a limited capacity therefore, there is a risk to forget the task and specific details about them [34]. Consequently, it is vital to externalise the memory to deal with interruptions and variety of tasks. Hence, in USWAM, externalisation of tasks stored in human memory is suggested via a `pool'. The pool represents the externalisation of tasks stored in worker's memory graphically on a UI. In Fig. 1, the two pools namely First Level (FL) pool and Second Level (SL pool) are depicted that contain both event tasks and planned task in the form of a pile known as queue task in the form of a pile known as queue. The principle this queue works is FIPO (First In Prioritised Out) meaning all planned tasks are piles and events received during a work day are piled on top. But the way these tasks are processed depend on the prioritisation judgement of the support workers.

If there are N levels in a user support model then N level pools are possible. This *memory pool of an employee* is represented in the Fig. 1 for each of the employee that processes the tasks. The incident tasks are represented as light blue and planned tasks as dark blue in the Fig. 1. An employee processes these tasks based on his/her judgement. The employee's judgement is based on some background information and experience which makes up "a priority rule" to prioritize and process incidents, depicted in the Fig. 1 as a cloud (on the right bottom). Alternatively, this priority rule can be automated via an algorithm that can be introduced to a user support system for the facility of employee. However, designing a priority rule algorithm is set aside as a future work in this study.

Currently in ESGF governance or organisation, FLS position is not specified or fixed as yet but it is recommended to be specified soon. Furthermore, it is recommended that the position of FLS shall be given to multiple people (at least 6 distributed in different continents) who may be students or technicians. Their job is to process incidents and further develop user support system. Apart from processing incidents their job is to automate parts of user support process and make relevant help or support information available to users. It is not necessary for them to have a high profiled portfolio of top computer/climate scientists. Thus, dividing the simple and routine incidents to be treated by them and forwarding only the incidents which cannot be treated to the SLS with some diagnostic information (that probably may help in solving user's concern).

In USWAM, a point counter, which is a step towards gamification[4], is also embedded for both FLS and SLS but especially for the SLS. This is because SLS are top climate or computer scientists who on top of performing their core tasks related to their job description, may perform incident tasks referred to them by the FLS. So, if SLS processes incident tasks i.e. incidents they acquire recognition for their additional services i.e. supporting end-user concerns or problems. Since they put in additional effort they acquire additional recognition in the form of certificates of appreciation/ recognition, extra remuneration in the form of salary bonus, free hours or holidays, gifts, give-aways or promotions. So in case SLS has a free time, SLS can carry forward additional incidents from FLS thus releasing the burden of FLS, thus collecting extra points and working in a free time. Apart from the rewards mentioned above rich gamification techniques similar to can be applied at the UI level to experience support workers to experience gameness at a later stage. The reason for using gamification techniques in ESGF user support system is because there is empirical evidence that gamified system does produce positive effects on workers [35].

4.2 Integrating USWAM in the Bigger Picture of User Support System of CI

User-support-worker's activity model (USWAM) is designed after examining the current user support process in ESGF which is a use case of climate cyber-infrastructure. The data is collected from the stakeholders of ESGF in the form of interviews and survey questionnaires. It was found out that the current user support process in ESGF has some limitations and can be improved. Amongst the other changes suggested to improve the user support system, USWAM was also an outcome of this analysis.

It was suggested to introduce something like a user social networking & support system, in which the users can connect to other users and initiate incidents using a web-form. This web form once submitted transfers the incident to an employee or a worker who is supporting users. Now these support workers are employees of an organisation which is part of a CI. They have planned tasks as well as incidents. In order to manage these tasks and save time USWAM is suggested. Its visualization through GUI is meant to be part of the bigger user support system. This UI is normally visible to an employee or someone who is interested in processing/handling incident

---

[4] Gamification is "a process of enhancing a service with affordances for gamely experiences in order to support user's overall value creation."[36].

tasks. At a later stage, this can be done by users themselves too (who have a login and are verified).

5   Discussion and Future Work

At the moment, an ESGF user support system is under development where the employee-facing UI shall be integrated based on the USWAM to support employees in managing tasks (planned and incidents). Moreover, in the long run this UI can also be used by users who are willing to support other users. This will be made possible at a later stage. It is important to analyse the worksheets i.e. doing auditing in the longer run to determine user value from this model as well as cost of employees in processing tasks. It is vital to gauge or test USWAM that to up to what extent it promotes teamwork and arouses interest of support worker in the real environment. However, to accomplish these goals, further study is a must. Therefore, it is recommended to conduct experiments as a future work to prove or reject the predictions. In addition to it, computational methods such as simulation or multi-agent simulation can be applied to test the data gathered from the workers and their priority rules. The algorithm designed to re-prioritize or prioritize tasks can be designed in future and can be developed for a specific domain of a CI. This can be a dynamic simulation between a team of support workers.

Processing tasks enables the support workers to learn from processing incidents. More incidents a worker processes, more learning s/he gain in the longer period about user issues and in turn can contribute to the design and development of the CI. This is because the incidents comprise; information requests, problems such as system outages, data errors, data access failures, user feedbacks and requests for future features. The learning effect amongst support workers can further be observed in future.

Currently, application of USWAM in the user support environment in CI is intended to make the tasks manageable within a specified time thus knowing the priorities. It further facilitates better planning of tasks, providing visual assistance and motivation to process the incidents. USWAM can also be used as it is, or with some amendments to other fields such as patient treatment in medical science, servicing customers in government or commercial departments and other support areas.

6   Conclusion

In a nutshell, it is anticipated that implementation of USWAM in a dynamic, team-oriented, distributed environment such as cyber-infrastructures makes planned tasks as well as incidents more manageable. However, this claim is needed to be tested in the real environment, which is proposed as a future work. Application of USWAM in a use case of a climate cyber-infrastructures; ESGF, intends to create motivation and interest amongst the support workers using gamification. This can be achieved by introducing the point assignment system along with a reward system that would push employees to work efficiently and process incidents in their free time. Therefore, USWAM tends to optimize the schedule of support workers. Consequently, the introduction of USWAM is aimed at creating value and effectiveness for the whole user support system or service-desk. In future, the authors will refine this model and test it further. Finally, they will validate it through actual data and system development in the real environment.

References

1. Soehner, C., Steeves, C., Ward, J.: E-Science and Data Support Services. DC, USA, Washington (2010)
2. Taylor, K.E., Stouffer, R.J., Meehl, G.A.: An overview of CMIP5 and the experiment design. Bull. Am. Meteorol. Soc. **93**(4), 485–498 (2012)
3. Jäntti, M.: Lessons learnt from the improvement of customer Support processes: a case study on incident management. In: Bomarius, F., Oivo, M., Jaring, P., Abrahamsson, P. (eds.) PROFES 2009. LNBIP, vol. 32, pp. 317–331. Springer, Heidelberg (2009)
4. Chunpir, H.I.: Enhancing User Support Process in Federated E-Science, University of Hamburg (2015)
5. Chunpir, H.I., Ludwig, T., Badewi, A.: A snap-shot of user support services in Earth System Grid Federation (ESGF): a use case of climate cyber-infrastructures. In: Proceedings of the 5th Applied Human Factors and Ergonomics (AHFE) Conference, July 2014
6. Chunpir, H.I., Badewi, A.A., Ludwig, T.: User support system in the complex environment. In: Marcus, A. (ed.) DUXU 2014, Part IV. LNCS, vol. 8520, pp. 392–402. Springer, Heidelberg (2014)
7. Chunpir, H.I., Ludwig, T., Badewi, A.A.: Using soft systems methodology (SSM) in understanding current user-support scenario in the climate science domain of cyber-infrastructures. In: Marcus, A. (ed.) DUXU 2014, Part III. LNCS, vol. 8519, pp. 495–506. Springer, Heidelberg (2014)
8. Vu, L.: Earth system grid federation: A modern day 'silk road' for climate data, Energy Science Network (2013). https://es.net/news-and-publications/esnet-news/2012/ESGF/. Accessed 20 Aug 2014
9. Williams, D.N., Drach, R., Ananthakrishnan, R., Foster, I.T., Fraser, D., Siebenlist, F., Bernholdt, D.E., Chen, M., Schwidder, J., Bharathi, S., Chervenak, A.L., Schuler, R., Su, M., Brown, D., Cinquini, L., Fox, P., Garcia, J., Middleton, D.E., Strand, W.G., Wilhelmi, N., Hankin, S., Schweitzer, R., Jones, P., Shoshani, A., Sim, A.: The earth system grid: enabling access to multimodel climate simulation data. Bull. Am. Meteorol. Soc. **90**(2), 195–205 (2009)
10. Chunpir, H.I, Ludwig, T.: Reviewing the governance structure of end-user support in e-science infrastructures. In: Mastering Big Data Complexity, Informatik 2014 Proceedings. Lecture Notes in Informatics (LNI), vol. 232 (2014)
11. Chunpir, H.I., Ludwig, T., Williams, D.N.: Evolution of e-research: from infrastructure development to service orientation. In: Marcus, A. (ed.) DUXU 2015. LNCS, vol. 9188, pp. 25–35. Springer, Heidelberg (2015)
12. Chunpir, H.I, Ludwig, T., Curri, E.: Improving processes for user support in e-science. In: IEEE 10th International Conference on e-Science (e-Science), vol. 2, pp. 87–90 (2014)
13. Chunpir, H., Moll, A.: Analysis of marine ecosystems: usability, visualization and community collaboration challenges. Procedia Manufact. **3**, 3262–3265 (2015)
14. Freeman, P.A.: Is 'Designing' Cyberinfrastructure - or, Even, Defining It - Possible? First Monday **6**(12) (2007). http://firstmonday.org/ojs/index.php/fm/article/view/1900/1782. (Accessed on 11 October 2015)

15. Chunpir, H.I., Rathmann, T., Ludwig, T.: The need for a tool to support users of e-science infrastructures in a virtual laboratory environment. Procedia Manufact. **3**, 3375–3382 (2015)
16. Chunpir, H.I., Rathmann, T.: E-mail analysis of a user- staff communication in e-research, pp. 1–26, Hamburg (2015)
17. Chunpir, H.: C3Grid - INAD : Support centre with semi-automatic notification andcoordination for experts work, pp. 1–10, Hamburg (2013)
18. Chunpir, H., Williams, D., Cinquini, L., Kindermann, S.: Third Annual ESGF and Ultrascale Visualization Climate Data Analysis Tools Face-to-Face Meeting report. Livermore, CA (2013)
19. Williams, D.N.: Earth System Grid Federation (ESGF): Future and Governance. Livermore, CA, USA (2012)
20. Bernholdt, D., Bharathi, S., Brown, D., Chanchio, K., Chen, M., Chervenak, A., Cinquini, L., Drach, B., Foster, I., Fox, P., Garcia, J., Kesselman, C., Markel, R., Middleton, D., Nefedova, V., Pouchard, L., Shoshani, A., Sim, A., Strand, G., Williams, D.: The earth system grid: supporting the next generation of climate modeling research. Proc. IEEE **93**(3), 485–495 (2005)
21. Cinquini, L., Crichton, D., Mattmann, C., Bell, G.M., Drach, B., Williams, D., Harney, J., Denvil, S., Schweitzer, R.: The earth system grid federation (ESGF): an open infrastructure for access to distributed geospatial data. In: 8th IEEE International Conference on E-Science, pp. 1–10 (2012)
22. OMG, OMG Unified Modeling Language (OMG UML) (2010)
23. Havey, M.: Essential BPM (Business Process Modeling). O Reily Media, Sebastopol (2005)
24. Card, S.K., Moran, T.P., Newell, A.: The model human processor: an engineering model of human performance. In: Boff, K.R., Kaufman, L., Thomas, J.P. (eds.) Handbook of Perception and Human Performance, vol. 2, pp. 1–35. Wiley-Intersience, New York (1986)
25. Watanabe, K., Nishimura, T.: Interpersonal service support based on employee's activity model. In: Yamamoto, S. (ed.) HCI 2013, Part III. LNCS, vol. 8018, pp. 401–409. Springer, Heidelberg (2013)
26. Kendall, H.: Prehistoric Help Desk!. Support World. Help Desk Institute, Colorado Springs, CO, USA, pp. 6–8, October–November 2002
27. Williams, D.N., Bell, G., Cinquini, L., Fox, P., Harney, J., Goldstone, R.: ESGF: federated and integrated climate data from multiple sources. In: Hiller, W., Budich, R., Redler, R. (eds.) Earth System Modelling, vol. 6, pp. 61–77. Springer, Heidelberg (2013)
28. Hey, T., Trefethen, A.E.: Cyberinfrastructure for e-science. Science **308**(5723), 817–821 (2005)
29. Earth System Grid Federation, ESGF research and development report (2010)
30. ENES, The ENES portal: European network for earth system modelling (2013). https://verc.enes.org/. Accessed 02 Dec 2014
31. Yin, R.: Case Study Research: Design and Methods, 5th edn. Sage Publishing, Thousand Oaks (2013)
32. Rocco, T.S., Bliss, L.A., Pérez-Prado, A., Gallagher, S.: Taking the next step: mixed methods research in organizational systems. Inf. Technol. Learn. Perform. **21**(1), 19–29 (2003)
33. Buchanan, D.A.: Case studies in oranisational research. In: Symon, G., Cassel, C. (eds.) The Practice of Qualitative Organisational Research: Core Methods and Current Challenges, pp. 373–392. Sage Publishing, London (2012)
34. Chunpir, H.I., Curri, E., Zaina, L., Ludwig, T.: Improving user interfaces for a request tracking system: best practical RT. In: Chunpir, H.I., Curri, E., Zaina, L.A.M., Ludwig, T., (eds.), Human Computer Interaction International (HCI) Proceedings. LNCS, vol. 9735, pp. 391–401. Springer, Heidelberg (2016)

35. Hamari, J., Koivisto, J., Sarsa, H.: Does Gamification Work? – A Literature Review of Empirical Studies on Gamification. In: 2014 47th Hawaii International Conference on System Sciences, pp. 3025–3034, January 2014
36. Huotari, K.: Defining Gamification - A Service Marketing Perspective (2012)

Improving User Interfaces for a Request Tracking System: Best Practical RT

Hashim Iqbal Chunpir[1,2,3(✉)], Endrit Curri[2], Luciana Zaina[1],
and Thomas Ludwig[2,3]

[1] Department of Computer Science,
Federal University of São Carlos, São Carlos, SP, Brazil
lzaina@ufscar.br
[2] Faculty of Informatics, University of Hamburg,
Vogt-kölln-Straße 30, Hamburg, Germany
lcurri@informatik.uni-hamburg.de
[3] German Climate Computing Centre, Bundesstr. 45a, Hamburg, Germany
{chunpir,ludwig}@dkrz.de

Abstract. User Interface (UI) design guidelines have not been adequately applied towards the design of UI of request tracking systems. Moreover, UI of request tracking systems in particular have not been researched in federated e-Science organisations. These systems, however, play a central role for the collaboration in e-Science. The users of e-Science infrastructures that constitute data and High Performance Computer (HPC) facilities interact with the cyber-infrastructures to use their features mainly for research purposes. The incoming problems and information queries i.e. user requests are shown using a Graphical User Interface (GUI) of the Request Tracking System (RTS) – like other software systems. In this paper, a field study has been conducted and it has been found out that in the process of using a cyber-infrastructure the users face problems on one hand as well as the people who process incoming user requests also need better UI of RTS on the other hand. From this field study observations were made and amendments in the current UI of RTS were proposed. Moreover, the UI of RTS has been evaluated and recommendations have been made to improve it in a federated e-Science environment using a field study.

Keywords: User interfaces · Trouble ticketing systems · Time management · UI enhancement · Service desk interface · Incidents · User queries

1 Introduction

Trouble tickets is a well-known phenomenon in service oriented industries whether commercial or non-commercial [1]. Trouble tickets are created once a user or a customer has a trouble interacting with an information system. To counter customer troubles, companies provide help known as help-desk or service desk. This paper explores the interaction of employees of an organisation who provide support, known as user-support-staffs (also known as help-desk staffs) with the User Interface (UI) of

© Springer International Publishing Switzerland 2016
S. Yamamoto (Ed.): HIMI 2016, Part II, LNCS 9735, pp. 391–401, 2016.
DOI: 10.1007/978-3-319-40397-7_37

a trouble tracking system. The trouble tracking system observed in this paper was Best Practical Request Tracking (RT), version 4.0 at the German Climate Computing Centre (DKRZ)[1]. The study was conducted by observing the technicians engaged in user support (help-desk) activities using an ethnographic field research in real settings [2]. DKRZ is a High Performance Computing (HPC) as well as a data centre. It is one of the governmental organisations participating in the ongoing international project of Earth System Grid Federation (ESGF) [3, 4]. ESGF is a global climate e-Science infrastructure that offers climate data projects, computing and visualization facilities to climate scientists. ESGF is currently also being extended to serve other domains such Biology, Chemistry and Astronomy.

The User Interface (UI) of trouble ticketing systems, also known as request tracking systems in general have not been adequately researched [1] and particularly not in the field of e-Science. These request tracking systems, however, play a central role for the success of e-Science as e-Science is considered a new paradigm in doing research and helps to fulfill the Science 2.0 vision. Science 2.0 is a term under which more col-laboration amongst scientists using technology especially Web 2.0 is expected as opposed to traditional laboratory science which is termed as Science 1.0. The end-users of ESGF experience problems in getting the data needed and send requests in a hope to get their problems solved. Therefore, establishing an efficient support in a wider scope is one of the major exercises that lies ahead to make e-Science a central scientific method in the highly digitalized and linked up world-wide society of the 21st Century.

This paper supported by this observation study evaluates the usability of UI of User Request Tracking System: Best Practical RT and attempts to provide recommendations to enhance the UI of RT. This paper is structured as follows: In the Sect. 2 the background of the context and terminologies of e-Science, UI and User Support is provided. Also in this section an overview of related work to the research question is given. Subsequently the research steps taken to generate recommendation are explained in Sect. 3. The results of this research study are then shown and explained in Sect. 4. Future work and conclusion are elaborated in Sects. 5 and 6, respectively.

2 Background and Related Work

e-Research is conducted via e-Science infrastructures that are deployed to access and share the data, high performance computing (HPC) facilities and human resources to facilitate interdisciplinary and inter-disciplinary research to harvest knowledge [3–6]. Users need an interface to access its resources usually data. The interface includes command line tools, web portals and Graphical User Interface (GUI) to access data assets which are the main resources hosted [7, 8]. However, during an interaction of a user with an e-Science infrastructure, a user may require help due to outages of some resources e.g. servers or any other anomaly. In other case: a user requires particular scientific or technical information [9]. In order to meet these user support challenges, CI offers user support in the form of a help-desk, which even being a core activity has not received adequate attention since inception of cyber-infrastructures [10–12].

---

[1] DKRZ (www.dkrz.de) is a key partner institution in Earth System Grid System (ESGF) initiative.

Nevertheless, the aspect of interaction with UI of an e-Science infrastructure is not limited to the end-users. Indeed, it has been observed that also other stakeholders, especially the support worker's, need better UI of a request tracking system to properly support the users of an e-Science infrastructure [4, 13–15]. This is also due to a reason that there is often no or just a single real working position for a user support worker in e-Science organization [4, 13]. Moreover, e-Science infrastructure is mostly a decentralized structure of multiple organizations worldwide and there are many participants (user support workers) interested in supporting users at multiple sites world-wide rather than a single site [5, 16]. These employees are generally scientists and they contribute to user support on a voluntary basis [5, 13]. All these facts lead to study the current UI of RTS in place in ESGF.

Earth System Grid Federation (ESGF) is an important practical use-case in the field of climate science cyber-infrastructure project. ESGF facilitates to study climate change and impact of climate change on human society and Earth's eco-system [21, 27]. In a case study of ESGF, user support concept covers "helpdesk" or "service-desk" of a distributed, multi-organizational research-oriented, non-commercial, collaborative environment. The current user support in ESGF is being performed by human support agents i.e. employees, that include top scientists [1]. Better the user experience of GUI of the tracking system is, quicker it is to handle user requests.

There are many books as well as articles that provide guidelines to design an effective Graphical User Interface (GUI) in order to enhance the user experience and the usability e.g. [17–19]. Xie et al. evaluated many trouble ticketing systems in 2004, however, all had design problems. Unluckily, the UI guidelines have not been applied in the current request tracking systems [1], including Best Practical RT System. Jiri Janak investigated UI of five request tracking systems [20]. Moreover, apart from better usability, User eXperience (UX), the possibilities of UI customization, UI as well as software extension, and collaboration features amongst user support staffs are very important in choosing the right help desk system. Another factor that should not be undermined is the distribution politics as well as community support.

In the last decade, the user-support in ESGF has been evolving mainly due to the changes in ESGF CI. For instance, looking at the history of ESGF development, due to the technological plus organizational changes and especially the introduction of new data projects served by the ESGF data archive system, the number of users and their needs have been on constant rise [6, 19–21, 24–27]. Consequently, up until now the employees of ESGF are performing the user support by handling incidents, on a free will basis, on top of their core infrastructure development activities/tasks. A recent survey questionnaire and mailing list analysis conducted revealed that up to 15 % of the incidents were ignored by the employees. Therefore a need to enhance ESGF user support was felt and as a part of result USWAM is suggested amongst other changes in the organisation and governance of ESGF.

3   Research Methods

The field studies were conducted at the German Climate Computing Centre (DKRZ) by eight groups of participants i.e. Masters students of Human Computer Interface (HCI) from the department of Computer Science of the University of Hamburg who agreed to conduct it. Field study is a systematic investigation of groups in their natural research area. In this case, it is the working environment of the support staffs at DKRZ. The field researcher must be integrated in the natural environment of the subjects to be observed. It is important that the researcher disrupt or interfere the workflow of the subjects (in our case: DKRZ support employees) as little as possible. Fieldwork is primarily descriptive. Fieldwork is a holistic view of the research object by discovering the overall context and existing relationships in it.

Each group comprising of four students, observed the support staffs (also known as user support workers) involved in processing user requests. The groups noted the advantages and disadvantages of GUI of the user request tracking software that the user support staffs interacted with in order to support users. The duration of observation was two hours. Based on their observations they criticized the current User Interface (UI) in practice and suggested enhancements in the UI of the requesting tracking system (RTS) in the form of a paper prototype (see Fig. 1 and Table 1). The groups had to follow the following research steps indicated in Fig. 1.

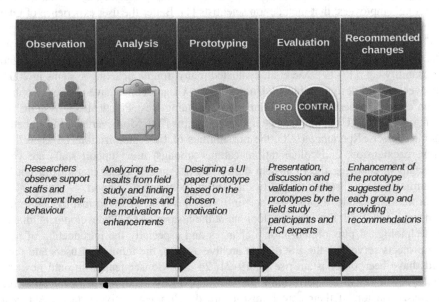

Fig. 1. The figure shows the four steps that the groups went through during this research.

In Table 1 the input to each step is shown in the second column under input and the research outcomes of each step is also shown. Each step is further described in Subsects. 3.1 to 3.5, respectively:

3.1 Observation

Researchers had to find out the advantages and disadvantages of the actual User Request Tracking Interface. The student researchers observed the working environment

Table 1. The table shows the steps of research process, the input and output to each research step.

No.	Input (observation)	(Research) process	Output/research outcomes
1	Workflow of user support staff	Observation	Notices
2	Notices	Problem analysis	Problem description
3	Problem description	Prototyping	Paper prototype
4	Paper prototype	Presentation and evaluation	Critique
5	Critique	Change	Recommendations for enhancements
6	Recommendations for enhancements	Documenting	Published results

and the atmosphere of the user support unit at the German Climate Computing Centre (DKRZ), in which the user support staffs performed their work using the actual UI used in a particular Request Tracking System. The researchers observed the support staffs completing their tasks by especially paying attention to their individual behavior as they supported end-users by following a noted protocol of actions performed by user support staffs. The students noted their observations that became the basis for the prototypes. During the observation, important points were noted down in the form of notes.

3.2 Analysis

Right after the observation, notes were analyzed again to re-construct the advantages and disadvantages of the current RTS interface in use. The possible problems were described based on the information. Moreover, motivation to change the current interfaces in use was also noted.

3.3 Prototyping

Based on the experiences and knowledge which were gained in the first step a paper prototype was drafted. It focused on:

- Handling the main problems of the current UI of RTS
- Enhancing the actual functionalities of RTS based on, and
- Proposing new functions

3.4 Evaluation

After prototyping, each group presented their prototype. The HCI student groups evaluated the prototypes of other groups by observing the proposed prototype carefully in guidance with Nielsen's 10 heuristics for UI design [21] while the group presented the prototype to other groups. The groups then provided recommendations to improve the suggested UI prototype presented by each group.

The student groups went through the process of evaluating their own and each other's prototype as well. Consequently, they had to enumerate advantages and especially the disadvantages of the presented prototypes in the form of a critique.

3.5 Recommended Changes

Based on the evaluation results, the participating research groups provided recommendations to improve their own as well as other's paper prototype. This provided them an opportunity to share their ideas with other groups and integrate these ideas and perspectives they learned from other groups' results.

Eventually, these recommendations were derived from each prototype to improve the interface of RTS. These recommendations are described in detail in the next section.

4 Results and Discussion

The authors observed the whole process of the groups and summarized the ideas of groups in the form of recommendations, grouped into the five sections shown in the Fig. 2.

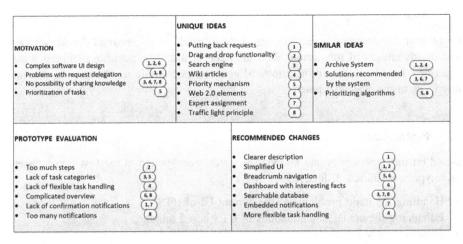

Fig. 2. The figure shows the five areas. These areas depict the motivation of groups behind proposed UI prototypes, the unique as well as similar ideas that the groups had. "Prototype Evaluation" lists the problems with the UI prototypes that were made evident after the evaluation of each prototype belonging to a group. And finally the changes recommended by each group.

4.1 Motivation

After looking at the results, the authors were able to find the basis of a *motivation* to change the current UI that was observed by the groups during the field study. The proposed prototype UI design by groups were based on the problems categorized as "no knowledge sharing", "complex software UI design", "problems with request delegation" and "prioritization of tasks."

Group number 3, 4, 7 and 8's prototype was based on knowledge sharing concepts. These groups were of the opinion that the user support staffs that use Request Tracking Systems (RTS) in a federated organization need to share more knowledge with other staff members and the RTS must provide such facilities. For example, a knowledge base can be made available about problems and incidents of users that can be shared with other staff members.

Similarly, group 5 based their UI porotype on priority of requests. They were of the opinion that the support staffs should be able to order the priorities of the user requests in an easy manner while interacting with the UI of an RTS. Alternatively, prioritization mechanism can be provided automatically in RTS. Group 1 and 8's prototype was mainly based on the features of re-directing or delegating user requests to other federated partner institutions of ESGF.

Finally, groups 1, 2 and 6 were of the opinion that the UI design of RTS was very complex as right from the beginning it exposes its user to plethora of functions. Moreover, they suggested that simple UI design with lesser functions may be replaced e.g. like Google search engine.

4.2 Unique Ideas

Each group had their unique idea in their proposed prototype; these ideas are listed in the Fig. 2 under "Unique Ideas."

- Group number 1 had an idea of *putting back requests* that can be marked solved or unsolved by the direct intervention of users via a proposed interface to the RT system
- Group number 2 introduced a *drag and drop functionality* in their paper prototype. The rationale for a drag and drop function was that it saves clicks and eliminates the complexity of interlaced or nested drop down menus
- Group number 3 suggested a *search engine* where one can input the keywords defined by user support staffs or the keywords suggested by the users to find the solutions, workarounds in the database. These keywords can be symptoms that may be mentioned in a user request, based on which the matching solutions can be proposed or shown as search results. The examples are shown in Fig. 2. In Fig. 2, the mockup shows that a keyword was given and a solution was proposed by the system that had a relevance probability of around 99 %.
- Group number 4 proposed that all requests and respective responses should be automatically saved into a *wiki article,* which can be used for learning or lookup purposes. This feature is however partially provided by the RT version 4.0.

398 H.I. Chunpir et al.

- Group number 5 came up with the proposal to introduce *an inbuilt priority mechanism* based on possible priority algorithms to prioritize tickets automatically and show those tickets in the form of visualization. The priority of tickets must be done according to relevant importance.
- Group number 6 introduced *various Web 2.0 elements* in their prototype. The tickets are shown under each other which gave the UI a blog-like interface. Also support workers are able to give quick replies to a selected ticket (see Fig. 3)

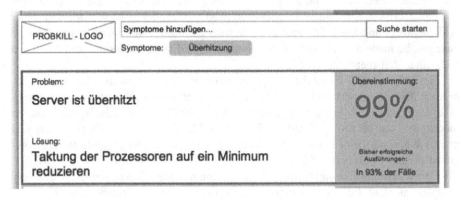

Fig. 3. A sample of the prototype made by a group of participants.

- Group number 7 had the idea that tickets should be *assigned and delegated to a respective expert* of a federated partner within ESGF
- Group number 8 suggested a *traffic light principle*. Green in a traffic light visualization stands for the workers with less requests, yellow for the ones with a lot of unanswered tickets and red for workers who are currently not able to handle user requests. Moreover, using this mechanism tickets are automatically delegated to the user support staff.

4.3 Similar Ideas

It was also noted that the groups had similar ideas that the system should *automatically recommend a solution*; *a request priority algorithm* can be introduced or embedded in RTS and finally *an archive system* or knowledge base that contains work arounds or solutions may also be introduced.

4.4 Prototype Evaluation

However, the prototypes designed by each group had some deficiencies in them which were pointed out by other groups in the evaluation phase. They are listed in the Figs. 1 and 2 under "evaluation" and "prototype evaluation" respectively. The changes recommended in the design of the UI prototype of each group are provided in the Fig. 2.

It is expected that the changes in the UI and the back-end functionality of an RTS can help the user support staffs to perform better.

- Group 2 was criticized for "too much steps" to complete a user interaction. This means that the user needed too many clicks until he performed a desired function.
- The prototypes of group 3, 5 and 7 were both criticized for their lack of task categories, in a way that no classification of the tickets into categories was possible.
- Group 4 was criticized for a lack of a flexible task handling
- The UIs of the prototypes of group 6 and 8 were seen as too complicated, because of appearance of too many functions at once.
- In the prototypes of group 1 and 7 confirmation notifications or other types of feedback when an action was performed, were absent. Consequently, the user would never know 100 %, whether his action has actually been successful.
- On the other hand, group 8 attracted attention by his high number of confirmation notifications (even after simple and often repeated actions), which has effects the work flow of supporting a user. A reduction of the number of notifications shall be improving the user experience and UI.

4.5   Recommended Changes

The last phase the recommended changes about their own prototypes were collected from the student groups. It is necessary to add that these recommendations were mostly, but not always, based on the critique of phase 4 (prototype evaluation). In this way the student groups sometimes also adopted ideas of other groups which they got to know during the presentations in phase 4.

- Group 1 suggested to build a clearer description so that functions are immediately comprehendible for a user
- Group 1 and group 2 were of the opinion to enhance the UI of their prototype by simplifying it. Moreover, they reiterated that only the most important functions shall be immediately visible in a particular UI
- Group 5 and 6 suggested breadcrumb *navigation*. This shall provide the support staff the ability to see the history of invoked functions and to possibly return to a previous step
- Group 6 suggested a dashboard with interesting facts and figures about the summary status of current user support situation (e.g. average response time) on the initial screen. This could for example include the number of requests answered today, a ranking of the user with the most solved tickets and other pertinent facts that may increase the motivation of the user support staffs.
- Groups 3, 7 and 8 recommended adding a searchable database to their prototype. This is an idea that was possibly borrowed from other groups after the presentation of each prototype
- Also group 7 suggested implementing embedded confirmation notifications after the user completes an action. They are clearly shown within the RT web UI, but do not appear as a separate window.
- Group 4 suggested a more flexible task handling.

5 Future Work

In future a complete prototype that integrates all the interesting and important features of other prototypes as recommended by the groups shall be built as a mock-up and finally implemented in the form of a software prototype. Furthermore, this software prototype shall be tested with the user support staffs of ESGF before putting into production.

6 Conclusion

In this paper the field study method was applied to observe the user support staffs using UI of the best practical RT trouble ticketing system in a federated e-Science environment. The study was conducted by eight groups of students of HCI. After conducting field observations, each group had their unique idea in their proposed prototype. Examples include: Drag and drop, search engine, wiki articles and others. These ideas are listed in Fig. 2 under "Unique Ideas." It was also noted that the groups had similar ideas e.g. the RT system should automatically recommend a solution, see Fig. 3. Moreover, a request priority algorithm can be introduced or embedded in RTS and finally an archive system that contains solutions or work arounds may also be introduced. Yet, the prototypes designed by each group had some deficiencies in them which were pointed out by other groups. The changes recommended in the design of the UI prototype of each group are summarized at the bottom of the Fig. 2. In a nutshell, the changes in the UI and the back-end functionality of an RTS can help the user support staffs to perform better.

Acknowledgement. We appreciate the sincere participation and support of the students of the Informatics department at the University of Hamburg and Prof. Martin Kindsmüller.

References

1. Xie, M., Bodenheimer, B.T.M.: Interface design for a modern software ticketing system. In: Proceedings of the 42nd Annual Southeast Regional Conference, pp. 122–127 (2004)
2. Broadhead, R.S., Agar, M.H.: The professional stranger: an informal introduction to ethnography. Contemp. Sociol. **10**(6), 785 (1981)
3. Chunpir, H.I., Ludwig, T., Curri, E.: Improving processes for user support in e-Science. In: IEEE 10th International Conference on e-Science (e-Science), vol. 2, pp. 87–90 (2014)
4. Chunpir, H.I.: Enhancing user support process in federated e-Science, University of Hamburg (2015)
5. Chunpir, H.I., Ludwig, T., Williams, D.N.: Evolution of e-Research: from infrastructure development to service orientation. In: Marcus, A. (ed.) DUXU 2015. LNCS, vol. 9188, pp. 25–35. Springer, Heidelberg (2015)
6. Chunpir, H.I., Ludwig, T.: Reviewing the governance structure of end-user support in e-science infrastructures. In: Informatik 2014 Proceedings of the Mastering Big Data Complexity. Lecture Notes in Informatics (LNI), vol. 232 (2014)

7. Chunpir, H.I., Rathmann, T., Ludwig, T.: The need for a tool to support users of e-Science infrastructures in a virtual laboratory environment. Procedia Manuf. **3**, 3375–3382 (2015)
8. Chunpir, H.I., Rathmann, T.: E-mail analysis of a user-staff communication in e-Research, Hamburg (2015)
9. Freeman, P.A.: Is it possible to define cyberinfrastructure? First Monday **6**(12) (2007)
10. Chunpir, H.: C3Grid – INAD: support centre with semi-automatic notification and coordination for experts work, Hamburg (2013)
11. Chunpir, H., Williams, D., Cinquini, L., Kindermann, S.: Third annual ESGF and ultrascale visualization climate data analysis tools face-to-face meeting report, Livermore, CA (2013)
12. Soehner, C., Steeves, C., Ward, J.: e-Science and data support services, Washington, D.C., USA (2010)
13. Chunpir, H.I., Ludwig, T., Badewi, A.: A snap-shot of user support services in Earth System Grid Federation (ESGF): A use case of climate cyber-infrastructures. In: Proceedings of the 5th Applied Human Factors and Ergonomics (AHFE) Conference, July 2014
14. Chunpir, H.I., Ludwig, T., Badewi, A.A.: Using soft systems methodology (SSM) in understanding current user-support scenario in the climate science domain of cyber-infrastructures. In: Marcus, A. (ed.) DUXU 2014, Part III. LNCS, vol. 8519, pp. 495–506. Springer, Heidelberg (2014)
15. Chunpir, H.I.: Prioritizing tasks using user-support-worker's activity model. In: Yamamoto, S. (ed.) HIMI 2016, Part II, LNCS 9735, pp. 379–390. Springer, Cham (2016)
16. Chunpir, H.I., Badewi, A.A., Ludwig, T.: User support system in the complex environment. In: Marcus, A. (ed.) DUXU 2014, Part IV. LNCS, vol. 8520, pp. 392–402. Springer, Heidelberg (2014)
17. Shneiderman, B.: Designing the User Interface, vol. 2, no. 2, 1–97 (1998)
18. Nielsen, J.: Iterative user-interface design. Computer (Long. Beach. Calif) **26**(11), 32–41 (1993)
19. Finstad, K.: Interacting with computers the usability metric for user experience. Interact. Comput. **22**, 323–327 (2010)
20. Janak, J.: Issue Tracking Systems, Universitas Masarykiana (Masaryk University) (2009)
21. Nielsen, J.: 10 usability heuristics for user interface design. In: Conference Companion on Human Factors in Computing Systems, CHI 1994, pp. 152–158 (2005)

Strategic Knowledge Management for Interdisciplinary Teams - Overcoming Barriers of Interdisciplinary Work Via an Online Portal Approach

Tatjana Hamann, Anne Kathrin Schaar, André Calero Valdez[✉],
and Martina Ziefle

Human-Computer Interaction Center, RWTH Aachen University,
Campus-Boulevard 57, Aachen, Germany
{hamann,schaar,calero-valdez,ziefle}@comm.rwth-aachen.de

Abstract. Interdisciplinary collaboration and its success is still not fully understood. In two explorative studies we examine both the existence of benefits and barriers of interdisciplinary collaboration as well as the leverage of a social portal to support benefits and lower the barriers of such cooperations. As core issues we identified problems of language and missing depth as the strongest barriers in a triangulation of qualitative (N=6) and quantitative results (N=45). In contrast we found intrinsic motivation and widening of one's horizon as well as the combination of knowledge as key benefits of interdisciplinary collaboration. In the second interview study (N=5) we found that our social platform approach could address theses barriers and leverage the benefits from the first study.

Keywords: Interdisciplinarity · Knowledge management · Collaboration support · Online portal · Web 2.0 technologies

1 Introduction

Since the 1980 s interdisciplinary research is considered a "mantra for change" [1]. Especially when research focuses global challenges interdisciplinary cooperation is perceived as an appropriate measure. Yet, still several challenges exist and its benefits are critically discussed. A central question is how to support scientific cooperation successfully. Therefore this paper focuses on research regarding benefits and barriers of interdisciplinary work and the evaluation of a knowledge management tool "Scientific Cooperation Portal" (SCP), which was designed to support interdisciplinary cooperation in a large interdisciplinary research project in Germany[1].

Successful interdisciplinary work is still a black box, this paper focuses on an empirical evaluation of benefits and barriers of interdisciplinary work and

---

[1] www.produktionstechnik.rwth-aachen.de.

© Springer International Publishing Switzerland 2016
S. Yamamoto (Ed.): HIMI 2016, Part II, LNCS 9735, pp. 402–413, 2016.
DOI: 10.1007/978-3-319-40397-7_38

the derivation and evaluation of adequate measures to support interdisciplinary innovation management. To work out the character of interdisciplinary work Sect. 1.1 reviews known benefits and barriers. Section 2 presents general information about the research cluster "Integrative Production Technology for High-Wage Countries" (IPTHWC) and its specific interdisciplinary situation (see Sect. 2.1). There we also present the first part of results — a qualitative and a quantitative evaluation of benefits and barriers of interdisciplinary work. Afterwards the concept of the SCP is portrayed (see Sect. 3) as our measure for strategic knowledge management in interdisciplinary teams. In Sect. 3.1 a second quantitative study investigating knowledge management for interdisciplinary teams is presented. This study focuses on the impact of the online portal on perceived benefits and barriers of interdisciplinary work. Concluding in Sect. 4, the results of both studies are discussed and triangulated, while taking into account the lessons learned in the context of social media based knowledge management. Section 5 addresses limitations and gives an outlook on future research activities.

1.1 Benefits and Barriers of Interdisciplinary Cooperation

There is no widely accepted definition of interdisciplinarity, although the importance of a common definition should be taken seriously [2]. Different researchers focus different aspects of this phenomenon. Key definitional components are the qualitatively different modes of interdisciplinary research and different forms of collaboration. Other definitions focus on the outcome of the collaboration or outline the existence of a continuum of collaboration [3]. We understand interdisciplinarity as a coordinated collaboration between researchers from at least two different disciplines, which can manifest itself in a simple exchange of ideas to the point of integration of methods, concepts and theories. The goal is primarily to solve problems and optimize research on certain topics by continuously conducting exchange [4]. Since knowledge about interdisciplinary success criteria or working guidelines are as fuzzy as the definition itself, we first shortly present the status-quo of benefits and barriers in interdisciplinary work.

Benefits. Since the 1980 s various (research) projects and cooperations were labeled "interdisciplinary", based on the promise of being preferable. But which benefits of interdisciplinarity really exist or are aspired? Nissani [5] stresses the *creative breakthroughs* of interdisciplinary work [6,7]. Hübenthal [8] calls it *fertilization* when researchers break out of standardized questions and approaches and look beyond the borders of their discipline. They *widen their own horizon* by getting insights into foreign disciplines and develop ideas they would have never had by staying in their field. Repko [6] criticizes that disciplinarity promotes a tunnel vision and blinds researchers from seeing the bigger context. Especially in times of *dead ends* a foreign discipline can help to expose mistakes or to balance weaknesses and borders of a single discipline [4]. Moreover, *interesting, exciting, and satisfying work* [7] can be a *personal benefit* and cause intrinsic motivation for the scientist. Experts have come to the agreement that global challenges, e.g. climate change, demographic changes, etc., are far too complex to be studied by only one discipline. Although it seems that the sole reliance on disciplinarity and profound technical knowledge are criticized, they are nevertheless considered the most important factors for successful interdisciplinary collaboration.

We can say that it is especially the perceived innovation potential to overcome dead ends in science that makes interdisciplinary cooperation so attractive. But besides this goal-oriented view on benefits, there is another component of interdisciplinary work that is highly correlated to the success of such cooperation – the personal motivation of people involved. It is not until the intrinsic motivation and persuasion of involved researchers are known that such cooperation can be beneficial.

Barriers. Beside the aforementioned positive attributes of interdisciplinary work, there are just as much critics as proponents. Negative associations of interdisciplinary cooperation address different facets of the interdisciplinary working process, which are often a result of disciplinary differences. Differences become relevant in the way methods are used and also organizational barriers can interfere with the collaboration. Jacobs and Frickel [9] appoint the *missing reputation and acknowledgements* for researchers that work interdisciplinarily as a meaningful factor. But almost the hardest part of interdisciplinary cooperation is in most cases *communication*. Even if researchers try to agree on one definition or expression the disciplinary assumptions and epistemology standing behind the terms cannot be "carried over" easily along the definition [10]. To simplify communication and avoid misunderstandings researchers use simplifications, which can lead to *falsifications*. Moreover there is the risk of staying on a *superficial* level during interdisciplinary work [4]. Another factor that is important in interdisciplinary cooperations is *time*. Interdisciplinary work is described as immensely time-consuming [11]. Additionally several studies on interdisciplinary work have shown that *spatial distance* is a central aspect of successful cooperation, which contributes to the generation of knowledge. In this context Toker and Gray revealed that the innovation potential in research is often negatively influenced by the distance between involved researchers [12]. More barriers that can have a negative impact on interdisciplinary work are *coordination costs* and *effort* of the single researcher [13]. In the following section, we present an evaluation of benefits and barriers of interdisciplinary work within an exemplary research cluster. Derived from identified benefits and barriers the need for a strategic knowledge management within interdisciplinary teams is depicted.

2   Benefits and Barriers of Interdisciplinary Work

We investigated benefits and barriers in two studies as a start to identify measures that should support researchers and serve as a baseline for the investigation of effectiveness of conceptualized measures. To ensure a deep insight into these aspects, quantitative and qualitative methods were used. At first, qualitative semi-structured interviews were conducted with a total of $N = 6$ participants.

All participants work in the Cluster of Excellence IPTHWC at RWTH Aachen University. Then, the results of the interviews were used to create a questionnaire to verify the findings quantitatively. $N = 45$ participants completed the questionnaire. In the following sections we first present the context, then the design and results of the qualitative study. Afterwards the design and results of the questionnaire study are presented.

2.1 The Interdisciplinary Research Cluster "Integrative Production Technology for High-Wage Countries"

The research cluster consists of more than 25 institutes of material and production technology at RWTH Aachen University in Germany. Since 2006 this project is funded by the Excellence Initiative of the German federal and state governments, integrated into the RWTH Aachen's concept of an integrated interdisciplinary university of technology. The main focus of the cluster is to assure the production in high-wage countries considering principles of sustainable production strategies and theories, as well as approaches for technologies that are needed to realize them. This challenge is worked on in four cluster domains that address different emphases (individualized production, virtual production systems, integrated technologies, self-optimizing production systems). The cluster domains are flanked by so-called "Cross Sectional Processes" (CSP), which were implemented to support the (interdisciplinary) work within the cluster. The topics *scientific cooperation engineering*, *production theory*, and *technology platforms* were conceptualized "cross-sectionally" and are supporting but also investigating the three aspects people, theory, and technology transfer. This paper is a product of the field of *scientific cooperation engineering* with a special focus on *interdisciplinary innovation management*, which aims to investigate and conceptualize measures that support the interdisciplinary cooperation.

2.2 A Qualitative View on Benefits and Barriers of Interdisciplinary Work

The semi-structured interviews (N=6) were conducted face-to-face. All participants were visited at their workplace. We started with warm-up questions, e.g. what the interviewees had studied or how long they had been working in interdisciplinary projects. The following questions focused on the experiences and general impressions concerning barriers and benefits of interdisciplinary work. The interviews took between 16 and 43 min. The interviews were analyzed in order to identify potential benefits and barriers of interdisciplinary work, using the qualitative content analysis method according to Mayring. [14] In the following subsections the results for revealed benefits and barriers are presented.

Barriers. As Fig. 1 shows, *language* and *missing depth* were identified as the central barriers of interdisciplinary work. The participants named problems and misunderstandings due to the use of different definitions or the use of different words (i.e. synonyms) to describe the same thing. Another aspect, mentioned in this context, was the experience that *discussions about the research subject stay on the surface* due to the fact that no one can learn a completely foreign and remote discipline in a short time and communication is simplified.

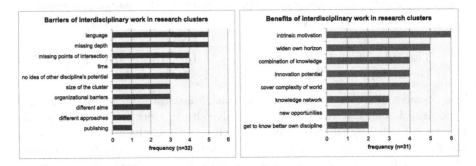

Fig. 1. Barriers and benefits of interdisciplinary work within the cluster according to their number of mentions

Three aspects that were mentioned by four participants were *missing points of intersection, no idea of other discipline's potential* and *time*. The first two aspects are addressing challenges that arise directly from the character of interdisciplinary cooperation. *Time* as another factor can have different influences on interdisciplinarity: on one hand it can be an organizational aspect and on the other it can stand for the workload that arises with the time that is needed to get to know and understand other disciplines. On the third rank there were mentioned further two barriers: *size of the project* and *organizational barriers*. Both complicate the collaboration between researchers of different disciplines. Organizational barriers can be e.g. a missing structure or even an oversized administrative organization. The size of the team can also have a negative influence on collaboration. As less important barriers *different aims in the research process*, *different approaches* and *publishing* in interdisciplinary teams were mentioned. These aspects are related to the aforementioned barriers that address the different workflows and rules of disciplines, which can hinder a smooth cooperation.

Benefits. In contrast to the presented barriers this study also revealed benefits that come up in the context of interdisciplinary teams. The most important benefit in the context of interdisciplinary work in this study was *intrinsic motivation*. All participants reported that the spiking of their own interest in the interdisciplinary scope of the project is the most important benefit for them. In line with intrinsic motivation the benefit *widening of the own horizon* ranks No. 2 of the mentioned benefits. The three benefits that follow on rank 3 are: *combination of knowledge, innovation potential,* and the potential of *covering complexity of global challenges* (four mentions each). The benefits to work in a *knowledge network* and *new opportunities* that arise from interdisciplinary work were each named by three participants. The network of scientists from various disciplines allows the single researcher to find an expert for a specific task whom he can ask for help. The last benefit that could be identified was *getting to know better one's own discipline*. Through interdisciplinary work and the comparison with other disciplines researchers got an impression of advantages and disadvantages of their own disciplines.

A follow up study in a different context has been also performed and published [15]. Based on the first explorative findings a questionnaire was designed and distributed among the members of the cluster. Results are presented in the next section.

2.3   A Quantitative View on Benefits and Barriers of Interdisciplinary Work

Based on the results of the qualitative study we designed a questionnaire study. The questionnaire was paper-based and conducted during a meeting of the members of the research cluster. It was divided into three parts. Part one asked for personal data, part two asked for a evaluation of the identified benefits and barriers on a 4-point scale ("correct" to "incorrect"), and part three focused on the emergence of new barriers by introducing the portal. A total of 45 participants answered the questionnaire.

Results. In the following subsection the results for benefits and barriers are presented separately. Results were conducted using descriptive mean analysis.

In the context of evaluated barriers, we found that the biggest barrier is the presence of *different approaches*, based on different disciplinary cultures and backgrounds. The *lack of a unified language and terminology* was followed by the *size of the cluster*. According to the participants, research group size can be a barrier for interdisciplinary work (in what aspect is not further investigated). *Time* resources that have to be applied for this kind of cooperation were also evaluated as an existing barrier. *Organizational barriers* as well as problems in the *publishing* process in interdisciplinary teams are less strongly experienced as barriers.

For the evaluated benefits we could reveal that *widening of the own horizon*, *innovation potential* of interdisciplinary teams and the *combination of knowledge* were considered as the main benefits of interdisciplinary collaboration among the members of the excellence cluster. The other benefits were all confirmed with means ranging from $M = 2.81$ for *intrinsic motivation* to $M = 2.38$ for *new opportunities* (see Tables 1 and 2).

2.4   Triangulation of Qualitative and Quantitative Findings and Derivations for Strategic Knowledge Management

Triangulating both studies a trend is visible: *Organizational barriers, different aims*, and *publishing* are of minor importance in the analyzed research cluster.

Table 1. Evaluation of barriers on a four-point Likert scale (1=incorrect to 4=correct).

Barriers	M	SD
Different approaches	2.77	0.71
Language	2.65	0.83
Size of cluster	2.65	0.91
Time	2.64	0.95
Missing points of intersection	2.55	0.82
Missing depth	2.54	0.63
No idea of other discipline's potential	2.54	0.76
Different aims	2.47	0.86
Publishing	2.42	0.80
Organizational barriers	2.11	0.85

Additionally we can say that the barriers are almost in line in both studies: *language* was rated as the biggest barrier in the qualitative study, while it is the second important barrier in the quantitative study. *Time* and the *missing points of intersection* are on the middle ranks in both studies. Striking is the barrier of *different approaches in the research process*, which is highly rated in the quantitative study ($M = 2.77$, $SD = 0.71$) but very low in the qualitative. Only one participant experienced it during interdisciplinary work. Concerning benefits there is clear agreement: the first four benefits are ranked similarly in both studies: *widening of the own horizon, innovation potential, combination of knowledge*, and *intrinsic motivation*. In the qualitative interviews intrinsic motivation was mentioned by all interviewees. It is not certain that especially in this case the interview situation has had some influence on the participants' statement. The *new possibilities* arising from interdisciplinary work and *getting to know better the own discipline* are the last two benefits in both cases.

Table 2. Evaluation of benefits on a four-point Likert scale (1=incorrect to 4=correct).

Benefits	M	SD
Widen own horizon	3.23	0.64
Innovation potential	3.11	0.69
Combination of knowledge	3.06	0.72
Intrinsic motivation	2.81	0.65
Knowledge network	2.77	0.74
Cover complexity of global challenges	2.74	0.75
Get to know better own discipline	2.74	0.72
New opportunities	2.38	0.78

Based on the findings of the presented study we can say that, for the case of research cluster IPTHWC, there are special needs and difficulties that should be supported by strategic (knowledge) management. Central aspects in this context are measures that address a better understanding of the involved disciplines. These address on one hand the need for enhancing the communication of disciplinary skills (methods, approaches etc.) and on the other one steered definition and discussion of/about central terminologies. Our findings support prior studies on interdisciplinary work within this research project [16] which also underline the necessity to manage interdisciplinary cooperation strategically. In the next section the SCP is portrayed, which is the product of a cooperation of the CSP within this cluster.

3   Strategic Knowledge Management for Interdisciplinary Teams - the Scientific Cooperation Portal (SCP)

As presented in the section above, interdisciplinary cooperation reveals a need for measures addressing strategic exchange of knowledge and knowledge management across disciplines. In order to cope with the demands of integrating knowledge in interdisciplinary teams a social portal approach (SCP [15]) was designed, which addresses different requirements i.e. knowledge management, communication, and target support for interdisciplinary topics (e.g. terminologies, publications, project and project management). The underlying software architecture is a social networking site with added collaboration tools specifically suited for interdisciplinary scientific research. The functions reach from employee profiles with specific competences to a virtual meeting-point, which allows scheduling of appointments, exchange of documents and storage of results. In addition, target solutions are provided to support the interdisciplinary collaboration [17]. These are a project management tool, a tool for cluster specific terminologies [16], a technology-platform [18], and a publication visualization tool [15,19], which should foster the understanding of interconnectedness based on publication data.

3.1   Evaluation of the Scientific Cooperation Portal (SCP)

In order to find out whether the implementation of an online portal leads to a perceived improvement of interdisciplinary cooperation we initiated a first study with focus on the scientists' opinion about the technical solution.

Methodology. The aim of this study was to evaluate the SCP with regard to the identified barriers and benefits. For this purpose we conducted an exploratory interview study with five members of the cluster of excellence. During the interviews they were shown the results of the qualitative evaluation of benefits and barriers (see Fig. 1) and logged in into the SCP. Afterwards they were asked for every single barrier (derived from the studies presented above) whether they think that the portal could reduce or compensate for the barriers. Equally they were asked whether the portal could support the benefits and at the same time interdisciplinary collaboration. The last (open) question asked if the participants saw new problems or barriers arise traceable to the use of the portal.

Results. Results of the semi-structured interviews show that especially simple functions of the portal lead to an improvement of interdisciplinary work. Figure 2 illustrates the connection between specified benefits and barriers and the range of services within the SCP. Benefits and barriers are presented according to the level of confirmation from the highest level of confirmation to the lowest (see Tables 1 and 2).

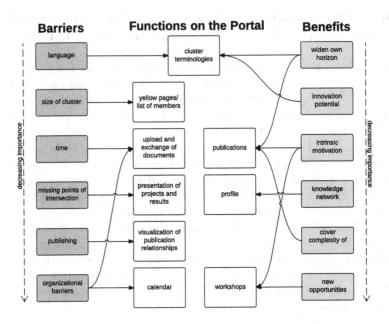

Fig. 2. Connections between possible barriers or benefits and functions of the SCP

Impact of the Scientific Cooperation Portal on Barriers. According to the question whether the functions of the portal could reduce existing *barriers* we revealed that *organizational barriers* and *time* were evaluated as the two factors that benefit most from the SCP. Our participants stated that these barriers are tackled by the functions *upload and exchange of documents* and *calendar.* In this context only one participant clearly denied this benefit. This person stated that he already had two calendars and does not need more. According to the exchange of documents (and chat-function) participants think these will save *time* and thus reduce time pressure in interdisciplinary cooperation. For the more specific barriers that arise specifically from the interdisciplinary exchange (*language* and *publishing*) the developed tools *cluster terminologies* and *visualization of publication relations* are evaluated as semi-helpful. The barriers *missing points of intersection* and *size of the cluster* are on the minor important ranks in the context of evaluating the fit and functionality of portal tools for interdisciplinary cooperation. In the interviews *missing points of intersection* were named in the context of function *presentation of projects and results*. *Size of the cluster* was interlinked with the function *yellow page/member list*.

Impact of the Scientific Cooperation Portal on Benefits. In regard to the question whether a social portal could enhance benefits of interdisciplinary work we found that this is true for the benefit *knowledge network*. From the point of view of four participants the knowledge network of interdisciplinary cooperations is enhanced by the function *profile*. Additionally the benefit *new opportunities* is supported by the offering of workshops, which are no technical component, but an offer provided via the portal. *Cover complexity of the world* was interlinked with the function *publications*. One participant stated in this context that concerning the *publishing* process different requirements from institutes and universities play a more important role. At most the implemented visualization tool [19] can be a help in the publication process as it supports finding neighboring disciplines where e.g. certain methods are applied and ease citation from neighboring publications. The benefit *intrinsic motivation* was named in the context of two functions of the portal *workshops* and *publications*. On minor important ranks we found *widen own horizon* and *innovation potential* both mentioned in the context of *cluster terminologies*.

Although we found a positive impact of functions of the portal, there are still limitations. At least three of five participants think that the portal cannot help to get an impression of the *other disciplines potential* at all.

4 Discussion

The presented paper shows that interdisciplinary research cooperations have both benefits and barriers. Main *benefits* were in our case study mostly seen in *personal benefits* (widen own horizon, intrinsic motivation) and *innovation potential* arising from the *combination of knowledge*. In contrast to that *barriers* were predominantly seen in the *differences between the disciplines* (different approaches, language). Additionally *size* and *time* for the interdisciplinary work were evaluated as central barriers. Based on the findings of the study on benefits and barriers we have conducted another study with focus on the impact of the SCP, an online portal approach, designed for an interdisciplinary research cluster in Germany on benefits and barriers of interdisciplinary work. Findings of this study let us say that the concept of an online portal as a measure for strategic knowledge management is on a good way. We could identify a first positive impact on *organizational barriers* and *time*. Additionally the approaches that were especially designed to tackle interdisciplinary communication – and thus support cooperation – the applications *cluster terminologies* and *visualization of publication relationships* were evaluated with a positive connotation.

But although the tone was positive, there is no doubt that there is still research to do, especially when recognizing that even new barriers arise in the context of a social portal. Open questions and to-do's basically address to big topics: *Usability issues* and *organizational implementation of the portal into the workflow*. It seems that the challenges that emerge through the portal can easily be tackled by technical measures. To face the usability issues it is necessary to evaluate the portal according to established usability testings to optimize the interface corresponding to user needs.

The most complex challenge from our point of view is user acceptance as a multifactorial construct. In this context aspects of motivation and rewarding should be evaluated and considered to find out more about the individual aspects of usage. Only if the personal benefits become tangible it is possible to overcome the fact that the portal is not a "bottom-up" approach, as social media applications often are. It must be considered that the working context comes up with special needs that influence the usage [20] and the personal willingness to disclose information [21].

5   Limitations and Outlook

Our studies were explorative in nature. So far we do not have a full-sample or time-series data for the impact of the portal on strategic knowledge management and on interdisciplinary work. The following steps will be considered in future work. To maximize acceptance and foster optimal usage conditions next steps should happen iteratively. This allows simultaneous evaluation and optimization. Other mechanisms considered for control of success of the SCP are key performance indicators. Those are: performance of the cluster in form of publications, which are supported by the portal (disciplinary and interdisciplinary), but also user statistics, and qualitative insights in form of perceived level of interdisciplinary integration in meetings. For the realization of this research model a mix of qualitative and quantitative methods but also technical components (usage statistics) will be used to get deeper insights into interdisciplinary knowledge sharing and appropriateness of the used solutions.

Acknowledgments. The authors thank the German Research Council DFG for the friendly support of the research in the excellence cluster "Integrative Production Technology in High Wage Countries".

References

1. Klein, J.T.: Creating Interdisciplinary Campus Cultures: A Model for Strength and Sustainability. Wiley, New York (2009)
2. Repko, A.F., Szostak, R.R., Buchberger, M.P.: Introduction to Interdisciplinary Studies. Sage Publications, New York (2013)

3. Aboelela, S.W., Larson, E., Bakken, S., Carrasquillo, O., Formicola, A., Glied, S.A., Haas, J., Gebbie, K.M.: Defining interdisciplinary research: conclusions from a critical review of the literature. Health Serv. Res. **42**(11p1), 329–346 (2007)
4. Lattuca, L.R.: Learning interdisciplinarity: sociocultural perspectives on academic work. J. High. Educ. **73**(6), 711–739 (2002)
5. Nissani, M.: Ten cheers for interdisciplinarity: the case for interdisciplinary knowledge and research. Soc. Sci. J. **34**(2), 201–216 (1997)
6. Repko, A.F.: Interdisciplinary Research: Process and Theory. Sage Publications, New York (2011)
7. Lyall, C., Bruce, A., Tait, J., Meagher, L.: Interdisciplinary Research Journeys: Practical Strategies for Capturing Creativity Ebook. FT Press, New York (2011)
8. Hübenthal, U.: Interdisziplinäres Denken. Franz Steiner Verlag, Stuttgart (1991)
9. Jacobs, J.A., Frickel, S.: Interdisciplinarity: a critical assessment. Ann. Rev. Sociol. **35**, 43–65 (2009)
10. Deinhammer, R., Group, U.S.P.R., et al.: Was heißt interdisziplinäres Arbeiten?: FWF (Austrian Science Fund): Research project Y 164. University of Salzburg/Poverty Research Group (2003)
11. Böhm, B.: Vertrauensvolle Verständigung - Basis interdisziplinärer Projektarbeit. vol. 4. Franz Steiner Verlag (2006)
12. Toker, U., Gray, D.O.: Innovation spaces: workspace planning and innovation in US university research centers. Res. Policy **37**(2), 309–329 (2008)
13. Cummings, J.N., Kiesler, S.: Who collaborates successfully?: prior experience reduces collaboration barriers in distributed interdisciplinary research. In: Proceedings of the 2008 ACM Conference on CSCW, pp. 437–446. ACM (2008)
14. Mayring, P.: Qualitative Inhaltsanalyse. Beltz Pädagogik (2003). ISBN: 978-3407255334
15. Valdez, A.C., Schaar, A.K., Ziefle, M., Holzinger, A.: Enhancing interdisciplinary cooperation by social platforms. In: Yamamoto, S. (ed.) HCI 2014, Part I. LNCS, vol. 8521, pp. 298–309. Springer, Heidelberg (2014)
16. Vaegs, T., Welter, F., Jooß, C., Leisten, I., Richert, A., Jeschke, S.: Cluster terminologies for promoting interdisciplinary scientific cooperation in clusters of excellence. In: Proceedings of INTED2013, IATED, pp. 5805–5812 (2013)
17. Brecher, C., Wesch-Potente, C.: Exzellenzcluster Integrative Produktionstechnik fürHochlohnländer – Perspektiven interdisziplinärer Spitzenforschung. Auflage: 1 edn. Apprimus Verlag, May 2014
18. Schuh, G., Aghassi, S., Calero Valdez, A.: Supporting technology transfer via web-based platforms. In: Proceedings of the PICMET 2013 Conference on Technology Management in the IT-Driven Services (2013)
19. Valdez, A.C., Schaar, A.K., Ziefle, M., Holzinger, A., Jeschke, S., Brecher, C.: Using mixed node publication network graphs for analyzing success in interdisciplinary teams. In: Huang, R., Ghorbani, A.A., Pasi, G., Yamaguchi, T., Yen, N.Y., Jin, B. (eds.) AMT 2012. LNCS, vol. 7669, pp. 606–617. Springer, Heidelberg (2012)
20. Valdez, A.C., Schaar, A.K., Ziefle, M.: Personality influences on etiquette requirements for social media in the work context. In: Holzinger, A., Ziefle, M., Hitz, M., Debevc, M. (eds.) SouthCHI 2013. LNCS, vol. 7946, pp. 427–446. Springer, Heidelberg (2013)
21. Schaar, A.K., Valdez, A.C., Ziefle, M.: The impact of user diversity on the willingness to disclose personal information in social network services. In: Holzinger, A., Ziefle, M., Hitz, M., Debevc, M. (eds.) SouthCHI 2013. LNCS, vol. 7946, pp. 174–193. Springer, Heidelberg (2013)

Data Integration and Knowledge Coordination for Planetary Exploration Traverses

Jordan R. Hill[1]([✉]), Barrett S. Caldwell[1], Michael J. Miller[2],
and David S. Lees[3]

[1] Purdue University, Industrial Engineering, West Lafayette, IN, USA
{hill265, bscaldwell}@purdue.edu
[2] Kennedy Space Center, NASA, Titusville, FL, USA
michael.j.miller@nasa.gov
[3] Ames Research Center, CMU/NASA,
Moffett Field, Mountain View, CA, USA
david.s.lees@nasa.gov

Abstract. In order to implement an ambulatory physiological monitor in a free-range environment, a number of human performance sensing, human-computer interaction, data visualization, and wireless transmission technologies must be effectively and unobtrusively integrated. The Zephyr BioHarness™ is being integrated into NASA's Biologic Analog Science Associated with Lava Terrains (BASALT) Mars simulation in order to monitor and transmit crewmember health and activity information during "extravehicular activity" (EVA) sample collection tasks. The structure of the simulation and the different types of data and knowledge coordination are described. The importance of physiological monitoring in extreme environments, the selection of the BioHarness™ for use in the project, the process of integrating the monitor into the simulation, and the anticipated results from the analysis of the gathered data are also discussed.

Keywords: Physiological monitoring · Extravehicular activity · Human performance · Extreme environments · Distributed task coordination

1 Introduction

Ambulatory physiological monitoring has been shown to be effective in experiments in a variety of fields. However, nearly all of these experiments have taken place in controlled, enclosed environments, such as a hospital [1], or research laboratory [2–4]. With the desire of the space community to send humans to Mars and conduct necessary extravehicular activity (EVA), it is necessary to move ambulatory physiological monitors out of the lab and into free-range, extreme environments to collect data in situ and to transmit that data to a secondary location to allow for real-time monitoring.

In an attempt to fill this gap in research, a commercially available physiological monitor was selected and integrated into NASA's Biologic Analog Science Associated with Lava Terrains (BASALT) Mars simulation. The BASALT simulation was designed to test concepts of operations and sample collection protocols for human planetary exploration, while performing actual geological and geobiological science in

S. Yamamoto (Ed.): HIMI 2016, Part II, LNCS 9735, pp. 414–422, 2016.
DOI: 10.1007/978-3-319-40397-7_39

scientifically interesting terrestrial settings. The lava terrains involved in the BASALT study include geologically recent (< 2000 years) and currently active lava flows in Idaho and Hawai'i, respectively.

The architecture as well as the data and knowledge coordination demands of the BASALT simulation are described below. The importance of physiological monitoring in extreme environments, such as the Martian climate and long duration spaceflight, is also discussed. Different physiological monitors were examined for integration into the BASALT simulation before the Zephyr BioHarness™ was eventually chosen; that process and the steps taken to integrate the selected monitor into the simulation are described in Sects. 4.1 and 4.2. Finally, the anticipated analyses to be performed on the collected data and the implementation of the results of those analyses are discussed.

2 BASALT

2.1 BASALT Architecture

BASALT is a NASA-organized research study simulating mission coordination and science achievement within the communication limitations caused by transmission lags of 5–20 min between Earth and Mars. The first BASALT deployment is scheduled for June 18th–30th, 2016 on the Eastern Snake River Plain (ESRP) in Idaho. This site was investigated as an analog to lava plains on Mars. A second BASALT deployment is planned during autumn 2016 on the Big Island of Hawai'i near Kilauea volcano. Crew information coordination and knowledge sharing in both Idaho and Hawai'i deployments are structured similarly, as shown in Fig. 1. An extravehicular (EV) crew left the simulated Mars habitat to perform scientific experiments and collect biological and geological samples on the lava flows. An intra vehicular (IV) crew remained in the

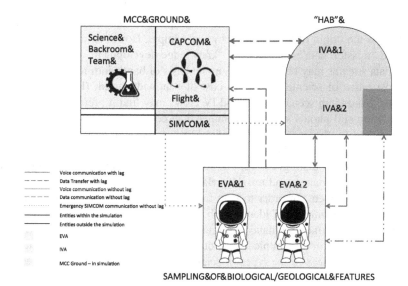

Fig. 1. BASALT simulation architecture

habitat to coordinate with the EV crew, monitor their progress, and to communicate with the Mission Control Center (MCC) stationed in a different location.

MCC consists of the capsule communicator (CAPCOM) and the flight controller, as well as the simulation communicator (SIMCOM), who monitors the simulation in real-time to ensure crew health and safety. The science backroom team is composed of individuals who have some scientific interest in the simulation, whether in its use as a Mars analog, or in the geological or biological samples taken from the site.

EV and IV crews can communicate with each other in real-time. Communication channels between the IV crew and the MCC, with the exception of the SIMCOM, are lagged 5–20 min to simulate real communication from Mars to Earth. MCC can also receive EV crew communication transmissions but their ability to respond to those communications was limited to sending messages through the IV crew; this was done in order to minimize distractions to the EV crew in the field.

2.2 Varieties of Data and Knowledge Coordination Demands

In order to fully capture the range of scientific mission achievement and knowledge coordination demands associated with the BASALT mission, comprehensive concepts of operations must be developed that enable and support a wide variety of data exchange and information alignment capabilities. The widely multidisciplinary nature of the BASALT research teams means that no two researchers will be necessarily focused on the same sources of engineering status, science achievement, or technology performance data flows. Nonetheless, the BASALT Simulation Architecture must be able to support this variety of flows, and remain robust to experimentally induced lags in data availability, as well as unintentional dropouts in communications.

The physiological monitoring of EV crew must be considered one of these data flows; however, such data does not map directly to a geologist's interest in infrared spectral analysis data of a basaltic structure, or proper GPS-based location tagging and annotation of the origin of a particular physical sample. However, all of these may be considered "mission data" or sources of "knowledge development" or "achievement". Further, data streams may be prioritized on the basis of bandwidth requirements or net benefit/cost ratios of scientific value to cost of bandwidth used. (For this reason, in constrained bandwidth scenarios, EV and IV crews may find it preferable to exchange high-resolution still photos with MCC, rather than continuous motion video.)

In addition to the technology requirements associated with constructing and maintaining the BASALT Architecture, members of the BASALT team have also found it important to distinguish various forms of science achievement, engineering status, human performance, and mission-related analog operational experience data or knowledge development. In order to help facilitate this distinction, the second author developed the following set of identifiers based on prior BASALT preparation meetings and initial deployment in Idaho in August, 2015. Rather than focusing on technical aspects of bandwidth or communication protocol requirements, the following identifier list addresses differences in the types of scientific and mission activities served:

- **Sample Artifact Direct (SAD):** physical artifacts collected for later transport and processing (e.g., rock piece or powdered material in sample bag);
- **Processed Artifact into Data (PAID):** use of instruments to conduct on-site analysis of artifact characteristics for immediate transmission via communication architecture (e.g., diffraction or infrared spectra);
- **Context-Relevant Instrument Measurements and Elaborations (CRIME):** instrument data important in defining or describing location, elevation, or composition of physical location (e.g., LIDAR or GPS instrument, visuals from aerial vehicles);
- **Activity, Communication, and Execution as Data (ACED):** human performance and mission task completion used for studies of time- and location-based crew capability and task activity (e.g., voice communication, physiological monitoring);
- **Artifacts for Later Processing Offline (ALPO):** a subset of SAD objects must be sent for further processing (e.g., thin sections of rocks for crystallography) long after the analog deployment is completed;
- **Experiential Learning and Knowledge (ELK):** a variety of lessons learned, updates to task protocols, or changes in understanding of scientific domains based on field experience (e.g., considerations of new lava types or different communication protocols after a week of field deployment).

Full details of the mapping of BASALT Architectures to data flow types is beyond the scope of this paper. However, future studies of human-computer interaction and distributed knowledge coordination for similar mission designs will require conceptual and operational (if not technological) sensitivity and differentiation of the benefits and costs of obtaining different types of information resources in a constrained planetary science mission configuration. For the purposes of this paper, the remaining discussion will focus on the BioHarness physiological monitoring as a form of ACED data; further work will emphasize analyzing BioHarness and terrain information (integrating ACED and CRIME data sources) for further insights into proper crew scheduling and health monitoring strategies (creating new ELK mission operations baselines).

3 Physiological Monitoring in Extreme Environments

EVA offers a level of operational flexibility that will be paramount during long duration space flights and planetary exploration [5]. However, space and non-Earth planetary environments are arguably the most extreme environments humans have ever ventured to explore. Mars in particular combines the challenges of working in a very cold environment as well as in space.

Due to its thin atmosphere, Mars does not retain heat in the same way Earth does and therefore can reach temperatures as cold as $-125°C$ near the poles in winter [6]. It is for this reason that arctic environments on Earth are often used as analogs for Mars. In an environment that can reach such low temperatures, there is a high dependence on technical systems to keep astronauts warm, especially when they are required to perform EVA. It is also important to note as the temperature of the body decreases, there is an increase in human metabolic rate in order to keep warm [7].

Along with its frigid temperatures, Mars offers other challenges specific to planetary exploration. The reduced gravity on Mars presents significant challenges. Studies of human locomotion hypothesize that energy expenditure increases in lower gravity environments due to the increased amount of effort required to self-stabilize and the decrease in traction with the reduced gravitational force. Large, cumbersome space suits also reduce mobility [8, 9]. The reduced gravitational force on Mars will also deteriorate weight-bearing bones and muscles, and cause pressure changes within the cardiovascular system, which could significantly impair an astronaut's ability to perform EVA. In addition to this, psychological parameters such as isolation, confinement, dependence on technical systems, and the high risk of the environment could present themselves physiologically and affect EVA efficiency [7, 10, 11].

Though data on the effects of long term spaceflight has increased since the establishment of the International Space Station (ISS), there will still be many unknowns and risks when it comes time to send the first manned crew to Mars or the Moon for a long-duration mission [7]. It is for this reason that remote and real-time physiological monitoring will be such a critical capability during these missions. Even early American and Soviet space programs recognized the importance of being able to physiologically monitor the first astronauts and cosmonauts that were sent into space [8–10]; it allows identification of anomalies and early reactions to potentially dangerous situations, which is invaluable in such an extreme environment [15, 16].

In order to overcome the lack of knowledge surrounding long term spaceflight and planetary explorations, simulations such as BASALT are used in order to attempt to fill some of the gaps in research. While it is not possible to simulate reduced gravity or cold climates during this simulation, Idaho and Hawai'i offer their own extreme environmental factors. The black lava flow at the Craters of the Moon National Monument & Preserve can reach temperatures of 77°C in the summer due to solar radiation [17] and Hawai'i is a tropical climate with high levels of humidity at sea level, but mountain sites may be more desert-like at altitude, with high solar incidence. More specifically, the active fumaroles in the BASALT target site can release toxic gases at any time. Both of these environments could cause EVA crewmembers problems with core body temperature cooling. In this situation physiological monitoring is also critical to ensure crew health and safety as the EVA crew may not recognize when they are overheating or dehydrated [7, 18].

4   The Zephyr BioHarness™

4.1   Selection

Unlike the early Russian and American space programs, computing power and mass is no longer a restricting factor in determining which physiological parameters can be monitored in space [12, 13]. There are many commercially available, wearable technologies that monitor a variety of physiological parameters and transmit the data in real-time.

When considering which physiological monitor to implement into the BASALT simulation, multiple wearable technologies were evaluated. Due to the variety of parameters that it can measure, the reliability with which it measures those parameters, and the unobtrusive placement of the device, the Zephyr BioHarness™ was chosen (Fig. 2).

Fig. 2. The Zephyr BioHarness™ worn around chest [19]

The BioHarness™ is worn on a strap around the wearer's chest, as shown above, and is able to measure heart rate, respiration rate, posture, activity levels, and estimated core temperature, among others [19]. This is a larger variety of physiological parameters than many other available monitors, which will give a more accurate indication as to the exertion of the EV crew. Also, the placement of this device is not only unobtrusive, but it also allows for more accurate measurements of vital signs than a wrist wearable technology. A monitor worn on the wrist would make accurate body posture and acceleration measurements impossible, due to the hands-on tasks crewmembers perform during EVA. The BioHarness™ also comes with its own live-monitoring and post-activity analysis software, which reduced the amount of work required to implement the device into BASALT.

The BioHarness™ has been used in a variety of laboratory studies including experiments simulating spaceflight [15], healthcare experiments [1, 2, 20], and sports settings [3, 4]. These experiments have shown the BH to be an accurate and reliable method to measure physiological parameters however they have all taken place in laboratory settings. There was no available literature on its use in extreme environments or in simulations such as BASALT.

4.2   Integration in BASALT

The BioHarness™ is worn by both EVA crewmembers while they complete the scheduled EVA tasks. When it is worn, the device automatically logs the wearer's physiological data internally for future download and analysis.

The IV crew and SIMCOM are responsible for monitoring the EVA crew's physiological parameters in real-time in order to ensure their health and safety at all times during an EVA. The data is also transmitted to the MCC with a time delay for observational purposes.

A key challenge of the BASALT mission architecture is the requirement to transmit real-time data to the IV crew, SIMCOM, and MCC. While the BioHarness™ transmits data over a Bluetooth or IEEE 802.15.4 connection, this only supports short range remote monitoring. Because of the challenging environment at the BASALT field sites, the IV crew, SIMCOM, and MCC can be located several miles away from EV crewmembers. Instead, the data will be locally linked to a Bluetooth relay device at the field site (Zephyr Echo Gateway). Then, the USB output from the gateway will be converted to an Ethernet data stream to be transmitted over BASALT's wireless Local Area Network (LAN) to IV and SIMCOM. This LAN provides a backbone for all communication (voice, video, data) between EV crewmembers, IV, and MCC. At the IV or MCC sites, the data stream can be received from the network and monitored with the standard software provided with the BioHarness^{TM}.

5   Anticipated Use of Physiological Data

The sampling rate of the BioHarness^{TM} provides large amounts of data to analyze, enabling a variety of different human performance aspects to examine.

First, the physiological data will be paired with EVA tasks to ensure that crewmembers did not need to overstress in order to keep to the scheduled timeline. This could eventually lead to the creation of guidelines for task scheduling. There are currently few standards applied to EVA scheduling, although studies suggest that the order in which tasks are arranged can have some effect on human performance. For example, performing repetitive tasks can be fatiguing and the longer an EV crew needs to be performing a task increases the risk of error, which could lead to injuries [9, 21]. This demonstrates the need for efficient scheduling of EVA tasks.

Gaining a base understanding of the workload requirements of different EVA tasks could also help allocate the appropriate amount of resources for each task [9] and could optimize crewmember performance by keeping individuals within defined performance parameters that ensure they are not expending too much energy [22]. Ultimately, strategic task scheduling and performance optimization will increase the robustness of planetary exploration missions.

Comparing the frequency and duration of communication transmissions against the measured physiological parameters could also ensure that communication was not compromised during particularly strenuous tasks. As a critical aspect of EVA, if a certain sequence of tasks causes a critical reduction in EV crewmember communication then that sequence of tasks will need to be reevaluated.

6   Conclusion

Physiological monitoring in an environment as extreme as Mars is critical for crew survival. Even in an analog (but scientifically valid for other purposes) field deployment environment, there are considerable needs for ongoing health monitoring of field crew/scientists during deployments at the science site. However there have been few implementations of ambulatory physiological monitors outside of controlled environments capable of providing reasonable or real-time performance data in such a challenging, "free-range" setting. The implementation of the Zephyr BioHarness^{TM} into

NASA's BASALT Mars simulation demonstrates the possibility of integrating a commercially available monitor into an extreme environment. One of the largest challenges of this implementation is getting the real-time data to transmit over the simulation's internal network.

It is anticipated that the analysis of the collected data will lead to EVA task scheduling guidelines that will ensure EV crewmembers do not need to overstress to keep to task timelines and that communication is not compromised during strenuous tasks.

References

1. Claudio, D., Velazquez, M.A., Bravo-Llerena, W., Okudan, G.E., Freivalds, A.: Perceived usefulness and ease of use of wearable sensor-based systems in emergency departments. IIE Trans. Occup. Ergon. Hum. Factors **3**, 177–187 (2015)
2. Stenerson, M., Cameron, F., Payne, S.R., Payne, S.L., Ly, T.T., Wilson, D.M., Buckingham, B.A.: The impact of accelerometer use in exercise-associated hypoglycemia prevention in type 1 diabetes. J. Diab. Sci. Technol. **9**, 80–85 (2015)
3. Kim, J.-H., Roberge, R., Powell, J.B., Shafer, A.B., Williams, W.J.: Measurement accuracy of heart rate and respiratory rate during graded exercise and sustained exercise in the heat using the Zephyr BioHarness^{TM}. Int. J. Sports Med. **34**, 497–501 (2013)
4. Hailstone, J., Kilding, A.E.: Reliability and validity of the Zephyr^{TM} BioHarness^{TM} to measure respiratory responses to exercise. Meas. Phys. Educ. Exerc. Sci. **15**, 293–300 (2011)
5. Newman, D., Barratt, M.: Life support and performance issues for extravehicular activity (EVA). In: Fundamentals of Space Life Science. (1997)
6. Sharp, T.: What is the Temperature of Mars? (2012). http://www.space.com/16907-what-is-the-temperature-of-mars.html
7. Gunga, H.-C.: Human Physiology in Extreme Environments. Elsevier, Burlington (2015)
8. Chappell, S.P., Klaus, D.M.: Enhanced simulation of partial gravity for extravehicular activity. Hum. Perform. Extrem. Environ. 10 (2013)
9. Chappell, S.P., Norcross, J.R., Abercromby, A.F.J., Gernhardt, M.L.: Evidence Report: Risk of injury and compromised performance due to EVA operations, Houston (2015)
10. Bishop, S.L.: Evaluating teams in extreme environments: from issues to answers. Aviat. Sp. Environ. Med. **75**, 14–21 (2004)
11. Le Pape, M.A.: Human-computer interaction in extreme environments: interaction effects between field dependency-independency and altered ± Gz accelerations on end-user performance. University of Hawai'i (2009)
12. Karandeyev, K.B.: Biological measurements in space (1965)
13. Holt, T.W., Lamonte, R.J.: Monitoring and recording of physiological data of the manned space flight program. In: IEEE Trans. Aerosp., pp. 341–344 (1965)
14. Fei, D.-Y., Zhao, X., Boanca, C., Hughes, E., Bai, O., Merrell, R., Rafiq, A.: A biomedical sensor system for real-time monitoring of astronauts' physiological parameters during extra-vehicular activities. Comput. Biol. Med. **40**, 635–642 (2010)
15. Rai, B., Kaur, J.: Human factor studies on a mars analogue during crew 100B international lunar exploration working group EuroMoonMars crew: proposed new approaches for future human space and interplanetary missions. N. Am. J. Med. Sci. **4**, 548–557 (2012)

16. Cermack, M.: Health and safety monitoring in extreme environments. J. Ocean Technol. **7**(3), 28–38 (2012)
17. Craters of the Moon - Weather. National Park Service (2016). http://www.nps.gov/crmo/learn/nature/weather.htm
18. Peacock, C.A., Glickman, E.L., Sanders, G.J., Pollock, B.S., Burns, K.J., Kakos, L., Gunstad, J.: Assessing a monitoring scale of physiological health and risk assessment among those exposed to heated environments: a brief report. Hum. Perform. Extrem. Environ. 12 (2015)
19. Zephyr Technology Corp.: Zephyr BioHarness 3 User Guide (2015)
20. Rodes, C.E., Chillrud, S.N., Haskell, W.L., Intille, S.S., Albinali, F., Rosenberger, M.E.: Predicting adult pulmonary ventilation volume and wearing compliance by on-board accelerometry during personal level exposure assessments. Atmos. Environ. **57**, 126–137 (2012)
21. Whitmore, M., McQuilkin, M.L., Woolford, B.J.: Habitability and performance issues for long duration space flights. Hum. Perform. Extrem. Environ. **3**, 64–74 (1998)
22. Cermack, M.: Monitoring and telemedicine support in remote environments and in human space flight. Br. J. Anaesth. **97**, 107–114 (2006)

Gauging the Reliability of Online Health Information in the Turkish Context

Edibe Betül Karbay[1](✉) and Hashim Iqbal Chunpir[2,3,4](✉)

[1] Faculty of Communication, Galatasaray University,
Ciragan Cad. no. 36, Ortakoy, 34357 Istanbul, Turkey
ebkarbay@gsu.edu.tr
[2] Department of Computer Science,
Universidade Federal de São Carlos, São Paulo, Brazil
chunpir@dkrz.de
[3] Faculty of Informatics, University of Hamburg,
Vogt-Kölln-str. 30, Hamburg, Germany
[4] German Climate Computing Centre (DKRZ),
Bundesstraße 45a, Hamburg, Germany

Abstract. It is hard to gauge the reliability of health information that is provided on the internet as there are plethora of medical firms and other organizations promoting their massive marketing campaigns to sell their products and services. However, an initiative; Health On the Net (HON) foundation claims that it is possible to observe the credibility and trustworthiness of health information on the websites internationally by following HON-code principles. Keeping with the principles set by the HON foundation, we analyzed the credibility of Turkish health websites and portals related to health information seeking behavior from the point of view information seeker's benefit. We selected and analyzed 56 websites within three categories which are "psychology", "aesthetics and beauty" and "motherhood, baby and children". We then evaluated their credibility of health information as according HON principles. We found out that most of the selected websites do conform to the basic principles set by the HON foundation, in Turkey. However, this information of conformance to the standards has not been listed explicitly, as opposed to the health portals in the US. Furthermore, we observed that accessibility of health information for patients and other information seekers is another topic that is needed to be dealt with separately.

Keywords: Participatory health decision making · Patient-web portal interaction · Health information seeking behavior · Reliability of online health information · Seeking health advice on the web

1 Introduction

There hardly be any internet user who has never searched for information online. It is seen that there has been a constant growth in the community of people who seek health related information also known as health information seekers through the internet [1]. This community has been on the constant rise with the enormous population growth in the online world by 832.5 % between 2000–2015, as according to [1].

© Springer International Publishing Switzerland 2016
S. Yamamoto (Ed.): HIMI 2016, Part II, LNCS 9735, pp. 423–433, 2016.
DOI: 10.1007/978-3-319-40397-7_40

Nonetheless, there has been a burning issue pertaining to this behavior of health information seeking that is: How health information quality can be defined that is presented at online platforms? To answer this issue, there was an initiative called Health On the Net foundation (HON) [2]. Founded in year 1995, it is also currently working on this problem. This foundation has been doing research and establishing guidelines within international standards for health information seekers and web publishers, inspired by many professional websites and studies that provide measurement tool for information quality with a trustworthy score [2].

This paper analyzes the credibility and trust standards of health information websites from the point of view of health information seekers keeping with HON principles in the Turkish context. In this paper the authors try to answer the research question: *Do the platforms that host health information in Turkish language on the internet conform to international standards of credibility as defined by HON?* This paper is organized as: Background and literature review is given in Sect. 2, research methodology is elaborated in Sect. 3, results are discussed in Sect. 4 and finally, conclusion and future work are provided in Sect. 5.

2 Background and Literature Review

Internet is seen as a great opportunity for patients especially, patients with chronic diseases are one of the major health information seekers due to possibility it offers by hosting a number of health portals. These portals allow more personal paths towards a better outcome through the chance of doing own diagnoses, treatments, symptoms and doing comparisons with many other similar cases [3]. There has been a plenty of research starting from accepting the notion that health information websites play an important role on disseminating health related messages, and focus on the quality of information. However, credibility of websites, considering the usability and reliability issues, are expostulated due to having lack of sufficient health information sources such as core concepts and guidelines related to diseases [4, 5].

Turkey, at this point, is not disparate from the world trends and there is hardly any study conducted to find out the trustworthiness of online health information. The aspect of health information in Turkey is of pivotal nature due to number of facts. 55.9 % of Turkish population claims that they use internet connection [6]. In Turkey, the internet is mostly used for social media 89 % as well as reading news, online journals or magazines, 70.2 %, respectively [6]. In 2013, 49 % of mobile applications were downloaded for health and sport activities [7]. Turkish ministry of health as according to Health Development Report of Turkey [8, p. 46] indicated that 70.5 % of the population aged 18 years and above gathers health information from mass media channels. Television has the highest rate in mass media to collect health information which is 76.4 % [8, p. 46]. It is followed by the internet (26.8 %), newspapers (10 %), smart phones (8.3 %), radio (3.2 %) and a category that includes banners, leaflets, journals, books, billboards (11.5 %), respectively. It is noteworthy to mention here that information seeking on internet is a purposeful and a goal oriented activity that is critical for a shared decision-making [9] and it is quite distinct from passively being exposed to traditional media such as TV etc.

The idea of providing a guide for online health information was first floated at the conference: "The use of internet and World-Wide Web (WWW) for Telematics in healthcare" in 1995 and 60 participants from 11 countries gathered under the same roof of non-profit organization which is called Health On The Net foundation (HON), and then they developed guidelines and tools for health related websites [2]. 250 % augmentation of HON code supply in almost 3 years after its foundation shows the need for guidelines of online health related information both for the web site developers and users [10].

HON code is based on 8 principles that are authoritative, complementary, privacy, attribution, justifiability, transparency, financial disclosure, advertising policy. There are guidelines for three separate categories for patients or individuals seeking medical information, medical professionals and web publishers. Whereby, it is possible to analyze the website quality according to a related checklist. According to HONcode checklist for patients, a website is credible, hence trustable, if on the website:

1. The qualifications of the authors are indicated,
2. The doctor-patient relationship is supported,
3. Personal data and privacy regulations are respected,
4. Sources of the information and dates are indicated,
5. Claims of the information is justified,
6. Contact information of the information providers are transparent,
7. Financial disclosure is identified,
8. Editorial content and advertisement is clearly distinguished.

There is a checklist that specifies those qualifications with a checklist form which occurs from 15 questions. It then provides a trustworthy score depending on the patient's observation with the help of this check list that ensures the health information quality in international standard (See Fig. 1).

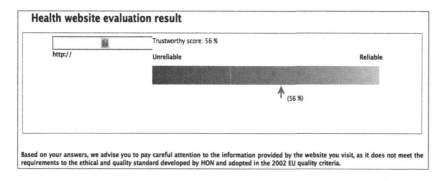

Fig. 1. A health website evaluation result taken from HON [11]

There are so many institutions and researchers that actually take advantage of HONcode criteria [10]. For instance, National Institute of Health (NIH), sets a highlighted path for elders on finding reliable health information on the web as if someone is asking the questions and an authority is answering. NIH [12] also gives its quick checklist questions as below:

1. Is the sponsor/owner of the website a federal agency, medical school, or large professional or non-profit organization, or is it related to any one of these?
2. If not sponsored by a federal agency, medical school, or large professional or non-profit organization; does the website refer to one of these trustworthy sources for its health information?
3. Is the mission or goal of the sponsor clear?
4. Can you see who works for the agency or organization and who authored the information? Is there a way to contact the sponsor of the website?
5. When the information written or the webpage was last updated?
6. Is your privacy protected?
7. Does the website offer unbelievable solutions to your health problem(s)? Are quick, miracle cures promised?

3   Research Methodology

It is vital to consider the fact that the internet presents a huge varied platform for health information seekers. However, it is very challenging and hard to know the whole picture of health information websites and know the total number of such portals in Turkey. This is because, there is no specific standardized health websites if we search in a health web browsers such as Kreshmoi (http://everyone.khresmoi.eu/hon-search/), mednar.com, health sciences online (hso.info) in Turkey by putting in keywords related to diseases or health information.

In Turkey, specifically, there are as much as 30,176 medical institutions both private and state [13] and most of them have websites. The private and state institutions include pharmaceutical companies, newspapers and journals as most of them have health related websites in addition to social media accounts, health professional personal websites and general health information websites. A keyword search was made with Google search engine because Google is the top search engine with 96.84 % rate in Turkey [14]. The search was made by providing keywords such as "psychology", "health beauty", "diet", "mother and baby health", "family health", "health", "disease and treatments", "alternative treatments", "general health", "doctors" and "medicine." The keyword search resulted in diversified amount of list including newspaper's health pages, journals in different languages. The first three pages given by Google search engine were only taken into account in this study.

After the search, the authors created a list of 497 health websites that also included the sites that are registered and supported by Turkish authorities such as: Chambers of Medicine, Chambers of Pharmacists, Chamber of Dentistry, and Turkish Republic local health authorities of 81 provinces of Turkey. The list of 497 health websites were further filtered based on the websites that focused on the patient's view or the health information seeker's context. The state or hospital websites that are already thought to be credible by the Turkish authorities were excluded from the list. The websites that presented the technical information were also excluded.

Finally, the list became limited to 138 health information websites whose raison d'etre is presenting health related information, treatments, advises and so on. Finally, for this paper, we analyze 56 websites pertaining to three categories or keywords only which are "psychology", "aesthetics and beauty" and "motherhood, baby and children."

4 Results and Discussion

In this section, the chosen 56 health information websites in Turkey have been analyzed as well as discussed, as according to 8 principles of Hon code criteria [15]. Just to recapitulate, these 8 principles are mentioned in Sect. 2 and include concepts of: Authority, complementing and mission orientation, privacy, attribution, justifiability, transparency, financial disclosure and finally advertising policy.

Principle1 "Information must be Authoritative": This principle points out the qualifications of the authors that provide health related or medical information in a web portal i.e. whether the authors are trained and qualified professionals or not. Most of the chosen health information websites conform to the first principle of HON i.e. the information emanates from a competent and professional authority. This is evident because author's credentials are mentioned in 33 out of the 56 websites, if we see the first question of the principle 1 of HON Code website evolution form.

If we see the second question of the principle 1 of HON Code website evolution form, 23 health websites have medical advice given by professional who have their credentials listed. In 11 websites a clear statement (e.g. a disclaimer) is made whenever medical/health information or advice is offered by non-medical professionals or organizations. However, 22 of the websites contain some health/medical information that is not attributed to an author.

Principle 2 "Complementarity, Mission and Assistance": Principle 2 indicates that the information provided on the health website should support the doctor-patient relationship instead of replacing it. In our sample of 56 websites, 32 of the websites made a statement declaring that information provided on the site is meant to complement and not replace any advice or information from a health professional (see Fig. 2). Moreover, 33 of them are describing the intended mission of the site is provided on the site and 36 of the health websites clearly mentions the intended audience of the site.

Principle 3 "Privacy and Confidentiality": This principle refers to conformance to the visitor's privacy and confidentiality through meeting the legal requirements. Out of 56 websites, 20 of the websites have a complete privacy and confidentiality policy regarding e-mail addresses, personal, non-personal and medical information that is displayed on the website.

If we look at a check list of HON Code patient/individual "website evolution form" which has 15 items (questions). There are "yes, no, and I don't know" options for the item "Do my site and its mirrors respect the legal requirements, including those concerning medical and personal information privacy, that apply in the country and state of their location?" question. There were 11 websites that we could clearly answer as "yes". Generally people do not know legal requirements unless it is specifically mentioned. For the rest of 41 websites the answer was "I don't know" that means they

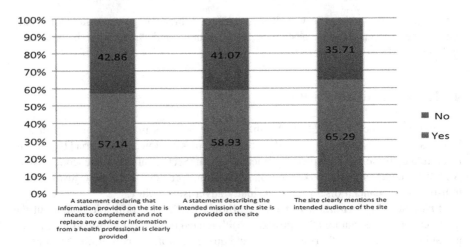

Fig. 2. Principle 2 "Complementarity, Mission and Assistance" results (Colored figure can be found in the online version of this paper)

haven't got any information telling about meeting any legal requirements and it is hard for us to say that whether they are meeting them or not.

Principle 4 "Information must be Documented, Referenced and Dated": This principle is the attribution part, focuses on modification date and external sources. Out of 56 websites, 14 of the websites do not have a modification date neither for a page or the content nor for website as a whole. Only for 5 of the websites, a bibliographic reference to the source data was given while 33 of the content of the sites were original, written by the editorial person/s. On the other hand we don't if any of the information was copy and pasted from another website.

Principle 5 "Justification of Claims": This principle stipulates that a health website must back up claims relating to benefits and performance. Consequently, it interrogates whether the site makes claims relating to the benefit or performance of a specific medical treatment, commercial product or service or not. Out of 56 websites, 35 websites had claims that were based on the author's personal research or opinions. Moreover, 16 of the claims were supported by clear references to scientific research results and/or published articles. And only in 5 websites didn't have any claims.

Principle 6 "Website Contact Details": This criterion is about transparency which is needed for accessible presentation, accurate email contact. It requires a valid email address for the webmaster or a link to a valid contact form is easily accessible throughout the site. 47 of 56 websites provided a contact link, form or information of the specialist (a doctor or a health professional who may be a writer of the website).

Principle 7 "Disclosure of Funding Sources": This criterion is for identifying funding sources of the website including commercial or non-commercial organizations, for personal or private sites, or those hosted without charge. Out of 56 websites, 48 of the websites do not have any explanations about funding.

Principle 8 "Advertising Policy": The most important thing for this criterion is to distinguish advertising from editorial content clearly. Out of 56 websites, 10 of the websites have a page that provides a description of the advertising policy (see Fig. 3). In 3 websites there were no description but a separation between editorial content and advertising was clearly stated. For 27 of the websites there were no explanation regarding banner advertising was given. Therefore, it was not possible to understand if the content is a display of an advertisement or a claim from a personal experience. There were advertising, however, those were not identified as such in 16 websites and this is dangerous for patients (see Fig. 3).

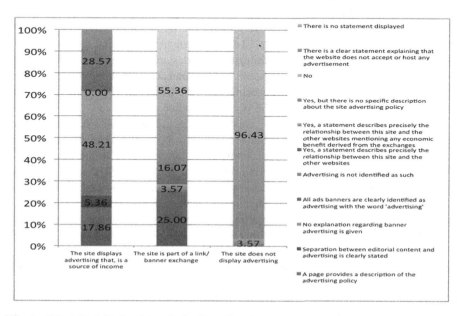

Fig. 3. Principle 8 "Advertising Policy" results (Colored figure can be found in the online version of this paper)

The other issue was whether the site was part of a link/banner exchange or not. 41 of the websites did not have an exchange banner or link (see Fig. 3). 14 of the sites have a statement that describes precisely the relationship between this site and the other websites. Only 2 of them have a statement that describes precisely the relationship between this site and the other websites mentioning any economic benefit derived from the exchanges, whilst in 9 of the websites had an exchange banner or link but there is no specific description about the site advertising policy. In total, only 2 of the 56 websites had a clear statement explaining that the website does not accept or host any advertisement while 54 websites had no statement displayed.

From the analyses of the results as according to HON code criteria, it can be stated that the Turkish websites conform well to the requirements and expectations of following principles: Authoritative (Principle 1), complementarity (Principle 2), attribution (Principle 4) and transparency (Principle 6). On the other hand, there needs to be more diligence for determining the policies of privacy (Principle 3), justifiability (Principle 5), financial disclosure (Principle 7) and advertising policy (Principle 8).

In the observed websites there were no explanations of patient rights, advertisement policies, the sources of information, privacy of the individuals and state policies among webmasters.

HON principles do not include any rules or requirements about accessibility and usability issues even though it is lethal for patients. Nielsen [16], for example, gains attention to medical usability issue that matters not only for online health information but also for a wider perspective from hospital systems to medicine prescriptions that even cause deaths because of bad design. Actually HON Foundation also conducted a survey online to find out the most important user requirements and the problems of getting health related information on web within the frame of Khresmoi EU Project. There were 385 answers collected from 42 different countries [17]. The results revealed the need for helpful tools, medical dictionary, well designed Information Architecture (IA), easiness and directions for navigation to find content, and risk factor tools. If the ads are clear and controlled, they are acceptable on the web pages. There was a need to separate qualified information from the poor information as well.

These findings also indicate the importance of accessibility. No matter what information is available, how it is explained and shown online is also another pivotal issue to acquire comprehensible health knowledge corresponding to the accessibility for a user-friendly web environment. Eighmey and McCord [18] asserts that it is important to build a user-friendly web environment that considers cognition effects, motor skill diminishment, loss of hearing, vision decline and so forth, for disseminating preventive health information, forestalling mislead health information, balancing medical information gap and so on. In this way, it is also possible to examine reactions of web audience' needs about health related issues.

Web Content Accessibility Guidelines 2.0 -WCAG 2.0- [19], for example, provides all the directions for website builders for developing user-friendly websites for the relevant audience and public. The list of requirements include providing text alternatives for any non-text content; supporting time-based media; presenting an adaptable content; the content must be distinguishable for users to see and hear; all functions must be accessible from keyboard; there must be enough time for content to be seen and used; seizures must be avoided, the pages must be easily navigable, readable and appearing predictable; the input assistance must be provided, and the pages should be compatible for current and future user agents. Every single item of those criteria makes a website clearly comprehensible, measurable and testable. For a future study, there should be a study measuring the accessibility of those 56 websites to extrapolate a deeper analysis.

There are two important questions here: First, are web site developers aware of the standards of the HON code and do the developers consider those standards while developing the web platforms? Second, can we trust this information if it is credible? For the first question a future study, having a research with health website developers to understand their point of view is important.

The second question about credibility must be reflected up for participating health decisions because even doctors make mistakes [20]. According to Doctors Union of Germany, it was learnt about 2243 malpractices during the treatment of patients; 1864 incidents caused permanent damage whereas 77 patients passed away due to malpractice of doctors were confirmed in Germany [21]. Many people became concerned about their treatments increasingly [22] i.e., health issue is not just about authority.

Trustworthiness about health information concept is quite ambiguous as health and health systems vary from person to person. Moreover this concept is full of uncertainty. It is complex and can also be manipulated by a rant [23]. This may be the reason why people try to find their own solutions or look for more information on the internet. Thus the most important thing that needs to be paid attention to is transparency, credibility and accessibility of the health information on the websites to help individuals to find and distinguish the most suitable information for themselves or for the ones whom are cared by them. There can be some studies to structure the information seeking behavior as it was done before [26–29] for the information seekers would be helpful for general public as well.

5   Conclusion and Future Work

Internet is seen as a high hope for empowerment of patients for participated health decisions through shared health information and experiences, showing parallelism with increased health information seeking world trends. An objective criterion for measuring or observing the standards of health information on the internet is yet needed to be decided. What treatment, doctor, service or environment is better for an individual is also a question mark for modern medicine, health professionals and medical services actually. In our paper, we keep with the claim of HON principles; they work internationally to define standards for credible and trustworthy health information. Based on HON principles and Hon code website evaluation form for patients/individuals or any information seekers, we conducted this research to see whether Turkish health websites were meeting the requirements of credibility or not.

We found out that most of the websites relatively conform to the HON principles. However, the matter of health information and health information on the internet is a much deeper subject that we cannot identify them with 8 principles as HON code asserts. We need to see it with a wider perspective because health is not just about the absence of disease; it is about a complete wellbeing of humans, physically, mentally and socially [24]. [25] What is also needed to be done about health information on the internet is to create accessible, user-friendly and transparent web environment to facilitate information seekers on decision making which is already an uphill battle in medical everyday life. Moreover, it is important for policy makers as much as for patients to support or built well-controlled websites for avoiding manipulation of health information. Because health information seeking on Internet is a very popular phenomenon in Turkey as it is for many other countries.

References

1. Internet World Stats: World Internet Users and 2015 Population Stats, 30 November 2015. http://www.internetworldstats.com/stats.htm. Accessed 23 Feb 2016
2. HON: About HON, 14 October 2015. http://www.hon.ch/Global/. Accessed 14 Feb 2016
3. Johnson, J.D., Case, D.O.: Health Information Seeking. Peter Lang Publishing, New York (2012)
4. Hendrick, P.A., Ahmed, O.H., Bankier, S.S., Chan, T.J., Crawford, S.A., Ryder, C.R., Welsh, L.J., Schneiders, A.G.: Acute low back pain information online: an evaluation of quality, content accuracy and readability of related websites. Manual Ther. 17(4), 318–324 (2012)
5. Nagappa, A.N., Sam, K.G., Zarrin, F., Saurabh, H., Partha, G., Pathak, K.: Evaluation of web sites for quality and contents of asthma patient education. J Young Pharm. 1(3), 278–283 (2009)
6. TUIK: Use of Informatics by Households, 18 August 2015. http://www.tuik.gov.tr/PreHaberBultenleri.do?id=18660. Accessed 1 Feb 2016
7. Çalışkan, K.: Mobil uygulamaların kullanım oranları 2013 yılında yüzde 115 arttı, 14 January 2014. http://webrazzi.com/2014/01/14/mobil-uygulamalarin-kullanim-oranlari-2013/. Accessed 20 May 2015
8. Bakanlığı, T.C.S.: Sağlık istatistikleri yıllığı. Sentez Matbaacılık ve Yayıncılık, Ankara (2013)
9. Anker, A.E., Reinhart, A.M., Freeley, T.H.: Health information seeking: a review of measures and methods. Patient Educ. Couns. 82(2011), 346–354 (2011)
10. Boyer, C., Baujard, V., Scherrer, J.R., Appel, R.D.: The health on the net code of conduct for medical and health-related web sites: Three years on, 19 September 1999. http://www.jmir.org/1999/suppl1/e99. Accessed 13 Feb 2016
11. HON: Health website evaluation result (2016). Accessed 11 Feb 2016
12. NIH: Online health information: Can you trust it?, December 2014. https://auth.nia.nih.gov/health/publication/online-health-information. Accessed 4 Feb 2016
13. Ministry of Health: Number of medical institutions, total hospital beds and number of hospital beds per 1000 population, 1967–2014, 15 December 2015. http://www.turkstat.gov.tr/Start.do;jsessionid=bZVyWNIVldKvWp2xMcNpbx942n4GsSN2y6rbV6FsRpvhLt2txZnT!519585183. Accessed 24 Feb 2016
14. StatCounter: Top 5 search enginees in Turkey from Feb 2015 to Jan 2016 (2016). http://gs.statcounter.com/#all-search_engine-TR-monthly-201502-201601-bar. Accessed 4 Feb 2016
15. HON: The HON Code of Conduct for medical and health Web sites (HONcode), 19 September 2013. https://www.healthonnet.org/HONcode/Conduct.html. Accessed 26 Mar 2016
16. Nielsen, J.: Medical usability: how to kill patients through bad design, 11 April 2005. https://www.nngroup.com/articles/medical-usability/. Accessed 13 Feb 2016
17. Khresmoi: Requirements for general public health serach, ICT Theme of the 7th Framework Programme (2011)
18. Eighmey, J., McCord, L.: Adding value in the information age: uses and gratifications of sites on the world wide web. J. Bus. Res. 41, 187–194 (1998)
19. WCAG: How to Meet WCAG 2.0, 16 September 2014. http://www.w3.org/WAI/WCAG20/quickref/#guidelines. Accessed 7 Feb 2016
20. TED: Director, doctors make mistakes. Can we talk about that?. [Film]. TED (2011)

21. Dotmund: Almanya'da geçen yıl 77 kişi doktor hatasından hayatını kaybetti, 23 June 2014. http://www.haberler.com/almanya-da-gecen-yil-77-kisi-doktor-hatasindan-6184606-haberi/. Accessed 28 Mar 2016
22. Welch, G., Schwartz, L.M., Woloshin, S.: Sağlık adına hasta etmek. İNSEV, Istanbul (2013)
23. Deppe, H.-U.: Sağlık hizmetlerinin doğası: Metalaştırmaya karşı dayanışma. In: Panitch, L., Leys, C. (eds.) Kapitalizmde Sağlık Sağlıksızlık Semptomları, pp. 43–53. Yordam Kitap, İstanbul (2009)
24. Irwin, S.O.: A Conceptual Framework for Action on the Social Determinants of Health. World Health Organization, Geneva (2010)
25. Chunpir, H.I.: Enchancing user support in federated e-science, University of Hamburg (2015)
26. Chunpir, H.I., Ludwig, T., Badewi, A.: A snap-shot of user support services in Earth System Grid Federation (ESGF): a use case of climate cyber-infrastructures. In: Proceedings of the 5th Applied Human Factors and Ergonomics (AHFE) Conference, Krakow, Poland (2014a)
27. Chunpir, H.I., Ludwig, T., Badewi, A.A.: Using soft systems methotology (SSM) in understanding current user-support scenario in the climate science domain of cyber-infrastructures. In: Marcus, A. (ed.) Design, User Experience, and Usability. LNCS, vol. 8519, pp. 495–506. Springer, Cham (2014b). doi:10.1007/978-3-319-07635-5_48
28. Chunpir, H.I., Ludwig, T., Badewi, A.A.: User support in the complex environment. In: Marcus, A. (ed.) Design, User Experience, and Usability. LNCS, vol. 8520, pp. 392–402. Springer, Cham (2014). doi:10.1007/978-3-319-07638-6_38
29. Chunpir, H., Moll, A.: Analysis of marine ecosystems: usability, visualisation and community collaboration challenges. Procedia Manuf. 3, 3262–3265 (2015)

How to Improve Research Data Management

The Case of Sciebo (Science Box)

Konstantin Wilms[1(✉)], Christian Meske[1], Stefan Stieglitz[1],
Dominik Rudolph[2], and Raimund Vogl[2]

[1] Department of Computer Science and Applied Cognitive Science,
University of Duisburg-Essen, Essen, Germany
{konstantin.wilms,christian.meske,
stefan.stieglitz}@uni-due.de
[2] ZIV-Centre for Applied Information Technology,
University of Muenster, Münster, Germany
{d.rudolph,r.vogl}@uni-muenster.de

Abstract. The digitalization of research processes has led to a vast amount of data. Since third-party funding institutions progressively set standards and requirements regarding the handling of such data, research data management has become important in the context of international research collaboration projects. Simultaneously, adequate collaboration systems are needed to support scientists in this context. In this paper we discuss existing standards for research data management in the context of third-party funding and how cloud technology could support the fulfillment of existing provisions.

Keywords: Cloud computing · Usability · Research data management · Technology adoption

1 Introduction

Malcom Read, executive secretary of the Joint Information Committee (JICS), stated that "We need to move away from a culture of secrecy and towards a world where researchers can benefit from sharing expertise throughout the research lifecycle" [20].

Whether in the social, behavioral, physical or computer sciences, data have always been the source of all empirical knowledge. For researchers their data are essential since they are required to prove, disprove or replicate empirical statements. For this reason, research data need to be managed professionally, in order to support efficient and effective research projects. Today, there are plenty of documented cases in which researchers lost their data or refused to disclose their research data (e.g. [32]). This is problematic, since the reproducibility of data plays a key role in many scientific fields and moreover is the only source of credibility. Although adequate data management has been an issue for a while, the responsibility for storing and disclosing data still lies with the researcher. To avoid the discussion of questionable results e.g. generated by impure data or the well-known publication bias [9], several journals now require authors to share their data sets as condition of publication [19, 27]. At the same time

S. Yamamoto (Ed.): HIMI 2016, Part II, LNCS 9735, pp. 434–442, 2016.
DOI: 10.1007/978-3-319-40397-7_41

third-party funding institutions started to set up guidelines establishing management policies for research data. Different guidelines and requirements from different funding institutions have made it difficult for the researchers to practice proper research data management (RDM). Although the number of platforms supporting the data management process is increasing, various studies indicate that there is still a lack of adoption among researchers [10]. One reason might be, that numerous departments and universities already run their own infrastructures (e.g. [11, 13, 26, 31]). While these infrastructures are generally used to provide cloud technologies, features which help researches to improve their data management are still missing.

In our paper, we focus on existing standards for RDM in the context of third-party funding and how cloud technology could support the fulfillment of existing provisions. We compare three major research funding institutions from North America (USA), Australia and Europe (Germany) in terms of requirements regarding RDM. In this first investigation we analyzed documents published by the National Science Foundation (NSF), Australian Research Council (ARC) and the German Research Foundation (Deutsche Forschungsgemeinschaft, DFG) with regard to requirements for research proposals for funding. Furthermore, we take the users perspective into account and focus on factors and barriers diminishing the acceptance of such systems. Additionally, we analyze, if and how sciebo ("science box"), an on-premise cloud service hosted by universities and used by over 5,000 researchers in Germany, can support scientists to meet existing RDM requirements. We especially focus on the following research questions: Which claims result from the guidelines of third-party funding institutions and from the needs of researchers for dealing with research data? How could an infrastructure like sciebo be implemented to deal with these requirements?

The remainder of the paper is structured as follows. In the next chapter the authors present some basic definitions and background knowledge about RDM and the sciebo cloud service, Following, the requirements of three different RDM standards are described and it is discussed how a system such as sciebo could support the fulfillment of the requirements. The paper ends with a conclusion.

2 Literature Review

2.1 Research Data Management

So far, there is no uniform definition of RDM on which researchers of all disciplines do agree on. One common definition describes RDM as "the organization of data, from its entry to the research cycle through to the dissemination and archiving of valuable results" [33]. RDM is strongly related to the notion of "scientific data curation" which means to "collect, organize, validate and preserve data so that scientists can find new ways to address the grand research challenges that face society" [14]. According to [7] "research data" cover "any research materials resulting from primary data collection or generation, qualitative or quantitative, or derived from existing sources intended to be analyzed in the course of a research project". Data are the base of scientific communication and cover numerical data, textual data, digitized materials, images recordings or modeling scripts [7].

RDM has the potential to facilitate the entire research process and to support the efficient utilization of research data. By the disclosure of the data, the process becomes more transparent [15]. This is a basic imperative, to support the reproduction of research processes, which is a core principle in scientific research. Transparency in research helps researchers to become more resistant against the allegation of misconduct [15]. Providing access to research data has proved to be useful for scientists as sharing research data with the community may result in higher citation rates [23]. Furthermore it helps to overcome bottleneck effects, which for example could show up, if research data are only represented in the narrow context of a specialized topic [34]: "For example, a dataset collected by agronomists who are researching water quality may also be used by earth and atmospheric scientists to improve the accuracy or to validate the output of climate models" [34].

According to the Long Tail theory described by [21], shared research data have the potential to provide endless knowledge as the data are discovered and used by new audiences. Currently, there is a growing market, where several research teams migrate to basic platforms, allowing them to perform RDM and to share their data with the scientific community [1].

While the number of scientist practicing RDM is increasing [8, 17], different publications indicate, that there is still a huge mistrust when it comes to record, preserve, and share research data [5, 24, 25]. In a study of [10], the majority of researchers claimed to miss appropriate technical infrastructures for RDM, fitting all their needs. [2] found out, that a significant number of researchers need up to 100 GB of storage capacity, in order to store all their research data. Researchers also concern about ethical aspects [2]. Despite the advantages that arise from outsourcing data, public data storage services could not used without risk. Today there are still uncertainties about how data copyrights are protected in public cloud storages [12]. It is legally questionable to share or store data externally when these data are collected on the basis of the waiver of disclosure to third parties.

In addition to technical and ethical barriers there are non-technical barriers regarding a structured RDM [10]. Such non-technical barriers are for example the fear of having to compete with colleagues as well as the loss of control over the own data. Also a lack of trust to the operator of the system was reported as common reason for rejection [10]. While researchers see the added value of systematic backups and long-term storage, as they are given in cloud systems, there is still a huge number of researchers rejecting the concept of shared research data [10].

2.2   Sciebo – The Campus Cloud

The history of sciebo started in 2013 when [30] found out, that the academic community in North Rhine-Westphalia (Germany) expressed the need for an in-house cloudservice. At this time, the market was already dominated by commercial cloud services, founded by American companies like Google, Dropbox or Microsoft. Researchers expressed their concerns about privacy issues and asked for a private infrastructure placed within Germany. As a consequence the cloud infrastructure 'sciebo' was built up. Today sciebo, which is short for 'science box', is a running infrastructure providing access to 23 academic institutions. The service is free to use and provides 30 GB storage capacity for individuals such as students as well as the academic and administrative staff of the participating institutions. In addition, project groups can apply for work boxes of up to 1 TB [28]. Up to 500,000 potential users have access to the platform. The data are stored under German data protection law. Besides the opportunity to store data, sciebo offers functions for sharing folders or set them public. Public data can also be seen and downloaded by persons who have no sciebo-account. The system, which is based on ownCloud open source software, does not offer data management functions yet. Students who finish their academic careers are given six months transfer time before their data are deleted.

3 Requirements of a Research Data Management System

3.1 Current Requiremements for Research Data Management

The following literature review takes the requirements of the three major foundation institutions into account. One of the institutions we looked at in this review is the National Science Foundation (NSF). The NSF is the largest science foundation in the United States with a promotional volume of 6.9 billion US Dollar in 2010 [29]. For Europe the 'Deutsche Forschungsgemeinschaft' (DFG) is the major funding institution in academia with a promotion budget of 2.73 billion Euro (approx. 3 billion US Dollar) in 2014 [25]. The third institution taken into account is the 'Australian Research Council' (ARC) which belongs to the major research councils in Australia [24]. Each funding institution has set up individual guidelines dealing with the topic of how RDM should be realized. In this work, we analyze the guidelines and compare the requirements. By overseeing the guidelines, twelve categories were identified (see Table 1). In the following part we show how the individual guidelines deal with the topics of data management plans (DMP), duration of storage, sharing of primary data, approaches for information collection, data standards, data security, collaboration tools for data, education in RDM, and ethics & legislation.

Table 1. Comparison of the guidelines of DFG, ARC and NSF

	Technical aspect	DFG	ARC	NSF
Data Management Plan		x	x	x
Replicability/Sharing of primary data	x	x	x	x
Duration of storage	x		x	
Approaches for information collection	x	x		
Data standards		x	x	
Data security and safety	x		x	
Collaboration tools for data	x	x		
Education in research data management		x	x	
Ethics and legislation		x	x	x

The documents comprising grant conditions and funding rules define the sharing of primary data as mandatory unless ethical or confidentiality issues prevent this. A comprehensive document labeled DMP is a required part of any proposal at the NSF including e.g. types of data, policies for access and sharing as well as plans for archiving data. Also DFG states that such a document should be included and additionally ask for e.g. data quality management, storage place, duration of access to research data, and conditions of re-use for other researchers. In contrast, the ARC considers data management planning as important but does not specify the need for a DMP. Rather, it strictly defines that research data must be retained for at least five years and should be made available for use of other researchers. The identified documents published by the DFG cover some other aspects that could not be found for the other institutions. For example, the DFG does not only require the publication of primary data, they also ask for suitable repositories and databases. Furthermore, the DFG asks as part of the proposal what implementations and techniques will be used for research data collection and processing. While the ARC emphasizes the role of researchers holding primary data including security and confidentiality aspects, the DFG maintains the education of staff in RDM but does not defer to security questions. A last example unique to the DFG is the requirement of internal collaboration tools to enable research data sharing, which is not mentioned by either ARC or NSF.

3.2 Cloud-Based Research Data Management Systems - The Case of Sciebo

This section deals with the question if and how standard cloud services among universities can support the RDM process. Since cloud services are generally based on different solutions and infrastructures, we use sciebo as an example and check if the cloud has the potential to fit the requirements pointed out in Sect. 3.1. To fit the requirements, cloud services like sciebo need to fulfill at least the technical requirements.

The first technical requirement is 'Replicability/Sharing of primary data'. Sciebo does support two main functions which allow the user to share the data. The first function enables the users to share data among each other within sciebo. The second feature enables the user to set data public and share the data with non-sciebo-users. This option of external access is provided by sending out an http-link pointing to the data archive. Both features fit the concept of the requirements set by the three institutes. In terms of 'duration of data' sciebo misses the requirements. As a cloud service, sciebo provides all the technical requirements which are necessary to store long-term data. Since the service is limited to students and employees only, the users lose the right to use sciebo after e.g. graduating. Yet it is not possible to create internal relations between data stored in the system as it is required by the DFG (approaches for information collection). When it comes to 'Data security', as it is required by ARC, sciebo is well-positioned. The service is running under a restrictive national data protection law and uses high level security standards. Here the cloud service meets all the goals set up by the funding institute. The last technical aspect required by DFG is the need for collaboration tools. This means especially the possibility to use wikis, blogs or data tracking tools. Sciebo currently does not support collaborative functions. However, technically there already exist some collaboration features that could be enabled in the near future.

Overall sciebo, which is representing the concept of an academic in-house cloud service, does already support some basic requirements which are necessary for being used as an RDM tool.

3.3   How to Support User Adoption

While the technical requirements are essential to fulfill the guidelines set by DFG, NSF and ARC, there are also requirements set up by the users. According to the findings of [10] the user expects that tools and services of the given RDM system are aligned to researchers discipline specific workflow. Often users require various functionalities that could be selected based on a 'cafeteria model' which allows the user to pick and choose from a set of services. Another crucial aspect is, that the researchers need to be set in a state of mind where they have the feeling of being in control over the process. They need to be awarded of 'what happens to their data, who has access to it, and under which conditions' [10]. 'Consequently, they want to be sure that whoever is dealing with their data (data centre, library, etc.) will respect their interests' [10]. To overcome the problem [2] is recommending a motivation system, where the user gets benefit by practicing RDM.

4   Discussion

RDM is a growing topic within scientific debates. According to the Horizon 2020 report the current debate is mostly focusing on the aspects of open data access and long term data storage [6]. While scientist demand improvements, it seems that universities and higher education institutes have mostly ignored the boat of this current trend. Yet RDM is mostly discussed in disciplines like medicine and microbiology [4]. However, this is a step forward to create a multirelational system among all disciplines and different workflows used by different disciplines.

[3] sees the responsibility to press ahead the implementation of such systems for the libraries. As the main competences for the librarians [3] sees the knowledge in archiving data for a long-term period and as well the competence of standardizing meta-data. Another important aspect pointed out by [3] is the implementation process. Information Systems (IS) as a discipline is therefore challenged to bring in their knowledge and competencies in order to design adequate RDM-systems. When it comes to user adoption problems or to design specific usability questions, IS researchers should develop concepts how to push up the implementation process. As a third party administrators of running academic infrastructures need to be involved in the process as well. Since the universities normally run their own in-house infrastructures, which already fulfill technical requirements partly, these could be used to support the development process. Platform or software services could be set up on the base for running infrastructure services. To foster these collaborative development processes, universities need to make investments in the future and improve their infrastructures.

Another crucial problem in RDM is the negative attitude of researchers towards an open data process. As shown in this paper, there is still a huge number of researchers which avoid to share their research data among the scientific community. It is important that the researchers join the RDM process as early as possible to gain trust in the system and overcome mentally barriers [10]. Another idea which should be considered when it comes to user adoption is to support motivational processes by incentive systems [2]. An exemplary instrument could be gamification, which has been proved to increase the activities of employees in new systems [18].

5 Conclusion

Summarizing, RDM becomes increasingly relevant for researchers. Nevertheless, the requirements differ in terms of the level of detail. Also, clear standards (e.g. for storage repositories) that can support researchers are mostly lacking. The NSF focuses mainly on the Data Management Plan (DMP), which allows (even forces) applicants to define most details themselves. The ARC does not require a formal DMP but defines a few necessities (e.g. duration of data retention). However, the ARC seems to make least requirements for research funding in terms of RDM. On the other hand, the DFG includes more aspects that are not considered by the other institutions (e.g. data management education, collaboration, as well as data collection and processing techniques) and hence, gives more weight to data management in its funded projects. Since sciebo suits several of these requirements pointed out in this research, it has the potential to provide a suitable infrastructure, through which RDM can be effectively supported.

References

1. Amorim, R.C., Castro, J.A., de Silva, J.R., Ribeiro, C.: A comparative study of platforms for research data management: interoperability, metadata capabilities and integration potential. In: Rocha, A., Correia, A.M., Costanzo, S., Reis, L.P. (eds.) New Contributions in Information Systems and Technologies. AISC, vol. 353, pp. 101–111. Springer, Heidelberg (2015)
2. Bauer, B., Ferus, A., Gorraiz, J., Gründhammer, V., Gumpenberger, C., Maly, N., Mühlegger, J. M., Preza, J. L., Sánchez Solís, B., Schmidt, N., Steineder, C.: Forschende und ihre Daten. Ergebnisse einer österreichweiten Befra-gung–Report 2015. Version 1.2
3. Ball, R., Wiederkehr, S. (eds.) Vernetztes Wissen. Online. Die Bibliothek als Management aufgabe: Festschrift für Wolfram Neubauer zum 65. Geburtstag. Walter de Gruyter GmbH & Co KG (2015)
4. Benson, D.A., Karsch-Mizrachi, I., Lipman, D.J., Ostell, J., Wheeler, D.L.: GenBank. Nucleic Acids Res. **36**(1), D25–D30 (2008)
5. Bukavova, H.: Supporting the initiation of research collaborations. In: Jena Research Papers in Business and Economics, vol. 64 (2009)
6. Commission, E.: Guidelines on open access to scientific publications and research data in horizon 2020. Technical report (2013)

7. Corti, L., Van den Eynden, V., Bishop, L., Woollard, M.: Managing and Sharing Research Data: A Guide to Good Practice. Sage Publications Ltd, New York (2014)
8. da Silva, J.R., Barbosa, J.P., Gouveia, M., Ribeiro, C., Lopes, J.C.: UPBox and DataNotes: a collaborative data management environment for the long tail of research data. In: iPRESS2013: Proceedings of the 10th International Conference on Preservation of Digital Objects, Lisbon, Portugal (2013)
9. Easterbrook, P.J., et al.: Publication bias in clinical research. Lancet **337**(8746), 867–872 (1991)
10. Feijen, M.: What Researchers Want. SURF-foundation, Utrecht (2011)
11. Hager, R., Hildmann, T., Bittner, P.: Ein Jahr mit ownCloud – von der Planung bis zur Neustrukturierung. In: Kao, O., Hildmann, T. (eds.) Cloudspeicher im Hochschuleinsatz: Proceedings der Tagung "Cloudspeicher im Hochschuleinsatz" am 05. und 06. Mai 2014 am IT-Service-Center (tubIT) der Technischen Universität Berlin, Universitätsverlag der TU Berlin (2014)
12. Hilber, M., Reintzsch, D.: Cloud Computing und Open Source-Wie groß ist die Gefahr des Copyleft bei SaaS? Comput. Und Recht: Forum für die Praxis des Rechts der Datenverargeitung, Inf. und Autom. **30**(11), 697–702 (2014)
13. Hildmann, T., Kao, O.: Deploying and extending on-premise cloud storage based on ownCloud. In: 2014 IEEE 34th International Conference on Distributed Computing Systems Workshops. IEEE (2014)
14. Johns Hopkins University. http://www.dataconservancy.org/home. Accessed 4 Mar 2009
15. Joshi, M., Krag, S.S.: Issues in data management. In: Spier, R.E., Bird, S.J. (eds.) Science and Engineering Ethics, vol 16:4, pp. 743–748. Springer, Heidelberg (2010)
16. Library Trends, vol. 57:2, pp. 191–201. Johns Hopkins University Press, Illinois (2008)
17. Lyon, L.: Dealing with Data: Roles, Rights, Responsibilities and Relationships. Consultancy Report (2007)
18. Meske, C., Brockmann, T., Wilms, K., Stieglitz, S.: Gamify employee collaboration – a critical review of gamification elements in social software. In: ACIS (2015)
19. Nature Journal. Authors & Referees, Editorial Policies, Availability of data & materials. http://www.nature.com/authors/editorial_policies/availability.html. Accessed 4 Mar 2009
20. 'New advice for universities in light of the Climate Change Emails Review' JISC news release July 2010. http://www.jisc.ac.uk/news/stories/2010/07/opendata.aspx
21. Palmer, C.L., Cragin, M.H., Heidorn, P.B., Smith, L.C.: Data curation for the long tail of science: the case of environmental sciences. In: Third International Digital Curation Conference, Washington, DC (2007)
22. Peterson, M., Zasman, G., Mojica, P., Porter, J.: 100 year archive requirements survey. In: SNIA's Data Management Forum, p.1. SNIA (2007)
23. Piwowar, H.A., Day, R.S., Fridsma, D.B.: Sharing detailed research data is associated with increased citation rate. PLoS ONE **2**(3), e308 (2007)
24. Savage, C.J., Vickers, A.J.: Empirical study of data sharing by authors publishing in PloS journals. PLoS ONE **4**(9), e7078 (2009)
25. Sayogo, D.S., Pardo, T.A.: Exploring the determinants of scientific data sharing: understanding the motivation to publish research data. Gov. Inf. Q. **30**, 19–31 (2013)
26. Schlitter, N., Yasnogorbw, A.: Sync&Share: a cloud solution for academia in the state of Baden-Württemberg. In: Kao, O., Hildmann, T. (eds.) Cloudspeicher im Hochschuleinsatz: Proceedings der Tagung "Cloudspeicher im Hochschuleinsatz" am 05. und 06. Mai 2014 am IT-Service-Center (tubIT) der Technischen Universität Berlin, Universitätsverlag der TU Berlin (2014)
27. Science Magazine. General Information for Authors. Conditions of Acceptance. http://www.sciencemag.org/about/authors/prep/gen_info.dtl#datadep. Accessed 4 Mar 2009

28. Stieglitz, S., Meske, C., Vogl, R., Rudolph, D.: Demand for cloud services as an infrastructure in higher education. In: Icis (2014)
29. Suresh, S.: Biography. http://www.nsf.gov/news/speeches/suresh/suresh_bio.jsp Accessed 10 Jan 2016
30. Vogl, R., Angenent, H., Bockholt, R., Rudolph, D., Stieglitz, S., Meske, C.: Designing a large scale cooperative sync&share cloud storage plattform for the academic community in Northrhine-Westfalia. In: Proceedings of EUNIS 2013 Congress 1(1), (2013)
31. Vogl, R., Rudolph, D., Thoring, A., Angenent, H., Stieglitz, S., Meske, C.: How to build a cloud storage service for half a million users in higher education: challenges met and solutions found. In: HICCS 2016 Proceedings of the 49th Hawaii International Conference on System Sciences, pp. 5328–5337 (2016)
32. Voorbrood, C.M. Voer voor psychologen. Archivering, beschikbaarstelling en hergebruik van onderzoeksdata in de psychologie, Aksant Academic Publishers (2010)
33. Whyte, A., Tedd, J.: Making the case for research data management. Digitar curation centre, edinburgh (2011)
34. Witt, M.: Institutional repositories and research data curation in a distributed environment. In: Library Trends, vol 57:2, pp. 191–201. John Hopkins University Press and the Graduate School of Library and Information Science, Illinois (2008)

Information in Health and Well-being

Well-Being and HCI in Later Life - What Matters?

Arlene J. Astell[1,2(✉)], Faustina Hwang[3], Elizabeth A. Williams[1],
Libby Archer[4], Sarah Harney-Levine[1], Dave Wright[5],
and Maggie Ellis[6]

[1] University of Sheffield, Sheffield, UK
{a.astell,e.a.williams}@sheffield.ac.uk
[2] Ontario Shores Centre for Mental Health Science, Whitby, Canada
astella@ontarioshores.ca
[3] University of Reading, Reading, UK
f.hwang@reading.ac.uk
[4] Age UK, London, UK
libby.archer@ageuk.org.uk
[5] University of Brighton, Brighton, UK
d.wright2@brighton.ac.uk
[6] University of St. Andrews, St. Andrews, UK
mpe2@st-andrews.ac.uk

Abstract. As part of the Challenging Obstacles and Barriers to Assisted Living Technologies (COBALT) project, we developed the COBALT Tools for Engagement[TM], a number of innovative techniques to engage older people in all stages of the technology development process. In the present study we used Technology Tours of the homes of eight older adults to look at their daily usage and examine the ways in which technology influences well-being. All of the participants use multiple technologies every day both inside the home and out. The data highlighted how technology contributes to well-being in a number of ways, including enabling them to maintain current activities; providing a means of staying in touch with families and friends; being easy to access and learn to use; and enhancing their lives. These can be divided into two types of factors: ones that relate to the direct outcomes of technology use and how these contribute to feelings of wellbeing and factors that relate to meeting an individual's needs, which if met contribute to their well-being. The findings indicate that well-being is a multi-faceted construct that includes autonomy, i.e. remaining independent, competence both in continuing to complete activities and learning new ones, and communication with other people. The study also indicates that Technology Tours provide an easily applicable and accessible means for enabling older adults to speak as 'experts' on technology.

Keywords: Ageing · Well-being · Technology · Methods

1 Introduction

Age is a major risk factor for many illnesses and with life expectancy increasing across all world regions [1] there is an urgent need to improve health and tackle age-related conditions. Since 1948 the World Health Organization has defined health as "...a state

© Springer International Publishing Switzerland 2016
S. Yamamoto (Ed.): HIMI 2016, Part II, LNCS 9735, pp. 445–453, 2016.
DOI: 10.1007/978-3-319-40397-7_42

of complete physical, mental and social well-being and not merely the absence of disease or infirmity". Therefore, improving understanding of well-being and ways to promote it is vital for developing new approaches to supporting the growing numbers of older people.

'Positive psychology' provides a context for studying well-being as it is concerned with the aspects and qualities that promote and provide a positive and meaningful existence – essentially the things that make life worth living. Positive psychology considers the human experience from the individual to the social group, highlighting the "valued subjective experiences [of] well-being, contentment and satisfaction (in the past); hope and optimism (for the future); and flow and happiness (in the present)" [2]. This approach recognises that people do not exist and operate in isolation and thus the satisfaction of an individual's needs occurs within the social context, acknowledging the importance of interaction and relationships with others in achieving this.

There is no reason to believe that satisfying our human needs for well-being, achievement, hope, etc., lessen as we age. Additionally, there is a strong preventive argument to be made for assisting and supporting people to keep experiencing a meaningful and fulfilling life for the benefits this can bring [3]. However, well-being is a complex concept to describe and measure. Like quality of life, well-being is largely subjective and a feeling of well-being arises in relation to many different aspects of a person's life. It is also a transient state, reflecting changes in health, wealth and social situation across the life-course [4]. Crucial for improving our measurement of well-being is the need to increase our understanding of what elements contribute to feelings of well-being in later life, how they can be characterized and why they are important.

1.1 COBALT Project

The COBALT (Challenging Obstacles and Barriers to Assisted Living Technologies) project set out to work with older adults across the UK to explore what factors, including well-being, influenced their decisions about technology adoption. To achieve these aims, partnerships were established with groups of older adults and a set of tools put together to extend data gathering beyond existing methods, such as focus groups. Building on previous projects working in partnership with older adults to create a digital conversation support [5], activity package [6] and multidimensional assessment tool [7], the COBALT team adopted an approach we term 'user as expert'. From this starting point we set out to identify ways to capture data from older adults about their existing technology use. This included reviewing existing methods used for exploring attitudes towards technology such as focus groups [8], and cultural probes [9].

The COBALT Tools for Engagement[TM] included an adapted version of Technology Tours [10], a method for documenting the range of deices a person uses in their daily life, which we combined with a semi-structured interview to find out how participants came to choose and learn about the various technologies. During the tour we also looked for any adaptations they had made and probed the reasons why. Additionally, we also developed new interactive methods including "Show & Tell" and

"Technology Interaction" [11]. Of these COBALT tools, we found that Technology Tours and Show and Tell provided means of exploring well-being and here we report the findings from Technology Tours of eight older adults' homes.

2 Method

2.1 Participants

Ethical approval was granted by the ethics committees of both the University of St Andrews and the University of Sheffield. The inclusion criteria specified that the participants should be native English speakers over age 65 years with no known cognitive impairment.

Eight participants, including two couples, aged between 76–82 years of age, were recruited for the Technology Tours of their homes. All participants lived in the community either in their own homes or in assisted living apartments. Two were wheelchair users and one used a walking frame and electric scooter. Informed consent to take part in the study and to be audio and video recorded was obtained from all participants.

2.2 COBALT Approaches

Technology Tours: We developed a two-stage process with a paper 'technology log' (Stage 1) followed by a one-on-one tour (Stage 2) of their home. The technology log was a blank paper log with space for the participant to write the time of usage, technology used and additional comments which was to be used by participants to record their technology use in a timely manner over a 24-hour period.

2.3 Procedure

Six Technology Tours were conducted.

Stage 1. Participants were asked to list the technologies they used over a 24-hour period in the technology log. This was designed in table format with time slots of one hour to enter technology and to add comments when desired i.e. brand of technology.

Stage 2. Participants were asked to give the researcher a tour of technologies in their home. This lasted for one hour on average. The technology log was used as a starting point for the tours During the tour the older adults were encouraged to explain the value and importance of the items in their life, including how they used them, why they were acquired, whether they were self-purchases or gifts, and what they liked and disliked about each item.

All sessions were video or audio recorded and these were transcribed and analysed using nVivo 9 software.

3 Results

During the Technology Tours the older adults highlighted how technology contributed to well-being in a number of ways. These included (1) enabling them to maintain current activities, such as cooking or shopping or hobbies; (2) providing a means of staying in touch with families and friends; (3) being easy to access and learn to use and often an improvement over older items; and (4) enhancing their lives as solutions, such as e-readers or low vision aids, or offering new opportunities, such as Internet surfing and email. In addition, self-identity appeared as a factor that interacted with well-being, particularly in relation to how older adult's view themselves as users of technology and how their technology use is viewed by other people.

1. Maintaining current activities

This 78-year old lady described how her different mobility aids assisted her to keep going out and about:

> **I: "I'm just going to ask you how you came to own your electric wheelchair, your normal wheelchair and your scooter."**
> AC: "Well the normal, this one's not mine, this is the NHS issue. I've had one for, I suppose about 15 years now. I had it before I came to live in S… Then I bought a scooter for getting round and going out, because I'm heavy. I was a lot heavier when I bought it. Pushing me is not easy so I bought a scooter so I could get around better. And the indoor one, I just thought I'd like one, because even for me in a place like this (extra care housing), up and down the corridors, it's heavy work on the carpet, so I found the electric one gets me about nicely." (Lines 625–633).

2. Staying in touch

In the Technology Tours, seven participants used a mobile phone and the eighth owned one but had reverted to the landline as they went out from home less often. Going through their Technology Tour log, this couple (T&J) described their use of the computer for social media:

> T: "You look at Facebook."
> J: "Oh, I was looking at Facebook last night with the children and the grandchildren, keeping in touch with what's going off there. Catch up with all of that." (lines 357–360).

Later in the Technology Tour interview J described the usefulness of her mobile phone:

> J: "…then my other daughter, er granddaughter, she's teaching at C… (neighbouring town), and I go swimming with her and she, I'll get a text, "Grandma, want to go to, want to go swimming tomorrow, the day after, such-and-such a time?" Then I'll just send "yes, okay", and that saves a lot of trouble, doesn't it, and so. That's it to keep in touch with everybody, and my friend, I might just send: "Do you want to come up for a meal in the evening?" (Lines 1141–1145).

In addition to staying in touch and simplicity, another participant noted among the benefits that having a mobile phone gave her a sense of security but also how it had become a part of her life:

> **Interviewer: "What made you buy a mobile phone, why did you want one?**
> Mrs C: "Getting stuck on dark roads at night"
> **I: "Had that happened to you?"**
> Mrs C: "No, but I used to baby-sit for my family when they were up at K…, and I'd be coming back midnight or something, along the dark roads, and kept thinking it would be nice to be able to, in case of breakdown. I think you'll find a lot of us oldies get one for when we're travelling. So it began from that, and then I used to only use it when I went, took it out in the car. Now I keep it on all the time so my use has changed, and it goes everywhere with me."
> **I: "So has it become more important to you as the time's gone on?"**
> Mrs C: "Yes, yes."
> **I: "But how do you think that happened?"**
> Mrs C: "Familiarity with it, usage, and its general usefulness really. But it's not as useful as one of those [indicating interviewer's smartphone], obviously, but just having it with you, it gives you a sense of security I suppose, that's really what it comes down to."
> **I: "Yeah, and when you started using it a bit more, was it for things like texting and …"**
> Mrs C: "Yes, and also if I'm meeting people. That's often where it, somebody can be standing in the wrong place, and that's when you can link up. It's, getting my older friends, we all have them now, or most of us do, and it's if your train has broken down or anything like that, and you've got an appointment, that's when I think we switch on our mobiles, and as I say, I have mine on all the time, but some people don't, and if they're meeting you they'll put their mobile on and, yeah, just general helpfulness." (Lines 160–189)

3. Easy to access

This participant explained that she enjoyed watching television and had two in the house. Here she describes the process of acquiring her new television and Freeview box. Freeview is the UK's digital terrestrial television platform which requires a 'tuner' (either built in or as a set-top box) to view:

> **I: So I see you have a got a grey television there, a silver television, is that a Freeview box you have got?**
> Mrs A: Oh it is a Freeview, it is yeah.
> **I: Did you buy that yourself?**
> Mrs. A: "Let me think now, oh I think I approached my son in law. And he looked on his computer and decided that it was a good thing to go to a certain shop in town, so I went on my own, saw the one that I wanted and the size and everything. They delivered it".

This gentleman (L) who had developed an essential tremor which reduced his ability to use a mouse and keyboard, used a large button calculator (Fig. 1) and had recently acquired speech to text software. Here his wife (M) describes the process of getting it up and running:

Fig. 1. Large button calculator to overcome problems with fine motor movements

I: [You've] been trying to use this software for just a couple of weeks now, isn't it? So I'm just about to see a sample.
F: It's getting the enunciation correct, which is a problem.
I: I see, right
F: So if you run words together you get a real jumble
(Laughter)
I: But you have to train it, don't you?
M: Yes.

This 78-year old lady uses multiple technologies and keeps her pill box buy the toaster as a reminder (Fig. 2).

 She describes how she updated her devices over the years, moving from a typewriter to a word processor:

I: Do you remember why you got one in the first place, what you wanted it for?
Mrs C:" Well, it was a word processor I wanted first, definitely. Because I was a secretary so, gradually I've gone from the old original Remingtons, from the manual to the electric, to what was the next stage up and then a computer, so I've gone through the whole process."
I: So do you think, am I right in thinking you were working when you got your first one?

Fig. 2. MrsC's pillbox kept by the toaster

Mrs C: "No, because I've been retired quite a few years now. No I would think it was after, afterwards."
I: So were you using it to produce documents for
Mrs C: "I think I just had a word processor, and then graduated to a proper computer and a server. I think."
I: So did you move onto email and things after that?
Mrs C: "Yes."
I: So how would you say your usage of your PC's changed over the years?
Mrs C: "Well I've learned the basics of, I can email, I can now research, I can get on the internet, I can order stuff from Amazon, I can tinker around to that extent. I can print off something, if somebody puts a photograph on it I can get a copy. But that it is just about as far as I go with it." (lines 294–321).

4. Life enhancing

This 78- year old lady describes how she acquired her Kindle and the features she appreciates:

I: How did you come to own it?
AC: "I'd seen it advertised on TV and thought, that sounds like a good idea, because I've always been a big reader, and I'd had mountains and mountains of books, which I've now got rid of. And they're expensive, and getting them onto Kindle the most you pay is a fiver, so it appealed to me. So I got the girls to look on the Internet because there are several different ones, and I thought Kindle sounded, and I like Amazon, I think they're good, so that's why I got it."
I: I know you use it for reading, do you use any of the larger fonts?

AC: "Yes. I've got it on a large font at the moment because my eyes have been so bad, but I'll get K... to get a smaller font now I don't need it quite so big. But I'll wait till I've got my new glasses and see how I cope then." (Lines 325–338).

Finally, this couple sum up the reasons they search for and acquire new technologies:

"Well, we suddenly realised when we retired, I didn't retire until I was over 70, I was just 70 and a half when I stopped work, and then we started buying all things that we realised that we need now that we're older. It suddenly dawned on us, and we started buying things to make life easier". (T&J, Lines 1223–1225)

4 Discussion

Technology Tours are an approach to capturing detailed information older adults' currently use of technology. We adapted this existing approach by combining a Log with a semi-structured interview. The eight participants all utilized a range of technologies in their daily lives that they demonstrated to the researcher. These included many everyday items including kettles, showers, stoves, washing machines, and televisions. Most of the items they used were self-purchases or gifts, with many instances of people researching the items before purchasing, to get the best features or price.

Two of the participants who had physical challenges had both purchased items to enhance their well-being and also made adaptations. For example, one lady who lived in extra care accommodation used an electric scooter and electric wheelchair, both of which she purchased herself. She had also adapted her wheelchair by putting marker pens in the arms so it can hold her shopping bags. She said it is difficult to use on carpets so she purchased an indoor scooter online with the help of her daughter and regards this is a luxury. She also purchased her outdoor electric scooter online. She said this was a key purchase for keeping her independence. An older gentleman with essential tremor had purchased speech-to-text technology to overcome his problem with typing and a large button calculator to assist in calculations as he was no longer able to make fine motor movements.

The technology log was found to act as a memory aid for participants both in terms of filling it in and as a prompt for the Tour. It also helped to assess which types of technology are of interest to the participants, and to focus on these in the technology tour. The tours enabled the COBALT team to see technology in context, see technology in use, see any modifications made to the home, and use the technological objects as a visual prompt for conversation.

The findings highlight that well-being is as important in later life as at any other time. As the participants went around their homes and talked through how they spent their days, they gave many examples of how technology impacted on their well-being. From a positive psychology perspective, the participants selected and used technologies to enable them to keep doing activities that are important to them, help them keep in touch with family and friends, are easy to use or an improvement on existing devices and generally enhance their lives.

The factors that contribute to well-being fall into two groups: Those relating to the direct outcomes of technology use, i.e. enabling continued activities, participation and socialization and how these contribute to feelings of wellbeing. The second set refer to indirect factors such as technology use meeting needs for competence and autonomy, which along with connectedness (i.e. being in contact with others) have been proposed as the three basic human needs [12]. Together, these findings enhance our understanding of the multiplicity of factors that produce feelings of wellbeing in older adults from using technology. These could be used as the basis for developing comprehensive approaches to sensitively elucidate, describe and measure the impact of HCI on wellbeing in later life.

References

1. Prince, M., Wimo, A., Guerchet, M., Ali, G.-C., Wu, Y.-T., Prina, M.: World Alzheimer Report 2015: The Global Impact of Dementia. Alzheimer's Disease International, London (2015)
2. Seligman, M.E.P., Csikszentmihalyi, M.: Positive psychology: an introduction. Am. Psychol. **55**, 1–14 (2000)
3. Astell, A.J.: Technology and fun for a happy old age. In: Sixsmith, A., Gutman, G. (eds.) Technology for Active Aging. Springer, New York (2013)
4. Adams, K.B., Leibbrandt, S., Moon, H.: A critical review of the literature on social and leisure activity and well-being in later life. Ageing Soc. **31**, 683–712 (2011)
5. Alm, N., Astell, A., Ellis, M., Dye, R., Gowans, G., Campbell, J.: A cognitive prosthesis and communication support for people with dementia. Neuropsychol. Rehabil. **14**(1–2), 117–134 (2004)
6. Astell, A., Alm, N., Dye, R., Gowans, G., Vaughan, P., Ellis, M.: Digital video games for older adults with cognitive impairment. In: Miesenberger, K., Fels, D., Archambault, D., Peňáz, P., Zagler, W. (eds.) ICCHP 2014, Part I. LNCS, vol. 8547, pp. 264–271. Springer, Heidelberg (2014)
7. Astell, A.J., Hwang, F., Brown, L.J.E., Timon, C., Maclean, L.M., Smith, T., Adlam, T., Khadra, H., Williams, E.A.: Validation of the NANA (Novel Assessment of Nutrition and Ageing) touch screen system for use at home by older adults. Exp. Gerontol. **60**, 100–107 (2014)
8. Barrett, J.: Running focus groups with elderly and disabled participants. Appl. Ergon. **31**, 621–629 (2000)
9. Wherton, J., Sugarhood, P., Procter, R., Rouncefield, M., Dewsbury, G., Greenhalgh, T., Hinder, S.: Designing assisted living technologies "in the wild": preliminary experiences with cultural probes. BMC Med. Res. Methodol. **12**, 188 (2012)
10. Maguire, M.: Methods to support human-centred design. Int. J. Hum.-Comput. Stud. **55**, 587–634 (2001)
11. Astell, A.J., Hwang, F., Williams, E.A., Archer, L., Harney-Levine, S., Wright, D., Ellis, M. P.L Ageing and technology – what factors influence use and abandonment? (Submitted)
12. Ryan, R.M., Deci, E.L.: Self-determination theory and the facilitation of intrinsic motivation, social development, and well-being. Am. Psychol. **55**, 68–78 (2000)

Improving Sense of Well-Being by Managing Memories of Experience

Mark Chignell[1]([⊠]), Chelsea de Guzman[1], Leon Zucherman[1],
Jie Jiang[2], Jonathan Chan[3], and Nipon Charoenkitkarn[3]

[1] The University of Toronto, Toronto, Canada
chignell@mie.utoronto.ca
[2] TELUS Communications Company, Toronto, Canada
[3] King Mongkut's University of Technology Thonburi (KMUTT),
Bangkok, Thailand

Abstract. Memories of experience are influenced by a peak-end effect [13]. Memories are modified to emphasize the final portions of an experience, and the peak positive, or negative, portion of that experience. We examine peak-end effects on judged Technical Quality (TQ) of online video. In two studies, sequences of different types of video disruption were varied so as to manipulate the peak-end effect of the experiences. The first experiment demonstrated an end effect, plus a possible peak effect involving negative, but not positive, experience. The second study manipulated payment conditions so that some sessions were structured as requiring payment to watch the video. The second study also distinguished between a peak effect and a possible sequence effect. Evidence was again found for an end effect, with a secondary effect of sequence, but no evidence was found for a peak effect independent of sequencing.

Keywords: Technical quality · Over-The-Top video · Peak-End effect

1 Introduction

Memories of experience are disproportionately influenced by the end of the experience (the end effect), and by the most intense (positive or negative) portion of the experience (the peak effect), a finding first demonstrated by Frederickson and Kahneman [1] and confirmed in a number of subsequent studies [2]. Since measures of well being, such as user experience and satisfaction, are based on memories of experience, rather than on experience per se, design to improve satisfaction needs to consider how to improve peak and end experiences.

Quality of Experience (QoE) has become a key concern and competitive differentiating feature in the telecommunications industry [3]. In this paper we assess whether or not the peak-end effect applies to cumulative QoE after viewing sequences of Over-The-Top (OTT) videos. If the peak-end effect applies for services such as online video, then the service provider can better estimate customer experience based on peak-end effects in the Technical Quality (TQ) of viewed video.

In the following section we briefly review past work on QoE and its measurement. We discuss how QoE is related to frustration and satisfaction, and how it accumulates

© Springer International Publishing Switzerland 2016
S. Yamamoto (Ed.): HIMI 2016, Part II, LNCS 9735, pp. 454–465, 2016.
DOI: 10.1007/978-3-319-40397-7_43

over time to form memories of experience, and attitudes towards the application or service being experienced. We then report on two studies that tested peak-end effects with online video. The first study is briefly summarized here and is reported more fully elsewhere [4], while the second study is reported here for the first time. Both studies used ethics protocols that were approved by the University of Toronto IRB.

2 Background

Quality of Experience (QoE) for the customer is a key differentiator of business success between service providers [5]. Overall QoE of video streaming is influenced by criteria such as video quality, audio quality, speed of service access, and frequency of service interruption. These elements of TQ are particularly important, and may be the only aspect of QoE that is under the control of service providers [6].

The Mean Opinion Score (MOS) [7] is commonly used to measure perceived video TQ. MOS provides a rating of subjective service quality, typically using the following scale anchors: 1 (bad); 2 (poor); 3 (fair); 4 (good); 5 (excellent). Other methodologies have been proposed for measuring TQ, including Session MOS [8], physiological measures such as skin conductance [9], behavior-based measures such as cancellation rates [10], and user acceptability of service quality [11].

A considerable amount of research has shown that a divergence between actual experiences and memories of those experiences [1, 12–14]. Although the memory of emotional experience is not objectively accurate, it is a powerful predictor of behavior [13].

Chignell et al. [15] carried out a subjective QoE study where videos with different types of impairments and disruptions were compared under different assumed payment conditions. As expected, the free service was most preferred, but no significant interaction was found between payment type and disruption type. Thus, the relative ordering, in terms of TQ, of different types of disruption such as freezings or failure to play all the way through, did not change between the free and paid condition.

The first study summarized below examined the applicability of the peak-end effect to TQ ratings of online video. The second study sought to replicate the peak-end effect found in the first study and to determine whether or not the peak-end effect is influenced by the type of payment (free vs. paid).

3 Study 1

Twenty-four participants (10 female, 14 male) each saw three blocks of eight videos (24 videos in total). Videos were modified to have four different levels of disruption. Some of the videos played without any impairment or disruption (I0), some videos had either one (I1) or three (I3) impairments (incidents of freezing) but still played all the way through to the end, and some played only part way through before stopping and failing to complete (NR1). Videos that had no more than one instance of freezing (I0 and I1) were labeled as "good", while the I3 and NR1 videos were labeled as "bad". After each video was shown, a TQ rating was made using the following question and response options. "Your evaluation of the technical quality in the video is: Excellent (5), Good (4), Fair (3), Poor (2), Bad (1)."

Videos consisted of short film trailers and popular YouTube videos. After each block of eight videos participants were asked two further questions. The first question was "How would you rate your level of satisfaction with the viewing experience provided by the brand?" (Response options were 0-Completely Satisfied, 1-Mostly Satisfied, 2-Somewhat Satisfied, 3-Neither Satisfied nor Dissatisfied, 4-Somewhat Dissatisfied, 5-Mostly Dissatisfied, 6-Completely Dissatisfied). The second question was "How would you rate your level of frustration with the viewing experience provided by the brand?" (Response options were on an 11-point scale ranging between 0-Not at all Frustrated and 10-Extremely Frustrated). After viewing the three sequences of four videos within the first half of each block participants were also asked: How would you rate your overall experience after viewing the last four videos? (Response options for this question were: 5-Excellent, 4-Good, 3-Fair, 2-Poor, 1-Bad, 0-Terrible).

Each group of four videos was comprised of one of six sequences of "good" (1) and "bad" videos (2). Each participant saw each of the sequences once, and the ordering of the sequences was counterbalanced between participants. As can be seen in Fig. 1, there seems to be some evidence for an end effect, with the two sequences ending in good videos (2111 and 2211) having a higher overall rating than the sequence ending with two bad videos (1122) or one bad video (1112). In terms of the peak effect, the sequence with two bad videos in the middle of the sequence has relatively low quality of experience, even though the sequence ended with a good video. However, the sequence with two good videos in the middle did not have relatively higher quality of experience. In summary, there is evidence for an end effect on judged QoE involving both a bad ending and a good ending to the sequence. However, for the peak effect, the evidence in Fig. 1 suggests that it may only apply with respect to bad videos.

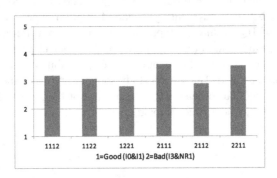

Fig. 1. Impact of Good/Bad sequences of 4 videos on judged QoE

Figure 2 shows mean frustration and satisfaction ratings with respect to sequences of four videos. As expected with the end effect, the sequence with three good videos and one bad video had more associated frustration, and lower satisfaction when the bad video was at the end of the sequence than it did when the bad video was at the beginning of the sequence. Similarly, for sequences for two bad, and two good videos, frustration was lower, and satisfaction was higher when the two good videos were at the end of the sequence.

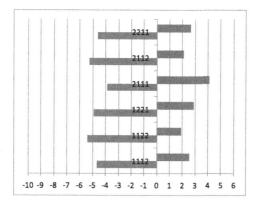

Fig. 2. Mean frustration and satisfaction for different sequences of last four videos in a block (bars on the right show satisfaction, bars on the left show frustration).

Regression analysis with frustration as the criterion was carried out, with the list of predictors including: the number of bad videos in the block; the maximum number of back to back bad videos in the block; the number of the first two videos (in the block) that were bad, and whether or not the last video (or two last videos) was/were bad. The analysis suggested a significant peak effect ($r = 0.372$, $p < .05$) with the two predictors in the derived model being the last video, and the number of bad videos in the second half of the block (the respective beta coefficients were 0.303, and 0.22, respectively). Additionally, ratings of satisfaction were significantly higher (t $[61.7] = 2.68$, $p < 0.01$), with a mean increase of 0.84 on the 7-point satisfaction rating scale, when the last video in the block (of eight videos) was good rather than bad.

4   Study 2

Study 2 considered two issues that had not been addressed in Study 1. First, Study 1 did not distinguish between peaks (i.e., videos with exceptionally high or low TQ) and sequences, i.e., sequences of two or more videos that were relatively "bad", or "good". Second, Study 1 did not consider the issue of payment. Would peak-end effects also be found, and would an effect of payment type interact with the peak-end effect?

Study 2 had two classes of disruption (impairments, and non-retainability failures where the video failed to play through to the end) and nine types of disruption in total (see Table 1, where the first row represents undisrupted video, the next four rows are impairments and the last four rows are failures). The nine disruption types were randomly assigned to each video. In addition, where the disruptions occurred and how long the freezing impairments lasted was randomized within the constraints shown in Table 2.

The study was broken down into 8 blocks of videos, with each block lasting approximately five minutes. There were two experimental groups – one that could terminate videos and one group that could not terminate the videos. Each video was approximately 1–1.5 min long, and once the participant had watched 4.5 min of video

Table 1. Description of disruption types used

Disruption	Description
I0	No impairments; video plays fully with no interruptions
I1	One freezing impairment
I2	Two freezing impairments
I3	Three freezing impairments
I4	Four freezing impairments
R0	Non-retainability failure with no freezing impairments
R1	One freezing impairment followed by a non-retainability failure
R2	Two freezing impairments followed by a non-retainability failure
R3	Three freezing impairments followed by a non-retainability failure

Table 2. Constraints for randomizing video disruption

Constraints
Freezing impairments were between 1 and 4 s long
For non-retainability failures, the video buffered for 0–2 s before displaying the network failure message
No impairments were inserted in the first 10 s of video
Non-retainability failures did not occur in the first 20 s or last 5 s of video
There was a minimum of 5 s between disruptions

within a block, the video they were watching at that time would be the last video they would watch for that block. For users who could terminate, another video would come up if they decided to stop watching a video, and they would keep watching videos until they reached the 4.5 min mark. This method ensured that the total viewing time for each block would be approximately the same for all participants.

The users had 14 categories of videos to choose from (e.g., sports, nature, entertainment, etc.) and chose 8 categories of interest (one category per block). Four of the blocks were "free" and the other four were "paid". The payment type was manipulated using e-tokens that represented the amount of money participants would receive at the end of the study. At the beginning of the study, participants were told they had 30 tokens that would reflect their payment for the study and that each token was equal to one dollar. They were also told that some blocks would require payment of 2.5 tokens (but were not told how many paid blocks there were), which meant that money would be deducted from their eventual compensation. According to the design of the study, each participant would pay 2.5 tokens for each of the four paid blocks, resulting in a loss of 10 tokens (i.e., $10), therefore, the participants ended up with 20 tokens at the end of the study, resulting in a payment of $20. After the experiment the participants were told that everyone received $20 and that the tokens were just used to give the illusion that the participants had to pay, or give up money, for the paid videos.

The sequences of video disruptions varied randomly within blocks. Some blocks tended to have more failures at the beginning or end, and some blocks included the most severe failure (R3), allowing an assessment of the peak-end effect to be made by comparing blocks with appropriately contrasting sequences of disruption types.

Each video clip contained audio, and the content was not graphic in nature (i.e. no horror, gore, violence, nudity or emotionally disturbing content). Videos consisted of short film trailers and a selection of popular YouTube videos. Disruptions to the video included freezing during play back and videos that did not play all the way to the end (sometimes with periods of freezing prior to the failure to complete).

Participants provided ratings of TQ, Quality of Experience (QoE), and Accept-ability after each video. At the end of each block, participants also provided ratings of overall TQ (Block TQ), and Overall Experience (Block OE), with respect to the block of videos just viewed. Response options were Yes or No for acceptability, and for all other ratings the following six point scale of response options was used: 6-Excellent, 5-Good, 4-Fair, 3-Poor, 2-Bad, 1-Terrible. After viewing all 8 blocks of videos, par-ticipants also filled in a short post-questionnaire that asked them to rate their overall experience of viewing videos in the experiment.

4.1 Results

The TQ ratings provided by participants confirmed our hypotheses that I0 and I1 videos would be rated most favourably, non-retainability failures would be rated least favourably, and the I2, I3, and I4 impairments would have ratings between the two extremes (see Fig. 3). Because of this trend, we created a new factor called Expected Technical Quality (Expected TQ) that classified the disrupted videos into three groups: Good (I0, I1), Medium (I2, I3, I4), and Poor (R0, R1, R2, R3).

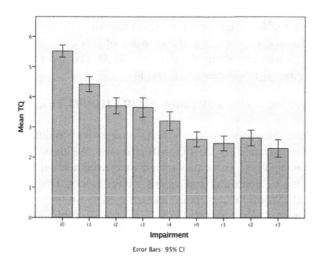

Fig. 3. Mean TQ ratings by disruption type

Repeated measures ANOVA was carried out with payment type (PayType) and Expected TQ as the experimental factors, and TQ as the independent variable. Mauchly's test was used to test for sphericity, and degrees of freedom were adjusted using the Greenhouse-Geisser criterion where necessary (as described in [16]). There was a significant main effect of Expected TQ (F [2, 22] = 106.8, p < .001), but the main effect of Pay Type, and the interaction of Pay Type with Expected TQ were non-significant (F < 1 in both cases). As can be seen in Fig. 4, the mean TQ across the three levels of Expected TQwas almost identical for the two Pay Types.

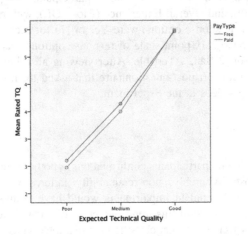

Fig. 4. Effects of pay type and expected technical quality on mean TQ (Color figure online)

We developed a GoodBad measure to assess sensitivity to differences in degree of impairment (number of freezings) of the videos. Equation 1 below shows the formula for the GoodBad measure, which reflects the mean of four difference scores between rated TQ for videos with few if any impairments (I0, I1, I2), and rated TQ for videos with a higher number of impairments (I3, and I4).

$$\text{GoodBad} = \text{MEAN(I0DiffI4, I0DiffI3, I1DiffI4, I2DiffI4)} \qquad (1)$$

We screened out three participants who had low sensitivity to differences in number of impairments, as indicated by their GoodBad scores. We then carried out further analyses on the remaining 11 participants. First we created a set of features to capture different sequencing of good and bad videos within blocks. Disruption types were classified as "good", "medium", or "poor" as explained above (beginning of Sect. 4.1) and these types were coded respectively as 1, 2, and 3. Table 3 shows the coding scheme then used for the First2 and Last2 features. For instance, if the first two videos were both good the value of First 2 would be 1, and similarly for the last two videos and Last2. As another example of the coding (fourth row of the table), if the first video in the pair was good and the second video in the pair was poor, then the corresponding score for First2 or Last2 would be 4.

Table 3. Coding for First2 and Last2 feature

First two videos (First video code, second video code) OR Last two videos (Second last video code, last video code)	Feature score
1, 1	1
1, 2 or 2, 1	2
2, 2	3
1, 3 or 3, 1	4
2, 3 or 3, 2	5
3, 3	6

Table 4 provides an overview of the peak and sequence features. We then carried out two multiple regression analyses to determine which block features influenced Block TQ, and Block OE, respectively. The Pearson correlation between the Block TQ and Block OE was .587. Other correlations between the two outcome measures and the predictors are shown in Table 5. All of the correlations between the features used as predictors (below) were below .4 except for the correlation between First and First2 (r = .709), and the correlation between Last and Last2 (r = .695).

Table 4. Peak and Sequence Feature Descriptions

Feature	Description
PosPeak	Binary variable that codes whether a positive peak (I0 or I1 video) is present in the block, excluding the first and last videos
NegPeak	Binary variables that codes whether a negative peak (R2 or R3 video) is present in the block, excluding the first and last videos
Longest.bad. sequence	Count of the number of consecutive Poor videos (R0, R1, R2, R3) within a block, excluding the first and last videos

Table 5. Predictor and outcome measure correlation table

	First	First2	Last	Last2	PosPeak	NegPeak	Longest.bad.sequence
Block TQ	0.069	0.131	.426**	.494**	−0.09	.224*	.270**
Block OE	0.001	0.056	.356**	.339**	−0.16	0.103	.294**

**p < .01

The predictors in the multiple regression analysis were First, First2, Last, Last2, positive.peak, negative.peak, and longest.bad.sequence. As recommended by Field et al. [16] for an exploratory analysis, backward stepwise removal of the predictors was used. For Block TQ, the backward stepwise analysis removed all the predictors except Last2. The correlation of Last2 with Block TQ was .538.

For Block OE, Last and longest.bad.sequence were the two predictors in the selected model (adjusted R-squared as reported by IBM SPSS was .253). Since one of the Last (Last or Last2) predictors was part of the chosen model for both the outcomes, and Last2 was almost as highly correlated with Block OE, and more highly correlated with Block TQ than Last, we selected Last2 as a predictor for the next analysis along with Longest Bad Sequence, which had the next highest correlation with the two outcomes. Two forced entry regression analyses were carried out. In the first analysis (with Block OE as the dependent measure), adjusted R-squared for the model was .197, and both predictors were significant (p < .05, Table 6).

Table 6. Forced entry regression summary for the model Block OE as the dependent measure

Model	B	Std. Err	Beta	t	Sig.
(Constant)	2.401	0.326		7.371	0
Last2	0.255	0.074	0.344	3.439	0.001
Longest.bad.sequence	0.318	0.139	0.228	2.278	0.025

For the model predicting Block TQ, the adjusted R-square was .282, and only Last2 was a significant predictor (Table 7).

Table 7. Forced entry regression summary for the model with rated Block TQ as the dependent measure.

Model	B	Std. Err	Beta	t	Sig.
(Constant)	2.133	0.272		7.842	0
Last2	0.333	0.062	0.509	5.377	0
Longest.bad.sequence	0.125	0.116	0.101	1.071	0.287

Figure 5 shows Last2 and Longest Bad Sequence (the number of "bad" videos in the longest sequence) plotted against Block OE. The "f" and "p" labels stand for free or paid service in the block. There was a strong end effect with Block OE scores tending to increase as the Last2 score increased. Block OE scores were ranked from best to worst, so a higher score reflected a more negative opinion. Thus, as the Last2 score increased (i.e., the end of the block had worse TQ), Block OE became less favourable. There was also a sequencing effect where longer bad sequences were associated with lower Block OE. In contrast, there was no tendency for these effects to differ between the "free" and "paid" blocks, which were inter-mixed throughout the scatterplot.

Figure 6 shows Last2 plotted against Block TQ. The "f" and "p" labels in the figure again indicate whether the block corresponding to that data point was represented as a free or paid service. It can be seen that there is a strong end effect with block TQtending to increase as the Last2 score increases. Block TQ satisfaction was rated using a Likert scale from Strongly Agree to Strongly Disagree (coded from 1 to 5), meaning that higher scores reflected less satisfaction with the TQ of the block. Figure 6 shows that blocks with "bad" ends are associated with less satisfaction. Again, there is no tendency for this effect to differ between the "free" and "paid" blocks, which are inter-mixed throughout the scatterplot.

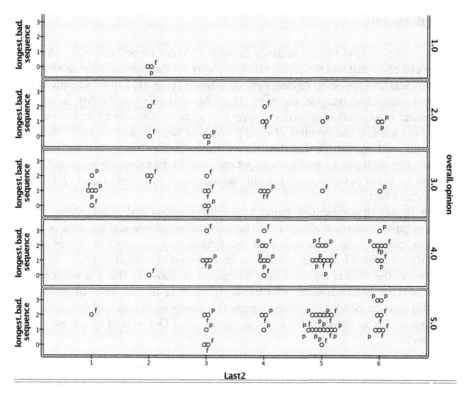

Fig. 5. Last2 and longest.bad.sequence features plotted against Block OE

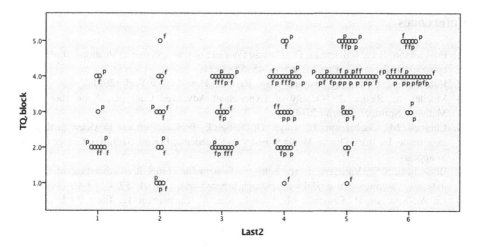

Fig. 6. Last2 feature plotted against Block TQ

5   Conclusions

Payment effects were not found in Study 2, nor did payment type interact significantly with the end effect that was observed. One possibility for this non-intuitive result is that people are less susceptible to payment effects when judging TQ if they actually watch the video rather than imagine the experience. An alternative possibility is that the experimental manipulation of payment type was unsuccessful either because the participants did not find the amounts of money involved large enough to worry about, or because they did not believe that they were actually having to pay since the payment was concerned with money they had not yet received. Further research is needed to pin down the impact of payment type, not only on judgments of technical quality, but also on peak-end effects.

Both studies discussed here found a reasonably strong end effect. Study 1 also found a negative "sequence effect" involving pairs of bad videos in the middle of block sequences. Study 2 found an effect of the longest bad sequence in the block on Block OE, but longest bad sequence did not have a significant effect on rated block TQ. In summary, the studies reported here succeeded in showing that the sequence of disruption types within a block of viewed videos does in fact have an impact on Block TQ, and on Block OE. This suggests that peak-end effects will influence customer experience for online video and that estimation of QoE should take these effects into account.

Acknowledgment. The authors would like to thank KanmanusOngvisatepaiboon for his assistance in developing the software used in the experiment. This research was funded by a grant from TELUS Communications Company, and by an NSERC Collaborative Research Development Grant, both to the first author.

References

1. Fredrickson, B.L., Kahneman, D.: Duration neglect in retrospective evaluations of affective episodes. J. Pers. Soc. Psychol. **65**(1), 45–55 (1993)
2. Kahneman, D.: Thinking Fast and Slow. Random House, New York (2011)
3. Moeller, S., Raake, A.: Quality of Experience: Advanced Concepts, Applications and Methods. Springer, Cham (2014)
4. Chignell, M., Zucherman, L., Kaya, D., Jiang, J.: Peak-end effects in video quality of experience. In: IEEE Digital Media Industry and Academic Forum, Santorini, Greece (2016, to appear)
5. Bharadwaj, S.G., Varadarajan, R., Fahy, J.: Sustainable competitive advantage in service industries: a conceptual model and research propositions. J. Mark. **57**(4), 83–99 (1993)
6. Li, W., Spachos, P., Chignell, M., Leon-Garcia, A., Zucherman, L., Jiang, J.: Impact of technical and content quality of overall experience of OTT Video. In: 2016 IEEE Consumer Communications and Networking Conference (CCNC) (in press)
7. ITU-T.: Subjective Video Quality Assessment Methods for Multimedia Applications. Recommendation P. 910, Telecommunication Standardization Sector of ITU (2008)

8. Leon-Garcia, A., Zucherman, L.: Generalizing MOS to assess technical quality for end-to-end telecom session. In: Globecom Workshops (GC Wkshps), pp. 681–687. IEEE, New York (2014)

9. Laghari, K., Gupta, R., Arndt, S., Antons, J-N., Schleicher, R., Möller, S., Falk, T.H.: Neurophysiological experimental facility for quality of experience (QoE) assessment. In: Proceedings of the First IFIP/IEEE International Workshop on Quality of Experience Centric Management, pp. 1300–1305. IEEE, New York (2013)

10. Khirman, S., Henriksen, P.: Relationship between quality of service and quality of experience for public internet service, In: Proceedings of Passive and Active Measurement (PAM 2002), Fort Collins, Colorado, (2002)

11. Spachos, P., Li, W., Chignell, M., Leon-Garcia, A., Zucherman, L., Jiang, J.: Acceptability and quality of experience in over the top video. In: 2015 IEEE International Conference on Communication Workshop (ICCW), pp. 1693–1698. IEEE, New York (2015)

12. Lottridge, D., Chignell, M., Jovicic, A.: Affective interaction understanding, evaluating, and designing for human emotion. Rev. Hum. Fact. Ergon. 7(1), 197–217 (2011)

13. Kahneman, D.: New challenges to the rationality assumption. In: Kahneman, D., Tversky, A. (eds.) Choices, Values, and Frames, pp. 758–774. Cambridge University Press, Cambridge (2000)

14. Baumgartner, H., Sujan, M., Padgett, D.: Patterns of affective reactions to advertisements: the integration of moment-to-moment responses into overall judgments. J. Mark. Res. 34, 219–232 (1997)

15. Chignell, M., Kealey, R., DeGuzman, C., Zucherman, L., Jiang, J.: Using visualizations to measure SQE: individual differences, and pricing and disruption type effects. Working paper, Interactive Media Lab, University of Toronto (2016)

16. Field, A., Miles, J., Field, Z.: Discovering Statistics Using R. Sage, Thousand Oaks (2012)

Towards Understanding Senior Citizens' Gateball Participations Behavior and Well-Being: An Application of the Theory of Planned Behavior

Chia-Chien Hsu[1], Yu-Chin Hsu[2], and Ching-Torng Lin[2(✉)]

[1] Leisure and Recreation Management, Kainan University, Taoyuan, Taiwan
hsu127@mail.knu.edu.tw
[2] Department of Information Management,
Dayeh University, Changhua County, Taiwan
charllin@mail.dyu.edu.tw

Abstract. Successful aging is expected goal for every older adult. Well-being has been considered an important indicator of successful aging. Thus the aim of this study is applying the Theory of Planned Behavior to investigate senior citizens' leisure participation behavior and their perceived psychological well-being of participating in gateball-playing activities. We analyze a survey of 614 Taiwanese senior citizens gateball players to test the hypothesized. The results indicated that perceived behavioral control, attitude, and subjective norm have significant positive effects on gateball participation behavior, and ultimately significant positive impact on senior citizens' perceived psychological well-being. Perceived usefulness and perceived ease of use have positive and significant effects on attitude. Friend/co-worker influences have significant positive effects on subjective norm. Both resource facilitating conditions and self-efficacy have significant positive effects on perceived behavioral control. Managerial implications and suggestions are also discussed in this study.

Keywords: Theory of Planned Behavior (TPB) · Gateball · Exercise behavior · Psychological well-being

1 Introduction

Population aging is a common trend in the world. Successful aging is expected goal for every older adult in Taiwan and other countries. It is also one of the main objectives of the government policy. Well-being has been considered an important indicator of successful aging. Thus, how to help senior citizens aging actively for the purpose of increasing their quality of life has profoundly become a social phenomenon [27] and identifying factors that promote well-being perceived by senior citizens is of growing importance. In the past there have been some researchers focused in elderly leisure activities on well-being. Silverstein and Parker [33] note that engaging in friendship-type leisure activities lead to the highest quality of life perceived by Swedish elders. In a literature review addressing social and leisure activity and well-being in older people,

© Springer International Publishing Switzerland 2016
S. Yamamoto (Ed.): HIMI 2016, Part II, LNCS 9735, pp. 466–477, 2016.
DOI: 10.1007/978-3-319-40397-7_44

Adams et al. [1] indicate that joining informal social activity (e.g., club going) is most likely to benefit their well-being. In an analysis of the health and retirement study, Chen and Feeley [13] conclude that individual well-being improves with higher levels of social relationship.

Although many studies have focused on identifying various factors influencing older adults acceptance behavior of leisure participation factor and their well-being, researchers are still developing leisure participation evaluation techniques, using subjective approaches based on individual preferences, or simply to find the factors that influence participation leisure behavior, lack of well-constructed theoretical models for the connection between cause and accepted understanding of behavioral and psychological mechanisms, in addition to its findings can only be answered "What" questions, but cannot understand the behavior of the elderly to accept the reasoning of perception and feeling process, while there will be an unstable situation. As a result, although subjective researchers have made some contributions to overview concept of the development of leisure activity, they may not have adequately required direct evaluations through perceptive reasoning processes. So a deep understanding of the problem and treatment is not sufficient. Theory of Planned Behavior (TPB) is the use of a personal attitude, subjective norm and perceived behavioral control to predict the behavior of individuals to participate in a particular activities, TPB is widely accepted and has been successful used in various fields of study includes leisure activity. Furthermore, gateball-playing is a good elderly leisure activities and it has increasingly become popular leisure activity for the older adults in Taiwan.

Thus based on TPB, an integrated model was developed to explore the behavior of the elderly to participate in gateball and well-being. Also, through reviewing of gateball activities literature, authors identified several antecedents contributing to playing gateball behavior and those affecting attitude, subjective norm, and perceived behavioral control. For example: the two exogenous factors "perceived ease of use" and "perceived usefulness" to replace the original exogenous factors, behavior belief and outcome evaluation; "Family/friend/co-worker influences" to replace the original exogenous factors, normative belief and motivation to comply. And "self-efficacy" and "resource facilitating conditions" to replace the original exogenous factors, control beliefs and perceived facilitate.

2 Literature Review and Hypothesis Development

2.1 Theory of Planned Behavior

Human behavior tends to be goal-oriented. Based upon this tenet, Ajzen and Fishbein [4] propose the Theory of Reasoned Action (TRA) which addresses that most human behaviors follow a certain pattern and therefore are predictable. According to TRA, individuals consist of a high degree of volitional control and are capable of making logical choices among alternatives. As one of intention-based models, TRA uses behavioral intention to predict subjects' actual behaviors. Behavioral intention correspondingly leads to actual behavior and is a function of attitude toward a behavior and subjective norm. Attitude is correspondingly correlated with behavioral belief and subjective norm is associated with normative belief [4].

Based on theoretical framework of TRA and incorporates a new dimension, perceived behavioral control, as one of the determinants of behavioral intention, TPB is established for predicting human behavior [2, 21]. The applicability of TRA, however, has drawn concerns from researchers. This is because the performance of a particular behavior may require the presences of opportunities and resources which are non-volitional in nature [2]. That is, TRA is unable to fully explain certain situations if the availability of resources and opportunities are limited. For example, although a senior citizen has positive attitude and is aware of general supports toward participating in playing gateball, he/she cannot join the leisure activity if the playing ground is not conveniently located or the opportunity cost for this particular person is high. The application of TPB, in this case, would be appropriate in predicting the senior citizen's behavior. It is clear that senior citizens' decision making can include a variety of non-volitional factors that can diminish their opportunities or capabilities to play gateball. Thus, TPB fits the conceptual framework of the study because it offers a well-developed structure which enable researchers to conduct a thorough examination of the formation of senior citizens' gateball playing behavior and their psychological well-being by considering both volitional and non-volitional factors.

2.2   Relationship of Leisure Participation Behavior and Psychological Well-Being

The psychological benefit of leisure participation is one of the most frequently pursued topics in the field of leisure study [27]. This is because researchers generally believe that psychological benefit is considered a useful evaluation criterion pertaining to leisure activity participation [29] and is correlated with perceived quality of life [32]. The common interpretation of leisure participation and psychological well-being is that both are positively correlated. That is, leisure participation can be an important behavior in increasing one's health and psychological well-being. Prior research has shown that positive emotional state or subject well-being can be a promoting agent for individual health [37]. Lawton indicates that there is a positive relationship between leisure activity participation psychological well-being. Hassmen et al. [22] emphasize that regular exercise has been characterized as a positive leisure participation behavior which may yield psychological benefits. In their study, a consistent positive association between psychological well-being and regular exercise is found. The results of a meta-analysis show that participation in physical activity is linked to individual strength, functional capacity, and psychological well-being [30].

By referencing the results of prior studies, we believe that participation in gateball is beneficial for players, particularly for senior citizen players. This is because gateball is a game of strategic deployment which offers exercise for the mind as well as for the body [24]. Through such leisure activity, players may view the activity as a means for maintaining a clear mind and body fitness. In addition, players may consider playing field as a place for social interaction [24]. As stated above, research has shown that the relationship between leisure participation behavior and psychological well-being is positive and leads the following hypothesis:

Hypothesis 1: Senior citizens' gateball-playing behavior has a positive influence on their psychological well-being.

2.3 Relationship of Attitude, Subjective Norm, Perceived Behavioral Control and Leisure Participation Behavior

The Theory of Planned Behavior (TPB) proposition has been indicated that the behavioral intention is a determinant of actual behavior, and this behavioral intention is determined by three antecedent beliefs, attitude, subjective norm and perceived behavioral control [6, 7]. Similar results were also found in the field of sports, leisure, and recreation studies [5, 28]. Continuing the TPB proposition, this study revalidates constituent relationships in the context of senior citizens' gateball-playing with the following hypotheses:

H2: Attitude has a positive influence on senior citizens' gateball-playing behavior.
H3: Subjective norm has a positive influence on senior citizens' gateball-playing behavior.
H4: Perceived behavioral control has a positive influence on senior citizens' gateball-playing behavior.

2.4 Relationship of Perceived Ease of Use, Perceived Usefulness and Attitude

The Technology Acceptance Model (TAM) has been indicated that behavioral attitude is determined by two antecedent beliefs, perceived usefulness and perceived ease-of-use [15]. Similar results were also found in the field of sports, leisure, and recreation studies [12, 26]. In our context, if senior citizens perceive that gateball is not difficult to learn and play, they are likely to have a positive attitude toward gateball-playing behavior. If senior citizens perceive that playing gateball is useful for keeping their mind sharp, maintaining their physical fitness, or providing opportunities for social interaction, they are likely to have a positive attitude toward gateball-playing behavior. Continuing the TAM proposition, this study revalidates constituent relationships in the context of gateball-playing with the following hypotheses:

H5: Perceived ease of use is positively associated with senior citizens' attitude toward gateball-playing behavior.
H6: Perceived usefulness is positively associated with senior citizens' attitude toward gateball-playing behavior.

2.5 Relationship of Family/Friend/Co-worker Influences and Subjective Norms

Subjective norm is a function of salient normative belief [6]. In TPB, normative norm is defined as a person's perception concerning social pressures or other individuals' beliefs that he/she should or should not conduct a particular behavior [17]. Motivation to comply, accordingly, refers to a person's choice of whether he/she follows instructions and reaches outcomes desired by important referents [17]. In fact, normative belief is basically a concept of social influence which refers to accepted standards or unwritten rules of behavior existing in a particular group, community, or culture. It is assumed that important referents in combination with the individual's motivation to comply constitute the prevailing subjective norm. In real life situation, all individuals have important referents or groups around them. Those important referents generally consist of spouse, family members, friends, supervisors, or coworkers. If persons are aware that those important referents endorse a particular behavior, they are more likely to perform such behavior [6]. In our context, if important referents encourage or provide advice to senior citizens by indicating that playing gateball is good for them, they are likely to follow their advice to participate in gateball playing and games. In this study, the important referents include family members, friends, and peers. Family members and friends are two significant groups of people who may have impact on individual decision making. Researchers [19] have pointed out that family members and friends are usually the most influential persons in shaping a particular person's views. We also consider that viewpoints provided by peers are important for senior gateball players in this study. As stated above, gateball is a group activity. Interacting with teammates and other players is a part of the game. In this study, teammates and other gateball players are considered as peers. In fact, peers' encouragement is can play a key role for the participation in the leisure activity. Therefore, the following hypotheses are developed.

H7:   Family members' influence is positively associated with subjective norms as perceived by senior citizens.

H8:   Friends' influence is positively associated with subjective norms as perceived by senior citizens.

H9:   Peers' influence is positively associated with subjective norms as perceived by senior citizens.

2.6   Relationship of Self-efficacy, Resource Facilitating Conditions and Perceived Behavioral Control

In TPB, perceived behavior control is a function of control belief. Control belief refers to the presence of factors which may either facilitate or hinder the performance of a particular behavior [3]. If the participation of a leisure activity, for instance, is convenient (e.g., location, low cost) for an individual, he/she is more likely to join that activity, and vice versa. Facilitation conditions, thus, may play a pivotal role of whether a person is willing to participate in a leisure activity. In addition, Ajzen [2] notes that perceived behavioral control is conceptually compatible to the concept of self-efficacy. Self-efficacy is defined as the belief in one's capabilities of "how well one can execute courses of action required to deal with prospective situations" [9]. Researchers have addressed that individual confidence in his/her ability is the key to have such person performing a particular behavior [34]. Self-efficacy can not only influence individual selection of activities, but also reflect determinations and efforts expanded during the execution process [2]. We believe that control belief is constituted by the internal force of self-efficacy and external factor of facilitation conditions. In this context, if senior citizens perceive that they have confidence in playing gateball well, they are more likely to engage in more efforts and time for this activity. If playing gateball can be cost efficient and based on individual time availability, as well as convenient locations for participation, senior citizens are more likely to involve in the gateball-playing behavior. Previous studies have indicated that both self-efficacy and facilitation conditions have positive relationships with perceived behavioral control [31]. Therefore, the following hypotheses are developed.

H10:   Self-efficacy is positively associated with perceived behavioral control as perceived by senior citizens.

H11:   Facilitation conditions are positively associated with perceived behavioral control as perceived by senior citizens.

3   Method

3.1   Measures

The questionnaire development was based on theory, recreation management-related literature review and psychology literature review. Perceive ease of use was measured using four items adopted from [11]. Perceived usefulness was measured by six items adopted from [36]. The construct of normative belief was categorized into three dimensions including family members' influence, friends' influence, and peers' influence. Each dimension was measured by four statements [14]. Control belief consists of self-efficacy and Facilitation conditions. Self-efficacy was measured by four statements. The development of these statements was based on [10]. Facilitation conditions were measured using three statements adopted from [2, 34]. Drawing upon previous studies [7], five statements were used to measure attitude. The subject norm statements were adopted from [16], and Curtis et al. (2010). Three statements were used to measure the construct of subjective norm. Based on the prior studies [2, 34], three statements were used to measure perceived behavior control. Leisure participation behavior was measured by four statements. The development of these statements was based upon the works of. Psychological well-being statements were adopted from [2, 23]. A total of eight statements were used to measure this construct. The wordings of the measurement were modified for the purpose of being appropriate for this study. The refinement of the instrument was also reviewed by a panel of experts.

3.2   Data Collection

Purposeful sampling was employed in this study because a complete population list concerning senior gateball players was unable to be obtained. Subjects were senior gateball players who were 60 years old or above. Empirical data were collected via the assistance of Chinese Taipei Gateball Association (CTGA). The period of data collection lasted about four and a half months from July 16 to November 30, 2014.

3.3 Data Analysis

SPSS and AMOS were used to analyze the data. Drawing on approach, an estimate of a measurement model was first developed using confirmatory factor analysis (CFA). After assessing the adequacy of the model, structural equation modeling (SEM) was employed for the purpose of testing hypothesized relationships and theoretical model. For model testing, SEM is a multivariate technique which combines factor analysis and multiple regressions and, accordingly, enables researchers to assess a series of independent/dependent relationships simultaneously [20].

4 Results

4.1 Descriptive Statistics

A total of 614 usable responses were received and used in data analysis. Of the 614 respondents, 60.4 % were male (n = 371). Female respondents accounted for 39.6 % (n = 243). Respondents' age ranged from 60 to 83 years and their average age was 68.3 years. Respondents who had graduated from middle school (29.7 %, n = 184), high school or vocational school (25.6 %, n = 157), and elementary school (25 %, n = 151) were the major groups categorized by their educational levels. The majority of the respondents indicated that they currently lived with their family members (92.2 %, n = 566). Approximately 93 % of the respondent (n = 569) revealed that the have played gateball for at least a year. Among them, about 60 % of respondents (n = 371) had at least five-year experiences in playing gateball.

4.2 Testing of the Measurement Model

Table 1 presents an overview concerning the means, standard deviations, and correlation among the constructs. The CFA results revealed that the model fits the data (χ^2/df = 1.528, GFI = .881, AGFI = .868, RMSEA = .029, CFI = .953, NFI = .859). The loadings of all statements were above .70 on their assigned constructs. These results indicated that all statements were significantly related to their specified constructs and the unidimensionality of each scale was satisfactory. Composite reliability of the underlying constructs ranged from .782 to .982. The values exceeded the recommended value of .70 suggested by [8]. Average Variance Extracted (AVE) was also performed to examine the convergent validity of the measures. The AVE values, ranging from .525 to .903, exceeded the recommended value .50 suggested by [18]. Additionally, the square root value of AVE from each construct was larger than the correlation between each construct, As listed in Table 1. Such value indicated that discriminant validity was satisfactory.

Table 1. Measure correlations, reliability coefficients, and AVE

	PEOU	PU	FMI	FI	PI	SE	FC	ATT	SN	PBC	LPB	PWB
PEOU	.86											
PU	.80	.95										
FMI	.69	.65	.79									
FI	.61	.52	.71	.83								
PI	.60	.51	.78	.71	.82							
SE	.59	.42	.77	.81	.79	.85						
FC	.63	.53	.72	.74	.73	.76	.81					
ATT	.82	.75	.64	.53	.51	.44	.54	.85				
SN	.64	.58	.73	.70	.71	.72	.71	.58	.74			
PBC	.59	.48	.77	.73	.72	.82	.80	.49	.73	.83		
LPB	.69	.65	.76	.69	.68	.72	.79	.68	.72	.82	.88	
PWB	.61	.57	.67	.61	.60	.63	.70	.59	.63	.71	.69	.72
Mean	5.76	5.51	5.84	5.79	5.79	5.95	5.96	5.77	5.71	6.00	6.14	6.11
SD	.76	.76	.71	.73	.75	.60	.62	.86	.72	.61	.59	.68
CR	.916	.982	.868	.901	.893	.911	.855	.926	.782	.866	.934	.898

Note. PEOU = perceived ease of use; PU = perceived usefulness; FMI = family members' influence; FI = friends' influence; PI = peers' influence; SE = self-efficacy; FC = facilitation conditions; ATT = attitude; SN = subjective norm; PBC = perceived behavioral control; LPB = leisure participation behavior; PWB = psychological well-being; CR = composite reliability; The diagonals represent the square root of average variance extracted (AVE).

4.3   Structural Model

The results of hypotheses testing are presented in Table 2. As indicated in this table, except hypothesis 7, the results supported the other relationships hypothesized at a significance level of 0.05. The findings for these hypotheses showed that senior citizens' psychological well-being is positively correlated with their participation in gateball-playing behavior, and their attitude toward playing gateball, subjective norms, and perceived behavioral control all have impact on such participation behavior. In addition, as shown in Table 2, the estimates of the standardized coefficients revealed that the effect of perceived behavioral control on leisure participation behavior was greater than attitude and subjective norm. The effect of perceived usefulness on attitude was greater than perceived ease of use. The effect of friends' influence on subjective norm was greater than peers' influence. Finally, the effect of self-efficacy on perceived behavioral control was greater than facilitation conditions.

5   Discussion

In combination of TAM as a part of TPB model, this study was an effort to test the appropriateness of TPB in explaining senior citizens' decision making process concerning gateball playing behavior and the effect of such behavior on individual psychological well-being. In this model, the predictive constructs were validated as determinants of leisure participation behavior and psychological well-being. Overall, the results of the study verified that proposed constructs can be the primary reasons for

Table 2. Structural equation modeling results (N = 614)

Paths	Coefficient	Hypothesis
H1: LPB → PWB	.807***	Supported
H2: ATT → LPB	.148*	Supported
H3: SN → LPB	.105*	Supported
H4: PBC → LPB	.730***	Supported
H5: PEOU → ATT	.296***	Supported
H6: PU → ATT	.671***	Supported
H7: FMI → SN	.178	No supported
H8: FI → SN	.598***	Supported
H9: PI → SN	.194*	Supported
H10: SE → PBC	.532***	Supported
H11: FC → PBC	.439***	Supported

senior citizens' participation in gateball-playing behavior and the possibility of such behavior contributing to their psychological well-being. In addition, the findings of the study also verified the roles of belief constructs (e.g., friends' influence, peers' influence, facilitation conditions, self-efficacy) and TAM applied constructs (i.e., perceived usefulness, perceived ease of use) which served as antecedent variables to specifically explain the path of the proposed model.

The study provides theoretical implications for a better understanding of the determinants of senior citizens' leisure participation behavior (i.e., gateball-playing behavior). First, TPB is a theoretical model that attempts to explain the decision making process for a particular behavior. An extension of TPB was developed in this study. Psychological well-being was applied in order to comprehend the effect of leisure participation on senior citizens' psychological well-being. Although prior research has reported that leisure participation behavior has positive effect on individual psychological well-being, the application of the link for senior gateball players enables investigators to extend previous research on TPB. Not surprisingly, the finding revealed that gateball-playing behavior has a significant effect on psychological well-being. This finding also implies that, through the participation in leisure activities, individuals may perceive a higher degree of psychological well-being. Accordingly, they may be happier, more confident, and more satisfy with their current life.

Second, embedding TAM in TPB, to our knowledge, is the first attempt in the field of leisure and recreation studies. Senior citizens possess life experiences in making logical choices among alternatives. When engaging in a particular leisure activity (i.e., gateball), they would assess how the activity is useful for them and whether the activity is easy to comprehend and get involved. In this case, based on the examination of the estimated standardized coefficients, perceived usefulness had a greater level of impact on attitude. This implies that, to enhance senior citizens' attitude to engage in gateball activities, having them understand the usefulness of such activity can be an effective promotional strategy which emphasizes social interactions, communication, or medium level of physical exercises/fitness.

Third, the findings of this study indicated that perceived behavioral control had a greater level of impact on leisure participation behavior (i.e., gateball-playing behavior) than attitude and subjective norm. This implies that senior citizens are more likely to join gateball activities if they have a higher level of the belief in their abilities. In addition, having more spare time, economic sufficiency, and convenient locations for playing gateball all plays an important role of helping senior citizens to engage in such leisure activity.

Fourth, the findings of this study also revealed that friends' influence is the primary factor to have impact on individual decision making for engaging in gateball activity. Though family members and peers are all significant referents, friends are the most influential persons in shaping senior gateball players' view. A plausible reason is that a majority of respondents' friends may consider gateball is a good leisure activity for senior citizens. Encouraging them to participate in such activities can be good for them. This is because gateball is a group activity and having opportunities to interact with others is a part of the game. Through these interactions senior citizens are able to enhance their social connectedness which, in turn, helps reduce social isolation [35]. Prior research also show that better self-reported individual health is positively correlated with higher frequency and number of participating in leisure activities promote health [12].

Several limitations exist in this study. First, due to being unable to obtain a complete population list, purposeful sampling was employed in this study. Therefore, the results of this study cannot be generalized to the entire senior gateball players. Second, the respondents of this study were exclusively senior gateball players. The results of the study are not applicable for other leisure activities. Finally, the levels of gateball activity involvement can be different in skill sets and years of experiences in playing or practices. Therefore, the perception of playing gateball is easy or difficult can be varied. Using perceived ease of use as an example, a player with several years of experiences may consider this leisure activity is easy, but it may not be an easy task for a new player. In fact, such topic has not been fully investigated. Researchers can focus on this direction to develop further investigations.

References

1. Adams, K.B., Leibbrandt, S., Moon, H.: A critical review of the literature on social and leisure activity and wellbeing in later life. Ageing Soc. **31**, 683–712 (2011)
2. Ajzen, I.: The theory of planned behavior. Organ. Behav. Hum. Decis. Process. **50**, 179–211 (1991)
3. Ajzen, I.: Nature and operation of attitudes. Annu. Rev. Psychol. **52**, 27–58 (2001)
4. Ajzen, I., Fishbein, M.: Understanding Attitudes and Predicting Social Behavior. Prentice Hall, Englewood Cliffs (1980)
5. Ajzen, I., Driver, B.L.: Application of the theory of planned behavior to leisure choice. J. Leisure Res. **24**, 207–224 (1992)
6. Armitage, C.J., Conner, M.: Efficacy of the theory of planned behavior: a meta-analytic review. Br. J. Soc. Psychol. **40**, 471–499 (2001)

7. Armitage, C.J., Christian, J.: From attitudes to behaviour: basic and applied research on the Theory of Planned Behaviour. Curr. Psychol. **22**(3), 187–195 (2003)
8. Bagozzi, R.P., Yi, Y.: On the evaluation of structural equation models. J. Acad. Mark. Sci. **16**, 74–94 (1988)
9. Bandura, A.: Self-efficacy mechanism in human agency. Am. Psychol. **37**, 122–147 (1982)
10. Bandura, A.: Self-efficacy: The Exercise of Control. W.H. Freeman, New York (1997)
11. Cardinal, B.J.: Assessing the physical activity of inactive older adults. Adap. Phys. Act. Quart. **14**, 65–73 (1997)
12. Chang, C.M., Chen, N.C., Lin, C.L.: The study on the differences of elementary school students' technological acceptance models between Wii and XBOX-360 KINECT's sports games. J. Sport Leisure Hospitality Res. **7**(2), 103–118 (2012)
13. Chen, Y., Feeley, T.H.: Social support, social strain, loneliness, and well-being among older adults: an analysis of the health and retirement study. J. Soc. Pers. Relat. **31**(2), 141–161 (2014)
14. Curtis, J., Weiler, B., Ham, S.: Identifying beliefs underlying visitor behaviour: a comparative elicitation study based on the Theory of Planned Behaviour. Ann. Leisure Res. **13**(4), 1–22 (2010)
15. Davis, F.D.: Perceived usefulness, perceived ease of use, and user acceptance of information technology. MIS Q. **13**(3), 319–340 (1989)
16. Downs, D.S., Hausenblas, H.A.: Elicitation studies and the Theory of Planned Behavior: a systematic review of exercise beliefs. Psychol. Sport Exerc. **6**, 1–31 (2005)
17. Fishbein, M., Ajzen, I.: Belief, Attitude, Intention, and Behavior: An Introduction to Theory and Research. Addison-Wesley Publishing, Reading (1975)
18. Fornell, C., Larcker, D.F.: Evaluating structural equation models with unobservable and measurement error. J. Mark. Res. **18**, 39–50 (1981)
19. Gallant, M.P., Spitze, G.D., Prohaska, T.R.: Help or hindrance? How family and friends influence chronic illness self-management among older adults. Res. Aging **29**(5), 375–409 (2007)
20. Hair, J.F., Anderson, R.E., Tatham, R.L., Black, W.C.: Multivariate Data Analysis. Prentice Hall, Upper Saddle River (1998)
21. Han, H., Hsu, L.T.J., Sheu, C.: Application of the Theory of Planned Behavior to green hotel choice: testing the effect of environmental friendly activities. Tour. Manag. **31**, 325–334 (2010)
22. Hassmen, P., Koivula, N., Uutela, A.: Physical exercise and psychological well-being: a population study in Finland. Prev. Med. **30**, 17–25 (2000)
23. Hills, P., Argyle, M.: The Oxford happiness questionnaire: a compact scale for the measurement of psychological well-being. Pers. Individ. Differ. **33**, 1073–1082 (2002)
24. Kalab, K.A.: Playing gateball: a game of the Japanese elderly. J. Aging Stud. **6**(1), 23–40 (1992)
25. Lawton, M.P.: Personality and affective correlates of leisure activity participation by older people. J. Leisure Res. **26**, 138–157 (1994)
26. Lay, Y.L.: The effectiveness of how TAM theories enhanced the "perceived playfulness" - a case study of university students' participation of tennis activities for verification. J. Sport Recreat. Res. **2**(4), 122–137 (2008)
27. Leitner, M.J., Leitner, S.F.: Leisure in Later Life. Sagamore Publishing, Urbana (2012)
28. Milne, S., Orbell, S., Sheeran, P.: Combining motivational and volitional interventions to promote exercise participation: protection motivation theory and implementation intentions. Br. J. Health Psychol. **7**(2), 163–184 (2002)

29. Minhat, H.S., Rahmah, M.A., Khadijah, S.: Continuity theory of aging and leisure participation among elderly attending selected health clinics in Selangor. Int. Med. J. Malays. **12**(2), 51–58 (2013)
30. Netz, Y., Wu, M.J., Becker, B.J., Tenenbaum, G.: Physical activity and psychological well-being in advanced age: a meta-analysis of intervention studies. Psychol. Aging **20**(2), 272–284 (2005)
31. Park, C.H., Elavsky, S., Koo, K.M.: Factors influencing physical activity in older adults. J. Exerc. Rehabil. **10**(1), 45–52 (2014)
32. Riddick, C.C., Daniel, S.N.: The relative contribution of leisure activities and other factors to the mental health of old women. J. Leisure Res. **16**(2), 136–148 (1984)
33. Silverstein, M., Parker, M.G.: Leisure activities and quality of life among the oldest old in Sweden. Res. Aging **24**, 528–547 (2002)
34. Taylor, S., Todd, P.A.: Understanding information technology usage: a test of competing models. Inf. Syst. Res. **6**(2), 144–176 (1995)
35. Toepoel, V.: Aging, leisure, and social connectedness: how could leisure help reduce social isolation of older people? Soc. Indic. Res. **113**, 355–372 (2013)
36. Venkatesh, V., Davis, F.D.: The theoretical extension of the Technology Acceptance Model: four longitudinal field studies. Manage. Sci. **46**(2), 186–204 (2000)
37. Xu, J., Roberts, R.E.: The power of positive emotions: it's a matter of life or death – subjective well-being and longevity over 28 years in a general population. Health Psychol. **29**, 9–19 (2010)

Video Recommendation System that Arranges Video Clips Based on Pre-defined Viewing Times

Mitsuhiko Kimoto[1,2(✉)], Tomoki Nakahata[1,2], Takahiro Hirano[1,2],
Takuya Nagashio[1,2], Masahiro Shiomi[2], Takamasa Iio[2,3],
Ivan Tanev[1], and Katsunori Shimohara[1]

[1] Graduate School of Science and Engineering, Doshisha University,
1-3 Tatara Miyakodani, Kyotanabe-shi, Kyoto 610-0321, Japan
{kimoto2013,nakahata2013,hirano2015,
nagashio2015}@sil.doshisha.ac.jp,
{itanev,kshimoha}@mail.doshisha.ac.jp
[2] Intelligent Robotics and Communication Laboratories,
ATR, 2-2-2 Hikaridai, Seika-cho, Soraku-gun, Kyoto 619-0288, Japan
{m-shiomi,iio}@atr.jp
[3] Graduate School of Engineering Science, Osaka University,
1-3 Machikaneyama-cho, Toyonaka-shi, Osaka 560-8531, Japan

Abstract. The popularization of video-viewing systems enables both adults and children to endlessly watch countless video clips. But such long-time video viewing might cause health problems especially for children, but rule-making tendencies are weaker among video-viewing systems than for watching television. Children have difficulty voluntarily curbing their watching of rich video clips because they are so attractive. In this study, we propose a video recommendation system that arranges video clips based on pre-defined times to support parental-mandated video-viewing stops. Our proposed system enables parents to limit the video-viewing time in advance and provides video clips that are arranged to finish exactly at pre-defined times. In this paper, we targeted adults to confirm the effectiveness of our approach. The results suggest that our proposed system increases post-viewing satisfaction.

Keywords: Childcare · Recommendation system · Motivation · Smartphone · Voluntary

1 Introduction

Smartphones are becoming a childcare support device used by parents. For example, they often give their smartphones to children as a video viewer, which even toddlers can control to watch YouTube videos by themselves. In fact, in Japan as of March 2014 the diffusion rate of smartphones among adults in their 20s was 83.7 % [1]. They are also spending more time on the internet than watching television [2]. Their lifestyles are also changing their childcare styles.

However, giving smartphones to children is creating several childcare issues. It is difficult to assume that children will voluntarily curb their smartphone use. Eyesight

S. Yamamoto (Ed.): HIMI 2016, Part II, LNCS 9735, pp. 478–486, 2016.
DOI: 10.1007/978-3-319-40397-7_45

might be harmed by long-sustained smartphone use, which is one serious problem for both parents and children. Even if parents set rules to prevent long-sustained use, such a tendency is more weakly applied to smartphone use than watching television [2]. Japanese mothers are relatively reluctant to intervene in the television-watching habits of their children [3]. The number of children using smartphones is also increasing more and more. It is also difficult to realize punctual smartphone use by children and planned stops. The unlimited contents provided by smartphones are too enticing for children. Such video contents are generally used with smartphones by children [2]. In this study, we propose a system with which parents can limit the duration of the video content watched by children on smartphones, tablets, and other digital devices in a video-viewing context.

Our study has three objectives. Objective one, providing uninterrupted viewing for children. For example, our system engages children's attention while their mothers are busy with housework and unable to give attention to their children. Objective two, children should stop viewing at a pre-set time. Children have difficulty turning off smartphones, and parents often fail to set rules to prevent long-sustained use. Therefore, our system encourages children to stop watching videos. Objective three, they must satisfied. Although it is also possible to mandatorily stop video-viewing, we disagree with such a method.

2   Related Works

Many video recommendation systems have been studied. For example, Deng et al. [4] proposed a personalized video recommendation system based on cross-platform user modeling. Xu et al. [5] proposed a personalized recommendation algorithm for online contents including videos and predicted user interest based on attention times to online contents acquired by eye-tracking. These systems improved recommendation accuracy and provided many suitable videos to users. In contrast, we propose a recommendation system that considers waiting time to discourage children from excessive video viewing.

Some research has focused on the time limitations of video-viewing. CastOven [6], which is a microwave oven with a LCD display that enables people to watch videos while they are cooking dinner, automatically delivers media contents for leisure time. Although they focused on the time limitations of video-viewing, they didn't focus on the video-viewing ending time. We focused on the ending time and self-motivated video-viewing stops for children.

3   Voluntary Stop Support

As mentioned in the introduction, parents are concerned about preventing long-sustained video viewing for various health concerns for their children. Without usage rules for smartphones or other digital devices, many children will constantly use them. We believe that one factor that explains why children cannot stop video viewing is the well-designed recommendation systems of video-sharing websites, whose endless recommendations are designed to encourage more video-viewing based on viewing histories. If we stop using such well-designed systems, children might stop watching videos; however, such an approach would not encourage voluntary stops and children would not be satisfied. We must consider the satisfaction of both parents and children.

Based on these considerations, we developed a system with two approaches to support parental-mandated video-viewing stops. In one approach, a system displays to users appropriate videos that respond to their viewing times. Our proposed system, which reduces endless video-viewing by establishing automatic time limits, is the opposite of existing video recommendation systems that encourage video-viewing. In our second approach, our system makes a video playlist based on keywords and video-viewing time durations input by a parent and provides playlists to children. This function is elaborated in Sect. 4. Our system encourages voluntary stops within limited times set by parents.

4   System Architecture

Figure 1 shows the architecture of our system that uses the YouTube API to show videos to children. This system consists of a controller for parents and a viewer for children. First, the controller sends requests to the viewer to make playlists based on inputted keywords and time durations controlled by parents. Second, based on such information, the viewer searches for appropriate video candidates by accessing You-Tube. Finally, the viewer makes an appropriate playlist, which includes videos based on keywords (Fig. 2). The controller and viewer are directly connected to each other, i.e., a peer-to-peer approach. Moreover, we use HTML and JavaScript to build a platform-independent system. The parents control the playlist properties through the system, which has functions to control the volume and to search for candidate videos using keywords and time durations through YouTube's API. Since the system shows a

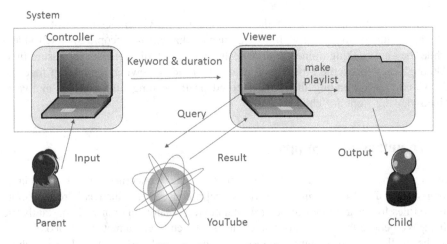

Fig. 1. System architecture

Duration = 10 (minutes)

1-minute video	3-minutes video	2-minutes video	1-minute video	1-minute video	2-minutes video

Fig. 2. Example of playlist

snapshot image of the video being played on the controller, parents can stop the video if its content is inappropriate. The system displays the duration and the playback status of the playlist in the controller. Parents can determine the remaining playback time and decide when the playback will end. For this purpose, the system stores the current playback time and a playlist's ending time. Figure 3 shows a snapshot of our system.

The system also has a function that dynamically remakes the playlist if network delays or video interruptions occur by storing the current playback and the ending times (Fig. 4). If such stoppages happen and the end time of the playback exceeds the playlist's inputted time duration, the system remakes the part of the playlist that was played-back after the interruption and compares the playback's ending time and the playlist's inputted time duration when each video playback is almost finished. If the playback's ending time exceeds the playlist's inputted time duration, the system remakes it and restarts its playback. Since users cannot detect such remaking, they can still enjoy seamless playlist playback. The ending time of the playback doesn't exceed the time duration of an inputted playlist.

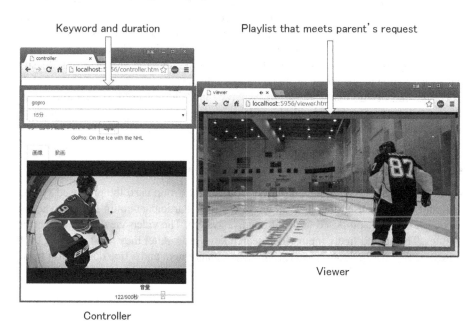

Fig. 3. Snapshot of system

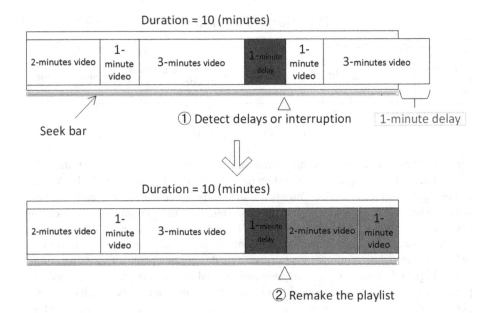

Fig. 4. Remaking playlist due to information delays

5 Experiment

We experimentally targeted adults to confirm our approach's effectiveness. Our participants were 22 college students who viewed videos for ten minutes with both the proposed and alternative systems. Our proposed system makes a playlist based on the inputted time duration and its playback ends at a specified time. The alternative system makes a playlist without considering the inputted time duration and playback doesn't end at a specified time. Instead, users of the alternative system are told the end of video-viewing during playback by the experimenter. Our experiment examined whether participants are satisfied with the video-viewing ending time. To investigate their impressions, we prepared the following 7-point scale questionnaire item and a free description form.

- Were you satisfied with the video-viewing end-timing?

We evenly split the participants into two groups. One group used the proposed system first, and the other used the alternative system first. Participants didn't know whether they were using the proposed or the alternative system. The video-viewing time was ten minutes. They could freely input video search keywords. After they finished using each system, they answered the 7-point scale questionnaire item and a free description form.

6   Results

Figure 5 shows the questionnaire item results for which we conducted a paired t-test. We identified a significant difference among the conditions ($t(21) = -2.493$, $p = .021$, $d = 0.72$), indicating that participants were satisfied with the video-viewing ending time.

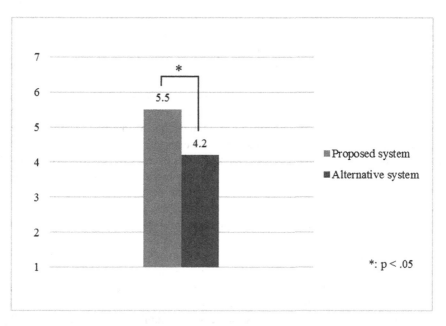

Fig. 5. Questionnaire item: Were you satisfied with the video-viewing end-timing? (Color figure online)

We gathered much free description feedback that contained many favorable remarks about the video-viewing ending time, including "The ending time of the video-viewing was good," and "The ending time felt neither too quick nor too slow."

7   Discussion

7.1   Implications

We experimentally verified the effectiveness of our proposed system that encourages video-viewing stops. It received favorable feedback about the ending time of the playback: "The playlist ended with nice timing" and "The ending time of the playback was good, because it was nicely timed as the video finished." Participants seemed to have such feelings because the proposed system made a playlist based on the inputted time duration and its playback ended at a specified time. The alternative system condition received much negative feedback: "I didn't like being forced to stop viewing in the middle of a video" and "I wanted to see the rest of the video." Participants seemed to have such feelings because they were told the end of video-viewing while they were watching the video. These results suggest that our proposed system creates good ending time for viewing and increases post-viewing satisfaction.

7.2   Limitations

We also got much feedback about the similarity of the displayed videos. Our system doesn't include identical videos in a playlist and it doesn't evaluate such contents. Although some children will repeatedly watch the same video, the viewing motivation of adults might decrease. Future work will consider video contents when making playlists.

In addition, we got feedback about the poor relationships between the inputted search keywords and the displayed videos. Two main causes might explain this problem. First, there were not enough suitable videos for the inputted search keywords on YouTube. The duration of videos often depends on keywords, and if the time duration of many well-related videos to the keywords exceeds the set times of playlists, the candidate videos don't include enough appropriate videos. If there are insufficient well-related videos, YouTube includes poorly related videos in the search results. The system also includes the result in the playlist and displays videos that are unrelated to participant demands. To prevent this problem, we must consider not only a keyword but also a category that provides broader information about user demands while the system makes playlists. The system also uses too many candidate videos to make a playlist. Candidates consist of videos that are ranked in the top 100 YouTube search results, and low-ranked videos are often poorly related to keywords. As a result, playlists sometimes have too few well-related videos that depend on keywords. To prevent this problem, the system must decrease the number of candidate videos for making playlists. If it decreases the number of candidate videos, playlists are more likely to have many well-related videos.

If the number of candidate videos is insufficient, a playlist is more likely to have many well-related videos, but the temporal accuracy of making playlists decreases. Machines face difficult problems achieving good balance between increasing the satisfaction level of playlists and temporal accuracy.

7.3   Future Work

Future works will investigate the effects of video durations and the number of video contained in a playlist toward children's satisfaction. In our experiment, since the system randomly selects videos and makes playlists based on pre-set times, no effects of video duration and number were revealed. Moreover, using the video-viewing history of each child to control playlists might be useful to find appropriate videos. By gathering and analyzing these data, our system could make improved playlists. Related to this topic, sensing children's emotions and behavior might be useful for personalizing videos services. If children are strongly interested in specific videos, the system might recognize them and change playlists.

Another future work is to investigate our system's social acceptance. Shiomi et al. reported that the social acceptance of childcare support systems with sensing or robotics technologies is lower than such popular childcare support technologies as anesthesia during labor and baby food. But they also reported that the experiences of actually using new technologies increased their social acceptance [7]. We believe that the social acceptance of our proposed system will be relatively low during its initial situations, but the actual using experiences will also increase it.

8 Conclusion

We developed a system that restricts children's video-viewing based on parental time limitations and focused on video viewing using YouTube. Our system, which consists of a controller for parents and a viewer for children, makes and shows an appropriate playlist based on keywords and time durations input by parents. Unlike traditional recommendations for video-viewing systems, our proposed system arranges video clips based on pre-defined times to support parental-mandated video-viewing stops.

In this paper, we experimentally targeted adults and identified a significant difference among the conditions, proposed and alternative system, in satisfaction with the video-viewing ending time. This result indicates that our proposed system increases post-viewing satisfaction needed to encourage voluntary stop of video-viewing. We are set to experimentally target children and their parents and verify the effectiveness of our proposed system.

Acknowledgements. This research was supported by the Strategic Information and Communications R&D Promotion Programme (SCOPE), Ministry of Internal Affairs and Communications (132107010).

References

1. MIC, Communications Usage Trend Survey (2013). http://www.soumu.go.jp/johotsusintokei/tsusin_riyou/data/eng_tsusin_riyou02_2013.pdf. Accessed 22 Dec 2015
2. Survey on Media Access of Parent and Child in Japanese. http://berd.benesse.jp/jisedai/research/detail1.php?id=4105. Accessed 22 Dec 2015
3. Komoya, M., Bowyer, J.: College-educated mothers' ideas about television and their active mediation of viewing by three- to five-year-old children japan and the U.S.A. J. Broadcast. Electron. Media **44**(3), 349–363 (2000)
4. Deng, Z., Sang, J., Xu, C.: Personalized video recommendation based on cross-platform user modeling. In: 2013 IEEE International Conference on Multimedia and Expo, San Jose, pp. 1–6 (2013)
5. Xu, S., Jiang, H., Lau, F.C.M.: Personalized online document, image and video recommendation via commodity eye-tracking. In: The 2008 ACM Conference on Recommender Systems, Lausanne, pp. 83–90 (2008)

6. Watanabe, K., Matsuda, S., Yasumura, M., Inami, M., Igarashi, T.: CastOven: a microwave oven with just-in-time video clips. In: The 12th ACM International Conference Adjunct Papers on Ubiquitous Computing, Copenhagen, pp. 385–386 (2010)
7. Shiomi, M., Hagita, N.: Social acceptance of a childcare support robot system. In: 24th IEEE International Symposium on Robot and Human Interactive Communication, Kobe, pp. 13–18 (2015)

Diminished Agency: Attenuating a Sense of Agency for Problem Finding on Personal Physical Performance

Sho Sakurai[1,2(✉)], Yuki Ban[2], Nami Ogawa[3], Takuji Narumi[2], Tomohiro Tanikawa[2], and Michitaka Hirose[2]

[1] Graduate School of System Design,
Tokyo Metropolitan University, Tokyo, Japan
[2] Graduate School of Information Science and Technology,
The University of Tokyo, Bunkyō, Japan
{sho,ban,narumi,tani,hirose}@cyber.t.u-tokyo.ac.jp
[3] Graduate School of Interdisciplinary Information Studies,
The University of Tokyo, Bunkyō, Japan
ogawa@cyber.t.u-tokyo.ac.jp

Abstract. A feeling that "I controlling this" is called as the sense of agency (SA). Recently, there have been many studies for improving motor skill through making perception that the passive bodily movement caused by observation of the other's movement or a machine operation as active movement. However, these methods cannot impress the problems of self-motion. In this regard, we hypothesize that observation of himself/herself from third-party's point of view and improving skill of finding problem of self-motion is possible when self-motion is perceived as an other person's motion based on mechanism of SA. In this paper, we propose "Diminished agency" to attenuate SA from observing self-motion for the finding problem involved motor-skill based on the findings a sense of ownership (SO) influences SA. This paper summarizes finding mechanism of SA and discusses the feasibility of "Diminished agency."

Keywords: Diminished agency · Sense of agency · Sense of ownership · Problem finding skill

1 Introduction

To enhance a skill of the sports or passing traditional techniques, learners have to be aware of good or bad points of their motions [1]. If we are aware of a problem in our motions, we can revise them effectively and can get the skills.

As the previous method of behavior analysis, two types of method are mainly used for analyzing ourselves, an introspection and an observing others. The latter is the method in that a professional outsider for some motion techniques observes our motions, and reveals the problems. In this method, the lack of skills or knowledge of these specialists is possible to decrease the quality of training and to make learners' motions worse. Therefore with this method we need a specialist with high skills, so it is not easy to use this method in our daily life. On the other hand, introspection is a

© Springer International Publishing Switzerland 2016
S. Yamamoto (Ed.): HIMI 2016, Part II, LNCS 9735, pp. 487–493, 2016.
DOI: 10.1007/978-3-319-40397-7_46

method in that learners observe themselves objectively using a video recording, and reveal the wrong points of their physical exercises. This method does not need a specialist and is useful in a daily life. In the phase in that we reveal our good or bad points by observing ourselves, It is important that we can observe us as others. However, for our own performances, the cognitive bias can be occurred with which it is hard to analyze or to evaluate our performance precisely. Especially, it is difficult to aware of self-problem for learners who have gotten a skill to some extent.

In this regard, recently the engineering field has tried to research for getting a motor skill by focusing on the sense of agency (SA). SA means the subjective feeling that we do some work by ourselves [2].

These main studies use the method that informs the motion by making users perceive passive motions directed by some machines, as their own active motion. For example, Mizushina et al. proposed the method that evokes the sense of agency by making users relive a motion of playing the badminton from the first-person view [3]. This system displays the vibration stimuli on the racket that a leaner has in actual, when a specialist hit a shuttle on his or her racket in the video. These stimuli makes users feel as if they can perform and hit a shuttle like a specialist, by evoking the sense of agency to the motion of a specialist in a video. Ikei et al. also propose a system named "five sense system" for making a feeling as if a user walks actively although the user sitting on a chair by presents vestibulohaptic and vibration sensation resembles walking bodily movements [4].

However, simulating all the movements of an expert is inefficient when a learner's skill is more excellent than the expert up to a certain phase. These methods also can not solve the fundamental problem for finding problem of self-motor skill since it is difficult to impress the reason of changing self-motion.

We hypothesize that cognitive bias caused by SA at the time of self-motor skill analysis would be removed by not enhancing SA toward external person's motion but diminishing SA from self-motion. Based on the hypothesis, we propose "Diminished agency" for attenuating SA from self-motion reflected picture images.

First, this paper digests findings about the mechanism of SA. Then this paper introduces the concept of "diminished agency" for improving problem finding skill and discusses the feasibility of our proposed concept based on our past works.

2   The Senses of Agency and Ownership as Foundation of Self-recognition

The sense of agency (SA) is a mechanism of recognizing the agent of behavior or action as ownself. During working state or movements, SA is considered that evokes when perceived deep sensation and visual feedback caused by intentional movement and matches the prediction of its [2].

SA has close relationship with the sense of ownership (SO). SO is a mechanism of distinguishing oneself from the external environment [5]. In other words, SO is the subjective feeling that "This is myself." SA and SO are regarded as the principal of self-awareness [6].

In general, SO is felt only for self-body. However, SO has been known to also occur for the things outside the body. As a representative example, it has rubber hand illusion well known. Rubber hand illusion is a phenomenon that a rubber hand front of the eye has come to be perceived as a part of a self-body when self-hand and rubber hand are traced with a brush at the same time with covering self-hand [7].

However, SO is less likely to occur if the appearance of the observed object is different from self-hand. For example, SO does not occur when the rubber hand with hand consisted tree branches or when the rubber hand placed in the direction from the rotation 90° of the self-hand [8].

These phenomena occurs since SO is perceived by matching of visual and deep sensation obtained through bodily movement. Generally, the core sensation for a range of self-body is deep sensation. The body perceived by the deep sensation is referred to as "body schema" [9, 10]. However, the range of body recognized in the brain flexibly changes due to the interaction of visual and deep sensation. In this regard, it is clarified that five factors, including spatial continuity, skin texture, shape, coherency of visual-tactile sensation and coherency of visual-motion influence in evoking SO.

Various studies also confirmed the influence of SO in SA. For example, when hitting the virtual drum with image-based computer graphic (CG) hand reflects the movement of the self-hand motion in a virtual environment, the CG-hand is felt as not to reflect the movement of self-hand if the color of the CG-hand is significantly different from the actual hand color [11]. Also, the perception of momentum and position of self-hand in the virtual environment is also influenced by the apparent momentum and position CG hand [12].

In this way, the apparent characteristics and movements of the body affect not only SO but also SA. Based on these findings, in this paper, we propose a method for eliminating SA by modifying apparent bodily characteristics or movement during exercise that are visually observed (Fig. 1).

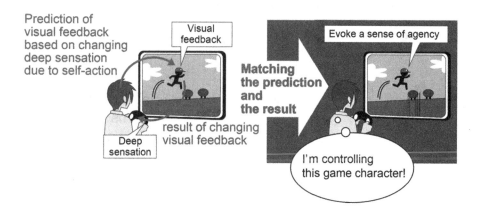

Fig. 1. The sense of agency

3 Diminished Agency

3.1 Concept of Diminished Agency

The concept of the "Diminished agency" shown in Fig. 2. "Diminished agency" is a method for attenuating SA by modifying the apparent cues of self-body that affect a SO. As described in Sect. 1, the main purpose of the conventional method for improving performance skill through controlling SA is to understand bodily movement of an expert as if the bodily movement of the learner. However, the purpose of "Diminished agency" is improving the skill of finding problem of the learner's bodily movement by making the learner realized that oneself s/he looks is not myself by the use of the mechanism of SA.

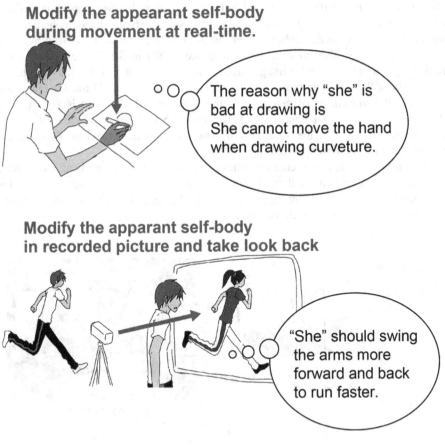

Fig. 2. Diminished agency

As they say "you can better yourself by observing others," many people would be able to find problems of oneself by standing in a position to teach to a third party.

In this paper, we discuss the feasibility of "Diminished agency" for improving the skill of finding problem and acquiring a user's motor skill.

3.2 Findings Obtained from Previous Works

Researchers have discussed that how these factors affect each other and which factor affect stronger than others for a long time. However, it has not been revealed that the range of expansion of the body schema and how we can control it concretely. Besides, the effect of the Rubber Hand Illusion like [7] is individuality, so the how the SO changes is different person to person although the condition of these factors are same.

In this regard, we are now trying to investigate the effect in the SO and its relationship between these factors described above, when some factors are completely different from what a subject actually has. For this investigation, we constructed an artwork called "Metamorphosis Hand", which provides users with a pseudo-experience of playing a virtual piano with a dynamically transforming body [13]. This system enables users to play a virtual piano, and gives users an illusion as if their own hands' shape or texture are modified by synchronizing a user's motion and an audiovisual feedback to evoke a pseudo haptic sensation.

The pattern of deformation for a CG-hand that this system displays are following four patterns: texture of a skin, modification of a shape, a visuo-motor asynchrony and modification of a shape with a visuo-motor asynchrony.

Through the exhibition, we investigated that how these modifications affect the sense of body ownership for the CG-hand. More than 400 people experienced the system. Overall, most people seemed to have bizarre or peculiar feelings because even though the shapes differed considerably from their own, they felt a strong sense of body ownership. On the contrary, when the movements of the left and right hands were exchanged, most people could not understand what happened to their virtual hands and they seemed to have difficulty in completely controlling their virtual hands at will. Therefore, in this pattern, they did not feel the sense of body ownership to the CG-hands.

In this exhibition, we also asked users that *"Do you feel that you playing the piano with your own hand?"*. Many of the users told positive answer to this question when they tried with virtual hands, which texture or shape was modified. However, when the visuo-motor synchronization was broken, they did not feel the sense of body ownership.

This study suggested that modification of the CG-hand's shape or texture does not reduce the sense of body ownership, even if the visuo-motor synchronization is remaining. However, to realize "Diminished Agency," it can be hard to analyze a body motion or to extract points for revising the behavior, if the difference between actual body motion and virtual body motion. Therefore, we should precisely consider the range of modification of physical feature with which the system can show oneself in a video as others while keeping the features of a body motion.

Furthermore, we will consider how the reality of the virtual body affects the sense of body ownership and agency, especially the difference of effect between an image based virtual hand and a CG-hand. Argelaguet et al. revealed that there is no specific need to provide realistic avatar representation to increase the sense of agency [14]. Besides, they also revealed that the sense of ownership is dependent on the virtual representation of the virtual hand and the need of morphological resemblance is required to increase the sense of ownership. As this study, we should consider which method is more suitable for diminishing agency, using an image-based body or a CG-body.

There is also need to examine the effect of our proposed method on the changes in SA and SO and the skill of finding problem of self-motion. In this regarding of the evaluation of SA and SO, various rating scales have been proposed [7, 12, 15, 16]. Besides, we will evaluate our proposed method on the skill of finding problem of self-motion by comparing the numbers of found problems when a user watch actual picture of self-motion with the numbers when the user watch picture of modified appearance bodily characteristics. We also plan to conduct the same experience on expert of the skill for following investigations: whether our proposed method does not obstruct correctly observation of self-motion and whether there are differences in finding problem skill due to the skill of the observer.

Our proposed method might have little effect on evoking SA. For example, there is a report that the morphological resemblance is not the decisive factor for changing SA [17]. However, it is highly predictable that modified the appearance of the bodily characteristics changes the impression in skill s/he has. In this regard, Suzuki et al. shown that converting the sonority of a male operator's voice into a female's voice improves impression of the operator and increases during simple task even if the actual operator's gender is understood [18]. Considering based on this finding, our proposed method would have an effect on problem finding ability due to changes in the self-impression even if the SA is completely removed from observed self-motion. Therefore, evaluation of the proposed method is given to the impact the problem finding the ability to give to the SA and SO will be going performed in parallel.

We will evaluate and demonstrate the effect of "Diminished agency" through these experiments.

4 Conclusion

In this paper, we proposed "Diminished agency," that is a method for finding problems of self-motion. Our approach attenuates a sense of agency from observing self-motion by changing apparent bodily characteristics, which can influence on a sense of ownership based on findings about SA, SO and feedback for our past work.

In the future, we will advance the implementation and evaluation of the method we developed. We will also investigate other methods for eliminating SA by the use of factors related SA and SO. In addition, we are planning to investigate how attenuate not only SA from self-hand motion but also motion of other parts of the body or the full body. Through these investigations, we aim for the realization of "Diminished agency."

References

1. Zimmerman, B.J.: Becoming a self-regulated learner: an overview. Theory Pract. **41**(2), 64–70 (2002)
2. Jeannerod, M.: The mechanism of self-recognition in human. Behav. Brain Res. **142**, 1–15 (2003)
3. Mizushina, Y., Fujiwara, W., Sudou, T., Fernando, C.L., Minamizawa, K., Tachi, S.: Interactive instant replay: sharing sports experience using 360-degrees spherical images and haptic sensation based on the coupled body motion. In: Proceedings of the 6th Augmented Human International Conference, AH 2015, pp. 227–228. ACM, New York (2015)
4. Ikei, Y., Abe, K., Hirota, K., Amemiya, T.: A multisensory VR system exploring the ultra-reality. In: Proceedings of the 18th International Conference on Virtual Systems and Multimedia (VSMM 2012), pp. 71–78 (2012)
5. Gallagher, S.: Philosophical conceptions of the self: implications for cognitive science. Trends Cogn. Sci. **4**, 14–21 (2000)
6. Tsakiris, M., Schütz-Bosbach, S., Gallagher, S.: On agency and body-ownership: phenomenological and neurocognitive reflections. Conscious. Cogn. **16**, 645–660 (2007)
7. Botvinick, M., Cohen, J.: Rubber hands 'feel' touch that eyes see. Nature **391**(6669), 756 (1998)
8. Tsakiris, M., Haggard, P.: The rubber hand illusion revisited: visuotactile integration and self-attribution. J. Exp. Psych. **31**(1), 80–91 (2005)
9. Ramachandran, V., Blakeslee, S.: Phantoms in the Brain. William Morrow, New York (1998)
10. Schwoebel, J., Coslett, H.B.: Evidence for multiple, distinct representations of the human body. J. Cogn. Neurosci. **4**(17), 543–553 (2005)
11. Kilteni, K., Bergstrom, I., Slater, M.: Drumming in immersive virtual reality: the body shapes the way we play. IEEE Trans. Vis. Comput. Graph. **19**(4), 597–605 (2013)
12. Armel, K.C., Ramachandran, V.S.: Projecting sensations to external objects: evidence from skin conductance response. Proc. R. Soc. B, Biol. Sci. **270**, 1499–1506 (2003)
13. Ogawa, N., Ban, Y., Sakurai, S., Narumi, T., Tanikawa, T., Hirose, M.: Metamorphosis hand: dynamically transforming hands. In: Proceedings of the 7th Augmented Human International Conference 2016, AH 2016. ACM, New York (2016). Article 51:2
14. Argelaguet, F., Hoyet, L., Trico, M., Lécuyer, A.: The role of interaction in virtual embodiment: effects of the virtual hand representation. Proc. IEEE VR **2016**, 3–10 (2016)
15. Honma, M., Koyama, S., Osada, Y.: Double tactile sensations evoked by a single visual stimulus on a rubber hand. Neurosci. Res. **65**, 307–311 (2009)
16. Asai, T., Sugimori, E., Tanno, Y.: Schizotypal personality traits and atypical lateralization in motor and language functions. Brain Cogn. **71**, 26–37 (2009)
17. Short, F., Ward, R.: Virtual limbs and body space: critical features for the distinction between body space and near body space. J. Psychol. Hum. Percept. Perform. **35**(4), 1092–1103 (2009)
18. Suzuki, K., Yokoyama, M., Kinoshita, Y., Mochizuki, T., Yamada, T., Sakurai, S., Narumi, T., Tanikawa, T., Hirose, M.: Enhancing effect of mediated social touch between same gender by changing gender impression. In: Proceedings of the 7th Augmented Human (AH 2016) (2016). Article 17:8

Evaluating Hedonic and Eudaimonic Motives in Human-Computer Interaction

Katie Seaborn[(⊠)]

University of Toronto, Toronto, Canada
kseaborn@mie.utoronto.ca

Abstract. New measures of well-being are drawing the attention of researchers and practitioner in human factors generally and human-computer interaction (HCI) in particular. Following in the footsteps of previous scholarly endeavours in hedonic well-being (HWB), this paper argues for the adoption of eudaimonic well-being (EWB) in explorations of well-being in HCI. To this end, I report on initial findings from research in which I have evaluated the impact of hedonic and eudaimonic motives on gaming experience using a validated instrument developed by psychologists and adapted for use in HCI contexts.

Keywords: Human factors · Human-computer interaction · Interaction design · Quality of life · Well-being · Hedonia · Eudaimonia · Motivation · Theory

1 Introduction

Well-being, or quality of life, is a multifarious term that is often used loosely—without operationalization or theoretical or conceptual backing—within human-computer interaction (HCI) research. The term, however, has a rich and complex history in psychology, where it has been conceptualized, operationalized, and validated within several complementary frameworks. Taking inspiration from this domain, some scholars in HCI and the broader domain of human factors/ergonomics (HF/E) have adopted theory, conceptual frameworks, and measures from psychology to explore how design can and does impact well-being factors. As yet, the greater part of this work has focused on the hedonic, or pleasure-oriented [1], perspective. However, another perspective within the philosophical tradition of well-being as well as more recently established in psychological research needs to be considered: the eudaimonic, or personal growth and realization, perspective [2]. In the first half of this paper, I discuss the nature of this new measure, its history and conceptualization within psychology, and its relevance to HF/E and HCI. In the second half, I present and discuss the results of the use of a validated psychological instrument for evaluating hedonic and eudaimonic motives in an HCI context; these findings are an extension of those reported in [3]. The main contributions are: (a) a theoretically- and empirically-backed rationale on the importance of including a eudaimonic perspective in studies of well-being in HF/E and HCI, and (b) a demonstration of how a psychological tool that assesses hedonia and eudaimonia can be successfully adapted for use by human factors researchers in HCI contexts.

© Springer International Publishing Switzerland 2016
S. Yamamoto (Ed.): HIMI 2016, Part II, LNCS 9735, pp. 494–500, 2016.
DOI: 10.1007/978-3-319-40397-7_47

2 Well-Being in Psychology

In psychology, hedonic and eudaimonic perspectives on well-being have been associated with several theories and measured using different instruments. I discuss the most well-known and often used here; see Huta and Waterman [4] for an in-depth review. Waterman [2] developed a scale of personal expressiveness to distinguish eudaimonia from hedonia, and was successful in this regard. Ryan et al. [5] made parallels between self-determination theory (SDT) and eudaimonia, concluding that living a eudaimonic life involves pursuing intrinsic goals, positive relationships, and competency, while being autonomous and mindful. Ryff and Singer [6] drew from the philosophical roots of eudaimonia to argue for conceptualizing Ryff's psychological well-being scale as a eudaimonic measure. Most recently, Huta and colleagues developed an activity-based, individual-level instrument for measuring hedonic and eudaimonic motives [7]; it is this instrument that I have adopted in my research, as discussed further in this paper.

In response to this diversity of approaches and measures, Huta and Waterman [4] created a framework for understanding the differences and incongruities among these and other applications of hedonic and eudaimonic well-being. In particular, they noted that well-being has been approached as orientational (including values and motives), behavioural (shown through activities), experiential (affective and cognitive states), and functional (based on evaluations and mental health status), leading to different outcomes that are hard to compare or conceptualize across studies. Additionally, different approaches have evaluated either state (in the moment or with a given activity) or trait (typical, underlying patterns) levels, which can make comparisons difficult. They conclude that consciously choosing and stating one's choice of approach using this framework will increase conceptual congruity, illuminate relationships between different measures, and more easily allow for cross-study comparisons. As researchers in HCI, it would behoove us to follow suit when adopting psychological measures of hedonic and eudaimonic well-being in our own research.

3 A Brief History of Well-Being in HF/E and HCI

Researchers in HF/E drew on the philosophical roots and namesake of hedonia in the creation of a new domain of study and model of human factors called "hedonomics." Since then, hedonomics has followed a somewhat tumultuous path: initially broadly conceptualized as affective human factors [8, 9], it was then constrained to maximizing pleasurable experiences through design [10], but subsequently broadened again into an affective design framework [11], and presumably eclipsed by other efforts in affective design over the last decade, perhaps due to conceptual imprecision. Recently, my colleagues and I have proposed a return to adopting psychological measures of well-being in HF/E by revisiting the hedonomics model: revising the model for conceptual congruency with the psychological literature on hedonia, and expanding the model to account for a newly advanced, complementary perspective—eudaimonia—for a robust model of well-being [12]. Eudaimonia, first proposed by Waterman over two decades ago [2], addresses the personal growth side of well-being: personal expressiveness, self-actualization, and realizing one's full potential [1]. However, it has not received the same amount of attention in psychology as hedonia, and the view that both (if not other) perspectives should be considered jointly in studies of well-being is relatively recent, appearing shortly after the creation of hedonomics [1, 4]. As such, eudaimonia is a new measure in HF/E with great potential to enliven and strengthen research on well-being within our domain.

4 Evaluating Eudaimonia and Hedonia in HCI: A Case Study

For my research, I have adopted the Hedonic and Eudaimonic Motives for Activities (HEMA) scale [7] as a tool to measure the impact of well-being motives on various factors in an HCI context. Here, I discuss how the instrument was adapted, the nature of the particular context of use, and initial statistical results.

4.1 The HEMA Scale

The HEMA scale assesses the subjective effect of hedonic and eudaimonic motives following a particular activity, event, or experience. The scale uses the most common conceptualizations of hedonia and eudaimonia in psychology; see Table 1.

Table 1. A comparison of hedonia and eudaimonia in the HEMA scale

Subscale	Hedonia	Eudaimonia
Operationalizations	Pleasure	Authenticity
	Absence of pain (seeking rather than avoiding)	Excellence
		Growth

The HEMA scale takes an orientation approach to assessing well-being: it assesses the impact of well-being motivation rather than well-being as an outcome. Additionally, unlike other instruments, it presents hedonia and eudaimonia as parallel concepts in the form of subscales that are distinct and can be compared. The revised version of the scale (HEMA-R) allows for state-level (current, activity-based) and trait-level (typical, overarching) evaluations [13]. It has been successfully deployed in several studies, e.g., [14, 15], but as it has not, beyond the case study discussed in this paper, been used in HCI research. Even so, the scale is ideal because the delivery of the scale is flexible, with instructions and items being easily adapted for use in evaluations that involve an HCI context. For instance, we can take "During the [activity], how much were you seeking enjoyment?" and adapt it to read "During the game, how much were you seeking enjoyment?" without losing the original meaning of the item. The recommended response scale is the Likert scale, which is well-known among HCI researchers and well-used in HCI research, thus allowing comparisons among disparate constructs. The full instrument is available for download on Dr. Huta's website.

4.2   Context of Use: Cooperative Puzzle Game

For my research, I am developing a mixed reality gaming platform designed to improve the well-being of older adults who use powered chairs, such as mobility scooters and electric wheelchairs. The platform requires power mobility and the participation of someone who does not use a powered mobility aid. This setup allows me to address the well-being of the older adult group in two ways: internally, through performance mastery, and externally, through empathy training of a non-powered chair user who is a friend, family member, or stranger. In the present paper, I focus on the game prototype stage, which features networked web-based gameplay in the traditional interaction paradigm of desktop computing.

The game is a cooperative puzzle game with a space setting (Fig. 1). The goal of the game is to create a constellation by drawing lines between paired stars. The challenge is that each player can only see their own stars, and thus only has access to paired star information for their own stars. Thus, the gameplay strongly encourages cooperation between players so that they can achieve the common goal of constellation formation by sharing information about their stars.

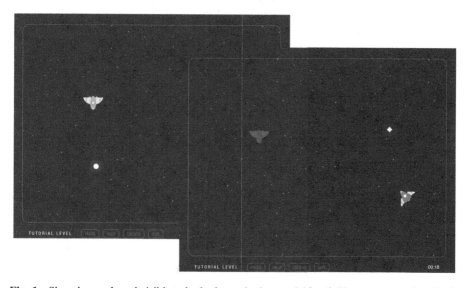

Fig. 1. Shared game board visible to both players in the tutorial level. Players can see the other's position through a ghostly image on their own screens, but cannot see each other's stars. Notice the absence of the blue player's star (right) on the red player's screen (left). (Color figure online)

In the web-based game prototype, two laptop computers are networked through a Node.js- and Socket.io-powered server that passes along information about the game and players in realtime. The game was developed using an HTML5 game engine powered by jQuery, a JavaScript library. In this version, players use the arrow and enter keys on their respective keyboards to control their spaceship avatars. The mixed reality version will feature a shared game board projected in physical space on the floor, over which players will move in their powered chairs; display of private star information and selection of stars will be facilitated by a tablet attached to each chair.

4.3   Case Study

Methods. As part of the larger usability study on the efficacy of the game prototype, well-being motives were gathered using the HEMA scale and compared to usability items (ease of use, ease of learning, and satisfaction); see [3] for initial results gathered by the halfway point with about half of the participants. The present data set includes nineteen participants in ten pairs comprised of older powered chair users and a friend, family member, or stranger; one participant did not have a partner and instead participated with one of the principal investigators, hence one missing data point. The procedure involved participants completing a pre-questionnaire, playing the game together, and filling out a post-questionnaire, in which the HEMA scale was included.

Results. A summary of the results for the HEMA scale are presented graphically in Fig. 2. Descriptive statistics are presented in Table 2.

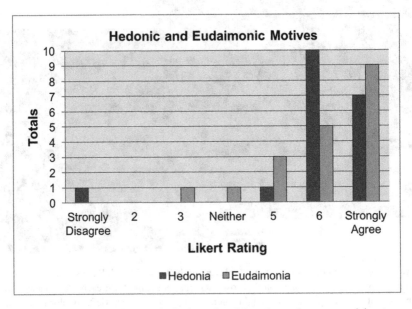

Fig. 2. Bar graph showing hedonic and eudaimonic motives per participant

Table 2. Descriptive statistics for hedonic and eudaimonic motives

Variable	Median	Range	Min	Max	Kurtosis	Skew
Hedonia	6	6	1	7	12	−3.2
Eudaimonia	6.5	4	3	7	1.5	−1.3

Kolmogorov-Smirnov tests of normality indicated that hedonic $(KS(19) = .36, p > .001)$ and eudaimonic motives $(KS(19) = .26, p = .001)$ were not normally distributed. A related-samples Wilcoxon Signed Rank test indicated that hedonic and eudaimonic motive scores were not significantly different.

A Kendall's tau test showed that hedonic and eudaimonic motives are significantly correlated, $r_\tau = .64, p = .002$. In comparing to usability items, Kendall's tau tests found significant correlations between hedonic motives and ease of use, $r_\tau = .72, p < .001$, eudaimonic motives and ease of use, $r_\tau = .69, p < .001$, hedonic motives and ease of learning, $r_\tau = .42, p = .006$, eudaimonic motives and ease of learning, $r_\tau = .59$, $p = .009$, and hedonic motives and satisfaction, $r_\tau = .69, p = .003$.

Discussion. These results suggest that most participants were strongly motivated by hedonic and eudaimonic factors. This makes sense in the context of an entertainment platform that involves a shared performance-based task, i.e. solving a puzzle cooperatively. Individual participants tended to be motivated by hedonic and eudaimonic well-being in the same way; additionally, a strong, statistically significant relationship was found between hedonic and eudaimonic motives. These results are congruous with the psychological literature, which expects a correlation between these constructs and for individuals to score each in the same way [7].

Well-being motives correlated to two of the measures of usability assessed in this study: ease of use and ease of learning. Given that hedonic and eudaimonic motives are expected to have some overlapping effects [7], this outcome is not unexpected. However, only hedonic motives correlated with satisfaction, the third usability measure. One way this result might be understood is by interpreting satisfaction as a measure of affect; this way, this result matches previous findings in psychology that found similar correlations between well-being motives and positive affect [7]. However, we cannot be sure of this interpretation of satisfaction. Additionally, the psychological outcome of life satisfaction, which refers to a general sense or longitudinal satisfaction with one's life, may be translated into an HCI context as satisfaction in general with the technology or experience under study. If this is valid, then we would expect hedonic and eudaimonic motives to correlate with satisfaction; however, in this study, they did not. More research is needed to explicate the notion of satisfaction as a usability outcome before we can draw conclusions on the nature of these correlations compared to potentially parallel constructs evaluated in the psychological literature.

5   Conclusions

While they may be new concepts to many HCI researchers and practioners, the hedonia and eudaimonia have a solid history in the domain psychology. Further, initial efforts to incorporate hedonia into HF/E models and frameworks have set the stage for a wider view of well-being in research on human-technology interactions. In particular, there is room and precedent for extending existing models to include eudaimonia, hedonia's conceptual pair in philosophical tradition and modern empirical work. As demonstrated through the case study of a cooperative puzzle game, existing instruments developed by psychologists can be easily adopted for use in studies of HCI. Future work will explore the efficacy of these tools in assessing the role of well-being and the impact on well-being in other HF/E and HCI contexts, as well as clarify the relationships, if any, between HF/E and HCI variables (e.g., usability) and well-being motives/outcomes.

Acknowledgements. I would like to thank Drs. Peter Pennefather and Deb Fels for their help with exploring the psychological well-being literature. I would also like to thank Variety Village for recruitment assistance and providing the study space. Finally, I thank the participants for their interest and involvement. This work was funded in part by the National Sciences and Engineering Council of Canada (NSERC).

References

1. Deci, E.L., Ryan, R.M.: Hedonia, eudaimonia, and well-being: an introduction. J. Happiness Stud. **9**, 1–11 (2008)
2. Waterman, A.S.: Two conceptions of happiness: contrasts of personal expressiveness (eudaimonia) and hedonic enjoyment. J. Pers. Soc. Psychol. **64**, 678–691 (1993)
3. Seaborn, K., Fels, D.I., Pennefather, P.: A cooperative game for older powered chair users and their friends and family. In: Proceedings of the 7th IEEE Consumer Electronics Society Games, Entertainment, Media Conference, pp. 52–55. IEEE, Toronto (2015)
4. Huta, V., Waterman, A.S.: Eudaimonia and its distinction from hedonia: developing a classification and terminology for understanding conceptual and operational definitions. J. Happiness Stud. **15**, 1425–1456 (2013)
5. Ryan, R.M., Huta, V., Deci, E.L.: Living well: a self-determination theory perspective on eudaimonia. J. Happiness Stud. **9**, 139–170 (2008)
6. Ryff, C.D., Singer, B.H.: Know thyself and become what you are: a eudaimonic approach to psychological well-being. J. Happiness Stud. **9**, 13–39 (2008)
7. Huta, V., Ryan, R.M.: Pursuing pleasure or virtue: the differential and overlapping well-being benefits of hedonic and eudaimonic motives. J. Happiness Stud. **11**, 735–762 (2010)
8. Helander, M.G.: Hedonomics—affective human factors design. In: Proceedings of the Human Factors and Ergonomics Society 46th Annual Meeting, pp. 978–982. SAGE, Baltimore (2002)
9. Helander, M.G., Tham, M.P.: Editorial: hedonomics—affective human factors design. Ergonomics **46**, 1269–1282 (2003)
10. Hancock, P.A., Pepe, A.A., Murphy, L.L.: Hedonomics: the power of positive and pleasurable ergonomics. Ergon. Des. **13**, 8–14 (2005)
11. Helander, M.G., Khalid, H.M.: Underlying theories of hedonomics for affective and pleasurable design. In: Proceedings of the Human Factors and Ergonomics Society 49th Annual Meeting, pp. 1691–1695. SAGE, Orlando (2005)
12. Seaborn, K., Fels, D.I., Pennefather, P.: Eudaimonia in human factors research and practice: foundations and conceptual framework applied to older adult populations. In: Proceedings of the 1st International Conference on Information and Communication Technologies for Ageing Well and e-Health, pp. 313–318. SCITEPRESS, Lisbon (2015)
13. Huta, V.: The complementary roles of eudaimonia and hedonia and how they can be pursued in practice. In: Joseph, S. (ed.) Positive Psychology in Practice: Promoting Human Flourishing in Work, Health, Education, and Everyday Life, 2nd edn., pp. 216–246. Wiley, Hoboken (2015). (Chap. 10)
14. Asano, R., Igarashi, T., Tsukamoto, S.: The Hedonic and Eudaimonic Motives for Activities (HEMA) in Japan: the pursuit of well-being. Japan. J. Psychol. **85**, 69–79 (2014)
15. Huta, V., Pelletier, L.G., Baxter, D., Thompson, A.: How eudaimonic and hedonic motives relate to the well-being of close others. J. Positive Psychol. **7**, 399–404 (2012)

Personalized Real-Time Sleep Stage from Past Sleep Data to Today's Sleep Estimation

Yusuke Tajima[1(✉)], Tomohiro Harada[2], Hiroyuki Sato[1],
and Keiki Takadama[1]

[1] The University of Electro-Communications, Tokyo, Japan
y_tajima@cas.hc.uec.ac.jp, sato@hc.uec.ac.jp,
keiki@inf.uec.ac.jp
[2] Department of Human and Computer Intelligence,
Ritsumeikan University, Kyoto, Shiga, Japan
harada@ci.ritsumei.ac.jp

Abstract. This paper focuses on the real-time sleep stage estimation and proposes the method which appropriately selects the past sleep data as the *prior knowledge* for improving accuracy of the sleep stage estimation. The prior knowledge in this paper is represented as the parameters for estimating the sleep stage and it is composed of 26 parameters which give an influence to the accuracy of the real-time sleep stage estimation. Concretely, these parameters are acquired from the heartbeat data of a certain *past* day, and they are used to estimate the heartbeat data of a *current* day, which data is finally converted to the sleep stage. The role of the proposed method is to select the appropriate parameters of the heartbeat data of a certain *past* day, which is similar to the heartbeat data of a *current* day. To investigate the effectiveness of the proposed method, we conducted the human subject experiment which investigated the accuracy of the real-time sleep stage estimation of two adult males (whose age are 20 and 40) and one adult female (whose age is 60) by employing the appropriate parameters of the different day from three days. The experimental results revealed that the accuracy of the real-time sleep stage estimation with the proposed method is higher than that without it.

Keywords: Sleep stage estimation · Real-time monitoring · Evolutionary computation

1 Introduction

We often take various actions according to past experience in the same situation. For example, when we decide a menu of the dinner, the choice of the meal of the dinner is affected by the meal of several days. This example describes the conscious action, but it is unclear whether it is true in the unconscious action such as sleep. Concretely, we do not know how the sleep of the current day is affected by the sleep of several past days. If some kinds of relationship are found between the sleep of the current day and that of the past days, the sleep stage (which indicates the deepness/lightness of the sleep) can be estimated by using such a relationship. More importantly, if the current sleep stage is estimated by the past sleep data, the accuracy of the *real-time* sleep stage estimation

© Springer International Publishing Switzerland 2016
S. Yamamoto (Ed.): HIMI 2016, Part II, LNCS 9735, pp. 501–510, 2016.
DOI: 10.1007/978-3-319-40397-7_48

can be improved. From this fact, this paper focuses on the real-time sleep stage estimation and proposes the method which appropriately selects the past sleep data as the *prior knowledge* for improving accuracy of the sleep stage estimation.

This paper is organized as follows. The next section introduces the real-time sleep stage estimation method. The method of personalized the prior knowledge is described in Sect. 3. Section 4 conducts the experiment and discusses the results. Finally, our conclusion is given in Sect. 5.

2   Real-Time Sleep Stage Estimation

2.1   Overview

The sleep that is the action that we take much time and do routinely, but many people will spend it whether own sleep is healthy without knowing it. If we want to know own sleep, we are necessary many processes [4]. Because to know own sleep is difficult unlike knowing the numerical value like the weight, blood pressure, temperature. Specifically, we obtain sleep data by attaching innumerable electrodes to the head, and we can finally know the sleep for the day by the specialists diagnose the provided data. To reduce those impossibility with the metering equipment of the unconstraint type, the technique that estimates for a sleep stage by using fast Fourier transform is devised by provided data [2, 3, 6, 8]. However, we know own sleep of the day after having got up and are not provided in real time. If the sleep stage is obtained in real time, the sound and the smell to lead a deep sleep using the real-time sleep stage, and am applicable to the monitoring in the nursing facility. In late years the study of the estimate attracts attention elsewhere for a real-time sleep stage because it is applicable to many fields.

2.2   Using Trigonometric Function Regression Model Parameters Express the Wave Which Assumes the Full Time of Heartbeat Data Letting Be Similar from One Period to n Period

Harada proposed the real-time sleep stage estimation method using trigonometric function regression model [1]. This method approximates the shape of heartbeat data acquired in real time by the expression (1), and estimates the sleep stage. In the expression (1), a_n and b_n are the parameters to show the wave of heartbeat data are similar, and those parameters express the wave which assumes the full time of heartbeat data letting be similar from the wave of one period to the wave of n period. In addition, c is a parameter to express the relative numerical high value of wave, and takes around 60 values if it is heartbeat data of healthy adults. N is a parameter to decide the frequency ingredient of the wave to use for approximation, and usually uses the parameter with $N = 13$ for the real-time sleep stage estimation. Because the frequency ingredient is approximated by the parameter of $N = 13$ shows the middle frequency of heart beat, and the middle frequency is tended to similar to the figure of the sleep stage [7].

$$f(t) = c + \sum_{n=1}^{N} \left(a_n * cos\frac{2\pi t}{L/n} + b_n * sin\frac{2\pi t}{L/n} \right) \qquad (1)$$

The Fig. 1 shows the sleep data of the phrase subject. In the Fig. 1, the cross axle shows the sleep time, and the vertical axes show the heart rate numerical value and the sleep stage. The number 5 of the sleep stage value shows wake of the sleep stage, the number 4 shows REM of the sleep stage, the number 3 to 0 show stage 1 to 4 of the sleep stage. The solid line (color is blue) shows the heart rate value which measured with measuring instrument, and the small dotted line (color is red) shows the approximate value which it was similar to by this method. In addition, the rough dotted line (color is green) shows the value which is discretized the approximate value, and it also shows the sleep stage.

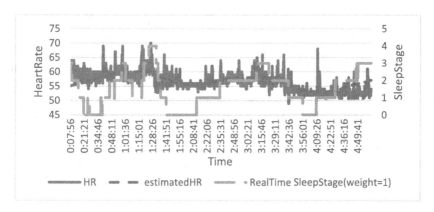

Fig. 1. Heart rate approximation using trigonometric function regression model (Color figure online)

This method can get the sleep stage using heart rate data. But this method needs quantity of enough heart rate data which is from the time of falling sleep to the time of the getting up. Therefore, when there is less heart rate data as immediately after the beginning of sleep, there is the problem that is too difficult to have the good approximation.

2.3 Real-Time Sleep Stage Estimation Using the Prior Knowledge

In order to solve the problem in the previous chapter, expression (1) is added the approximate expression such as expressions (2) and (3). Those parameters that are $\hat{a}_n$, $\hat{b}_n$, $\hat{c}_n$ in expression (2) are correction parameter called "the prior knowledge", those prevent excessive approximation in less heart rate data and has the effect to promote to the appropriate approximation. λ is a parameter of indicating the correction degree, and the value of the parameter shows the approximate degree. Further, ΔT is a parameter that shows setting a time to function correction, and it is set at 1.5 h in the general real-time sleep stage estimation. This means that there is no correction to the prior knowledge after 1.5 h. This equation makes it possible to estimate the sleep stage in real time only by the heartbeat data.

$$P(\phi) = \frac{\lambda s(t)}{N} \left\{ (c - \hat{c})^2 + \sum_{n=1}^{N} \left\{ (a_n - \hat{a}_n)^2 + (b_n - \hat{b}_n)^2 \right\} \right\} \qquad (2)$$

$$s(t) = \begin{cases} -\frac{T[hour]}{2\Delta T_s[hour]} + 1 & T < 2 * \Delta T_\gamma \\ 0 & otherwise \end{cases} \qquad (3)$$

2.4   Problems

There are the problems that are not decided which should use the prior knowledge on day for a real-time sleep stage estimation. Figure 2 shows the estimated rate of the real-time sleep stage of one certain subject. There is no prior knowledge from the left and is the figure where used the knowledge which is obtained from the different day for as prior knowledge. The stick of each figure expresses the rate of agreement of the sleep stage in each time called 0–5 min, 5–10 min, 10–20 min… The rate of agreement is the numerical value in comparison with the sleep stage measured by an electroencephalograph (wake, REM, stage1–4). The result of using the prior knowledge no. 1 shows the real-time estimated rates always become higher than the result of not using the prior knowledge. However, the rate of agreement falls in the figure of using the prior knowledge no. 2 than using the prior knowledge no. 1 same way as a case of not using the prior knowledge. Therefore it is necessary to choose the prior knowledge that can appropriately attain a high rate of agreement, but there are ignorance and problems to say which standard we should choose it in.

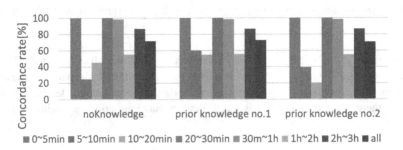

Fig. 2. The concordance rate in having the prior knowledge parameters or not (Color figure online)

3   Selection of Personalized the Prior Knowledge

3.1   Overview

The appropriate selection of the personalized data as prior knowledge is important because estimated precision drastically changes down as spoke in the second sections when the appropriate choice of the prior knowledge is not selected do the choice that various, is appropriate by not only the individual but also the estimated day. We pay our attention on the shape of heartbeat data provided in real time and employ the subsequent knowledge on a day to resemble the heartbeat data provided from the past sleep as prior knowledge. The prior knowledge is implemented by the parameter of the heartbeat data which a shape resembles most for an estimate. When the shape of the heartbeat is different from the estimated heartbeat shape in real time from past prior knowledge, we can follow it quickly and it is big with estimate precision and becomes able to in this way prevent that I fall down.

3.2   Determination of Similarity of Heartbeat Data

We calculate the difference degree with the heart rate at the time to measure a heartbeat and the similarity with heartbeat data in past sleep estimating and demand the mean. Specifically, we find similarity by a flow to show in Fig. 3. At first we find the heartbeat data between 60 s and the data which it was similar to for the past sleep data number. By a well-thought value, we use the small prior knowledge of the value for choice as a thing having high similarity and estimate it at that point. The next does a similar calculation between 120 s and decides prior knowledge. We become able to choose appropriate prior knowledge in real time by performing this for a sleep.

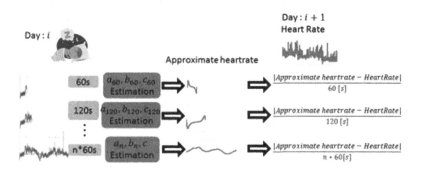

Fig. 3. Calculation flow of the similarity

4   Experiment

4.1   Experiment Setting

I inspect whether you can choose appropriate prior knowledge using sleep data for 9th for three adult male *3 day in total in an estimate for a real-time sleep stage. The sleep data use the thing which converted the data which I obtained from an apparatus and the electroencephalograph apparatus which can acquire a heartbeat, the body movement data of the unconstraint type for a sleep stage.

4.2   Evaluation Criteria

The rate of agreement for a sleep stage provided by a sleep stage and the electroen-cephalograph which estimated by choice of the prior knowledge for a real-time sleep stage becomes higher; watch it whether can choose it. More specifically, the estimated rate that is calculated by the prior knowledge having good fitness which is selected by the proposed method is compared with the estimated rate that is calculated by the other prior knowledge. Here evaluation value in the means is the difference the heart rate that is approximated using the selected prior knowledge and the heart rate is measured, and this lower value is high similarity.

4.3   Results

Figures 4, 5 and 6 are estimated results about subject A. The left figure shows the value of the gap with the approximate heartbeat, and the right figure is the result estimated for a sleep stage in real-time. In addition, the result of having been surrounded in a red line is the result which is chosen the prior knowledge of being calculated lower fitness as a thing having high similarity. Subject A knows what can choose the prior knowledge to start the estimated percentage that is higher that there is no knowledge in than this. Figures 7, 8 and 9 are estimated results about subject B. It can attain the estimated percentage that is higher that there is no the prior knowledge in subject B. Figures 10, 11 and 12 are estimated results about subject C. In subject C, the result not to use the prior knowledge for improves, and the estimated precision becomes low even if I use either the past prior knowledge.

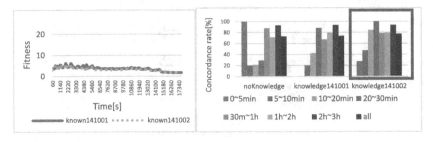

Fig. 4.   Result of Subject A in 140930 (Color figure online)

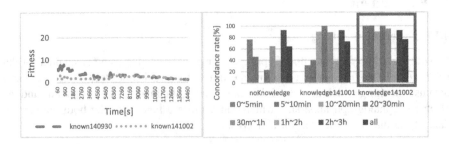

Fig. 5.   Result of Subject A in 141001 (Color figure online)

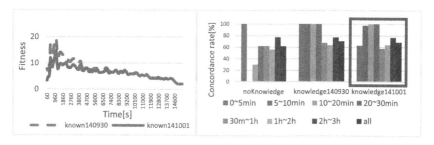

Fig. 6. Result of Subject A in 141002 (Color figure online)

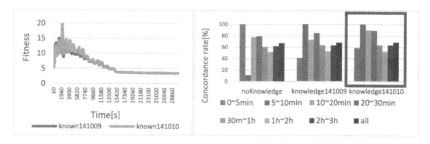

Fig. 7. Result of Subject B in 141003 (Color figure online)

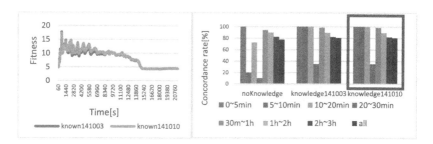

Fig. 8. Result of Subject B in 141009 (Color figure online)

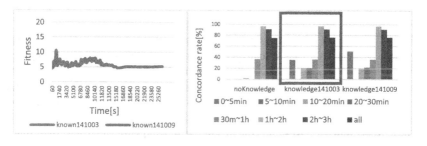

Fig. 9. Result of Subject B in 141010 (Color figure online)

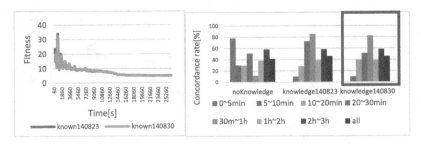

Fig. 10. Result of Subject C in 140821 (Color figure online)

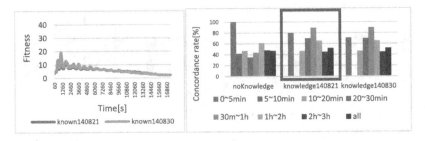

Fig. 11. Result of Subject C in 140823 (Color figure online)

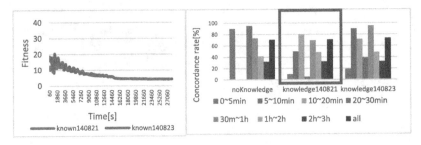

Fig. 12. Result of Subject C in 140830 (Color figure online)

4.4 Discussion

In subject C, the result of estimating is not higher than the result of not using the prior knowledge, because we thought that it is different from the past heartbeat shape in the heartbeat shape of the day. In other words precision has worsened because the heartbeat shape of the day was not similar the heartbeat shape of estimating. It is necessary to estimate in real-time without using the prior knowledge from the past sleep data when there is not similar thing to solve this problem. Also the estimated rate in each times (0–5 min, 5–10 min, 10–20 min…) are different in each subject. It is shown that it is necessary to change to other the prior knowledge or no need to use the prior knowledge. Therefore, to tackle the problem is necessary to change the value of the some prior knowledges in the real-time estimation or to use the weighted average value of the some prior knowledges.

5 Conclusion

This paper focused on the real-time sleep stage estimation and proposes the method which appropriately selects the past sleep data as the *prior knowledge* for improving accuracy of the sleep stage estimation. The prior knowledge in this paper is represented as the parameters for estimating the sleep stage. Concretely, these parameters are acquired from the heartbeat data of a certain *past* day, and they are used to estimate the heartbeat data of a *current* day, which data is finally converted to the sleep stage. The role of the proposed method is to select the appropriate parameters of the heartbeat data of a certain *past* day, which is similar to the heartbeat data of a *current* day. Such a role clarifies the relationship of the past sleep (and heartbeat) and the current sleep (and heartbeat), which contributes to estimating the current sleep stage from the heartbeat data of a different past day which is similar to the data of the current day. To investigate the effectiveness of the proposed method, we conducted the human subject experiment which investigated the accuracy of the real-time sleep stage estimation of two adult males (whose age are 20 and 40) and one adult female (whose age is 60) by employing the appropriate parameters of the different day from three days. The experimental results revealed that the accuracy of the real-time sleep stage estimation with the proposed method is higher than that without it.

What should be noticed here is that the effectiveness of the proposed method has been shown in only two adult males and one adult female with three days. Therefore, further careful qualifications and justifications, such as an increase of the number of human subjects or sleep days, are needed to generalize our results. Such important directions must be pursued in the near future in addition to the following future research: (1) an investigation of the accuracy of the sleep stage estimation in the case of not finding appropriate parameters; and (2) a classification of the relationship with the current and past sleep data.

References

1. Harada, T., Takadama, K.: A real-time sleep stage estimation from biological data with trigonometric function regression model. In: AAAI Spring Symposium: Wellbeing Computing: AI Meets Health and Happiness Science (2016)
2. Harper, R.M., Schechman, V.L., Kluge, K.A.: Machine classification of infant sleep state using cardiorespiratory measures. Electroencephalogr. Clin. Neaurophysiol. **67**, 379–387 (1987)
3. Matsushima, H., Hirose, K., Hattori, K., Sato, H., Takadama, K.: Sleep stage estimation by evolutionary computation using heartbeat data and body-movement. Int. J. Adv. Comput. Technol. (IJACT) **4**(22), 281–290 (2012)
4. Otsuka, K., Ichimaru, Y., Yanaga, T.: Studies of arrthythmias by 24-hour polygraphic records. II. Relationship between heart rate and sleep stages. Fukuoka Acta. Med. **72**(10), 589–596 (1991)
5. Rechtschaffen, A., Kales, A. (eds.): A Manual of Standardized Terminology, Techniques and Scaring System for Sleep Stage of Human Subjects, Public Health Service U.S. Government Printing Office (1968)

6. Shimohira, M., Shiiki, T., Sugimoto, J., Ohsawa, Y., Fukumizu, M., Hasegawa, T., Iwakawa, Y., Nomura, Y., Segawa, M.: Video analysis of gross body movements during sleep. Psychiatry Clin. Neurosci. **52**(2), 176–177 (1998)
7. Watanabe, T., Watanabe, K.: Estimation of the sleep stages by the non-restrictive air mattress. Sensor Trans. Soc. Instrum. Control Eng. **37**, 821–828 (2001)
8. Watanabe, T., Watanabe, K.: Noncontact method for sleep stage estimation. IEEE Trans. Biomed. Eng. **51**(10), 1735–1748 (2004)

Exploring Dance Teaching Anxiety in Japanese Schoolteachers

Rina Yamaguchi[1], Haruka Shoda[1,2], Noriko Suzuki[3],
and Mamiko Sakata[1(✉)]

[1] Graduate School of Culture and Information Science, Doshisha University,
Tataramiyakodani 1-3, Kyotanabe, Kyoto 610-0394, Japan
shoda@fc.ritsumei.ac.jp, dip0010@mail4.doshisha.ac.jp
[2] Global Innovation Research Organization, Ritsumeikan University,
Nojihigashi 1-1-1, Kusatsu 525-8577, Japan
[3] Faculty of Business Administration, Tezukayama University,
Tezukayama 7-1-1, Nara 631-8501, Japan

Abstract. The purpose of the present study is to understand Japanese school-teacher anxiety when teaching dance and how such anxiety differs according to the teachers' individual characteristics. We focused on "teaching anxiety," which we defined as teachers' concerns regarding physical education curricula. We conducted a questionnaire survey of teachers from randomly selected public junior high schools ($N = 143$). Our text-mining analysis showed that teaching anxiety is classified into five groups: anxiety over teaching methods, his/her own dance skills, lack of knowledge, student interest, and general teaching. Multiple correspondence analysis showed that teaching anxiety differed according to age, sex, dance experience, and dance teaching experience.

Keywords: Teaching anxiety · Dance education · Text mining · Multiple correspondence analysis

1 Introduction

In 2008, Japan's Ministry of Education, Culture, Sports, Science and Technology (MEXT) revised the Course of Study for Junior High Schools. This revision in physical education focused mainly on "dance" and "*Budo*," which became mandatory, rather than elective, courses [1]. Nakamura (2009) predicted that many teachers would be anxious due to their lack of experience in these subjects [2]. In addition, Hamashima and Muto [3] reported that a revision in 1994 increased teacher anxiety in homemaking education because they had no background in gender-unbiased methods of teaching.

The aforementioned literature shows that compulsory revision of the Course of Study causes tremendous problems for teachers in terms of instruction, curricula, detailed teaching methods, and more. Our focus in the present study is to understand the components of "dance teaching anxiety" in teachers for their classroom practices.

Yamaguchi, Shoda, Suzuki, and Sakata (2015) [4] defined "dance teaching anxiety" as teachers' concerns about physical education curricula and conducted a questionnaire survey for teachers participating in training seminars given by the Nippon

S. Yamamoto (Ed.): HIMI 2016, Part II, LNCS 9735, pp. 511–517, 2016.
DOI: 10.1007/978-3-319-40397-7_49

Street Dance Studio Association (NSSA). Based on this survey, the authors defined five categories of teaching anxiety: anxiety over lack of knowledge (a), lack of teaching experience (b), curricula (c), students (d), and teaching methods (e). In the present study, we explored the replicability of this structure in another population: teachers in public junior high schools. As in our previous study [4], we explored how the categories of teaching anxiety correspond to teacher characteristics, such as sex, age, previous dance experience, and previous dance teaching experience.

2 Method

2.1 Respondents

The respondents were physical education teachers in randomly selected public junior high schools in Japan. Responses were collected from 143 teachers in 74 schools (the collection rate was 24.67 %), 131 out of which were valid. Only questionnaires in which all questions were answered were included. The remaining 131 responses consisted of 95 men and 36 women, with a mean age of 37.66 years old ($SD = 11.05$).

2.2 Procedure

We provided five sets of questionnaires to each school to be answered by multiple teachers within the school. We enclosed the details of the study and asked all teachers to sign a consent form. The questionnaire asked:

1. Do you have any anxiety teaching "dance?"
2. If your answer is "yes" to Question 1, describe the details of your anxiety.
3. Please provide your sex, age, previous dance experience, and previous dance teaching experience.

We asked one of the teachers from each school to return the answered questionnaires by mail.

2.3 Analyses

The answers (free descriptions) to Question 2 (provided when the answer to Question 1 is "yes") were analyzed using KH Coder [5], a text-mining software. We extracted the co-occurrence network with KH Coder to visualize automatically the relationship among the divided words, as well as categorize them based on the connectivity of the words. Subsequently, the correspondence between the categories and the teachers' characteristics was visualized on a two-dimensional map by multiple correspondence analysis.

3 Results and Discussion

3.1 The Relationship Between the Presence of Teaching Anxiety and Teacher Characteristics

We created a contingency table for the relationship between the presence of anxiety and each of the respondents' characteristics (sex, age, previous dance experience, and previous dance teaching experience for Tables 1, 2, 3, and 4, respectively). For example, 54 % of men and 64 % of women answered that they have experienced some teaching anxiety (Table 1). Similarly, 68 % of young teachers (in their 20s, Table 2), 57 % of teachers who had previous dance experience (Table 3), and 66 % of teachers who had no dance teaching experience (Table 4) were likely to answer that they have teaching anxiety. For each table, we conducted a χ^2 analysis showing that the presence of anxiety was associated significantly with age ($p = .05$). The post-hoc residual tests revealed that older teachers (over 40) tended to be less anxious than younger teachers (in their 20s and 30s) about dance education.

Table 1. Sex and teaching anxiety ($\chi^2(1, N = 131) = 0.730$, $p = 0.393$ Cramer's $V = 0.092$)

	Anxiety-absent	Anxiety-present	Total
Man	44 (46.32 %)	51 (53.68 %)	95
Woman	13 (36.11 %)	23 (63.89 %)	36
Total	57	74	131

Table 2. Age and teaching anxiety ($\chi^2(2, N = 131) = 5.886$, $p = 0.053$ Cramer's $V = 0.150$)

	Anxiety-absent	Anxiety-present	Total
20s	12 (31.58 %)	26 (68.42 %)	38
30s	9 (34.62 %)	17 (65.38 %)	26
Over 40	36 (53.73 %)	31 (46.27 %)	67
Total	57	74	131

Table 3. Previous dance experience and teaching anxiety ($\chi^2(1, N = 131) = 0.003$, $p = 0.958$ Cramer's $V = 0.005$)

	Anxiety-absent	Anxiety-present	Total
Dancing-experience-absent	51 (43.59 %)	66 (56.41 %)	117
Dancing-experience-present	6 (42.86 %)	8 (57.14 %)	14
Total	57	74	131

Table 4. Previous dance-teaching experience and teaching anxiety ($\chi^2(1, N = 131) = 0.809$, $p = 0.369$ Cramer's $V = 0.097$)

	Anxiety absent	Anxiety present	Total
Dance teaching-experience-absent	10 (34.48 %)	19 (65.52 %)	29
Dance teaching-experience-present	47 (46.08 %)	55 (53.92 %)	102
Total	57	74	131

3.2 Co-occurrence Network: Teachers' Anxiety to Dance Teaching Anxiety

Figure 1 shows the co-occurrence network extracted from the teachers' free descriptions about their anxiety over teaching dance. The details of anxiety were classified into five groups based on hierarchical cluster analysis. We focused on groups including more than two words in the following analyses. We named the group in blue, which includes *boys*, *can*, *whether*, and *method,* the anxiety over teaching method (f). We named the group in yellow, which includes *my*, *example*, and *good,* the anxiety over

514   R. Yamaguchi et al.

his/her own dance skills (g). The group in green, which includes *knowledge, better way,* and *no idea,* was named the anxiety over lack of knowledge (h). The group in red, which includes *interest, class,* and *modern rhythm dance,* was named the anxiety over student interest (i). Finally, we named the group in purple, which includes *teaching, dance,* and *experience,* general teaching anxiety (j). We hereafter refer to these groups as "anxiety components."

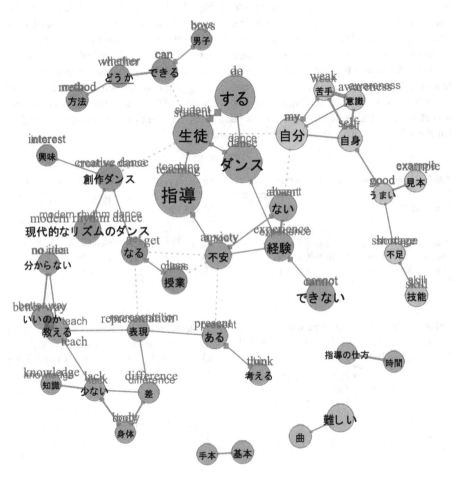

Fig. 1. The co-occurrence network for the reasons of anxiety (in English and Japanese) (Color figure online)

3.3   Correspondence Between the Anxiety Components and Teacher Characteristics

We conducted multiple correspondence analysis (Fig. 2) to understand the relationship between each of the teacher characteristics (summarized in Sect. 3.1) and each of the anxiety components (found in Sect. 3.2). In the horizontal direction, groups (f), (g),

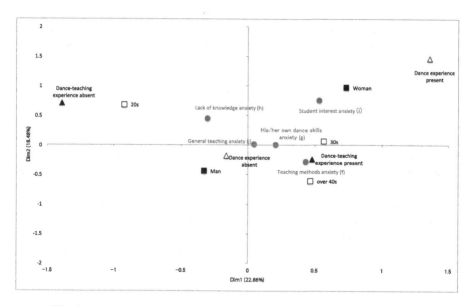

Fig. 2. Two-dimensional map generated by multiple correspondence analysis

and (i) were plotted positively, whereas group (h) were plotted negatively. In the vertical direction, groups (h) and (i) were plotted positively and group (f) were plotted negatively. Group (j) was plotted near zero so that the general anxiety divergently corresponded with all of the teacher characteristics.

Based on these interpretations, we can describe how each of the teacher's characteristics was positioned. For teaching method (f) anxiety, teachers with dance teaching experience plotted closest. In addition, older teachers (30s and over 40) plotted near the teaching methods anxiety (f). No characteristic was positioned near his/her own dance skills anxiety (g). Moreover, younger teachers in their 20s and teachers without dance teaching experience plotted in the same direction as the lack of knowledge anxiety (h). Female teachers and teachers with dance experience plotted in the same direction as student interest anxiety (i).

3.4   Discussion

We clarified that teaching anxiety is comprised of five categories, specifically, anxieties regarding teaching methods (f), his/her own dance skills (g), lack of knowledge (h), student interest (i), and general teaching (j). In line with the categories found in our previous study [4], we extracted the anxiety over lack of knowledge (h) and teaching methods (f), demonstrating that teaching methods and teacher knowledge are common stressors with compulsory revision of the Course of Study. The result is also in line with the previous studies by Nakamura [2], and Hamashima and Muto [3], who advised caution in revising the Course of Study for physical and homemaking education. In addition, anxiety over student interest (i) was reported, which is similar to the student anxiety (d) in Yamaguchi et al. (2015) [4]. The anxiety for students (d) included anxiety for students' dance skills, but not for student interest (i). Interestingly, we found his/her own dance skills anxiety (g) instead of that of lack of teaching experience (b) in the previous study [4]. The teachers in our previous study [4] answered our survey at a training seminar designed to teach a more efficient method of *teaching* dance. The teachers at the seminar therefore might have been describing the anxiety in relation to *teaching* rather than their own dance skills.

Moreover, we discovered a correspondence between the teachers' characteristics and the anxiety components. First, older (30s and over 40) and experienced teachers are likely to be anxious about teaching methods (f). Perhaps, they have already experienced some specific anxiety while actually teaching students from which the anxiety might be manifested. Next, female and dance experienced teachers were anxious about student interest (i). One reason is the relationship between the teacher's sex and previous dance experience. In our study, female teachers had more dance experience than male teachers, resulting in the female teachers focusing on teaching the *students* rather than on their own skills and/or knowledge of dance. In other words, female teachers with dance experience might feel anxiety on a higher level. Finally, young (20s) and inexperienced teachers reported anxiety regarding lack of knowledge (h). In this context, knowledge includes knowledge both of dance and teaching, so this kind of anxiety is specific to young and inexperienced teachers.

4 Conclusion

In the present study, we investigated the anxiety structure of Japanese schoolteachers over teaching dance using a co-occurrence network and subsequent multiple correspondence analysis. The results were as follows:

- The teachers' age was associated with the presence of the anxiety. Older teachers (over 40) tended not to have teaching anxiety.
- Teaching anxiety consists of five categories: anxiety over teaching methods, his/her own dance skills, lack of knowledge, student interest, and general teaching anxiety.
- The teaching anxiety varied with the teachers' characteristics. For example, dance experienced teachers feel anxiety at a high level and all teachers have general teaching anxiety and anxiety regarding his/her own dance skills.

In our future study, we would like to construct a standardized questionnaire to measure teacher anxieties aimed at solving the teaching anxiety discovered in the present study.

References

1. The Ministry of Education, Culture, Sports, Science and Technology: A Handbook of the Course of Study for Health and Physical Education (in Japanese), pp. 5–13. Higashiyama-shobo, Kyoto (2008)

2. Nakamura, K.: A research on the problem of the new guideline about coeducational required dance classes in junior high schools: on the basis of a study which deals with junior high school teachers (in Japanese). J. Health Sports Sci. Juntendo **1**(1), 27–39 (2009)
3. Hamashima, K., Muto, Y.: A change of consciousness on the teaching of homemaking education by the new course of study of senior high school teachers (in Japanese). Japan Assoc. Home Econ. Educ. **40**(3), 41–48 (1997)
4. Yamaguchi, R., Shoda, H., Suzuki, N., Sakata, M.: Analyses of the teacher's anxiety structure in accordance with the introduction of the compulsory dance education (in Japannese). In: Proceedings of the 32nd Annual Meeting of the Japanese Cognitive Science Society, pp. 309–312 (2015)
5. Higuchi, K.: Quantitative Text Analysis for Social Researchers: A Contribution to Content Analysis (in Japanese). Nakanishiya-shuppan, Kyoto (2014)

Case Studies

Sensory Evaluation Method with Multivariate Analysis for Pictograms on Smartphone

Naotsune Hosono[1,2(✉)], Hiromitsu Inoue[3], Miwa Nakanishi[1], and Yutaka Tomita[1]

[1] Keio University, Kanagawa, Japan
naotsune@mx-keio.net
[2] Oki Consulting Solutions, Co., Ltd., Tokyo, Japan
[3] Chiba Prefectural University of Health Sciences, Chiba, Japan

Abstract. New technologies have the potential to be used by anyone irrespective of age, gender, location, nationality, disability or time considerations. The session topic of well-being is close in meaning to User Experience (UX) which is considered a broader category under which usability and accessibility fall and is concerned with human perceptions and responses related to system attractive and comfortable use. To measure one quality of well-being, this paper discusses an original method: the Sensory Evaluation method. This method is demonstrated using multivariate analysis with the example of creating pictograms/icons of daily used signs from seven national sign languages on a smartphone. A usability evaluation test on its effectiveness and efficiency revealed that communication speed by tapping pictograms/icons on the smartphone was about five times more efficient than text message .

Keywords: Human computer interface · Usability · Accessibility · User experience · Human-Centred design · Sensory evaluation

1 Introduction

It is often said that we are living in the Information and Communication Technology (ICT) age, where complex information must be quickly and easily accessed. This is shown through the emergence of smartphones and how new and sophisticated electronics allow for smaller and more powerful technologies in daily use. These new technologies have the potential to be used by anyone irrespective of age, gender, location, nationality, disability or time considerations [1].

This paper discusses the Sensory Evaluation method which may be used to measure one aspect of a happy life based on the session theme: "New Well-Being Measures in HCI."

2 Well-Being and User Experience

Recent discussions in the field of ergonomics have shifted from usability into User Experience (UX) [2]. The session topic of well-being may be close in meaning to this concept. UX can generally be considered a broader category under which usability of

S. Yamamoto (Ed.): HIMI 2016, Part II, LNCS 9735, pp. 521–530, 2016.
DOI: 10.1007/978-3-319-40397-7_50

the user interface (UI) falls. UX depends on human perceptions and responses that result from the use or anticipated use of a system, product or service of before, during and after use. It includes user emotions, preferences, perceptions, physical and psychological responses behaviours and accomplishments. It is affected by prior experiences, attitudes, skills, personality and the context of use [3]. In this sense, well-being measures may be used as criteria to assess aspects of user experience.

Figure 1 explains the potential relationship between well-being and user experience. The ISO defines usability as the extent to which a system, product or service can be used by specified end-users to achieve specified goals with optimal effectiveness, efficiency, and satisfaction in a specified context of use [3]. Accessibility is the usability of a product, service, environment or facility by people with the widest range of capabilities [4]. Universal design as well as inclusive design consists of usability and accessibility. User experience is a person's perceptions and responses that result from the use and/or anticipated use of a product, system or service [5]. In summery accessibility includes physical factors like reliability and functionality of use; usability is cognitive and perceptual factors, like usefulness and effectiveness of use; and UX includes emotional factors [6] like attractiveness and comfort of use. Hence well-being involves all of these expressions of use; functional, reliable, effective, useful, comfortable and attractive. Sensory Analysis, the method discussed in this paper, focuses on the attractive, comfort, and useful aspects of human emotion in evaluation of user experience.

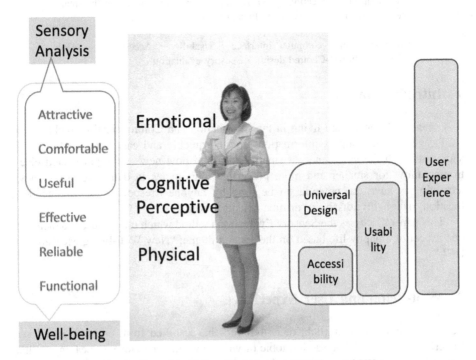

Fig. 1. Potential relationship between well-being and UX

3 Human-Centred Design

Product design in industry must start from an initial perception of user needs. However at the present, original design resources tend to be derived from proprietary technologies. For example, the smartphone is an all-purpose machine with a lot of features and functions; however, only a limited number of users will be able to use these functions thoroughly. This is because the experimental and manufacturing development stages tend to be based on the predetermined target specification solely created and measured by experts. Then the products are refined by Value Engineering (VE) for the cost factor [7] and shipped into the market, which may be the first opportunity that actual users have to examine and determine the usability of the machine. Therefore, needed feature requests and vital feedback from end users are only available to the designers after the machine has been introduced into the real market.

Human-centred design (HCD) is especially relevant to the usability, accessibility and user experience of products. HCD became an international standard as ISO 9241, Ergonomic requirements for office work with visual display terminals (VDTs), part 210: 2010 (former ISO 13407) [5]. Nowadays many manufactures have applied it to the development processes bringing innovative concepts to production plans and designs to gain up-to-date feedback from end users for gathering requirements earlier in the design process. HCD is based on the context of use and now standardized as ISO 9241 Part 11: 1998, - Guidance on usability. The context of use is combination of specified users, tasks, resources, environment and goal as an intended outcome [3].

4 Sensory Evaluation Method

In this study, the Sensory Evaluation (SE) method was applied to examine human emotional and perceptible attributes for products [6]. This research was started in order to measure the context of universal communication through local sign languages by applying the correspondence analysis (CA) of multivariate analysis (MVA) in SPSS [8]. Sign languages are originally designed for use by hearing-impaired people, and they include semantic expressions in their scope.

In this project, an original method to create pictograms based on seven multiplex local sign languages, Japanese (JSL), American (ASL), British (BSL), French (FSL), Spanish (ESL), Korean (KSL), and Chinese (CSL), using the HCD concept of context of use on dialogue, and by applying MVA [9, 10], is discussed.

In this paper, "thank you" in several multi-national sign languages will be presented and discussed as an application example. The overall research is initially focused on the creation of pictograms or icons to support dialogues, since the fundamentals of sign language are hand shape, location and motion. References are made to a collection of animation figures, extracted from seven local sign languages used by a deaf architect. This architect provided enthusiastic support for this research by supplying and permitting these references to be added to the database [11].

To evaluate this approach, the SE method was applied through following three steps. The first step was to measure the similarity of a selected word "thank you" among seven different local sign languages using MVA (Fig. 2). In the experiments,

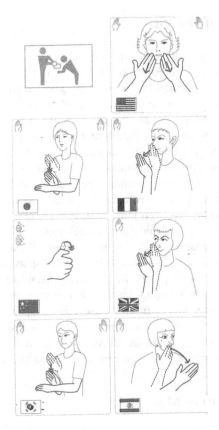

Fig. 2. Sign figures for "thank you."

the participants were first shown an expression with the collection of animation figures extracted from seven local sign languages. Subsequently, the participants were informed of the meaning of the sign, and then they were requested to vote with 19 tokens to express which of the seven different local sign language expressions (samples) best coincided with the original image. They were asked to use all 19 tokens, but they were permitted eventually to use zero voting on some samples (Figs. 3 and 4). The first experimental participants were 13 students in their twenties. Some had experience living overseas as well as sign language interpreting.

For the analysis, correspondence analysis (CA) of MVA in IBM SPSS Statistics Ver. 18 [8] was applied. The outcome was plotted on a plane such that similar local sign languages were plotted close together (Fig. 5). The outcome of CA of MVA indicates fundamentally no dimension in Eigenvalue axes. Because of the characteristics of CA, the participants who have general and standard ideas are positioned near the centre, whereas those who have extreme or specialized ideas are positioned away from the centre. The centre crossing point (0.0) of the first and second Eigenvalues is also called "centre of the gravity" or "average". In this way, CA generates a graphical examination of the relationships between local sign languages and participants [12].

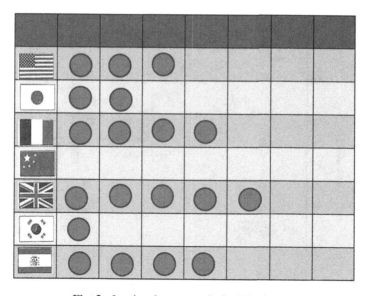

Fig. 3. Inquiry sheet example for "thank you"

Fig. 4. A view of the experiment and a participant

Figure 5 is a plot diagram for the "thank you" results and represents the relations between the seven sign languages (samples) and participants. Notably, there were two split sample groups. One group consisted of the elements; BSL, ESL, FSL and ASL which are western sign languages. The other group consisted of the elements; JSL, KSL and CSL, which are Asian sign languages.

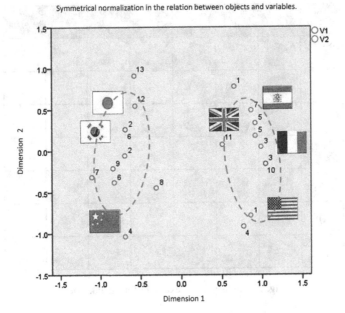

Fig. 5. A plot for the "thank you" results with seven sign languages

The second step was to help a pictogram designer to create a new common pictogram by exploiting and summarizing expressions resulting from the MVA analysis conducted in the first step. Figure 6 is a newly created pictogram referring to only the BSL and FSL sign languages.

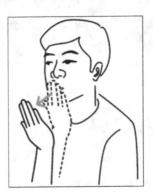

Fig. 6. A newly created pictogram: "thank you" that combines BSL and FSL

5   Results and Consideration

The final step was to validate the newly created pictogram with MVA. The outcome, including the newly designed pictogram, was plotted with the other seven local sign languages in order to measure whether the newly created pictogram was representative of the dominant cluster. The second experiment participants were 20 engineering department students in their twenties including two female students. Almost all except three were different participants from the first experiment. After voting with 23 tokens this time, all the participants were again asked to rate their confidence level using the Semantic Differential (SD) method [9, 10].

Figure 7 is an example of an outcome chart where the new and old "thank you" sign result set is plotted. The newly designed symbol has a coloured green flag and represented the FSL and BSL sign languages because they were plotted close to those two sign languages. As the figure showed ASL and ESL positioned closer to the green flag, whereas JSL, KSL, and CSL were plotted further down. As with the first step, two split sample groups emerged.

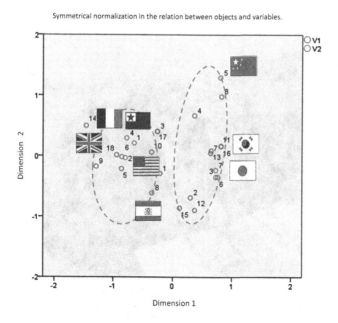

Symmetrical normalization in the relation between objects and variables.

Fig. 7. A supplementary treatment plot of the new "thank you" showing 7 + 1 sign languages

6   Application for Smartphones

The resulting pictograms/icons were implemented as an application on smartphones that have touch screens (Fig. 8). The final system was evaluated by hearing-impaired participants and foreigners, to compare qualitative and quantitative measures of effectiveness, efficiency, and satisfaction based on context of use (Fig. 9). This

Fig. 8. Pictograms on a touchscreen-based smartphone

Fig. 9. The evaluation experimental setup

evaluation focused particularly on efficiency by comparing two task groups. Initial results suggest that applying tapping pictograms/icons on the smartphone is about five times quicker than text message by e-mail.

7   Conclusions and Future Work

This work shows how the Sensory Evaluation (SE) method can easily make relative comparisons between the seven expressions of local sign languages. It is more effective than the Ordering Method or Pair Comparison Method [12], because of the characteristics of applied CA of MVA in SPSS, the participants who have common and/or standard ideas are positioned near the centre, whereas those who have extreme or specialized ideas are positioned away from the centre. In this way CA establishes a method to graphically examine the relationship between local sign languages and the preferences of the participants.

Through the SE method, the relationships between selected words and local sign languages were initially explained by a sensory evaluation of the participants. Although this paper discussed the SE method as used for the analysis of multiplex local sign languages, it can be extensively applied to the other systems, products or services as well, where future work will explore. For instance, Customer Satisfaction Index (CSI) [13] may be another approach to measure some aspect of well-being. Future research issue could explore how create complementary representations using SE and CSI together.

Acknowledgement. The original idea of this research was proposed by a hearing impaired architect, Mr. M. Suzuki of Architectural Association of Japanese DEAF (AAJD). A collection of local sign language database is supplied and permitted for research use by Mr. M. Akatsuka. Doctorate candidate K. Seaborn discussed this research with the author and kindly performed a native check for this proceeding.

References

1. Beavan, N.: User Interfaces for All. Lawrence Erlbaum, Mahwah (1999)
2. Hartson, R., Pyla, P.S.: The UX Book: Process and Guidelines for Ensuring a Quality User Experience. Morgan Kaufmann Publishers, San Francisco (2012)
3. International Organization for Standardization: ISO9241-11, Ergonomic Requirements for Office Work with Visual Display Terminals (VDTs). Guidance on usability, Geneva (1998)
4. International Organization for Standardization: ISO 9241-171:2008, Ergonomics of Human-system Interaction – Part 171: Guidance on Software Accessibility, Geneva (2008)
5. International Organization for Standardization: ISO9241-210 (former ISO13407:1999): Ergonomics Human-centred Design Processes for Interactive Systems, Geneva (2010)
6. Mukhopadhyaya, A.K.: Value Engineering: Concepts Techniques and Applications. Sage Publications, Thousand Oaks (2003)
7. Norman, D.: Emotional Design: Why We Love or Hate Everyday Things. Basic Books, New York (2005)
8. Field, A.: Discovering Statistics Using SPSS, 3rd edn. Sage Publications, Los Angeles (2009)
9. Hosono N., Inoue H., Tomita Y.: Sensory analysis method applied to develop initial machine specification, measurement. In: IMEKO, vol. 32, pp. 7–13. Budapest (2002)

10. Hosono, N., Inoue, H., Nakanishi, M., Tomita, Y.: Pictogram creation with sensory evaluation method based on multiplex sign languages. Int. J. Adv. Intell. Syst. IARIA **8**(3&4), 233–244 (2015). http://www.iariajournals.org/intelligent_systems/
11. Akatsuka, M.: Seven Sign Languages for Tourists: Useful Words and Expressions. Chinese-Japanese-American Working Group, Osaka (2005)
12. Inoue, H.: Sensory Evaluation, Juse-P, ISBN978-4-817-9435-0. Japanese version, Tokyo (2013)
13. ACSI LLC: National ACSI score, Ann Arbor MI (2010). http://www.theacsi.org/about-acsi/the-science-of-customer-satisfaction

Exploring Information Needs of Using Battery Swapping System for Riders

Fei-Hui Huang[(⊠)]

Department of Marketing and Distribution Management,
Oriental Institute of Technology, Pan-Chiao 22061, Taiwan, ROC
Fn009@mail.oit.edu.tw

Abstract. In order to improve penetration in Taiwan's electric two wheeler (E2W) market to decrease emissions of pollutants generated by scooters, a battery swapping model is proposed to overcome battery limitations (e.g., expensive purchase price, short lifetime, limited driving range per charge, long charging time, and inconvenient charging). This study aims to understand individuals' information needs of using battery swap station (BSS) and, furthermore, providing several suggestions to improve BSS service for enhancing their willingness to accept a battery swapping system. In this study, a sample of 2,100 riders who had experienced a battery swapping service and filled out a post-experience questionnaire. The questionnaire elicited their traffic demands, the system acceptability, and purchase intention. The results showed that approximately 79.9 % of riders adopted the battery swapping system, but only 3.9 % were willing to purchase an e-scooter. Riders identified a number of problems with the self-service BSSs, including 42.8 % usability, 33.1 % environment, 18.7 % utility, and 5.4 % price. Finally, these problems were discussed, and addressed several recommend ways of resolving them.

Keywords: Electric two wheelers (E2Ws) · Battery swapping model · System acceptability · E-scooter · Information needs

1 Introduction

Taiwan has a population of 23 million, of which about 13.7 million are scooter users. Thus, one in every 1.67 people is a scooter commuter, which is the highest density in the world, and New Taipei City has the highest density in Taiwan. According to Taiwan's Environmental Protection Administration (EPA) report, emissions generated by scooters account for 330,000 tons of carbon monoxide and 90,000 tons of chemical compounds containing carbon hydroxide per year. The real-world operation of motorcycles/scooters results in a significant contribution of road transport CO and HC emissions, reaching 38 % and 64 %, respectively, to the total emissions from road transportation [1]. In order to improve the air quality, the Taiwanese government is dedicated to promoting an eco-environmental protection policy. Increasing the penetration level of electric two wheelers (E2Ws), including electric scooters (e-scooter), electric bicycles (e-bike), and electric-assisted bicycles, is one of the aims of the policy. The widespread adoption of E2W brings potential social and economic benefits, such

© Springer International Publishing Switzerland 2016
S. Yamamoto (Ed.): HIMI 2016, Part II, LNCS 9735, pp. 531–541, 2016.
DOI: 10.1007/978-3-319-40397-7_51

as reducing the quantity of fossil fuels and greenhouse gas emissions, as well as environmental benefits. However, limitations on E2Ws batteries, including an expensive purchase price, short lifetime, limited driving range per charge, long charging time, and inconvenient charging, have meant that many people are unwilling to buy the related products. In spite of the incentives offered by Taiwan's government, the penetration level of E2W in the market is not encouraging. Only 29,942 e-scooters and 108,602 e-bikes were sold between 2009 and 2014. A battery swapping model is proposed to overcome the battery charging and driving range limitations in order to improve the penetration of E2Ws in Taiwan. The purpose of this study is to understand individuals' information needs of using battery swap station (BSS) and, furthermore, providing several suggestions to improve BSS service for enhancing their willingness to accept a battery swapping system.

2 Literature Reviews

2.1 Battery Swapping Model

A battery swapping model may provide a faster charging service than even the fastest recharging stations and lower the charging cost by charging depleted batteries overnight at a discounted electricity price. In this study, the battery swapping system is providing a separation of the ownership for the battery and the E2W. Using a battery leasing service may also reduce the expense incurred by E2W owners. The model provides self-service BSSs, where an owner can ride to the nearest BSS and swap to a fully-charged battery within two minutes. The concept of an exchangeable battery service was first proposed as early as 1896 in order to overcome the limited operating range of electric cars and trucks [2]. In addition, BSS is one of the solutions to the limitations of the E2W battery [3–6]. The battery swapping system comprises four industries: battery swapping system operators, E2W battery manufacturers, E2W manufacturers, and E2W retailers. In order to effectively integrate the industries and adopt the battery swapping system, battery certification specifications for E2Ws have been drafted to formulate a size standard for 48 V/10 Ah–15 Ah lithium-ion batteries, interchangeable interface standards to link batteries and vehicles, and a Taiwan E-scooter Standard (TES) for performance and safety. The draft was announced by Taiwan's EPA on December 9, 2013, to ensure the consistency of battery and vehicle quality. Here, E2Ws include e-scooters and e-bikes. According to E2W traffic laws, e-scooters are limited to 1,000 W output, and cannot travel faster than 45 km/h on motor power alone on level ground. A driver's license and helmet are required to ride an e-scooter. E-bikes cannot travel faster than 25 km/h. There is no lower age limit, so anyone can legally ride an e-bike on roads. Furthermore, based on the swapping service availability, the construction cost of the system is the primary problem for investors. Taiwan's EPA approved grants to encourage related industries to become members of the system by, for example, subsidizing a US$50,000 for each BSS to battery swapping system operator in order to establish as much as BSSs. Because the construction of BSSs and their infrastructure is expensive, there are 30 operational BSSs open to the public in limited locations in New Taipei City, Taiwan. These have been set in seven of New Taipei City's 29 districts. The average distance between each station is about 3.5 km.

2.2 System Acceptability

One of the challenges that face the designers of human-computer interaction (HCI) systems is to produce a final system that responds to the expectations of its end-users. In other words, it has to respond to its users' needs in order to be acceptable. The production of a suitable system for end-users requires knowledge of users' needs and the environments in which they work. Furthermore, in HCI research, it is important to pursue user satisfaction and system usage. In the battery swapping system, a BSS is the only way E2W riders can use a battery swapping service. Furthermore, the battery swapping system services require the support of the above-mentioned four industries. This highlights the importance of industrial integration and user acceptance for the battery swapping system. Moreover, system acceptability is the major issue addressed in this study.

Nielsen's system acceptability model may provide an overview of the issues that influence the service acceptance of a system. Nielsen [7] defines acceptability as "whether the system is good enough to satisfy all the needs and requirements of the user." System acceptability is the goal designers should aim for and can be achieved by meeting the social and practical acceptability objectives of the system. Hence, the Nielsen system acceptability model is a combination of social acceptability and practical acceptability. Social acceptability recognizes the broader social issues that affect system users [7]. The concept of social acceptability is needed to understand the social context of users, why the activity is performed in a certain way, and how tools can be adapted or designed to support it. Social aspects may influence the adoption [8] and manner of using the product and service. Individuals evaluate social acceptability when their motivation to use technology competes with social restrictions. Individuals make decisions on the social acceptability of their actions by gathering information about their current surroundings and using their existing knowledge [9]. In addition, practical acceptability is a combination of the characteristics of the system, including its usefulness, cost/price, compatibility, reliability. Usefulness has been identified as a key objective of practical acceptability. Usefulness refers to how well a system achieves a desired goal, and is divided into two subcategories: utility and usability [10]. Here, utility refers to whether appropriate functionality is at hand, and usability refers to how well users can apply that functionality. With regard to the definition of usability, Bevan et al. [11] focus on how usability should be measured, with a particular emphasis on either ease of use or acceptability. Then, Nielsen [7] further defines a usable system as a quality attribute that assesses how easy user interfaces are to use, and outlines five usability attributes: learnability, efficiency, memorability, error recovery/few errors, and satisfaction. The International Organization of Standards (ISO) [12] defines usability as the extent to which a product can be used by specified users to achieve specified goals with effectiveness, efficiency, and satisfaction in a specified context of use. The two concepts of usability and utility are highly interrelated. A usable user interface may contribute to a service being perceived as having the utility to provide appropriate functionality. Conversely, if a service has the utility to provide appropriate functionality, but can only be used or consumed via a badly designed user interface, users may avoid using the product or service.

3 Methods

A battery swapping system is an innovative service to provide a convenient charging service to E2W riders. The purpose of this study is to understand individuals' information needs of using BSS, and to further provide suggestions to improve BSS service. The Taiwan Electric Scooter Development Association (TESDA) provided ten services centers to individuals to have a free trial ride on an e-scooter. Individuals could sign up for an immersive experience for a maximum trial period of fourteen days (two weeks). These experiences gave trial riders an opportunity to understand, adapt, and overcome any battery charging and driving range limitations. After returning the e-scooters, each trial rider filled out a questionnaire and obtained a bag of polished rice as a reward. System acceptability and purchase intention were measured using a paper-and-pen survey. The survey was used to elicit feedback from the trial riders in order to improve BSS service.

The paper-and-pen questionnaire for the post-experience feedback contained the following four sections:

- Personal information: five items designed to collect socio-demographic data on age (<20, 20–29, 30–39, 40–49, 50–59, 60–69, and ≥70), sex (male and female), education (elementary, junior high, high school (senior), college, master's degree, and other), name, and phone number.
- Individual traffic demands: two items designed to collect categorical data on transportation usage (scooter, bike, walk, car, public transportation, and other) and daily commuting distance (<10, 10–19, 20–29, 30–39, and ≥40 km).
- System acceptability evaluation: two items designed to collect categorical data on practical acceptability—"Which factors made you unsatisfied with the battery swapping system and why?" (utility, usability, environment, and price)—and social acceptability—"Is the system convenient?" (yes or no). Here, social acceptability is identified as the convenience factors that influence users' willingness to use the battery swapping system, but does not provide insight into what those factors are or how they might influence riders' opinions.
- Purchase intention: three items designed to collect categorical data on respondent's willingness to own an e-scooter (yes, maybe, and no), reasons for not wanting to own an e-scooter (speed, appearance, performance, price, driving range per charge, BSS services, and other), and e-scooter usage (sports and leisure, shopping, picking up a child from school, commuting, long-distance travel, and other).

The study was conducted over a thirteen-month period between February 2014 and March 2015.

4   Results

Of 2,213 surveys, 113 involved material data omission, and the effective response rate was 95 %. Summarized demographic information of the 2,100 riders is shown in Table 1.

Table 1. Demographic information of the trial riders (N = 2, 100).

Items	Frequency (n) & Sequence	1	2	3	4	5	6	7
Gender	Item	Male	Female					
	Total	1,134	966					
	%	(54.0%)	(46.0%)					
Age	Item	30-39	40-49	50-59	20-29	60-69	≥70	<20
	Total	531	525	413	381	151	41	55
	%	(25.2%)	(25.0%)	(19.6%)	(18.1%)	(7.1%)	(2.5%)	(1.9%)
Education	Item	College	Senior	Junior	≥Master	Elementary	Other	
	Total	953	664	258	63	143	19	
	%	(45.4%)	(31.6%)	(12.3%)	(3.0%)	(6.8%)	(0.9%)	

4.1   Descriptive Statistics

The results showed that approximately 81.3 % of trial riders were using high air-polluting road vehicles as their major means of transport, including scooters (61.6 %), cars (10.0 %), and buses (9.7 %). Approximately 74.8 % of trial riders commuted less than 20 km (one way) per day. After riding the e-scooter, there were several unsatisfied checks for practical acceptability from the 2,100 trial riders, including usability (42.8 %), environment (33.1 %), utility (18.7 %), and price (5.4 %). However, approximately 79.9 % riders were still willing to use the battery swapping system, with 20.1 % of riders not finding the system convenient. With regard to the purchasing intention, approximately 3.9 % riders were willing to own the e-scooter and 76.0 % were willing to consider purchasing the e-scooter. Approximately 98.2 % would ride the e-scooter as means of transport for short-distance travel (e.g., shopping, picking up children from school, commuting to work, and sports). A more detailed analysis of the results is presented below.

4.2   Chi-Square Test

The chi-square test results (see Table 2) indicated that trial riders' one-way daily commuting distances differed significantly according to educational level, sex, and age. The results showed significant differences in the purchase intentions of e-scooter according to age. The results indicated significant differences in the BSS locations according to educational level and sex. The trial riders aged 60 to 69 years displayed a higher percentage of one-way daily commuting under 10 km (3.7 %; AR = 3.4) relative to those aged 40 to 49 years (9.4 %; AR = −1.3). Trial riders who had received college degree displayed a higher percentage of one-way daily commuting ≥40 km (1.0 %; AR = 3.9) relative to those with a junior high education (0.0 %; AR = −2.9). Men exhibited a higher percentage of daily commuting 30 to 40 km (4.1 %; AR = 3.9) relative to women (1.7 %; AR = −3.9). Women displayed a higher percentage of daily commuting under 10 km (20.5 %; AR = 4.3) relative to men (19.0 %; AR = −4.3). In addition, trial riders aged 60 to 69 years displayed a higher intention to purchase an e-scooter with the BSS (6.0 %; AR = 2.2) relative to those aged 20 to 29 years (13.2 %; AR = −2.8). With regard to BSS location, riders who had received elementary education displayed a higher percentage of satisfying with the locations (0.6 %; AR = 2.4) relative to those with a senior education (0.8 %; AR = −3.0). Riders who had received a senior high education showed a higher percentage of neutral with the locations (18.0 %; AR = 3.7) relative to those with college degree (9.0 %; AR = −2.3). The trial riders aged 60 to 69 years displayed a higher percentage of satisfying with locations (0.6 %; AR = 2.7) relative to those aged 50 to 59 years (0.5 %; AR = −2.2).

Table 2. Summarized Chi-square results

Items	Factors	Pearson's χ2	p value
Daily commuting distance	Age	39.422	.025
	Education	42.835	.002
	Sex	40.396	.000
Purchase intention	Age	24.012	.020
BSS location	Age	48.301	0.002
	Education	40.685	0.004

4.3   Cross-Tabulation

With regard to most often used transportation of different age ranges, most of them would ride scooters; riders aged <30 would take bus as their second options; trial riders aged e-scooter usage ≥30 would drive cars to be their second options. Men most often used scooters, followed by cars, buses, bikes, and walking. Women most often used scooters, followed by buses, bikes, walking, and cars.

5   Discussion

This study results in 2,100 riders who experienced the e-scooter products and the BSS service. After they were educated about the battery swapping system, BSS, E2W, the benefits and potential drawbacks by the person who work at service center, and had experienced the system for a maximum trial period of two weeks, 79.9 % of the trial riders were willing to adopt the system.

5.1 Purchase Intention

Results showed that approximately 79.9 % trial riders were more likely to adopt e-scooter products and the BSS service, with 3.9 % of riders willing to purchase an e-scooter and 76 % riders willing to consider becoming an e-scooter owner. Only 82 trial riders were willing to buy an e-scooter. During the study period, most of the e-scooter buyers needed to buy a scooter or bike. Of the 1,596 trial riders who were willing to consider buying e-scooter, approximately 1,306 (62.2 %) were scooter riders. In Taiwan, the density of scooter owners, one in every 1.67 people, is high. Because scooters are a relatively economical way to commute, the majority of scooter-based commuters are from middle- and low-income families. Even though an e-scooter is half the price of a regular scooter, most people prefer to ride their original scooter, and not to replace it with a new e-scooter. Then, 210 trial riders (10 %) were car owners, and may be willing to purchase an e-scooter if they found them practical and convenient. Of the 2,100 trial riders, 422 (20.1 %) were not willing to purchase an e-scooter and the BSS service. The results indicated that the major reason of not willing to become an e-scooter owner was driving range per charge (25.3 %), followed by e-scooter speed (14.6 %), BSS usability (14.2 %), e-scooter performance (13.9 %), e-scooter price (10.8 %), BSS service fee (8.7 %), and e-scooter design (8.5 %).

5.2 Individual Needs

Individual differences in the daily commuting distance, the purchase intentions, and BSS location of trial riders were observed. The average one-way daily commuting distance differed according to educational levels, age, and sex. The results showed that men displayed a higher percentage of daily commuting of ≥10 km relative to women. Moreover, the most used means of transport by men was a scooter, followed by a car, bus, and bike. Compared with women, their most used means of transport was a scooter, followed by a bus, bike, and walking. In addition, trial riders with a higher level of education (e.g., a college's degree), displayed a higher percentage of daily commuting of ≥40 km relative to other rider groups. Riders aged 60 to 69 displayed a higher percentage of daily commuting of under 10 km relative to other age groups. In other words, riders who were women, who had a lower level of education, or who aged more than 60 tended to travel a shorter distance in their daily lives.

Purchasing intentions differed according to age. The results showed that trial riders aged 60 to 69 years exhibited a higher intention to purchase an e-scooter relative to other rider groups.

BSS locations differed according to age and educational level. The results showed riders with a lower level of education displayed a higher percentage of satisfying with BSS location relative to other rider groups. Riders aged 60 to 69 displayed a higher percentage of satisfying with BSS location relative to other age groups.

The results may be summarized as that women, less educated people, and people aged 60–69 years could be target customers for the current e-scooter with battery swapping system market.

5.3   Information Needs

The high degree of willingness to adopt the battery swapping system (79.9 %) also indicated that the service may satisfy most of the needs and requirements of riders, but several parts of the service still need to improve. Here, two issues were discussed: social acceptability and practical acceptability. In terms of social acceptability, the convenience factor was identified as influencing riders' willingness to use the BSS. The results showed that most trial riders (86.7 %) found the proposed system convenient. The remaining 13.3 % of trial riders found that the system did not satisfy their needs. The major reason for the latter result is that 30 BSSs are not sufficient, especially when the BSSs are located far from home. In other words, the density of BSSs needs to be increased to improve the convenience to riders. Suggestions have been proposed based on these results, for example, identifying target e-scooter customers and setting up BSSs on frequently traveled routes. In addition, BSSs may be set up at nearby residential, shopping, elementary school, tourist, and sport parks. Furthermore, BSSs may be set up on routes from communities to the above-mentioned areas. The BSS infrastructure, including battery swapping machines, battery chargers, and many extra batteries, is expensive to build. Thus, further research on developing an optimal BSS choice location model is suggested.

With regard to practical acceptability, 42.8 % usability problems, 33.1 % environment problems, and 18.7 % utility problems were found and 5.4 % of trial riders were not satisfied with the price. These problems were discussed based on the trial riders' qualitative feedback. Firstly, the usability of the proposed system needs to be improved to provide more useful information on the BSS. Since the batteries stored in the station are expensive, the battery swapping system operator preferred to stock the stations with as few batteries as possible. Riders needed extra information to provide them with numbers of fully charged batteries in the BSS, because some riders found there were no fully charged batteries available. Even though the location of the 30 BSSs were summarized and posted at each BSS to help riders decide where next to go, they doubted whether there were batteries available at the next BSS. Such doubts caused them to stop trying. Therefore, it is important to develop an ideal number of batteries for the station model, battery reservation service, or innovative service in the near future to lead to better battery swapping system adoption. In addition, several riders were unable to swap their battery on their first try because they found the BSS operating procedure did not match their cognition. They also suggested displaying step-by-step information on the BSS screen while swapping their battery. The above-mentioned information suggests displaying information on the BSS screen, as well as multiple ways of retrieving integrated information technology and communications technology. For example, a 7/24 call center service is suggested to satisfy the information needs of E2W owners, especially for riders who are not part of the network generation. It is expected that riders will receive information via interphone on the BSS, telephone, or mobile phone. In addition, an application service is suggested to satisfy the information needs of riders who have internet connections. It is expected that riders will retrieve information or search for the nearest available BSS via a BSS screen, smartphone, tablet PC, or PC. This also reveals an important issue of BSS capacity limitations, which should be investigated in the near future. Secondly, the BSS environment should be improved by considering the setting location. In this study, self-service BSSs were set up at public spaces, such as gas stations, scooter parking lots, parks, and sidewalks. Several BSSs set at parking lots, parks, or sidewalks had been skipped by trial riders. The reasons were that BSSs set on sidewalks had a long distance between the e-scooter and the BSS, making it difficult to exchange batteries. Some riders could not use the BSS service because of noncompliance with parking regulations after parking the scooter right in front of the BSS. BSS settings in these locations are limited by local governments. Applying for a public space for a BSS must go through many audit requirements. Therefore, to have full support from local governments and to plan appropriate locations jointly are suggested. Of course, renting private space, such as gas stations and convenience stores, is also an option. The major reason why the battery swapping system operator did not choose this option is to avoid rent expenses. Thirdly, the system utility needs to be improved by enhancing the design of the connection interface between the battery and the BSS, as well as considering weather problems. Several trial riders could not swap their battery successfully because the connection interface between was not designed properly, causing BSS to not sense the battery after riders dropped the battery off at the station. In such cases, most of the riders did not know what happened. Then, they try to reinsert the battery again. In order to increase riders' understanding and BSS life, the connection interface and usability (e.g., providing information or signals on BSS screen or battery track to illustrate problems and solutions, or to show whether the battery is placed correctly) should be improved. In addition, most of BSSs were set in open spaces. To provide a good service, self-service BSS should be designed to be applicable in any place and any weather. However, some trial riders encountered were unable to read information on BSS screen because of strong sunlight. Some riders did not want to swap a battery during a rainy day because there was no rain shelter. Hence, waterproofing and anti-glare are important issues in the design of a BSS. Finally, trial riders needed to know the charging standard before using the BSS service and the charging fee at the time swapping battery. Most trial riders would like to compare the charging fee to the oil price when deciding on the affordability of the swapping service. However, as oil prices have continued to fall in recent years, a new challenge is created by battery swapping fees gradually becoming higher than oil prices. This also shows the importance of finding good countermeasures to overcome the impact of oil prices in the near future. In addition, trial riders were wondering why the charging fee was not shown on BSS screen. After they had been told that they may receive the charging fee and detail information the next time, most of them found the service acceptable. Of course, they further addressed the need to receive immediate information on charging fees. This is another issue that needs to be improved.

5.4 Study Limitations

The current study is limited in the New Taipei City, Taiwan. The sample is also limited to individuals who have a scooter driver's license to allow them to have a short test drive on an e-scooter. Based on traffic law, individuals must have a scooter driver's license to ride on an e-scooter. The longest trial period provided by the program was two weeks. Many people were unwilling to trial ride on an e-scooter. Therefore, the 2,100 trial riders were more open minded and willing to adopt a new product or service.

6 Conclusion

In this study, ten service centers were provided by Taiwan Electric Scooter Development Association to individuals with a free trial ride on an e-scooter and a paper-and-pen questionnaire was provided to elicit rider's feedback including personal information, individual traffic demands, system acceptability, and purchase intention after he/she had a long period of using the battery swapping system. The results indicate that battery swapping system may provide e-scooter owners with a convenient charging service and high degree of system adoption. The viability of this charging service scheme had been demonstrated. However, several problems of BSS were found and needed to be improved. BSS location, sufficient battery at stations, and ease of use should be investigated further.

Funding/Support. The author would like to express her gratitude to Taiwan Electric Scooter Development Association for assistance this study and Environmental Protection Administration of Taiwan for the funding under the grant number EPA-102-FA13-03A291.

References

1. Tsai, J.H., Hsu, Y.C., Weng, H.C., Lin, W.Y., Jeng, F.T.: Air-pollution emission factors from new and in-use motorcycles. Atmos. Environ. **34**, 4747–4754 (2000)
2. Kirsch, D.A.: The Electric Vehicle and the Burden of History, pp. 153–162. Rutgers University Press, New Brunswick, London (2000)
3. Li, J.Q.: Transit bus scheduling with limited energy. Transp. Sci. **48**(4), 521–539 (2014). http://dx.doi.org/10.1287/trsc.2013.0468
4. Liu, J.: Electric vehicle charging infrastructure assignment and power grid impacts assessment in Beijing. Energ. Policy **51**, 544–557 (2012)
5. Worley, O., Klabjan, D.: Optimization of battery charging and purchasing at electric vehicle battery swap stations. In: IEEE Vehicle Power and Propulsion Conference (VPPC), Chicago, IL, 6–9 September 2011, pp. 1–4 (2011)
6. Lombardi, P., Heuer, M., Styczynski, Z.: Battery switch station as storage system in an autonomous power system: optimization issue. In: IEEE Power and Energy Society General Meeting, Minneapolis, MN, 25–29 July 2010, pp. 1–6 (2010)
7. Nielsen, J.: Usability Engineering. Academic Press, Cambridge (1993)
8. Malhotra, Y., Galletta, D.F.: Extending the technology acceptance model to account for social influence: theoretical bases and empirical validation. In: Proceedings of HICSS 1999. IEEE Computer Society (1999)
9. Goffman, E.: The Presentation of Self in Everyday Life. Penguin Books, London (1990)
10. Grudin, J.: Utility and usability: research issues and development contexts. Interact. Comput. **4**(2), 209–217 (1992)

11. Bevan, N., Kirakowski, J., Maissel, J.: Proceedings of the 4th International Conference on HCI, Stuttgart (1991). http://www.nigelbevan.com/papers/whatis92.pdf
12. ISO 9241-11: International standard first edition. Ergonomic requirements for office work with visual display terminals (VDTs), Part 11: Guidance on usability (1998). http://www.idemployee.id.tue.nl/g.w.m.rauterberg/lecturenotes/ISO9241part11.pdf

Detecting Multitasking Work and Negative Routines from Computer Logs

Hirofumi Kaburagi[✉], Simona Vasilache, and Jiro Tanaka

University of Tsukuba, Tsukuba, Japan
{kaburagi,simona,jiro}@iplab.cs.tsukuba.ac.jp

Abstract. Multitasking on digital media has a negative effect on mental health and concentration. At the same time, the negative effects of computer usage are not immediately obvious to most people. We suggest that people can improve their daily experience on the computer if they pay closer attention to their multitasking activities. To this end, we have constructed a system that detects multitasking work and periodic negative multitasking routines from computer logs. We created two indicators: relax rate and multitasking rate. The relax rate is defined on the basis of heart rate variability information and the multitasking rate is derived from how often users switch their computer windows. We analyze whether users' multitasking is negative or not and whether or not negative multitasking is part of a periodic routine. We logged the computer activities and heart rate data of one participant for six days.

Keywords: Human factors · Activity tracking · Computer log · Multitasking · Stress · Time management · Digital lifestyle · Lifelog

1 Introduction

As computers are becoming increasingly ubiquitous, people are spending more and more time on computers. Information and communication technology has greatly improved, to the point that users can read the news, write reports, play games, or watch sports events while easily switching between these tasks on the same computer. People's lives' are made easier this way, but as stated in [1], multitasking is an activity that distracts users and generally has a negative effect on the brain.

For instance, as reported in [5], one college student stated: "I spend so much time on social network sites every day and play games on it that I have to work at night, which increases my stress." This shows that he cannot control his activities on his computer, even though this lack of control induces irritation. Doidge [4] points out that brains keep their neurons' routines whether these routines are positive or negative.

It is often said that we become more knowledgeable through obtaining a variety of information from the Internet. However, as part of this process we are often forced to perform quick task switching and multitasking during Web

© Springer International Publishing Switzerland 2016
S. Yamamoto (Ed.): HIMI 2016, Part II, LNCS 9735, pp. 542–549, 2016.
DOI: 10.1007/978-3-319-40397-7_52

browsing. Small et al. show that the human brain is rapidly changed through Web searching [2,3]. According to Small's experiment, users improve some of their capabilities, such as scanning or quickly multitasking. Yet, Ophir et al. state that digital media heavy multitaskers are more likely to be distracted by irrelevant environmental stimuli than light multitaskers [7]. This research indicates that their capabilities, such as concentrating or memorization, are diminishing.

Hence, multitasking and negative routines have a negative effect on users. However, most users are not aware of this effect. We intend to develop a system that analyzes user activity on a computer and then provides users with a visual representation of the results.

2   System Description

Our system has the following two main functions.

- detecting multitasking and negative routines,
- visually representing results on a graph.

Figure 1a shows an overview of our system. First, it records computer activity data (using free software such as Manictime [11] or Kidlogger) and at the same time monitors the user's heart rate using a ready-made activity tracker. Next, it analyzes the collected data.

2.1   Logging Computer Activity

We log the user's computer activity using an application such as Kidlogger or Manictime [11,12]. The software generates a log every time a user opens a new window or switches between already opened windows. Each log record includes the starting time and duration of the active window, the name of the application, and a URL (if the window is a Web browser tab), as well as the duration of inactivity. We export raw data as a csv file and use it in our system. Figure 1b shows sample computer logs.

2.2   Observing Heart Rate Using an Activity Tracker

The computer works in conjunction with an activity tracker to gather heart rate information. We use the Fitbit Charge HR, as this device can send heart rate information through a wireless network.

2.3   Detecting Multitasking and Negative Routines

We propose a method of detecting multitasking and negative routines. Two indicators are used for this: relax rate and multitasking rate.

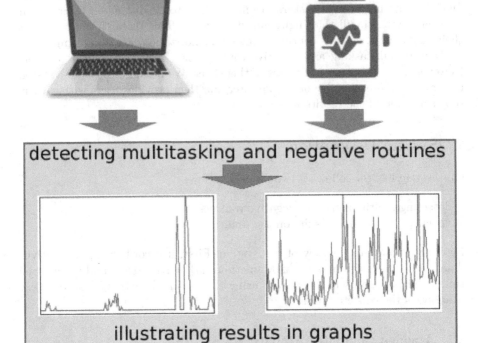

(a) Overview of the system

Name	Start	End	Duration	Domain
http://www.msn.com/ja-jp/?pc=SK2M&ocid=SK2MDHP8	19:44:18	19:44:23	0:00:05	www.msn.com
https://toefl-registration.ets.org/TOEFLWeb/profile/sel	19:45:58	19:46:04	0:00:06	toefl-registration.ets.org
https://toefl-registration.ets.org/TOEFLWeb/order/subr	19:46:04	19:46:10	0:00:06	toefl-registration.ets.org
https://toefl-registration.ets.org/TOEFLWeb/order/subr	19:46:15	19:46:23	0:00:08	toefl-registration.ets.org
https://toefl-registration.ets.org/TOEFLWeb/order/subr	19:46:23	19:46:33	0:00:10	toefl-registration.ets.org
https://toefl-registration.ets.org/TOEFLWeb/order/subr	19:46:33	19:46:41	0:00:08	toefl-registration.ets.org
https://toefl-registration.ets.org/TOEFLWeb/order/subr	19:46:41	19:46:49	0:00:08	toefl-registration.ets.org
https://toefl-registration.ets.org/TOEFLWeb/order/can	19:46:55	19:47:03	0:00:08	toefl-registration.ets.org
https://toefl-registration.ets.org/TOEFLWeb/order/sear	19:47:03	19:47:08	0:00:05	toefl-registration.ets.org
https://toefl-registration.ets.org/TOEFLWeb/order/disp	19:47:08	19:47:19	0:00:11	toefl-registration.ets.org
https://toefl-registration.ets.org/TOEFLWeb/order/subr	19:47:19	19:47:29	0:00:10	toefl-registration.ets.org
https://toefl-registration.ets.org/TOEFLWeb/order/disp	19:47:29	19:47:35	0:00:06	toefl-registration.ets.org
https://toefl-registration.ets.org/TOEFLWeb/account/s	19:47:35	19:47:49	0:00:14	toefl-registration.ets.org
https://production.ets-hosted.cybersource.com/ets-ho	19:47:49	19:48:02	0:00:13	production.ets-hosted.cybersource.com
https://production.ets-hosted.cybersource.com/ets-ho	19:48:02	19:49:02	0:01:00	production.ets-hosted.cybersource.com
https://production.ets-hosted.cybersource.com/ets-ho	19:49:02	19:49:12	0:00:10	production.ets-hosted.cybersource.com
document 1	19:49:25	19:49:39	0:00:14	document 1
https://www.google.co.jp/search?q=We+are+unable+to+|	19:50:05	19:50:26	0:00:21	www.google.co.jp
https://www.drupal.org/node/941216	19:50:26	19:50:51	0:00:25	www.drupal.org
https://www.drupal.org/node/941216	19:51:00	19:51:37	0:00:37	www.drupal.org
https://www.google.co.jp/search?q=We+are+unable+to+|	19:51:37	19:51:48	0:00:11	www.google.co.jp
https://www.google.co.jp/search?q=We+are+unable+to+|	19:51:53	19:52:01	0:00:08	www.google.co.jp
https://www.google.co.jp/search?q=We+are+unable+to+|	19:52:01	19:52:08	0:00:07	www.google.co.jp
https://production.ets-hosted.cybersource.com/ets-ho	19:52:22	19:52:29	0:00:07	production.ets-hosted.cybersource.com
https://production.ets-hosted.cybersource.com/ets-ho	19:52:34	19:52:48	0:00:14	production.ets-hosted.cybersource.com

(b) Computer activities

Fig. 1. Overview and computer activities

Heart Rate Variability and Relax Rate. We use heart rate information to measure stress. Heart rate variability (HRV) is considered a valid indicator of mental stress in clinical studies [9,10]. One of the variables used to calculate HRV is the standard deviation of the NN interval (SDNN). NN interval is the interval between two consecutive beats. In medical research, NN intervals per beat are observed by biosensors. However, we do not use precise NN intervals in our research. If we want to observe precise NN intervals, we need to use a large sensor (e.g., one that requires a chest strap), however this is likely to be burdensome for most users. A wrist-worn activity tracker such as Fitbit Charge HR is better, yet this tracker cannot observe NN interval directly. Thus, we use the mean of the heart rate over 60 s (heart rate over the course of 60 s divided by 60). Consequently, we define the relax rate as the standard deviation of the mean of the heart rate interval over 60 s. The relax rate is similar to SDNN and is used to measure stress. Generally, the lower the HRV value, the higher the degree of stress. Therefore, in our research, the lower the relax rate value, the higher the degree of stress.

Computer Logs and Multitasking Rate. We analyze how users multitask and define the multitasking rate as read by computer logs. Logs have the starting time of the active window and include the name of the application or a URL. We calculate the times of switching windows from the logs. Our concept is that the more frequently a user switches the active window, the more that user is multitasking. MR, NA and SW refer to the multitasking rate, the number of applications (and URL, if user is browsing), and the number of times of switching windows, respectively. Then, we define an equation, $MR = \sqrt{NA * SW}$ For example, if we browse three pages and switch windows four times, the multitasking rate is $\sqrt{3 * 4} = \sqrt{12}$.

Detecting Negative Multitasking by Multitasking Rate and Relax Rate. We construct a theory to detect negative multitasking with the relax rate and multitasking rate. First, we define conditional equality with the relax rate and multitasking rate (requirement 1). If a multitasking activity satisfies the following requirement 1 (where RR represents relax rate), we regard it as a negative multitasking.

$$RR < C_{RR} \text{ and } C_{MR} < MR \quad \text{(requirement 1)}$$
$$C_{RR} : \text{median of Relax rate}$$
$$C_{MR} : \text{median of Multitasking rate}$$

Detecting Periodic Negative Multitasking Routines. We detect not only negative multitasking activities but also whether these multitasking activities are periodical or not. If a multitasking activity satisfies requirement 1, and if it always takes place at the same time, we consider it a periodical negative multitasking routine.

2.4 Visualizing Results on a Graph

We visualize the relax rate, the multitasking rate, and our analysis of the data on a graph.

3 Experiment

3.1 Overview of Experiment

We tracked the heart rate data and the logged computer activity of one participant over a period of six days. The participant installed our system on his laptop computer and he wore an activity tracker all day, except during taking a shower and charging the battery of the device. We monitored his activities and heart rate for most of the day. We performed an experiment in which our system attempted to detect negative multitasking and periodical negative multitasking routines.

3.2 Results

We show the results of calculating the relax rate and multitasking value, as well as our analysis of negative multitasking. We also observe whether negative multitasking activities are periodical negative multitasking activities or not. Figure 2a shows the relax rate for February 3. As we can observe, the relax rate presents lower values than median on February 3 between 19:00 and 20:00. We deduce from this observation that the user feels stressed during this interval.

The multitasking rate is plotted in Fig. 2b. According to the computer activity data (Fig. 1b), the user tends to perform multitasking between 19:00 and 20:00.

Similarly, Fig. 2c shows the relax rate value over a period of six days, and the multitasking rate is drawn in Fig. 2d. According to Fig. 2d, the participant has the habit of multitasking between 19:00 and 21:00, and then he tends to feel stressed, as suggested in Fig. 2c. Figure 2e and f show the results of our analysis, specifically, whether the user's multitasking activities are negative or not. From Fig. 2f, we can observe negative multitasking between 19:00 and 21:00 on several of the six days, leading us to conclude that the user has a periodical negative multitasking routine between 19:00 and 21:00.

3.3 Considerations

We detect multitasking activities and negative multitasking routines through observing six days of data gathered by our system. We should, however, consider external factors. For example, the participant in our experiment ate breakfast at 10:00 and dinner at 18:00. We can guess that the reason for a significant increase in the relax rate (HRV) is breakfast and dinner. Thus, we need to investigate whether external events, such as dinner or exercise, affect the results or not, even though they are separate from multitasking time.

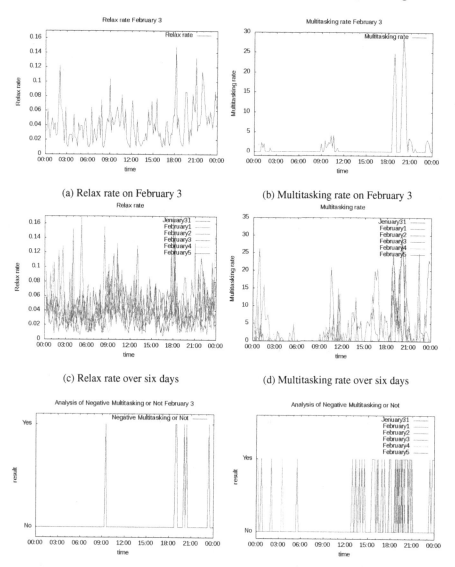

(a) Relax rate on February 3

(b) Multitasking rate on February 3

(c) Relax rate over six days

(d) Multitasking rate over six days

(e) Analysis of negative multitasking on February 3   (f) Analysis of negative multitasking over six days

Fig. 2. Results (Color figure online)

Yet, we could also state that the multitasking activities influence on relax rate. We could assume that the user wants to relax after dinner by surfing the Internet (according to the logs, he often watches sports news). However, our system detects this routine as stressful. In fact, we suggest that he was not relaxed during this routine.

In addition, we also need to solve a problem related to logging. For example, in our experiment, we can observe that on February 4 the multitasking rate is very low. Our system, which uses Manictime running on Windows, logged a low number of activities. This occurred because the participant used a different OS on February 4. In the future, we intend to use other software programs (e.g., Kidlogger[1]) that work on various OSs (Mac, Android).

Graphical Interface and Feedback. We intend to collect more data and receive more feedback in order to improve the reliability of our system. Moreover, we are going to develop a graphical interface to visualize our graphs. We found that our results, such as those in Fig. 2c, f, are too complicated for the average user to easily comprehend, meaning they cannot be used to obtain precise feedback. Hence, we will try to reconsider requirement 1 or the way in which we show the results. Finally, we intend to experiment and research the extent to which users realize the nature of their habits (negative, periodic etc.), as well as evaluate the usability of our system.

4   Related Work

4.1   Influence of Multitasking

Lottridge et al. examined how "heavy" and "light" digital multitaskers differ in analytical writing [6]. They observed that "heavy" multitaskers write low quality essays when faced with task-irrelevant distractors and write high quality essays when faced with task-relevant distractors. Lottridge pointed out that multitasking does not cause problems in focusing on the right things; rather, multitaskers have trouble ignoring the wrong things.

Ophir et al. found through examining cognitive tests that heavy multitaskers tend to be distracted by irrelevant environmental stimuli [7]. In their experiments, participants viewed two consecutive exposures of an array of rectangles. First, they memorized an image, and next, they looked at a second image and pointed out whether or not a red target rectangle had changed from the first, while ignoring a blue distracting rectangle. Results showed that heavy multitaskers had less accurate selection than light multitaskers under given condition.

4.2   Analysis of Multitasking

Mark et al. investigated the relationship between computer and mobile activity [5]. Participants installed a logging software (Kidlogger [12]) and logged their computer or smartphone activities. They also wore heart rate monitors to collect heart rate variability, which is a measure of stress. The authors found a positive relationship between window-switching frequency and stress.

---

[1] Manictime can export richer logs and is more useful than Kidlogger, which is why we adopted Manictime initially.

Dabbish et al. suggested that self-interruption increases depending on the external environmental [8]. They found that people in open office environments interrupt themselves frequently.

5   Conclusion

Digital media multitasking is increasingly common and can negatively affect user memory and concentration. We consider periodic multitasking as having a particularly strong negative influence. In response to this issue, we created a system that detects multitasking routines and visualizes the results of analysis to users. By seeing the results, we believe that users can become aware of the negative impact on their health and possibly give up their negative routines. Our system is effective in the detection of multitasking activities; however, we feel it can be improved further. In our future work, we will gather feedback from more users and analyze their observations and the data we obtain from them.

References

1. Patricia, M.: Greenfield.: technology and informal education. Science **323**(5910), 72–75 (2009)
2. Small, G., Vorgan, G.: iBrain: Surviving the Technological Alteration of the Modern Mind. Collins, New York (2008)
3. Small, G.W., Moody, T.D., Siddarth, P., Bookheimer, S.Y.: Your brain on google: patterns of cerebral activation during internet searching. Am. J. Geriatic psychiatry **17**(2), 116–126 (2009)
4. Doidge, N.: The Brain That Changes Itself: stories of personal Triumpb from the Frontiers of Brain Science. Penguin, New York (2007)
5. Mark, G., Wang, Y., Niiya, M.: Stress and Multitasking in Everyday College Life. In: Proceedings of CHI2014, pp. 41–50. ACM, New York (2014)
6. Lottridge, D.M., Rosakranse, C., Oh, C.S., Westwood, S.J., Baldoni, K., Mann, A.S., Nass, C.I.: The Effects of Chronic Multitasking on Analytical Writing. In: Proceedings of CHI2015, pp. 2967–2970. ACM, New York (2015)
7. Ophir, E., Nass, C., Wagner, A.D.: Cognitive control in media multitasker. PNAS **106**(37), 15583–15587 (2009)
8. Dabbish, L., Mark, G., Gonzalez, V.: Why do i keep interrupting myself?: environment, habit and self-interruption. In: Proceedings of CHI2011, pp. 3127–3130. ACM, New York (2011)
9. Acharya, U.R., Joseph, K.P., Kannathal, N., Lim, C.M., Suri, J.S.: Heart rate variability: a review. Med. Bio. Eng. Comput. **44**(12), 1031–1051 (2006)
10. Malik, M.: Heart rate variability; standards of measurement, physiological interpretation, and clinical use. Ann. of Noninvasive Electrocardiol. **1**(2), 151–181 (1996)
11. Manictime. http://www.manictime.com
12. Kidlogger. http://kidlogger.net

A Leader and Media Spot Estimation Method Using Location Information

Koya Kimura[1]([X]), Yurika Shiozu[2], Ivan Tanev[1], and Katsunori Shimohara[1]

[1] Graduate School of Science and Engineering, Doshisha University, Kyoto, Japan
{kimura2013,itanev,kshimoha}@sil.doshisha.ac.jp
[2] Faculty of Economics, Aichi University, Nagoya, Japan
yshiozu@vega.aichi-u.ac.jp

Abstract. This research aims to characterize the system of local resident-based regional activations using ICT. It verifies the hypothesis that an individual participates aggressively in the local community planning only when the main activity does not take place in the home and workplace. Verification was conducted by employing a proposed leader estimation method that uses kernel density estimation (KDE) and evaluated questionnaire results. This method was applied to location information gathered between August 1 and 31 in 2015. This research finds that KDE can serve as a visualization method to promote awareness.

1 Introduction

After the Tohoku Earthquake, the structure of regional communities in Japan was challenged. Japan is the first country to have a super-aging society, first noted in 2007. Having strong leaders who would lead the community for the locals' regional activation was deemed necessary. Non-profit organizations and municipalities provided leadership training courses to train the regional leaders. According to the latest Annual Health, Labour and Welfare Report, the number of people who want to help in the community increased despite an observed weakening of the connections among members of the communities [1].

Over the past few years, information and communications technology (ICT) has become more familiar to people, owing to the spread of smartphones. The Cyber Physical System (CPS) has become an active area of research in the field of computer science. CPS is a system that collects data on both inanimate objects and humans and then integrates and analyzes them for application in the community. In its Strategy Proposal for 2012, the Japan Science and Technology Agency proposed the usage of CPS to promote community involvement among the elderly [2].

The research on "constructing" the system has been successful, but that on its "usage" is in the developing stage. Moreover, the introduction of the system does not always guarantee regional activation, which always depends on the locals who will notice their problems and act to solve them. As such, the present research aimed to characterize the system of local resident-based regional activations using ICT.

© Springer International Publishing Switzerland 2016
S. Yamamoto (Ed.): HIMI 2016, Part II, LNCS 9735, pp. 550–559, 2016.
DOI: 10.1007/978-3-319-40397-7_53

In this research, the hypothesis that an individual participates aggressively in local community planning only when the main activity does not take place in the home or workplace was verified. A leader estimation method using kernel density estimation (KDE) and evaluated questionnaire results was proposed to be the method of verification. Such method was applied to location information gathered between August 1 and 31 in 2015. The appropriateness of the estimation method was evaluated by comparing estimation and questionnaire results using a name generator form.

2   Research Concept and Related Research

2.1   Resident-Centered Vitalization of the Local Community

Ushino's research (1982) on local resident-based regional development explained the importance of such concept and proposed a system called "Kande System" [3]. Ushino said that after the industrialization and urbanization in the 1950s, the village communities in the rural areas were divided by the agricultural policy and then re-integrated in the 1970s to create a new regional system. The importance of local resident-based regional development has already been a significant research topic since the 1980s.

Meanwhile, Yoshizumi's case study (2013) analyzed the way for locals to develop regions sustainably and suggested the "Eco Card System" [4]. In this system, the locals are given a stamp card called "Eco Card" that promotes environmental activities, thereby creating a setup for the locals to be involved in the region. This system highlights the importance of visualizing or making the locals notice the problems for them to manage local resident-based regional development.

2.2   Importance of Regional Leaders

Hayashi (2007) focused on the importance of regional leaders [5]. In particular, he looked into one of the leaders who made a huge success at a village by promoting green tourism. He analyzed why the program worked and how the leader became one. He concluded that the leader's huge success was attributed to the vast human network between the farmers and the government.

The Handbook of Training Regional Development Leaders issued by the Statistical Research and Training Institute in 2014 [6] says that a leader needs to meet the following criteria:

- Be passionate and have belief of improving the region
- Be able to develop and harmonize many kinds of opinions from the locals

The handbook also says that the organization needs to do the following to keep the leader at a sustained position:

- Excavate and develop
- Develop a successor and division of roles

Hence, having a big human network and sophisticated communication skill are needed to become a regional leader. The organization also needs to develop a successor at an early stage to attain a sustained village development.

2.3 Research Concept

The above discussion explained how local resident-based regional development is tightly connected with the presence of a leader; developing a successor at an early stage is important for a sustained village development. Visualizing or making the locals notice the problem for them to be able to manage local resident-based regional development has also been emphasized. The research examples and the government's approaches, such as that of the Statistical Research and Training Institute, indicate a society that aspires to promote local resident-based regional developments.

All these analyses on successful cases and proposals to the regions have existed independently. However, the following three steps must be done continuously to be able to achieve successful village developments:

- A proposal for a better region
- A practice of the proposal
- An analysis on the practice

A region will most likely not practice a proposed plan that has never been tried or has failed. A successful village development plan does not always work in different regions. Hence, attention has been given to "community designers" or "facilitators" who make the three-step sequence into a cycle and help in regional activations [7].

This type of social situation has prompted the development of several approaches from the computer science field, including the Strategy Proposal of 2012 mentioned above. The person-watching system for the elderly and smart city system are examples of these approaches. Despite the need for these approaches in many regions, most regions lack the system that allows them to work on regional activation. Having a facilitator to extract the region's problem and solve it with the locals is how a community design works.

However, it is difficult at times to solve a new problem as a facilitator cannot do the problem extraction at the same region all the time. At the same time, the computer science field has no available research on ways to solve regional problems, only proposals for the usage of such systems. In terms of connections in regions, most research works focus on virtual connections, such as regional social networking services.

Hence, more studies that are directly related with real-world connections are needed. As such, the present research focuses on residents and the promotion of ICT-aided visualization, or making the locals notice their community's problems using ICT. ICT was used as a tool to help the locals, who are the subject of problem solving. The visualization of a new leader was selected as the first step to help the locals.

3   Experiment Method

This section presents the hypothesis on a local leader, inspection method, and demonstration experiment conducted for the inspection.

The researchers performed KDE using location information acquired from the smartphones given to experiment cooperators. By deriving the local maximums, the researchers extracted the place where each person was usually found. The extracted locations were compared with the hypothesis and then analyzed.

3.1   Hypothesis and Inspection Method

The hypothesis was that "an individual participates aggressively in local community planning only when the local activity does not take place in the home or workplace." The first step was an estimation of "the place where the person was usually found" to inspect this hypothesis. The researchers used KDE, a nonparametric technique to estimate probability density function. It is not necessary to set a boundary. The estimated kernel probability density function is expressed as follows.

$$\widehat{f}_h(x) = \frac{1}{Nh} \sum_{i=1}^{N} K\left(\frac{x - x_i}{h}\right) \tag{1}$$

$K(x)$ is a kernel function and h is a bandwidth. The researchers used (2) Gaussian kernel for a kernel function.

$$K(x) = \frac{1}{\sqrt{2\pi}} e^{-\frac{1}{2}x^2} \tag{2}$$

In addition, the researchers applied Scott's Rule expressed in (3) to the bandwidth.

$$h = \frac{1.06\sigma}{n^{0.2}} \tag{3}$$

$$\sigma = min\left\{S.D., \frac{q(0.75) - q(0.25)}{1.34}\right\} \tag{4}$$

where n is the number of dimensions, $S.D.$ is standard deviation, and $q(0.75) - q(0.25)$ is four-quantiles acquired by subtracting first four-quantiles from third four-quantiles.

The two-dimensional (2D) location information (the point showing a position) consisted of latitude and longitude that recorded a person's action at a specific time. The point that showed many positions at the spot where the person stayed in will be plotted, and then density would become higher. The part that is high in density appears as the maximum value. Subsequently, the researchers derived the probability density function of this location information using KDE and then estimated the place where each person was usually found by counting the number of maximum value locations. The inspection of the hypothesis followed. A media spot was defined as the place where communication is active in an area. "Active communication" refers to the place where many residents gather in an area. The media spot estimation method entailed the following steps:

- Find the local maximums using KDE from each person's location information.
- The local maximums show places who was usually found as it shows density of location information.
- Delete location information around the global maximums, which are expected main activity places such as the home and workplace.
- Collect the dataset with deleted information on the home and workplace.
- Apply KDE to the collected dataset and then find the local maximums as media spots.

The researchers also used Numpy and Scipy, which are libraries for high-level scientific calculations of Python for the inspection.

3.2   Summary of the Proof Experiment

The field experiments were conducted in the Makishima area in Uji City, Kyoto Prefecture, Japan, in cooperation with members of the non-profit corporation Makishima Kizuna-no-Kai. Through the experiments, information related to community activities was collected using the smartphones provided to the participants. Table 1 presents the data on experiment cooperators. Tables 2 and 3 present the data on experimental installation. The activity data included "location information," "email exchanges," and "passing information using Bluetooth."

The action data were analyzed using location information. The location information was acquired every minute, except for the following situations:

- The researchers announced that "the experiment cooperator can switch off the smartphone when he/she does not want to inform his/her location information."
- The smartphone has run out of battery/the experiment cooperator forgets to carry the smartphone.
- The smartphone cannot transmit location information as it is out of range.
- The timing when the Android finishes to acquire location information is not determined exactly.

3.3   Evaluation of the Appropriateness of the Estimation Method

The researchers designed a questionnaire using a name generator form and conducted a survey before the field experiment. The name generator form is a method for identifying a respondent's relationship with the names of persons in the questionnaire entries. The questionnaire included an item that asks for the name of the person who is thought to be the leader in an area. The questionnaire results were evaluated. The proposed method was applied to location information between August 1 and 31 in 2015.

Table 1. Field experiment data

Area	Makishima, Uji, Kyoto, Japan
Number of experiment cooperators	20–50 persons
Age	30–70yo
First period	November 11 to December 10, 2013
Second period	February 11 to March 27, 2015
Third period	July 11, 2015 to January 11, 2016

Table 2. Experimental installation (first period)

Network career	NTT docomo
Manufacturer of smartphone	Fujitsu
Model number of smartphone	ARROWS Kiss F-03E
OS	Android 4.0.4

4   Results of the Analysis and Discussion

4.1   Leader Estimation

Figure 1 shows a portion of the results of applying KDE to location information (left) and leader estimation (right). The upper side shows 2D figures. The vertical and horizontal axes represent latitude and longitude, respectively. The blue part is the place of the point's high density. Meanwhile, the bottom side shows three-dimensional (3D) figures. The left and right axes represent latitude and longitude, respectively. The upper axis represents density. The red part means the place of the point's high density.

Figure 2 presents a scatter diagram for the comparison of peaks of leader estimation method and the total number of points for the question "Who do you think is the leader?" The correlation coefficient ($r = 0.0046$) does not show a correlation peaks of leader estimation method and the total number of that question. The following are reasons for such low correlation:

The following are reasons for such low correlation:

- The experiment cooperators comments:
  - The person who does community involvement in his/her home

Table 3. Experimental installation (second & third periods)

Network career	IIJ mobile
Manufacturer of smartphone	ASUS
Model number of smartphone	ZenFone 5 A500KL
OS	Android 4.4.2

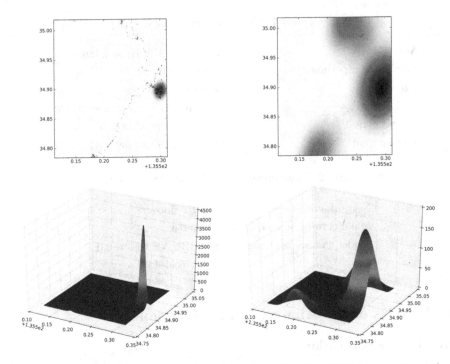

Fig. 1. Left: The results of applying kernel density estimation (KDE) to location information; right: the results of leader estimation (a portion). (Color figure online)

- - The person who works at the place where he/she has become active in the local community such as hosting an event
- – Analysis algorithms
  - From computational resource, the researchers used the reduced data.
  - The location information was not accurate.
  - The time information of location information was not collected.

As regards the comments of experiment cooperators, it is necessary to judge whether location information shows local community activation. A versatile data analysis method that accounts for the use of information sent to other participants via Bluetooth needs to be developed.

Analysis algorithm is a prototype and must be optimized. The kernel function and bandwidth in KDE are fixed in a given datum. When considering the accuracy of the individual location information, the estimated result can be improved by applying accuracy as the bandwidth. Moreover, the present research did not take into account the time when the location information; it was assumed that the local community would not be active in the middle of the night. Thus, an analysis technique that considers the time information would provide improved estimation results.

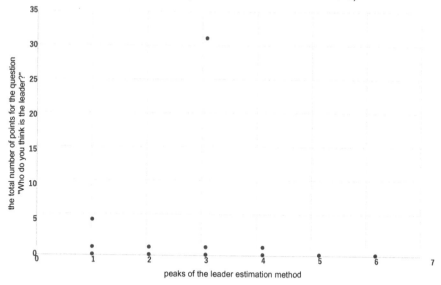

Fig. 2. Scatter diagram for comparison of peaks of the leader estimation method and the total number of points for the question "Who do you think is the leader?"

4.2   Media Spot Estimation

Figure 3 presents the results of executing the media-spot estimation. The upper side shows a 2D figure. The vertical and horizontal axes represent the latitude and longitude, respectively. The blue part is the place of the point's high density. Meanwhile, the lower side is a 3D diagram. The left and right axes represent latitude and longitude, respectively. The upper shaft indicates the density, whereas the red part means the place of the point's high density.

The longitude and latitude of the highest density place are below:

$$(latitude, longitude) = (34.9015292, 135.7827344)$$

This point is close to a meeting place and community center. Hence, an activity place could take place here.

However, this might not be the only place where communication is active in the region. As such, estimating the next media spot is possible by removing location information in the periphery of the densest part of this dataset and then performing the KDE again. However, developing a mechanism to verify the validity of the media spot is necessary as meaningless location information might be visualized as portions having high density.

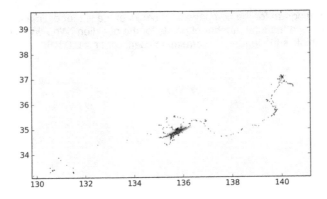

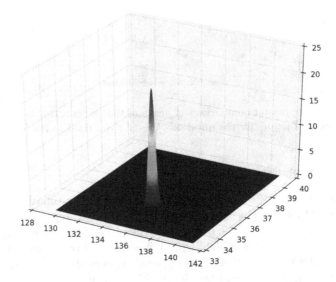

Fig. 3. Results of the media spot estimation (Color figure online)

5   Conclusion

The present research verified the hypothesis that an individual participates aggressively in the local community planning only when the main activity does not place in the home or workplace. Previous studies suggested that this idea is dependent on the importance of the leader who leads the local community. It also promoted resident-centered vitalization of local communities by visualizing the leader and being realized states of local community.

The leader estimation method using KDE and evaluated questionnaire results was proposed to verify the hypothesis. This method was applied to location information between August 1 and 31, 2015, involving the following steps:

- Find the local maximums using KDE from each person's location information.
- The local maximums show places who was usually found as it shows the density of location information.
- Delete location information around the global maximum points, which are assumed main activity places such as the home and workplace.
- Apply KDE to the dataset with deleted location information around the main activity place and then find the local maximums. Compare each person's local maximums and estimate the leader of the local community as the one who has the most local maximum

The research defined a media spot as the place where communication is active in an area. It estimated media spots through the following steps:

- Find the local maximums using KDE from each person's location information.
- The local maximums show places who was usually found as they show the density of location information.
- Delete location information around the global maximums, which are assumed main activity places, such as the home and workplace.
- Collect the dataset with deleted information on the home and workplace.
- Apply KDE to the collected dataset and then identify the local maximums as media spots.

The estimation did not yield good comparative result but KDE was found to be a valid visualization method to promote awareness. From a viewpoint of resident-centered design, data that seem insignificant should be important for residents. As such, the researchers propose that the visualization method of location information by nonparametric method is significant.

Acknowledgement. This work was supported by Grant-in-Aid for JSPS Fellows.

References

1. Ministry of Health: Labour and Welfare: Annual Health. Labour and Welfare Report 2013–2014 (2014)
2. Japan Science and Technology Agency: Research and development on fundamental technologies of cyber physical systems and their social implementation-A case study on promoting aged people to social activities, CDS-FY2012-SP-05 (2013)
3. Ushino, T.: Comprehensive district plan by inhabitants and "Kande" system. J. Rural Plann. Assoc. 1(3), 19–29 (1982)
4. Yoshizumi, M.: A study on actively community-based environmental town planning toward sustainable communities: a case study on the Eco-community program in Nishinomiya, Hyogo, Japan. J. City Plann. Inst. Jpn. 48(3), 831–836 (2013)
5. Hayashi, T.: Development factors of agritourism in Nagawa district, Nanbu town, Aomori prefecture: role of local leaders. Geog. Rev. Jpn. 80(11), 635–659 (2007)
6. Statistical Research and Training Institute (Jinzairyoku Kasseika Kenkyujo), Ministry of Internal Affairs and Communications: Handbook of training regional development leaders (Chiiki Zukurijin Ikusei Handobukku) (2014). http://www.soumu.go.jp/main_content/000352864.pdf. Accessed 24 Dec 2015
7. Yamazaki, R.: "Community Design", Gakugei Shuppansha (2011)

What Kind of Foreign Baseball Players Want to Get Japanese Baseball Team?

Hirohito Matsuka[✉] and Yumi Asahi

Department of Management Systems Engineering,
School of Information and Telecommunication Engineering,
Tokai University, Tokyo, Japan
m0657h@gmail.com, asahi@tsc.u-tokai.ac.jp

Abstract. We want to know what kind of foreign baseball player were hired in Japanese Baseball League. We used the data that is from Nippon Professional Baseball (NPB). We only used the result which is batter for one year. At first, we want to know about characteristics which is the team current situation. Then we used the way that is principal component analysis. The ingredients are a hit, 2-base hit, 3-base hit, Home run, Run batted in, Stolen base, Sacrifice, Four balls, Dead ball, Struck out and Double play hitting. We could find the two components. First, it is power hitter that is a lot of home run. Second, it is short hitter that is difficult to become out. We used the result which show a graph which is team current situation. That mean, we could easy to understand that is team characteristics, because we could see the graph. We compared between current team situation and except foreign baseball players. The reason is because we want to know the position that the role of foreign baseball players. We could find reason that the role of foreign baseball players. There is one reason for this. Foreign baseball players are needed to power. That is why Japanese team don't have a lot of power hitter. Therefore Japanese team need to hire foreign baseball players for the win.

Keywords: Decision support systems · Principal component analysis

1 Introduction

1.1 About Japanese Baseball League

We used the data that is from Nippon Professional Baseball (NPB) at that site. NPB have two leagues. There are Pacific League and Central League. The two leagues have six teams of each, NPB has total 12 teams. The 12 team have a home ground around Japan. The way how to become champion in Japanese baseball league for one year. At first, the team have to win the league for one year as much as possible, the team is decided to belong the league which are Pacific League or Central League. The battle is held 143 for a year. The team keep winning in the top three for one year each leagues. After the season, the battle would start between second rank of team and third rank of team. The team which is winner that the team could battle first rank of team. As a result, the team is won the league each of Pacific League and Central League, Both of winning team fight baseball game to be become Japanese champion. Major League

S. Yamamoto (Ed.): HIMI 2016, Part II, LNCS 9735, pp. 560–568, 2016.
DOI: 10.1007/978-3-319-40397-7_54

Baseball (MLB) also have two leagues. There are American League and National League same as NPB system, but MLB have a lot of teams. There are 15 of each leagues. MLB has total 30 teams and there are divided three in the league. Consequently there are five teams for each. They are different between NPB and MLB, This is the number of people that could be registered in the regular team. Regular team means that first team. For example, MLB has the Major League and the Minor League. Regular team means Major League. In NPB, it could register 25 players for one year, but it is limited to register foreign baseball players. NPB is decided to register up to four players who are from except Japanese player. They have rules to admit foreign baseball players or not. There are four rule. Firstly, the players go to school which is junior high school, high school or junior college at least for three years. Secondly, the players go to university at least for four years. Thirdly, the players live in Japan for three years, in addition the players play baseball in the company at least for five years. Forth, the players could be gotten the right which is Free Agent (FA). FA means that the player could play baseball in NPB at least 8 years, then the player could be gotten a FA. If you would like to go to foreign country though getting FA, the player could play baseball in NPB at least for 9 years. After 8 or 9 years, you could be gotten FA, the player could go anywhere. If there are team, the team want to be gotten you, the player could move that team. If the players full at least one rule, the players could be allowed Japanese players. Furthermore, NPB couldn't be allowed to register only pitcher and batter. If the team want to register four foreign baseball players, the team should register both pitcher and batter at least one players. In contrast, MLB could register 28 players for one year, MLB doesn't have limitation to register foreign baseball players. Therefore the Japanese team want to get successful players who is from foreign baseball players. The team want to search the players who will be successful foreign baseball players in Japan.

1.2 Date Used for the Analysis

The data that could be used for Japanese Baseball Team. The team should be hired foreign baseball player for the win. There is a data that could be used Japanese Baseball team.

1.3 Explain the Data

The team data used for the analysis.

It is used 670 player who is playing in Japanese Baseball league in 2015. The data include foreign player. Table 1 is shown the rank of league on 2015. This season HOWKS became a champion on 2015.

The result that baseball player were played for a year in Japan.
Term: 27th March 2015–7th October 2015

Table 2 means a number of people who is played regular team. NPB has rules which are limited to register on the regular team. The number are 28 players. In addition, if the players are moved from regular team to second team, the player could

Table 1. The rank of league on 2015

Rank	Central League	Pacific League
1	SWAROWS	HOWKS
2	GIANTS	FAITARS
3	TIGERS	MARINES
4	CARP	LIONS
5	DRAGONS	BAFFALOWS
6	BAYSTARS	EAGLES

Table 2. A number of register on the regular team on 2015

Team	Member
EAGLES	66
DRAGONS	60
BAFFALOWS	60
TIGERS	57
BAYSTARS	57
FAITARS	57
GIANTS	54
MARINES	53
LIONS	52
HOWKS	52
CARP	51
SWAROWS	51

not register on regular team for 10 days. second team means that Minor league in case of Japan.

Tables 3 and 4 means salary on Japanese Baseball League of each club. Japanese League were gotten a salary less than Major League Baseball. From this result, the Japanese baseball player want to go Major baseball league.

1.4   The Team's Home Ground

The map is shown where home ground of each team. The 12 teams are scattered in Japan. Mainly Pacific league are scattered in Japan. Pacific league is a local contact type more than Central League. The rectangular is showed Pacific league (Fig. 1).

Table 3. Average annual salary (Unit: Dollar)

Team	Average annual salary
GIANTS	482,270
BAFFALOWS	441,977
HOWKS	439,573
TIGERS	402,182
SWAROWS	328,892
MARINES	307,917
LIONS	290,838
FAITARS	290,009
DRAGONS	285,946
CARP	284,454
BAYSTARS	272,267
EAGLES	258,338
Average	340,389
Median	299,378

Table 4. Average annual salary

		(Unit: Dollar)
Country	Japan	Major
Average annual salary	340,389	3,952,252

(1 dollar = 112 yen in February)

2   Result of Analysis

2.1   The Data to Analyze

The Table 2 is shown that a number of foreign baseball players in each team. Japanese Baseball League has total 72 foreign baseball players. The league has 6 foreign baseball player in average. It mean that there are 6 foreign baseball players in each club. However the team could be registered 4 foreign baseball player in the regular team. Some of the foreign baseball players could not play baseball in regular team that the player will be left the team next year. In addition, the team was spent a lot of money to be hired foreign baseball players and also the tem was spent a lot of money that to be used searching about many foreign baseball players who is the better player for the team (Table 5).

Table 5. Result of principal component analysis

Ingredients	1	2
a hit	0.979	0.32
2-base hit	0.953	-0.9
3-base hit	0.589	0.501
Home run	0.847	-0.372
Run batted in	0.954	-0.218
Stolen base	0.643	0.546
Sacrifice	0.412	0.715
Four balls	0.943	-0.057
Dead ball	0.741	-0.125
Struck out	0.944	-0.045
Double play hitting	0.862	-0.201

A hit means that the batter hit the ball from the pitcher, the batter run to first base and stop the base. 2 base hit means that the batter hit the ball from the pitcher, the batter run to second base and stop the base. 3 base hit means that the batter hit the ball from the pitcher, the batter run to third base and stop the base. Home run means that the batter hit the ball from the pitcher, the ball over the fence with no bound or the batter run to fourth base. Run batted in means that the batter hit the ball from the pitcher, besides the runner run to the fourth base. Stolen base means that the runner run to next base such as from first base to second base during the pitcher is throwing the ball to catcher. Sacrifice means that the batter is advanced the runner to next base by the batter's sacrificed. Four balls means that the pitcher is thrown the four balls and then the batter is advanced to first base. Dead ball means that pitcher hit the ball to the batter's body. And then the batter advanced to the first base. Struck out means that the pitcher is gotten three stories from the batter. The batter is out. Double play hitting means that the batter hit the ball from the pitcher, the batter is gotten the double out.

2.2   Role of Foreign Baseball Player

This figure is shown that the foreign baseball player were given big effect in the team. The players are power hitter because the upper graph is shown the two players in the circle. The circle means power hitter. The bottom graph were shown except the two players. Others teams were show same as EAGLES Japanese Baseball League.

Fig. 1. Japanese map

2.3   The Result of Foreign Player

Table 6 is shown that result of two foreign baseball players on 2015. The data shown that the players hit a lot of home run. Therefore Fig. 2 shown that result.

Table 6. The result of two foregin players on 2015

Name	Wily Modesto Peña	Zelous Lamar Wheeler
Official Game	125	91
Plate Appearance	492	313
At Bats	406	274
Run	51	28
A Base Hit	109	70
2 Base Hit	20	12
3 Base Hit	1	0
Home Hun	17	14
Base Hit	182	124
Runs Batted In	40	50
Stolen Base	1	1
Caught Stealing	3	0
Sacrifice	0	0
Sacrifice fly	0	3
Four Balls	70	30
Intentional Walk	0	0
Dead Ball	16	6
Struck Out	111	63
Double Play Hitting	5	6
Batting Sverage	0.268	0.255
Slugging Percentage	0.448	0.453
On Base Percentage	0.396	0.339

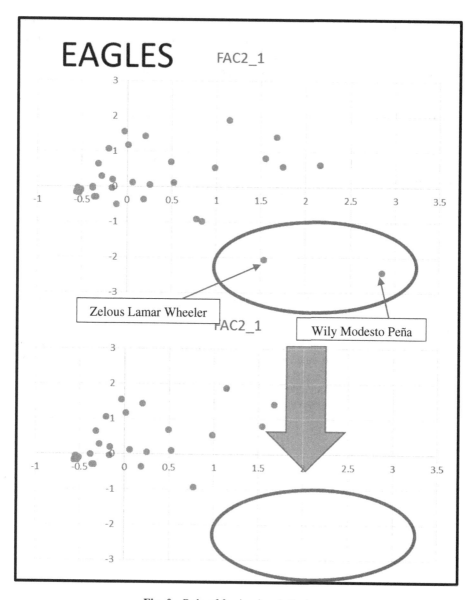

Fig. 2. Role of foreign baseball player

3   Conclusion

3.1   The Data's Conclusion

In the future we have to use the data which is from Major League Baseball (MLB) because if we use the data we more collect answer about who is the supporter for the team. On 2016, EAGLES was left Wily Modesto Peña, the team is not enough long hitter. Therefore the team was hired Japhet Isidro Amador in 2016. The player is from Mexico and the player was gotten an award in Mexican baseball league. EAGLES expect to success in Japanese baseball league. As a result of subject, almost Japanese baseball teams were helped foreign baseball player who are meant power hitter.

4 Further Task

As a result of subject only were used batter's data. We could be included pitcher's data. If we could be used the data, we could be gotten detail information. In addition, we were used data which is only for one year. If we were used for several year's data, we could know player's growing or decline. In conclusion, the team could be easy to decide to hire the player who will expect to success in the team.

References

1. Itoh, E., Katsumi, U.: Yakyu No Saiteki Dajun ni Tuite (On the Optimal Batting Orders of Baseball) (2002)
2. Nabeya, S.: Statistical Analysis of Baseball Data (2007)
3. Takashi, Y., Asami, T., Katoh, Y.: yakyu no dasya type no tigai ni yoru syoukuturyoku Ashi power no tokusei ni tuite (A different type of batter by the effect which are palmar flexion and legs) (1997)
4. Japanese Baseball Association. http://npb.jp/. Accessed 29 Feb 2016
5. Data Freak. http://baseball-data.com/. Accessed 29 Feb 2016

Effect of Changes in Fresh Vegetables Prices Give Consumers

Ryota Morizumi[1](✉) and Yumi Asahi[2](✉)

[1] Course of Information and Telecommunication Engineering,
School of Information and Telecommunication Engineering,
Tokai University, Tokyo, Japan
cm230025@gmail.com
[2] Department of Management Systems Engineering,
School of Information and Telecommunication Engineering,
Tokai University, Tokyo, Japan
asahi@tsc.u-tokai.ac.jp

Abstract. On October 6, 2015, TPP (Trans-Pacific Strategic Economic Partnership Agreement) has reached a basic agreement. TPP benefit in the industrial sector of Japan. However Japanese are wary about agriculture sector. As mountains account for 80 % of country, it cannot be efficient agriculture on a large scale in Japan. It is disadvantageous in the price side too. Furthermore, it becomes the problem that the area under tillage decreases by the aging of the scholar of agriculture. Among in this environment, the freshness vegetables are indispensable to a domestic dining table every day. Therefore, it is necessary that the freshness vegetables are supplied qualitative, price mark and quantitatively. It is the purpose that changes in the price of fresh vegetables is to analyze whether give how to affect the purchasing behavior of consumers.

As the analysis, changes in price and quantity were classified into three features.

Feature 1 is "two peaks of quantity". Feature 2 is "The difference in the Hall vegetables and cut vegetables". Feature 3 is "The difference in the way of price declines".

From the analysis, the authors clarified what kind of influence the change of the price of freshness vegetables had on the purchasing action of consumers. In addition, it was found that there is a difference market transaction price and store price.

Keywords: Comparative analysis · TPP · Time-series data

1 Introduction

1.1 About TPP

On October 6, 2015, TPP (Trans-Pacific Strategic Economic Partnership Agreement) has reached a basic agreement. TPP is diversified economic partnership agreement with the aim of liberalization of the economy by the countries of the Trans-Pacific. TPP was started in among Singapore, Brunei, Chile, and New Zealand on June 3, 2005. After

S. Yamamoto (Ed.): HIMI 2016, Part II, LNCS 9735, pp. 569–578, 2016.
DOI: 10.1007/978-3-319-40397-7_55

that, due to an increase in participating countries, it has joined 12 countries. In addition to this, it is said that Korea and China and Thailand and Taiwan show interest (Fig. 1).

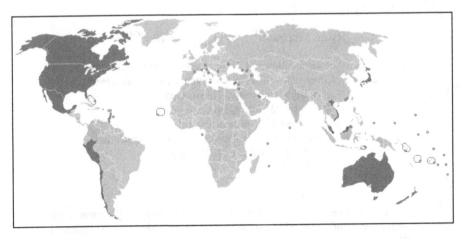

Fig. 1. Negotiations participating countries and Expressed an interest in the past the country (Color figure online)

1.2   Trends in Japan's Agriculture

Approximately 80 % of Japan are mountainous districts. This is attributed that Japan belongs to the Ring of Fire. Therefore, it is difficult for farmer to secure large-scale farmland. Table 1 shows area per farmer review. Farmland area of Japan is about one two-thousandth as small as that of Australia which is a big exporter of farm produce. Being narrow farmland area per one farmhouse is reduced farm production effi-ciency. Therefore, farm production price of Japan is higher than Australia's it.

Table 1. Area per famer review

	Farmland area per one farmhouse	Comparison with Japan
Japan (2006)	1.8ha	-
U.S. (2005)	180.2ha	99times
EU (2005)	16.9ha	9times
Australia (2004)	3,423.8ha	1,902times

In addition, it is for farmers of Japan to be aging and decrease. Figure 2 shows the configuration of the age agriculture employment population. Percentage in this figure shows composition ratio each year and Ave. in figure shows average of age of famers each year. It shows that agriculture employment population in 2015 is less than half compared to that in 1995 and Average age goes on increasing year after year. In particular, the proportion of the agriculture employment population of over 65 years old in 2015 is 63.5 %, and average age in 2015 is 66.3 years old; it is very high.

As a background, there is two reasons that it is policy of the Japanese government and low wages of farmer. About first reason, it has been promoted the policy of reducing

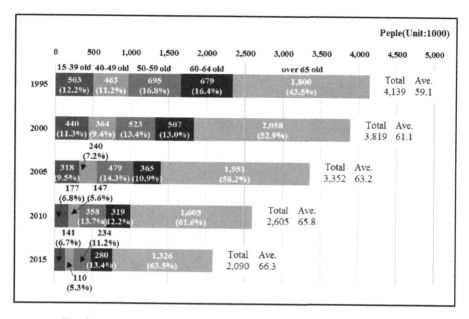

Fig. 2. The configuration of the age agriculture employment population

crop acreage by Japanese government. Japanese major production of agriculture is rice. However, Japanese no longer eats rice by westernizing of eating habits compared to before. For this reason, Japanese government has kept product prices by promoted the policy of reducing crop acreage. For this reason, Japanese government has kept product prices by promoted the policy of reducing crop acreage. At the same time, Japanese government has protected farmers by imposing duties from foreign countries. About second reason, as mentioned previously, there is inefficient farm production. Also, it is thought that the primary industries such as the agriculture and forestry marine products industry continue declining in the country which is high in wages like Japan widely. Furthermore, it is one of the reasons that there is a uniquely Japanese distribution system of production of agriculture. That system is commonly to be through JA (Japan Agricultural Cooperatives). At first, JA was made in order to protect farmers. It was purpose of JA to stabilize shipping prices by shipping together the products. However, in the case of system of JA had to ship all products of making. Therefore, even if farmers thought to want to sell by myself a part of products of making, they weren't able to do it. This means that famers can't decide product prices himself. Accordingly, in recent years, it has become the problem regarding system of JA.

1.3 Trends of Vegetable's Price in Japan

Vegetable's price in Japan is varies greatly. As a background, there is for seasons in Japan. There are the four seasons, and the severe change of the climate is not stable in its production of vegetables. Therefore, vegetable's price is not stable too. Figure 3 shows market transaction price of vegetables in Tokyo. The vertical line in Fig. 3

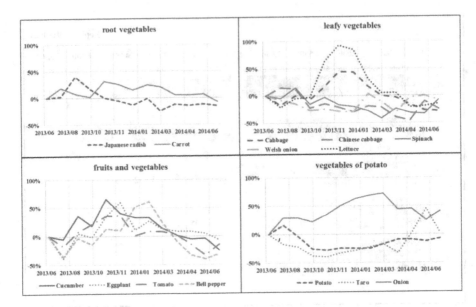

Fig. 3. Market transaction price of vegetables in Tokyo (Color figure online)

shows percentage of increase or decrease of the quantity standard of July 1, 2013. The price of vegetables, as can be seen from this figure change up to twice.

1.4 The Effect of TPP Gives to Japan

As mentioned previously, Japanese agriculture is having various problems. Therefore, it was divided Japan whether she will join or not to TPP. Especially, agricultural group including JA declared opposite opinion. On the other hand, TPP brings profit to manufacturing industry by being rescinded tariff of shipping country. Especially, it has brought about great effect for Japan which exports a lot of industrial products. Finally, Japanese government declared to join TPP on the condition that protect of rice, wheat, dairy products, beef, pork, sugar cane 5 items.

2 Data Used for the Analysis

The analysis was carried out using the purchasing data was offered from All Japan Foods Co., Ltd. which be supplied by Joint Association Study Group of Management Science of all customers who visited stores.

2.1 Store Data Used for the Analysis

It is used 5 stores in Hokkaido area and Tokyo area respectively to analysis. Data of store shows in Table 2.

Figure 4 shows position in Area of Hokkaido and Kanto. Area of Hokkaido is located in the north of Japan. Public transportation of Hokkaido is not much development. Therefore, motorized society is developing into Hokkaido in Japan relatively. On the contrary, public transportation of Tokyo is highly developed to be the center of Japan. Therefore, there are a lot of people who don't have a car.

Also, it is found that shop area is proportional to the daily turnover.

Fig. 4. Position in area of Hokkaido and Kanto

Table 2. Store data

Area	Adress	Shop area	1\$=115yen(February,2016) Daily turnover
Hokkaido	Higasi-ku, Sapporo City, Hokkaido	879m²	¥221,000
Hokkaido	Higasi-ku, Sapporo City, Hokkaido	1,285m²	¥3,140,000
Hokkaido	Kita-ku, Sapporo City, Hokkaido	879m²	¥1,740,000
Hokkaido	Bunkyodai, Ebetsu City, Hokkaido	244m²	¥280,000
Hokkaido	Asabu, Ebetsu City, Hokkaido	482m²	¥440,000
Tokyo	Higasimurayama, Kanamiku-ku, Tokyo	125m²	¥390,000
Tokyo	Mihasekaido, Sakado City, Saitama	330m²	¥570,000
Tokyo	Higasidai, Midorigo City, Chiba	115m²	¥290,000
Tokyo	Yasio, Shinagawa-ku, Tokyo	214m²	¥490,000
Tokyo	Kuramawa, Tonanka-ku, Yokohama City, Kanagawa	198m²	¥400,000

2.2 Purchasing Data of All Customers

It is indicated below about the outline of data.

Term: Jul. 2013–Jun. 2014
Area: Hokkaido area and Tokyo area, 5 each
Number of data: about 18.6 million cases

Data is receipt data. Including information is sale date, sale time, membership number (members only), large classification code, middle classification code, jan-code, using coupon flag (members only), and coupon number (members only).

3   Procedure of Analysis

3.1   The Selection of Kind of Vegetables for Analysis

Firstly, the authors selected vegetables for analysis. As research object, it is targeted the 14 items listed in "About the growth situation and price outlook of vegetables" that are announced every month by Ministry of Agriculture, Forestry and Fisheries. These 14 items are popular items and are eaten in Japan. Table 3 shows vegetables which is selected for analysis.

Table 3. Slected vegetables for analysis

Genre	Item Name	Genre	Item Name
root vegetables	Japanese radish	fruits and vegetables	Cucumber
	Carrot		Eggplant
leafy vegetables	Cabbage		Tomato
	Chinese cabbage		Bell pepper
	Spinach	vegetables of potato	Potato
	Welsh onion		Taro
	Lettuce		Onion

3.2   The Selection of Kind of Items for Analysis

Secondly, the authors selected items for analysis. As a reference Jan-code, it targeted things that are sold more than 250 days corresponds to two-thirds of the year were included. Table 4 shows items that are selected for analysis. Looking at the figure, there is "1/2 off", "1/4 off" or "1 pice" in item name. This shows purchasing style of Japanese. The Japanese tends to purchase it many times little by little. Therefore, supermarket in Japan sells the item which was subdivided. Additionally, about Taro, it was excluded from items for analysis because it didn't exist items were sold more than 250 days.

3.3   Ranking for Items Price

Thirdly, the authors was the ranking of the items price. At first, we seek Dairy price each item. If same item sells at plurality of stores in same day, daily price was the average of the price of each store. Next, it was classified as a price per day the 22 stage from less than 100 yen to more than 300 yen as shown in Table 5. Finally, we aggregated number of sales each rank.

4   Result of Analysis

As the result of analysis, it was found three characteristics.

Table 4. Selected items for analysis

Vegetables	Area	Jan-Code	ItemName
Japanese radish	Hokkaido	210010000000	Japanese radish
		210020000000	Japanese radish 1/2Off
		250010000000	Japanese radish
		2000020318138	Japanese radish(1Pice)
		4963717129401	Japanese radish(Top)
	Tokyo	210010000000	Japanese radish
		210020000000	Japanese radish 1/2Off
Carrot	Hokkaido	210050000000	Carrot(1Pice)
		250150000000	Carrot
		2000020413178	Carrot(1Pice)
		2000020413253	Carrot(in Bags)
		2000020413338	Carrot(in Bigbags)
	Tokyo	210050000000	Carrot
		210051000000	Carrot
Cabbage	Hokkaido	210322000000	Cabbage(1Pice)
		210325000000	Cabbage 1/2Off
		251000000000	Cabbage
		2000020305183	Cabbage(1Pice)
		2000020305268	Cabbage 1/2Off
	Tokyo	210322000000	Cabbage
		210325000000	Cabbage 1/2Off
Chinese cabbage	Hokkaido	210192000000	Chinese cabbage 1/4Off
		2000020324313	Chinese cabbage 1/4Off
	Tokyo	210192000000	Chinese cabbage 1/4Off
Spinach	Hokkaido	210100000000	Spinach
		216018000000	Spinach(bundle)
		250400000000	Spinach
		2000020101143	Spinach(bundle)
	Tokyo	210100000000	Spinach
Welsh onion	Hokkaido	210240000000	Welsh onion(1Pice)
		250700000000	Welsh onion
		250710000000	Welsh onion
		2000020112033	Welsh onion
		2000020321008	Welsh onion(1Pice)
		2000020321183	Welsh onion(1Pice)
	Tokyo	210241000000	Welsh onion
		210251000000	Welsh onion
Lettuce	Hokkaido	210330000000	Lettuce
		251110000000	Lettuce
		251120000000	Sunny Lettuce
		251180000000	Other Lettuce
		2000020326133	Lettuce(1Pice)
		4571129876105	Lettuce
	Tokyo	210330000000	Lettuce
Cucumber	Hokkaido	210490000000	Cucumber(1Pice)
		210491000000	Cucumber(5Pices)
		251500000000	Cucumber
		2000020312198	Cucumber(1Pice)
		2000020312358	Cucumber(3Pices)
	Tokyo	210490000000	Cucumber
Eggplant	Hokkaido	210432000000	Eggplant(1Pice)
		2000020310118	Eggplant(3Pices)
		2000020310293	Eggplant(5Pices)
		2000020311023	Eggplant(1Pice)
	Tokyo	210430000000	Eggplant

Vegetables	Area	Jan-Code	ItemName
Tomato	Hokkaido	210410000000	Tomato(Pack)
		210411000000	Tomato(1Pice)
		210412000000	Tomato(Pack)
		210426000000	Mini Tomato
		251200000000	Tomato
		251203000000	Fruit Tomato
		251240000000	Cherry Tomato
		251241000000	Mini Tomato
		2000020221353	Mini Tomato
		2000020302038	Tomato(in Box)
		2000020302113	Tomato(1Pice)
		2000020302458	Tomato(4Pices)
		2000020304193	Midi Tomato
		2000020304278	Tomato(in Box)
		4993839072262	Fruit Tomato
		4993839072521	Tomato
	Tokyo	210411000000	Tomato
		210412000000	Tomato
		210420000000	Midi Tomato
		210426000000	Mini Tomato
Bell pepper	Hokkaido	210460000000	Bell pepper(small bags)
		251400000000	Bell pepper(small bags)
		2000020315168	Bell pepper(Pack)
	Tokyo	210460000000	Bell pepper
		210461000000	Bell pepper
Potato	Hokkaido	210636000000	Potato
		210641000000	*Mekuin(in bags)*
		251900000000	Potato
		251910000000	Potato
		251930000000	*Mekuin*
		2000020405333	Potato(big bags)
		2000020410108	*Mekuin(big bags)*
		2000020454904	*Kitaakari(big bags)*
		4946666904015	*Mekuin*
		4946666904022	*Bareisyo*
		4988559800080	*Kitaakari*
	Tokyo	210631000000	Potato
		210636000000	Potato
Onion	Hokkaido	210700000000	Onion
		210710000000	Onion
		210711000000	Onion(in bags)
		252200000000	Onion
		2000020203038	Onion(Big bags)
		2000020401113	Onion(Midi bags)
		2000020401298	Onion(3Pices)
		2000020401373	Onion(Big bags)
		2000020401601	Onion(1Pices)
		4946666904039	Onion
	Tokyo	210710000000	Onion
		210711000000	Onion(in bags)

Note: Italic type of Item Name in Table.5 shows

4.1 Characteristic 1: There Was Two Peaks

The first characteristic, it was found two peaks in low-price rank. As the background, there is sale of supermarket. It is commonly that the supermarket in Japan performs a sale in once a week. Thereby, vegetables also are often on sales items. Therefore, these two peaks is conceivable that one is normal selling price and the other is sale selling price. Figure 5 shows Specific examples that belong to characteristic 1.

Table 5. Ranking for item price

Rank	Daily price
1	0 yen or more less than 100yen
2	100 yen or more less than 110yen
3	110 yen or more less than 120yen
4	120 yen or more less than 130yen
5	130 yen or more less than 140yen
.	.
.	.
.	.
18	260 yen or more less than 270yen
19	270 yen or more less than 280yen
20	280 yen or more less than 290yen
21	290 yen or more less than 300yen
22	300 yen or more

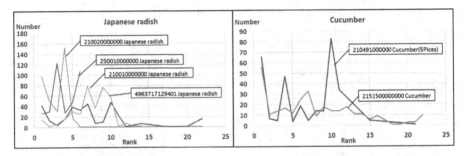

Fig. 5. Specific examples that belong to characteristic 1 (Color figure online)

4.2 Characteristic 2: Difference of Hole Vegetables and Cut Vegetables

The second characteristic, it was found difference of hole vegetables and cut vegetables. Hole vegetables sales volume is greatly changed with the rise of the price. Reduces the quantity and price of the hole vegetables increases. The quantity of cut vegetables rises. This tings is conceivable that there have been switching to cut vegetables from the Hall vegetables with an increase in price. Figure 6 shows Specific examples that belong to characteristic 2. Market price shows market transaction price in Tokyo, and its unit is "Yen". Otherwise shows percentage of increase or decrease of the quantity standard of July 1, 2013.

4.3 Characteristic 3: Difference of Way of Decline in the Items Price

The third characteristic, it was found difference of way of decline in the items price. Even if these products are the same products, the change of the price is not similar. For the reason, it is conceivable difference of sales specifications. Figure 7 shows Specific examples that belong to characteristic 3.

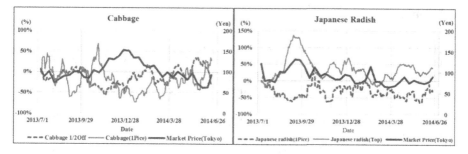

Fig. 6.   Specific examples that belong to characteristic 2 (Color figure online)

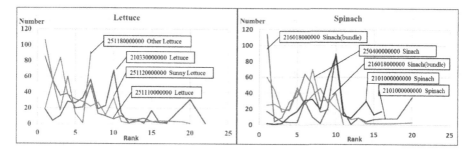

Fig. 7.   Specific examples that belong to characteristic 3 (Color figure online)

5   Conclusion

5.1   Conclusion

The authors analyzed changes in sales volume with respect to a change in price using purchasing data of all customers. The purpose of the analysis was to clarify effect of changes in fresh vegetables prices give consumers.

As a result of the analysis, it was clarified that the change in the price of fresh vegetables had three features.

The result of the study is able to predict the influence that the change of the price of vegetables gives demand. By using this prediction, the farmers can be maintained prices by exported overseas, when the supply is too large relative to demand. As mentioned previously, farmers of Japan has disagreed to TPP. However, the famers can utilize TPP in what they export abroad positively in this way effectively.

5.2   Further Task

As a result of the analysis, it was clarified that the change in the price of fresh vegetables had three features. However, using the analysis as for the data which I used for analysis this time, standard information suffered a loss. Therefore, it is necessary to analyze considering standard information. Also, because there is season in vegetables, a price fluctuates by a season. It is necessary to analyze considering seasons too.

References

1. Izumi, S., Yumi, A., Yamaguti, T.: Analysis of the factor to affect the reception price of domestic vegetables. In: The Operations Research Society of Japan Autumn Research Workshop Abstracts, Tokyo (2011)
2. Ministry of Agriculture, Forestry and Fisheries: About the growth situation and price outlook of vegetables, Tokyo (2015)
3. Ministry of Agriculture, Forestry and Fisheries: Food, agriculture and rural white paper, Tokyo (2007)
4. Ministry of Agriculture, Forestry and Fisheries: Census many years statistics of Agricultural and forestry, Tokyo (2016)
5. Ministry of Agriculture, Forestry and Fisheries: Census of agricultural and forestry, Tokyo (2015)
6. Morizumi, R., Asahi, Y.: Analysis using purchasing data in Japan. In: HCI International 2015, CA (2015)

Tacit Skills Discovery by Data Mining

Makoto Oka$^{(\boxtimes)}$ and Hirohiko Mori

Tokyo City University, Tokyo, Japan
{moka,hmori}@tcu.ac.jp

Abstract. The aim is to extract only experts' "skills" without "individual habits" by extracting data of postures and actions of expert Japanese drum players and then conducting data mining of the collected data. In order to discover the skills of the experts, we obtain data of postures and actions of novices to compare them with the data of the experts to extract skills. As a stage before automated skill extraction, in the present study, we examined whether it is possible to extract skills from limited data. We found that recording the positions of joints, grip strengths, and the accelerations of the drumstick allowed extraction of Japanese drum playing skills. By comparing the experts' movements with the novices' ones, we also found skills common to the experts. Further, we could create a model of automated skill extraction from experts' movements and body dimensions.

Keywords: Expert-Novice · Tacit skills · Tacit knowledge

1 Background

In recent years, expert skill persons (experts) are decreasing year by year in traditional performing arts in Japan due to the aged society and the year 2012 problem, i.e., the concurrent retirement of the postwar baby-boom generation. The falling birth rate affects the decrease in heirs to the traditional performing arts. These situations raise a concern about the danger of decline and disappearance of experts' skills in the Japanese traditional performing arts.

Skills encompass tacit knowledge acquired through experience or by intuition. Tacit knowledge cannot be expressed with characters or figures. It is knowledge difficult to be conveyed in the form of character information. When learning skills, an heir (novice) is required to "hear, see, and learn" them without being taught by a expert. When a novice copies the postures and actions of a expert, his/her skill acquirement begins. Skills are handed down through bodily learning experience just like a novice repeatedly copies the actions of a expert to acquire a skill without even noticing. Since experts have skills obtained through bodily experience, it is difficult to express such skills in the form of explicit knowledge such as characters and figures. This makes it difficult to hand down skills to novices. This is considered to be the cause of loss of skills. Another problem is that it takes a long time to hand down skills because it is necessary to repeatedly copy the skills.

As a solution to this problem, many studies have tried to convert skills into explicit knowledge in the preservation and handing down of skills. The idea here is converting

© Springer International Publishing Switzerland 2016
S. Yamamoto (Ed.): HIMI 2016, Part II, LNCS 9735, pp. 579–588, 2016.
DOI: 10.1007/978-3-319-40397-7_56

individuals' tacit knowledge into clearly-expressed explicit knowledge to hand down skills. However, it is also difficult to extract skills that are tacit knowledge to convert them into explicit knowledge.

2 Related Work

Ando et al. [1] created a performance teaching aid using motion capture and virtual space. They proposed a method based on virtual reality using 3-D space on the basis of "performance observation" and "watching video teaching aids" that have been basic methods in conventional performance teaching. Specifically, they created a teaching aid based on a motion-capture technology that allows learners to observe an action from a desired angle. They used a motion capture system to shoot actions for the teaching aid, calculated 3-D joint coordinates, and generated a human model. This human model made it possible to see the difference in actions between a novice and a expert from various angles. This study showed that the teaching aid was useful as a performance teaching aid because the motion-capture technology made it possible to compare difference in actions between a novice and a expert.

Yamaguchi et al. [2] conducted a study to compare the Japanese drum playing skills between a expert and a novice. They compared arm actions that a expert and a novice took when playing the Japanese drum. As for the arm actions, they shot the movements of the head, shoulder, elbow, wrist, and waist on the right side of each test subject and the movement of a drumstick to analyze them using image processing. Besides, they used surface electromyography to measure muscle activities of the anterior deltoid, biceps, triceps, extensor carpi radialis, and extensor carpi ulnaris on the right side of each test subject.

As a result of the analysis, the expert had large angle variations at joints from the shoulder to the wrist whereas the novice had small ones. The expert's drumstick swing was fast. The analysis thus revealed that drumming actions varied between the experts and novices.

As for the expert, muscle activities were detected from all the measured muscles. By contrast, as for the novice, only the upper arm muscles were active. This study thus showed that their upper arm actions were different in playing the Japanese drum, and they had different skill levels.

These studies started with recording the actions of a novice and a expert with the use of various sensors etc. Then, researchers analyzed recorded data by using knowledge on analysis subjects and various analysis tools to extract the skills of the expert. However, researchers cannot extract all skills. They can extract only part of skills that they focus on.

3 Research Target and Proposal

The Japanese drums are broadly classified into the following three types: most common ones called long trunk drums (imperial drum) whose trunk is made of a hollowed-out log; those with a relatively lightweight trunk called tub drums; and tight drums for high-pitched sound. As a drum for the present study, we chose a tight drum that plays a role in keeping overall rhythm. Since tight drums are responsible for overall beats, players are required to have the highest skills and there is a large skill difference between experts and novices.

If it is possible to record the movements of experts and novices in traditional performing arts to discover movements common to many experts, they are considered to be skills in the traditional performing arts. We aim at automated skill extraction so that skills can be extracted without researchers.

The aim is to extract only experts' "skills" without "individual habits" by extracting data of postures and actions of expert Japanese drum players and then conducting data mining of the collected data. In order to discover the skills of the experts, we obtain data of postures and actions of novices to compare them with the data of the experts to extract skills. As a stage before automated skill extraction, in the present study, we examine whether it is possible to extract skills from limited data.

4 Pre-survey

At the beginning of the present study, we asked cooperation from three Japanese drum organizations to conduct a pre-survey to collect information on Japanese drums including basics. The survey items were "difference between experts and novices," "time required for mastering Japanese drum playing," and "first practice for novices."

4.1 Difference Between Experts and Novices

In order to find if a player is a novice, experts check "how to hold the drumstick," "how to swing the drumstick," and the "posture for playing the drum." The basic way to hold the drumstick is holding it without strain and holding it tightly right before the drumstick hits the drumhead. The way to swing the drumstick is swinging the drumstick down without strain and with surrendering to the gravity. By using the wrist to snap a stroke like whipping right before the drumstick hits the drumhead, you can make a large sound. The posture for playing the drum is keeping your feet apart about 1.5 times the shoulder width and keeping your waist stably when hitting the drumhead. Besides, we learned that players consciously hold the upper body basically with a straight back.

4.2 Time for Mastering Japanese Drum Playing

This varies depending on the frequency of practice and a sense of a player. We obtained an answer stating that at least 5 years are required in a case of two practices per week. In the present study, players with over five years' playing experience are defined as experts.

4.3   First Practice for Novices

We were told that a main practice method is orally teaching novices the aforementioned three items: "hot to hold the drumstick," "how to swing the drumstick," and the "posture for playing the drum," and then making them actually play the drum to correct their play.

5   Overview of Recording System

The system recorded "how to hold the drumstick," "how to swing the drumstick," and the "posture for playing the drum" that we learned in the interview with experts. By reference to the studies of skill extraction using motion-capture technology by Ando et al. and Fujimoto et al., we used an acceleration sensor, pressure sensor, motion capture sensor, etc. to record the experts' drum beating actions. These sensors made it possible to accurately record their actions [3].

5.1   Recording Method and Measurement Sites

The postures and actions of the experts were measured by use of a motion capture sensor in the form of 3-D spatial coordinate data. Obtaining the 3-D spatial coordinates of persons allows grasping accurate positional relations such as depth. This was considered to improve skill acquisition. With the use of the 3-D special coordinate data extracted with the motion capture sensor, skeletal data of the persons was generated.

Besides, the speed of drumstick swings and grip strength data were measured with the acceleration and pressure sensors since they cannot be obtained only from information from the motion capture sensor.

As data of an action that a expert takes when beating the drum, the angle of the raised arm, the movements of the wrist joint and elbow joint, and the speed of a drumstick swing were extracted. These parameters were determined by reference to the study of Yamaguchi et al. Yamaguchi et al. stated that these parameters showed a significant difference between the experts and novices. Besides, Japanese drum instructors also stated that these parameters were most likely to show a difference between the experts and novices. We further measured lower body postures. We then extracted standing positions and waist positions relative to the drum from the lower body postures. Although Yamaguchi et al. analyzed muscle activities with an electromyograph, we did not use it because muscle activities are considered to show in actions.

5.2   Motion Capture Sensor

We adopted Microsoft's motion capture sensor "Kinect" to obtain the 3-D spatial data of actions. These sensors calculate depth information with a near-infrared camera to estimate the 3-D coordinates of joints of the body. Kinect can build skeletal information on the basis of the 3-D coordinates to track a skeletal structure in real time.

Kinect makes it possible to easily obtain a person's 3-D joint data in real time without using a marker etc.

Kinect for Windows SDK was adopted as the driver for Kinect. This driver allows obtaining videos with a video camera, obtaining depth images, and tracking skeletal information. This driver has the following sufficient performance for the present study: Frame rate 30 fps; Maximum pixels of depth images 640 × 480; Distance for capturing persons from 0.8 m to 4.0 m; and capable of tracking skeletal data of six persons simultaneously.

5.3 Acceleration Sensor

A triaxial acceleration sensor (KXM52-1050) was used in measuring the speed of drumstick swings. This acceleration sensor can measure x, y, and z-way accelerations and inclinations. It detects accelerations between -2G and + 2G.

5.4 Pressure Sensor

A pressure sensor (FSR406) was used in measuring grip strengths. This is a 43.69 mm square sensor. It is attached to the grip of the drumstick so that grip strengths are measured. These sensors are controlled by Arduino.

6 Evaluation Methodology

The figure shows how apparatuses were set up. Kinect was set up in a position 2.25 m ahead of the player on the left by 45 degrees. Kinect was set up at a height of 0.8 m from ground. The video camera shot the player's beating action. The player played the Japanese drum with a drumstick to which the acceleration and pressure sensors were attached. We instructed the player to play the drum so that the acceleration sensor attached to the drumstick faced upward. The frame rate for video shooting was 30 fps and the sampling rate for sensors was 30 Hz.

We recorded actions during playing of 22 players (experts) with over 5 years' experience from four organizations including the three organizations that cooperated with us in the pre-survey. We also recorded actions during playing of 22 novices after orally teaching them "how to hold the drumstick," "how to swing the drumstick," and the "posture for playing the drum." We asked both experts and novices to play the drum at a speed of BPM = 60 for 30 s. We adopted a frame rate of 30 fps for the pressure, acceleration, and motion capture sensors. Obtained data was saved separately as experts' data and novices' data.

6.1 Analysis Method

After adjusting data, we visualized and analyzed them. Then, we formed a hypothesis on the basis of the analysis and conducted detailed analysis.

6.2 Adjustment of Data

Although the actions of the players were recorded with the sensors, part of data was missing. In a case where occlusion occurs for example, the motion capture sensor cannot record joints. In addition, the sampling rate showed the unstable values: 26 Hz ± 4 Hz due to various causes.

Therefore, we made up for the missing values and converted data so that the sampling rate became 30 Hz (30 data per second).

1. Calculating the difference between data "n" and "n + 1" (n ≥ 0) with respect to each pair
2. Finding a pair of "n" and "n + 1" having the largest difference
3. Inserting an average between the found data "n" and "n + 1"
4. Repeating 1 to 3 above until the number of data per second reaches 30

We performed this procedure so that the number of data became 30 in every second.

7 Result

7.1 Visualization of Data

On the basis of the adjusted data, we performed 3-D plotting of 3-D coordinates of the joins. In the Fig. 1, the X, Y, and Z axes represent right and left, height, and depth, respectively. Besides, depth was visualized so that the far side and near side were expressed in red and blue, respectively. Although the pre-survey appeared to show that skills could be extracted from postures, the figure does not show significant characteristics.

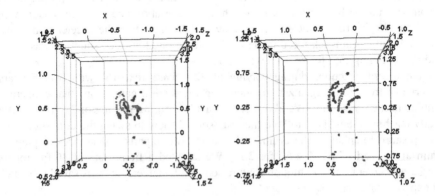

Fig. 1. 3-D plotting of the joints (Left: Expert, Right: Novice) (Color figure online)

3-D plotting of the joints throughout the body showed the most significant differences in wrist movements. The graph of right wrist joints (Fig. 2) shows the following facts.

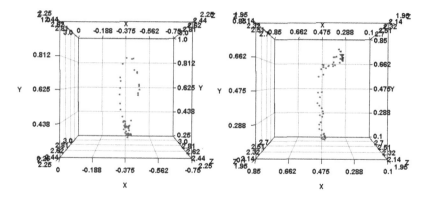

Fig. 2. 3-D plotting of the right wrist joints (Left: Expert, Right: Novice)

1. Experts bend the wrist up and down at different speeds.
2. Experts' wrist strokes depict an elliptical shape.

We examined each fact in order to see if these characteristics apply to part of experts or all the experts.

7.2   Characteristics of Wrist Joints

We here examine the difference between bending up and bending down movements of the wrists. "Wrist joint speeds," "grip strengths," and "Y-axis accelerations" were used in the examination. All of these values were normalized (maximum value = 1). The graph of wrist joint speeds (Fig. 3) shows that experts maintained high speeds. By contrast, novices lacked regularity.

In order to examine in what case experts speed up, we overlaid grip strength data thereon. The Fig. 4 shows wrist joint speeds on which the grip strength data were overlaid. This graph shows that experts increased the grip strength when the wrist joint speed increased. The graph also shows that they tightly held the drumstick in a short period, and in other periods, held the drumstick loosely.

Lastly, in order to examine the relation between timing when the drumstick hits the drumhead, speed, and grip strength, we overlaid the graph of Y-axis accelerations thereon. This Fig. 5 shows that there were moments when the direction of acceleration changed regularly. This seems to be because the drumstick hit the drumhead and bounced. The graph showed that speed and grip strength were high when the drumstick hit the drumhead. Besides, the speed was maintained even after the drumstick hit the drumhead. This shows that experts used bouncing power to shift to the next posture.

From these findings, we can show that "capability of controlling power to swing the drumstick" is one of the skills of experts.

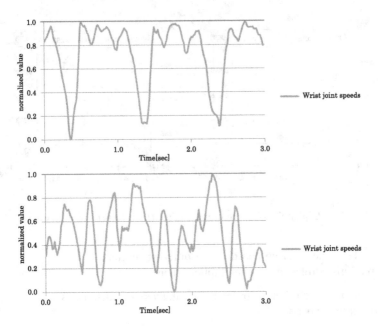

Fig. 3. Right wrist joint speeds (Above: Expert, Below: Novice)

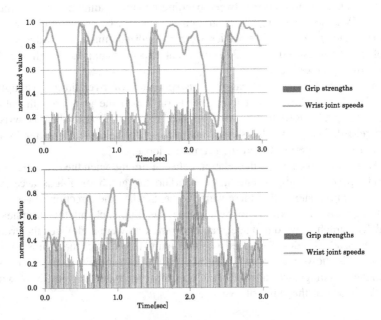

Fig. 4. wrist joint speeds and grip strengths (Above: Expert, Below: Novice) (Color figure online)

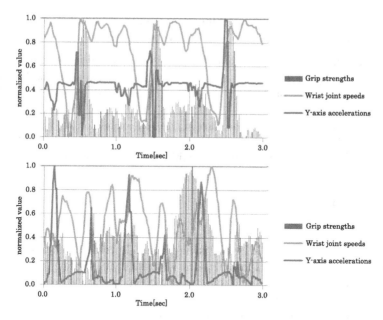

Fig. 5. wrist joint speeds, grip strengths and Y-axis accelerations (Above: Expert, Below: Novice) (Color figure online)

7.3 Examination of Trajectories of Wrist Joints

We adopted the method of least squares to examine if the trajectories of wrist joint movements had an elliptical shape. If it is possible to express the wrist trajectories with approximate ellipses, we can conclude that the wrist joints depicted elliptic trajectories. The Fig. 6 shows the result obtained by the method of least squares. Red indicates recorded wrist joint trajectories and blue indicates the approximate ellipses.

The Fig. 6 shows that although the experts' wrist joint movements depict approximate ellipses, the novices had different movements from the approximate ellipses.

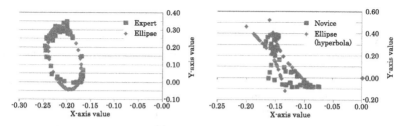

Fig. 6. Plotting of wrist trajectories and approximate ellipses (Above: Expert, Below: Novice) (Color figure online)

We further found approximate ellipses from all the subjects' data. As a result, the wrist joint trajectories of 21 out of 22 experts were elliptic shapes. This shows that experts' right wrist joints have elliptic movement.

7.4 Examination of Approximate Ellipses in Consideration of Body Dimensions

Although we found that the experts' wrist joint trajectories were close to elliptic shapes, the sizes of them varied depending on experts. Under the assumption that the sizes of the elliptic shapes depend on the body dimensions of the experts, we estimated ellipses from their dimensions.

From arm lengths, we could find three regression expressions of the major axis, minor axis, and inclination at a multiple correlation of 0.7. This shows that body dimensions and the parameters of ellipses highly correlated with each other.

8 Conclusion

We established a system for recording actions of players for the purpose of extraction and handing down of Japanese drum playing skills. Recorded data allowed us to discover characteristics of the experts. Besides, we found that recording the positions of joints, grip strengths, and the accelerations of the drumstick allowed extraction of Japanese drum playing skills.

By comparing the experts' movements with the novices' ones, we also found skills common to the experts. Further, we could create a model of automated skill extraction from experts' movements and body dimensions.

9 Future Work

Since the automated ellipsis extraction model has somewhat insufficient accuracy, it is necessary to improve it. Also in areas other than automated ellipsis extraction, at the same time, we consider adding other movement parameters such as holding timing and holding strength to automatically extract many other skills.

References

1. Ando, A., Sumikawa, T.: Development and function evaluation of teaching materials for "sawing" observation by using motion capture and the virtual world. Jpn. Soc. Educ. Technol. **36**(2), 103–110 (2012)
2. Yamaguchi, M., Horikawa, M., Okai, R., Fujiwara, M.: Japanese society of physical education. Health Sport Sci. **61**, 157 (2010). (in Japanese)
3. Oka, M., Mizukoshi, A., Mori, H.: Transferring tacit skills of WADAIKO. In: Proceedings of Human-Computer Interaction International 2013 Conference, pp. 118–125 (2013)

Basic Observation About the Difficulty of Assembly Wood Puzzle by Wooden Joint

Takamitsu Tanaka[1(✉)], Masao Tachibana[1],
Thongthai Wongwichai[1], and Yen-Yu Kang[2]

[1] Iwate University, Morioka, Japan
{taktak, tatimasa}@iwate-u.ac.jp,
Pang_design@hotmail.com
[2] Kaohsiung Normal University, Kaohsiung, Taiwan
yenyu@nknu.edu.tw

Abstract. In order to understand the manner to develop what type of teaching material from wooden puzzle by combining the aspect of "easy to understand models" and "fun to assemble" for learning how to measure volume, this paper discuss about what is variable that impact to different degree of assembly difficulty in cube puzzle. The experiment is conducted by 3 characters of cube puzzle which have different condition such a picture print, many color, and no image or color. All puzzles were composed by third and sixth grade student. Each experiment spent 15 min for observation. It was designed for 2 times for observation and each time students experienced the different sizes to evaluate for difficult assembly. The result showed that the easiest in degree of assembly difficulty due to the large size. Further, since students found assembly difficult for shapes with deep joints, we notice that the color provided a helpful hint when selecting joints.

Keywords: Wooden joint · Interlock · Puzzle

1 About 3D Wooden Puzzles

Three-dimensional (3D) wooden puzzles are produced worldwide. Most are solid shapes based on cuboids and cubes. Since wood shrinks as it dries, the dimensions begin to differ from the designer's original intention as the months and years pass after the user's purchase. Above all, when fitting pieces of a wooden puzzle together, parts can be interlocked by employing an approach similar to configuring traditional wooden joints. However, while interlocking wood into complex wooden joint configurations may be appropriate for buildings not intended to be taken apart, it is not suitable for a 3D wooden puzzle intended as a toy. Therefore, wooden puzzles are assembled with simple wooden joints, allowing them to be disassembled repeatedly, and many are designed so that they can be easily put back together. However, as seen in Figs. 1, 2 and 3, most wooden puzzles are designed with simple wooden joints. Although some wooden puzzles have fewer parts, many are difficult to solve [1–3]. The author noted this fact during his experimental observation in 2012 [4]. One reason assembly is difficult is that while wooden puzzles possess the functions of a puzzle, they are often used as objets d'art.

© Springer International Publishing Switzerland 2016
S. Yamamoto (Ed.): HIMI 2016, Part II, LNCS 9735, pp. 589–598, 2016.
DOI: 10.1007/978-3-319-40397-7_57

There are 3D wooden puzzles, such as the one in Fig. 4, that blend the functions of a toy with those of art and design education. This puzzle is made of resin, and magnets hold the parts together, without wooden joints [5]. Painted in three colors, it is devised such that children can easily assemble it according to the shape of the pieces and their color. With this puzzle, children use its given form. As mentioned above, puzzles are mainly "3D wooden puzzles intended for adults" and "3D wooden puzzles incorporating educational functions intended for children." This study aims to develop 3D wooden puzzles so that children can learn to calculate volume while having fun, utilizing shapes of wooden joints mostly built with straight surfaces such as cuboids and cubes, which are characteristic of 3D wooden puzzles. This paper includes basic observations in order to gain necessary information to effectively use wooden puzzles as teaching materials.

Fig. 1. 3D wooden puzzle designed by Gregory Benedetti

Fig. 2. 3D wooden puzzle designed by Hirokazu Iwasawa

Fig. 3. 3D wooden puzzle designed by Bill Cutler

2 Teaching Children to Calculate Volume: The Current Circumstances

In Japanese schools, the two methods of instruction for teaching children to measure volume are: "Instruction measuring volume with an instrument and expressing the volume" and "Instruction determining volume based on calculations." Furthermore,

Fig. 4. 3D resin wooden puzzle for educational purposes

there are two subcategories under the latter: (1) learning formulas to determine the volume of a solid (such as cuboids, cubes, cylinders, pyramids and spheres); and (2) calculating the volume of complex figures that represent a combination of basic shapes (cuboids and cubes).

Students learn to calculate volume in fifth grade (elementary school) when they learn the concepts and units for measuring volume. During this time, they learn the concept of 1 cm^3, and quantify volume based on the number of 1 cm^3 cubes, which leads to the formulas for the volume of cuboids and cubes. In fifth grade, when students recall what they previously learned about area, they discover that volume can also be expressed in terms of the number of universal units. As a result, they are able to grasp this area of learning and compute volume in an integrated way. During instruction on volume, exercises are devised to find out how many 1 cm sided cubes it takes to fill a cuboid or cube. Through these exercises, students learn formulas such as the following: "volume of a cuboid = length × width × height" and "volume of a cube = side × side × side." In 2001, the National Institute for Educational Policy Research conducted a survey presenting problems to sixth grade students, asking whether they could "express the volume of the solid as a formula."

The percentage of correct answers was 79.5 %. The report of the Curriculum Implementation Survey for elementary and junior high schools pointed out that, "One example is actively adopting operational and experiential arithmetic activities, such as ones where solids of the size of a unit are prepared; students construct various cubes and cuboids by actually stacking and arranging them, then find their volumes. Students can understand the meaning of units and how to measure volume. Creating instruction that enhances students' feel for the size of volume is important."

The question on volume in the elementary school arithmetic section for the upcoming 2014 national survey is as follows. While the question is different than the one from 2001, which asked about units and measurement, the percentage of correct answers was 81.3 %. We can see that approximately 20 % of students were still unable to understand how to quantify volume. While the preceding manuscript mentions the current situation, whereby 20 % of students do not understand how to calculate volume, we believe this is due to inadequate teaching materials for calculating the volume of 3D objects. Textbooks are two-dimensional (2D), but in practice, students have to imagine 3D objects for calculations. While it is important to also learn problems from the textbook that are simply made 3D, in the next chapter "Observations," we decided to see what types of teaching materials were possible by combining the aspects of "easy to understand models" and "fun to assemble" for learning how to measure volume.

3   Observations

In order to understand the manner in which wooden puzzles balance the combination of the two aforementioned elements ("easy to understand models" and "fun to assemble"), we carried out basic observations on February 18 and 19, 2014.

We used three types of wooden puzzles for the observation, as shown in Fig. 5; they were made of ABS resin with a 3D printer and designed by us. Puzzle A was a wooden puzzle with pictures printed on the ABS resin. Puzzle B was painted such that the surfaces of pieces that come into contact with each other at the joints were the same color. Puzzle C was made of white ABS resin with a 3D printer and lacked any images or colors.

Fig. 5. The 3D wooden puzzles used during observations

However, the number of pieces and assembly methods of the three types of puzzles were designed based on the author's previous experience of the puzzle having nearly the same degree of difficulty. A professional designer performed the data design, based on 3D CAD. However, as seen in the comments in Tables 1, 2, 3 and 4, some students perceived difficulty due to size.

Over two days, third and sixth grade students were each given 15 min to put the puzzles together, for a total of two times.

Time and other details were as follows. We observed different students on both days. While third grade students have not yet learned how to measure volume, sixth grade students already have.

February 18, 2014:

"10:15–10:35 3 third grade students"
"12:55–13:10 3 sixth grade students"

February 19, 2014:

"10:15–10:35 3 third grade students"
"12:55–13:10 3 sixth grade students"

Table 1. February 18, 2014, first observation

Time (min)	Third grade, Student A	Third grade, Student B	Third grade, Student C
0–3	Works on Puzzle A. Has nearly constructed the form after 1 min, and completes after 2 min. Works on Puzzle C next, and finishes in about 30 s	Works on Puzzle B. It appears to be taking shape after about 1 min. However, afterward, student can be seen struggling and the puzzle remains incomplete	Works on Puzzle C. Begins to take shape in approximately 1.5 min, and is completed in 2 min. Next, works on Puzzle A. Assembles the pieces without any problems
4–6	Appears to struggle more with Puzzle B than the previous ones and remarks that the pieces are "difficult to insert." Completes this in approximately 2 min	Still unable to find pieces that fit after 5 min, exchanges for Puzzle C. Completes this in about 1 min	Completes Puzzle A in about 1 min
7–9		Starts on Puzzle A after about 6.5 min, and is able to complete in about 2 min	Assembles Puzzle B last. Appears to have difficulty initially, but is able to complete it in about 2 min after figuring out a section
10–12	Responded that Puzzle C was the easiest as it had few pieces	Felt that Puzzle C was the easiest because the pieces were large	Responded that Puzzle C was the easiest as it had few pieces, the same response as Student A
13–15	Conversely, remarked that Puzzle B was complex and the most difficult	Puzzle B was the most difficult as it had difficult parts	Remarked that Puzzle B was the most difficult as its shapes were uneven, strange, and hard to figure out

Table 2. February 18, second observation

Time (min)	Sixth grade, Student A	Sixth grade, Student B	Sixth grade, Student C
0–3	Starts assembling Puzzle A very smoothly, and completes it after approximately 2 min. Begins assembling Puzzle C and finishes it in about 1 min	Works on Puzzle B. Assembles the corners during the first 3 min. Appears to be having difficulty	Begins assembling Puzzle C from the bottom up. Completes in about 3 min
4–6	Lastly, works on Puzzle B. Quickly assembles this one as with the earlier puzzles, and is nearly finished	Work on Puzzle B is halted after 5 min, and we have the student assemble Puzzle C. Student smoothly assembles this, starting at the bottom, and completes it in a little over 1.5 min	Divides the pieces for Puzzle A into two groups, assembles them separately, and combines them at the end. Time required is about 1 min
7–9	Completes Puzzle B at the early 7 min mark	Can be seen assembling Puzzle A while looking at the pictures. Completes in less than 1 min	Completes Puzzle B in roughly 2 min
10–12		Attempts Puzzle B again. Remarks something to the effect that it might be possible to match pieces of the same color. Completes the puzzle with about 5 min remaining	
13–15	Selected Puzzle A as the easiest since it could be assembled by looking at the pictures. Responded that Puzzle B was the most difficult due to the myriad shapes of the pieces	Responded that Puzzle A was the easiest, for the same reasons given by Student A. Also stated that the most difficult was Puzzle B because comparatively, its parts had a lot of contours	Also responded that Puzzle A was the easiest for the same reasons. Selected Puzzle B as the most difficult due to the difference in the inner and outer colors

Table 3. February 19, first observation

Time (min)	Third grade, Student A	Third grade, Student B	Third grade, Student C
0–3	Can be seen assembling Puzzle A while looking at the pictures. Finishes in about 3 min	Assembles Puzzle B in sections	Begins to assemble Puzzle C, but appears unable to assemble evenly in sections
4–6	Works on Puzzle B. Student is seen tilting his head in confusion and appears to struggle with assembly	After 5 min, pieces are still dispersed and far from resembling a cube. Student leaves it as is and moves on to Puzzle C	Incrementally taking shape in sections, but unable to complete. Next, student assembles Puzzle A
7–9	Unable to complete the puzzle after 5 min, student trades it in for Puzzle C	Unable to complete it after 5 min, student trades it in for Puzzle A	Completes Puzzle A in about 2 min
10–12	Begins to assemble Puzzle C. After 1 min, the student is seen looking around	Student works on Puzzle A. Appears to assemble the puzzle by looking at the pictures. Completes in about 1.5 min	Begins assembling Puzzle B, but it shows no sign of taking shape
13–15	Nearing completion of Puzzle C. Completes after 14 min. Responded that Puzzle A was the easiest because each part was large. Conversely, responded that Puzzle C was the most difficult because it lacked pictures and was uneven	Stated that Puzzle A seemed the easiest as it had printed pictures, making it easy to assemble. Puzzle B was the most difficult because it was painted with many colors and lacked pictures	Completes the puzzle with about 10 s remaining. Also said that Puzzle A was the easiest as it had pictures printed on it. Stated that Puzzle B was the most difficult since it lacked pictures, had an uneven surface, and a lot of white space

Table 4. February 19, second observation

Time (min)	Sixth grade, Student A	Sixth grade, Student B	Sixth grade, Student C
0–3	Student can be seen assembling Puzzle A by looking at the pictures. Completes in about 1 min. Next, works on Puzzle B. Makes comments such as, "Uh-uh, no way…" Appears to find it difficult	Works on Puzzle B. Completes this in about 1 min. Works on Puzzle C next	Works on Puzzle C. Just as the student appears to have completed it, the student begins to disassemble and reassemble by trial and error. Completes in about 2.5 min. Works on Puzzle A next
4–6	Completes Puzzle B shortly before the 5 min mark. Student reassembles while waiting for the next puzzle	Has difficulty with 2 pieces remaining. Dismantles the puzzle for the moment	Completes Puzzle A in about 1.5 min
7–9	Works on Puzzle C. Gets a section to take shape, but is unable to make much progress	Completes Puzzle C Works on Puzzle A and completes in about 1.5 min	Assembles Puzzle B. Completes this in about 30 s
10–12	Finds some pieces that fit. Unable to complete it, student takes it apart again.		
13–15	Not much progress until the end, and time runs out, without being able to finish Felt that Puzzle A was the easiest as the pictures could be matched up, and responded that Puzzle C was the hardest as there were no patterns or colors, making assembly difficult	Responded that Puzzle A was the easiest for the same reasons given by Student A. Responded that Puzzle C, lacking any colors or pictures and complex in shape, was the most difficult	Also responded that Puzzle A was the easiest due to the printed pictures. Felt that Puzzle C was the most difficult because there were no colors to offer any hints

The three students each assembled all of the 3D puzzles (i.e., A, B, and C). We measured the time required for assembly. Upon completing the 3D puzzles, we interviewed the three students and asked them which puzzle was the easiest, which was the most difficult, and their reasons.

As C was clearly difficult, we stopped the students once 5 min had elapsed and then had them assemble A or B.

As a result of the observations, we found that Puzzle A, with the printed pictures, had a low degree of difficulty, except during the first observation on February 18, 2014. Additionally, we noted that even when presented with a complex structure, if students were able to recognize the rule that the surfaces of pieces were the same color where they meet, they were able to assemble the puzzle easily. However, since students found assembly difficult for shapes with deep joints (described by students as being "rugged," i.e., uneven, in shape), we believe that the color provided a helpful hint when selecting joints.

4   Future Developments

Unlike planar materials, the size of teaching materials for measuring volume is important to students (i.e., when holding the object in one's hand). Thus, the size of wooden puzzles must be determined from an alternative ergonomic perspective. We plan to create models resembling the same 3D objects found in textbooks, and perform an experiment on the differences between students who use 3D teaching materials versus those who learn by using traditional 2D textbooks.

The reason behind having professional designers devise the data of the 3D CAD was to understand under which types of processes modeling would occur. According to the designer, shapes were constructed by combining cubes or cuboids with each other, depending on the shape's degree of difficulty. Another method was to take a large cube

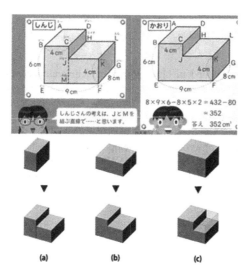

Fig. 6. Methods for solving volume calculation as shown in textbooks

or cuboid and subtract cubes and/or cuboids from it. These processes are the same as the basis for calculating volume that children learn in textbooks, as shown in Fig. 6 [6]. This figure shows that in textbooks, there is not just one method for calculating volume; rather, there are several. In addition, the 3D CAD data have all been recorded. In the future, we believe the 3D-CAD can be put to practical use as an application on tablets; for example, as shown in Fig. 7.

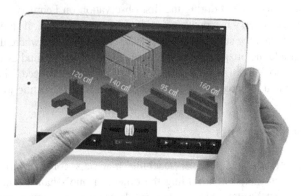

Fig. 7. Example of an application of volume calculation

Acknowledgements. We received support from Professor Masao Tachibana of Iwate University regarding the educational portion of arithmetic volume calculation, and from Mr. Ichiro Hirata of Hyogo Prefectural Institute of Technology regarding methods of observation. We also received support from Mr. Toru Sasaki and Ms. Eriko Yanagimura of the Elementary School that is attached to the Department of Education at Iwate University, undergraduate student Asami Kashiwagi, and graduate student Suleeporn Kamchompoo. Thank you, everyone.

References

1. Designed by Gregory Benedetti. https://www.cubicdissection.com/html/purchase/discont/2halves4.html
2. Designed by Hirokazu Iwasawa. http://www.puzzle-place.com/wiki/Iwahiro%27s_Apparently_Impossible_Cube_No.1
3. Designed by Bill Cutler. http://www.puzzle-place.com/wiki/The_Binary_Burr
4. Tanaka, Takamitsu: Basic observation to develop a wood puzzle having a volume calculation function using a wood joint. J. Soc. Art Educ. Univ. **46**, 181–188 (2014)
5. Puzzle by Beverly Enterprises Inc. https://www.be-en.co.jp/upload/save_image/nt010_1.jpg
6. Fuji, T., Iitaka, S., et al.: New mathematics 5 part 1, Tokyo Shoseki Co., Ltd. (2011)

Livelog: Sensing and Inducing Japanese Idol Fan Activities with Smartphone

Tomohiro Tanikawa[(✉)], Rihito Hashido, Takuji Narumi,
and Michitaka Hirose

7-3-1 Hongo, Bunkyo-Ku, Tokyo, Japan
{tani,hashido,narumi,hirose}@cyber.t.u-tokyo.ac.jp

Abstract. In this study, we propose and implement method for sensing the excitement action of the participant by using smartphone. Also we propose and demonstrate method for inducing fan activities to Japanese idol by using gamification through smartphone-based communication in and out live concerts. We measured the acceleration of live concert participants can be measured with their own smartphone, and revealed that the acceleration data can be used as barometer of participants' excitement by utilizing the relationship between the known heart rate and emotion. Based on this concept, we carried out long-term experiments by implementing and distributing our smartphone application via internet with promoting in live concerts, and evaluated the effectiveness of proposed inducing methods of fan activities by analyzing log data from our smartphone application.

Keywords: Live concert · Acceleration · Gamification · Excitement · Mobile computing

1 Introduction

In the music industry, while the value of production of a music title hangs low, the sales of a live concert market increase every year, annual sales proceeds will exceed 270 billion yen in 2014, and the live concert market is an important market in recent years, when making a profit. The meaning which raises a spectator's degree of satisfaction for the further development of a live concert market is large. In the live concert in the subculture field, since it becomes an important element in which a spectator heaps up and action determines a spectator's degree of satisfaction, I can mainly raise a spectator's degree of satisfaction by heaping up and promoting action.

The research for realizing a better live concert has so far been made by making a spectator use application [1]. However, in the environment which surrounds a live concert, it is thought possible to raise a spectator's degree of satisfaction by change of a business model or the spread of SNS(s), using [2] and this, since communication between a performer and a spectator and between spectators is active.

The purpose of this research is to propose the technique of heaping up by using gamification technique on communication of those which participate in a spectator's technique and live concert which heap up and carry out sensing of the action by a simple method, and inducing action.

© Springer International Publishing Switzerland 2016
S. Yamamoto (Ed.): HIMI 2016, Part II, LNCS 9735, pp. 599–606, 2016.
DOI: 10.1007/978-3-319-40397-7_58

2   Experiment 1: Sensing Excitement in Live Concert

We carried out experiment to measure psychological climax that occurs when live concert participants performing the excitement behavior by using a smartphone.

2.1   Procedure of Experiment

Humans it is known that the heart rate is changed when in the excited state [3]. Therefore, it is possible by measuring heart rate to carry out sensing of a spectator's climax. Furthermore, if acceleration is measured simultaneously with heart rate and both value is interlocking, it will become possible to measure climax by carrying out sensing of the acceleration.

In order to verify this, I attach the smart phone with which the heart rate meter was carried in the accelerometer by the breast to one subject at the thigh in the actual live concert, and acquire heart rate and acceleration. Moreover, I gave one more set of a smart phone to the hand, when it rose, I acquired mental climax time because I have a tap of the screen carried out, and I conducted the experiment which analyzes each relationship.

2.2   Results and Discussion

The time series data of the size and the heart rate and the climax time of acceleration shown in Fig. 1. From Fig. 1, the magnitude of heart rate and acceleration increases during swelling, it can read the magnitude of heart rate and acceleration are interlocked.

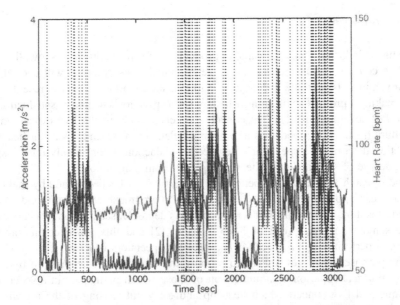

Fig. 1. Time series data of acceleration, heart rate and exciting feeling

Therefore, separate the experimental time every 30 s, the average value of each parameter included in each section was analyzed by normalizing. The correlation coefficient between the magnitude of the normalized acceleration and heart rate and at each interval is 0.725, a strong correlation was observed (Fig. 2).

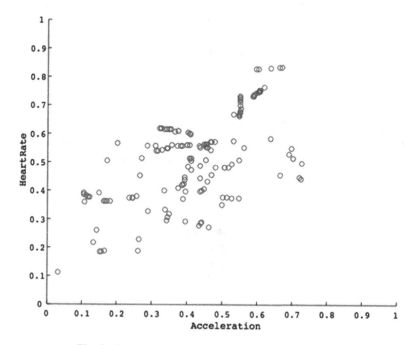

Fig. 2. Correlation between heart rate and acceleration

Furthermore, the difference value between the whole period and data including the swelling time was examined using the t-test, significant differences in any magnitude of the acceleration and heart rate were present. In other words, psychological excitement and heart rate and acceleration can be verified to be linked.

The results show that in the live concert, the magnitude of the acceleration and heart rate are linked, the size of the heart rate and the acceleration is higher than the normal state at the time of climax. Therefore, it may be possible to measure the behavioral heaped by sensing accelerations. The results utilizing, in the following chapters, using the sum of the magnitude of the acceleration as a measure of the size of excitement behavior of the participant.

3 System for Sensing and Inducing Excitement

We implement a system for sensing and inducing excitement action of the participant as a smartphone application "Livelog".

3.1   Sensing Sub-system

"Livelog" is an application which records the log which participated in the live concert. If the application is started during the public performance, from the acceleration obtained from the accelerometer carried in the smart phone, I will compute the "excitement point" in the public performance which heaped up and turned a fixed quantity of actions, and will be referred to as one of the parameters of the log of a live concert.

We calculate as a value specifically proportional to total of the absolute value of the acceleration which acquired at intervals of 0.5 s during a live concert performance.

3.2   Inducing Sub-system

In order to realize the induction of excitement action, we implemented the following three types of Gamification technique. It is because these techniques can be presumed that appropriate as motivation for the participant to participate in a live concert performed by the stimulus to liven up by action the emotions that get in communication with other fans and performers (Fig. 3).

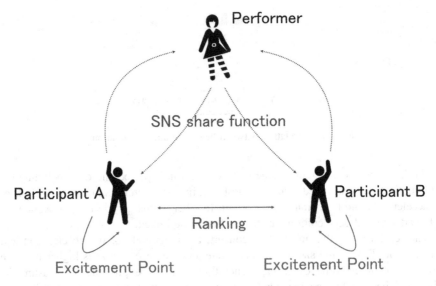

Fig. 3. Gamification technique to inducing fun activities

- Point function to present the amount of the action as a "excitement point"
- User ranking function that crowd each other using that you have a competitive spirit against each other
- SNS share function that spectators were using the feeling that I want to recognize their support to performers

In addition, the performer so that the small-scale target office is supervising the contribution to Twitter which is one of the SNS(s) by this research, and this function is realized in the origin of the premise that the spectator also recognizes it.

An overview of the typical screen transition diagram of "Livelog" shown in Fig. 4.

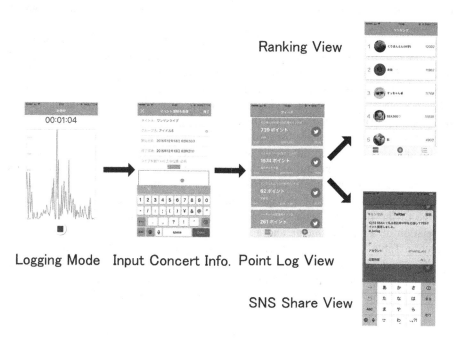

Fig. 4. Screen transition diagram in "Livelog"

4 Experiment 2: Inducing Excitement in Live Concert

4.1 Procedure of Experiment 2

The constructed the system "Livelog" distributed to subjects 42 people, Gamification approach taking into account the characteristics to compete with properties and other spectators to absolute view of the performers in the crowd, to verify that induce excitement behavior of participant the experiments were carried out over four weeks from December 13, 2015 until January 9, 2016. Delimited period by two weeks, to the period 1 and 2. Apply the only presentation of the support points in all subjects in the period 1, in the period 2, the subject, group (P group) to apply the only presentation of the support point, the group also applied presentation of user rankings (R group), divided into three groups of the group (S group) be applied granting Twitter sharing function, and analyzed changes in each user support points is indicative of excitement action. In addition, a questionnaire was examined individual characteristics of each user.

4.2   Results and Discussion

The number of live concert log that was recorded in the experimental period through our application was total 115. The number of the valid user who participated in ones or more live concerts during period 1 and 2 is 4 persons out of 14 persons of P group, 4 persons out of 14 persons of R group, and 4 persons out of 14 persons of S group, respectively.

First, in order to investigate the effects of induction by presentation of the point, for the entire effective user, with respect to the severity index in points earned per second, which is of the excitement behavior of the participant, from the period 1 to period 2, 3 where the difference between the rate of change was verified by t-test, no significant difference was observed. In addition, the difference between the change in the ratio of the support points per second of the three groups, was verified by Tukey-Kramer test, no significant difference was observed.

In addition, we carried out seven steps of questionnaires, "Are you aware of how much the evaluation from the performers", "whether you are aware of how much the other spectators" to investigate the characteristics of communication consciousness of each user and the effect of the gamification technique. Therefore, the situation of change of the point per second in each group was shown in Fig. 5. Moreover, the correlation of a rate of change and a questionnaire result was shown in Table 1. As shown in Table 1, for a user to be aware of the performer the SNS share function was effective, and ranking function was also effective for the user to be aware of either performers and other participant. In addition, strong positive correlation also between the point of Post count and per second to Twitter shown in Fig. 6 was observed.

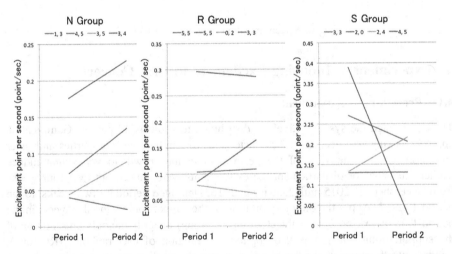

Fig. 5. Change of average point of each user in 3 experimental groups (Color figure online)

It results from, in order to increase the intensity of the crowd of excitement, that there is no effect on the presentation of the point has been suggested. In addition, the user to be aware of strong performers is effective sharing function and ranking, to the

Table 1. Correlation between average score and personal character for each experimental group

	Aware of performers	Aware of others
N group	No correlation	No correlation
R group	Strong positive correlation	Week positive correlation
S group	Strong positive correlation	No correlation

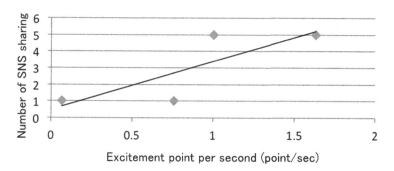

Fig. 6. Relation between the number of share and average point for group S

user to be aware of the other participant was found that the ranking is valid. Then, the difference in rate of change of points per second during the 3 groups did not occur, without taking into account the individual characteristics of the user is considered to be because the allocated users to experimental groups randomly.

5 Conclusion

In the present study, the excitement action of the participant in the live concert, a method for measuring by acceleration obtained by using a smart phone, was devised through the verification experiment. In addition, the experiments carried out to distribute the application to the general user, suggesting that it is not sufficient to present the only point in the induction of excitement action, we do not apply the Gamification method in accordance with the individual characteristics of the user shall possibility has been shown.

In the future, I want to induction of excitement action utilizing other Gamification techniques to verify whether valid or not. In addition, in the experiment, increasing the number of subjects by the general public of the application, to lengthen the duration of the experiment, devising to increase the valid data, such as lowering the withdrawal rate by reducing the burden on the application of the user.

References

1. Kazuma, H., Katsuhiko, O.: Live concert annotation system by penlight application. In: The proceedings of Information Science and Technology Forum, vol. 12, no. 3, pp. 619–620 (2013). (In Japanese)
2. Uno, T.: Contention of Japanese Culture, pp. 61–71. Chikuma Shobo, Tokyo (2011). (In Japanese)
3. Appelhans, B.M., Luecken, L.J.: Heart rate variability as an index of regulated emotional respond-ing. Rev. Gen. Psychol. 10(3), 229–240 (2006)

Author Index

Printed in the United States
By Bookmasters